AFRICAN HISTORICAL DICTIONARIES
Edited by Jon Woronoff

1. *Cameroon,* by Victor T. LeVine and Roger P. Nye. 1974. Out of print. See No. 48.
2. *The Congo,* 2nd ed., by Virginia Thompson and Richard Adloff. 1984
3. *Swaziland,* by John J. Grotpeter. 1975
4. *The Gambia,* 2nd ed., by Harry A. Gailey. 1987
5. *Botswana,* by Richard P. Stevens. 1975. Out of print. See No. 44.
6. *Somalia,* by Margaret F. Castagno. 1975
7. *Benin [Dahomey],* 2nd ed., by Samuel Decalo. 1987. Out of print. See No. 61.
8. *Burundi,* by Warren Weinstein. 1976
9. *Togo,* 2nd ed., by Samuel Decalo. 1987
10. *Lesotho,* by Gordon Haliburton. 1977
11. *Mali,* 2nd ed., by Pascal James Imperato. 1986
12. *Sierra Leone,* by Cyril Patrick Foray. 1977
13. *Chad,* 2nd ed., by Samuel Decalo. 1987
14. *Upper Volta,* by Daniel Miles McFarland. 1978
15. *Tanzania,* by Laura S. Kurtz. 1978
16. *Guinea,* 3rd ed., by Thomas O'Toole and Ibrahima Bah-Lalya. 1995
17. *Sudan,* by John Voll. 1978. Out of print. See No. 53.
18. *Rhodesia / Zimbabwe,* by R. Kent Rasmussen. 1979. Out of print. See No. 46.
19. *Zambia,* by John J. Grotpeter. 1979
20. *Niger,* 2nd ed., by Samuel Decalo. 1989
21. *Equatorial Guinea,* 2nd ed., by Max Liniger-Goumaz. 1988
22. *Guinea-Bissau,* 2nd ed., by Richard Lobban and Joshua Forrest. 1988
23. *Senegal,* by Lucie G. Colvin. 1981. Out of print. See No. 65.
24. *Morocco,* by William Spencer. 1980
25. *Malawi,* by Cynthia A. Crosby. 1980. Out of print. See No. 54.
26. *Angola,* by Phyllis Martin. 1980. Out of print. See No. 52.
27. *The Central African Republic,* by Pierre Kalck. 1980. Out of print. See No. 51.
28. *Algeria,* by Alf Andrew Heggoy. 1981. Out of print. See No. 66.
29. *Kenya,* by Bethwell A. Ogot. 1981
30. *Gabon,* by David E. Gardinier. 1981. Out of print. See No. 58.
31. *Mauritania,* by Alfred G. Gerteiny. 1981
32. *Ethiopia,* by Chris Prouty and Eugene Rosenfeld. 1981. Out of print. See No. 56.
33. *Libya,* 2nd ed., by Ronald Bruce St John. 1991
34. *Mauritius,* by Lindsay Rivière. 1982. Out of print. See No. 49.
35. *Western Sahara,* by Tony Hodges. 1982. Out of print. See No. 55.

HISTORICAL DICTIONARY OF BENIN
Third Edition

by
SAMUEL DECALO

African Historical Dictionaries, No. 61

The Scarecrow Press, Inc.
Lanham, Md., & London

SCARECROW PRESS, INC.

Published in the United States of America
by Scarecrow Press, Inc.
4720 Boston Way, Lanham, Maryland 20706

4 Pleydell Gardens, Folkestone
Kent CT20 2DN, England

The first edition of this book was published in 1976 under the title *Historical Dictionary of Dahomey* (People's Republic of Benin), and is now out-of-print.

The second edition of this book was published in 1987 under the title *Historical Dictionary of Benin,* and is now out-of-print.

British Cataloging in Publication Information Available

Library of Congress Cataloging-in-Publication Data

Decalo, Samuel.
Historical dictionary of Benin / by Samuel Decalo. — 3rd ed.
p.   cm. — (African historical dictionaries ; no. 61)
Includes bibliographical references.
1. Benin—History—Dictionaries. I. Title. II. Series.
DT541.5.D4   1995   966.83'003—dc20   94–17082

ISBN 0–8108–2905–3 (cloth ː alk. paper)

Printed in the United States of America

The author wishes to acknowledge the generous financial support of the University Research Committee of the University of Natal, without which this third edition could not have been completed.

This book is dedicated to my wife, Roma.

CONTENTS

v

EDITOR'S FOREWORD

When the first edition of this Dictionary was published, I mentioned that few African countries had undergone ''more history'' in such a short time. In just over a decade since independence, what was then known as Dahomey passed through a rapid succession of regimes, sometimes relatively democratic, occasionally radical, more often conservative, and various forms of military rule, first by senior, then by junior officers. This progression has since slowed down and there is considerably more stability, although changes within the regime continue. Thus, anyone who wants to know who is who in Benin will still find this handy guide essential.

The Benin Historical Dictionary, of course, does more than keep track of a broad cast of political personalities. It looks at leading figures in the economic, social and cultural life of the country and, last but not least, the military. It considers significant events in these other sectors as well. This time, nothing is more important than the economic sphere. For none of the different approaches to development has solved the underlying problems that continue to plague the economy. Until greater progress is made here, the political future of the country remains uncertain.

As for many French-speaking countries, this Dictionary is still one of the rare sources of material in English. Not only does it provide a broad range of information, a look at the past and present and an inkling of what the future may bring, it contains a substantial bibliography. This directs readers to more specific references—to the extent that they exist.

This volume was extensively revised and updated by the original author, Samuel Decalo. He is one of the foremost authorities on French-speaking Africa and also on military regimes, a particularly useful combination in this case. His most recent books on these subjects are *Military Rule in Africa: Motivations and Constraints* (1990) and *Psychoses of Power: African Personal Dictatorships* (1989)

Jon Woronoff
Series Editor

NOTE ON SPELLING

Historical and anthropological studies dealing with the precolonial kingdom of Dahomey frequently use the following terms interchangeably: Dahomey, Danhomé, Dahome, Dahomi, Dauxome, the Fon kingdom, Abomey, the Abomey kingdom, etc. In this volume "Dahomey kingdom" is employed when referring to the historical kingdom and "Dahomey" for the entire territory or state prior to its 1975 name-change to Benin.

With respect to other terms or names, the most common French spelling has been followed, since it is in this language that most of the research on Benin has been published. Where important variants exist or when the English form is significantly different they are cross-referenced to avoid confusion.

RECENT POLITICAL CHRONOLOGY

Dec. 4, 1958	Proclamation of the Republic.
May 21, 1959	Investment of a National Assembly with Maga as prime minister.
Aug. 1, 1960	Proclamation of Independence.
Sept. 20, 1960	Admission to the United Nations.
Dec. 11, 1960	Election of National Assembly with Maga as president and Apithy as vice-president.
Oct. 28, 1963	Coup d'etat of Colonel Soglo.
Jan. 5, 1964	Constitution of the Second Republic approved by referendum.
Jan. 19, 1964	Presidential and legislative elections: Apithy and Ahomadégbé elected president and vice-president, respectively.
Aug. 1, 1965	Inauguration of the completed Port of Cotonou.
Nov. 29, 1965	Coup d'etat of General Soglo. Congacou appointed interim president.
Dec. 22, 1965	Second takeover by General Soglo. Military administration established.
Dec. 17, 1967	Coup d'etat of Major Kouandété.
Dec. 19, 1967	Interim military administration established under Colonel Alley.

March 31, 1968	New constitution approved by referendum.
May 5, 1968	Presidential elections held with 74-percent abstentions.
May 9, 1968	Presidential elections and victory of President-elect Dr. Adjou Moumouni annulled.
July 17, 1968	The military appoints Dr. Zinsou as president.
July 28, 1968	Zinsou confirmed by a plebiscite.
Dec. 10, 1969	Coup d'etat of Colonel Kouandété.
Dec. 12, 1969	Interim Military Directorate formed under clairmanship of Colonel De Souza.
Dec. 26, 1969	Adoption of a provisional constitution.
March 9, 1970	Staggered region-by-region presidential election commences.
April 3, 1970	Presidential elections ''suspended'' prior to the vote of the last region, Atakora.
May 1, 1970	Presidential Council formula agreed upon.
May 7, 1970	Maga inaugurated as first chairman of the Presidential Council.
Feb. 23, 1972	Abortive anti-Maga coup d'etat.
May 7, 1972	Maga transfers chairmanship of the Presidential Council to Ahomadégbé.
May 11, 1972	Kouandété and several plotters sentenced to death.
Oct. 26, 1972	Coup d'etat of Major Kérékou.

Feb. 28, 1973	Colonel Alley and several plotters arrested for preparing a countercoup.
Feb. 11, 1974	Decree announcing new decentralized local administrative structures.
Nov. 30, 1974	Proclamation of a "Marxist-Leninist" state, followed by a series of partial nationalizations, including of the educational establishment.
Jan. 21, 1975	Attempted coup by the Minister of Labour and Civil Service, Captain Assogba.
Jan. 21, 1975	Key junta officer, Major Aikpé, liquidated. Major riots erupt in coastal cities.
Nov. 30, 1975	Name of Dahomey changed to the People's Republic of Benin. Establishment of the Benin People's Revolutionary Party.
June 1976	Delegalization of all religious holidays in Benin.
Oct. 1976	Major reorganization of the Benin armed forces. Major educational reforms announced.
Jan. 16, 1977	Mercenary assault on Cotonou airport. Benin maintains France, Gabon, and Morocco are directly implicated in the conspiracy.
Aug. 30, 1977	New Constitution adopted.
June 1978	Administrative reorganization of Benin creates 84 local districts.
Nov. 20, 1979	Elections for a new National Revolutionary Assembly.
Feb. 6, 1980	First Session of the National Revolutionary Assembly elects Kérékou as president of the

People's Republic. The regime regards itself constitutionalized and civilianized.

Aug. 1978   Expulsion of 9,000 Beninois from Gabon in retaliation for continued friction since the 1977 mercenary assault on Cotonou.

April 1981   The political triumvirate is released after nine years of house detention.

May 1981   Decision to denationalize part of the State sector due to massive deficits and inefficiency.

Feb. 17, 1982   Visit to Benin by Pope John Paul II.

April 1982   Fifteen State companies dissolved; others placed under ''strict probation.''

Feb. 1983   Massive expulsions of non-nationals from Nigeria seriously affect Benin.

Dec. 1983   The parastatal sector, still highly deficitory, requires major fiscal subsidies. Direct French aid to the Benin budget recommences.

Jan. 1984   Oil exploitation by Saga Petroleum finally comes on stream.

Feb. 13–18, 1984   Extraordinary Session of the National Revolutionary Assembly modifies the Basic Law of 1977, reducing the number of deputies to be elected and increasing the term of the Head of State.

June 10, 1984   Elections for a new National Revolutionary Assembly.

Aug. 1, 1984   Kérékou reelected as President of Benin for a term of five years.

May 1985	Student demonstrations against the regime are dispersed by the armed forces. The entire educational establishment is closed down.
June 1985	Cabinet reshuffle in which Colonel Alladaye is purged of all cabinet and party duties.
Mar. 26, June 1988	Military coup attempts; 150 personnel arrested.
1988–1989	Massive intermittent strikes by labor, unpaid for up to 18 months.
Dec. 1989	Marxism-Leninism renounced.
Feb. 19–28, 1990	National Conference held, ushering in an interim government.
Aug. 1, 1990	Independence Day celebrated under the old tricolor ''Dahomean'' flag.
Oct. 10–11, 1990	Competitive local elections.
Dec. 2, 1990	National referenda ratifies new constitution that bars presidential bids by the Old Guard.
Feb. 17, 1991	Legislative elections contested by 1,800 delegates and 36 parties.
Mar. 10, 24, 1991	Presidential elections in which Nicéphore Soglo beats in the second round Kérékou by 67 percent to 31 percent.
June 1992	Soglo's political hold consolidated by the emergence of a 34-deputy Le Rénouveau coalition backing him.
Aug. 2, 1992	Natitingou garrison briefly seized by a military mutiny headed by Captain Tawès.

TABLES

TABLE 1: ETHNIC GROUPS

Fon	39.2%
Adja	11.1%
Bariba	8.5%
Yoruba	11.9%
Aizo/Houéda	9.8%
Somba	1.8%
Fulani	5.6%
Kotokoli	1.7%
Dendi	2.1%
Others	8.3%

TABLE 2: BASIC LANGUAGE GROUPS

Adja-Fon:	Adja, Aïzo, Fon, Houéda, Popo, Mahi, Mina, Ouéménou
Yoruba:	Holli, Mahi, Dassa, Ife, Savé
Mossi:	Pila Pila, Tanéka
Mande:	Bariba
Paragurma:	Somba
Others:	Dendi, Fulani, Djérma, Hausa, Kourtey

TABLE 3: PRINCIPAL COMMODITIES MARKETED, 1990

Cotton	104,660
Karite	7,000
Palms	9,000
Tobacco	322

Latest figures, in tons.

TABLE 4: PRINCIPAL STAPLE CROPS PRODUCED, 1990

Maize	424
Millet, sorghum	129
Rice	9
Beans	55
Igname	1,010
Manioc	977
Sweet potatoes	37

Latest figures, in 1,000 tons.

TABLE 5: IMPORTS/EXPORTS, 1960–1991

Year	Imports	Exports	Exports as % of Imports
1960	7,643	4,513	59
1961	6,275	3,579	57
1962	6,627	2,699	40.6
1963	8,249	3,155	38.3
1964	7,762	3,254	42
1965	8,491	3,367	39.8
1966	8,270	2,585	31.2
1967	11,983	3,750	31.2
1968	12,211	5,505	45
1969	14,129	6,693	47.3
1970	17,660	9,062	51.3
1971	21,202	11,648	54.9
1972	23,510	9,189	39
1973	24,859	9,794	39.4
1974	35,530	10,240	28.8
1975	42,080	6,791	16.1
1976	50,528	9,053	17.9
1977	65,789	10,115	15.4
1978	70,197	6,140	8.7
1979	68,100	9,773	14.4
1980	69,969	13,272	19.0
1981	147,499	9,141	6.2
1982	152,553	7,837	5.1
1983	112,032	25,351	22.6
1984	125,903	72,822	57.8
1985	152,763	67,824	44.4
1986	133,850	36,013	26.9
1987	104,980	34,266	32.6
1988	168,913	24,821	14.7
1989	135,312	35,111	25.9
1990	147,900	30,618	20.7
1991	179,688	34,218	19.0

ABBREVIATIONS AND ACRONYMS

AB	Air Bénin
ABP	Agence Bénin-Présse
ADD	Alliance Démocratique Dahoméenne
ADP	Alliance Démocratique pour le Progrés
AGB	Société d'Alimentation Générale du Bénin
AMIBEF	Amicale des Béninois en France
ANR	Assemblée Nationale Révolutionnaire
AOF	Afrique Occidentale Française
ASYNB	Association des Syndicats du Bénin
ASYNDA	Association des Syndicats du Dahomey
BBD	Banque Béninoise de Développement
BCB	Banque Commerciale du Bénin
BCEAO	Banque Centrale des Etats de l'Afrique de l'Ouest
BDD	Banque Dahoméenne
BELIMINES	Société Bénino-Arabe-Libyenne des Mines
BELIPECHE	Société Bénino-Arabe-Libyenne de Pêche Maritime

BGP	Batallion du Garde Présidentielle
BGR	Batallion de la Garde Républicaine
BIBE	Banque Internationale du Bénin
CA	Convention Africaine
CARDER	Centres d'Action Regionale pour le Développement Rural
CCCE	Caisse Centrale de Coopération Economique
CCFOM	Caisse Centrale de la France d'Outre Mer
CCOE	Comité Central d'Organisation Electorale
CCR	Conseil Communal de la Révolution
CDC	Caisse des dépôts et Consignations
CDR	Comités Pour la Défense de la Révolution
CDTC	Confédération Dahoméenne des Travailleurs Croyants
CEA	Comité d'Etat d'Administration
CEB	Communauté Electrique du Bénin
CEN	Conseil Executif National
CFA	Communauté Financiére Africaine
CFDT	Compagnie Française pour le Développement des Fibres Textiles
CIB	Céramique Industrielle du Bénin
CIMBENIN	Ciments du Bénin

CMR (1967)	Comité Militaire Révolutionnaire
CMR (1972)	Comité Militaire pour la Révolution
CMV	Comité Militaire de Vigilance
CNCA	Caisse Nationale de Crédit Agricole
CND	Convention Nationale Dahoméenne
CNER-TP	Centre National d'Essais et de Recherches des Travaux Publiques
CNR	Conseil National de la Révolution
CNSL	Conseil National des Syndicats Libres
COBENAM	Compagnie Béninoise de Navigation Maritime
COCODA	Compagnie des Commerçants Africains du Dahomey
CODANAM	Compagnie Dahoméenne du Navigation Maritime
CPR	Conseil Provincial Révolutionnaire
CPS	Cour Populaire Suprême
CRD	Conseil Révolutionnaire du District
CRL	Conseil Révolutionnaire Locale
CRN	Comité de Rénovation Nationale
DIE	Défense des Intérêts Economiques
DS	Démocratic et Solidarité
ECA	Economic Commission for Africa

EDF	European Development Fund
EEC	European Economic Community
ENA	Ecole Nationale d'Administration
FAB	Forces Armées du Bénin
FAC	Fonds d'Aide et de Coopération
FACEEN	Front d'Action Commune des Elèves et Etudiants du Nord
FAD	Front d'Action Démocratique
FAO	Food and Agriculture Organization (UN)
FEANF	Fédération des Etudiants de l'Afrique Noire en France
FED	Fonds Européen de Développement
FIDES	Fonds d'Investissement pour le Développement Economique et Social des Territories d'Outre Mer
FLERD	Front de Libération et de Réhabilitation du Dahomey
FND	Front National pour la Démocratie
FUD	Front Unifié Démocratique
GEN	Groupement Ethnique du Nord
GEND	Groupement Ethnique du Nord Dahomey
GIBA	Groupement Interprofessionnel des Enterprises du Benin

GMB	Grande Moulin du Benin
GRVC	Groupements Révolutionnaires de Vocation Coopérative
HCRB	Haut Conseil de la République du Benin
IBETEX	Industrie Béninoise des Textiles
ICODA	Industrie Cotonnière du Dahomey
IDATEX	Industrie Dahoméenne de Textile
IESB	Institut d'Enseignement Supérieur du Bénin
IFAC	Institut Français de Recherches Fruitières Outre Mer
IFAN	Institut Français d'Afrique Noire
IHEOM	Institut de Hautes Etudes d'Outre Mer
IOM	Indépendants d'Outre Mer
IPN	Institut Pédagogique National
IRACT	Institut de Recherches Cotonnières et Textiles
IRAD	Institut de Recherches Appliquées du Dahomey
IRHO	Institut de Recherches pour les Huiles et Oleagineux
JUD	Jeunesse Universitaire du Dahomey
MABECY	Manufacture Béninoise des Cycles
MBLD	Mouvement Béninois pour la Liberté et la Démocratie

MDD	Mouvement Démocratique Dahoméen
MLDS	Mouvement pour la Liberté et le Développement Social
MLN	Mouvement de Libération Nationale
MNDD	Mouvement Nationale pour la Démocratie et le Développement
MRD	Mouvement de la Rénovation du Dahomey
MSA	Mouvement Socialiste Africain
NCC	Notre Cause Commune
OAE	Office d'Approvisionnement de l'Etat
OBA	Office Béninois des Arts
OBAR	Office Béninois d'Aménagement Rural
OBEMAP	Office Béninois des Manutentions Portuaires
OBEMINES	Office Béninois des Mines
OCAD	Office de Commercialisation Agricole du Dahomey
OCAMM	Organisation Commune Africaine, Malgache et Mauritienne
OCBN	Organisation Commune Bénin-Niger des Chemins de Fer et des Transports
OCDN	Organisation Commune Dahomey-Niger des Chemins de Fer et des Transports
OFRB	Organisation des Femmes Révolutionnaires du Bénin

OJRB	Organisation de la Jeunesse Revolutionnaire du Bénin
ONAB	Office National du Bois
ONATHO	Office National du Tourisme et de l'Hôtellerie
ONC	Office National de Céréoles
ONEPI	Office National d'Edition, de Presse, et d'Imprimerie
ONP	Office National de Pharmacie
ORTB	Office de la Radiodiffusion et de Télévision du Bénin
PANACO	Pan Ocean Oil Company
PCD	Parti Communiste Dahoméen
PDD	Parti Démocratique Dahoméen
PDU	Parti Dahoméen de l'Unité
PND	Parti des Nationalistes Dahoméens
PNDD	Parti National pour la Démocratie et le Développement
PPD	Parti Progressiste Dahoméen
PRA	Parti du Regroupement Africain
PRD	Parti Républicain Dahoméen
PRD	Parti de Rénouveau Démocratique
PRPB	Parti de la Révolution Populaire du Bénin

PRSB	Parti de la Révolution Socialiste du Bénin
PSD	Parti Sociale-Democrate
RAVINAR	Régie de Ravitaillement des Navires
RDA	Rassemblement Démocratique Africain
RDD	Rassemblement Démocratique Dahoméen
RFD	Rassemblement des Forces Démocratiques
RIN	Rassemblement de l'Imipératif National
RND	Rassemblement National pour la Démocratie
RRN	Régie de Ravitaillement des Navires
RTPA	Régie des Transports de la Province de l'Atlantique
SABLY	Société Agro Animale Bénino-Libyenne
SADEVO	Société d'Aménagement de Développement de la Vallée de l'Ouémé
SAGB	Société d'Alimentation Générale du Bénin
SBEE	Société Béninoise d'Electricité et d'Eau
SCB	Société des Ciments du Bénin
SCD	Société des Ciments du Dahomey
SCIEB	Syndicat des Commerçants Importateurs et Exportateurs du Bénin
SCO	Société des Ciments d'Onigbolo
SDB	Société Dahoméenne de Banque

SDEE	Société Dahoméenne d'Electricité et d'Eau
SBS	Société Béninoise de Sidérurgie
SDI	Service de Documentation et d'Information
SIEIB	Syndicat Interprofessionel des Enterprises Industrielles du Bénin
SMDN	Société Miniére du Dahomey-Niger
SNAFOR	Société Nationale pour le Développement Forestier
SNAHDA	Société Nationale des Huileries du Dahomey
SNE	Société Nationale d'Equipement
SOBEK	Société Béninoise du Kenaf
SOBEPALH	Société Béninoise de Palmiér à Huile
SOBETEX	Société Béninoise des Textiles
SOBRADO	Société des Brasseries du Dahomey
SOCAB	Société du Car du Bénin
SOCAD	Société de Commercialisation et de Crédit Agricole Dahoméenne
SODAIC	Société Dahoméenne d'Importation et du Commerce
SODAK	Société Dahoméenne Agricole et Industrielle du Kenaf
SODATEX	Société Dahoméenne de Textiles
SODIAC	Société Dahoméenne pour le Développement de l'Industrie et le Commerce

SODIMAS	Société de Distribution de Fournitures, Matériel Administratif et Scolaire
SOFITEX	Société des Fibres Textiles
SOGADA	Société Générale d'Approvisionement du Dahomey
SOGECOB	Société Générale du Commerce du Bénin
SOGEMA	Société de Gestion des Marchés Autonomes
SONAC	Société Nationale de Ceramique
SONACEB	Société Nationale de Commercialisation et d'Exportation
SONACI	Société Nationale des Ciments
SONACO	Société Nationale Agricole pour le Coton
SONACOP	Société Nationale de Commercialisation des Produits Pétroliers
SONACOTRAP	Société Nationale de Construction et des Travaux Publiques
SONADER	Société Nationale pour le Développement Rural
SONAE	Société Nationale d'Equipement
SONAFEL	Société Nationale pour le Développement des Fruits et Légumes
SONAFOR	Société Nationale pour le Développement Forestière
SONAGIM	Société Nationale de Gestion Immobilière

SONAMEEN	Société Nationale de Matériel Electrique et Electroménager
SONAPA	Société Nationale pour la Production Animale
SONAPAL	Société Nationale de Papeterie et de Librairie
SONAPECHE	Société Nationale de Pêche
SONAPRA	Société Nationale pour la Promotion Agricole
SONAR	Société Nationale d'Assurances et Réassurances
SONARAF	Société Nationale de Raffinage
SONATA	Société Nationale de Transport Aérien
SONATRAC	Société Nationale de Transit et Consignation
SONIAH	Société Nationale d'Irrigation et d'Aménagement Hydro-Agricole
SONIB	Société Nationale d'Importation du Bénin
SONICOG	Société Nationale pour l'Industrie des Corps Gras
SOTRACOB	Société de Transit et de Consignation du Bénin
SPB	Société des Produits Plastiques du Bénin
SSS	Société Sucrière de Savé
STRB	Syndicat des Transporteurs Routiers
SYNACIB	Syndicat des Commerçants et Industriels Africains du Bénin
SYNACID	Syndicat National des Commerçants et Industriels Africains du Dahomey

SYNES	Syndicat des Enseignants du Supérieur
TAB	Société Nationale de Transport Aérien du Bénin
TRANS-BENIN	Société de Transports Routiers du Bénin
UDD	Union Démocratique Dahoméenne
UFP	Union des Forces de Progrés
UGDO	Union Générale pour le Développement d'Oiudah
UGEED	Union Générale des Etudiants et Elèves Dahoméens
UGSD	Union Générale des Syndicats du Dahomey
UGTAN	Union Générale des Travailleurs d'Afrique Noire
UGTD	Union Générale des Travailleurs Dahoméens
ULD	Union pour la Liberté et le Développement
UNB	Université Nationale du Bénin
UND	Union Nationale Dahoméenne
UNDP	Union National pour la Démocratie et le Progrès
UNEED	Union National des Etudiants et Elèves Dahoméens
UNFP	Union Démocratique des Forces du Progrès
UNIDAHO	Union des Indépendants du Dahomey

UNSP	Union Nationale pour la Solidarité
UNSTB	Union Nationale des Syndicats des Travailleurs du Bénin
UNSTD	Union Nationale des Syndicats des Travailleurs du Dahomey
UPD	Union Progressiste Dahoméenne
URD	Union pour le Renouveau du Dahomey
USN	Union Syndicale Nationale
UTR	Union pour le Triumphe du Rénouveau Démocratique

INTRODUCTION

The People's Republic of Benin, until 1975 known as Dahomey, is one of Africa's smaller countries with an area of 112,665 square kilometers spreading out from a 181-kilometer Atlantic Ocean coastline to the Niger river 675 kilometers to the north. The country is nestled between Togo in the west and Nigeria in the east and has common borders in the north with Burkina Faso and Niger. It has five natural regions: (1) the coastal area, which is a flat lagoon region (with sea outlets only at Grand Popo and Cotonou) dotted with coconut palms; (2) beyond the coastal area, the fertile clay barre country reaching to Abomey; followed by (3) the plateaus of Abomey, Zagnanado, Ketou and Aplahoué; the northern regions (4), composed of the quartzite Atakora mountains in the west (highest altitude 654 meters) that continue into Togo; and (5) the Niger river drainage plains in the northeast.

Climatically, there are two zones, one in the north and one in the south. In the north there are two seasons, with the rains falling between May and September (averaging between 96 centimeters in the far north and 135 centimeters along the Atakora or to the south). During the dry season temperatures may rise to a high of 110 degrees (in January) with the dry hot Harmattan wind blowing from the north between December and March. In the south there are four seasons. The main ("big") rainy season falls between March and July, followed by a short dry season (through mid-September), a short rainy season (through mid-November) and the main dry season of November-March. Temperatures in the south fluctuate between 72 and 94 degrees and total rainfall increases as one progresses eastward, from 32 inches in Grand Popo to 50 inches in Porto Novo (the capital) and Cotonou (the de facto capital).

The natural drainage system includes the Niger river and its tributaries in the north, and the Mono, Ouémé and Couffo rivers, which flow southward. Much of the original rain forest in the

1

south has been cleared so that the country's vegetation is a mixture of palm plantations, light forests, and savanna land. The basic food crops grown include maize, cassava, and manioc while oil palms (in the south) and cotton (in large quantities since the 1970's) and peanuts (in the north) are grown for the cash economy.

Benin's population of 4,850,000 (1992) is more highly concentrated in the south where population density reaches 240 per per square kilometers (Atlantique) vs. 12 per square kilometer (Borgou). Since independence the population has increasingly become urbanized, from less than 7 percent (1960) to 15 percent (1980), and an estimated 38 percent in 1992. The rate of population increase has been relatively high (3 percent); were it not for the heavy outflux during the "Revolutionary era" (1972–1990), the population would have been higher today.

Benin's population is composed of 46 ethnic groups. Several of these originated from outside the current territory of Benin and—as elsewhere in Africa—are artificially divided by the country's international borders. The ethnic groups that figured most prominently in Benin's history are the Fon and Adja of the west and central part of the country; the Yoruba (also called Nagot locally) along the eastern littoral, and the Bariba of the north (see map of Ethnic Distribution). Historically the Bariba were isolated from developments in the south. In the nineteenth century they were organized in several small but powerful and much-feared kingdoms of which Nikki was the most important. The region was not seriously affected by Fulani invasions from the north and hence remained largely animist. Its geographical isolation and traditional outlook have placed it in a disadvantageous position vis-a-vis the south, breeding regional frustrations that were exploited by modern political elites in the pre- and post-independence eras.

The precolonial history of the south is closely tied to the rise of the Fon kingdom of Dahomey (Danhome), with its center in Abomey. The dynasty expanded to the south and west, eventually (1724) conquering Allada (known to European traders as Ardra), which according to oral legends was the "parent-state" of both the Dahomey and later the Porto Novo kingdoms. In 1727 the key port of Ouidah (Whydah) was conquered, giving Dahomey direct access to the gun market through European slave traders who were

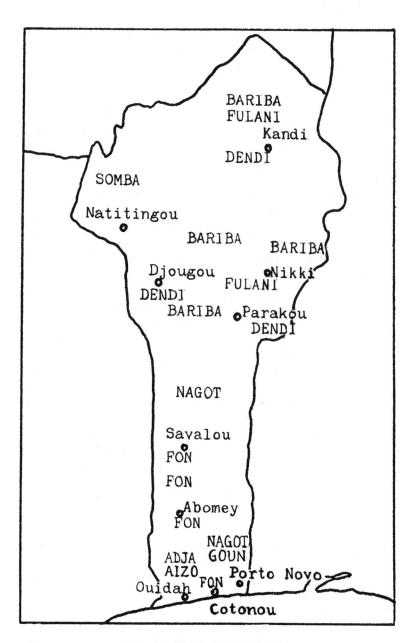

ETHNIC DISTRIBUTION

established all along the coast. The destruction of Allada power ushered in a long era of invasions from the Oyo Empire (to which Allada had been a tributary state) and the subjugation of Dahomey to nominal Oyo suzerainty. In 1818 Oyo domination was thrown off in the wake of a resurgence of Dahomean power and expansion under two of the kingdom's most illustrious kings, Ghézo and Glélé. At the height of its power, Dahomey became widely known in European capitals, gaining further fame for its elite women's military units (the Amazons) and its ritual human sacrifices (Anubomey).

Growing Dahomean military power and the kingdom's refusal to curtail the slave trade, which was elsewhere being suppressed, ushered in the British annexation of Lagos (1861) and the establishment of a French protectorate over Porto Novo (1863) and Cotonou. Though forced out of their two coastal footholds for several years, the French soon returned, seizing Cotonou under a much disputed treaty and establishing their second protectorate over Porto Novo (1882). Dahomey's repudiation of the treaty ceding Cotonou to France and a renewed flare-up in the perennial hostilities with Porto Novo (one of Dahomey's principal enemies) rapidly mobilized public opinion in France behind a Franco-Dahomean campaign. In 1893 Abomey was captured and the following year King Béhanzin (who had assumed the throne in 1889) surrendered and was exiled to Martinique. In 1900 his brother, Agoli-Agbo, was also deposed and exiled to Gabon, having been elevated as France's puppet king in Abomey. No new kings were allowed to assume the Dahomean throne and with the death of King Toffa of Porto Novo all the major thrones in the country became vacant.

The period of French colonial rule saw the expansion in missionary and educational facilities in the country (though highly concentrated in the south) and efforts to bring about a better utilization of the country's agricultural potential. Unfortunately for Benin, most of its meager known mineral resources lie in isolated pockets far from the coast and uneconomical for exploitation.

Until the 1970's, when a surprisingly vibrant cotton cultivation program took place, and the small Sémé offshore oilfields (near the international maritime boundary with Nigeria) came on-stream in the 1980's, Benin's principal exports had been linked to its palm plantations and palm by-products, revenues from which have always been insufficient to satisfy the voracious appetites of the urban population for social services and public employment. Hence the paradox that in the post World War II years Dahomey acquired the reputation of being both Africa's "Latin Quarter" and the "enfant terrible" of French West Africa: the former referring to the large number of intellectuals, authors, and professionals produced by the small country's very upwardly mobile southern populations, and the latter a testimony to the high turnover of French governors in Cotonou—partly a consequence of the rapid pace of events in Dahomey and the country's social vibrance and turbulence.

Dahomey became independent on August 1, 1960, with a weak economy, a poorly integrated society rife with ethnic and regional cleavages, and a splintered political elite. Though for a brief time the country's nascent political leadership had been united within a single party, the Union Progréssiste Dahoméenne, interpersonal conflicts, power gambits, and the inherent societal and ethnic cleavages rapidly polarized political allegiances into three ethnically/regionally-based movements. In the southeast, Sourou Migan Apithy, the country's most veteran politician, emerged as the leader of the Yoruba peoples of the Porto Novo region. Justin Ahomadégbé, a descendant of one of the Dahomey kingdom's royal families, developed an electoral stranglehold over the Fon and Adja areas along the Abomey-Cotonou axis in the center and southwest of the country. And Hubert Maga, a Natitingou schoolteacher turned master politician, succeeded in putting together an array of Bariba and other notables in the north who periodically delivered him the combined vote of the two northern regions.

Much of Dahomey's history until the 1972 "Revolution" was the story of the various interactions of this political triumvirate (able neither to unite in a stable coalition nor to purge each other effectively) interspersed by trade union and student strikes (largely but not solely consequent to fiscal austerity) and increasingly punctuated by coups, attempted coups, mutinies and military regimes. Apithy had been the preeminent territorial leader in the early postwar years. His reputation had been tarnished, however, by the corruption and ineptness of his pre-independence administration; consequently he was slowly eclipsed by the two other regional leaders and at independence Dahomey emerged under the leadership of Maga with Apithy in a very secondary position. Apithy was subsequently totally squeezed out of the leadership—in favor of an opportunistic Maga-Ahomadégbé campact—only to reemerge as Vice President after the September-October 1960 events in which Ahomadégbé attempted to ride to power in the wake of union strikes in the south. The latter and his principal lieutenants were eventually imprisoned on trumped-up charges, and their party banned, as Maga—following electoral engineering—declared a uniparty state. Apithy himself, increasingly powerless and isolated in the preponderantly northern-staffed party and governments, left for Paris where, still Dahomey's Vice President, he served as Ambassador to France.

On October 28, 1963, Dahomey's First Republic collapsed following massive unionist demonstrations in the south over the "Bohiki Affair" and the corruption and ostentatious expenditures of the regime that was simultaneously promulgating austerity policies. The army under Colonel Christophe Soglo presided over the creation of a new government (January 1964) under the bicephalous leadership of Apithy and Ahomadégbé. This second ruling coalition pitched together two mismatched personalities and was equally short-lived. It became hopelessly deadlocked in a dual power gambit over the "Supreme Court Affair." On November 29, 1965, Chief of Staff General Soglo again intervened in the turbulent political arena, dismissing both President Apithy and Vice President Ahomadégbé, and confided the creation of a new government to Tahirou Congacou, President of the National Assembly. (In the background of the coup was Ahomadégbé's attempt to influence Soglo's deputy to support his bid for power.) When Congacou proved incapable of forging a stable political alliance Soglo assumed the reins of power (December 22, 1965) and set up his own administration.

The curious pattern of a coup d'etat during the dry season of alternate years continued through 1969, except that now the assaults on the center of national authority came from ambitious factions in the armed forces that seized power for reasons rooted in the internal state of the army. Dahomey's armed forces had traditionally been divided on a variety of planes. The creation of Soglo's military regime exacerbated internal tensions and polarized the army into competing power formations only nominally under control of the de facto senior army hierarchy. In 1967 a clique of junior officers coalesced around ambitious Somba northerner Major Maurice Kouandété and toppled Soglo's regime. Unable to generate sufficient support for his presidential bid, Kouandété was forced to relinquish ultimate power to Soglo's popular Chief of Staff, Alphonse Alley, who had initially been placed under house arrest together with other senior officers.

The interim administration proceeded with new presidential elections (May 5, 1968) in which the former political triumvirate and their lieutenants were banned from competing. The elections were a fiasco when over 73 percent of the voters shunned the polls—heeding calls for a boycott by two of the three exiled regional-ethnic leaders. In desperation, and in the midst of a dangerous power struggle within the army command, the military administration invited Emile Derlin Zinsou, former foreign minister and veteran politician, to assume power. Shortly after the latter was confirmed in power by the popular plebiscite he had requested, the military tug-of-war was temporarily resolved with the purge of Alley and the rise of Kouandété as Chief-of-Staff.

Zinsou's administration was equally short-lived, lasting until December 10, 1969, but was marked by the first serious attempt to tackle forthrightly some of Dahomey's perennial economic problems. Yet the solidarity (25 percent) tax inherited from the Soglo era (and in a form different from Maga's 1960–1963 administration) weighed heavily on the urban population, even as many of Zinsou's policies further eroded his weak claim to the political throne. For, as a member of the "Brazilian" elite (i.e. detraditionalized former slaves from the Americas or uprooted and fully assimilated coastal elements), Zinsou had neither an ethnic nor a regional power base. His main props were the urban masses and their leaders, and the army. The former he thoroughly alienated by his tough anti-smuggling decrees (which hit at a healthy source of income along the Dahomey-Nigeria border) and his no-nonsense stand on the issue of student strikes, a perennial problem in Dahomey. At the same time Zinsou's independent posture and unwillingness to bend to the "suggestions" of the man who had helped bring him to power alienated Kouandété, whose political ambitions remained unabated.

On December 10, 1969, Kouandété again moved into the limelight with a coup that saw Zinsou spirited to the northern garrison town of Natitingou. An extremely tense meeting of the officer corps (still highly packed with southerners) again refused Kouandété's bid to become interim president. Instead a Military Directorate was set up, composed of the heads of the army (Kouandété), gendarmerie (Colonel Benoit Sinzogan), and Department of National Defense (Colonel Paul Emile de Souza), under the chairmanship of the latter, the most senior Colonel in the army hierarchy.

Since the army was totally incapable of resolving its own highly factionalized disputes, let alone of reaching a consensus regarding the political future of the country, all political exiles (including the civilian triumvirate) were invited back to Dahomey. Originally assured that the latter were finally reconciled and would unite behind one candidate for the scheduled presidential elections, the army watched helplessly as this "reconciliation" fell apart and all four (inclusive of Zinsou) prepared for the campaign. The staggered region-by-region elections were a farce. They very much resembled elections for regional leaders, with Apithy, Ahomadégbé and Maga scoring heavily in their ethnic fiefdoms with percentages practically identical to those of a decade earlier, and with Zinsou's candidacy confirmed as virtually irrelevant in a race where ethnicity and regionalism were the prime criteria. (He obtained barely 3 percent of the vote and did not even carry his home-town, Ouidah.) Moreover, abuses were rife and different factions of the army openly participated in campaigning or promoting their preferred candidates.

Dahomey's checkered political evolution nearly came to a disastrous ending when the Military Directorate (citing electoral abuses and violence) abruptly suspended and then cancelled the elections just before the Atakora region could deliver to Maga its vote confirming his expected victory. While the command hierarchy of the army again assembled to clash behind closed doors (with armed contingents of the opposing factions warily confronting each other), Maga and his lieutenants announced from the northern capital, Parakou, the creation of an Assembly of the Northern Populations that would declare its secession from Dahomey unless Maga was confirmed as President. In Porto Novo, Apithy allowed his lieutenants to issue threats of a secession to Nigeria, while he tried to arrange a military putsch in which he would share power with a military leader. The tense April 1970 events were finally resolved as the triumvirate agreed to form a Presidential Council in which all three would share power as "Co-Presidents" under the two-year (executive) Chairmanship, first of Maga (1970–1972), followed by Ahomadégbé and Apithy.

The unique power formula was no major success though it did bring Dahomey its first peaceful transfer of power in May 1972, when Ahomadégbé replaced Maga as Chairman of the Presidential Council. Maga's term in office was marked, however, by the same forms of fiscal excesses, immobilism, nepotism and corruption that had characterized his 1960–1963 administration. Moreover, though the abolition of the onerous solidarity tax removed a major source of urban unrest, at the expense of continued French budgetary subsidies, new radical political sentiments were beginning to sweep through the armed forces and the urban masses. The easygoing nonideological tempo of the 1960s—when bread and butter issues had provided the background for power clashes— had slowly given way to more highly ideologically-charged rhetoric among unionists, politicized youth and the army's junior officers. The armed forces, restructured into different commands under the overall leadership of De Souza, were in particular a major source of instability. Already, in 1970, Kouandété had been purged for a haughty armed attempt to free a prisoner held by the police. Late in 1971 and early in 1972 the country was rocked by two mutinies in the Ouidah garrison which included an ambush for Ahomadégbé and an attempted assassination of De Souza. On February 23, 1972, a large number of military men (including Kouandété) and civilians were arrested for their part in an extremely convoluted multiple motive two-stage attempted coup. (Poignantly, Dahomey's judiciary refused to try the defendants, arguing that their own lives were in danger since any sentences they imposed would not be implemented, and the mutineers would very likely soon bounce back to power.) Thus it was with little surprise that the country greeted the army's sixth coup d'etat on October 26, 1972.

The 1972 coup was not perceived at the outset as much different from any of the preceding military interventions, though in due time it was to change the face of Dahomey. Concocted by a quartet of southern officers from the key Ouidah garrison who convinced the Somba Major Mathieu Kérékou to lead the new regime, the coup immediately swept from command positions, and into retirement, the entire ethnically politicized senior officer corps, and placed under house arrest (in military camps away from their home-regions) the country's political triumvirate. The latter were only released in 1981, when they were regarded, if only due to old age and their ideological sterility, as politically irrelevant. Paradoxically, though one of them (Apithy) was to die in 1989, the other two continued to play an active political role after the reversal of Marxism in Benin in 1990, and might have tried to reclaim their political throne were it not for a constitutional age-restriction that was ratified by referendum.

Though initially in 1972 the ideological rhetoric emanating from Cotonou was mild, sophomoric, and often contradictory, by 1974–1975 the grand outlines of a definitive leftward shift in orientation were clear. A series of nationalizations in 1974 (originally seemingly largely symbolic), coupled with the renaming of the country to the People's Republic of Benin, were but the tip of the iceberg. By 1977 large segments of the economy, and many social activities, had been placed under the control of the State. Foreign risk capital—always a modest trickle and still assiduously courted by Kérékou, Marxist rhetoric notwithstanding—dried up completely as the country moved into the Socialist orbit.

Simultaneously, structural reorganizations brought changes in the armed forces, administrative, legal and educational system, and in the array of political power in the country. Ultimately a new Constitution codified the nature of the new order in Cotonou, decreeing a fusion of civil and military authority and sanctioning Kérékou's stranglehold over the new Marxist-Leninist party (PRPB) and the National Assembly of People's Commissioners "elected" from a single list based on corporatist lines. Ideologically and diplomatically aligned to the East, Benin began to receive infusions of State capital and technical assistance from a host of donors, previously not even diplomatically present in Cotonou. Throughout, however, despite contrary pressure from the ultra-Left (the Ligue clique pressure group; later, the underground foreign-based Parti Communiste Dahoméen) relations with France remained on a relatively even keel. Ironically, France even picked up the tab for compensating the Beninois nationalizations. Though the 1977 Bob Denard mercenary assault on Cotonou airport (in which several conservative African States were implicated) strained Franco-Beninois relations, these were eventually patched up.

The Beninois Revolution—as referred to in Cotonou—was attained at the cost of severe socio-economic and political strains, was replete with "tactical" ideological retreats, and very rapidly brought the country to its knees through massive wastage of scarce resources. Always a blend of radical dogma and pragmatism, militant socialist utopianism and jaded crass elite opportunism, fire-eating Marxist vituperation and naive crypto-Troskyite deviationism, the "Revolution" had at least the distinction (not always obvious) of being relatively devoid of the harsher aspects of similar experiments in other parts of the world. In 1981 Amnesty International, for example, estimated that the number of political prisoners in Benin jails was only 100, in a country with a human rights record superior to that of states with less controversial political systems. This was to change in the mid and late 1980's, however, as a fiscally and morally bankrupt beleaguered military regime, visibly plundering the coffers of the State, found it increasingly necessary to sustain itself in office by force.

The harshness of Kérékou's iron rule (compared to prior military interregnums) and its overall failure, camouflages a number of attainments, most of which, however, had little to do with the regime's new ideological tenor. Thus it was the northern leadership of the regime, and its permanence in office, that brought the first even-handed approach to the economic development of the country—with roads, tourist facilities, cottage and agro-industry, and mechanized agriculture extended to the hitherto neglected northern regions; in like manner the significant spurt in cotton production, (starting under civilian rule), was more a function of the fact that this was a "northern" (Borgou) crop encouraged by a northern regime.

The adoption of Marxism itself did not result in any major fiscal bonanzas (though some projects, such as the Chinese-built sports stadium could not have been constructed otherwise) with in essence only the source and nature of funding changing, but not the total amount. Nor did the new ideology bring much societal tranquility in the country, though during the preceding civilian era, unionists, intellectuals and youth had provided a vocal Left opposition to every regime. Indeed Kérékou, who turned out to be a centrist, pragmatically juggling ideological and ethnic cliques,

came under attack from both Left (for lack of "Socialist recti-
tude" and not proceeding with vigorously revolutionary goals)
and Right (for ideological repression and economic *étatism.*)

The regime did gain the distinction of being by far Benin's
longest-lasting. But this was not the result of its securing any
major sources of legitimacy through the adoption of Marxism
(though that did tap anti-colonial resentments) or the satisfaction
of societal needs (which could not be met in light of Benin's
abject poverty), but rather due to the greater generational cohe-
siveness of the officer corps, its willingness to employ brute force
to remain in office, and the erection of an array of control and
Intelligence structures to ferret out opposition.

Notwithstanding this, and the clean sweep (into prison, house
arrest, early retirement or self-exile abroad) of the senior political,
ethnic and military elites of yesteryear, the new ideology more
often than not polarized the elites, and sporadic plots and coup
attempts punctuated the rhythm of the new Republic. Innovations
that accompanied the nationalization of the educational system,
for example, resulted in a massive exodus of trained teachers to
neighboring states, bringing a serious deterioratation in educational standards. Similar desertions from the public administration resulted in 1975 (and later on, in the mid-1980's) in exit visas
being imposed for civil servants wishing to leave the country.
While the number of those who fled Benin for ideological reasons
has not been determined, their weight was considerable, for the
country's population growth slowed down for nearly a decade
despite a high birth rate.

Unionists and university students, hitherto espousing radical
stands and a thorn to all regimes, were ambivalent about Kérékou
after the 1975 liquidation of the popular southerner Captain
Michel Aikpé, which triggered massive demonstrations in the
coastal areas. The emergence of the Ligue pressure group and later
the Albanian-inspired Canadian-based Communist Party of Dahomey that totally rejected Kérékou's socialist credentials, further
polarized labor and youth, precluding even unity of society's
radical groups behind the regime.

The military clique in office, united solely by opposition to a
return to civilian rule, also slowly fell apart. Actual fist-fights
erupted during some cabinet meetings; mutual bickering between
military (later civilian and military) ministers spilled into the civil

administration as supporters were mobilized behind one or another of the protagonists. And one by one all the key architects of the 1972 coup—Assogba, Aikpé, Alladayé—fell by the wayside, to be joined by others in 1987–1988 when Kérékou was faced by generalized rebellion from within his most trusted control units.

Partly due to the effects of adverse climatic conditions that brought drought to coastal areas in West Africa, but mostly consequent to massive patronage and the mismanagement of an expanded public sector—Benin's prime employer—Benin's economy rapidly crumbled in the 1970's. The proliferation of state enterprises, some (e.g. Air Benin) erected without even cursory concern for "capitalist" cost-efficiency considerations, replete with redundant administrative personnel and offering opportunities for graft and embezzlement, piled up deficits even in sectors inherently profitable. In rapid order the supposed "motor of the revolution" (the nationalized State sector) became the anchor keeping the economy at a standstill, syphoning off what few scarce resources were in the country.

Despite a balanced budget in 1975, a freeze on salaries, general austerity, and a satisfactory 11.6 percent rise in GNP between 1970 and 1975, and 18 percent in 1977 alone, Benin remained one of the poorest countries in the world ($118.4 per capita income) with exports often covering less than 18 percent of imports. Corruption, always prevalent to some extent under the civilian era, rapidly became a way of life under military rule. Without any fiscal accountability, or the administrative muscle to monitor the mushrooming parastatals, the State sector became a private trough for civil and military influentials. Kérékou himself bitterly complained in 1981 that "the government and revolutionary structures no longer exist in reality, for the bureaucrats have virtually seized power on the government's back." (*Africa Confidential*, May 6, 1981).

With the economy collapsing in 1981 under onerous State payrolls (92 percent of the budget) and parastatal deficits, for all practical purposes the "Revolutionary" experiment was over. Several State companies were closed down in 1982, others were privatized and yet others reorganized as mixed economy companies, with Kérékou pledging a restricted State role in the economy, and actively courting Western risk capital, assuring all and sundry of the future sanctity of private enterprise in Benin.Other privatizations were to follow.

The bleak economic picture of the 1980's was only slightly alleviated by the coming on-stream of the Sémé offshore oil wells. Not exploited since they were discovered in 1968 (due to their limited reserves), the wells brought in $100,000 per day in royalties. So thin was the razor-edge between stability and economic collapse in Benin that Sémé—until 1985 under a Norwegian-Beninois company immune to the chaos of the public sector—was one of the regime's key fiscal lifelines. Benin's withdrawal of the concession in favor of a Swiss consortium (that offered better terms) led to litigation and a freeze of foreign guarantees as well as decline in production only recently reversed.

Cotonou's extremely dire fiscal straits in the mid-1980's explains why a nuclear disposal agreement was signed at fees up to one-tenth what other African states were able to negotiate. At the same time revelation of Kérékou's intention to bury the waste (the deal fell through after a global outcry about such contracts) near Abomey, drove Fon officers into rebellion, ushering heightened instability, a number of dangerous military plots (e.g. in 1988) and growing pressure for the army to step down. In the politicized south the regime had lost all credibility and was viewed as a corrupt northern militocracy with no redeeming features; the fact that delays in public salary payments were becoming increasingly frequent added to the truly revolutionary brew in the coastal cities. (One of the army plots, involving elements in the elite Presidential Guard, partly stemmed from rumors the military was also not to be paid on time.)

The year 1989 saw waves of demonstrations in coastal cities, State salaries now between eight and 18 months in arrears and the Treasury literally empty. The banking sector, looted by Kérékou aides (e.g. Cissé, a personal sorcerer and security aide), collapsed and neither France nor the World Bank/IMF were willing to throw a saving fiscal line (though Nigeria did) in the absence of basic political and economic reform. Global Marxism was dead and pressures for democratization were sweeping the world. Within this context what is at times referred to as Benin's "civilian coup" took place.

Aware that repression (employed in the past without qualms) could not restore order in the absence of fiscal resources, Kérékou reluctantly yielded to pressure (by southern aides, France, the Archbishop of Cotonou) to assemble a meeting of the "Country's

Living Forces'' (i.e. a National Convention, at the time a novel idea) to openly debate and propose solutions to Benin's economic morass. Participation in the nine-day 460-odd Convention was along corporatist lines, favoring the regime and the armed forces, but included self-exiled opposition groups including the banned Communist Party, ex-Presidents, and indeed delegates from the Beninois community abroad. (Later the elections allowed absentee voting, a novel thing in Africa.)

Once the principle of a governmental-societal forces dialogue was conceded, Kérékou's fate was for all purposes sealed, though he was unaware of this, shedding tears of frustration when the sincerity of his good intentions while in office was rejected by the conference, as was an interim executive role. The debate, carried live on radio and TV, turned out to be a total indictment of every aspect of Kérékou's 18 year rule. In short order the Convention arrogated to itself the role of a constituent assembly charged with preparing a constitution and ushering in multiparty elections and civilian rule.

Some scholars give credit to Kérékou for not heeding counsel of some northern aides at this juncture to arrest all assembled opposition elements and govern under a harsh State of Emergency. Benevolent assessments of Kérékou's behavior are difficult to accept, however, since he well knew there were no funds with which to even meet the military payroll and that his regime was barely clinging to power in face of constant riots and demonstrations. Any temporary retention of power that repression might have allowed would have been at the cost of civilian casualties for which Kérékou might be held accountable. Moreover, both France and World Bank/IMF officials then in Cotonou were warning of an immediate pull-out from ongoing aid negotiations unless basic economic reform and political democracy ensued. Kérékou accepted the inevitable, and Benin surprised Africa again to become among the first of the "new democracies." Marxism was renounced, the PRPB was dissolved (to compete in subsequent elections under a new name, but not winning a single seat), a general amnesty was declared and political prisoners released, with the normalization bringing in fiscal succor, debt-forgiveness and grants from global donors.

The interim new executive (under Kérékou's titular head, and the Fon Premier Nicéphore Soglo's actual leadership—the latter for long a World Bank director well-regarded in the West) came up with a novel constitution that was ratified by referendum. Among its clauses was one allowing any citizen to call for international assistance in case of non-democratic usurpation of power and another setting a maximum age for Presidential elections, specifically aimed at precluding the old triumvirate and Zinsou, who (apart from Apithy who died in 1989) had renewed presidential ambitions and had erected political parties. (Voters were allowed to express reservations about this clause, but over 73 percent of them ratified the eclipse of the old hierarchy.)

A large number of political parties and/or personal machines competed in the legislative elections for the much smaller Assembly. Indeed 34 parties and some 1,400 aspirants (for 65 seats) registered and/or ran in the elections that reflected ethnic voting. Many of those who won seats in the Assembly formed electoral alliances or compacts to maximize their influence: the largest such group, committed to Soglo, originally included 12 deputies; expanding to 34 by 1993, the bloc was renamed Le Renoveau.

Fourteen candidates sought the Presidency in the 1991 elections that followed. Some were inheritors of (or were backed by) the old triumvirate (e.g. Joseph Kéké, Moise Mensah), or were seasoned pre-1972 politicians (e.g. Bertin Borna, Albert Tevoédjré); others were relative newcomer aspirants or political unknowns. Among the latter some revealed a surprisingly strong following (especially Adrien Houngbédji, currently Speaker of the House) while others clearly only possessed a surplus of funds to sustain a political campaign. Though Tevoédjré revealed an impressive following (14 percent of the vote), the only viable candidates were Soglo and Kérékou, the latter surprisingly tendering his candidacy. As no candidate scored a majority in the first ballot, the next round was between the two front-runners, Soglo (who got 36 percent in the first round) and Kérékou (27 percent). Each scored a very high percentage of the vote in "his" (i.e. north/south) region, with Soglo elected President of Benin after winning 67.73% of the vote.

Since 1991 Benin has been engaged in an effort, full of pitfalls, at (a) restructuring and subordinating the armed forces (that though purged of its Kérékou Fulani Presidential Guard in 1991 has been rocked by a number of mutinies), (b) reviving the devastated economy (a painstakingly slow process) and attracting foreign risk capital (always difficult in Benin) and (c) ensuring political stability. Surprisingly the latter task has been somewhat easier, if only because of (a) the lengthy catharsis of the Kérékou dictatorship, (b) the general consensus among the political strata about the pressing need for an economic recovery, and (c) the coming of age of a newer, younger, better trained and more technocratic political generation than the old giants of the past.

Yet Benin's future is by no means rosy. Multiparty democracy has not changed an iota of Benin's always nefarious and multifaceted social, economic and political travails. The continued paramountcy of ethnic considerations, politics and subnationalism into the fourth decade of independence have already been amply confirmed, with Soglo's cabinets a delicate balance of ethnic and regional leaders. In the armed forces disgruntled northern elements have already flexed their muscles several times. Student and civil servant strikes and demonstrations continue to erupt against the new democracy, lambasting Soglo over the same bread-and-butter issues as they have in all preceding regimes, civil, military, radical or conservative. Above all else the economy remains weak, exports continuing to only cover a fraction of imports. The bloated civil service and its payroll—which global donor agencies demand be severely pruned—is resilient to cuts. Only a handful of entrepreneurs have shown interest in entering the country, while international aid, significant compared to Kérékou days, is nowhere near the Marshall Plan levels realistically needed by most African states, and certainly their weaker components such as Benin.

Indeed, were it not for the international environment that does not tolerate backtracking, Benin might already have stumbled. The future has yet to pass its verdict as to whether the process of democratization currently methodically transforming the face of Africa is just a fleeting vogue or an internationally-sustainable commitment. If the latter, Benin with its amiable, vigorous, hardworking and upwardly-mobile population has more than a fair chance at forging its niche among the stable and economically developing countries of the world.

THE DICTIONARY

ABDOU, ABDERAHMANE (Captain). Deputy-head of Kérékou's (q.v.) personal bodyguard, arrested in June 1988 for involvement in the murky Libyan-backed coup attempt. He was released in the general amnesty accompanying the end of military rule in Benin.

ABEOKUTA. Powerful Yoruba (q.v.) kingdom that supplanted Oyo (q.v.) as the prime threat to Abomey (q.v.), and against which the Dahomey Kingdom (q.v.) fielded several massive assaults in the nineteenth century. Formed by the Egba around 1830 and centered around the city of Abeokuta (in contemporary Nigeria) a Dahomean assault of 18,000 troops dispatched by King Ghézo (q.v.) on March 3, 1851, was repulsed with heavy Dahomean losses. A second assault on March 15, 1864, by King Glélé (q.v.), ended in a Dahomean rout, and a final attack in 1873 likewise failed.

ABIKANLOU, PASCAL ADJIBADE, 1935– . Movie producer and director. Born on April 21, 1935, in Pobé in southeast Dahomey, his father, who descends from the local royal family, was imprisoned by the French for four years for espousing the secession of Pobe to Nigeria. Abikanlou studied locally and in Dakar, Senegal, where he also worked for several years as a newspaper photographer and photography instructor. On his return to Dahomey, Abikanlou directed a variety of documentaries and the weekly news series "Actualités Dahoméennes." He directed the highly acclaimed film "Under the Sign of the Voudou" that received wide international praise.

ABIODUN, LALEYE. Director General of the Office National d'Edition, de Presse, et d'Imprimérie (q.v.), Benin's state publishing house.

ABIOLA, ADEBAYO FRANCOIS, 1950– . Veterinary surgeon. Born in 1950, and educated in veterinary sciences, Abiola taught between 1979 and 1981 at the National University of Benin (q.v.) before going to Dakar, Senegal, to teach at the Toxicology Laboratory of the Ecole Inter-Etats des Sciences et Médecine Veterinaire. He has published works on agro-industrial pollution and the effects of pesticides on fish.

ABOMEY. Capital of the Zou departement (q.v.) in the center of a palm and peanut agricultural area about 100 kilometers north of Cotonou (q.v.). Founded in the early seventeenth century, Abomey was the capital of the powerful Fon (q.v.) kingdom of Dahomey except for a few years (during the Oyo (q.v.) invasions) when the center of the Fon dynasty was Allada (q.v.). Abomey—Benin's third largest city—currently has a population of around 58,000 and is one of Benin's greatest tourist attractions on account of the royal palace compounds and tombs, transformed into a historical museum (which include the stools of Dahomey's kings.) Politically the region has been the political stronghold of Justin Ahomadégbé (q.v.). See also DAHOMEY, KINGDOM OF; FON.

ABOMEY-CALAVI. Small town ten kilometers from Cotonou (q.v.), site of the National University of Benin (q.v.).

ABOUDOU, SALIOU. Former Minister of Justice and Parastatals, joining Kérékou's (q.v.) cabinet in February 1987. Aboudou was unable, like his predecessors, to stem the massive deficits of the State sector or halt the wholesale plunder of its assets.

ABOUDOU TOURE, ALASSANE, 1941– . Civil Administrator. Born in 1941 and educated locally and in Ivory Coast, Aboudou Touré studied administration and economics, returning to Benin in 1965 to join the High Commission for the Plan as Director of Human Resources. In January 1967 he became Director of the cabinet of the Minister of Finance and Economics, and in September 1968, financial director of the state company SNAHDA (q.v.). Following 1972 Aboudou

Touré served in similar administrative capacities in the State sector companies.

ACAKPONI, ALBERT, 1942– . Ecologist and biologist. Acakponi was trained in biology and ecology (obtaining degrees in 1969, 1970 and 1972) and joined the Ministry of the Plan where he has served in a variety of duties. Since 1978 he has been Head of Benin's Environmental Services. He has written on encroaching desertification in Benin and has been a UNESCO consultant on this issue.

ACCROMBESSI, GEORGES COFFI, 1946– . Academic. Born in 1946 and educated at home and at Montpellier and Poitiers where he obtained a doctorate in chemistry, Accrombessi currently teaches at the University of Yaoundé in Cameroun.

ADAM, KOLAWOLE SIKIROU, 1948– . Academic. Born on October 14, 1948, and educated at home and in Paris where he obtained a doctorate in geography and cartography, Adam currently teaches at the National University of Benin (q.v.).

ADAMON, LAMINOU, 1897– . Traditional Chief of the Adjohon canton in the Ouémé prefecture, appointed under the French in 1937 and active through the late 1980's. A powerful ethnic broker, he has been on several advisory committees, including the Conseil Economique et Social (q.v.).

ADAMOU-N'DIAYE, MAMA, 1945– . Agronomist and zootechnologist. Born on April 21, 1945, and trained in France in stockbreeding in which he obtained his doctorate, Adamou-N'Diaye then returned home to join the Faculty of Agronomy at the National University of Benin (q.v.). He currently serves there as Vice-Dean of his Faculty.

ADANDE, ALEXANDRE SENOU, 1913– . Ethnologist, archivist and former Minister. Born in Porto Novo (q.v.) on March 12, 1913, to a princely Yoruba (q.v.) family, Adandé studied in Lomé, Togo, and at Senegal's Ecole William Ponty (q.v.). He completed his studies in art and ethnology in Paris, doing research in the Netherlands and Belgium. Between 1938–1948 he was archivist/librarian at the Institut Français d'Afrique Noire (IFAN) (q.v.) in Dakar, and from 1948 to 1960 Head of its Ethnology Department. During this period Adandé wrote extensively, organized art exhibitions in Europe and Africa, served on the editorial board of the Paris-based journal *Présence Africaine,* and edited the Gbédjinovi review, organ of the Benin Union of Dahomeans and Togolese residents in Dakar.

Combining academic pursuits with political activity Adandé was an early member of the militant interterritorial party Rassemblement Démocratique Africain (RDA) (q.v.), serving on its steering committee during 1946–1951. In September 1947, on leave from IFAN, he helped set up an RDA branch in Porto Novo which later became the Union Démocratique Dahoméenne (UDD) (q.v.), political vehicle of the Fon Justin Ahomadégbé (qq.v.). An internationalist and eschewing ethnic politics, Adandé spurned an early offer by Sourou-Migan Apithy (q.v.) to join the latter's Yoruba-based party, continuing his links with Apithy's rival, Ahomadégbé, even setting up a UDD branch in Dakar. In 1956 Adandé returned home to run with Ahomadégbé in that year's election, but was defeated. In 1956–1957 he served as Secretary General of the interterritorial Convention Africaine (q.v.) party, while also on the Executive Bureau of Senegal's ruling party, the Union Progréssiste Sénégalaise.

Returning to Cotonou prior to independence, he served in succession as Secretary General of the Parti Progréssiste Dahoméen (q.v.) and Treasurer General of both the Parti Dahoméen de l'Unité (q.v.) and later the Parti Démocratique Dahoméen (q.v.). In 1958–1959 he was Minister of Agriculture in Apithy's cabinet, but resigned over Apithy's change of heart regarding joining the projected Mali Federation (q.v.). He served as Minister of Finance (1960–1962) and of Rural Development (1962–1963) in Hubert Maga's (q.v.) first presidency, and after Maga's overthrow joined the 1964–1965 Apithy-Ahomadégbé government as Minister of Justice. Under the military regime of Gen. Christophe Soglo (q.v.), Adandé was appointed Director General of the State

SODAK (q.v.) company. Widely admired for his personal honesty and integrity, Adandé was considered for the presidency by the 1967–1968 interim military administration of Lt. Col. Alphonse Alley and Major Maurice Kouandété (qq.v.), only to be skipped over in favor of Emile Derlin Zinsou (q.v.). Since then Adandé has been in Niamey, Niger, as FAO representative, finally retiring in the mid-1980's.

ADANDE, JACQUES, 1940– . Diplomat. Born in Cotonou (q.v.) on July 4, 1940, and educated in France and England, where he obtained a degree in English and worked as a B.B.C. journalist. On his return home Adandé joined the Ministry of Foreign Affairs as Director of Economic Relations and Commercial Agreements (1962–1963), and of the Department of Political Affairs (1963–1968). In 1968 he was appointed First Counsellor at Dahomey's Embassy in France, accredited also to Italy and Great Britain. In 1972 he was appointed Ambassador to Nigeria and two years later he became Dahomey's first Ambassador to Japan. In 1977 he returned to Cotonou to become Director of Technical Cooperation at the Ministry of the Plan, and in 1979 became Director of the European Division of the Foreign Ministry.

ADANDEJAN, KING (1797–1818) OF DAHOMEY. Adandéjan ascended the throne in Abomey (q.v.) following a dynastic war accompanying the assassination of his father, Agonglo (q.v.), in 1797. Agonglo's lineage emerged victorious, and Adandéjan, still a minor, was proclaimed king, until 1804 under the guidance of a regent. Like his father before him, Adandéjan attempted to increase state revenues through the slave trade (q.v.). His policy of harassing traders using the preferred Porto Novo (q.v.) slave entrepot was cut short by pressures from the Oyo (q.v.) kingdom, Porto Novo's protector. After the abolition of the slave trade in 1808, he tried to shift the attention of the population to agriculture but to no avail. His last few years in office were troubled by growing popular resentments and he was overthrown in 1818 by a coup headed by a rival royal lineage that brought Ghézo (q.v.) to the throne. Adandéjan's fate is not known, though Sir Richard Burton (q.v.), visiting the area in 1861, heard reports that he was still alive at that time.

ADANDEJAN, BENOIT (Major). Influential Fon (q.v.) officer and former head of the Security Services. Great-grandson of King Ghézo (q.v.) descending from the lineage of King Adandéjan (q.v.), Major Adandéjan was part of the inner circle of Fon officers in the senior hierarchy of the armed forces during 1965–1967. As Director of the Security Services (to which he was appointed in July 1965), Adandéjan was ruthless and widely feared, acquiring the nickname "Dahomey's Beria." In May 1967 he was appointed commander of the Presidential Palace guard and head of Gen. Christophe Soglo's (q.v.) military cabinet. He was purged from the army several months later, after the junior officers' coup of 1967 (q.v.), and is currently in retirement.

ADASSIN, AHANOOGBIN, 1932– . Educator. Adassin teaches at the National University of Benin (q.v.), having obtained degrees in physics in France in 1966, 1973 and 1975.

ADELAKOUN, VICTOR, 1947– . Animal scientist. Born in 1947, and educated at home and abroad, Adelakoun commenced his academic career as research associate at the University of Sherbrooke in Canada (1978), following which he was promoted to Associate Professor of Biochemistry and Animal Physiology (1980). In 1982 he returned to Africa as Senior Lecturer in Animal Science at the Federal University of Technology in Bauchi, Nigeria.

ADEOUSSI, PIERRE, 1938– . Educator and administrator. Born on October 25, 1938, in Savé (q.v.), and educated at home and abroad, Adéoussi became a teacher of classics. He joined the interim Minister of Public Works' personal staff in December 1967 as Director of Cabinet, and was retained in the same capacity until August 1968. Transferred to the Ministry of Foreign Affairs as administrative head of a division, he reverting to educational duties after the 1972 coup d'état (q.v.).

ADIMOU, CHRISTOPHE, 1916– . Former Archbishop of Cotonou (q.v.). Born in Cana in 1916 Adimou was educated at the Ouidah (q.v.) seminary (1936–1942), following which he taught there himself (1942–1944). He was ordained a priest in 1951 and was Vicar of Cotonou until April 1968. In July he was named Bishop of Lokossa and shortly later Archbishop of Cotonou. During the mid-1970's Adimou clashed with the Marxist regime of President Kérékou (q.v.), publicly ridiculing the faulting of witchcraft and sorcerers for the crop failures and the disastrous 1974–1976 drought. He was ordered by a nervous Vatican to stop his lashings at the regime, and was replaced as Archbishop in 1978.

ADJA. Major ethnic group in southern Benin, numbering over 400,000, an offshoot of the Yoruba (q.v.) migration out of Nigeria in the thirteenth century, a branch of which settled in Tado (or Adja-Tado [q.v.]), currently in Togo. According to tradition, around the sixteenth century the Adja migrated back east, establishing the Ardra (Allada) kingdom (q.v.), which, following a succession dispute in the seventeenth century, gave birth to the Dahomey and Porto Novo (qq.v.) dynasties. The Adja are thus closely related to the Fon, Yoruba (qq.v.), and Togo's Ewe ethnic groups. A rich mythology, often contradictory, surrounds accounts of the dispersal from Tado and the establishment of the three kingdoms. See also ALLADA; DAHOMEY, KINGDOM OF; KETOU.

ADJALARA PROJECT. Second hydro-electric project on the Mono river (q.v.), aimed at supplementing the electricity output of the Nangbéto dam (q.v.) that only provides some 20 percent of the needs of Benin and Togo.

ADJA-TADO. A small village in southern Togo, also called Tado, the origin of the Adja (q.v.). Founded by elements migrating from Kétou (q.v.), originally from Ile-Ife (in Nigeria), in the sixteenth century, a dispersal from Adja Tado took place that led the Adja back west.

ADJAHOSSOU, SIMPHORIEN, 1926– . Public works engineer and civil administrator. Born on December 4, 1926, in

Abomey (q.v.) and trained as a civil engineer, Adjahossou served in the early 1960's on the board of the OCDN (q.v.) before becoming Deputy-Director of the Port of Cotonou (q.v.). During the Gen. Soglo (q.v.) regime, he also served on the Comité de Renovation Nationale (q.v.) in the Zou (q.v.) department. After the 1972 coup (q.v.) Adjahossou was attached to the central Ministry of Public Works as administrative head of division, until his retirement.

ADJAHOUTO. Leader of the Agasuvi (q.v.) who migrated from Adja-Tado (q.v.) to found the kingdom of Allada (q.v.). Different versions have the name meaning either "the one who killed Adja" (King of Adja-Tado and hence the reason for the move to Allada), or referring to his superiority over the leader and original population of Allada that was vanquished. After Adjahouto's death, he became deified as the ancestor of the Agasuvi of Allada, and, by extension also, of the kingdoms of Porto Novo and Dahomey (qq.v.) that split off from Allada. Annual ceremonies at Adjahouto's tomb in Allada to this day are attended by descendants of the royal lineages of all three kingdoms. See also ADJA; ADJA-TADO; ALLADA.

ADJANOHOUN, AUGUSTIN (Captain). Former Deputy-Commander of the gendarmerie (q.v.). Commissioned second Lieutenant in 1966, and first Lieutenant in 1968, Adjanohoun served during this period as deputy-commander of the gendarmerie. Following the 1968 coup (q.v.) he replaced Major Johnson (q.v.) as Director of the Sûreté Nationale (q.v.) but was replaced by a Kouandété (q.v.) loyalist in May 1968. A year later, in May 1969, Adjanohoun—by now Captain—was arrested for an anti-Zinsou (q.v.) plot (concocted with Héssou and Lozès [qq.v.]), but was reinstated in the gendarmerie after Zinsou's eclipse. In 1972 he headed the Commission of Inquiry into the triumvirate's (q.v.) conduct in office during 1970–1972. In 1975 Adjanohoun was once again involved in a conspiracy, this time in support of Captain Assogba's coup attempt (qq.v.), and was imprisoned on a life sentence that was commuted in 1984.

ADJANOHOUN, MARIUS S., 1947– . Development planner. Born in 1947 and trained at home and in France in development planning, Adjanohoun joined the Beninois Ministry of the Plan in 1976 as a development planner and became Head of the State Comptroller Office of Plan Expenditures in 1981, a post he still occupies today.

ADJARRA. River, flowing into the Porto Novo lagoon, that separates Benin from Nigeria. Also large village, 15 kilometers north of Porto Novo (q.v.), with a big market every four days. The village is renowned for its fine drums, producing 50 different kinds of tam-tams, attracting buyers from Nigeria.

ADJIBADE, TIAMIOU, 1937– . Former Foreign Minister. A Fon (q.v.) born in Porto Novo (q.v.) on July 15, 1937, Adjibadé studied at the University of Dakar in Senegal, and was briefly an instructor before joining Dahomey's Foreign Ministry. He served as Head of the Department for International Organizations and Technical Assistance (1961–70), and Secretary-General of the Ministry (1970–1973). After the 1972 coup (q.v.), though both a Fon and a member of the JUD (q.v.) he rallied to the northern military regime of Kérékou (q.v.), for which he was rewarded with the March 1973 appointment as Permanent Representative to the United Nations. In 1975 he gained notoriety when he defended Uganda's dictator Idi Amin against criticism of U.S.'s Patrick Daniel Moynihan. Shifted in 1978 to head Benin's Embassy to West Germany, in 1982 Adjibadé was appointed Foreign Minister, though his tenure was brief, until 1984. Returning to teaching duties at the National University of Benin (q.v.), and disenchanted with Kérékou, in January 1989 he was arrested, and briefly imprisoned, for inciting anti-regime rioting in the south. He is currently retired.

ADJO, PHILIPPE. Secretary-General of the Union Nationale des Syndicats de Travailleurs du Bénin (UNSTB) (q.v.). Adjo assumed leadership of the union after the eclipse of Romain Vilon Guézo (q.v.). He was hard pressed to retain the pro-government line of the UNSTB in face of multiple pressures from the Left—and especially members of the Ligue (q.v.)—who threatened to break the trade union (q.v.) unity of Benin. Adjo also served as First Vice-President of the National Assembly (q.v.), posts he lost after the eclipse of the Kérékou (q.v.) regime in 1990.

ADJO BOCCO, IGNACE, 1940–1982. Former President of the National Assembly (q.v.). A relatively little-known Deputy who rose through the administration, Adjo Bocco was flown to Havana in 1982, suffering from a terminal illness. He died there in November that year.

ADJOU MOUMOUNI, BASILE, 1922– . Physician, international civil servant and one time political aspirant. Born in Cotonou (q.v.) on October 5, 1922, and educated in France, Adjou practiced medicine in Cotonou until 1959. At independence he became Cabinet Director for the Minister of Public Health. Early in 1963 he joined the regional secretariat of the World Health Organization in Brazzaville, Congo. In 1968 he returned to Cotonou to run for President in the military-sponsored elections from which all previous heads of state were barred, being regarded as a UDD (q.v.) stalwart and stand-in for the latter's Justin Ahomadégbé (q.v.). Since Dahomey's other two regional leaders (Hubert Maga and Sourou-Migan Apithy [qq.v.]) called for an electoral boycott (which was heeded), Adjou emerged the victor, with 241,273 of the 287,392 valid votes cast. The election results were, however, voided by the army and shortly after Emile Derlin Zinsou (q.v.) was appointed President (see ELECTORAL BOYCOTT, 1968). Following the annulled elections, Adjou returned to his post in Brazzaville where he has been Deputy-Director for Africa (1968–1972), Head of WHO projects in Cameroun (1971–1976), and Director of the WHO Training Center since 1976. He was retired in the mid-1980's.

ADJOVI, JEAN-VINCENT, 1924– . Trade Unionist. Born in Ouidah (q.v.) on April 6, 1924, and a railway security officer, Adjovi has been a union activist. He has been Secretary of the Syndicat National des Commerçants et Industriels Africains du Dahomey (SYNACID) (q.v.), director general of the Compagnie des Commerçants Africains du Dahomey (COCODA), and a member of the Conseil Economique et Social (q.v.). He has been retired since the mid-1980's.

ADJOVI, ROGER, 1930–1967. Educator and former Minister. Born in Ouidah (q.v.) on June 1, 1930, and educated locally and in Porto Novo (q.v.), Adjovi's superior academic achievements gained him a place at the Ecole Technique Superièure in Bamako, Mali, where he studied mathematics. He continued his studies in science in Dakar, Bordeaux, and Aix-en-Marseilles, returning to Benin in 1957 to teach physics at the Lycée Béhanzin in Cotonou (q.v.). Briefly in Gen. Soglo's (q.v.) 1963 interim government, Adjovi became Minister of Education in 1964, a post he retained until the 1965 coup d'état (q.v.). He was in France during 1966–1967, to complete his Ph.D. work, when he died on March 30, 1967.

ADJOVI, SEVERIN. Presidential candidate. A rich building contractor originally from Ouidah (q.v.), Adjovi attained notoriety when he became one of the 14 Presidential candidates in the 1991 elections. He won only a minimal percentage of votes, though earlier he secured a seat in the National Assembly.

ADMINISTRATIVE ORGANIZATION. Under colonial rule Dahomey was divided into a number of *cercles* (q.v.), which in turn were subdivided into smaller units. In 1938 there were, for example, nine *cercles:* Abomey, Cotonou, Kandi, Natitingou, Ouidah, Parakou, Porto Novo, and Savalou (qq.v.), and Athiémé. The subdivisions, of which there were 20, consisted of *cantons,* each of which encompassed a number of villages, headed by a member of the local ruling (royal) family under French supervision. In the consolidation of administrative districts after World War II the country was divided into *départements* (q.v.), each with a central government Prefect, *sous-préfectures* (with Deputy Prefects), and the basic administrative unit, the *arrondissement* (q.v.). This

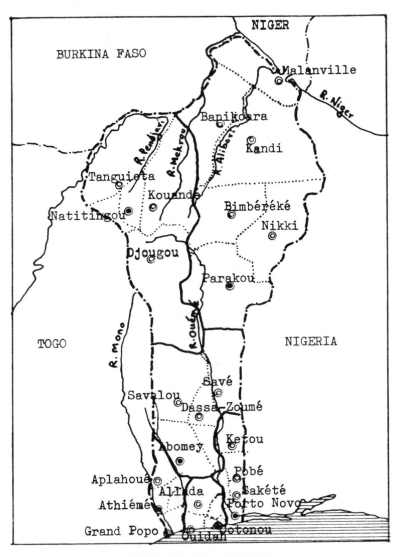

ADMINISTRATIVE DIVISIONS

structure was carried over into the independence era. In 1972 there were six *départements:* Atakora, Atlantique, Borgou, Mono, Ouémé, and Zou (qq.v.), and 35 sous-préféctures and 75 arrondissements.

On February 11, 1974, and again in June 1978, the military regime of Colonel Kérékou (q.v.) decreed an administrative reorganization of the country and a change in the nomenclature of the regional and local structures. The *départements* were renamed *provinces,* though with their old territory and headquarters, the same was done for *sous-départements,* renamed *districts* (q.v.). A June 1978 edict increased the latter's number to 84. The six *provinces* and their administrative headquarters are: Ouémé (Porto Novo), Atlantique (Cotonou), Borgou (Parakou), Mono (Lokossa), Zou (Abomey), and Atakora (Natitingou) (qq.v.).

The administrative reorganization of Benin aimed at revitalizing government and bringing it closer to the masses. Toward this end a number of new structures were set up, with advisory and executive powers, and local government was, in theory, decentralized. On the level of each of Benin's 404 *communes* (q.v.), a Conseil Révolutionaire Locale (CRL) (q.v.) was set up with heavy emphasis on representation of youth. At the level of the country's post-1978 84 *districts* (including four urban *communes*) a Conseil Révolutionnaire du District (q.v.) was set up with advisory powers vis-a-vis the District Chief (formerly the *sous-préfet*). All executive secretaries of the CRDs also sat on the national CNR (q.v.)—the highest administrative body in Benin. On the provincial level, six Conseil Provinciales de la Révolution were set up to assist/advise the Prefect, with the assistance of the Regional Council for Development and Planification (that had existed previously under a slightly different name).

In theory, significant decision-making powers devolved onto the advisory bodies, especially with respect to policy-making, finance and local development. In reality, the communal councils fell under the sway of either traditional elements (conservative) or youth, the latter exploiting them for upward mobility and/or rhetoric and, in both instances, ossified. The ''Revolutionary'' constitution of Benin also stipulated that in order that congruence exist between the masses and the leaders, the provincial Prefects should be members of the cabinet of Benin, though this was more of a control mechanism.

After the collapse of the People's Republic all the revolutionary structures were annulled, with a major reform of the administration envisaged. This has not happened to date (July 1993); it is widely assumed, however, that the reorganization would split every one of the country's regions into two. Allegedly to aid decentralization, it is hoped also to place in the northern regions representatives of the Soglo (q.v.) regime, the replacement of former Kérékou (q.v.) appointees being judged as too explosive an option.

ADMINISTRATIVE REORGANIZATION OF 1974 AND 1978 see ADMINISTRATIVE ORGANIZATION

ADOTEVI, MICHELINE, 1936– . Botanist. Born on September 29, 1936, to the influential Quénum family, and educated in Ivory Coast Senegal, and France (Sorbonne) where she completed her degree in botany in 1961, Mrs. Adotevi returned to Benin to teach at the Lycée Béhanzin and Lycée Toffa before joining IRAD (q.v.) in 1963 as Research Associate in Botany. She has published on Benin's flora and taught at the local university. For some time also the Secretary-General of the Mouvement National des Femmes du Dahomey, Mrs. Adotevi led a women's delegation to the 1964 Monrovia Pan African Women's Conference and served on several consultative boards. She currently lives abroad.

ADOTEVI, STANISLAS SPERO, 1934– . Schoolteacher, politician and former Minister. Born in Lomé, Togo, on February 4, 1934, of mixed Togolese-Dahomean parentage. After studies in France and teaching at the Béhanzin Lycée in Porto Novo (q.v.), Adotevi was appointed Cabinet Director for the Ministry of Foreign Affairs. He resigned his position in September 1965 over policy disagreements. Shortly after, when Gen. Christophe Soglo (q.v.) came to power and formed his cabinet of "technocrats," Adotevi was appointed Minister of Information, Youth and Sports. He served in that capacity from February 1966 to March 1967, when he again resigned over policy disagreements. In October 1967 Adotevi was appointed head of the Institut de Récherches Appliquées du Dahomey (q.v.), a position he occupied until April 1969 when he reentered the cabinet as Minister of Youth and Sports. He remained in that post until the 1972 coup d'état (q.v.). Following the coup, Adotevi left the country and has taught at several lycées in Togo and Senegal.

AFFO, FREDERIC ASSOGBA. Former Minister of Foreign Affairs under Kérékou (q.v.). Formerly Benin's Ambassador to the People's Republic of China, Affo joined the cabinet in August 1984 and served for three years.

AFFOUDA, JOSIAH (Captain). Junior Fon (q.v.) officer who played an aggressive role during the tenure of the Comité Militaire Révolutionnaire (CMR) (q.v.) from December 1967 to May 1968. Affouda served as CMR Second Vice-President and was one of a clique of young officers urging a permanent political role for the armed forces (q.v.). In 1972 he was arrested for an attempted putsch against the regime and sentenced to death. He was released from prison after the 1972 coup d'état (q.v.), and retired from the armed services.

AFFOYON, DIDIER, 1937– . Agronomist. Born in Porto Novo (q.v.) in 1937, Affoyon was educated at home and at the University of Toulouse as an agronomical engineer, completing his studies in 1961, and continuing on for several years as a pedalogist trainee with ORSTOM. In 1963 he was appointed Director of Agricultural Education and Training in Porto Novo, and in 1965 assumed the post of Director of Agriculture, serving in that capacity until 1969. Already his country's representative on OCALAV (the regional anti-locust and anti-birds organization), in 1969 he assumed related FAO research and coordination, based in Zinder, Niger. In 1976 he became OCALAV's Technical Director, based in Dakar, Senegal.

AFON. Another name for the Ouémé river (q.v.).

AFRIQUE OCCIDENTALE FRANCAISE (AOF). French West Africa, one of France's two colonial African federations, encompassing the colonies of Ivory Coast, Niger, Upper Volta, Mauritania, Senegal, French Soudan, Guinea and Dahomey. Established between 1895 and 1904, the organizational structure of the AOF changed over the years. In the post-World War II era, the AOF was headed by a Governor General in Dakar, Senegal, responsible for the federation to the Ministry of Colonies in Paris. He was assisted by a Council of Government with consultative powers, composed of five delegates from each territory. Each colony had its own Governor (responsible to Dakar) and a territorial assembly, also with limited deliberative authority. For the list of the AOF governors see GOVERNORS, FRENCH WEST AFRICA.

AGAJA, KING 1673–1740. One of Dahomey's greatest kings and military commanders. Ascending to the throne in 1708 in succession to his brother, King Akaba, he expanded Dahomey's territory from the Abomey plateau to the coast. In March 1724 Agaja crushed the kingdom of Allada (q.v.) and in February 1727 Whydah (q.v.) was sacked and conquered, giving Dahomey a major seaport. The conquest of Allada and Whydah opened the era of direct Dahomean contacts with Europe and control over the slave trade (q.v.). On the other hand, the assault on Allada nearly spelled the end of the Dahomey kingdom for it brought upon Agaja the wrath of the powerful Oyo Empire (q.v.) and its famed cavalry. Between 1726 and 1740 Abomey was repeatedly invaded and razed, with Agaja and his army retreating into the forests and marshes until Oyo forces withdrew. In 1730 Dahomey sued for peace and acknowledged Oyo suzerainty, a tributary status that was not shaken off until the reign of King Ghézo (q.v.). At the same time Agaja was forced to renounce the royal monopoly over slave trade under pressure from European traders. The concession was futile since traders had already left Whydah for more attractive slave ports, a development that depressed state revenues. After further Oyo invasions in 1739, Agaja died, succeeded by his son, Tegbesu, and is considered one of Dahomey's strongest and most expansionist kings. See also DAHOMEY, KINGDOM OF.

AGASU see AGASUVI

AGASUVI. "Children of Agasu," the founder of the Adja (q.v.) clan that later, under Adjahouto (q.v.) migrated from Adja-Tado (q.v.) to found Allada (q.v.). See also ADJA; ADJA-TADO; ADJAHOUTO; ALLADA; FON.

AGBAHE, GREGOIRE. Trade union (q.v.) leader and former Minister. A Fon from Ouidah (qq.v.), and an important union leader among the numerous transport workers, Agbahé was in the 1960's Treasurer of the Chambre du Commerce et d'Industrie du Dahomey. After the 1972 coup d'etat (q.v.) he became a member of the extreme-Left Ligue (q.v.) and was brought into Kérékou's (q.v.) cabinet in February 1980 as Minister of Tourism and Handicrafts, and between May 1981 and December 1982 as Minister of Public Works. He expanded his unionist base as deputy Secretary General of the UNSTB (q.v.), and became the union's head after the collapse of the Marxist regime in 1990.

AGBAHOUNGBA, LUDOVIC, 1924– . Former Principal Agricultural Works Engineer and union leader. Born in Abomey (q.v.) in 1924 and educated in agricultural engineering in Dakar and France, upon his return to Benin Agbahoungba was appointed to the Kandi and Porto Novo (qq.v.) sous-préfectures (1955–1959) and then headed agricultural services in the Central département (1959–1962). Since 1962 Inspector of Agricultural Services for the southern prefectures, and member of the Conseil Economique et Social (q.v.), Agbahoungba has throughout been deeply involved in union activities, becoming Secretary-General of the Syndicat National des Agents de l'Agriculture du Dahomey in 1964. He is currently in retirement.

AGBANGLA, CLAUDE 1943– . Educator. Born on July 18, 1943, and educated at home and at the University of Poitiers where he obtained a doctorate in physics, Agbangla currently has a teaching and administrative post at the University of Kinshasha in Zaire.

AGBANGLANON, BRUNO, 1930– . Senior Public Works Engineer. Born in Ouidah (q.v.) on December 12, 1930, Agbanglanon was educated at home and abroad acquiring a degree in engineering. He joined the civil service of Benin as head of engineering services in one of the subdivisions of the Ministry of Public Works, serving in that capacity between 1958 and 1967. After the 1967 coup d'etat (q.v.) he was appointed Cabinet Director of the Minister of Public Works, serving also as member of the Administrative Council of the Port of Cotonou (q.v.). In 1968 he was reassigned back to his technical and administrative duties in the ministry and in the port administration. He was recently retired from the civil service.

AGBANI, ASSEROU BENOIT 1941– . Educator. Specializing within physics on vibrations and sound, Agbani currently teaches at the National University of Benin (q.v.).

AGBANLIN. Founder of what was to become the Kingdom of Porto Novo (q.v.), originally known as Hogbonou ("large house") in reference to the large royal residence Agbanlin built himself. Following the conquest of Allada (q.v.) by Dahomey (1724), a large number of refugees migrated eastward settling in the Porto Novo region, strengthening what had been until then a minor chiefdom. Agbanlin's reign lasted between 1688 and 1729.

AGBO, CASIMIR, 1889?–1976. Civil servant, businessman and early historian. Born in Ouidah (q.v.) around 1889, Agbo had a varied life. Educated locally and in Porto Novo (q.v.), he worked for 12 years as a postal agent before becoming personal assistant to Georges Tovalou-Quénum (q.v.), a landowner and head of canton. In 1930 Agbo entered business on his own while immersing himself in the municipal affairs of his home town, Ouidah. Chief of one of its quarters, for several years editor of the monthly *La Tribune Sociale du Dahomey*, member of several self-improvement societies, Agbo served for eight years (1937–1945) as assistant to the local French administrator. Upon reaching retirement age (1945) he began writing his *Histoire de Ouidah de XVIe au XXe siècle* which, when published in 1959, won him wide acclaim as Ouidah's historian. During the years 1954–1956 Agbo also contributed to the daily press and continued deep involvement in Ouidah's municipal and civic affairs.

AGBO, ETIENNE TOGLOSSOU, 1905–1966. Early political militant. Born in Ouidah (q.v.) on June 30, 1905, and one of the colony's first physicians, Agbo was elected to the Territorial Council as representative from Ouidah in March 1952. He remained Ouidah's representative until 1964, running on the PPD, PRD and PDU (qq.v.) electoral tickets.

AGBOGBA, GERMAIN TOSSOVI, 1920– . Trade unionist. Born in Guézin on November 5, 1920, and educated in Porto Novo (q.v.) and at the Ecole William Ponty (q.v.) in Dakar, Agbogba trained as a postal inspector. He served as Treasurer of the Postal Workers' Union in Senegal, and upon his return home was the Propaganda Secretary of the equivalent local union between 1960 and 1963. He was elected PDU (q.v.) deputy to the National Assembly in 1960 and was a co-chairman of the assembly's social affairs committee. Agbogba is currently retired.

AGBOSSAHESSOU, VINAKPON, 1911– . Teacher, civil administrator and poet. His original name Vinakpon Gutemberg Martins, Agbossahéssou was born in Ouidah (q.v.) in 1911 of peasant origins. After primary studies in Dahomey he went to the Ecole William Ponty (q.v.) in Senegal (1930–1933), following which he taught for several years in Niger. After independence Agbossahéssou held a variety of administrative appointments, including Director of the National Center of Information (1964–1968). Retired since 1968, he published in quick succession (1969, 1971) two collections of poetry that were highly acclaimed.

AGBOTON, AMBROISE, 1923– . Civil administrator. Born in Zinvié on December 20, 1923, and educated in Paris in public administration, Agboton served in a variety of senior capacities in matters and structures relating to youth before entering the political world. He was Vice President of the World Youth Assembly (1958–1962) and Vice President of the Youth of the French Union (1956–1958). Between 1959 and 1961 he served as Cabinet Director of the Minister of Civil Service, and he later served as Deputy Director of the cabinet of Vice-President Ahomadégbé (q.v.). After the coup d'etat of 1965 (q.v.), Agboton was appointed Deputy Prefect of the Atlantique department (1966–1967) and later Prefect of Atlantique (1967–1968). He was then assigned administrative duties in the Ministry of Interior. Following the establishment of the Presidential Council (1970) Agboton was brought into the cabinet as Sourou Migan Apithy's (q.v.) personal choice and served as Minister of Labor until the 1972 coup (q.v.) toppled the Council. Reassigned other duties, and temporarily abroad, Agboton is currently retired.

AGBOTON, GASTON, 1935– . Educator and politician. Born in Porto Novo (q.v.) on April 24, 1935, Agboton obtained his education locally and at the University of Dakar, returning home to teach at Lycée Béhanzin in Porto Novo. In 1963 he was selected to be a member of the Constitutional Committee that prepared a new charter for Dahomey's second Republic. In the new administration he served as technical councillor to President Apithy (q.v.) (1964–1965). After the 1965 coup d'etat (q.v.) he was appointed manager of the government weekly *Aube Nouvelle* and technical advisor to the Ministry of Information (1966–1967). During this period he also served as Second Vice-President of the advisory Comité de Renovation Nationale (q.v.). Following the 1967 coup (q.v.) he was again appointed member of the constitutional committee preparing a new charter for Dahomey. Agboton also published two civics texts in 1968. After the 1972 coup (q.v.) Agboton established residence in France.

AGBOTON, YVES HILARION, 1938– . Educator. Born in 1938 and educated at home and abroad, Agboton is with the Institute of Public Health where he teaches public health and infectious pathology.

AGENCE BENIN-PRESSE (ABP). Press agency set up in Cotonou (q.v.) in 1961 as Agence Dahomey Presse, as a division of the Ministry of Information. It disseminates news internally and prepares data on local events for external publication. Between 1974 and 1990 ABP had cooperative links with the Soviet TASS under its director Innocent M. Lawson. Following the collapse of Marxism in Benin, ABP has adopted a moderate stance.

AGNAMEY, RENE, 1933– . Head of Benin's Topography Service in the Ministry of Public Works. Born in Abomey (q.v.) on February 9, 1933, and educated locally, in Dakar and in Paris, Agnamey was active during his student days in France in the association of Dahomean students, serving between 1956 and 1958 as first vice president of the association, and member of the Bursaries Commission. Upon his return home he joined the Ministry of Public Works and in 1962 was appointed head of the Topography/Cartography section, a post he still holds.

AGOLI-AGBO, KING. Last king of Dahomey (1894–1900). Agoli-Agbo (a self-adopted name—he was previously known as Goutchili) was Glélé's (q.v.) son and one of Béhanzin's (q.v.) brothers. He ascended to the throne on January 15, 1894, after the third Franco-Dahomean Campaign (q.v.) and the French expulsion and exile of King Béhanzin. Elevated essentially as a puppet king by the French, Agoli-Agbo nevertheless began acting independently, leading a series of punitive expeditions against "rebellious" provinces (de facto French possessions) and held ritual human sacrifices in memory of his father, in contradiction of French edicts. For these practices he was deposed by the French and exiled to Gabon. Unlike Béhanzin he was allowed to return to Dahomey in 1910, but only to a farm in Adi in the Savalou (q.v.) district, and under house arrest, since there was a movement among Abomey royalty to enthrone him as the King of the Fon (q.v.). Later, in 1925, he was allowed to move closer to his family in Abomey. The French did not allow the enthronement of any successor to the throne, though members of the royal families were appointed to regional administrative posts.

AGONGLO, KING (1766–1797) OF DAHOMEY. Like his father, King Kpéngla (q.v.), whom he succeeded to the throne
of Abomey (q.v.), Agonglo was faced with the problem of
economic depression and the continued domination of the
region by the Yoruba Oyo Empire (qq.v.). Internal disunity
in Abomey negated efforts to throw off Oyo suzerainty,
despite the latter's slow decline in strength. Agonglo tried to
increase trade with Europe, specifically calling for more
contacts with Portugal; all he got, however, was a request for
his conversion to Christianity and priests to assist him in
proselytizing the new faith in his kingdom. When he ultimately converted, the act was very unpopular in Abomey and
he was assassinated. His son, Adandéjan (q.v.), succeeded
him on the throne.

AGOSSA HOMEVO, ANTOINE, 1936– . Former Prefect. Born
in Athiémé on June 13, 1936, and educated in Paris in Public
Law and Economics, Agossa Homevo returned to Benin to
assume the post of Cabinet Director of the Minister of
Commerce, Economics and Tourism (August 1961–August
1963). Following the 1963 coup (q.v.) he was reassigned to
the prefectural pool and served as Deputy Prefect of Atlantique (1963), sub-prefect, of Ouidah (1963–1965), and Prefect of Zou (1966–1970) (qq.v.), among others. Like many
other senior civil servants Aggossa Homevo left the country
during its Marxist interregnum, and remains abroad.

AGOUE. Coastal village a few kilometers west of Ouidah (q.v.),
founded in 1823 to become the site of the largest early
"Brazilian" (q.v.) settlement in the nineteenth century,
headed by Joaquim d'Almeida (q.v.), also referred to as Zoki
Azatou. Close to the Togolese border, Agoué was the site of
the first church constructed in what was to become Dahomey. Though the surrounding land is fertile, the town was
weak and was plundered and destroyed in 1861 by Pedro
Codjo (whose real name was Pedro Pinto de Silveira) of
Aného. In 1873 it was devastated by a smallpox epidemic
that killed 1,500 of its 6,000 population. The town was also
once considered as the possible site for a new joint Dahomey-Togo port. Many of the early political leaders of both

Togo and Dahomey were born or had roots in Agoué (including former Togolese President Sylvanus Olympio), which had also been the site of the first permanent chapel along the coast, built by Venessa de Jesus in 1835. The original village was founded by refugees from neighboring Glidji (Aného), currently in Togo.

AGUESSY, CYRILLE, 1905– . Physician, historian and early politician. Born in Ouidah (q.v.) on March 19, 1905, and a descendant, on his father's side, from the royal family of the Oyo Empire (q.v.) (in Nigeria), Aguéssy was educated locally and in Senegal's Dakar School of Medicine, where he received his diploma. He practiced medicine in Senegal and in various localities in Dahomey and authored/co-authored a number of medical, historical and cultural studies, several with Adolphe Akindélé (q.v.). Between 1946 and 1949 Aguéssy participated in the creation of Dahomey's first political institutions, being a member of Dahomey's first consultative organ, the Conséil Général (q.v.). Aguéssy has been in retirement since 1967.

AGUESSY, HONORAT, 1934– . Former educator. Born on May 11, 1934, and educated in Paris in philosophy and sociology, Aguéssy taught at the National University of Benin (q.v.), where he also served for several years as Dean of the Faculty of Letters, until his recent early retirement.

AHIVODJI, DESIRE AIME, 1936– . Former Prefect. Born in Porto Novo (q.v.) on September 14, 1936, and educated at home and abroad as a civil administrator, Ahivodji served in a succession of leadership positions. He has been Deputy Prefect of Mono (q.v.), SubPrefect of Bohicon, Deputy Prefect of Atlantique and Deputy Prefect of Borgou (qq.v.). In January 1968 he was promoted to Prefect of Ouémé (q.v.) and in 1972 reassigned to the Ministry of Interior in Cotonou (q.v.), where he served as Head of Division.

AHO, PHILIPPE (Lt. Col.), 1914– . Former Deputy Chief of Staff of the Dahomean army and briefly a Minister. Born on July 17, 1914, in Oumbégamé (in the Zou département), Aho traces his lineage to Dahomey's King Glélé (q.v.). Interested from an early age in a military career, Aho gave up his studies in 1931 to enlist in the French army. Attaining the rank of Sergeant-Major, he fought in France during the Second World War (1940–1941) and was for a short time a prisoner-of-war. After his release he joined the Resistance and gained a commission in 1944 for his heroism. In 1945 he was promoted to Lieutenant. Dispatched to fight in Indochina (1953–1955), Aho again distinguished himself, was seriously wounded twice and moved up the ranks to Captain, and later Major. With Dahomey's independence he joined the budding army, attaining the rank of Lieutenant Colonel and becoming Deputy Chief of Staff in 1964.

In the events preceding the 1965 coup d'etat (q.v.), Aho's close ties with Vice-President Justin Ahomadégbé (q.v.), also a Fon (q.v.) of royal lineage, served as an irritant to Chief of Staff Christophe Soglo (q.v.) and played a role in inclining the latter to seize power. Aho served as Soglo's Minister of Interior and Defense, a position he utilized to further southern regionalist interests. After the overthrow of Soglo in 1967 he was temporarily under house arrest. The compromise between the leaders of the 1967 coup (q.v.) and the senior ranks of the army saw Aho's rehabilitation and inclusion in the interim government of Col. Alphonse Alley and Major Maurice Kouandété (qq.v.), as Minister of Foreign Affairs. He was pensioned from the armed forces (q.v.) early in 1968.

AHOMADEGBE, TOMETIN JUSTIN, 1917– . Former President of Dahomey and dominant political leader of the country's Fon and Adja (qq.v.) ethnic groups. Born in Abomey (q.v.) in 1917, Ahomadégbé is a direct descendant from the Agonglo branch of Dahomey's royal family. He studied at Ecole William Ponty (q.v.) in Dakar, Senegal, and qualified as a dentist in Dakar's School of Medicine. After a brief period of service in the French army (with the rank of Sergeant), he opened private practice in Porto Novo (q.v.).

After the Second World War Ahomadégbé joined Dahomey's first political party, the Union Progréssiste Dahoméenne (q.v.), leaving it in 1946 to establish (together with Emile Poisson [q.v.]) the Bloc Populaire Africain (q.v.). In 1947 he was elected to the Conséil Général (q.v.), in 1952 he was elected to the Assemblée Territoriale (q.v.) and in 1956 he became Mayor of Abomey. The same year his party merged with the rump of the UPD under Emile Derlin Zinsou (qq.v.), changed its name to Union Démocratique Dahoméenne (UDO) (q.v.) and became affiliated with the interterritorial Rassemblement Démocratique Africain (q.v.), led by Ivory Coast's Felix Houphouét-Boïgny.

In the 1957 and 1959 legislative elections the UDD scored serious inroads in Sourou-Migan Apithy's (q.v.) control of the south, forcing the latter to cede the premiership to the northern leader Hubert Maga (q.v.). By now Senator to the Communauté Française (q.v.) and deputy to the AOF Council, Ahomadégbé formed a brief tactical alliance with Maga, becoming at the same time President of the Assemblée Nationale (q.v.). He failed, however, in his November 1960 gambit to displace Maga and ride to power in the wake of unionist strikes. Maga renewed his alliance with Apithy, changed the electoral rules to win total control of the National Assembly, banned the UDD, and had Ahomadégbé and several of his political lieutenants imprisoned.

Ahomadégbé was released from prison in November 1962. Following Maga's overthrow in 1963 he became Vice-President and head of government alongside his old enemy, Apithy, who assumed the Presidency. It was under this administration that the 20 percent solidarity tax (q.v.) was decreed, causing unrest in the urban centers. In November 1965, Ahomadégbé—whose relations with Apithy were notoriously poor—tried to oust his rival from power. In the ensuing governmental deadlock Ahomadégbé's attempts to utilize the army backfired and sparked off a coup d'etat (q.v.). See COUP OF 1965(a); SUPREME COURT AFFAIR.

In exile in Togo and France, Ahomadégbé was behind a series of plots to have himself reinstated in power. In the 1968 military-sponsored Presidential elections (in which the triumvirate [q.v.] was barred from running) Ahomadégbé's stand-in, Dr. Basile Adjou Moumouni (q.v.), was the victor but saw his victory annulled by the army. Finally, in 1970, the triumvirate was invited back to Dahomey by the country's Military Directorate (q.v.). In the four-cornered presidential elections that followed, Ahomadégbé came in second, after Maga. The army refused to accept the results, but, after a tense period during which calls for secession were raised in the north and east, a Presidential Council (q.v.) form of government was hammered out by the three main regional leaders. As front runner, Maga assumed the rotating chairmanship for the period 1970–1972, handing over power to Ahomadégbé in May 1972.

A hard and abrasive personality, espousing militant policies in the past and the only one of the triumvirate with any ideological pretensions, Ahomadégbé's brief tenure before the October 1972 coup (q.v.) was marked by compromises, a fact cited by Major Mathieu Kérékou (q.v.) in justification for the coup (see KOVACS AFFAIR). Placed under house arrest in the distant north (Natitingou [q.v.]) after the coup, Ahomadégbé was only freed—with the other two leaders—in 1981. After the downfall of the Kérékou regime, Ahomadégbé—having served on the transitional Haut Conséil de la République and denied a Presidential role by virtue of the Constitutional age-clause—set up a political party together with Joseph Kéké (the RND) (q.v.) and was elected to the new National Assembly in 1991.

AHOUANMENOU, MICHEL, 1916–1979. Politician, Minister, and diplomat. Born on December 23, 1916, to a very influential Porto Novo (q.v.) family, Ahouanménou served in the civil service in northern Dahomey before becoming a prominent supporter and principal lieutenant of Sourou-Migan Apithy (q.v.). In 1946 he was elected Deputy to Dahomey's first Conséil Général (q.v.) and continued to represent Porto Novo in all subsequent pre-independence assemblies. Ahouanménou was also deputy to the AOF Council in Dakar (1957–1959) and a Senator in the Communauté Française (q.v.) between 1959 and 1961. In 1959 he refused to join the groundswell of opposition to Apithy's (q.v.) leadership within the Parti Républicain Dahoméen (PRD) (q.v.) despite strong support for his own assumption of leadership.

During 1958–1959 Ahouanménou served on the Steering Committee of the Parti du Regroupement Africain (q.v.), between 1959 and 1960 he was president of the PRD and in 1960 he entered President Hubert Maga's (q.v.) first cabinet as Minister of Youth and Sports (1960) and later Minister of Education (1960–1963). With Maga's overthrow and the creation of the Apithy-Ahomadégbé government, Ahouanménou became director of Apithy's cabinet (1964–1965), reverting to his old Ministry of Education under the administration of General Christophe Soglo (q.v.) (1966–1967). Briefly imprisoned after the 1967 coup (q.v.) and absolved of charges of embezzlement of funds while in office, Ahouanménou was appointed Ambassador to France (1967–1971) and Great Britain (1969–1971). With the advent of the Presidential Council (q.v.) regime Ahouanménou was recalled to Dahomey to become Foreign Minister (1971–1972), a position he occupied until the October 1972 coup d'etat (q.v.).

AHOUANSSOU, CANDIDE PIERRE. Ambassador to the USA.

AHOUEYA, LEOPOLD (Lt.Col.). Senior military officer, former Minister and Prefect. As a young Fon (q.v.) officer who early on rallied to the northern regime of Kérékou (q.v.), Ahouéya was rapidly promoted through the officer hierarchy, and in October 1974 was integrated into the cabinet as Minister of Transport and Public Works. Later, between 1988 and 1990 he was Prefect of Zou (q.v.).

AHOUNOU, LEOPOLD, 1944– . Economist. Born on October 16, 1944, and educated in economics and accountancy in Dijon, Ahounou currently teaches at the University of Dakar.

AHOYO, JEAN ROGER, 1941– . Historian and educator. Born in 1941 and obtaining a doctorate in geography and history in France, Ahoyo taught at Lycée Béhanzin between 1966–1971 and then joined the National University of Benin (q.v.) where he taught until 1981. In that year Ahoyo was appointed Director of the Ecole Normale Supérieure which he still heads. He has written several books on the ancient Dahomey Kingdom (q.v.).

AHYI, RENE-GILBERT, 1943– . Physician. Born on November 12, 1943, and completing his studies at Dakar's School of Medicine in 1977, where he specialized in psychiatry and psychology, Ahyi remained at Dakar where he still teaches. His current research interests are in traditional medicine and parapsychology, including sorcery.

AIKPE, MICHEL (Major), 1942–1975. Former Minister of Interior and Security. Influential and very popular Fon (q.v.) junior officer. Born in Bohicon (q.v.) in 1942, he was educated locally, at Bingerville, Strasbourg and Steyr, becoming a paracommando instructor attached to the Ouidah (q.v.) garrison. Aikpé first came to attention in 1967 when he served as a member (later, Vice-President) of the Comité Militaire Révolutionnaire (q.v.) that tried to supervise the policies of the government of Gen. Christophe Soglo (q.v.). He also briefly served as Minister of Interior in the 1968 interim military administration. Following the 1969 coup d'etat (q.v.) by Major Maurice Kouandété (q.v.), Aikpé helped prevent the latter from assuming total powers, supporting the establishment of a three-man Military Directorate (q.v.) in which Kouandété's ambitions were effectively hemmed in. Major Mathieu Kérékou's (q.v.) rise to power in the October 1972 coup (q.v.) was to a large extent engineered by Aikpé, who subsequently assumed the key post of Minister of Interior and Security. Promoted to Major early in 1975 and also serving as Prefect of Borgou (q.v.)—allegedly in order to keep him away from supporters in the south— Aikpé had, by 1975, become the most popular leader in Benin. He was also extremely powerful, by virtue of the fact that he was the darling of the trade unionists and of Left-wing radicals, students and intellectuals.

Aikpé was liquidated on Kérékou's orders on June 25, 1975, allegedly shot during an assignation with Kérékou's estranged wife. His assassination triggered massive unionist upheavals in the south, which the military suppressed with great difficulty.

AINA, EUSTACHE, 1944– . Educator. Born in 1944 and trained in animal physiology (1976) and nutrition and metabolism

(1979) at the University of Bordeaux, Aina returned to a teaching post at the National University of Benin (q.v.) where he also serves as Deputy-Head of Animal Physiology.

AINANDOU, CYPRIEN. Former President of the Supreme Court (q.v.). Trained in law in Dakar and Paris, Ainandou was a magistrate until appointed Attorney General of Dahomey on February 22, 1968. In 1970, as the senior magistrate in the country, he was promoted to Chief Justice of the Supreme Court (q.v.), replacing Ignatio-Pinto (q.v.) who had just joined the World Court in The Hague. Ainandou currently resides abroad, having been replaced after the 1972 coup (q.v.) by Léandre.

AIR BENIN (TAB). Former State airline (properly known as the Transport Aérien du Benin), with headquarters in Cotonou (q.v.), flying mostly internal routes with two Fokker 27 planes. Set up on July 15, 1978 (with a 10-minute inaugural flight on December 9, 1978, between Porto Novo [q.v.] and Cotonou) with little planning and no feasability studies, the airline was in the red from the outset and was liquidated in the mid-1980's. See also TRANSPORT AERIEN DU BENIN.

AIZO. Possibly the only indigenous coastal ethnic group at the time of the Adja (q.v.) migrations from Adja-Tado (q.v.) that resulted in the rise of the Houéda, Allada, and later the Dahomey and Porto Novo kingdoms (qq.v.). An alternate historical reconstruction has the Aizo as an early Adja branch, also from Adja-Tado. Largely assimilated into the Fon (q.v.) and Adja population, the Aizo currently number around 130,000, scattered in small villages around Ouidah (q.v.). Frequently counted with the Aizo are the closely related Houéda (q.v.) (known also as Pédah, 15,000) many of whom are fishermen along Lake Ahémé.

AJASE see AJASE IPO

AJASE IPO. Name of territory with Ajasé as its capital that became in the nineteenth century the Kingdom of Porto

Novo (q.v.). Settled in 1730 by refugees from the Allada Kingdom (q.v.) after its conquest by Dahomey (q.v.), and under the direct protection of the Oyo Empire (q.v.) of which Ajasé Ipo was a tributary. The population continued to refer to Ajasé as Allada, and European traders consequently referred to it as Ardra (q.v.), even though the real Allada/ Ardra was 32 kilometers to the east. Historical records refer to Great Ardra (the inland Ajasé capital) as opposed to Little Ardra, the port of the kingdom, i.e., Porto Novo. See also PORTO NOVO.

AJIKI, KING, ? –1913. Brother of King Toffa (q.v.) and successor to the Porto Novo (q.v.) throne upon the latter's death in 1908. Ajiki was named to the by then largely symbolic throne in fulfillment of French promises to King Toffa— their ally in the conquest of Dahomey—to name a successor from his lineage. In accord with the rotational principle in effect in Porto Novo, Sohingbé Mékpon (q.v.), who twice lodged claims, had a greater right to the throne. After Ajiki's death, no new kings were enthroned, though members of the royal lineage were elevated to cantonal posts.

AKADIRI, SALIOU, 1950– . Diplomat. Born in Pobé in 1950, and a Yoruba (q.v.), after studies in Porto Novo (q.v.) (1957–1972) he completed higher studies in law (1972– 1976) at the National University of Benin (q.v.). After specialized diplomatic training in Cotonou (q.v.) he assumed his first appointment as Head of the African and European Division in the Foreign Ministry (1976–1984). In Paris during 1984–1985 for further training, he returned to his old post until 1987, when he became First Counsellor at the Benin Embassy to France. Since August 1990 he has been the Embassy's Chargé d'Affaires.

AKAN, FELIX. Chief Pharmacist. Trained abroad in pharmacology, on his return Akan was appointed Director of Supply and Purchases in the Ministry of Public Health (1966–1968) and in 1968 became Director of the Office National de la Pharmacie (q.v.).

AKINDELE, ADOLPHE, 1902– . Physician, historian, trade union leader and early political militant. Born in Porto Novo (q.v.) on July 29, 1902, of Goun and Yoruba (qq.v.) parents, Akindélé obtained his medical degree in Dakar, following which he served for 28 years in various postings in Dahomey. He was co-founder of a trade union of doctors, pharmacists, veterinarians and mid-wives, and was its Dahomean Secretary-General. Between 1945 and 1965 Akindélé was active in a variety of political parties headed by either Justin Ahomadégbé or Sourou-Migan Apithy (qq.v.). He was also active in Porto Novo municipal affairs, serving as municipal councillor between 1956–1962. Author of a variety of scholarly publications on Dahomey's history—some in collaboration with Cyrille Aguéssy (q.v.)—in 1954 Akindélé received the first Literary Prize of French West Africa. He has been in retirement since 1962.

AKINDES, ALBERT, 1912–1969. Schoolteacher, early politician and trade union (q.v.) leader. Born in Allada (q.v.) in 1912 and educated locally and at Dakar's Ecole William Ponty (q.v.), Akindès taught in various schools in Cotonou and Porto Novo (qq.v.). Deeply involved in unionist activities, he served between 1946 and 1959 as Secretary-General of the Union Nationale des Syndicats des Travailleurs du Dahomey (q.v.) and the Dahomean Teachers Union. A member of Dahomey's first (1946–1952) Conseil Général (q.v.), Akindès was an active member of several political groupings, including the Union Progréssiste Dahoméenne, the Parti Démocratique Dahoméen and Justin Ahomadégbé's Union Démocratique Dahoméenne (qq.v.), of which he was Social Affairs Secretary. In 1960 Akindès was briefly Cabinet Director to the Secretary of State in charge of information, following which he retired to direct a private school until his death in 1969.

AKINDES, KOCU CLOVIS, 1920– . Physician. Born in Allada (q.v.) in 1920, and a graduate of the Dakar School of Medicine, Akindès served with the clinic in Djougou and as Medical Inspector in Ouidah (q.v.). Attached to the Ministry of Public Health in Cotonou (q.v.), he has also been Head Physician of Epidemiology and Malaria, Head Physician of the Cové district, later also of Aplahoué, and Secretary-General of the Benin Red Cross.

AKO. Clan, in southern Benin, comprised of several lineages (*hénnou*) related to each other via a common ancestor, the head of which is the *akohosou* (king; chief), whose authority is also religious.

AKOHOSOU see AKO.

AKOHOUENDO, JEAN J., 1943– . Educator. Born on February 16, 1943, and educated in geography at the University of Dakar, Akohouéndo currently teaches at the University of Kisangeni in Zaire.

AKONDE, CHARLES. Head Veterinarian. Educated in Dakar and Paris, Akondé served as Deputy Director of Stockbreeding between 1960 and 1966, before being appointed to his current position. From 1966 to 1973 he was simultaneously also Director of Stockbreeding. He is based in the Ministry of Rural Development in Cotonou.

AKO SEWA, EMMANUEL, 1935– . Civil servant and administrator. Born in 1935 and educated in geography abroad, Ako Sewa served briefly as a lecturer and researcher with the Ministry of Higher Education before assuming the post of Director-General of the Ministry of Youth, Popular Culture and Sports. He has written extensively on issues relating to youth, and has served as a UNESCO and Economic Commission for Africa consultant on several occasions.

AKPLOGAN. Title, in most Adja (q.v.) kingdoms, of the official in charge of religious cults and for the veneration of the ancestors and the royal tombs. In Allada (q.v.), for example, the *Akplogan* was responsible for ceremonies honoring the kingdom's founders, religious rites, and all cults within the kingdom.

AKPO, PHILIPPE (Captain). Former Minister and key Kérékou (q.v.) supporter. Originally brought into Kérékou's cabinet as Minister of Rural Development, Akpo served later as President of SOBEPALH before returning to the cabinet in April 1982 as Minister of Public Health. In the August 1984 cabinet shuffle he was reassigned to head the Minister of Nursery and Primary Education. His value to Kérékou was that he was a southerner, President of the Ligue (q.v.), cousin of National Assembly Head Ignace Adjo Bocco (qq.v.), and one of the officers in the Ouidah (q.v.) battalion that prevented the latter from moving against Kérékou in the 1975 coup d'etat attempt (q.v.).

AKUESSON, MARIUS, 1922– . Former Treasurer-General of Benin. Born in Porto Novo (q.v.) on September 3, 1922, and trained as an accountant, Akuésson served in the French administration in a variety of top positions including as Treasurer of the AOF (q.v.) federation. Since independence he has been Inspector of Treasury Services (1961–1963) and Treasurer of Benin (1964–1968). Currently in retirement, Akuésson lives abroad.

ALADJI, BONI, 1926– . Important early party leader. Born in Nikki (q.v.) in 1926, and a teacher by training, Aladji was an early Maga (q.v.) supporter and party broker from the Borgou (q.v.). He was elected to the National Assembly (q.v.) as an Independent on March 31, 1957, and served as a PPD, later RDD/PDU (qq.v.), Deputy in subsequent elections. Chabi Mama's (q.v.) prime lieutenant, Aladji was a major power wielder in the party. He sat in the Assembly through 1964, concurrently PDU Parliamentary Party Secretary (1960–1963) as well as Chairman of the Assembly Public Works Committee. Shut out from political office after the 1965 coup d'etat (q.v.), Aladji has been out of political life on the national level.

ALAPINI, JULIEN LAURIANO, 1906–1967. Educator and novelist. Born in Abomey-Calavi near Cotonou (qq.v.) on August 28, 1906, and a schoolteacher by profession, Alapini studied in Ouidah (q.v.) and at the Ecole William Ponty (q.v.) in Senegal (1926–1929). Back in Dahomey he worked as a teacher, school principal (1929–1960), and later as Inspector of Primary Education. In the 1950 he attained major success as a novelist. Among his publications are seven novels and several other literary contributions. Between 1962 and 1964 he served as Dahomey's Minister of Education. Shortly before his death he was Inspector of Primary Education of Ouidah.

ALAPINI, PASCAL EMMANUEL, 1919– . Veterinarian and administrator. Born in Ouidah (q.v.) on March 15, 1919, and a veterinarian physician by training, Alapini returned to Dahomey to be appointed director of Stockbreeding Services. An early political actor, he became involved in the electoral committees emerging after the end of the Second World War, and in 1946 was elected Municipal Councillor of Cotonou (q.v.), remaining in office for several terms through 1953. An active trade union member and organizer, he also served as Treasurer of the UGTD (q.v.) between 1961 and 1968. He was also for one year the head of the cabinet of Bertin Borna (q.v.), but did not find administrative life at cabinet level attractive. Alapini is currently in retirement.

ALBY, MAXIMILIEN GUSTAVE, 1855–1921. Colonial military officer. Born in Marseilles on February 12, 1855, and commissioned in 1874, Alby served in Tunisia, Tahiti, Guinea, and briefly as Consul in Sierra Leone. In October 1894 he arrived in Dahomey and was charged with securing the Bariba (q.v.) areas and attaching them to the French sphere of influence. Later, in 1895, he was dispatched to Sansanné-Mango (currently Togo) and to Mossi regions in the Upper Volta with a similar task. He later left for Madagascar and Indochina, retiring from the French army in 1910.

ALIBORI. A 250-kilometer tributary of the Niger river, originating south of Sinéndi and flowing through very sparsely populated territory to join the Niger river between Malanville and Karimama.

ALIDOU, SALIFOU, 1939– . Geologist. Born in 1939 and obtaining a doctorate in sedimentary geology in France, Alidou teaches at the National University of Benin (q.v.) where he is also Dean of the Faculty of Science and Technology.

ALIHONOU, EUSABE, 1938– . Head of the department of Gyneocology at the National University of Benin (q.v.).

ALIMENTATION GENERALE DU BENIN see SOCIETE D'ALIMENTATION GENERALE DU BENIN

ALLADA. A small town 32 kilometers north of Cotonou (q.v.) on the main road to Abomey (q.v.), Allada (Ardra) was the capital of an important kingdom of the same name in the seventeenth and eighteenth centuries, until conquered by Dahomey in 1724. According to tradition, Allada was founded following the Adja (q.v.) migrations from Tado (q.v.), now in Togo (See ADJAHOUTO), and was—following a succession dispute—the "parent" state of the Dahomey and Porto Novo (qq.v.) dynasties. To this very day annual ceremonies in Allada in honor of its *tovodun* (q.v.) are attended by delegations from the royal families of Porto Novo and Dahomey, symbolizing the common links of the three former kingdoms and the sacred status of Allada, where Agassou's tomb rests.

Itself a tributary state to the mighty Oyo (q.v.) Empire (in Nigeria) since the 1680's, Allada came into contact with Portuguese slave traders at the turn of the century and aspired to become the sole middleman in the slave trade. Straddling the slave routes from the north to the coast, Allada imposed taxes on all slave caravans entering the kingdom and on all ships anchoring in Whydah (Ouidah) (q.v.), the main Atlantic port that Allada intermittently controlled. Allada, however, was neither sufficiently large (permitting caravans to bypass it when taxes became too onerous) nor powerful enough to suppress competitors for its role. It suffered from perennial intrigues by the various foreign powers trading in Whydah and fell to Dahomey's (q.v.) might in March 1724. Following the Dahomean conquest, much of the population relocated to the east, founding Ajasé Ipo (q.v.) that was, in due time, to become the kingdom of Porto Novo (q.v.). (See AJASE IPO.)

The conquest of Allada by Dahomey also set off a long era of hostilities between Allada's "protector," Oyo, and Dahomey. Despite this intense pressure, Dahomey's conquest of the coastal areas opened up the kingdom to outside contacts and influences and made it a prime power in the region. In the 1960's Allada has been the political fiefdom of Valentin Djibodé Aplogan (q.v.). The region has two important markets, at Avékpa (12 kilometers away) and at Dessa, 11 kilometers away, which has a spectacular night market. See also DAHOMEY, KINGDOM OF; OUIDAH; SLAVE TRADE.

ALLADA, KINGS OF. As with all king-lists there is some controversy about sequence and dates of reign; in the case of Allada, only a few dates are either non-controversial or fixed.

1. Adjahouto
2. Megnoron-Mayroyovo
3. Latamakanfinkpon
4. Houezé
5. Dé Kokpon (d. 1610)
6. Avéssou Dangawa
7. Kpokponou-Danvomadjé
8. Hounou Gouingoin
9. Gbaggoué
10. Atchadé (d. 1724)

ALLADAYE, MICHEL (Colonel), 1940– . Former Minister. Born in Abomey (q.v.) in 1940, and educated locally at the Lycée Victor Ballot and in Strasbourg, France, Alladayé studied at the Military Academy of St. Cyr (1960–1962), joining the Dahomean army in 1963 as Lieutenant and Commander of the First Engineering Company, headquartered in Kandi (q.v.) in the north. He was promoted to Captain in 1967 and received further training in Versailles at the Field Engineers School. Returning to Benin in 1969 he was attached to the Chief of Staff as Logistics Advisor. His absence abroad shielded him from the factional infighting in the military forces, and he was part of the core troika to engineer the 1972 coup d'etat (q.v.) that ushered in the Kérékou (q.v.) regime.

Supposedly the original choice for the Presidency, Alladayé was outmaneuvered by Kérékou and took over, instead, as Minister of Foreign Affairs, while also promoted in the army to Head of the Field Engineers Corps. A pragmatic technocrat and ideologically very centrist, Alladayé clashed several times in the cabinet with captain Azonhiho (q.v.), the abrasive and ideologically militant Minister of Propaganda who wished to politicize the army. On at least two occasions these conflicts resulted in fist-fights. Even though Azonhiho was regarded at the time as indispensable, Kérékou retained Alladayé in the cabinet as a counterweight to the radical faction, and also because Alladayé was the most senior of the Fon (q.v.) officers in a regime dominated by northerners. A close friend of Aikpé (q.v.), Alladayé nevertheless accepted the latter's liquidation when he became too big a threat to Kérékou.

Promoted to Major, and then to Lt. Colonel, Alladayé was shifted again, this time to occupy the second-ranking post in the regime, the Ministry of Interior and Security where he was in charge of the Police and Security Forces. He was downgraded in August 1984 to the post of Minister of Middle and Higher Education. In June 1985, after the massive disturbances in the educational establishment, Alladayé was dropped from the cabinet and purged of all his party and National Assembly (q.v.) posts, because the student grievances were seen as stemming from errors of judgment on his part.

ALLAGBADA, NOEL. Journalist and, between 1982 and 1988, Director of Propaganda and Information in the Ministry of Information.

ALLEY, ALPHONSE (Colonel), 1930– . Former Chief of Staff of the Dahomean armed forces (q.v.) and briefly Head of State. Born on April 9, 1930, in Bassila (in central Dahomey near the Togolese border), Alley followed in the footsteps of his father, who fought with the French forces in Syria (1942) and helped train Togo's police force. Alley attended schools in Togo, Ivory Coast and Senegal until 1950. Enlisting in the French Army he saw action in Indochina (1950–1953), being pulled out just prior to the Dien Bien Phu debacle. He next attended Saint Maxient Officers School in France and fought in Morocco (1955–1956) and Algeria (1959–1961), where he obtained his paratrooper insignia. When Dahomey became independent, he was transferred home, with the rank of Lieutenant, and built up the paratroop-commando unit in Ouidah (q.v.). He was promoted to Captain in 1962 and to Major in 1964. In that year he commanded a detachment of troops on the border during the Dahomey-Niger border dispute (q.v.). Both in 1963 and in 1965 Alley was instrumental in nudging his superior, General Christophe Soglo (q.v.), to intervene in the turbulent political arena. See COUP OF 1963; COUP OF 1965(a). After the latter seized power in 1965 and set up his administration, Alley became Chief of Staff of the Army, being promoted to Lieutenant Colonel following senior staff courses in France.

Known to disagree with several of Soglo's policies, Alley nevertheless remained loyal to the military Head of State. For this reason the coup of 1967 (q.v.) was planned behind his back by his own adjutant, Major Maurice Kouandété (q.v.). Following the coup that toppled Soglo, Alley was for two days under house detention until it was obvious to the putschists that they would have to bring him in to head the new interim military regime. Popular among southerners as well as northerners in the army officer corps, Alley was also trusted by the southern populations, though a northerner himself. His interim administration brought about the appointment of Emile Derlin Zinsou (q.v.) as President in 1968. Shortly prior to this Alley engaged in a series of maneuvers to purge his rival, Kouandété. For these he was removed from operational command of the armed forces and ordered to take up duties as military attaché in the U.S. When he refused to leave the country Alley was summarily retired from the army, with Kouandété becoming Chief of Staff.

In 1969 Alley was placed on trial for his life, following a convoluted plot against Kouandété. He was sentenced to ten years of hard labor, a sentence regarded so lenient by his antagonist that it drove a wedge between Kouandété and President Zinsou, who had intervened on Alley's behalf. In the wake of the subsequent 1969 coup d'etat (q.v.) by Col. Kouandété, Alley was released from prison, reinstated in the army with his full rank and appointed Secretary-General of National Defense. Kouandété, who had seriously overestimated his own control of the officer corps, was appointed deputy to Alley.

A jovial, dashing, easygoing and well-liked figure in Cotonou (q.v.) circles, Alley was frequently referred to in diplomatic circles as the "wine, women and song" officer. He once again courted official displeasure in 1971 by unilaterally going against government policy in granting Togolese political refugee Noé Kutuklui (q.v.) his personal protection and a military escort out of the country. In 1972, following the coup of Major Mathieu Kérékou (q.v.), Alley's hectic military career came to an end as the new regime disencumbered itself of all its senior officers. Alley was appointed government commissioner of the National Oil Mills (SNADAH [q.v.]), a sinecure position. On February 28, 1973, he was arrested and imprisoned for 20 years for plotting against the military regime. During the fierce riots following the liquidation of Aikpé (q.v.) in 1975, Alley was liberated from his cell by supporters and spirited away to refuge in France. He was formally amnestied in August 1984 and returned home after the fall of Kérékou.

ALLIANCE DEMOCRATIQUE DAHOMEENNE (ADD). Political party set up by Justin Ahomadégbé (q.v.) on December 10, 1965, as successor to the Union Démocratique Dahoméenne (q.v.) in existence between 1955 and 1961, and the Parti Démocratique Dahoméen (q.v.), which was a merger between Ahomadégbé's UDD and the Yoruba (q.v.)-based following of Sourou-Migan Apithy (q.v.). The ADD was established after Gen. Christophe Soglo's November 29, 1965, coup (qq.v.) and the appointment of Speaker of the House Tahirou Congacou (q.v.) as Interim President. When Soglo dismissed the latter and established his military administration (December 22, 1965) all political parties including the ADD were banned. See also COUP OF 1965(b); POLITICAL PARTIES.

ALLIANCE DEMOCRATIQUE POUR LE PROGRES (ADP). New political party set up in 1990 and headed by Gedeon Dassoundo (q.v.), urging voters to reject the proposed constitution in that year's referendum (qq.v.).

ALMEIDA, BENJAMIN D' 1928– . Lawyer. Born in Grand Popo (q.v.) on November 28, 1928, and educated in Senegal's Lycée Faidherbe (1942–1949), and Law School (1949–1950), and at the University of Paris (1950–1955), d'Almeida served as a barrister in Paris and Dakar between 1955 and 1959 before returning to practice law in Cotonou (q.v.). Coming from an extremely prominent "Brazilian" (q.v.) family with extensive enterprises in Benin and Togo, d'Almeida had connections with Emile Derlin Zinsou (q.v.) and was brought into the latter's government in 1968–1969 as Minister of Public Health. Earlier he was elected as UDD, and subsequently PDD, deputy to the National Assembly (qq.v.). He ran on the latter's ticket for a seat in the National Assembly in 1970, but lost. He currently continues his law practice in Cotonou.

ALMEIDA, JOAQUIM D'. Co-founder in 1823 of the originally Brazilian (q.v.) coastal community of Agoué (q.v.), and for long its prime leader. D'Almeida was also known as Zoki Azatou.

ALMEIDA, LESLIE EDOUARD D', 1933– . Deputy Dean of the Faculty of Letters at the National University of Benin (q.v.). Born on March 23, 1933, d'Almeida obtained his degrees in history from the University of Paris, studying Adja (q.v.) political structures.

ALOHENTO GBEFA TOFA, 1882–1976. King of Porto Novo (q.v.).

ALOTOUNOU, JEAN. Director of the Treasury and Public Accounts since 1980.

AMAH, EMMANUEL. Civil administrator and former Secretary-General of the Department of Economics and Finance. Trained as a civil administrator, Amah has been Director of the Civil Service (1963–1966) and Director of the Cabinet of the Minister of Finance (1966–1968), becoming Secretary-General of the Ministry in September 1968. In 1972 he was shifted to head another department in the Ministry, and he left for Paris in 1975, where he currently resides.

AMAZONS. Elite fighting force of women in the precolonial Dahomean army. Many recruited from the wives of the king, and personally loyal to him, by the 1880's the Amazons constituted a significant portion of Dahomey's army. Fully institutionalized by King Ghézo (q.v.), the Amazons fought their first major campaigns in the wars against the Nigerian Egba in the 1840's. The force was virtually annihilated in the Franco-Dahomean Wars (q.v.) 40 years later.

AMICALE DES BENINOIS EN FRANCE (AMIBEF). Conservative mutual-aid and opposition movement, mostly Fon (q.v.), based in France, composed of elements who fled Benin after the 1972 coup (q.v.), and especially after the declaration for Marxism. Among their leaders where Adolphe Memeveyrin, Lazare Déh, Couvi Sagbo and Yves Agbogbé. The movement has lost its political momentum and many members since the political normalization in Benin in 1990.

AMLON, LEANDRE. President of the Cour Populaire Suprême. A former Apithy (q.v.) supporter, Amlon was the magistrate who replaced Cyprien Ainandou (q.v.) at the head of the Supreme Court (q.v.) after the 1972 coup d'etat (q.v.).

AMOUSSOU, ALEXIS, 1919– . Neuropsychiatrist. Born in Grand Popo (q.v.) on November 20, 1919, a physician with specialization in both neuropsychiatry and in tropical medicine, Amoussou has been mostly in private practice. In 1968 he briefly accepted the post of Minister of Public Health in Zinsou's (q.v.) cabinet but reverted to private practice in 1969. He is currently in retirement.

AMOUSSOU, BRUNO, 1937– . Banker, administrator and political leader. Born in Aplahoué on July 2, 1937, and trained as an agronomist and civil engineer, after a brief period in the Department of Rural Development, Amoussou switched careers and has since been involved almost exclusively as an administrator. He was successively Division Head at the Banque Dahoméene du Développement, President of the Société Dahoméenne de Banque, Director of the Société Nationale des Huileries du Dahomey, Director General of the Société Nationale pour le Développement Rural du Dahomey, Director of the Société de Commércialisation et de Crédit Agricole Dahoméenne, and member of the Conseil Economique et Social (qq.v.). He was arrested and imprisoned by the Kérékou (q.v.) regime between 1984–1985. In 1991 he presented himself as a candidate in the Presidential elections but received a small minority of the vote. As the leader of the Parti Sociale-Democrate (q.v.) he was elected to the National Assembly (q.v.), however, where he currently serves.

AMOUSSOU, ISIDORE (Lt. Colonel). Former Minister of Finance. Formerly the Quartermaster General of the Benin army of Mina ethnicity, Amoussou headed a commission investigating the triumvirate's (q.v.) alleged fiscal irregularities following the 1972 coup d'etat (q.v.). A dogmatic technocrat, he joined the cabinet in October 1974 as Minister of Finance. He was replaced in August 1984 by Hospice Antonio (q.v.) after a groundswell of complaints about the incompetence reigning in the Ministry, and his growing personal fortune, including houses in France.

AMOUSSOU GUENOU, THEOPHILE. Former Prefect and civil administrator. Trained for an administrative career, Amoussou Guénou served as Prefect of Atakora (q.v.) between 1963–1967, Administrative Head Inspector (1967–1968) and then Prefect of Mono (q.v.) (1968–1972). In 1972 he was attached to the Ministry of Interior as head of one of its divisions, and has recently gone into retirement.

ANAGON, BARTHELEMY. Head of the Union Général pour le Développement d'Ouidah (UGDO), a cultural association set up in 1984 to stress Ouidah's (q.v.) interests.

ANDRE, ANTOINE GERVAIS, 1935– . Educator and former diplomat. Born in Grand Popo (q.v.) on June 20, 1935, André was educated at Catholic schools in Grand Popo and Cotonou (q.v.), and in 1952 attended the Lycée Victor Ballot in Porto Novo (q.v.). He then proceeded to the University of Dakar, where he obtained a License in English, and to Princeton University where he studied at its Woodrow Wilson School of International and Public Affairs, simultaneously serving as Counsellor at the Benin Embassy to the U.S. (1964–1967). He was then appointed Head of the Department of Economic Relations (1967–1970) and later of Consular Affairs (1970–1972) in the Ministry of Foreign Affairs. Between 1972 and 1975 he served as Principal Secretary to the Minister of Foreign Affairs, leaving the Ministry in 1975 to teach at the Lycée Béhanzin in Porto Novo.

ANIMISM. Animist beliefs are deeply ingrained in Beninois society, both in the northern, more Muslim provinces and in the southern, more Christianized ones. Statistically the majority of the population subscribes to animist cults, the specific deities venerated varying from region to region. The southern Benin pantheon includes 5–6,000 divinities (fetishes in the West), referred to as *Vodun* (q.v.) among the Fon (q.v.), *Orisha* cults among the Yoruba (q.v.), *Tron* among the Mina (q.v.) and other coastal groups along the border with Togo.

ANNUAL CUSTOMS. A series of elaborate and deeply significant religious ceremonies at the center of ritual life of the precolonial kingdom of Dahomey (q.v.). First probably instituted on a regular basis during King Agaja's (q.v.) reign, and grossly misunderstood abroad at the time, the annual customs symbolized a renewal of ties between the monarch and his subjects through the presence of chiefs from all the provinces, and the links between the past and present generations for which the king of Dahomey was responsible. Towards that end ritual human sacrifices were offered, the necessity for which impelled Dahomey into ceaseless slave-hunting wars with its neighbors. The veneration of deceased chiefs and human sacrifices were not a uniquely Dahomean custom; a cult of the royal dead existed in both Houéda and Allada (qq.v.), as did human sacrifices at royal funerals. In Dahomey, however, the magnitude of these was much greater, and they became an annual practice, symbolizing also the dynastic continuity, veneration of former kings, and Dahomean prowess.

ANTI-CORRUPTION TRIBUNAL. An all-military investigatory organ set up following the 1967 coup (q.v.) that toppled the regime of General Soglo (q.v.). Originally proposed and chaired by major Louis Chasme (q.v.), then also Minister of Justice, the tribunal was disbanded in April 1968. Created in order to investigate charges of corruption against the mostly-civilian Soglo administration, the tribunal foundered when it was discovered that many military officers were guilty of similar offenses. Indeed, its only victim was Major Chasme himself, later tried for embezzlement.

ANTONIO, HOSPICE. Former Minister of Finance and the Economy. A former professor of political economy at the National University of Benin (q.v.), Antonio joined the cabinet in August 1984 to replace the dogmatic Lt. Colonel Isidore Amoussou (q.v.). A technocrat, whose views were not taken seriously, and who was often bypassed by the military ministers, Antonio was dropped from the cabinet in 1987.

ANUBOMEY see ANNUAL CUSTOMS.

APITHY, CLAUDE-APOLLINAIRE, 1913– . Former Deputy-Chief of Posts. Born in Porto Novo (q.v.) on June 14, 1914, and educated locally and at the Limoges School of Postal Workers in France, Apithy served for long as Deputy-Chief of Posts. In 1958 he was integrated as head of the cabinet staff of Sourou-Migan Apithy (q.v.), but was dropped in 1963 with the eclipse of his mentor. Continuing in the postal service, he retired in 1974.

APITHY, FELIX MEDARD, 1948– . Entrepreneur. Born on June 8, 1948, in Porto Novo (q.v.), and educated in history at the University of Paris, where he obtained a Ph.D., Apithy is currently in private trade in Porto Novo.

APITHY, SOUROU-MIGAN, 1913–1989. Former President of Benin and for long political leader of the country's Goun and Yoruba (qq.v.). A major figure in his country's politics for over a quarter of a century, Apithy was born in Porto Novo (q.v.) on April 8, 1913, of modest origins, though linked to a formerly important Goun clan. He was educated in mission schools, acquiring a pro-Catholic bias for which he was later criticized. He also studied in Bordeaux and Paris, obtaining a diploma in accounting. In France between 1933 and 1945 (returning home only once in 1939), he was pushed into national prominence by the popular Catholic priest Francis Aupiais (q.v.) when the two were elected Deputies from Dahomey to the French Constituent Assembly (1945–1946). In 1946 he joined the interterritorial Rassemblement Démocratique Africain (q.v.), but left the formation under local Catholic pressure to join the Indépendants d'Outre-Mer (q.v.), of which he later became President. Apithy remained a Deputy to the National Assembly (q.v.) (1946–1958), becoming also Councillor to the AOF Grand Council (1947–1957), member of the French delegation to the United Nations (1953), deputy in Dahomey's Conséil Général and Assemblée Territoriale (qq.v.) (1946–1960), and the latter's President in 1956–1957.

A founding member of Dahomey's first political party, the Union Progréssiste Dahoméenne (q.v.), Apithy set up his own regional party in 1951. The party, the Parti Républicain Dahoméen (q.v.), underwent various changes of names (see POLITICAL PARTIES) and alliances. A consummate political opportunist, Apithy switched his political allegiances from one to another of various French and African interterritorial groupings. In 1959 he split his own party, renouncing solemn pledges, when he abruptly changed positions on the scheduled Mali Federation (q.v.).

Elected mayor of Porto Novo (1956), Apithy became Prime Minister of Dahomey's Provisional Government in 1958–1959. The upsurge of Fon (q.v.) support for his southern rival, Justin Ahomadégbé (q.v.), and revelations of the scandals of the notoriously corruption-ridden Apithy administration, forced him to cede the Premiership to Hubert Maga (q.v.), the northern leader. Nearly losing control over his party—elements in which were calling for his demise— Apithy became Minister of Finance in Maga's 1960 cabinet. Only Ahomadégbé's unsuccessful power gambit of 1960 raised the value to Maga of cooperation with Apithy. Their two parties soon after merged (forming the Parti Dahoméen de l'Unité [q.v.]), changed the electoral rules and, after winning control of the National Assembly, banned the UDD (q.v.) opposition of Justin Ahomadégbé. In the next government, Maga became President and Apithy, Vice President. Apithy was soon personally squeezed out of Dahomean politics and, while still officially Vice President, left the country early in 1963 to become Ambassador to France, Great Britain and Switzerland.

Following Maga's overthrow in 1963, Apithy returned to Dahomey and became President and Head of State, with his former rival Ahomadégbé as Vice President and executive Head of Government. The alliance lasted until 1965 when feuding between the two sparked off a governmental deadlock and a coup d'etat (q.v.). See COUP OF 1965(a); SUPREME COURT AFFAIR. Banned from the country during the regimes of General Christophe Soglo and Emile Derlin Zinsou (q.v.), Apithy returned in 1970 to contest the military-sponsored Presidential elections of that year. He ran a poor third after Maga and Ahomadégbé. The elections were annulled by the army and in the ensuing tumultuous situation in which civil war threatened to break out, Apithy encouraged calls for the secession of Porto Novo to Nigeria and backed another military takeover. In May 1970 he joined the other two members of the triumvirate (q.v.) in forming the Presidential Council (q.v.).

Since his own chairmanship of the Council was scheduled for 1974–1976, Apithy had no chance to exercise power prior to the coup d'etat of 1972 (q.v.). Placed under house arrest following the coup—as were the other members of the triumvirate—Apithy, now in poor health, was released only in 1981 when he went to Paris to write his memoirs. He was to witness the beginning of the end of the Kérékou (q.v.) regime, assisting in setting up a new Yoruba/Nago party, but died on November 12, 1989, before the full transition to civilian rule. The Kérékou regime decreed a four-day period of mourning on his passing away.

APLOGAN see AKPLOGAN

APLOGAN, DOMINIQUE, 1913–1970. Former Minister in several governments. Born in Abomey (q.v.) on April 25, 1913, to an influential chiefly family, Aplogan received medical training but entered politics after independence. Deputy to the National Assembly (q.v.) between 1959 and 1960, he joined the Maga (q.v.) government in February 1962 as Secretary of State in charge of Afro-Malagasy Affairs, later as Minister of Communications. Shut out of politics for the duration of the next government, he joined the Soglo (q.v.) military administration as Minister of State in charge of Defense (for two months) and as Minister of Communications, serving until the December 1967 collapse of Soglo. He died shortly thereafter.

APLOGAN-DJIBODE, FRANCOIS, 1917–1983. Former Minister of Finance. Born in Allada (q.v.) on October 4, 1917, of chiefly lineage, Aplogan-Djibodé was trained as a civil servant and served in a variety of low-level administrative posts until the Africanization of the administration, when he was sent to France for specialized training. He then filled in rapid succession the posts of Director of Finance (1957–1958), Secretary of State (and then Minister) of Finance (1959–1960), Commissioner General of the Plan (1961–1963), Minister of the Plan (1964–1965) and Minister of Finance and Economics (1965). Locked out of office by the 1965 coup (q.v.) Aplogan-Djibodé went to France in 1967, where he served as a public administrator until his death in Paris in April 1983.

APLOGAN-DJIBODE, VALENTIN, 1916–1976. Former President of the Supreme Court and of the National Assembly (q.v.), union leader and power-wielder in the Allada (q.v.)

region. Born to an influential chiefly family in Allada on February 14, 1916, Aplogan studied in Porto Novo (q.v.) and worked as a teacher in Cotonou (q.v.) for several years. During the Second World War he was appointed chief of a canton with the strong backing of the French administration. After the war Aplogan began playing a major political role in Dahomey. Always highly independent and opportunistic, Aplogan usually allied himself with Sourou-Migan Apithy (q.v.), but did not hesitate to change allegiances when it suited his interests. In 1951 he ran on the Bloc Populaire Africain (q.v.) ticket of Justin Ahomadégbé and Emile Poisson (qq.v.), deserting it in 1952 to rejoin Apithy. He served as deputy to the French National Assembly, the AOF Grand Council in Dakar, and Dahomey's Assemblée Territoriale (q.v.). He was Secretary-General of Apithy's Parti Républicain Dahoméen (PRO) (q.v.) until expelled from the party in February 1958 for supporting unionist strikes in the south. A year later he reentered the PRD on the condition that Apithy be barred from the leadership, which indeed temporarily occurred.

Commanding strong traditional support in Allada, Aplogan was elected to independent Dahomey's Assemblée Nationale (q.v.), becoming its President in 1960. He retained this position throughout the national Presidency of Hubert Maga (q.v.) (1960–1963). In June 1964 Aplogan was appointed President of the Supreme Court. As the crisis built up at the helm of the nation with the feuding between Apithy and Ahomadégbé (see COUP OF 1965(a)) Aplogan sided with Apithy and helped spread anti-government tracts in the urban areas. In June 1965 he was arrested for two plots against the regime and for setting up an opposition party in Allada, the Rassemblement de l'Impératif National (q.v.). Politically eclipsed in the years following the 1965 coup d'etat (q.v.), Aplogan was defeated in the 1970 elections to the consultative assembly set up by the Presidential Council (q.v.).

ARABA, FELIX GODONOU, 1910–1977. Civil administrator. Born in Porto Novo (q.v.) on February 18, 1910, Araba was Deputy-Chief of Government Receipts between 1938 and

1960, and head accountant for the Banque Commerciale Africaine in Cotonou (q.v.) between 1929 and 1933. Consultant to the UTD-UGTN trade movement, Araba has also been a guiding spirit of the ethnic association Ainoniv in Porto Novo, especially during the years between 1953 and 1958. He was brought into Sourou-Migan Apithy's (q.v.) internal cabinet (while the latter was Minister of Finance) and served as the latter's Cabinet Director between 1960 and 1961, later being attached in a similar capacity in Alexandre Adandé's (q.v.) cabinet (1961–1963). After 1963, Araba was shifted to administrative duties within the Ministry of Finance.

ARCHIVES NATIONALES. Benin's national archives, reorganized in 1976 in Porto Novo (q.v.) and under the administrative responsibility of D. K. M. Videgla. The archives include colonial, pre-colonial and post-colonial documentation, including the governmental gazette, some in acute state of decomposition, and some 50 periodicals. The archives are open mornings only.

ARDRA. Name by which the kingdom and town of Allada (q.v.) were sometimes referred to by the early slave traders and merchants. See ALLADA. A measure of confusion developed in the eighteenth century with the Dahomean conquest of Allada (1727) and the relocation of much of the latter's population to the east. The new kingdom that was to develop there, Ajasé Ipo (q.v.), with its capital in Ajasé, continued to be referred to by the population as Allada. European traders likewise referred to it as Ardra (q.v.), with a distinction developing between ''Great Ardra'' the capital, and ''Little Ardra'' its port—the future Porto Novo (q.v.).

ARMED FORCES see FORCES ARMEES DU BENIN

AROUNA, MAMA, 1925– . Former Minister of Interior and Defense. Born in 1925 in Parakou (q.v.) to an influential family, Arouna was, in Hubert Maga's (q.v.) first presidency, part of a conservative faction including also Assogba Oké and Chabi Mama (qq.v.). Arouna was frequently at odds with the latter, Hubert Maga's right-hand man and heir-apparent.

Arouna first entered the Assemblée Territoriale (q.v.) in 1957, becoming its Second Vice President in 1959. Earlier, in 1956, his traditional credentials gained him the mayoralty of Parakou, always his fief. Between May 1957 and April 1959 he served as Deputy to the AOF Council in Dakar and, in 1959, was elected Senator to the Communauté Française (q.v.). A powerful member of Maga's northern political party, the Rassemblement Démocratique Dahoméen (q.v.), Arouna was appointed Minister of Interior in May 1959 and Minister of Interior and Defense in 1962. He occupied that position until Maga's overthrow in 1963. Known for his strong anti-southern views, early in 1964 Arouna fomented pro-Maga disturbances and riots in Parakou, where he has a strong following, for which he was imprisoned by Gen. Christophe Soglo (q.v.). He was at the same time accused of embezzlement of funds while in office. In eclipse since then, together with many of Maga's lieutenants, he was forced to work as an educational inspector. Arouna promptly bounded back to his old post of Minister of Interior and Defense with the establishment in 1970 of the Presidential Council (q.v.) under Maga's chairmanship (1970–1972). After the 1972 coup d'etat (q.v.) he was again imprisoned and found guilty of embezzlement while in office. He was only released on December 31, 1973, after returning 6.6 million CFA francs.

ARRONDISSEMENT. The basic administrative unit in French Africa. See also ADMINISTRATIVE ORGANIZATION; DEPARTEMENT.

ASSANE, ALI. Former Second Vice President of the National Assembly (q.v.).

ASSEMBLEE CONSULTATIVE NATIONALE. Consultative Assembly specified by the 1970 Constitution (q.v.). Finally erected in July 1972 (a few months before the 1972 coup) with 36 members (as opposed to the 30 specified) divided into three sections dealing with social, economic, and general policy issues and under the presidency of Paul Darboux (q.v.). Both the delay in setting up the organ and its enlarged membership were a result of intensive horse-trading between the partners in the Presidential Council (q.v.) and pressures from their political lieutenants for a position in the Assembly. The Assembly was replaced after the October 1972 coup (q.v.) by a Comité National Consultatif (q.v.) with similar functions though different membership.

ASSEMBLEE LEGISLATIVE DU DAHOMEY. Interim legislative organ of Dahomey from 1959 to 1961. Known previously as the Assemblée Territoriale (q.v.), the renamed assembly transformed itself in February 1959 into a constituent assembly—Assemblée Nationale Constituante (q.v.)—in order to approve the February 15, 1959, Constitution (q.v.), and was renamed in 1961 the Assemblée Nationale (q.v.). Most of Dahomey's post-independence political leadership was represented in the Assemblée Legislative.

ASSEMBLEE NATIONALE. Name of the post-1990 multi-party assembly of Benin. The Assembly, composed of a drastically reduced number of delegates (64), has a number of powers that act as a check upon possible executive abuses. Legislative elections (q.v.) were held on February 17, 1991 with a turnout from a low of 40.6 percent in Borgou (q.v.) to 55.1 percent high in Atlantique (q.v.). Only 1,069,367 voters of a total 2,069,343 registered ones voted, or 51.7 percent. The Speaker of the Assembly is Adrien Houngbédji (q.v.), an implaccable foe of President Soglo (q.v.).

ASSEMBLEE NATIONALE CONSTITUANTE. In February 1959 Dahomey's Assemblée Legislative (q.v.) transformed itself into a Constituent Assembly in order to approve the new Constitution (q.v.) of February 19, 1959. The Assembly was later renamed the Assembée Nationale (q.v.).

ASSEMBLEE NATIONALE DU DAHOMEY. Dahomey's post-independence legislative organ of 60 Deputies (in 1964, 42) which in 1961 replaced the Assemblée Legislative (q.v.). In light of the presidential system of government adopted by Dahomey and reflecting the highly splintered balance of power in the country, the National Assembly did not play a major legislative role. It was dissolved on December 22,

1965, following the military takeover of General Christophe Soglo (q.v.). Though several consultative organs were created by subsequent regimes, the next national assembly was set up after the 1972 coup (q.v.).

ASSEMBLEE NATIONALE REVOLUTIONNAIRE (ANR). Benin's revolutionary National Assembly, the first popularly elected body since the 1972 coup d'etat (q.v.). Elected into office on November 1979 from a single PRPB (q.v.) electoral slate, representation was not on the basis of geographical constituencies, but based on corporative principles reflecting social classes and occupations. With its election and the official "merger" of the civilian and military elites, the regime in Cotonou declared itself civilianized and constitutionalized. The ANR formally replaced the CNR (q.v.) that was dissolved. Until June 1984 it had 336 People's Commissioners (Commissaires du Peuple [qv]) comprised of 84 peasants, 33 workers, 25 teachers, 42 workers in public service, 33 members of the armed forces (q.v.), 64 trade unionists (q.v.), 8 members of the capitalist middle class, 6 religious leaders, etc. Its mandate, due to expire in 1983 in accordance with the Constitution (q.v.), was extended by decree through June 30, 1984. The official reason given was the "disruption" of daily life that elections might cause. The Assembly's Vice President was Philippe Adjo (q.v.), the pro-government Secretary-General of the UNSTB (q.v.), who succeeded in keeping more radical factions at bay. In June 1984 the Party Central Committee adopted certain fundamental changes relating to the ANR and somewhat later—in accord with these changes—a smaller (196) ANR was elected for a term of five years. The latter, slightly expanded (206), was reelected in June 1989, but had its term of office disrupted by the collapse of Marxism, single party and military rule in 1990.

ASSEMBLEE TERRITORIALE. Dahomey's consultative territorial assembly between 1952 and 1959, previously known as the Conseil Général (q.v.). The Assembly had 50 delegates, 18 of whom were chosen by the first electoral college, 32 by the second electoral college (see DOUBLE ELECTORAL

COLLEGE). In 1957 the membership of the Assembly was enlarged to 60. Among the Deputies elected to the Territorial Assembly were Dahomey's future political triumvirate (q.v.), as well as politicians such as Michel Ahouanménou, Tahirou Congacou, Emile Derlin Zinsou, Assogba Oké, Paul Hazoumé, French missionary-ethnologist Jacques Bertho, and French administrator-historian Edouard Dunglas (qq.v.). Following the March 1957 elections, several other important personalities entered the assembly: Chabi Mama, Paul Darboux, Valentin Djibodé-Aplogan (qq.v.), et al. In 1959 the assembly changed its name to Assemblée Legislative du Dahomey (q.v.).

ASSEMBLY OF THE PEOPLES OF THE NORTH. A loose temporary grouping of northern Dahomey's political leadership organized in Parakou (q.v.) in April 1970 in support of Hubert Maga's (q.v.) claim to the Presidency following the elections annulled by the Military Directorate (q.v.). Several of the more militant members of the group called for the secession of the north, leading to a frightened exodus of southerners working in the northern regions, and a generalized feeling that the country was falling apart. Following intensive bargaining between Dahomey's regional political triumvirate (q.v.), a Presidential Council (q.v.) formula was agreed upon in which each leader would serve as President for two years. See also PRESIDENTIAL COUNCIL.

ASSIMILATION POLICY. Underlying theoretical tenet of French colonial policy in Africa which presumed a slow cultural assimilation of colonial populations. The status of *assimilé* or *évolué* (qq.v.) was granted to colonial subjects who acquired the accoutrements of French civilization—i.e., language, dress, education, religion, etc.—or who had served with distinction in the French colonial armies or civil service. The status conferred upon them the right to petition for French citizenship, a process so complex that in the entire AOF (q.v.) only 2,000 Africans acquired it (in 1934, only 78 in Dahomey). The advantages of being classified as an *assimilé* or *evolué* and attaining citizenship included voting rights, governance under French civil and penal codes, freedom from the *indigénat* (q.v.) code or *corvée* (q.v.) labor. See also INDIGENAT.

ASIMILE. Colonial subject who had assimilated the basic ingredients of all aspects of French culture and mannerisms (or had served with distinction in the army or civil service) and has consequently been granted French citizenship. See also ASSIMILATION POLICY.

ASSOCIATION DES ANCIENS. Deliberative organ created in October 1964 under the chairmanship of Paul Hazoumé (q.v.) with recommendatory powers. The Association's main function was to give the government the policy recommendations of Dahomey's elder generation of politicians and intellectuals. Though including several of Dahomey's most prominent and respected elder leaders, the splintered nature of Dahomean politics prevented the Association from exerting significant influence. Similar organizations existed prior to independence. Though popularly best known under this name, the official name of this organ was Chambre de Reflexion (q.v.).

ASSOCIATION DES ECRIVAINS ET CRITIQUES LITTERAIRES DU BENIN. Association of Benin's many authors and poets, set up in 1980 to compensate in part for the absence of either literary reviews, literary circles or, since the 1972 Revolution, even a literary page in the daily newspaper, Ehuzu (q.v.).

ASSOCIATION DES SYNDICATS DU BENIN (ASYNB). Interunion union syndicate headquartered in Cotonou (q.v.) and headed by Pierre Fourn.

ASSOGBA, AUGUSTE, 1930– . Former personal secretary and troubleshooter for Justin Ahomadégbé (q.v.) during the latter's tenure on the Presidential Council (q.v.). Born in Savalou (q.v.) in 1930, and long a government delegate to the CATC trade union, Assogba joined the staff of President Maga (q.v.) in 1959, serving as Cabinet Director. With Maga's ouster in 1963 Assogba continued as Government

Delegate to the CATC; in 1968 he was appointed Technical Consultant at the Ministry of Public Works, and in 1970 joined Ahomadégbé's staff. With the overthrow of the Presidential Council in 1972, Assogba was integrated in an advisory capacity in the Ministry of Public Works and recently went into retirement.

ASSOGBA, JANVIER CODJO (Captain). Former Minister of Civil Service and Labor. Relatively unknown Fon (q.v.) junior military officer who was part of the inner clique to bring about the 1972 coup (q.v.) following which he was catapulted into the government. Assogba first came to attention in 1968 when he served as Interim Minister of Civil Service and Labor, and in 1969 when together with other officers he blocked the efforts of Col. Maurice Kouandété (q.v.), author of the 1969 coup (q.v.), from seizing total power in the resultant military regime. In 1972 Assogba was on the Special Military Tribunal that condemned Kouandété to death (a sentence that was not executed). He was appointed Minister of Finance in Kérékou's (q.v.) government in April 1973, and in October 1974 he was transferred to head the Ministry of Civil Service and Labor. Shortly after, on January 21, 1975, he initiated an abortive coup against Kérékou after circulating a memo alleging Kérékou's implication in the Kovacs (q.v.) corruption affair. The coup fizzled out and he was purged and imprisoned until the August 1984 amnesties.

ASSOGBA, JEAN INNOCENT, 1947– . Former General Director of Economics in the Ministry of Finance and Economics. Born in 1947 and educated in law and economics, Assogba has served in a variety of capacities: as economic advisor to the Ministry of Interior, head of international relations at the Ministry of Commerce and senior lecturer at the National University of Benin (q.v.). He has written a number of books on Africa's economic problems.

ASSOGBA, MICHEL, 1936– . Health administrator. Born in Paouignan on July 20, 1936, Assogba was trained locally and abroad and obtained a degree in hospital administration. A brilliant student, he secured additional scholarships for further study in France. Upon his return to Benin, he served as director of the Porto Novo Hospital and as Secondary Schools Inspector (1965–1973). Since then he has been Senior Technical Consultant in the Ministry of Public Health.

ASSOUMA, AMADOU. Co-leader of the clandestine anti-Kérékou (q.v.) Paris-based Movément de la Rénovation du Dahomey (q.v.).

ATAKORA. Northwestern province (ex-*département*) of Benin (in French Atacora) with its administrative center in Natitingou (q.v.) and subdivided into the districts (ex-*sous-préfectures*) of Natitingou, Bassila, Bou-Kombé, Djougou (q.v.), Kouandé (q.v.), and Tanguéta. Atakora's population in the 1992 census was 539,000. It is ethnically comprised of Bariba, Dendi, Somba and Pila Pila (qq.v.).

ATCHADE, ANDRE (Major), 1941– . Former minister of Public Health. Born in 1941 in Abomey (q.v.), and educated locally and at Strasbourg, Atchadé pursued a military career and graduated from St. Cyr and Infantry School at Anger. Appointed Lieutenant and Deputy-Commander of the first Company of Parachutist Commandos, he was shortly promoted to Captain, and the Commander of the force. He later moved to occupy the post of Deputy-Chief of the Third Bureau of the army and than Deputy-Head (later Head) of the First Company of Field Engineers. Briefly Minister of Public Works in the interim 1968 military regime, after the 1972 upheaval Atchadé returned to this cabinet post, serving until 1974. He was then shifted to head the Ministry of Industry and Commerce (1974–1976) and the Ministry of Commerce and Tourism (1976–1980). In 1981 he was dropped from the cabinet and reverted to his military duties, to resurface again in August 1984 as Minister of Labor and Social Affairs. In the aftermath of the disturbances in the educational establishment in 1985, Atchadé was shifted to take over the Ministry of Public Health. In June 1988 he was implicated in a murky Libyan-backed coup attempt against the government and was dropped from the cabinet and imprisoned until the collapse of the Kérékou (q.v.) regime.

ATLANTIQUE. One of Benin's provinces (formerly *départements*) with its administrative center in Cotonou (q.v.). It consists of the *sous-préfectures* of Abomey-Calavi, Allada and Ouidah (qq.v.) with a population, recorded at the 1992 census, of just over 762,000.

ATTAKPA, JUSTIN (Commissioner). Head of Benin's urban police (q.v.) under President Kérékou (q.v.) and Chairman of the dreaded Permanent National Investigatory Commission on State Security (q.v.) charged with monitoring possible subversion against the military regime. Attakpa replaced Lt. Colonel Clément Zinzindouhé in 1988 after the latter's investigatory (i.e. torture) techniques with political prisoners had triggered too much negative publicity in French and other international circles.

AUBE NOUVELLE. Government-issued weekly newspaper (successor to the French daily *France Dahomey*) published in Porto Novo (q.v.) until August 1, 1969. At that date the widely read "New Dawn" was superseded by the government daily, the *Daho-Express* (q.v.). "Aube Nouvelle" was also the name of Benin's national hymn. After the end of Benin's Marxist era, and the collapse of the State paper *Ehuzu,* the newspaper was revived.

AUPIAIS, FRANCIS, 1877–1945. French Catholic missionary, educator, ethnologist, and early Dahomey representative in the French National Assembly. Born on August 11, 1877, near Saint Nazaire in France, Aupiais studied for the priesthood, joining the Missions Africaines de Lyon. After working briefly in Senegal he was dispatched to Dahomey. He served as Vicar of Abomey (q.v.) in 1903, following which he assumed various duties throughout the territory but especially in Porto Novo (q.v.). His 23 years of almost continuous residence (1903–1926) contributed heavily to the proselytizing of the faith in Dahomey. Aupiais was also very concerned with helping to develop the budding elite of the territory and among his protégés, whose careers he helped to advance, were the author Paul Hazoumé and the politician Sourou-Migan Apithy (qq.v.).

Sympathetic to Africa and its indigenous values and culture, Aupiais strove to bring it proper appreciation abroad, for which purpose he founded the review *La Reconnaissance Africaine*. His ethnological contributions brought about his 1939 election to the Académie des Sciences Coloniales. His love for Dahomey brought him back to Porto Novo numerous times, though his duties after 1926 were mostly in France. A liberal and one of the best loved and most respected Frenchmen in Dahomey, he was elected on October 18, 1945, to serve as Dahomey's representative from the first electoral college to the French Assembly in Paris. Prior to his election he was instrumental in making acceptable the candidacy of his protégé, Apithy, on the second roll. Shortly after the election Aupiais fell ill and died in France on December 14, 1945.

AUSTERITY TAX see SOLIDARITY TAX

AWANOU, PAUL. Minister of Inspection of Public Enterprises between December 1982 and August 1984. A civil administrator by profession, in 1982 Awanou was given a mandate to oversee the bloated and deficit-ridden public sector of Benin, to eliminate corruption and inefficiency and to supervise the pruning down of state involvement in unviable enterprises.

AWE BONI, ARISTIDE (Colonel). Recently appointed Chief of Staff of Benin's armed forces (q.v.), replacing Kérékou's (q.v.) Chief of Staff.

AWOUNOU, EMMANUEL, 1916– . Early supporter of Sourou-Migan Apithy (q.v.) and major financial contributor to the latter's electoral campaigns over the years. Born in Porto Novo (q.v.) on October 16, 1916, to a branch of a chiefly lineage, and a trader by profession, with extensive links across the border in Nigeria, Awounou was one of the early supporters of Apithy's political aspirations. He served as treasurer of the PRD (q.v.) and later the PDU (q.v.) Parliamentary Party (since 1959), and he was a deputy in the National Assembly (q.v.) until the 1965 coup d'etat (q.v.). Since then Awounou, in bad health, has been out of political life.

AYAYI, MANASSE. Former Minister of Commerce and, prior to that, Minister of State Enterprises. A civil administrator of Mina (q.v.) ethnicity, Ayayi was a radical member of Ligue (q.v.) opposing the continued French economic presence in Benin. He joined Kérékou's (q.v.) cabinet in February 1981 to supervise and oversee the State sector as minister of State Enterprises. He rapidly floundered in his post with the Air Benin (q.v.) fiasco (set up without minimal economic feasibility studies), his worst error, resulting in an intrinsically loss-making State company. Severely criticized for his inadequate administrative leadership, his role as supervisor of the entire State sector was compromised and, in April 1982, he was shifted to head the Ministry of Commerce, a post he also lost in 1984, following which he reverted to lower-level duties in the administration.

AYIVI FOLIAON, FLORENCE, 1935– . Director of the National Library of Benin since 1967. Born in Bohicon (q.v.) on December 12, 1935, and a university Supplies Director between 1962 and 1967, Mrs. Ayivi Foliaon was placed in charge of the National Library in 1967 and presided over its expansion in subsequent years. See also BIBLIOTHEQUE NATIONALE.

AZANGO, AUGUSTIN. Key early political leader, virtually forgotten today. Azango was an early militant and important organizer of the Electoral Committees erected in Dahomey in 1945. A writer and journalist by profession, Azango had been resident in Paris between 1927 and 1939, editing *La Métro-Mère,* a weekly. With the post-Second World War electoral reforms, Azango, together with Emile Derlin Zinsou (q.v.), set up the Union Progréssiste Dahoméenne (UPD) (q.v.), Dahomey's first political party. Azango served as its first President in 1946. Offered the party's nomination for the second electoral college vacancy, Azango turned it down. (Sourou-Migan Apithy [q.v.] eventually was appointed.)

Though he played a certain role in subsequent years, he was by temperament ill-suited to deal with the cleavages that soon beset the UPD, and he faded from political life in 1949.

AZATOU, ZOKI see JOAQUIM D'ALMEIDA.

AZONHIHO, MARTIN DOHOU (Colonel). Long the militant second man in the Kérékou (q.v.) military regime. A former loyal aide-de-camp to Kérékou, Azonhiho, a gendarmerie (q.v.) officer of Fon (q.v.) origins from Abomey (q.v.), was catapulted to prominence in October 1974 when he was brought into Kérékou's cabinet as Minister of Information and National Orientation. He rapidly transformed the Ministry into a bastion of the extreme Left, and his drive and stamina gained him the critical Ministry of Interior and headship of the gendarmerie in June 1975, in the aftermath of the liquidation of Major Aikpé (q.v.), with whom he had been on extremely bad terms. Indeed, according to some sources, Azonhiho may have instigated the sequence of events leading to the elimination of his ideological arch-competitor, who had the trust of labor in the urban areas. A tall, balding, extremely abrasive officer, who has been involved in several fist-fights during cabinet meetings (including with Aikpé), Azonhiho was promoted to Captain and Major within only six years, and he was much feared by both the masses and the officer corps. His tenure as Minister of Interior was subsequently short, and he was reassigned his old Ministry of Information, becoming the prime ideologue of the regime. By 1982, very much crowding and threatening Kérékou himself—a pragmatic middleman—and his blunt mannerisms having alienated even his ideological supporters, Azonhiho was summarily dropped from the cabinet and appointed Prefect of Mono (q.v.) province. Azonhiho remained one of Benin's powerful personalities, with a seat in the National Assembly (q.v.), and bounced back into Kérékou's graces as the latter slowly lost all his friends and allies. In 1987 he rejoined the cabinet as Minister of Rural Development and Cooperatives; within a year he had been promoted to Colonel and had moved to assume the Ministry of Labor and Social Affairs and, in August 1988, he became

Minister of Equipment and Transport. He lost the post with the political normalization of 1989.

-B-

BABA MOUSSA, ABOUBAKAR. Former Minister of Information and Propaganda. A very close personal friend of President Kérékou (q.v.), Baba Moussa, who comes from the north, was brought into the cabinet in 1979 as Minister of Planning and Statistics. He had previously been the Governor of the Banque Beninoise de Développement (q.v.). Very unpopular with the Left (civilian and military) Baba Moussa was used by Kérékou as a political counterweight to Leftist pressures upon him. Cautious, conservative and pro-West, Baba Moussa replaced the mercurial and radical Major Azonhiho (q.v.) in 1982 as Minister of Information and Propaganda, reflecting the more moderate course of the Beninois Revolution in the 1980's. He left the cabinet in 1984 to pursue private activities, more recently as President of the West African Bank of Development in Lomé, Togo. From there he counselled Kérékou on numerous occasions, including before the move to privatization of the economy and to multipartyism. Baba Moussa currently serves on the Bank of Africa-Benin administrative board.

BABA MOUSSA, AMIDOU. Northern PRPB (q.v.) militant. Brother of the influential Aboubakar Baba Moussa (q.v.) Amidou was a member of the Politburo until dropped in 1985.

BADAROU, DAOUDA, 1929– . Surgeon, diplomat and former Foreign Minister. Born in Porto Novo (q.v.) on January 7, 1929, Badarou studied locally, in Senegal, and at the University of Paris, where he obtained his M.D. in 1957, qualifying as a surgeon in 1961. A former member of the Executive Council of the World Health Organization in Geneva, and essentially apolitical and unattached to any of the political movements of Dahomey's triumvirate (q.v.), Badarou was appointed Minister of Health in General Christophe Soglo's (q.v.) cabinet (1966–1967). Following the 1967 coup d'etat (q.v.) and the rise of Emile Derlin Zinsou (q.v.) to the Presidency, Badarou was appointed Foreign Minister. He retained this position under the Presidential Council (q.v.) until 1971. In that year he was appointed Ambassador to France (1971–1973) and nonresident Ambassador to the United Kingdom, Italy and Spain. Currently he serves on the WHO Commission in Dakar, Senegal.

BALLOT, VICTOR, 1853–1939. Colonial administrator and early Governor of Dahomey. Born on October 11, 1853, in Martinique to a navy doctor's family, Ballot studied in Paris and was appointed Commander of Porto Novo (q.v.) in September 1887, French Resident in Benin in October 1889 and Lieutenant Governor of Dahomey in December 1891. He was responsible for the extensive fortification of Porto Novo and the preparations for the Franco-Dahomean campaigns (q.v.) of Gen. Alfred Amedée Dodds (q.v.). After the formal conquest of Dahomey, Ballot was appointed governor of the new colony (1894–1900) and in that capacity sent expeditions to the northern regions, blocking a German advance from Togo and a British effort to merge Dahomey's Borgou (q.v.) with the Borgu region of their Nigerian colony. Ballot later became Governor of Guadeloupe, retiring from active service in 1904.

BANGANA. Title of the King of Kouandé, a Bariba (qq.v.) state founded at the end of the eighteenth century by one of the sons of the King of Nikki (q.v.). The dynasty included eight kings up to the French conquest. The current Bangana is a retired gendarmerie Sergeant.

BANK OF AFRICA-BENIN. New bank set up with headquarters in Cotonou (q.v.) following the January 1990 economic normalization. Capitalized at one billion CFA francs, most equity (65 percent) is held by private shareholders and by subsidiaries of the West African Development Bank and the CCCE (q.v.). Its administrative board is headed by Gatien Houngbédji (q.v.) and includes Aboubakar Baba Moussa (q.v.).

BANKS. During 1988–1989 Benin's largely nationalized banking sector collapsed completely, several banks such as the Caisse Nationale du Crédit Agricole (q.v.) and Banque du Commerce et Dévelooppement looted wholesale or defunct due to unsecured loans to high government officials. Following the 1990 normalization a number of new banks opened operations in the country, with the following ones currently operating: Banque Centrale des Etats de l'Afrique de l'Ouest (BCEAO) (q.v.); Bank of Africa-Bénin (q.v.); Banque Béninoise de Développement (BBD) (q.v.); Banque Internatinale du Bénin (BIBE); Ecobank-Bénin (q.v.); Financial Bank (q.v.); Caisse Autonome d'Amortissement de Bénin. In February 1993 Credit Lyonais joined the stream of new banks to establish themselves in Benin, bringing the total to five new banks.

BANQUE BENINOISE DE DEVELOPPEMENT (BBD). Fully State-owned bank founded in Cotonou (q.v.) in 1962 with an original capitalization of 1,000 million CFA francs, raised in 1983 to 1,500 million. The BBD was engaged in financing development projects in the agricultural, industrial, and transportation sectors. The bank was previously known as the Banque Dahoméene du Développement (BDD) with the State's equity limited to 60 percent. The Bank went bankrupt in 1988 due to unsecured loans and/or looting by State officials, was closed down early in 1989, to reopen with new funds in 1990, but by 1993 was again in liquidation.

BANQUE CENTRALE DES ETATS DE L'AFRIQUE DE L'OUEST (BCEAO). French West Africa's central bank, established in Paris in 1958 with branches in all member states. Late in 1974 the headquarters of the bank was transferred from Paris to Dakar, Senegal. It is currently headed by Paulin L. Cossi.

BANQUE COMMERCIALE DU BENIN (BCB). Until the 1990 economic normalization Benin's only commercial bank, the BCB was the former Société Dahoméene de Banque that was nationalized in 1974. Originally founded in Cotonou (q.v.) in 1962 with 45 percent of State equity and capitalized at 1,000 million CFA francs, later augmented to 1,500 million. The bank handled all governmental banking transaction as well. In 1979 it was the target of a major embezzlement, running into hundreds of millions of CFA francs, caused by serious lapses in security procedures. Though rescued by governmental fiscal infusions, it continued at the brink of insolvency and most French businessmen would not accept checks drawn on it since 1985. In 1989 it was again rocked by scandals relating to systematic embezzlement by government ministers and officials, and it was allowed to go under on June 15, 1990.

BANQUE DAHOMEENNE DU DEVELOPPEMENT (BDD) see BANQUE BENINOISE DE DEVELOPPEMENT (BBD)

BANQUE INTERNATIONALE DU BENIN (BIBE). Joint Benin-Nigerian bank set up in July 1989 after the bulk of Benin's banking sector had collapsed due to insolvency. Private Beninois shareholders hold 30 percent of equity; their Nigerian counterparts 14 percent; and four Nigerian banks 56 percent. The President of the Board is Chief (Dr) Samuel O. Asabia.

BARABAKAROU. Royal trumpets, symbols of sovereignty and nobility in Bariba (q.v.) traditional society. Endowed with quasi-magical qualities, the four trumpets (two large, two small) are only used on special ceremonial occasions, especially during the inauguration or funeral of a king. Not to be confused with the other long trumpets used by Bariba cavalry to herald the impending arrival or passage of a prince, or nobility, that had no sacramental connotation.

BAREY. Small village in the Djougou (q.v.) area that is one of the key villages of the Pila Pila (q.v.) ethnic group.

BARIBA. Major and historically much-feared ethnic group in northern Dahomey, found especially in the Nikki, Kouandé, Parakou, and Kandi regions of the Borgou (qq.v.), and near Natitingou in the Atakora (qq.v.). Mostly animist, and in the nineteenth century fielding an army against the Fulani (q.v.) attack on Ilorin (now in Nigeria), the Bariba are slowly becoming Muslim in the contemporary era. According to legends the Bariba arrived in Bussa (q.v.) and Ile (both in Nigeria) from Arabia and are descendants of the legendary Kisira (q.v.). Anthropologically they are a Sudanic people, with a Gur family language of Voltaic and Mande origins and a culture deeply suffused with influences from the indigenous cultures and peoples they subdued in Borgou, including the Boko (q.v.).

Following dynastic disputes a branch migrated to found Nikki in Dahomey. Their name is probably a European corruption of the Yoruba (q.v.) word Barba, though the Bariba call themselves Batomba—"the people." They achieved autonomy from the Oyo Empire (q.v.) around 1782 and formed a series of hierarchically linked, typically feudal kingdoms in the Borgou. In this hierarchy, Bussa has always been accorded primacy consequent to its role as the Bariba "parent" state and origin of the nobility (see WASAN-GARI) even though Nikki emerged as the strongest militarily. Next in this hierarchy are Wawa and Ile, which are the southern and northern dependencies of Bussa, followed by Nikki, the biggest, strongest, and oldest Bariba kingdom in Dahomey. After Nikki come Kandi, Kouandé, and Parakou (in that order), all of which shook off in different degrees Nikki's authority following dynastic rivalries. Socially stratified, traditional Bariba society was an alliance of powerful landed clans, with *Wasangari* (q.v.) cavalry, dominating—through territorial conquests and slave-raids—large numbers of Gando (q.v.) slaves and Fulani herdsmen. Much feared throughout the area, right to the Togo border, it has been noted that not a single one of the early European explorers to penetrate their domain ever came out alive.

Largely isolated from European and other influences from the south, once the Bariba regions were integrated into the colony of Dahomey they collapsed economically. The abolition of slave raiding and domestic slavery eliminated the source of livelihood of the *Wasangari* and triggered a massive outflux of ex-slaves and manual labor from Bariba villages to new "freedom villages." The imposition of an artificial

Anglo-French border doomed traditional caravan trade. All the Bariba villages of today were major towns and commercial centers in the nineteenth century, booming with activity. European explorers estimated, for example, the population of Bussa (Nigeria) at 25,000 (today 1,500); Péréré, at 14,000 (now 1,400); Nikki, at 20,000 (today 1,100). Consequently the entire Borgou fell into neglect and decay and lagged in socioeconomic and political development. This factor began to constitute a major obstacle to nation-building efforts after independence. The development of regionalist sentiments in the north, the historic Nikki-Parakou friction, and a distrust of the Yoruba (see SERO KPERA ILORINKPUNON) have catapulted to national prominence such regional leaders as Hubert Maga, Paul Darboux (qq.v.), and Chabi Mama, and made more intense the north-south cleavage in Dahomey. Bariba mistrust of southerners is matched by continued feelings of superiority vis-a-vis other groups in the north, traditionally raided for slaves, such as the Somba (q.v.). This has especially complicated the Somba General Kérékou's (q.v.) efforts to secure a political base of support in the north (during 1972–1990) especially since he was rejected in the south as a northerner. See also KANDI; KOUANDE; NIKKI; PARAKOU; REGIONALISM.

There are currently an estimated 500,000 Bariba in Benin, most of whom are farmers. Cattle herds are still normally delegated to either ex-slaves or to Fulani, in exchange for permission to graze on Bariba lands. Most of the Gando remain isolated in their "freedom villages" throughout the Borgou.

BARRA, YACOUB FREDERICK, 1942– . Born in 1942 in Dassa-Zoumé, and educated locally, Barra obtained higher education at the Universities of Minnesota (1961–1964) and of Dakar (1967–1968), studying economics. In 1965 he became the Secretary-General of the Dahomean National Commission for UNESCO, a post he held until 1974. In that year he was shifted into the Ministry for Foreign Affairs, where he served as head of a division.

BASSABI, SOULEYMANE, 1941– . Opthalmologist and current Director of the National Medical-Social Institute of Benin.

BATAILLON DE LA GARDE PRESIDENTIELLE (BGP). President Kérékou's (q.v.) main armed prop against assaults from within the armed forces (q.v.). A batallion (450 men) of hand-picked, North Korean trained troops, all northerner and most Fulani (q.v.), equipped since 1986 with a dozen Panhard armored cars and under the direct command of Captain Sambo Soulé, a Fulani as well. The BGP was dismantled by President Soglo (q.v.) in 1991.

BATCHO-ATEGUI, LEONARD, 1920– . Early political militant. Born in Sokponta on August 20, 1920, an accountant by profession, Batcho-Atégui was active in union affairs, serving as President of the Association de Jeunesse de Dassa, and as both Treasurer and General Administrator of the Union Coopérative Agricole of Dassa-Zoumé. His grass-roots contacts gained him several offers of political affiliation, and in March 1952 he ran for and won the Savalou (q.v.) seat on the PRD, later PDD, PDU (qq.v.) party tickets. He served in the National Assembly (q.v.) for an uninterrupted period between 1952 and 1963. There he was the influential Speaker (1959–1963) and member of the Cotton Stabilization Committee. Following the 1963 coup (q.v.) Batcho-Atégui withdrew from political life, continuing a trading career.

BATOKO, OUSMANE. Former Minister of Culture, Youth and Sports, in 1988 Batoko was shifted to head the Ministry of Information and Communications, a post he lost with the change of regime in Benin.

BATOMBA see BARIBA

BAUDIN, NOEL, 1844–1887. Early missionary along the Benin coast. Born in Guizé in 1844, and joining the Missions Africaines de Lyon in 1864, Baudin was dispatched to Ouidah (q.v.) in December 1868. He suffered various indignities in this major fetishist center, and following intrigues and a spell of imprisonment, he was forced to leave the town. After recuperation in France he returned to Africa, this time to Porto Novo (q.v.), judged as more amenable to the missionary effort. He later also worked in Lagos. Baudin was in particular interested in preparing a catechism in the Nagot (q.v.) language. He mounted various prosletyzing efforts along the Ghana-Nigeria coast, until illness forced him back to France in 1887.

BEBEDA, CHARLES (Lt. Colonel). Former Minister of Transportation. Part Fon and part Mahi (qq.v.), Bébéda came into national prominence when he was appointed President of the CMR (q.v.). He was integrated into the Kérékou (q.v.) cabinet as Minister of Transport in August 1973 but returned to military duties in October 1974. During the Assogba (q.v.) January 1975 attempted coup, Captain Bébéda played an equivocal role for which he was arrested and placed on trial. He was later acquitted of any involvement in the putsch attempt, and rallying more convincingly to the regime was progressively promoted up the ranks becoming commander of the army in 1986.

BECOU. Small village, 35 kilometers east of Bémbéréké in the Borgou (q.v.), scene of the famous 1916–1917 uprising against the French. See also BIO GUERA.

BEHANZIN, KING OF DAHOMEY. King of Dahomey (1889–1894) during the Franco-Dahomean campaigns (q.v.). Son of one of the kingdom's most illustrious kings, Glélé (q.v.), Béhanzin was born in 1840 and assumed the throne in December 1889 at a time of numerous foreign challenges and encroachments as well as general unease in the kingdom. His attempts to assert his authority over rebellious provinces or tributary states in the traditional manner (i.e., via wars of conquest) brought him into direct conflict with France. He rejected the latter's claim on Cotonou (q.v.) (ceded probably without his knowledge by a local official) and maintained that Porto Novo (q.v.) was a tributary state. Since the latter, under King Toffa (q.v.), had requested and obtained Protectorate status from France, Béhanzin's policies inevitably led to war (see FRANCO-DAHOMEAN CAMPAIGNS). After his final defeat by France he escaped into the bush, ultimately surrendering to the French on January 25, 1894. The French elevated to the Abomey throne Béhanzin's brother,

Goutchili, who adopted the "strong name" (under which each monarch was to be known) of Agoli-Agbo (q.v.). Béhanzin was exiled to Martinique and died in Algeria of pneumonia in 1906. Agoli-Agbo suffered the same fate when he ran afoul of the French and was himself exiled to Gabon, ending the Dahomean monarchical dynasty. Béhanzin's remains were repatriated in 1928 and he was reburied with full military honors at Djimé, a quarter still inhabited to this day by his descendants.

BEHANZIN, LOUIS. Radical political ideologue. Tracing his descent from the Abomey (q.v.) kingdom's royal family, Béhanzin is also a cousin of Theophile Paoléti, the trade union leader with whom, in 1959, he attempted to set up a radical political alternative in the south, through the creation of the Parti de la Révolution Socialiste du Bénin (PRSB) which was affiliated with the Parti Africain de l'Indépendance (qq.v.). The attempt was not successful and only a few intellectuals and students were attracted by the PRSB's radical plank. After Dahomey's independence, Behanzin—a member of France's Communist Party—based himself in Conakry, Guinea, where he worked as an ideologue and instructor (1961–1974). After the 1972 coup d'etat (q.v.) in Dahomey and the consequent radicalization of politics he briefly returned home to play a small role in influencing Colonel Kérékou's (q.v.) emerging leftist policies. Béhanzin's influence rapidly waned, however, and he was forced to leave the country early in 1975.

BEHETON, NESTOR (Major). Radical gendarmerie (q.v.) officer. As a junior Second Lieutenant, Béhéton served as the Interim Minister of Labor and Civil Service in the December 1967–May 1968 cabinet of Alley-Kouandété (qq.v.). At the time he was also appointed Director of the Regie des Transports Cotonois. He sat on the military tribunal that tried his former Chief, Colonel Kouandété, for treason in 1972, and later joined the new Kérékou (q.v.) cabinet of 1972 as Minister of Transport, Posts and Telecommunications. Considered strongly anti-French, a rabble-rouser and unrestrainable, Béhéton was dismissed from the cabinet in August

1973 after constant feuding with another military minister, Rodriguez (q.v.), during which he called upon the Coutonou dock workers to go on strike against some of Rodriguez' administrative decisions. In 1984 he once again fell foul of Kérékou, being arrested for instigating the attempted coup at the Ouassa barracks 130 kilometers north of the capital.

BELIMINES see SOCIETE BENINO-ARABE-LIBYENNE DES MINES

BELIPECHE see SOCIETE BENINO-ARABE-LIBYENNE DE PECHE MARITIME

BELLO, TOYID, 1949– . Economist. Born on January 1, 1949, and with a Ph.D. in economics from the University of Paris, Bello teaches economics at the National University of Benin (q.v.).

BENIN-MAGAZINE. Popular cultural magazine issued in Benin for the first time early 1987 by the State publishing house ONEPI (q.v.). The print run was 5,000.

BENIN-NIGER BOUNDARY DISPUTE see DAHOMEY-NIGER BOUNDARY DISPUTE

LA BENINOISE. Popular name for the Société Nationale de Brasseries de la Republique du Bénin (q.v.).

BERTHO, JACQUES. French Catholic missionary, anthropologist, ethnologist, and former Dahomey Deputy to the French National Assembly. Apart from his long missionary work in Dahomey, Bertho is chiefly known for his numerous scholarly articles on the ethnology of southern Dahomey and Togo. After the 1945 death of Francis Aupiais (q.v.), who shortly before had been elected Deputy to Paris of Dahomey's second electoral college, Bertho was appointed as his replacement in the French National Assembly.

BHELY-QUENUM, OLYMPE, 1928– . Journalist, author and editor. Born on September 26, 1928, in Cotonou (q.v.), Bhely-Quénum is the nephew of anthropologist Maximilien

Quénum (q.v.). He studied locally between 1938 and 1942 and, after working in Cotonou for four years for the British firm John Walker & Co. (a branch of Unilever), Bhely-Quénum went to Caen University (France) where he graduated in literature in 1957. He also studied sociology and diplomacy in Paris and briefly served in the French consular services in Italy, writing a book on Italian reactions to African developments.

Between 1962 and 1965 Bhely-Quénum edited in Paris the short-lived journal *La Vie Africaine* and, after its demise, started publishing his own *L'Afrique Actuelle,* a bilingual literary and cultural journal that collapsed in 1968. During the 1960's, he also published two novels. The first, *Un Piège Sans Fin* (1960), won him wide acclaim, while the second, *Le Chant du Lac* (1965), won the Literary Grand Prize for Black Africa in 1966. Another of his novels remains unpublished due to its harsh depiction of Parisian slum conditions. Bhely-Quénum currently works in Paris for UNESCO, but is due for retirement shortly.

BIAOU, ADOLPHE (Colonel). Former Minister of Rural Development. Biaou, one of the junior gendarmerie (q.v.) officers brought into the Kérékou (q.v.) cabinet in October 1974, was Minister of Popular Culture, Youth and Sports. Promoted to Captain in 1975 and Major in 1981, he was shifted to head the Ministry of Rural Development in 1976, the Ministry of Labor and Social Affairs later the same year, and in October 1984 was appointed back to the Ministry of Rural Development. His long tenure in office has been a direct function of his ability to steer between the various ideological factions and to deal with unionists.

BIBLIOTHEQUE NATIONALE. National Library of Benin created in 1975 in Porto Novo (q.v.) and lodged in the former building housing the National Assembly (q.v.). For long under the administration of Noël Amoussou, the Library publishes (very irregularly) a *Bibliographie du Bénin,* and in 1985 had a collection of 4,000 volumes and 45 periodicals.

BIC. Processing plant producing farina for Benin's bakeries.

BIO, DANIEL. Former Minister. For two years the Minister of Public Health in the Ahomadégbé-Apithy (qq.v.) government (1963–1965), and intermittently abroad, Bio was appointed the Deputy-Director of the Caisse de Compensation de Préstations Familiales in Cotonou (q.v.). He served in that capacity until the 1972 cup d'etat (q.v.) when he left to live abroad.

BIO GUERA, d. 1918. Chief of Gbékou, east of Bémbéréké in the Borgou (q.v.), who led an anti-French Bariba (q.v.) uprising in September 1916. The immediate causes of the uprising were the ineptitude of an inexperienced French official coupled with a mutual misunderstanding of intentions; though the onerous taxation system, corvée labor and military recruitment during World War I (see UPRISINGS OF 1915–1918) were at the root of all unrest in the Borgou. Utilizing the disorganization of the local French administration, Bio Guéra succeeded in fomenting revolt throughout the Bémbéréké-Kandi region, with the support of the King of Nikki, Chabi Prouka (qq.v.). The revolt was finally crushed in Borgou in 1917, with Bio Guera being killed a year later on December 19, 1918.

BIO TCHANE, 1923– . Former cabinet minister. Born in Djougou (q.v.) of venerable chiefly lineage, and trained for a teaching career, Bio Tchané ran for the National Assembly (q.v.) and was elected Deputy from Djougou on March 31, 1957. He was reelected on the RDD (q.v.) ticket in 1959. Serving in the Assembly as Vice-President of the Finance Committee, Bio Tchané remained a Deputy until the 1965 coup d'etat (q.v.). Throughout this period he also served as Vice-President of the PDU (q.v.) parliamentary group, and Minister of Technical Education in the pre-independence Apithy (q.v.) cabinet, continuing on as Minister of Finance through 1959. After the 1965 coup (q.v.) he served for several years as a civil administrator in Djougou, before appointment as sous-préfet of Tanguiéta (1968), Savé (1970), and other localities. Bio Tchané is currently in retirement.

BIOKOU, SALOMON, 1912– . Political activist. Born in Porto Novo (q.v.) on January 7, 1912, and of direct royal lineage,

Biokou was trained for a teaching career, becoming involved in national politics in the late 1950's. He was persuaded to become PDU (q.v.) Secretary-General of the Porto Novo region and was elected to the National Assembly (q.v.) in 1959 where he was voted first Vice President of the Assembly. He remained in the National Assembly until the 1963 coup d'etat (q.v.), when he retired from national politics and concentrated on the municipal administration of Porto Novo, retiring in 1972. During his long political career Biokou has been municipal councillor for Porto Novo for several years, and Deputy Mayor of the city.

BLOC POPULAIRE AFRICAIN (BPA). Political party established in 1946 by Emile Poisson and Justin Ahomadégbé (qq.v.) after their dissatisfaction with the policies of the Union Progréssiste Dahoméenne (UPD) (q.v.). The BPA received support especially among the Fon (q.v.) of Dahomey. The party was the precursor of the Union Démocratique Dahoméenne (q.v.), established in 1956 following the merger of the BPA with the remnants of the UPD, led by Emile Derlin Zinsou (q.v.). See also AHOMADEGBE, JUSTIN; UNION DEMOCRATIQUE DAHOMEENNE; UNION PROGRESSISTE DAHOMEENNE.

BOCCO, EUGENE, 1927– . Educator. Born in Ouidah (q.v.) on September 6, 1927, and educated in the sciences, Bocco taught in several schools, including the Lycée Béhanzin. In 1963 he joined the central administration as Director of Youth and Sports in the Ministry of Education, and with the rise of the government of General Soglo (q.v.), he was appointed Minister of Education and Culture. With the overthrow of Soglo in 1967, Bocco remained in the government in an interim capacity as Cabinet Director of the new President of the Republic. In 1969 he was reassigned administrative duties within the Ministry of Education. He is currently retired.

BOCO, ROGER IMOROU. First Vice-President of the National Assembly until 1990.

BODJOGOUME, HILAIR (Lt. Colonel). Serving as military attaché at the Dahomean Embassy to France in Paris as Captain, Bodjogoumé was one of the architects of the 1972 coup (q.v.) and was recalled to Cotonou (q.v.) after Kérékou's (q.v.) rise to power to join the cabinet as Minister of Education, Culture and Youth. Considered overly anti-French, he was replaced in the cabinet by Captain Guézodjé (q.v.) and given military duties in the Djougou (q.v.) garrison. Prior to that Bodjogoumé had played a murky role in the anti-French riots that had rocked Cotonou. Though progressively promoted, he was twice involved in coup plots against the regime: in 1984 in connection with the plot in the Ouasso paracommando barracks 130 kilometers north of Cotonou, and in 1988 when, as Head of the critical Camp Guézo (q.v.), he was arrested together with Hountoundji (q.v.) for the plot of that year.

BOHICON. Growing commercial and industrial center near Abomey (q.v.) with which it now comprises a single urban sprawl. The town developed consequent to its being on the Cotonou-Parakou (qq.v.) railroad, the latter consciously constructed by the French some distance away from Abomey.

BOHIKI AFFAIR. The ultimate spark that ignited the October 1963 general labor strike in southern Dahomey, which in turn precipitated the fall of the regime of Hubert Maga (q.v.). Christophe Bohiki was a Yoruba Parti Dahoméen de l'Unité Assembly (qq.v.) delegate from Sakété who had been arrested for the murder of party militant Daniel Dossou, a Goun (q.v.) from Porto Novo (q.v.). The National Assembly decided not to lift Bohiki's parliamentary immunity, thus ensuring that he would not stand trial. This epitomized to the population in the south the total insensitivity of the regime to the plight of the common man. Ethnic strife consequently burst out in Porto Novo (q.v.) and Maga's belated decision to bring Bohiki to trial could not appease the crowds. Shortly after General Christophe Soglo (q.v.) intervened by dismissing the Maga regime. Bohiki was eventually brought to trial and received a stiff prison sentence. See also COUP OF 1963.

BOISSIER-PALUN, LEON, 1921– . Lawyer, diplomat and politician. Born in Djougou (q.v.) in 1921 to a French colonial administrator and his wife of the Savalou (q.v.) royal house. Educated locally and in France, Boissier-Palun qualified for the bar and made Senegal his adopted home. He served for five years as president of the AOF's (q.v.) Grand Council in Dakar, was head of the Senegalese bar and, after Senegal's independence, headed the latter's Economic and Social Council. A long-standing colleague of Senegal's President Léopold Sédar Senghor, Boissier-Palun also represented his adopted country as Ambassador to Great Britain (1961–1967). He returned to Dahomey in 1968 to contest that year's Presidential election in which former Presidents and cabinet Ministers were barred from presenting their candidacies. Boissier-Palun's petition to run for office was rejected by the interim military administration on the grounds of his "unfamiliarity" with Dahomean problems and he returned to Senegal. See also ELECTORAL BOYCOTT, 1968.

BOKO. The pre-Bariba (q.v.) population of the Borgou (q.v.), speaking a Mandingo dialect. The Boko had similar patterns of organization to the Bariba, and they were culturally absorbed by the Bariba. In the various kingdoms established in the Borgou the Boko always shared power with the Bariba princes. Currently they are found in small numbers scattered throughout the Beninois and Nigerian Borgou. There are an estimated 30,000 Boko in Benin. In Nigeria, the Boko have been superficially influenced by the Hausa as well.

BOKO, MICHEL, 1950– . Geographer. Possessing a Ph.D. in geography from the University of Bordeaux, Boko teaches at the National University of Benin (q.v.).

BOKONO see FA.

BONI, ARISTIDE AWE (Colonel). Chief of Staff of the Beninois armed forces (q.v.) since the civilianization of the government in 1991.

BONI, PIERRE (Captain). Military medical officer, surgeon and, briefly, Minister. A militant, little-known northern army officer, Boni first came to attention when he was appointed Minister of Health and Social Affairs following the 1967 coup d'etat by Major Maurice Kouandété (qq.v.). He was dropped from the cabinet in May 1968 because of friction between him and the regime's chief executive, Colonel Alphonse Alley (q.v.). In 1970, following the annulment by the Military Directorate (q.v.) of that year's presidential elections (in which Hubert Maga [q.v.] would have been declared victor), Boni was prominent in calling for the secession of the northern regions from Dahomey. The outcome of the crisis was the creation of a Presidential Council (q.v.) with Maga as first Chairman (1970–1972). Toward the end of the latter's term of office Boni was arrested for a complex anti-Maga mutiny-cum-conspiracy for which he was sentenced to 20 years' forced labor. Following the October 1972 coup d'etat (q.v.) Boni was released from prison together with other military conspirators, and he retired from the army. He currently operates a medical clinic.

BORGHERO, FRANCOIS, 1830–1892. Early Catholic missionary. Born in Italy, Borghero taught in a convent near Rome and was ordained in 1854. In 1860 he was named First Superior to the Apostolic Vicarat of Dahomey. He established his headquarters in the Portuguese fort of Ouidah (q.v.) in 1861 (while it was temporarily deserted) and a second center was later opened in Porto Novo (q.v.). The headquarters of the Apostolic Vicarat eventually was transferred to Porto Novo under the intense pressure of Ouidah's fetishists (q.v.). Borghero is credited with founding the first dispensaries and a large number of mission schools. He travelled extensively to various kings and helped mediate hostilities between several warring clans and villages. Throughout his Dahomean stay his life was made miserable by almost continuous fever, friction with other Christian denominations and the fierce opposition of fetishist leaders to his mission in Ouidah. Borghero died of stomach cancer in October 1892.

BORGOU. Geographical region artificially dissected by the Benin-Nigeria border and bounded by the Atakora mountains to the west, the Niger river to the north, and the Mahi (q.v.) regions to the south. Of the region, some 130,000 square kilometers are within Benin, and 52,000 in Nigeria. Benin's Borgou is a large province in the northeast of the country, with a 1992 population of about 534,000, but a low density of 10 per square kilometer. Parakou (q.v.) is Borgou's administrative capital and it has several important Bariba (q.v.) centers, of which Nikki (q.v.) has traditionally been the most significant. The population is only 50 percent Bariba with large minorities made up of their ex-slaves, the Gando (16 percent), Fulani (22 percent), etc. The area was contested by France and Britain, the latter incorporating part of Borgou in its Nigerian colony, splitting the Bariba among the two administrations. The Nigerian Borgou (Borgu) is currently within Kwara state. Effective French occupation occurred in 1895, though sporadic revolts continued up to the end of the First World War. See also BIO GUERRA; UPRISINGS OF 1915–1918.

The Borgou attained independence from the powerful Yoruba Oyo Empire (qq.v.) in 1783. It is one of the few regions in this geographical area not to have fallen to, or even felt, the Fulani invasions and, partly for this reason, is still largely animist (q.v.). It has also strongly resisted Christian missionary efforts. Despite proselytizing efforts at the turn of the century, the first permanent mission in the region was established only in 1937 (in Kandi [q.v.]), followed by one in Parakou in 1944; the first church was built in Nikki in 1940. During the pre-colonial era the population was organized into several quasi-feudal semi-autonomous states hierarchically linked and owing traditional allegiance to that of Bussa in Nigeria. See BARIBA. Within "French" Borgou, the kingdom of Nikki was preeminent. The region also straddled the traditional caravan trails (and slave routes), especially the Kano-Ashanti route, with important stops in Parakou, Kandi and Nikki. Benin's Borgou has lagged significantly behind the southern areas on most indicators of modernization, creating a serious regionalist cleavage which has exacerbated prospects of stability. During the early "civilian" era (pre-1972) the Borgou had been the principal electoral fiefdom of Hubert Maga (q.v.). See also REGIONALISM.

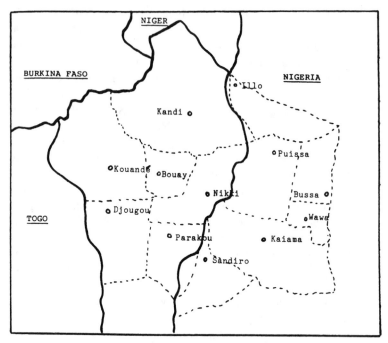

THE BARIBA STATES IN BORGOU

BORGU see BORGOU

BORNA, BERTIN, 1930– . Former Minister of Finance. Born on
November 20, 1930, in Tanguiéta, Borna studied abroad
obtaining a degree in law. A brilliant student leader and
agitator, he attended the Parakou Congress of 1957 at which
Hubert Maga's MDD (qq.v.) political party was transformed
into the Rassémblement Démocratique Dahoméen (RDD)
(q.v.). Joining that party he became representative to the 1958
PRA (q.v.) Cotonou Congress adopting a strongly militant
position. Secretary-General of the RDD parliamentary group
(April 1959–November 1960) and Vice-President of the National Assembly (q.v.) (1959–1960), Borna was a member of
the Maga-Apithy (q.v.) alliance that formed the Parti Dahoméen de l'Unité (q.v.), serving as the latter's Second-Deputy
Secretary-General in 1960. Borna joined the cabinet as Minister of Public Works (1958–1960) and of Finance, occupying

the latter post until the coup d'etat of 1963 (q.v.), when he was accused of gross abuses of fiscal responsibility. Borna reemerged in his old position in 1966 when he was brought into General Christophe Soglo's (q.v.) cabinet to represent the north. His entry into the government sparked the resignation of several of Soglo's "technocrats," and added to the dissatisfaction in the army that eventually led to the 1967 coup d'etat (q.v.). For some time representative of the UN Development Program (UNDP) in Dakar, Senegal, Borna was accused of complicity in the 1975 attempted coup (q.v.) (see ASSOGBA, JANVIER) and sentenced to death in absentia on March 7, 1975. He has remained in exile, mostly in Abidjan and Lomé, involved in international trade. In 1982 he became director of the regional UN bureau for the Sahel Region, and later a UNDP official. Borna returned to Benin after the 1990 normalization and was an unsuccessful Presidential candidate in the 1991 elections. He leads a small splinter-party with whose support he was elected in 1991 Deputy to the National Assembly.

BOSSOU, ALFRED AYMARD, 1923– . Early political leader and civil administrator. Born in Cové on October 23, 1923, and educated locally and in France as a senior civil administrator, Bossou served as the head of the French Governor's office staff between 1944 and 1947, followed by 11 years as Secretary-General of the Assemblée Legislative (q.v.) (1947–1958). After further training in France in 1958–1959, he returned home to become sous-préfet of Porto Novo (q.v.) (1960–1961) and Prefect of the Southeast Departement (1961–1966). During the transition from the Maga to the Apithy/Ahomadégbé (q.v.) government, he was appointed head of the Sûrété Nationale (q.v.) as well. His impartiality led to his being attached to the Presidency for two years (1964–1965) as security advisor, following which he became Prefect of Zou (q.v.) and, in 1966, Inspector of Administrative Affairs of Dahomey. In 1968 Bossou left for France where he currently resides.

BOUAY. Currently a very small village in the Borgou (q.v.), in the precolonial era Bouay was a small Bariba (q.v.) principality, the most ancient after Nikki (q.v.). Always allied with the latter, Bouay had been established by one of the sons of Sunon Séro (q.v.), the founder of Nikki.

BOUCHE, PIERRE BERTRAND, 1835–1903. Early missionary and writer on Dahomey. Born in Bagnere de Luchon in 1835, Bouche studied at the Toulouse Seminary, joining the Missions Africaines de Lyon, having been ordained in 1866. He was dispatched to Porto Novo (q.v.) the same year, served in Ouidah (q.v.) and, later, in 1868, founded the Lagos mission. Mindful of the spiritual needs of "Brazilians" (q.v.) along the coast, Bouche was the founder of the Agoué (q.v.) mission in 1874. He is the author of several early works on Dahomey including a basic study of the Nagot (q.v.) language. Bouche died in France on September 10, 1903.

BOURAIMA, YESSOUFOU (Major). Former Minister of Public Health. Yoruba (q.v.) officer, former aide-de-camp of Gen. Christophe Soglo (q.v.), Bouraima was arrested in 1969, together with Col. Alphonse Alley (q.v.) and several others, in connection with an alleged kidnapping plot against Col. Maurice Kouandété (q.v.), at a time of intense strife over control of the armed forces (q.v.). Sentenced to ten years, Bouraima was then released as part of a general amnesty after the December 1969 coup (q.v.) that toppled President Emile Derlin Zinsou (q.v.). Promoted to Captain shortly after, he was appointed military attaché to Dahomey's Embassy in Paris. In 1974 he returned to Cotonou (q.v.) and was appointed Minister of Public Health, a post he held until 1984 when he returned to military duties.

BOUSSARI, CORNEILLE TAOFIQUI, 1925– . Former Deputy Director of Administration of Benin. Born in Ouidah (q.v.) on July 17, 1925, and educated at Dakar's Ecole William Ponty (q.v.) and in Paris, Boussari joined the civil service and was appointed *sous-préfet* of Allada (q.v.) in 1960. He later served in a similar capacity in Kandi (1963) and in April 1964 was appointed prefect of Mono (qq.v.). Late in 1965 Boussari was integrated into the central administration and named Deputy Director of Administration, and briefly in

1967 he was administrative head of the Security Forces, attached to the Ministry of Interior. After the 1967 coup d'etat (q.v.), Boussari was shifted to the administrative chamber of the Supreme Court (q.v.), serving until his retirement in the mid-1980's.

BOYA, ANTOINE, 1918– . Civil administrator. Born in Cotonou (q.v.) on May 17, 1918, and a graduate of Dakar's Ecole William Ponty (q.v.) and the IHEOM of Paris, Boya joined the Ministry of Public Works in 1942 and served in a wide variety of administrative posts through 1961. Between 1956 and 1961 he was also assistant to the Mayor of Cotonou. In 1962 he was brought into the staff of the Minister of Foreign Affairs as Cabinet Director, serving concurrently as President of the Accounting Chamber of the Supreme Court (q.v.) (1961–1965). In 1966 he was appointed financial consultant of OCAM (q.v.), based in Yaoundé, Cameroun, returning in 1972 to assume the post of Director General of the Société Béninoise du Kenaf (q.v.), a post he held until his retirement in 1978.

BOYA, THOMAS, 1936– , Educator and diplomat. Born in Ouidah (q.v.) on February 6, 1936, and a graduate in philosophy (1956) and English (1961), Boya started his career as a teacher at the Lycée Béhanzin (1961–1974), and as headmaster of the Ouidah Secondary School (1974–1975). His knowledge of English and his contacts with the military regime secured him in January 1976 the key diplomatic posting of Ambassador to the United Nations. After he was replaced he was attached as head of one of the divisions in the Foreign Ministry.

BRAMOULLE, ADRIEN, 1924– . Colonial administrator. Born on June 23, 1924, in Saint-Yves-Finistére, Bramoulle joined the colonial civil service in 1946 and worked for 14 years in Dahomey, leaving his personal imprint upon the administrative structure of the colony. He served in Nikki (q.v.) and in Aplahoué before becoming head of the Abomey, and later, Porto Novo (qq.v.) cercles. Promoted Prefect of the entire southeast département, he continued serving the independent

Dahomey as technical consultant attached to the Ministry of Interior, and later as special advisor to the President of the Republic. Bramoulle left Dahomey in 1964 to assume administrative duties in a private company in Brest, France.

BRAZILIANS. Beninois of mixed Euro-African parentage; exiled or deported Africans at the time of Dahomey's dynastic wars; and slaves or descendants of slaves taken to Brazil and returning back to Dahomey in the nineteenth century. Many bear the names of the Portuguese aristrocracy or the Brazilian plantation gentry (d'Almeida, Paraiso, da Costa, de Madeiros, da Souza, de Campos, Oliveira, etc.). Among the first such families were those of Da Souza, Da Silva, Rodriguez and Martinez. Most settled in Ouidah (q.v.) or other coastal communities like Agoué, Grand Popo, Godomey and Porto Novo (qq.v.) and engaged in trade—usually as middlemen between the Africans and the Europeans. Of Porto Novo's 1898 population of 30,000, for example, 1,000 were Brazilian, headed for several generations by the Paraiso family. As late as the 1920's the town's main traders were all Brazilian—Badou, de Campos, Pinto, do Rego, Sodji, Chodaton, Tovalou-Quénum, Nicoué. Elsewhere, the original Da Souza, for example, became the powerful viceroy of Ouidah under King Glélé (q.v.), engaged in the slave (q.v.) and arms trade; Domingo Martinez settled in the 1820's in Porto Novo and became an important trader in palm oil, etc.

There were around 500 "Brazilians" in the late 1800's and among their descendants are to be found former President Emile Derlin Zinsou and former Chief of Staff Paul Emile De Souza (qq.v.). The group had split loyalties on the advantages of French over British tutelage, especially manifest, for example, in the bitter conflict between the pro-British Brazilian family of Lawson, and the pro-French family of Pedro Pinto de Silveira, both at Petit Popo (now Aného, across the border in Togo.) Mostly Catholic, Europeanized and well educated, Benin's Brazilians played a dominant role in the early days of French colonial rule (1900–1950), contributing disproportionately to their numbers to the cultural, professional and political life of the colony. With independence, their political significance rapidly declined because being totally "detribalized," they were devoid of ethnic networks, the building blocks of political power. Following the 1972 Revolution a significant number of them went into self-exile to France. See also FRANCISCO FELIX DA SOUZA; OUIDAH.

BRAZZAVILLE CONFERENCE. A conference of all senior French colonial administrators convened by General de Gaulle in Brazzaville, Congo, in January 1944 to set future policy regarding French Africa. The conference repudiated the possibility of self-rule or independence, but, recognizing Africa's contribution to the war effort, stipulated the end of the indigénat (q.v.) and corvée labor (q.v.). The Conference also recommended an administrative decentralization of French Africa that led to the creation of individual Territorial Assemblies for each colony with a common quasi-federal structure for France and its overseas territories.

BRETONNET, HENRI ETIENNE, 1864–1899. Naval colonial officer. Born in Mezières sur Seine on March 2, 1864, Bretonnet commanded several vessels in other colonial campaigns before being assigned to General Dodds (q.v.) as commander of the Mosca in 1893. He participated in the Franco-Dahomean campaigns (q.v.), assisting in the capture of King Béhanzin (q.v.) in January 1894. Later assigned to set up a series of posts from Parakou (q.v.) to Ilo, Bretonnet was instrumental in consolidating French rule in the Borgou (q.v.). He died on July 17, 1899, in the fighting against Rabah in Chad.

BURTON, (SIR) RICHARD F., 1821–1890. Famous British explorer, diplomat, soldier and writer. His career touched upon Dahomey when, in 1864, stationed as Consul in Fernando Poo, he made an official visit to Dahomey's King Glélé (q.v.) in an effort to persuade the latter to put an end to the slave trade (q.v.). After this visit Burton published his impressions of the mission.

BUSSA. Former kingdom, centered around the village of the same name, that is the cradle and traditional origin of the various Bariba in Benin's Borgou (qq.v.), from which the nobility, the Wasangari (q.v.), trace their lineage. Currently a small and very dilapidated village of 1,200 in Nigeria's Kwara state, whose location has been twice shifted, the total number of Bussa's Bariba population is less than 60,000. See also BARIBA; BORGOU; KISIRA.

BYLL-CATARIA, REGINA, 1946– . Historian. Born on October 3, 1946 and with a doctorate in history from the University of Grenoble, Byll-Cataria teaches at the National University of Benin (q.v.).

-C-

CADJA, GERMAIN. Former Minister of Nursery and Primary Education in the transitional August 1989 government of Kérékou (q.v.).

CFA FRANC. Common currency of the Communauté Finançiere Africaine—i.e., all territories of the former French West Africa (AOF, q.v.) and French Equatorial Africa federations except for those that opted to set up their own currency, including Madagascar and the former French mandatory territories of Togo and Cameroun. Established in 1946 as the Colonies Françaises d'Afrique franc, the currency's name was changed in 1962. Fully guaranteed by France, and pegged to the French franc into which it is freely convertible, CFA monetary reserves are held in Paris. Repeated and insistent requests from various African states that reserves be transferred to Africa and some of the fiscal treaties be modified finally led, in 1974, to the relocation of the BCEAO (q.v.) to Dakar, Senegal. Though a certain amount of decision-making authority accompanied this move, the CFAF is still tightly under the fiscal control of France.

CAISSE CENTRALE DE COOPERATION ECONOMIQUE (CCCE). Official French agency through which French governmental aid to Francophone Africa is channeled/ banked, and administered. Successor to the Caisse Céntrale de la France d'Outre Mer (CCFOM). In 1982 contributions amounted to 2,425 million CFAF.

CAISSE DES DEPOTS ET CONSIGNATIONS (CDC). Official French agency that serves as banker, administrator and manager of Francophone Africa's pension, national security and other social welfare programs.

CAISSE NATIONALE DE CREDIT AGRICOLE (CNCA). Defunct State organ, set up in Cotonou (q.v.) in 1975 and capitalized at 300 million CFA francs, aimed at providing credits for agricultural enterprises. The capital came from the government (51 percent) and from parastatal organs (49 percent). The CNCA took over some of the functions of SOCAD (q.v.) under its manager Bernard Tossou. Constantly under pressure and criticized due to its record of bad debts, massive embezzlement by government ministers and officials and a policy of granting unsecured loans for non-agricultural projects, the company, financially bailed out several times, finally went bankrupt in 1987 and closed down fully early in 1989.

CALMINA see KANA

CAMP BIO GUERA 1. Porto Novo (q.v.) staff headquarters of the gendarmerie (q.v.). Named after the early anti-French insurrectionist leader, Bio Guéra (q.v.).

CAMP GUEZO. Cotonou's (q.v.) main military camp, headquarters of the armed forces (q.v.). Named after one of Dahomey's most illustrious kings, Ghézo (q.v.).

CANTON see ADMINISTRATIVE ORGANIZATION

CAPO-CHICHI, GRATIEN TONAKPON (Captain). Former Minister of Literacy and Popular Culture and Benin's prime "Maoist" ideologue and labor leader. Coming from a politically active Mahi (q.v.) family, trained in Libya and popular in the armed forces (q.v.), Capo-Chichi was one of the guiding spirits of the ultra-Left Ligue (q.v.) faction that during 1972–1990 constantly prodded the government and the UNSTB (q.v.) to radicalize itself. Populist, pro-Chinese and very popular among unionists and intellectuals, Capo-Chichi on several occasions tried to expand his power base through the creation of parallel "vanguard" groups within the existing political, governmental and labor structures. He was brought into the cabinet in May 1981 in an effort to tame him with cabinet responsibility, but was dropped in 1984 when Kérékou (q.v.) veered to the Right. Capo-Chichi was arrested for his role in the 1988 attempted coup. After the normalization of 1990 he was appointed Ambassador to the UN and in 1992 was retired.

CARLOS, JEROME TOVIGNON. Revolutionary poet. Committed militant, Carlos wrote a collection of poems *Cri de Liberté* (1973) extolling the 1972 revolution, and the need for a violent uprooting of neocolonialism and capitalism from Africa.

CATHOLIC MISSIONS. Catholic missionary activities commenced practically as soon as Dahomey was "discovered." The first systematic evangelical effort occurred in 1634 in Whydah (Ouidah [q.v]), sponsored by the Breton Capucins who set up a mission in the slave port. The mission was a failure, and death from disease and fierce resistance from fetishists (q.v.) brought speedy ends to other similar efforts, including the mission established in Allada (q.v.) in January 1660 at the king's invitation. Only sporadic and individual evangelical efforts occurred until the middle of the nineteenth century when the Apostolic Vicarate of Benin and Dahomey was officially set up. In 1860 the Pères des Missions Africaines de Lyon commenced a concentrated effort in Dahomey with Father François Borghero (q.v.) being sent over to head their new mission in Ouidah. The first regular Catholic schools were opened at that time in Ouidah, Porto Novo and Agoué (qq.v.). The center of Catholic missionary efforts soon moved to Porto Novo, for Ouidah was the center of many fetish cults that exerted powerful influence at that time. New outposts were created at the turn of the century, in Ketou (1897), Abomey-Calavi

(1898), and Cotonou (qq.v.) (1901). See also SEMINARY OF OUIDAH.

The first Catholic mission in the north was set up in Kandi in 1937 with others in Nikki (1940) and Parakou (qq.v.) (1944), though the White Fathers and the Pères de Lyon had been engaged in proselytizing in Kouandé and Péréré (qq.v.) since the turn of the century. The Catholic missions and schools played a dominant role during the colonial era in educating Dahomey's future elite, and, as late as 1965, it was estimated that 45 percent of Dahomey's pupils were attending private Catholic schools. The Catholic archdiocese of Cotonou (which covers all of Dahomey and Niger) had, in 1974, 450 missionary schools with 2,500 personnel. Later these were all formally integrated into the State educational network, though many educators opted to leave the country. Around 12 percent of the population (according to the 1961 census) profess to be Catholic, with the majority (65 percent) holding a variety of animist (q.v.) beliefs. Official Church figures, however, based on more flexible criteria, give the following picture for 1980, broken down by diocese as in the table that follows. More recent estimates place the number of Catholics at roughly 20 percent less.

Diocese	Local Clergy	Foreign Clergy	Adherents
Cotonou	29	26	683,048
Porto Novo	20	5	139,520
Abomey	26	28	130,000
Lokossa	25	9	35,500
Parakou	2	20	15,420
Natitingou	4	35	9,750
Total	106	123	1,013,238

CENTRE NATIONAL D'ESSAIS ET DE RECHERCHES DES TRAVAUX PUBLIQUES (CNER-TP). Division of the Ministry of Public Works engaged in basic surveys and feasibility studies. At one time CNER-TP was given autonomy to recommend new projects aimed at raising the productivity of the economy.

CENTRES D'ACTION REGIONALE POUR LE DEVELOPPE-MENT RURAL (CARDER). Former regional rural development centers, set up in 1975 in all six regions in order to increase cultivated lands and agricultural yields, improve marketing arrangements and promote agroindustry. Due to inadequate financing, only four of the six centers were initially actually erected, all with external funding. The CARDERs fell under the jurisdiction of the Ministry of Rural Development and Cooperative Action.

CERAMIQUE INDUSTRIELLE DU BENIN (CIB). Former parastatal ceramic company set up in 1974 with 147.5 million CFA francs capitalization (80 percent government equity) to produce ceramic tiles, sanitary ware and other industrial products. Originally headed by shifting military State Commissioners (appointed to essentially sinecures), and later under the management of Emile Agbéhounkpon, as President and Théophile Glikou as Director General, CIB piled up large deficits as production plunged from 92 percent of capacity (995 tons in 1979) to 150 tons and 14 percent of capacity in 1985 when it was dissolved.

CERCLE. Francophone Africa's most basic administrative district in the period prior to the Second World War, it was governed by a *commandant du cercle* with the assistance of a hierarchy of local chiefs and a council of local notables appointed by him. In the early days of colonial rule, difficulties in communications resulted in commandants possessing tremendous and exceptional powers, some of which were abused. See also ADMINISTRATIVE ORGANIZATION; DEPARTEMENT.

CHABI GABA, 1731–1789. Founder of the Kouandé Bariba (qq.v.) lineage. Son of the 16th King of Nikki (q.v.), Sérou Tokorou, Chabi Gaba was, on all accounts, a very brutal and ambitious prince. Accused of killing one of his wives over a minor offense, he was chased out of Nikki. Together with members of his retinue (and some of the royal trumpets and other symbols of office), Chabi Gaba settled first in Kandé, then Banikoara, and finally south of Natitingou (q.v.). Marrying the daughter of the local chief and succeeding him upon his death, Chabi Gaba died in 1789. His son, Worou (who had accompanied him from Nikki), became the first king of Kouandé in 1799. The lineage survives to this day (the current "king" being a former gendarmerie sergeant) as does the historic friction with Nikki; the latter regards Kouandé as a subservient vassal state, at least for ritual and ceremonial purposes, while Kouandé—especially after its period of major military expansion in the nineteenth century—regards itself as coequal with Nikki.

CHABI-GONNI, DANIEL, 1947– . Chemical biologist. Born in 1947 and educated in chemical biology in Porto Novo (q.v.) and Ouagadougou, Chabi-Gonni has been employed mostly in Burkina Faso and since 1985 has served as Head of the Department of Hydrology.

CHABI IBRAHIMA (Major). Former Minister of Rural Economy. An unruly Bariba (q.v.) officer, of chiefly origins, who first entered the political limelight when appointed a member of Kouandété's (q.v.) interim military administration in 1967–1968. In 1970, after the electoral fiasco cut short Hubert Maga's (q.v.) drive for the Presidency, Chabi was prominent in threatening the secession of the north unless the military relented and nominated Maga to the Presidency. Retired from the armed forces (q.v.) in 1972, he was implicated the next year in an attempted coup against Kérékou in alliance with several other senior officers also purged after the 1972 military takeover (Alley, Ha chemé [qq.v.], etc.). Imprisoned for his role, he was released during the unionist riots of 1975 (associated with Aikpé's [q.v.] murder) and he fled abroad, where he currently resides.

CHABI KAO, PASCAL, 1935– . Northern politician and former Minister. Allegedly the illegitimate son of Hubert Maga (q.v.), Chabi Kao was born in Parakou (q.v.) on March 10, 1935. He studied at a Teachers' Training College in Ivory

Coast, at the University of Aix-en-Provence, France, and at the Paris Center of Financial, Economic and Banking Studies, obtaining a degree in law and economics. Upon his return home he was appointed Secretary-General of the Banque Dahoméenne de Développement (q.v.). One of Maga's trusted political lieutenants, he served in the cabinet during the latter's first Presidency (1960–1963) and was also appointed Minister of Labor in the administration of General Christophe Soglo (q.v.) (1966–1967). After the 1967 coup (q.v.) that toppled Soglo (about which he had foreknowledge), Cabi Kao was the only civilian minister (of Finance and the Civil Service) in the interim government of Colonel Alphonse Alley and Major Maurice Kouandété (qq.v.). In 1970, after the annulment of the Presidential elections that would have brought Maga back to power, Chabi Kao was one of several northern politicians who threatened the secession of the northern regions from Dahomey. When the Presidential Council (q.v.) was set up in May 1970, Chabi Kao entered the first Maga cabinet as Minister of Labor (later of Finance). Following the 1972 coup d'etat (q.v.) he was accused of various irregularities (see KOVACS AFFAIR). The unwillingness of the Presidential Council to purge Chabi Kao was cited as a prominent reason for the military intervention. Temporarily imprisoned, Chabi Kao was rearrested in 1973 for a plot against the military regime of Colonel Mathieu Kérékou (q.v.). Again released, he was attached to the Ministry of Finance, based in Porto Novo (q.v.). Chabi-Kao reemerged in 1989 when he joined Hubert Maga's PNDD (q.v.) political formation, and in the 1991 legislative elections was elected to the National Assembly (q.v.).

CHABI MAMA, 1921– . Important northern politician, former Minister in several governments and major power-wielder in the Parakou (q.v.) area. Of princely origins, Chabi was born in Parakou on July 15, 1921, and was among the first northerners to receive missionary education. He studied locally in Abomey and in Porto Novo (qq.v.), following which he entered the civil service. After the Second World War Chabi began his meteoric rise to power. At the age of 24 he became Secretary-General of the Parakou branch of Dahomey's first party, the Union Progréssiste Dahoméenne (q.v.). When Hubert Maga (q.v.) left that party in 1951 to form the Groupement Ethnique du Nord (q.v.), Chabi's support in Parakou was invaluable, though the two leaders had their differences. In 1956 Chabi was elected Deputy-Mayor of Parakou and in 1957 he became Deputy to the Assemblée Territoriale (q.v.). In that year Chabi—invariably regarded as the real power behind Maga's northern network of allegiances—became Secretary of the latter's Rassemblement Démocratique Dahoméen (q.v.), the temporary political alliance between Maga and Sourou-Migan Apithy, and Secretary-General of the RDD (qq.v.) following the split between the latter two. When Maga became President of Dahomey—following another alliance with Apithy and the merger of their parties—Chabi became Secretary-General of their joint party, the Parti Dahoméen de l'Unité (q.v.), a position he held until the overthrow of Maga in 1963. Member of Dahomey's Assemblies between 1957 and 1963, Chabi was also Second Vice-President of the Assemblée Nationale (q.v.), President of its Policies and Legislation Committee and Dahomean representative to the Senate of the Communauté Française (q.v.) (1959–1961).

Following Maga's overthrow (see COUP OF 1963) Chabi served in the interim administration of Gen. Christophe Soglo (q.v.) as Foreign Minister. When Maga was imprisoned and Soglo commenced preparations to turn over power to a southern coalition between Justin Ahomadégbé and Apithy (qq.v.), Chabi, completely shut out from any important position, returned to Parakou to foment massive and violent antigovernment demonstrations.

Sentenced to 20 years' imprisonment (which the government could not enforce due to his popularity in the north), Chabi's star declined until July 1968. On that date President Emile Derlin Zinsou (q.v.), seeking support in the north, appointed Chabi as Minister of Education, Youth and Sports. When Zinsou was overthrown in 1969 and Dahomey's triumvirate (q.v.) returned to power forming the Presidential Council (q.v.), Chabi was appointed Minister of Rural Development and Cooperation, a post he occupied until the

1972 coup (q.v.). He was briefly imprisoned at that time for fiscal irregularities connected with his chairmanship of Dahomey's National Company for Ceramic Crafts (SONAC), but was exonerated of embezzlement. He again reappeared in the spotlight in 1984 as a co-conspirator in the 1984 coup attempt at the Ouassa military barracks, but was released by a government unwilling to antagonize Borgou (q.v.).

One of the most powerful traditional Bariba (q.v.) leaders in Benin, Chabi Mama is not widely known outside his country. One of the undisputed leaders in the north, his traditional support there was the key to Maga's power. Chabi's rigidity, aggressiveness and traditional-conservative outlook, however, worked against his receiving either unofficial French support or anything but fierce resistance in the south to his Presidential ambitions; at the same time the historic Nikki (q.v.)-Parakou friction underscored the greater utility to the north of the mediatory leadership of a figure such as Hubert Maga.

CHABI PROUKA. King of Nikki (q.v.) who joined in the uprising of Bio Guéra (q.v.) against the French in 1916–1917. Following the collapse of the revolt, Chabi Prouka was arrested and exiled for five years in Guinea.

CHACHA OF WHYDAH see DA SOUZA, FRANCISCO FELIX

CHAMBRE DE COMMERCE, D'AGRICULTURE ET DE L'INDUSTRIE DU BENIN. Benin's Chamber of Commerce, Industry and Agriculture. Founded in Cotonou (q.v.) but with an increasingly influential Parakou (q.v.) branch, the Chamber is under the Presidency of the Minister of Commerce with two Vice-Presidents J.V. Adjovi and M.T. Laléye.

CHAMBRE DE REFLEXION. Consultative organ established by decree on August 17, 1964 (and set up in October) with 36 members (all over 50 years of age) appointed by Vice-President Ahomadégbé (q.v.) for a period of five years and under the Chairmanship of Paul Hazoumé (q.v.). The organ was divided into two sections, one dealing with political issues called Conseil des Anciens or Conseil des Sages, the other dealing with economic matters. The organ has often been referred to also as the Association des Anciens (q.v.).

CHASME, LOUIS JOSEPH (Lt. Colonel), 1929– . Former Quartermaster General of the Benin army and briefly Minister of Justice. Born on May 8, 1929, in Ouidah of Fon (qq.v.) origins Chasmé first came to prominence in the political arena late in 1967 after the coup d'etat (q.v.) that toppled the regime of General Christophe Soglo (q.v.). A member of the interim military government then established, Chasmé was appointed Minister of Justice. In that capacity he proposed, set up, and chaired an all-military ad hoc anticorruption tribunal (q.v.) investigating charges of fiscal abuses during the Soglo era. The only victim of the tribunal was Chasmé himself who was arrested in March 1968 and accused of two charges of embezzlement (totalling over 4 million CFA francs) while Quartermaster of the army. He was stripped of his commission and sentenced to 12 months in prison and confiscation of all his property. Later amnestied and reinstated in the army with his old rank, after the 1969 coup (q.v.) Chasmé was appointed to head the Security Services. In 1972 he presided over the all-military Court of Inquiry that condemned to death his rival Col. Maurice Kouandété (q.v.), who had purged him in 1968. After the October 1972 coup d'etat (q.v.) Chasmé was retired from the armed forces (q.v.).

CHEDO, AGBOMENOU GBENOU, 1943– . Born on June 2, 1943, and educated in physics and chemistry through the doctoral level, Chedo is provincial Director of Natural Science Education, and also teaches chemical thermodynamics at the National University of Benin (q.v.).

CHEF DU DISTRICT. New nomenclature for the pre-1974 *sous-préfet.* Responsible for his district (q.v.) to the Prefect (*préfet*) above him, the *chef du district* has always been assisted by an advisory committee. During the Revolutionary regime (1974–1990) this was the Conseil Révolutionnaire du District (CRD) (q.v.).

CHEKPO, ANDRE, 1936– . Educator. Born in Abomey (q.v.) and educated at home and abroad, Chékpo served briefly as technical counsellor in the Ministry of Education (late 1965) before becoming Cabinet Director of the Minister of Interior and Security (1965–1968). In September 1968 he was shifted to become Secretary-General of Education, a post he held through 1975. He then left for France and only recently returned to Benin.

CHODATON, LOUIS. Influential Cotonou (q.v.) freight and passenger transporter, Secretary-General of the Syndicat des Transports Portuaires, and a member of the Chambre de Commerce and the Conseil Economique at Social (qq.v.), Chodaton is a powerful commercial figure in Cotonou.

CIMENTS DU BENIN (CIMBENIN). The privatized, Scandi-navian-owned former Société Nationale des Ciments (q.v.) which see.

CISSE, MOHAMED AMADOU. Marabout, soothsayer, Kérékou (q.v.) confidant and coordinator of State Security. Of Malian origins, Cissé was Zaire's President Mobuto's personal soothsayer and advisor in the 1970's, as well as Zambia's President Kenneth Kaunda's aide before joining Kérékou's staff in 1980. Popularly known as the Djiné (devil), Cissé, a spiritual healer, is credited with having supernatural powers. He was appointed Minister Delegate to the Presidency in charge of Interior and Security where allegedly due to his occult powers he ferreted out several conspiracies against Kérékou. His Security duties were to coordinate the various intelligence services (such as the Service de Documentation et d'Information; the Permanent National Investigatory Commission on State Security) and report their findings and activities to Kérékou. Increasingly linked with international drug traders shipping out local marijuana, and with massive embezzlement in the Banque Commerciale du Bénin (BCB) (q.v.) (that collapsed in 1989), he escaped Benin in 1989 but was arrested in Paris on July 24th on charges of stealing 3.5 billion CFA francs from the BCB. He fled France despite posting a bond of $1 million, but was extradited to Benin from the Ivory Coast. On September 7, 1992, he was sentenced to ten years in prison and a 3 million CFA franc fine. Despite acute fears by Kérékou and his confidants that Cissé might reveal on trial details about the corruption of other members of the previous government (for which he was securely guarded, and his food monitored for poison) Cissé did not reveal any secrets.

CLUB DE L'ETOILE NOIRE. Early Dahomean social and cultural club. Created in 1912 in Porto Novo (q.v.), the only club open to all races, its purpose was to provide a congenial setting for cultural exchanges. Subscribing to many journals and possessing a good library, the club was quite prosperous and influential until 1924. Under its early officers (including Louis Ignacio-Pinto [q.v.]), the club maintained contacts with counterparts elsewhere (especially in Lagos) and with such pan-African speakers as Marcus Garvey. With the spread of education and social advances in the mid 1920's the Club lost its influence and closed down completely in 1927.

CODJOVI, JULIEN JEAN, 1942– . Lawyer. Born on January 27, 1942, and educated in law in France, Codjovi practices law in Cotonou (q.v.) and is the Director of the Center for Administrative Training of Benin.

COFFI, PIERRE (Colonel). Former Minister, Head of the Gendarmerie (q.v.) and Director-General of Defense. The former commander of a unit based in Cotonou (q.v.), Coffi first came to attention in 1969 when he was involved in, and convicted for, theft of arms linked to attempts to reinstate into the army the purged Lt. Col. Alphonse Alley (q.v.). He was released from prison in the 1969 amnesty following Col. Maurice Kouandété's (q.v.) coup. Promoted to Major at the same time, in 1970 Coffi became Deputy Head of the Service Civique (q.v.) under Major Jean-Baptiste Hachemé (q.v.). Following the 1972 coup Coffi was appointed head of the gendarmerie and Minister of Information. In a cabinet reshuffle in April 1974 he became Minister of Civil Service and Labor. In October 1974 he was dropped from the cabinet and returned to police duties. Shortly after, promoted to Colonel, he was appointed Director-General of the Ministry of Defense, a post he held to 1992.

COMITE DE RENOVATION NATIONALE (CRN). An advisory committee set up on December 24, 1965, by Gen. Christophe Soglo (q.v.), following the erection of his military regime (see COUP OF 1965(b)). Originally composed of 25 members (later enlarged to 36) from all walks of life, including three military officers, the "Committee for National Renewal" had few specified functions, and those, vague. With time, the Committee arrogated to itself quasi-legislative functions and, with the growing laxity of the Soglo regime, more militant members of the armed forces (q.v.) urged the creation of a military body to actually supervise the government. This occurred on April 6, 1967, when the CRN was dissolved and a Comité Militaire de Vigilance (q.v.) was established. The CRN had departmental, village and urban branches.

COMITE D'ETAT D'ADMINISTRATION (CEA). Seven-man executive committee during the Revolutionary era, set up at the provincial, district and local level, to head each level's Conseil Révolutionnaire (q.v.). The Comité d'Etat d'Administration was headed by a Secretary assisted by officers in charge of (1) propaganda, (2) security, (3) production, (4) cultural affairs, (5) social affairs and (6) fiscal matters. The Secretaries from each lower level are also deputies from their units to the higher level, culminating with the six Provincial Secretaries who are automatically members of the Conseil Executif National (q.v.).

COMITE DES 104. Clandestine 1965 antigovernmental faction centered around Valentin Aplogan-Djibodé (q.v.) and anchored in the latter's Rassemblement de l'Impératif National (q.v.), which, until banned, lashed out at Ahomadégbé's (q.v.) regime with a variety of seditious tracts.

COMITE MILITAIRE DE VIGILANCE (CMV). All-military organ set up on April 6, 1967, to replace the largely civilian

Comité de Rénovation Nationale (q.v.) and supervise the military regime of General Christophe Soglo (q.v.). The "Committee of Military Vigilance" rapidly assumed the role of a super-government to whom Soglo was ultimately accountable. Its first President was Major Benoit Sinzogan, head of the gendarmerie, with Major Maurice Kouandété (qq.v.) as Vice-President. From inception, the CMV was split on a variety of levels—age, rank, ethnic origin—and, as corruption seeped in, lost its utility. After Major Kouandété's 1967 coup (q.v.), Captain Hachemé temporarily assumed the MCV Presidency. See COUP OF 1967; COMITE DE RENOVATION NATIONALE.

COMITE MILITAIRE POUR LA REVOLUTION (CMR, 1972). A watchdog committee of 15 set up shortly after the 1972 military coup of Mathieu Kérékou (qq.v.), to provide the regime with advice and criticism and oversee the "morals" of administrative employees. The Committee's members were drawn from officers and NCO's in the army and gendarmerie (qq.v.) and included two of the government commissioners in charge of state industries (i.e., the former senior officer hierarchy, purged after the coup). The organ was dissolved with the institutionalization of the regime in 1978.

COMITE MILITAIRE REVOLUTIONNAIRE (CMR, 1967). A committee of military officers formed as the ultimate body to which the interim military regime set up after the 1967 coup d'etat of Major Maurice Kouandété (qq.v.) was responsible. The committee was dissolved when Emile Derlin Zinsou (q.v.) was appointed as Dahomey's civilian President in August 1968. Its first Chairman was Captain Hachemé (q.v.). The original composition of the CMR was 14 officers, of which only two were Majors, the remainder junior officers and NCO's.

COMITE NATIONAL CONSULTATIF. National advisory committee set up after the October 1972 coup d'etat (q.v.), replacing the Assemblée Consultative Nationale of the previous Presidential Council (qq.v.), with similar functions. The

CNC was a deliberative organ of 100 members representing all regions, ethnic groups and vocations, divided into three subcommittees dealing with (1) financial and economic issues, (2) social and cultural matters, and (3) general policy guidelines. Purges of "counter-revolutionaries" rapidly reduced its membership and the organ never played a meaningful role.

COMITES CENTRAUX D'ORGANISATION ELECTORALE (CCOE). Also known as Comités Eléctoraux, these were electoral committees that sprang up in Cotonou (q.v.) and other urban centers in 1945 to nominate and support political candidates and lists under the more liberal post-World War II representational system. Precursors of political parties (q.v.), and very much loosely organized machines—led by notables and intellectuals such as Paul Hazoumé, Augustin Azango (qq.v.), and Victor Patterson—the comitees played an important role so long as demands for regional equality of representation were kept at bay. Dahomey's first political party, the Union Progréssiste Dahoméenne (q.v.) was one product of cooperation of the comitees. The moment regionalism (q.v.) became a serious issue, as it did after 1950, both the comitees and efforts at forming "national" parties were to founder. See also POLITICAL PARTIES; REGIONALISM.

COMITES ELECTORAUX see COMITES CENTRAUX D'ORGANISATION ELECTORALE

COMITES POUR LE DEFENSE DE LA REVOLUTION (CDR). A series of committees, with managerial authority, established after the 1972 coup (q.v.) and the onset of the Revolutionary era, in all sectors of the Beninois economy to draw organized labor into a more productive (and less confrontational) stance vis-a-vis its employer, now mostly the State. Though the CDR's scored some successes, labor by and large remained in opposition to the regime on bread-and-butter issues, and was alienated as well by the strong northern and military composition of the Kérékou (q.v.) regime. The CDRs, like all revolutionary structures, were disbanded after the 1990 normalization.

COMMISSAIRES DU PEUPLE. Formal title of the Deputies to the Assemblée Nationale Révolutionnaire (q.v.). See also COMMISSIONERS.

COMMISSIONERS. The term "Commissioner" has been used in two different contexts in Benin during the 1972–1990 Revolutionary era. As Peoples' Commissioners (Commissaires du Peuple [q.v.]) it referred to the formal title of Deputies to the Assemblée Nationale Révolutionnaire (ANR) (q.v.). As State Commissioners it referred to the title granted to the senior military officers purged from the armed forces (q.v.) in 1972 and dispatched to head the various state industries.

COMMUNAUTE FINANCIERE AFRICAINE (CFA) see CFA FRANC

COMMUNAUTE FRANCAISE. Free association of autonomous republics set up with the adoption in France of the constitution of the Fifth Republic. In the referendum that ratified the constitution for France's colonies only Guinea opted for the alternative—independence. Within the Community, France retained jurisdiction in the fields of foreign policy, defense, currency and fiscal matters, and external communications. The structure set up for the Community included an executive (the French President) assisted by an Executive Council (all heads of the governments concerned and the French Minister of Community Affairs) and a Senate with representation from all republics in accord with their population. Early in 1960 an amendment to the French constitution was promulgated allowing associated republics to attain full independence while remaining in the Community.

COMMUNE. Basic administrative unit into which Benin is divided. The number of *communes* has varied over time but currently stands at 404. Mostly villages or rural areas, each *commune* had—since the 1974–1976 reorganization and until the 1990 normalization—a 25-man elected Conseil Communal de la Révolution (CCR) heavily weighted in terms of representation of youth. The Conseil Révolutionnaire Local (CRL) (q.v.) assisted in the administration of the *commune*. See also ADMINISTRATIVE ORGANIZA-TION.

COMPAGNIE BENINOISE DE NAVIGATION MARITIME (COBENAM). Joint maritime shipping line set up in 1974 between Benin (51 percent) and Algeria (49 percent) with headquarters in Cotonou (q.v.) under Director General Nouhoum Assouman. Capitalized at 500 million CFA francs, COBENAM took possession of its first (cargo) vessel—the *Ganvié*—in 1978. The company in theory had a monopoly over all imports and exports to Benin. Prior to the country's change of name to Benin, the company was known as Compagnie Dahoméenne du Navigation Maritime (CO-DANAM).

COMPAGNIE DAHOMEENNE DU NAVIGATION MARI-TIME (CODANAM) see COMPAGNIE BENINOISE DE NAVIGATION MARITIME (COBENAM).

COMPAGNIE ELECTRIQUE DU BENIN (CEB). Joint electric-ity consortium set up in 1968 between Benin and Togo, aimed at promoting the development of electric power in the two countries. Togo and Benin still receive much of their electricity from Ghana (the Volta River Hydroelectric Au-thority of Akossomba) with the CEB's function being to diversify sources of supply and develop internal sources. CEB has its headquarters in Lomé, Togo. It has been looking for new sources of power in the direction of Nigeria, at the same time aiding Beninois-Togolese hydroelectric develop-ments. In 1977 CEB's turnover was 835 million CFA francs. During the mid-1980's CEB's imports from Ghana were cut by 60 percent due to drought conditions that dropped water levels at Lake Volta below turbine operation levels. Power rationing (adopted in Ghana) did not spread to Benin, though outages were common. A new dam along their border is currently being jointly developed by Benin and Togo that, when completed in 1995, will decrease the two countries' dependence on external electricity by another 20 percent.

CONFEDERATION DAHOMEENNE DES TRAVAILLEURS CROYANTS (CDTC). Small trade union founded in 1952 and banned in November 1962, following the forcible merger by President Hubert Maga (q.v.) of all unions within the Union Générale des Travailleurs Dahoméens (q.v.). After Maga's collapse in 1964 the CDTC reemerged under the leadership of General-Secretary Gabriel Ahoué. The union, affiliated to the International Federation of Christian Trade Unions and with a membership of 1,000, disappeared as an autonomous organ with the centralization of unions in the 1970's.

CONFEDERATION NATIONALE DES SYNDICATS LIBRES (CNSL). Small trade union (2,250 members) founded in 1964 under Secretary-General Etienne Ahouangbé. It was merged into Benin's single trade union movement in 1974.

CONFERENCE DES FORCES VIVES see NATIONAL CONFERENCE.

CONGACOU, TAHIROU. Former President of the National Assembly (q.v.) and, briefly, Acting President of Dahomey. A Dendi (q.v.) of the royal house of Djougou, Congacou descended from the keepers of the oral traditions of the kingdom. During the colonial administration Congacou was Sub-Prefect in Nikki (q.v.) after an earlier teaching career. After the Second World War, he sat in Dahomey's first Conseil Général (q.v.) and was also Deputy to the Assemblée Territoriale (q.v.) (1952–1957). After the fall of the Maga (q.v.) government in 1963, Congacou was elected President of the National Assembly and Deputy Secretary-General of the new governmental party, the Parti Démocratique Dahoméen (q.v.). In 1965, after General Christophe Soglo's first coup d'etat (qq.v.), Congacou was entrusted with forming a new government. His inability to reconcile the various regional and personalist factions paved the way for Soglo's second coup several weeks later. Under President Emile Derlin Zinsou (q.v.), Congacou became President of the Conseil Economique et Social (q.v.) set up in October 1968.

Out of public life since the 1972 coup d'etat (q.v.), Congacou died in 1976.

CONSEIL COMMUNAL DE LA REVOLUTION (CCR). Revolutionary era Council set up at the level of all of Benin's urban *communes* (q.v.). Composed of 15 designated members and one delegate from each village (not necessarily the Chief), the CCR was headed by a seven-man committee with functions identical to those of members of the CPR (q.v.) committee. The chairman of the CCR was designated Mayor.

CONSEIL DE L'ENTENTE. The "Council of the Entente" is a regional organization encompassing Ivory Coast, Niger, Benin, Burkina Faso, and Togo. Created on May 29, 1959, under the auspices of Ivory Coast President Felix Houphouet-Boigny, as the latter's countermove to the then projected Mali Federation (q.v.), the Conseil de l'Entente provides for freedom of movement across state borders, coordination of policies in the fields of legal, communications, development and economic matters, and a Solidarity Fund aimed at fiscal redistribution in favor of weaker member states. Most of the goals of the Conseil de l'Entente have not been fulfilled because of the unwillingness of most states to renounce autonomous action in specified spheres, and also because of the overwhelming role within the Entente of one economic giant—Ivory Coast. Benin in particular has had continuous reservations about the utility of the association but has been kept within it through the disbursements of the Solidarity Fund. During 1963–1964 Dahomey actively boycotted Conseil meetings as a result of the border dispute with Niger and, periodically since 1972, Benin has claimed the collusion of some member-states in attempts to destabilize it.

CONSEIL DE NOTABLES. Advisory councils established on the *cercle* (q.v.) level and presided over by the French *commandant de cercle*. Participating members, appointed by the local *commandant,* included chiefs, local notables and "Brazilians" (q.v.). The Conseils were the major mode of participation in the decision-making process open to Africans until the end of the Second World War.

CONSEIL ECONOMIQUE ET SOCIAL. Consultative organ with recommendatory authority in the fields of economic and social policy. Originally set up by Gen. Christophe Soglo (q.v.) on November 8, 1967, it was suspended after the coup that toppled him and then reestablished by President Emile Derlin Zinsou (q.v.) on August 29, 1968. Meeting for the first time on October 12, 1968, under the Presidency of Tahirou Congacou (q.v.), the Social and Economic Council had 35 members representing all walks of life, especially labor. After Zinsou's overthrow in 1969 the Council, along with other political institutions, was suspended.

CONSEIL EXECUTIF NATIONAL (CEN). Formal name of the cabinet of Benin during the Revolutionary (1972–1990) era. Composed of the President, cabinet ministers and heads of the provincial administrative committees (See COMITE D'ETAT D'ADMINISTRATION.), the Council had a Permanent Committee composed of the President and other members, coopted by the Party Central Committee in consultation with the Council. In actual fact the Permanent Committee has been the CEN minus the six provincial secretaries, making the latter's presence at the national level somewhat superfluous.

CONSEIL GENERAL DU DAHOMEY. Consultative organ established under the colonial reforms and the decentralization of French Africa specified in the constitution of France's Fourth Republic. Renamed the Assemblée Territoriale (q.v.) in 1952, the Conseil Général was composed of 30 delegates. The first elections were held in January 1947 with 12 delegates elected by the first electoral college and 18 by the second college. Among these were many who played an important role in Dahomean politics, including Justin Ahomadégbé, Sourou-Migan Apithy, Tahirou Congacou, Michel Ahouanménou, Emile Poisson, Albert Akindès, Cyrille Aguéssy, and Françis Covi (qq.v.).

CONSEIL NATIONAL DE LA REVOLUTION (CNR). The "National Council for the Revolution" was a body of 67 individuals set up after the 1972 coup d'etat (q.v.) as

Dahomey's highest deliberative organ. Under the chairmanship of the Chief-of-Staff of the army and President of the Republic, Mathieu Kérékou (q.v.), the CNR included 33 military representatives of all ranks and 33 civilians, originally drawn from three so-called "fronts"—labor, youth and women, later representing the civil service, police, paramilitary and provincial administration. The CNR's function was to set policy guidelines for the government and watch for abuses of power. Late in 1974 the CNR was given an executive 13-man Political Bureau headed by Kérékou, and its composition came to include all the Executive Secretaries of the local District Councils. The membership, constantly shuffled and purged, was greatly decimated until in 1977 it was replaced by the new National Assembly (q.v.).

CONSEIL PRESIDENTIEL see PRESIDENTIAL COUNCIL

CONSEIL PROVINCIAL DE LA REVOLUTION (CPR). Revolutionary councils with significant administrative powers, set up in each province (q.v.) in the aftermath of the 1974 administrative reorganization (q.v.) of Benin, and disbanded in 1990. The CPR was the organ that assisted the Prefect of the province in the governing of the province and especially in planning the development effort there. The chairman of each provincial council—the Prefect—sat on the national cabinet in Cotonou (q.v.). The Council included the Prefect, heads of the army and gendarmerie (q.v.) units in the province, and five delegates from each of the province's districts (q.v.). It had a permanent executive committee with a secretary and six officials in charge of (1) propaganda, (2) security, (3) production, (4) cultural affairs, (5) social affairs, and (6) fiscal matters. This committee was called the Comité d'Etat d'Administration (q.v.).

CONSEIL REVOLUTIONNAIRE DU DISTRICT (CRD). District (q.v.) revolutionary councils set up as part of the administrative reorganization of Benin in 1974, and disbanded in 1990. They were above the 404 communal CRLs (q.v.) that sent delegates to the 39 districts (q.v.), four of which are urban. The CRD's had advisory powers vis-a-vis the district chief (ex-*sous-préfet*) and were composed of five delegates from each *commune* (q.v.), the heads of the army and gendarmerie (q.v.) in the district, and the District Chief. The CRD had a permanent committee composed of the District Chief and six officials that had functions identical to those members on the permanent committee of the CPR (q.v.).

CONSEIL REVOLUTIONNAIRE LOCAL (CRL). Local revolutionary councils established in 1975 at the level of the country's 404 rural communes (q.v.), disbanded after the 1990 normalization in Benin. Originally elected for an interim period, a full-scale review of the administrative reform (q.v.) in 1976 confirmed their compositions. The CRL's were supposed to bring the government closer to the people, sparking greater civic involvement and mobilization for the development drive. Their composition fluctuated somewhat, though they were supposed to be constituted of 25 members, 13 of whom were to be youth delegates, seven women and five elders. The CRL was headed by a seven-man Executive Permanent Committee headed by a Secretary and six officials, with functions identical to those members of the Permanent Committee of the CPR (q.v.). The Secretaries of the CRL provided a pool from which a certain number were integrated at the higher level of administration, the Conseil Révolutionnaire de District (q.v.).

CONSTITUTIONS OF DAHOMEY. Dahomey has had seven constitutions, promulgated in February 1959, November 1960, January 1964, August 1968, May 1970, August 1977 and December 1990.

(1) FEBRUARY 1959: Parliamentary system with a Prime Minister holding executive powers and a legislative assembly with legislative powers.

(2) NOVEMBER 1960: The "Independence" Constitution, different from those promulgated by Dahomey's partners in the Conseil de l'Entente (q.v.). A presidential system with a President assisted by a Vice-

President, neither of whom is responsible to a National Assembly (q.v.) with 60 Deputies, elected for five years. A Supreme Court (q.v.) was also created in 1961.

(3) JANUARY 1964: Two-headed executive with a President as head of state and chairman of the cabinet and a Vice-President—who countersigned all presidential acts—as head of government in charge of day-to-day administration. No solution for conflict between the two executives. Also, a National Assembly of 42 deputies, with generally restricted powers.

(4) AUGUST 1968: The constitution of the military-imposed presidency of Emile Derlin Zinsou (q.v.). Presidential system with wide powers and an Economic and Social Council (Conseil Economique et Social [q.v.]) with recommendatory powers.

(5) MAY 1970: The Presidential Council constitution, "guaranteed" by the army. Rotating two-year chairmanship of Presidential Council (with Hubert Maga presiding during 1970–1972, Justin Ahomadégbé 1972–1974, and Sourou-Migan Apithy [qq.v.] 1974–1976), a Consultative Assembly divided into social, economic, and general policy sections, and a Supreme Court.

(6) AUGUST 1977: The Loi Fondamentale set up an Assemblée Nationale Révolutionnaire (ANR) (q.v.) of 336 Commissaires du Peuple (q.v.), representing occupational classes and elected by universal suffrage for a term of three years. The Assembly in turn elects the President of the Republic. Conseils Révolutionnaires (q.v.) were set up at each level of the state—provincial, district, and local—headed by seven-man Permanent Committees and theoretically significant decision-making powers. A series of amendments in February 1984 reduced the ANR membership to 180,

while extending its term of office, as well as that of the President, to five years.

(7) DECEMBER 1990: Strong President (age 40–70) not accountable to parliament, restrained by an Assembly empowered to challenge him, and which cannot be dissolved. A constitutional court, Supreme Court, High Court of Justice, assisted by an Audio-Visual Authority and an Economic and Social Council. Maximum of two terms of five years for the President. Any citizen can appeal for international assistance to restore civilian legitimacy in case of a military coup.

CONVENTION AFRICAINE (CA). Interterritorial African political movement, inspired by Senegal's President Léopold Sédar Senghor, and successor of the latter's Indépendants d'Outre Mer (q.v.), which was more of an African caucusing-cum-pressure group in the French Assembly in Paris. Established in January 1957, Emile Derlin Zinsou (q.v.) set up a CA branch in Dahomey. Shortly after, it merged to form a larger grouping, the Parti du Régroupement Africain (q.v.). In light of the splintered political and ethnic picture in Dahomey, neither the Convention Africaine nor other interterritorial political movements succeeded in coalescing much political power or competing effectively vis-a-vis the regional-ethnic formations in the country.

CONVENTION NATIONALE DAHOMEENNE (CND). Political party set up by Sourou-Migan Apithy (q.v.) and Valentin Aplogan Djibodé on December 10, 1965, after Gen. Christophe Soglo's November 29, 1965 coup (qq.v.) and the appointment of Tahirou Congacou (q.v.), Speaker of the House, as Interim President. When Soglo dismissed the latter, setting up his own military administration (on December 22, 1965), all parties, including the CND, were banned. See also COUP OF 1965(b); POLITICAL PARTIES.

CONVERGENCE. Political party, formed in 1991 and winning six seats in the National Assembly (q.v.). The party joined in

1993 the parliamentary alliance Nouvelle République supportive of Nicéphore Soglo's (q.v.) Presidency.

COOVI, GASTON (Lt. Colonel). Military officer of mixed origin (Fon [q.v.] father, northern mother) who first came to prominence in 1972 when, as a Lieutenant, he was appointed to the Military Tribunal to try Major Kouandété (qq.v.). Rising up the ranks under Kérékou's (q.v.) regime, by 1985 he had become Commander of the Northern Military Region.

CORVEE. Forced labor, in lieu of taxes, mostly public construction and porterage. It existed in most Francophone colonies until the end of the Second World War, as part of the *indigénat* (q.v.) code applied to the traditional population. *Corvée* labor was the major complaint of colonial populations against French rule and sparked a variety of rebellions (see UPRISINGS OF 1915–1918).

COTONOU. Main port, largest town, center of commerce, capital of the Atlantique province (q.v.) and de facto capital of Dahomey. Originally part of the Dahomey kingdom (q.v.), Cotonou was ceded to France in 1878. The treaty was later repudiated by Dahomey, leading to the first Franco-Dahomean campaign (q.v.) and the full-scale occupation of Cotonou in 1890.

With an estimated population of 430,000 people, Cotonou is the commercial, political and modern center of the country, though Porto Novo (q.v.), 35 kilometers away, is still the official capital. The city is built on a narrow sandy spit between Lake Nakoué's navigable lagoon and the Atlantic Ocean. In its western part is the bulk of the town, while in the east is the industrial zone and Akpakpa quarter with its animated market. Dantokpa, next to the new bridge, is the national site of a market for all local and imported items. Construction of Cotonou's new port was completed in 1965 and has benefited from various grants including those from the EC's Fonds Européen de Developpement (q.v.). Cotonou is connected by excellent roads to Porto Novo (and from there with Lagos), Lomé in Togo (and on to Accra, Ghana) and Abomey (q.v.) to the north. The city is also connected to the east and west via railroad and is the terminus of the Benin-Niger railroad (see OCBN), which is one of Niger's main connections with the coast. The government's Supreme Court, radio station and National Assembly buildings are in Cotonou, as well as the Presidential Palace (q.v.), construction of which contributed to the social unrest that toppled President Hubert Maga (q.v.) in 1963. Cotonou's ethnic composition is a potpourri of groups, with the Adja and Fon (qq.v.) predominating, making it in the past a solid political bastion of Justin Ahomadégbé (q.v.).

COTONOU, PORT OF. Investigations regarding the construction of a new port to replace the lighterage port of Cotonou (q.v.) commenced in 1951 and led to the construction that ended in 1965. At the time 35 percent of tonnage arriving in Cotonou was destined for landlocked Niger, a percentage that has remained more or less constant. Cargo transitting through Cotonou rapidly increased in the next 15 years, from 351,000 tons to 1.5 million tons in 1979, necessitating further improvements to the port, carried out in 1983. These included new general cargo berths, an oil jetty and container and roll-on and roll-off terminals. In 1987 loans from the Islamic Development Bank and the World Bank were secured for further improvements in handling equipment. In the interim, however, traffic had declined to an average of 1.1 million tons per year. Some 88 percent of cargo handled is imports. Cargo to and from Niger use the OCBN (q.v.) rail-truck network passing via Parakou (q.v.) and Malanville.

COTTON. Though cotton had not been one of Benin's original important cash crops, its promotion in the north (Borgou [q.v.]) in the late 1960's met with unexpected success. A severe drought in the 1975–1976 season curtailed exports and production from the then all-time high of 50,000 tons (1972–1973), when cotton was Benin's prime export, to 20,000 tons in 1975–1976. The sudden eviction of the French marketing company CFDT and the allocation of its former responsibilities to the very inefficient state company SONA-GRI also played a role in depressing production and exports. The six cotton-ginning mills operated by SONAGRI were operating at the time at one-third of their capacity of 80,000 tons. Since 1980 production has steadily increased, reaching 65,000 tons in 1984 and 180,000 tons in 1991. There are high hopes for the future of the crop since the northern populations have seized at this rare opportunity to better themselves through its cultivation.

COUCHORO, FELIX, 1900–1968. One of West Africa's best-known authors. Born in Ouidah (q.v.) on January 30, 1900, Couchoro attended Ouidah's seminary (q.v.), following which he served as coach and instructor in several neighboring schools (1917–1939). In 1939 he moved to Aného (then Anécho) just across the border in Togo and tried his luck as a commercial agent, while at the same time seriously embarking upon his writing career. In exile in Ghana, 1952 to 1958, Couchoro returned to Togo in 1958 to become Assistant Director of the Ministry of Information. Couchoro's first novel (*L'Esclave*) was published in 1930. He published two more works in 1941 and 1950. It was essentially in Lomé, however, that he did most of his writing, publishing 12 more novels until his death in 1968. His writings made him one of Togo's most prolific authors and one of Africa's first regional writers. His works were always set in either Dahomey or Togo, dealt with themes understandable to the average person, and were written in simple language. He still enjoys wide popularity in both countries.

COUFFO. River, originating in Togo (between Glito and Agouma), and emptying—after a course of 125 kilometers—in Lake Ahémé, northwest of Ouidah (q.v.).

COUP (ATTEMPTED) OF JANUARY 21, 1975. A murky ill-prepared assault led by Captain Janvier Assogba (q.v.), the former Minister of Labor and Civil Service, who, deploying part of the key Ouidah (q.v.) armed division, was deserted by his troops at the approaches to Cotonou (q.v.). Assogba mounted his assault on the grounds that President Kérékou (q.v.) was directly implicated in the corrupt practices associated with the Kovacs affair (q.v.). A number of military officers, NCO's, and civilians were imprisoned for their role in the foiled putsch that allegedly aimed to bring back to office Emile Derlin Zinsou (q.v.). Assogba remained in prison until the amnesties of 1984, an abnormally long time for Benin, largely because as one of the original conspirators of the 1972 coup, he was personally an embarrassment to Kérékou.

COUP (ATTEMPTED) OF JANUARY 16, 1977. Often so misnamed, see MERCENARY ASSAULT ON COTONOU.

COUP (ATTEMPTED) OF 1988. Dangerous revolt against General Kérékou's (q.v.) regime of some of the most senior officers of his armed forces (q.v.). The plot had multiple motivations and grievances, foremost amongst which was discontent over paycuts and delays in payments of military salaries and fringe benefits by the cash-strapped regime. Southern Fon (q.v.) officers were further greatly aggravated by the news that the regime had negotiated a deal (at extremely low rates to boot) to bury millions of tons of European nuclear waste (q.v.) in Abomey (q.v.), something perceived as a sinister plot to exterminate the Fon people. The ringleaders of the plot were Lt. Col. François Kouyami (q.v.), Lt. Col. Hilaire Badjogoumi (close friend of Kérékou and Head of Public Security) and Captain Hountondji of the Presidential Guard (q.v.), and some 100 additional officers.

COUP OF 1963. The coup of October 23, 1963, was initiated by Col. Christophe Soglo (q.v.), Chief-of-Staff of the armed forces (q.v.), in the wake of widespread urban unrest in the south at the excesses and corruption of the Hubert Maga (q.v.) Presidency. Two specific incidents that sparked a great deal of resentment were the profligate spending on the new Presidential Palace in Cotonou (qq.v.) at a time of fiscal austerity, and the Bohiki Affair (q.v.). When Soglo intervened in the volatile situation, he first attempted to set up a ''unity'' government of the country's political triumvirate (q.v.), retaining Hubert Maga. Growing unionist demonstrations and the creation of ''revolutionary'' committees in the urban centers compelled him to place Maga under arrest and prepare for new elections. The new regime that emerged in

1964 was headed by the two-headed executive of Sourou-Migan Apithy and Justin Ahomadégbé (qq.v.).

COUP OF 1965(a). The two-headed executive set up in 1964 in the aftermath of Col. Soglo's (q.v.) first military coup broke down completely by the autumn of 1965. President Sourou-Migan Apithy and Vice-President Justin Ahomadégbé (qq.v.), each with separate constitutional powers, were of such different temperaments that under the best of conditions they would have found it difficult to get along. The final break between them occurred over the so-called Supreme Court affair (q.v.), and sharply divided the entire administration into antagonistic camps supporting one or the other of the two leaders. Ahomadégbé, more powerful in the parti unique set up in 1964 (the Parti Démocratique Dahoméen [q.v.]), was able to push through a resolution of questionable legality calling upon Apithy to resign. The latter retaliated by declaring Ahomadégbé dismissed from the Vice-Presidency. In the tumultuous situation that followed, Ahomadégbé tried to utilize his support in the armed forces (q.v.) to quell disturbances in Apithy's political fiefdom, Porto Novo (q.v.). His bypassing of the army's chain of command, especially its Chief-of-Staff, Col. Soglo (in favor of Lt. Col. Philippe Aho [q.v.]) was a further impetus for Soglo's military intervention on November 29, 1965. Dismissing both Apithy and Ahomadégbé, Soglo entrusted the formation of a new government to the President of the National Assembly, Tahirou Congacou (qq.v.).

COUP OF 1965(b). Dahomey's third military takeover followed in the wake of the second coup, in which Gen. Christophe Soglo (q.v.) dismissed the previous two-headed executive (Sourou-Migan Apithy and Justin Ahomadégbé [qq.v.]) and entrusted the formation of a new government to Tahirou Congacou, President of the National Assembly (qq.v.). The latter was unable to form a viable coalition in light of the volatility of the antagonistic ethnic-regional political formations. On December 22, 1965, Col. Soglo unilaterally withdrew Congacou's mandate and assumed full powers, setting up his own administration.

COUP OF 1967. The coup of December 17, 1967, was master-minded by a group of militant officers and NCO's, many from the north, who had coalesced around the dynamic leadership of Major Maurice Kouandété (q.v.). The group was disgruntled with the growing politicized and lax style of the regime of Gen. Christophe Soglo (q.v.), his ineffective-ness in coping with the country's problems and seeping corruption. Probably most rankling was the growing unrest in the urban centers at Soglo's austerity programs that were compromising the prestige of the army as a whole. The spark that ignited the coup was the government's indecisiveness in first issuing Decree No. 36 (q.v.) that banned trade union (q.v.) rights—only to rescind the decree a few days later under the threat of a general strike. This unmilitary "vacilla-tion" led to Major Kouandété's coup a few days later, Soglo finding refuge in the French Embassy. Most of the army's senior hierarchy were placed under house arrest. When Kouandété found he did not have sufficient support in the army to form his own administration, the senior officers were released and most were brought into the junta, forming an interim military regime under the leadership of Kouandété and Chief-of-Staff Col. Alphonse Alley (q.v.). The regime paved the way for elections, barring, however, Dahomey's triumvirate (q.v.) or their ministers, leading to the Electoral Boycott of 1968 (q.v.) and the annulment of the results. In despair the army then called upon the respected veteran politician Emile Derlin Zinsou (q.v.) to assume the Presi-dency, which he did.

COUP OF 1969. The coup of December 10, 1969, was the handiwork of a very small clique in the army under the leadership of Colonel Maurice Kouandété (q.v.), Chief-of-Staff of the armed forces (q.v.), and his trusted lieutenant, Arcade Kitoy (q.v.). The coup that toppled President Zinsou (q.v.) (whom the army had brought to power in 1968) occurred because of Kouandété's presidential ambitions and feelings that he had been slighted by Zinsou. In the back-ground was a history of interfactional struggle in the army, that had led to Colonel Alley's (q.v.) purge and imprison-ment, and efforts by his supporters to reinstate him.

Kouandété's largely unilateral action in 1969 brought about his own partial eclipse. The interim three-man Military Directorate (q.v.) set up by the officer corps invited back to Dahomey the country's Presidential "old guard"—Hubert Maga, Justin Ahomadégbé and Sourou-Migan Apithy (qq.v.). The four-cornered elections that followed (with Zinsou also running to vindicate his Presidency) were annulled when it appeared certain that Maga was about to become the victor, thanks to his solid control of the north. Following a tense period during which calls for secession were heard from both Apithy's and Maga's supporters, a Presidential Council (q.v.) formula was agreed upon, allowing each leaders a turn at the Chairmanship of the Council.

COUP OF 1972. The coup of October 26, 1972, followed by a few months the first peaceful political succession in Dahomey as Hubert Maga (q.v.) handed over the Chairmanship of the Presidential Council (q.v.) to Justin Ahomadégbé (q.v.). Two military mutinies and an attempted assassination of Chief-of-Staff Paul Emile De Souza (q.v.) had, however, preceded the coup that year. When Ahomadégbé did not move to correct the abuses of power and scandals of the Maga Presidency, the army under a troika (that coopted Major Mathieu Kérékou [q.v.], the northern Deputy Chief-of-Staff not a key conspirator) seized power. The army's senior officers (mostly southerners) were purged—initially appointed to administrative positions in the state enterprises—and all-military regime was set up with Kérékou as President. This regime in due course declared for Marxism-Leninism, and partly civilianized, remained in power until the 1990 rollback of military and single-party rule and Marxism. See also KOVACS AFFAIR.

COUPS. Dahomey has had six coups d'etat since independence, for some time the highest such incidence in subsaharan Africa. (Nigeria has since "overtaken" Benin.) These occurred in October 1963, November 1965, December 1965, December 1967, December 1969 and October 1972. (See under COUP OF. . . .) The country has also been rocked by numerous military mutinies and abortive coups, by one account numbering at least 15.

COUR POPULAIRE SUPREME (CPS). The Supreme Court (q.v.) of Benin in Cotonou during the Revolutionary era. Presided over by Léandre Amlon, the Court had four chambers: constitutional, judicial, administrative and accounting. See also SUPREME COURT.

COUTUMES. Rents paid by European trading agents to native chiefs and kings in the precolonial era in exchange for which they were permitted to anchor offshore, trade or build settlements and forts on the mainland.

COVI, FRANCIS MARINO MENSA, 1906–1966. Educator and politician. Born in Ouidah (q.v.) on February 5, 1906, Covi's early educational promise assured him a place in the Ecole William Ponty (q.v.) in Senegal, in 1919, following which he went to Aix-en-Provence, France, on a scholarship. Returning to Dahomey late in 1926 he was placed in charge of the educational system of Porto Novo and later Cotonou (qq.v.). Combining pedagogic pursuits with politics, Covi also served, prior to Dahomey's independence, as Councillor to the Conseil Général and later the Assemblée Territoriale (qq.v.) (acting as its President during 1957–1959), and as Senator of the Communauté Française (q.v.) (1959–1961). A powerful political figure after independence Covi was President of the ruling PDU (q.v.) parliamentary group in the National Assembly (q.v.) and President of the latter's key Finances and Budget Committees. He died in Porto Novo on November 14, 1966.

COWRIES. Local currency in precolonial Dahomey. Though the neighboring Ashanti federation used gold dust, Abomey (q.v.) maintained its cowrie-shell currency into the colonial era, with other kingdoms also maintaining a dual system in which cowries played a role. At Ouidah (q.v.), especially when the slave port was part of the Houéda (q.v.) kingdom, both gold dust and cowrie shells were acceptable as trade currencies. The rate of exchange, which did not change for nearly two centuries, was 32,000 cowries (strung in beads) for one ounce of gold, itself worth in England at the time four pounds sterling. Though most of the slave trade (q.v.) along the coast consisted of barter of trade goods for slaves, considerable amounts of shells were also imported by traders from the Indian Ocean.

COYSSI, ANATOLE, 1915–54. Early educator. Born in Ouidah (q.v.) on July 12, 1915, and educated in Porto Novo (q.v.) and at the Ecole William Ponty (q.v.) in Senegal Coyssi returned home in 1931 to teach in Porto Novo, later reassigned to Great Popo (q.v.), Cove, Ouidah (q.v.), and Tanguiéta. In the latter posting he completed one of the first studies of the Somba (q.v.) ethnic group. Coyssi received French citizenship in 1945, simultaneously with his promotion to the post of Principal of the Ouidah school. Later he was also in charge of Fon (q.v.) language radio programs of Radio Cotonou. He died in 1954 after a long illness.

CREOLES see BRAZILIANS

CROIX DU BENIN. Widely read Catholic bimonthly journal. Formerly the *Croix du Dahomey.*

CULT OF THE GREAT SERPENT. (Also PYTHON CULT.) Deity native to the precolonial kingdom of Houéda (q.v.) (Ouidah), with its main temple in the commercial capital and port of Houéda, Ouidah (q.v.). Its local name is Dangbé, with Ouidah specifically consecrated to its worship. Much of the early proselytizing effort of the Portuguese and French priests in Ouidah was hampered by the overwhelming attachment of the population in this specific area to the cult, and foreign priests were on several occasions chased out of town, their missions burned. The main temple of the cult, an unprepossessing complex, stands exactly across the modern cathedral, and many worshipers cross from one site to the other on Sundays. The temple and its huge defanged pythons is one of Benin's great tourist attractions. The cult was originally alien to the Fon (q.v.) of Dahomey but spread among them slowly, with python temples to be found today along the main road to Allada and Abomey (qq.v.).

-D-

DADJO, HOUEGBON MARCEL, 1925– . Engineer, politician and diplomat. Born in Savé on January 4, 1925, Dadjo was educated in Porto Novo (q.v.) and Dakar (1944–1948), graduating in 1952 as a public works engineer. Employed in Abidjan, Ivory Coast, for five years, he returned home in 1958. Rapidly involving himself in political activity in 1959 he was elected to the Assemblée Nationale on the PRD (qq.v.) list serving as Deputy until October 1963. In 1959 he was appointed Minister of Public Works (1959–1960), later of Transport (1960–1961). In January 1961 he left the cabinet to become Ambassador to the Federal Republic of Germany and (during 1961) representative to the European Economic Community (q.v.). In 1967 he rejoined the cabinet of Gen. Christophe Soglo (q.v.) as Minister of Public Works. Following the 1967 coup (q.v.), Dadja relocated to France.

DAHO-EXPRESS. Widely read daily government newspaper, successor (since August 1, 1969) to *L'Aube Nouvelle* (q.v.). Published in Cotonou (q.v.) by the Etablissement National d'Edition et de Presse, the name of the paper was again changed by the Revolutionary regime in 1975 to *Ehuzu* (q.v.) (Everything Has Changed) until 1990.

DAHOMEY, KINGDOM OF. Adja (q.v.) dynasty established at the beginning of the seventeenth century, probably in 1620. With its capital in Abomey (q.v.), Dahomey (or Danhome) became a powerful though small kingdom in nineteenth century West Africa. Of various legends relating to Dahomey's foundation, the most cited relates to a three-cornered fraternal succession struggle in Allada (q.v.), the victor retaining the throne while the other two brothers left the kingdom to establish Dahomey and Porto Novo (q.v.) (see DOGBAGRI). Another version recounts the request of their first king, Wegbadja (q.v.), for additional land from King Dan, a local ruler, who refused and upon whose grave Dahomey's royal compound was erected (Danhome—''on the belly of Dan''). Prior to this dispersal from Allada, the Adja traced their origins to Adja-Tado, Ketou (q.v.) and possibly Ile-Ife (Nigeria). A rich mythology surrounds this early period (see also ADJA; ADJA-TADO; KETOU; ADJAHOUTO).

Highly centralized, well-administered, and possessing able leadership and military skills, Dahomey commenced a period of rapid expansion in the eighteenth century, conquering Allada (in 1724) and Whydah (q.v.) (1727), thus gaining direct access to the coast and European trade. The conquest of Allada, however, led to the (Yoruba) Oyo (qq.v.) invasions, to whose kingdom Allada had been a tributary state. Partly sacked by Oyo several times, Dahomey became a tributary vis-a-vis the latter, only shaking this off 70 years later in 1818 under King Ghézo (q.v.).

In the nineteenth century Dahomey, with the best organized and largest standing army (20,000) in West Africa, reached its heights of strength and territorial expansion. Widely feared for its military might and slave raids—needed for its trade with Europe as well as for its ritual Annual Customs (q.v.)—Dahomey consolidated its control of the coast, mounted strong assaults in the direction of the Ashanti (in Ghana) and against its former Oyo suzerains. King Glélé's (and later Béhanzin's [q.v.]) efforts to reimpose Dahomey's suzerainty over Porto Novo (first established in the 1820's) at a time when the latter had obtained French Protectorate status, and Dahomey's repudiation of a dubious 1878 treaty ceding Cotonou (q.v.), led to the 1890–1894 Franco-Dahomean campaigns (q.v.). After Dahomey's defeat, the French exiled King Béhanzin to Martinique, enthroning his brother, Agoli Agbo (q.v.), as puppet king in Abomey. In 1900 the latter was also deposed (and exiled to Gabon), ending the Dahomean dynasty.

In the contemporary era feelings of Fon (q.v.) ethnic exclusiveness have remained, contributing to Dahomey's problems of regionalism (q.v.). Descendants from the royal families have been able to tap deep-rooted allegiances, transforming them into political power on the regional and national level. This especially occurred with Justin

Ahomadégbé (q.v.), who descends from the Agonglo lineage and has been the unchallenged political leader of the Fon and Adja populations between 1949–1972.

DAHOMEY, KINGS OF. Though some dates remain in dispute in the following king-list, there is a much higher degree of scholarly consensus about the Dahomean dynasty than about most other king-lists.

Wegbadja	?–1680
Akaba	1680–1708
Agaja	1708–1740
Tégbésu	1740–1774
Kpéngla	1774–1789
Agonglo	1790–1797 (murdered)
Adandézan	1797–1818 (deposed)
Ghézo	1818–1858 (direct descent from the Agaja lineage)
Glélé	1858–1889
Béhanzin	1889–1894
Agoli-Agbo	1894–1900

DAHOMEY-NIGER BOUNDARY DISPUTE. A boundary dispute, outstanding since 1960, which erupted in November 1963, involving the issue of ownership of the half-submerged Niger river border island of Lété. The issue evoked dispatch of Dahomean and Nigerien troops to the region. Underlying the confrontation were more pedestrian causes for hostility: Niger President Hamani Diori's displeasure at the 1963 coup and ouster of Hubert Maga (qq.v.), and fears that Dahomey would be sympathetic to Niger's Sawaba irredentist movement; also, Dahomey's annoyance at the Nigerien expulsion of resident Dahomeans. The conflict, which led to Dahomey's boycott of the 1964 conséil de l'Entente (q.v.) meeting, was resolved in 1965.

D'ALMEIDA, BENJAMIN see ALMEIDA, BENJAMIN D'

D'ALMEIDA, JOACHIM see ALMEIDA, JOACHIM D'

DALZEL, ARCHIBALD, 1740–1811. Slave trader and soldier of fortune. Born in October 23, 1740, in Kirkliston, Scotland, and trained as a surgeon, Dalzel joined the Africa Committee in 1763 and arrived in the Gold Coast the same year. He excelled in the slave trade (q.v.) and was named head of the British fort at Ouidah (q.v.) in 1767. Having made his fortune by 1770, he returned to London from where he continued his trading activities, including relations with Florida and Jamaica. In August 1778 he was seized, together with his ship, and ruined financially. He then engaged in tea and wine trade, returning to Africa in 1792 as governor of the Cape Coast and remaining in the area until 1802. During this time he wrote his *History of Dahomey*, which was more an amalgam of previous reports, and an apology for the slave trade, than his own original observations, but nevertheless remains a seminal work for the study of the origins of the Dahomey Kingdom (q.v.). He retired in 1802 and died several years later.

DANGBE. Ouidah's (q.v.) cult of the phython. See CULT OF THE GREAT SERPENT.

DANGOU, LEOPOLD, 1913– . Early Deputy to the Assemblée Territoriale (q.v.) and civil administrator. Born in Kouandé (q.v.) on October 8, 1913, Dangou served as a delegate to the joint administrative council of the OCDN (q.v.) and was attached to the civil administration of Djougou (q.v.). In 1957 he was elected as an independent deputy from Djougo, switching to the PDD/RDD (qq.v.) in 1958, remaining in the assembly through 1964. He retired from politics after the 1965 coup and remained with the civil administration of Djougo.

DANHOME see DAHOMEY, KINGDOM OF

DANKORO, SOULE (Colonel). Former Minister. An army doctor of Bariba (q.v.) ethnicity, Dankoré's support was politically invaluable to President Kérékou (q.v.) whose Somba (q.v.) origins had always been looked down upon in the north, where Somba had been regarded as slave-material. Dankoro served in Kérékou's regime in a variety of capacities virtually until its collapse: as Minister of Commerce and Tourism (1980–1987), Minister of Equipment and Transport (1987–1988) and Minister of Public Health (1988–1990).

DARBOUX, PAUL, 1919–1982. Important northern merchant, political leader and former Minister of Commerce. Born in Cotonou (q.v.) on May 10, 1919, to a family of the Djougou (q.v.) nobility, Darboux rapidly became a very successful trader. Though a northerner, his political ambitions and the ethnically mixed power balance in Djougou—with its strong Dendi and Wangara (qq.v.) population—allowed Darboux to play an important role as an independent, challenging the efforts of Hubert Maga (q.v.) to coalesce the north behind his own candidacy. In 1956 Darboux founded the Defénse des Intéréts Economiques (q.v.) party (at various times named Union des Indépendants du Dahomey and Indépendants du Nord [qq.v.]) as his own political vehicle. He won Djougou in the close 1957 election for the Assemblée Territoriale (q.v.) and his tactical alliance with Sourou-Migan Apithy (q.v.) gained him a cabinet position (Minister of Labor and Social Affairs) in the latter's 1958 government. Darboux also controlled the Syndicat des Commerçants Africains du Dahomey (q.v.) (a merchants union), using it as a supplementary vehicle for his political ambitions. Between April 1959 and November 1960 he was the RDD (q.v.) Parliamentary Secretary-General.

A powerful force in Atakora (q.v.), Darboux remained in the Hubert Maga (q.v.) 1960–1963 government, despite strong opposition from dissident elements in Djougou, as Minister of Economics and Commerce. After Maga's downfall, in 1963 Darboux was imprisoned for fiscal misappropriations. In eclipse for several years, during which he engaged in commerce, he joined the Conseil Economique et Social (q.v.) in 1968 and served as general director of the Société Générale d'Approvisionnement du Dahomey (SOGADA). In 1970 he represented Hubert Maga vis-a-vis the Military Directorate (q.v.) and, after the establishment of the Presidential Council (q.v.), Darboux was elected President of the Assemblée Consultative Nationale (q.v.). His political comeback was cut short by the 1972 coup (q.v.). Though he opportunistically tried to come to terms with the new regime—and even served as de-facto marketing agent for the State sector—he rapidly fell afoul of it. Until his death in 1982 in self-exile in Togo, he was one of the regime's most implacable enemies.

DA SILVA, KARIM URBAIN, 1930– . Muslim industrialist and merchant. Born in Porto Novo (q.v.) on November 2, 1930, of a Brazilian (q.v.) family, Da Silva owns the Grande Imprimérie Béninoise printing company and was President of the Syndicat National des Commerçants et Industriels du Dahomey (q.v.), a merchants and industrialists union. In the military-sponsored elections of 1968 (see ELECTORAL BOYCOTT, 1968) he competed for the Presidency, obtaining 19,319 of the votes cast. Da Silva has been active promoting Muslim causes in Benin and trying to mediate the constant friction in the country's Muslim leadership.

DA SOUZA, FRANCISCO FELIX. 1760(?)–1849. Portuguese drifter or political refugee who arrived in Whydah (q.v.) from Brazil around 1788. Of humble origins, Da Souza started off as a minor trader in a variety of commodities, including slaves, eventually prospering. While in Abomey (q.v.) attempting to collect a debt from Dahomey's King Adandozan, Da Souza was thrown into jail. In his efforts to free himself he cultivated a friendship with the next king of Dahomey, Ghézo (q.v.), and helped the latter seize power in 1818. Da Souza was then appointed chief customs collector (Chacha) and viceroy of Whydah, the personal representative of the Dahomey monarch, and director of Whydah's Portuguese Fort. Exercising a quasi-monopoly over all trade in that important slave port, Da Souza helped reorganize Whydah's customs system and convinced Ghézo to channel slave labor into the development of the royal palm tree plantations, which later became one of Dahomey's principal exports. Da Souza also was Ghézo's chief supplier of armaments from Europe. He prospered enormously and, upon his death (May 8, 1849), human sacrifices were offered for him in Whydah. His descendants continued to occupy important positions, until the sixth, Julian Felix da Souza, concluded a preferential treaty with Portugal against the wishes of Abomey, which led to the downfall of the privileged status of the Da Souzas.

DASSA. Yoruba (q.v.) ethnic group, arriving in Benin from Oyo (q.v.) but with an Egba royal dynasty. The clans settled in the vicinity of Dassa-Zoumé.

DASSI, DIDIER (Colonel). Former Minister. As a junior officer (Lieutenant) Dassi came into the public spotlight on two occasions: when appointed to the Military Tribunal (q.v.) of 1972, and in August 1973 when he was entrusted to take over Radio Dahomey and transform it into the Voix de la Révolution (q.v.). In 1975 Dassi was shifted to head a division in the Ministry of Defense, and in 1980 he was appointed Prefect of Mono (q.v.). In 1984 Dassi was recalled to the cabinet as Minister of Justice specifically charged with inspecting and overseeing public and semi-public companies that were crippling the Beninois economy with their inefficiency and deficits. It was under his aegis that much of the early privatization of the parastatal sector took place. In August 1988 he was named Minister of Finance, a post he lost with the normalization of 1990.

DASSI, SEBASTIEN, 1905–1975. Former President of the Supreme Court (q.v.) and Minister. Born in Cotonou (q.v.) on January 20, 1905, and educated at the prestigious Ecole William Ponty (q.v.) in Senegal, Dassi was an instructor and union leader before turning to politics. In 1952 he was elected to the Conseil Général (q.v.) on Apithy's PRD (qq.v.) list, and constantly delivered to Apithy the Aizo (q.v.) vote. In May 1957 he occupied the key Ministry of Interior, but with Apithy's subsequent eclipse he was shifted to head the Ministry of Agriculture (1959–1962). In March 1962 he was appointed President of the Supreme Court, serving in that capacity until November 1963, when he was retired.

DASSOUNDO, GEDEON. Former Director of the Société Nationale pour l'Industrie des Corps Gras (q.v.), Dassoundo was appointed in June 1982 as Minister of Development and Cooperative Action. His tenure was brief: he was dropped to a secondary post in the parastatal sector in December 1982. For the 1990 referendum (q.v.) he set up a party—the ADP (q.v.)—that urged voters to reject the constitution (q.v.). He was successful in getting elected to the National Assembly (q.v.) in the 1991 elections.

DATONDJI, COOVI INNOCENT, 1949– . Educator. Educated abroad and with a doctorate in African literature and a diploma in English language instruction, Datondji served during 1973–1977 as Director of Cultural Activities at CEMGI, Ouidah (q.v.), before his 1979 appointment as Head of Administration and Studies at Porto Novo's (q.v.) Ecole Normale Supérieure. He has published several books of fiction, and non-fiction, one in English.

DECREE NO. 36. Decree issued by Gen. Christophe Soglo (q.v.) on December 8, 1967—at the suggestion of the Comité Militaire de Vigilance (CMV) (q.v.)—suspending trade union (q.v.) activities, including public meetings, distribution of pamphlets, etc. These bans, issued in the light of growing urban unrest and unionist demonstrations, immediately resulted in the arrest of several trade union leaders and a massive general strike that Soglo was incapable of resisting or crushing. Decree No. 36 was promptly annulled, to the disgust of militant officers in the CMV, who two days later mounted their anti-Soglo coup d'etat (q.v.). See also COUP OF 1967.

DEFENSE DES INTERETS ECONOMIQUES (DIE). Temporary political movement established by Paul Darboux (q.v.) in the Djougou (q.v.) region in 1956 in his bid for power in the north against Hubert Maga (q.v.). In the 1957 elections for the Assemblée Territoriale (q.v.), Darboux won Djougou in a tight election and his support for Sourou-Migan Apithy (q.v.) brought him into the latter's 1958 cabinet as Minister of Labor. The DIE was defunct within a few years after its foundation. Darboux's control of the Djougou region continued, however, though under strong challenge from Maga and other political forces. The name of the pro-Darboux formation varied over the years, being, among others, Indépendants du Nord and Union des Indépendants du Dahomey (qq.v.).

DEGBE, MARCELIN. Leader of the Mouvement pour la Démocratie et le Progrès Social (MDPS), an original partner in the UTR (q.v.) parliamentary alliance formed in 1991 in support of President Nicéphore Soglo (q.v.). Degbé was elected to the National Assembly (q.v.) in 1991 on that ticket.

DEGBEY, ADRIEN, 1918– . Educator and former Minister of Labor. Born on May 10, 1918, in Honton, and trained as a teacher, Degbey was in due time appointed Inspector of Primary Education. He was an early participant in the electoral committees of Porto Novo (qq.v.) and was sent to the assembly to represent the capital in 1946. He served until 1952 and again between 1959 and 1960. Joining the interim cabinets of September–October 1963 (Minister of Labor and Social Affairs) and of January 1964–December 1965 (Minister of Rural Development), Degbey was appointed Director of Primary Education before retiring in 1978.

DEGLA, JOSEPH. Former Kérékou (q.v.) key aide. A PRPB (q.v.) militant, member of the arch-Left Ligue (q.v.), and one of the party's main ideologues, Degla was elected to the party Politburo in November 1985. He has also been President Kérékou's speech-writer.

DEGUENON, GABRIEL, 1930– . Educator. Born in Ouidah (q.v.) on January 25, 1930, and educated at Dakar's Ecole William Ponty (q.v.) and at Saint Cloud, Deguénon had been a teacher and principal (1952–1960) before being appointed, at independence, as Inspector of Primary Schools, based in Lokossa (q.v.). He served in that capacity until 1970 when he was transferred to the Ministry of Education as head of a division.

DE MEDEIROS, RICHARD, 1937– . Cinematographer and educator. Born on September 11, 1937, in Ouidah (q.v.), and educated at the Catholic Mission there, in Porto Novo (q.v.), at the prestigious Lycée Louis-le-Grand in Paris and the

University of Paris (1962–1964), De Medeiros has diplomas in both classics and international studies. He taught at a school in Soissons, France (1965–1967), at Algiers' School for Journalism (1967–1969) and at the University of Nantes (1969–1972) before returning to Benin in 1972 to teach art and literature at the National University of Benin (q.v.). He has both written fiction and produced a number of movies including "Le Roi et Mort en Exil" (1970) and "Téké-Hymne au Borgou" (1974).

DEMOCRATIE ET SOLIDARITE. Political party, formed in 1990, and gaining seven seats in the 1991 legislative elections (q.v.). The party is part of the parliamentary alliance Nouvelle République (q.v.) supportive of President Nicéphore Soglo (q.v.).

DENAGBE, SAMUEL JIJOHO, 1947– . Educator. Born on January 1, 1947, and trained in physics, Denagbé teaches at the National University of Benin (q.v.). He recently specialized abroad in nuclear physics and thermodynamics.

DENDI. Estimated at around 40,000 in number, the Dendi are a non-indigenous people, originally Mende from Songhay (many involved in trade), who are found dispersed in the urban areas of north Benin. Migrating through the Niger valley and especially via Gao (Mali), the Dendi tended to settle along the principal ancient caravan routes, offering middleman services. Today they are found especially in Parakou (q.v.), where most notables, successful merchants and urban chiefs are Dendi, and in Djougou (q.v.), Kandi, and Nikki (q.v.). In Djougou in particular they form a very powerful commercial and political elite. Intermarried with the local populace and no longer considered "strangers" by the Bariba (q.v.), the Dendi still speak their own language, a Songhay dialect, and are Muslim in the midst of largely animist (q.v.) country. Their precise number is difficult to estimate since they are indistinguishable from Bariba Muslims. In the contemporary era the Dendi concentrations in Parakou and Djougou have had a significant political impact upon regional politics.

DEPARTEMENT. Administrative regions into which Dahomey was divided until the reforms of 1974. Each *département* was headed by a Prefect who was the delegate of the central government. The *départements* were divided into *sous-préfectures* (with a Deputy Prefect) which in turn were composed of a number of *arrondissements.* Until 1974 there were six *départements:* Atakora, Atlantique, Borgou, Mono, Ouémé, and Zou (qq.v.); 35 *sous-préfectures;* and 75 *arrondissements.* In addition the country had five urban constituencies: Abomey, Cotonou, Ouidah, Parakou and Porto Novo (qq.v.). For the 1974 reforms see ADMINISTRATIVE ORGANIZATION.

DEROUX, RENE, 1913– . Physician. Born in Kassakperé near Nikki (q.v.) on June 15, 1913, and a graduate of the Dakar Medical School, Deroux joined the Assemblée Territoriale (q.v.) as Deputy from Borgou (q.v.), serving one term between 1952 and 1957. He was simultaneously Councillor of the French Union (1953–1958) and Minister of Public Health in the three governments between May 1959 and October 1963. Since the 1963 coup d'etat (q.v.) Deroux has been the chief OCDN (q.v.) physician, retiring in 1978.

DE SODJI, KING (1848–1864) OF PORTO NOVO. Dé Sodji's reign was historically a most important one for Porto Novo (q.v.), second only to that of Toffa (q.v.), the last independent ruler of the kingdom. Dé Sodji encouraged the French to establish themselves on the coast, to counteract British influence allowed in under his predecessor, and approved a French Protectorate relationship (the first) in 1863. Dé Sodji also encouraged the entry of Catholic and Protestant missionaries, helped curb the slave trade (q.v.) through Porto Novo, and made the first efforts to spread the cultivation of palm plantations and the export of palm oil (q.v.) and palm products. The French were forced to evacuate Porto Novo following Sodji's death, though they returned under the reign of the next king, Toffa (q.v.).

DE SOUZA, ISIDORE. Archbishop of Cotonou. De Souza served for a year (March 9, 1990–April 1991) as the "neutral"

Chairman of the interim legislature—the Haut Conseil de la République (q.v.)—that ushered in a new constitution and civilian elections (qq.v.). It was also he who helped persuade Kérékou (q.v.) of the need for a National Conference (q.v.) and a return to civilian rule.

DE SOUZA, PAUL EMILE (Lt. Col.). Former Chief-of-Staff and, as Chairman of the Military Directorate (q.v.) (1969–1970), Head of State of Dahomey. De Souza first came to public attention when he was appointed in 1966 Vice-President (and one of only three military officers) of the Comité de Rénovation Nationale (q.v.), Soglo's (q.v.) advisory committee. Following the overthrow of Soglo in 1967, De Souza became Director of Cabinet (Military Affairs) of President Emile Derlin Zinsou (q.v.). Essentially apolitical and loyal to Zinsou, De Souza was briefly under house arrest at the time of Col. Mathieu Kouandété's 1969 coup d'etat (qq.v.). When the latter proved incapable of consolidating power in his own hands, an interim Military Directorate (q.v.) was forged under the chairmanship of De Souza, the army's most senior officer. De Souza served in this position between December 1969 and May 1970, in effect Head of State and Minister of Defense. Shortly after the Presidential Council (q.v.) was formed in May 1970, De Souza was appointed Chief-of-Staff of the armed forces (q.v.), replacing Col. Kouandété (q.v.). In 1972 there was an assassination attempt on his life from within the armed forces. After the October 1972 coup d'etat (q.v.) De Souza was purged from the army, together with all senior officers. He was appointed government commissioner of Dahomey's national Agricultural Credit Bank (SOCAD [q.v.]), a sinecure, and later retired.

DE SOUZA, WILFRID RAOUL, 1935– . UN official. Born in Ouidah (q.v.) on April 18, 1935, De Souza was educated at the University of Paris, following which he served with the French Foreign Ministry (diplomatic internship) and in the French Embassy in Vienna (1960). After independence he progressed from Second Secretary at the Dahomey Embassy in West Germany (1961–1964) to First Secretary at the Embassy in France (1964–1968). During 1968–1970 he served as Secretary-General of the Dahomean Foreign Ministry under Minister Dr. Daouda Badarou (q.v.). In 1970 he was appointed Dahomey's Ambassador to the United States and Permanent Representative to the United Nations, and in 1973 Ambassador to France, Great Britain, Italy and Spain. De Souza currently is with the UN Secretariat.

DETIEN HONVO, MICHEL, 1935– . Former Deputy-Director of Radio Benin. Born in 1935 in Cotonou (q.v.), Détien Honvo holds a diploma in economic planning and is also a communications engineer. Upon his return from studies abroad, he first served as Cabinet Director of the Minister of Public Works (1966–1967), followed by a year as President of the Administrative Council of the Port of Cotonou (q.v.). In September 1968 he was named Director of Radio Benin and held that post until the coup of 1972 (q.v.). He is currently Senior Communications Consultant with the Ministry of Information.

DETTON, MONTCHO HILAIRE, 1919– . Physician. Born in Savalou (q.v.) on July 15, 1919, and married into the de Souza family, Detton was educated at Dakar's Ecole William Ponty (q.v.) and in Paris. He served in various localities in Ivory Coast as pediatrician (1948–1956), returning home in 1956 to serve in Kandi (q.v.) as Chief Medical Officer. In 1958 he became the Cabinet Director of the Ministry of Public Health and, in 1960, Director of Social Affairs in the Ministry of Public Health and Social Affairs. In 1962 Detton served for 18 months as Chief Medical Officer of Tanguiéta, following which he left for Abidjan, Ivory Coast, where he stayed three years. Returning home in 1969 he has since been Chief Medical Officer of Porto Novo (q.v.) (1969–1974) and of Adjohoun (1975–1982) before retiring.

DEUXA. Ritual site of importance to the Pila Pila of the Atakora (qq.v.) and funeral repository of their former Superior Chiefs.

DEUXIEME BUREAU. Military structure set up by the Kérékou (q.v.) regime, and in the reorganization of the Forces Armées (q.v.) du Bénin the Section Deux (its formal name), charged with political indoctrination. The organization has, however, largely operated as Military Intelligence, ferreting out military plots. Disbanded in 1991, it was ruthlessly commanded by the staunchly loyalist Lt. Isidore Laléye (q.v.).

DEVELOPMENT PLANS. Benin has had two development plans, and both had to be drastically scaled down, due to major shortfalls in anticipated internal or external investment funds. (1) The Three-Year Plan, 1978–1980: An ambitious plan envisioning 244 billion CFA francs of investments that had to be scaled down progressively to roughly 50 percent of its original estimates. Originally the plan carried provisions for an oil refinery (45,000 million CFA francs) that was later downgraded in priority. Some 70 percent of expenditures were slated for commerce and industry. Other important projects included a much needed expansion of the port of Cotonou (q.v.), extension of the railway from Parakou (q.v.) to Niamey, construction of the Savé sugar factory and a cement factory at Onigbolo. (2) The Five-Year Plan, 1983–1987: The plan included targeted expenditures from the previous plan that had been deferred, and the first part of an ambitious Ten-Year Plan, 1981–1990, that aimed at increasing by 50 percent per capita income by the end of the decade. It included diversification of food supplies and of the food industry in every region of Benin, with State farms set up in each involved in the processing of peanuts, tomatoes, cotton (q.v.), manioc, etc., and vegetable farms in the Atakora and Borgou (qq.v.). The plan also envisaged the expansion of Benin's fisheries in the coastal provinces and the setting up of canning plants for tomatoes in Malanville, insecticides and onion dehydrating plants, and other industrial efforts. Even more than with the Three-Year Plan, acute austerity prevented implementation of many of these projects, though a number of them reached fruition.

DISSOUDI, MACHOUDI. 1937– . PRPB (q.v.) militant. Born on June 11, 1937, and with degrees in agronomy (University of Algiers, 1960) and rural economics (University of Paris, 1970) Dissou taught in both a high school in Porto Novo (q.v.) and at the National University of Benin (q.v.). A PRPB member and political consultant, with the dissolution of the latter party Dissoundi appeared as the provisional Head of the Union des Forces de Progrès (q.v.) that was set up in April 30, 1990, in its place.

DISTRICTS. The post-1974 equivalent of the *sous-préfectures* (q.v.). Their number originally remained the same, at 35 rural and 4 urban, as did their administrative headquarters. Each is subdivided internally and is administered by a *chef du district* (q.v.), formerly the *sous-préfet,* assisted by a local advisory committee, during the Revolutionary era, the Conseil Révolutionnaire du District (CRD) (q.v.).

DJEKIN see JACQUIN

DJIBRIL MORIBA, MOUSSA (Lt. Colonel), 1934– . Former Minister of Justice. Born in Parakou (q.v.) in 1934, Djibril Moriba joined the army at an early age, in December 1950, after primary school at the Lycée Victor Ballot in Porto Novo (q.v.). He served in Morocco, Senegal and Guinea as an NCO and was repatriated to the Dahomean gendarmerie (q.v.) in October 1960 as a Sergeant. Sent to officers' school in France between 1962 and 1965, Djibril Moriba returned home in 1965 as Second Lieutenant and was promoted to First Lieutenant in October 1967. From 1968 to 1972 he was commander of the gendarmerie of the Atlantique province (q.v.). In 1971 he was promoted to Captain and joined the Kérékou (q.v.) government as Minister of Public Health and Social Affairs. In October 1974 he was shifted to head the Ministry of Rural Development and, in April 1975, the Ministry of Civil Service. In January 1976 he was again shifted to the post of Minister of Justice. He was dropped from the cabinet in December 1982.

DJOUGOU. Important town and key commercial center in the north-western Atakora (q.v.). Settled by the Dendi (q.v.), its name is a corruption of a Dendi word. The town—at times vassal to the Kouandé Bariba (qq.v.) kingdom—was one of the most important stops on the Kano (Nigeria)-Ashanti (Ghana) caravan routes and consequently prospered. It became the biggest market for kola nuts, though not of slaves, Nikki and Parakou (qq.v.) having gained that monopoly. Despite its alliances with Kouande (q.v.), Djougou always maintained excellent relations with Nikki, the "parent" Bariba state. Its peculiar geographical location at the periphery of the Bariba dispersion, its significant Dendi and other non-Bariba population and its continuing commercial interests, distinct from the rest of the Bariba centers, has given Djougou a maverick political orientation. During the civilian era, the region has been a difficult one to swing behind Hubert Maga's (q.v.) Presidential candidacy as the sole representative of the north, since the local political boss, Paul Darboux (q.v.), was frequently at odds with Maga. See also DENDI.

DJOUGOU, MAMA (Colonel). Former Chief of Staff. Originally President Maga's (q.v.) personal aide-de-camp until the 1972 coup d'etat (q.v.), Captain Djougou joined the subsequent military regime as Minister of Rural Development and Cooperation. He was shifted back to military duties in March 1974, and occupied a stream of important commands. By 1984, when he was already Commander of the North headquartered at the Kandi garrison, he rose to the pinnacle being appointed Army Chief of Staff.

DO. Small village near the Nigerian border in southern Benin, site of an important Oguéré Afokoyeri *vodun* (q.v.) shrine.

DODDE, SEPTIME. Civil administrator. Born in Cotonou (q.v.) and educated in Paris, Doddé is a graduate of IHEOM and served for several years (1958–1961) as technical consultant with the Ministry of Agriculture. In 1961 he was appointed Director of the Budget in the Ministry of Finance, and in 1962 he moved to head the Agence Dahoméenne de Presse, staying in that post until 1967. Attached to the Accountancy Chamber of the Supreme Court (q.v.) in 1967, Doddé was implicated in 1968 in an anti-Zinsou (q.v.) plot, for which he was arrested. Released some time later, he was shifted to consultancy duties in the Ministry of Information, and he left the country shortly after the 1972 coup d'etat (q.v.).

DODDS, ALFRED AMEDEE (General), 1842–1922. French General, ''conqueror'' of Dahomey. Born on February 6, 1842, in Saint Louis, Senegal, Dodds entered the Saint Cyr officers' school in 1862 and served in Reunion, Senegal and Indochina. In April 1982 he was appointed commander of the French forces in the Bight of Benin and ordered to mount the second campaign against King Béhanzin (q.v.) of Dahomey. At the outset on the defensive and with only 800 troops under his command, within a month Dodds broke the back of Béhanzin's crack Amazon (q.v.) units and entered Dahomey's capital, Abomey (q.v.) on November 18, 1892. On December 3, Béhanzin (who had escaped) was declared deposed, but resistance to the French occupation continued. In August 1893 a new campaign against Dahomey was mounted, following which Béhanzin surrendered and was exiled. His brother, Prince Goutchili, was elevated to the throne as King Agoli-Agbo (q.v.) and a treaty of protection was signed with France. Dodds died in Paris July 17, 1922. See also FRANCO-DAHOMEAN CAMPAIGNS.

DOGBAGRI (d. circa 1625). Quasi-mythical founder of the kingdom of Dahomey. According to tradition, he was deposed as ruler of Allada (q.v.) in a dynastic dispute between three brothers, and his clan migrated in 1620 to the vicinity of Abomey (q.v.), where they settled. Expanding on the modest lands, the kingdom was formally founded by Wegbadja (q.v.) who is thus viewed as Dahomey's first king.

DOGBEH, RICHARD, 1932– . Educator, poet and author, one of Dahomey's best-known contemporary writers. Born in Cotonou (q.v.) on December 31, 1932, of Peda (see AIZO) origins, Dogbéh was educated in Cotonou (1940–1950), Ivory Coast (1950–1953) and Senegal (1953–1954). His brilliant school record enabled him to continue his studies in psychology and child psychology in Toulouse, Bordeaux and Aix-Marseille (1954–1957). While in France he became involved in both the militant Black Africans' student movement FEANF (q.v.), and in the nationalist Mouvement de Libération Nationale (q.v.), branches of which he headed. Shortly after his return to Dahomey, Dogbéh was named

Cabinet Director of the Minister of National Education. He served in that capacity until 1966, concurrently also as Research Associate at IRAD (q.v.) and as head of the National Pedagogic Institute in Porto Novo (q.v.). Later he moved to Accra, as head of the French section and Deputy Editor of the Ghanaian Academy of Sciences' African Encyclopedia project. In 1968 Dogbéh began his association with UNESCO and since 1969 he has taught at a high school in Atakpamé, Togo. He has published numerous novels and collections of poems that have received international recognition as well as a large number of articles published in France and Benin.

DO REGO, BERNARDINE, 1937– . Diplomat. Born on August 20, 1937, in Dakar to Dahomean parents, Mrs. Do Rego was educated in Dakar and Paris, including at the University of Paris (1961–63) and IHEOM (1962–1964). Appointed Administrative and Consular Affairs Director at the Ministry of Foreign Affairs in 1964, she was shifted to the position of technical consultant to the Office of the Presidency in 1970. She served as consultant to the Office of the Presidency from 1970 until the 1972 coup d'etat (q.v.). After the coup, she was sent on diplomatic duties, as First Counsellor at the Benin Embassy in France (September 1973) and in a similar capacity several years later in the United States.

DORGERE, ALEXANDRE, 1855–1900. Early missionary. Born in Nantes on December 6, 1855, and joining the Missions Africaines de Lyon after seminary training, Dorgère was ordained in 1880, departing for Dahomey the following year. He first served in Agoué and in 1884 in Ouidah (qq.v.). Briefly arrested for treason and brought to King Béhanzin in Abomey (qq.v.), Dorgère later served as emissary in the negotiations of 1890 over French demands for trading rights in Cotonou (q.v.) and Ouidah. Regarded as a friend of the Dahomean kingdom, Father Dorgère returned to France in 1896; he died of black fever on February 23, 1900.

DOSSA, RENE, 1934– . Journalist. Born on September 28, 1934, in Grand Popo (q.v.), Dossa is best known for his editorship of *L'Aube Nouvelle* (q.v.) during its formative years (1961–

1963) and his arrest for ten days for a "seditious" article (during the Maga [q.v.] Presidency) attacking unipartyism. He moved from that post to Director of the Agence Dahoméenne de Presse (1963–1965), serving concurrently as manager of the Dahomean Cinematographic Society (SODACI), before being appointed General Director of Information (1967). In September 1968 he reverted back to being Secretary of the Ministry of Information, replacing Stanislas Adotevi (q.v.). Since 1974 Dossa has been President of SONACOP (q.v.), the State marketing company with a monopoly over petroleum products.

DOSSOU. Among the Fon (q.v.), the given name of children born immediately after twins. Among the Yoruba/Goun (qq.v.), the equivalent name given to children is Idowu.

DOSSOU, CHRISTIAN, 1937– . Zoologist. Born on July 24, 1937, and trained in biology, Dossou teaches biology and zoology at the National University of Benin (q.v.).

DOSSOU, FRANCOIS (Lt. Colonel). Former Minister of Justice. A Fon (q.v.) officer who rallied to the Kérékou (q.v.) regime, Dossou entered the cabinet in January 1976 as Minister of Planning and Foreign Aid. Promoted to Lieutenant Colonel in 1981 and shifted to head the Ministry of Transportation and Communications, in December 1982 he was again shifted, this time to head the Ministry of Justice, a post he held until August 1984.

DOSSOU, LEOPOLD. Head of SYNES (q.v.). A militant unionist, Dossou led his union in the 1989 massive demonstrations demanding increased salaries, political reforms and democratization in Benin. After the eclipse of the Kérékou (q.v.) regime he became head of the new confederation of trade unions (q.v.).

DOSSOU, ROBERT. Former Minister of Planning. By profession a brilliant lawyer, former President of FEANF (q.v.) in Paris, and at the time Dean of the Law Faculty at the National University of Benin (q.v.) and President of the Bar Association, Dossou was called into the Kérékou (q.v.) government after the 1989 elections as the key Minister of Planning. Previous to that he had cooperated with the Kérékou regime on legal issues, including those related to the privatization of State enterprises. He remained in the transitional period 1989–1990 as Chairman of the organizing committee of the National Conference (q.v.) that was to lead to multipartyism and civilian rule. Dossou contested both the legislative and Presidential elections, and was elected to the National Assembly on the ASD ticket.

DOSSOU-YOVO, EDMOND. Educator and trade unionist (q.v.). A strong supporter of former President Justin Ahomadégbe (q.v.), Dossou-Yovo served briefly in 1970 as Minister of Youth and Education. Earlier, in the 1963 urban riots that ushered in the country's first coup (q.v.) and the fall of the government of Hubert Maga (q.v.), Dossou-Yovo, a union leader, was instrumental in setting up and heading a Revolutionary Committee in Cotonou. During the regime of Kérékou (q.v.) he was an active member of the PRPB (q.v.) and head of one of its urban branches.

DOUBLE ELECTORAL COLLEGE. Electoral system existing in French colonial territories under which representatives were elected by two separate electoral colleges: one composed of metropolitan citizens (including *évolués* [q.v.]) and the second of African subjects satisfying certain lower criteria. Since quasi-equality of representation existed at the outset between the two rolls, the system was highly discriminatory against the African population. In the 1947 elections for the Dahomean Conseil General (q.v.) 12 delegates were elected by the first college and 18 by the second. The situation was somewhat improved by the 1950's when, in the elections to the Assemlée Territoriale (q.v.), 18 and 32 delegates were elected by the first and second colleges respectively. The electoral college increased from 54,208 in 1948 to 971,012 at independence in 1960.

DRAMANI, BAZINI ZAKARI, 1940– . Poet. Born on August 22, 1940, in Djougou (q.v.), and educated in Adjohoun and

Porto Novo (q.v.) before higher studies at the Universities of Dakar and Caen, Dramani teaches in a Lycée in Bayeux, France, and has published a number of volumes of poetry.

DUNGLAS, EDOUARD, 1891–1952. French physician, colonial administrator, important historian and geographer. Dunglas was born in Paris in 1891 and trained as a doctor, a profession he was shortly to drop to become colonial administrator in Ivory Coast and then Dahomey. He served most of his time in Ketou (q.v.), about whose history he wrote a highly acclaimed study. His geographical work on Natitingou (q.v.) also received acclaim from France's Geographical Society and, while stationed in Abomey (q.v.), he prepared a study of Fon (q.v.) traditions. His avid scholarly mind and solid academic contributions brought him after the Second World War the post of head of Dahomey's IFAN (q.v.) branch in Porto Novo (q.v.). In 1951 Dunglas commenced his brief political career when he ran for election together with Sourou-Migan Apithy on the Union Française (qq.v) ticket. Elected to the Assemblée Territoriale (q.v.), Dunglas died soon after in Porto Novo, where he is buried in the adopted country that he so loved.

DURAND, ALEXANDRE, 1933– . Magistrate. Born in Porto Novo (q.v.) on December 8, 1933, and educated at home and abroad in law, Durand served as president of the Court of Porto Novo since 1965. He has also been a senior technical consultant with the Ministry of Justice.

-E-

ECOBANK-BENIN. New commercial bank established in Cotonou (q.v.) with most of its equity (97.3 percent) owned by Ecobank Transnational Inc., the residual by local Beninois interests.

ECOLE WILLIAM PONTY. Prestigious school (originally on Gorée Island off Dakar, Senegal), to which the children of Francophone Africa's elite were usually admitted. Among

Beninois educated at William Ponty were: Alexandre Adandé, Justin Ahomadégbé, Michel Ahouanménou, Albert Akindès, Julien Alapini, Valentin Djibodé Aplogan, Francis Covi, Hubert Maga, Eustache Prudencio, Auguste Alfred Quénum, Abdou Sérpos Tidjani and Emile Derlin Zinsou (qq.v.)

EDUCATION. During colonial rule Benin had one of French Africa's relatively more advanced educational systems, and the large number of intellectuals and professionals of Dahomean origin gained it recognition as Africa's Latin Quarter. The first regular missionary schools in the country were established in the 1960's in Ouidah, Porto Novo and Agoué (qq.v) by the Missions Africaines of Lyon. Only some 40 years later were the first schools established in the north. School attendance has always been spread very unevenly, however, from 17 percent of school-age children in Tanguiéta in Atakora (q.v.) to over 90 percent in Cotonou (q.v.) in 1968, for example. In 1974, shortly before the nationalization of private schools, the State devoted 40 percent of the budget to education and, in 1972, 45 percent of schoolchildren went to private Catholic schools. Comparative enrollments in 1971–1972 and 1982–1983 (during which the most rapid educational advances were scored), broken down by level of instruction (with number of schools shown in parentheses), was as follows:

	1971–1972	1982–1983
Primary education	186,000 (852)	404,289 (1,661)
Secondary education	27,000 (60)	113,750 (1,215)
Technical education	2,000 (7)	3,725 (9)
Teacher training	2,553 (4)	3,433 (5)
University education	600 (1)	5,575 (1)

These strong school enrollment figures, coupled with traditional Beninois upward-mobility strivings, translated in the 1980's into massive increases in higher education registrations. In 1989 there were already 8,989 students at the National University of Benin at Abomey-Calavi (qq.v.)

alone (a 61 percent increase in six years), and in 1992 fully 13,000, with around 1,900 abroad, mostly in France.

Concerted efforts by the northern military regime of Kérékou (q.v.) to develop levels of scholarization in the far north only paid meager dividends at the expense of a lowering of academic standards. In 1978 educational figures were strongly skewed, with a spread from 25.7 percent in Atakora (with 17 percent for Tanguiéta in the far north) to 66.8 percent in the coastal Atlantique (q.v.), and over 90 percent in Cotonou itself. This uneven spread was little changed over the next decade despite the overall strong spurt in school registrations occasioned by the Educational Reform (q.v.) of 1975. Tanguiéta still retained the lowest scholarization rate in the country (now 35.6 percent), Atlantique still led with 78.3 percent, and school-attendance reached 99 percent in Cotonou.

The Beninois educational establishment has been plagued by periodic eruptions of strikes that have mobilized primary and secondary school pupils as well as university students. As often as not these have been motivated by bread-and-butter issues (stipends, living conditions, quality of food, etc) as by political considerations. Notwithstanding Kérékou's categorizing the National University as a center of ''anarcho-leftist agitation,'' students, though more volatile and prone to erupt in fits of violence, reflected widespread societal grievances. The most vehement strikes (after the incidents associated with the liquidation of Aikpé [q.v.] in 1975) took place throughout 1985. In February, and again in April–May, and in September, students were up in arms against the regime in protest over a variety of issues including the end of guaranteed State employment to all graduates. Because Minister of Education Alladayé (q.v.) expressed sympathy with the strikers, he was dismissed.

New strikes broke out in January 1989 and continued intermittently (in May, August, December) over non-payment of stipends (by the bankrupt regime), quality of food and demands for reinstatement of multipartyism. The fact that student strikes have not usually been politically motivated is best attested to by the continuing record of riots and demonstrations by Benin's student population even after the reinstatement of the popularly legitimated Nicéphore Soglo (q.v.) regime.

EDUCATIONAL REFORM, 1975. Heralded by some abroad as a major innovation of import to all Third World countries, the educational reforms of 1975–1976 aimed at lifting school attendance rates from 41.5 percent to 61.3 percent by 1983. Significant advances were indeed attained, with secondary school attendance (always lagging due to paucity of schools and qualified teachers) rising by 60 percent alone. The net result, however, was a gross decline in academic standards that even the military regime had not anticipated. This was compounded by a major exodus abroad of many qualified teachers (those who had remained in the country despite the nationalization of parochial schools in the former decade). Their main grievance was the further radicalization of politics coupled with the intolerable strains caused by the unscheduled and unbudgeted academic reform of 1975. An added inducement to their self-exile was the massive gap between Beninois salaries and those in neighboring countries. Currently a large number of the ''teachers'' in Benin's schools are high school graduates, with second-year university students allowed to head secondary schools. Other aspects of the otherwise quite innovative reform of 1975 included a change in the academic calendar to conform closely to the agricultural cycle—assuring that school does not cause economic and manpower hardship at home or at harvest/planting time. (This calendar was, however, unmanageable and in 1983 the normal school year was reintroduced.) All students were also required to work at the farms during school recesses. Age no longer was the criterion for either admission or promotion from grade to grade. Indeed, promotion was granted freely irrespective of performance or grades, which was deemphasized and disappeared. Marxist indoctrination was introduced at all levels with greater vigor, though the absence of textbooks made the actual indoctrination dependent on the teacher's inclinations and/or competence. At the post-secondary level, industrial and technical education was emphasized through three new polytechnics in

Pobé, Bohicon, and Natitingou (qq.v). Several others scheduled to be built were postponed due to financial constraints.

EGUE, GUILLAUME, 1922– . Educator. Born in Ouidah (q.v.) on June 25, 1922, and long a teacher and principal (1944–1962), Egué was appointed in 1962 Prefect of Lokossa (q.v.), and in 1964 was dispatched to France for specialized training. Upon his return he became Chief of Protocol at the Ministry of Foreign Affairs, serving in that capacity between 1964 and 1977, when he left the country.

EHOUMI, PIERRE. Magistrate. Former Judge presiding over the Parakou (q.v.) Court, Ehoumi was transferred to Cotonou (q.v.) in October 1968, where he served until his retirement in 1980.

EHUZU. Name of the former daily *Daho-Express* newspaper during the Kérékou (q.v.) regime. Published in Cotonou (q.v.), it had a circulation of over 10,000. The name meant ''everything has changed.'' On May 1, 1990, with the eclipse of Marxism in Benin, the name of the newspaper was changed to *La Nation* (q.v.).

EKUE, ALBERT-KANENI, 1936– . Historian and international administrator. Born in Porto Novo (q.v.) on April 8, 1936, and educated in Porto Novo and Dakar, Ekué continued his higher education at the Universities of Dakar (1955–1956), Toulouse (1956–1961) and Yaoundé (1959).He then served for two years as technical advisor to the Ministry of Information (1961–1962) and the Education, Culture and Information Division of the Secretariat of the African and Malagasy Union (1962–1964), before becoming Director of OCAM's (q.v.) Cultural and Social Affairs Division (1964–1973). In 1973 Ekué took the position of Director of the Ecole Internationale de Bordeaux in France and, after a year at the National University of Benin (q.v.) (1977), became Director of the OAU's Technical Cooperation and Aid office in Addis Ababa. In 1979 he assumed the post of Director of the OAU's Educational and Cultural Division also in Addis Ababa.

ELECTIONS OF 1979. On November 20, 1979, the first general elections since the 1972 coup (q.v.) were held throughout Benin.The 336 Commissaires du People (q.v.)—representing the various occupational classes in Benin—were elected on a single list, with a 97.5 percent vote among those going to the polls. The official figures listed 1,582,910 registered voters, 1,275,461 voting in the election, and 1,270,051 valid votes cast, of which 1,243, 286 were in favor of the list and 21,438 against, with 5,327 abstentions. A total of 307,449 registered voters did not appear at the polls to vote.

ELECTIONS OF 1984. The second elections in Benin since the 1972 coup d'etat (q.v.) were held on June 10, 1984, for a smaller Assemblée Nationale Révolationnaire (q.v.), composed of 180 Commissaires du Peuple (q.v.), representing, as before, various societal corporate groups. Official results indicate that 1,845,921 valid votes were cast out of 1,851,044 votes and a registered electorate of 1,987,173. Of these, 1,811,808 were cast in favor of the single slate of candidates, 27,720 voted against it, 6,397 abstained and 5,119 cast spoiled ballots. The next elections, following the modification of the Assembly's term of office, were held in 1989 but were already clouded by the imminent eclipse of Marxism and single partyism in Benin.

ELECTIONS OF 1990–1991. The series of elections that took place during 1990–1991 were heralded as the first truly free elections since independence in that multipartyism was given free reign.

(1) Primary elections of November 10, 1990. The elections for Village Chiefs and Mayors attracted a much higher voter turnout (70 percent) than for the legislative elections.

(2) Legislative elections of February 17, 1991. The elections for a smaller assembly of 64 Deputies attracted over 1,800 candidates representing 24 parties of which 17 secured seats; most of the victors were local influentials elected largely on ethnic grounds in their home constituencies. The electoral turnout was 52.15 percent.

National Assembly election results by region

	Atakora	Atlantique	Borgou	Mono	Ouémé	Zou	Total
UTR		6	1	1	1	3	12
PNDD-PRD	1	1	3	1	2	1	9
PSD-UNSP	2	1		4		1	8
RND		2		1	2	2	7
NCC		1	1	1	4		7
MNDD-MSUP-UDRN	3	1	1			1	6
UDS	1		3			1	5
RDL-Vivoten	1	1		1	1		4
ASD-BSD		1		1		1	3
ADP-UDRS			1			1	2
UNDP					1		1
Total	8	14	10	10	11	11	64

(3) Presidential elections of 1991. The Presidential elections took place in two rounds, since no candidate secured an absolute majority of the vote in the first. A total of 14 Presidential aspirants presented themselves for the first round. The front-runners were Nicéphore Soglo (36.87 percent of the vote), Mathieu Kérékou (26.04 percent) and Albert Tévoédjré (14.44 percent) (qq.v.). All the others scored below 6 percent of the vote. In the second round, Soglo easily defeated Kérékou, capturing 67.6 percent of the vote to the latter's 32.2 percent, most of which (80 percent) was from the north.

ELECTORAL BOYCOTT, 1968. Following the 1967 coup d'etat that toppled Gen. Christophe Soglo's (qq.v.) regime, the interim military administration sponsored Presidential elections in which both Dahomey's political triumvirate (q.v.) and their cabinet Ministers were barred from running. Both Hubert Maga and Sourou-Migan Apithy, the Bariba and Goun (qq.v.) political leaders respectively, appealed from abroad for a boycott of the elections by their supporters in Dahomey. Their appeal was successful, and about 75 percent of the eligible voters shunned the elections. Justin Ahomadégbé, the Fon (qq.v.) leader, did not call for a boycott and his stand-in candidate, Dr. Moumouni Adjo (q.v.), garnered most of the votes cast. The election results were promptly cancelled and, shortly after, the military declared that Emile Derlin Zinsou (q.v.), veteran politician and former Foreign Minister, would assume the Presidency. See also COUP OF 1967.

ELEGBE, AMOS. Former Minister. A Yoruba (q.v.) from the north, Elegbé is a geographer by training. Charged with town planning in the Cotonou (q.v.) municipality, he was appointed interim Minister of Trade and Tourism in August 1989.

ELEGBEDE, MOUSTAPHA. Civil administrator. Formerly Prefect of Zou (q.v.), in February 1988 Elegbédé was named prefect of Ouémé (q.v.).

EOUAGNIGNON, NICOLAS AMOUSSOU, 1915– . Physician, politician and diplomat. Born in Savalou (q.v.) on December 4, 1915, and a graduate of the Dakar School of Medicine and the University of Paris, as well as of the Dental Surgery School of Montreal University, Eouagnignon practiced in Ivory Coast (Gagnoa) until 1957 before returning home. There he was immediately elected to the Assemblee Territoriale (q.v.) as Deputy from Savalou, serving until 1960. He was also brought into the pre-independence cabinet as Minister of Public Health (1957–1959), between 1959 and 1960 serving also as Inspector General of School Medical Facilities. Dr. Eouagnignon was then a member of the Dahomey delegation to the UN (in 1961), following which he was appointed Ambassador to Haiti (1962–1964). In 1964 he was shifted to represent Dahomey in West Germany, Scandinavia, and Switzerland (1964–1969), before returning to private practice in Cotonou (q.v.).

ETCHRI, LEON. Civil administrator. Deputy Head of the Civil Service between 1962 and 1964, Etchri headed the Civil Service between 1964 and 1968. In 1968 he was shifted to administrative duties in the Ministry of Interior, serving first as sous-préfet of Porto Novo (q.v.) (1968–1972), then Adjohoun (1972–76), before joining the Ministry of Information as technical consultant charged with propaganda.

ETHNIC CONFLICT see REGIONALISM

ETHNIC GROUPS. Benin's population was 4,855,349 according to the January 1992 census, divided into some 40 ethnic groups. Of these, the following were numerically the most important:

In the north: the Bariba (8.5 percent), Fulani (5.6 percent), Djougou (3 percent), Dendi (2.1 percent, Pila Pila and Somba (1.8 percent) (qq.v.).

In the south and center: the Fon (39.2 percent), Yoruba (11.9 percent), Adja (11 percent) and Houéda (8.5 percent) (qq.v.).

ETUDES DAHOMEENNES. Former irregular publication of the Institut Français d'Afrique Noire (q.v.) of Dahomey and its successor, the Institut de Rechérches Appliqués du Dahomey (q.v.) in Porto Novo (q.v.). An extremely valuable scholarly publication carrying mostly articles on ethnology, anthropology, musicology, linguistics and history, *Etudes Dahoméennes* (which was issued from time to time in monograph form) commenced publication in 1948. In 1959, to mark its epistemologically new sponsorship with Dahomey's independence, it adopted a "new series" numerology. Lack of budgetary resources made the publication defunct by 1970.

EUROPEAN ECONOMIC COMMUNITY (EEC). Consequent to the Yaoundé conventions of 1963 and 1969, Dahomey has been an Associate Member of the EEC, receiving preferential tariff treatment for its commodity exports and partaking of the community's technical assistance fund, the Fonds Européen de Développement (q.v.).

EVOLUE see ASSIMILATION POLICY; ASSIMILE; INDIGE-NAT

EZIN ONVEHOU, JEAN PIERRE, 1944– . Mathematician. Born in 1944 and with a doctorate from the Institut d'Administration des Entreprises, Ezin Onvehou teaches at the National University of Benin (q.v.), having previously taught in Lille (France), Abidjan and Brazzaville.

-F-

FA. Fon word referring to destiny as willed by the spirits and gods. Fa can be foreseen by special diviners (*bokono*), who are highly respected in their villages. Divination may be accomplished in a variety of methods, the most common of which is the manipulation and examination of 16 palm kernels on a rectangular tray and their examination for signs of the solution or destiny of the issue or problem. Still extensively practiced in southern Benin. See also FETI-CHEURS.

FABO, PAUL, 1906–1973. Diplomat and journalist. Born in Porto Novo to a Goun (qq.v.) family on June 5, 1906, Fabo studied under Paul Hazoumé and Father Aupiais (qq.v.) before commencing his career as an agent for a Kinshasa-based commercial company. In the late 1930's he journeyed to Paris where he had a chance to complete his education, obtaining a degree in the humanities. He was then recruited into the French army and founded the periodical *L'Afrique et le Monde* in Brassels. He published a few books as well at the conclusion of the Second World War, commencing a literary life. With the independence of Dahomey, he was called home to serve in a diplomatic capacity and was named chargé d'affaires to Kinshasa (1961–1963) and later Ambassador to Zaire (1963–1973). Retiring from public life in 1973, he died soon after in Cotonou (q.v.).

FABOUMY, CYRILLE LAUREN OLAITOU, 1931– . Hydraulic engineer. Born in Cotonou (q.v.) to an influential chiefly family on December 23, 1931, and educated in Dakar, Paris and Grenoble, Faboumy graduated in hydraulic engineering and was appointed deputy head of the research division of the Organization for the Development of the Senegal River (1957–1979). He returned to Cotonou shortly before independence, occupying a series of similar posts until appointed Chief Engineer of the Hydraulic Service in 1963. During this period he was also tapped for administrative services, served as Cabinet Director of the Minister of Public Works, and was elected Regional Councillor of Cotonou (1959–1961). In

1967 he was shifted to diplomatic duties, being dispatched as Ambassador to the EEC, Belgium and the Netherlands. He served until after the coup in Cotonou and, in 1973 he was repatriated and appointed Director General of the Electric Company of Benin. Faboumy joined the newly formed RND (q.v.) party when it was formed, and was elected on its ticket in the 1991 legislative elections.

FAGBAMIGBE, GUILLAUME. Early trade union (q.v.) leader, editor and Minister. Leader of the radical and Communist-affiliated CGT, in the early 1950's Fagbamigbé headed the Syndicat des Employés du Commerce et de l'Industrie du Dahomey (SECID) and was editor of its newspaper, *Le Travail,* between 1947 and 1955. He was appointed Dahomey's first Minister of Labor after the Loi Cadre (q.v.) colonial reforms, serving until 1959.

FAGBEMI, MANOU ROFIOU. State Prosecuting Attorney. Previously attached to the Natitingou (q.v.) court, Fagbemi was transferred to Porto Novo (q.v.) in 1968 where he served until 1975. He is currently retired.

FAGNON, EMMANUEL. Inspector of Taxes for the Cotonou (q.v.) area. Fagnon has also been Deputy to the National Assembly (q.v.) (1959–1966) and first Vice-President of the Conseil Economique et Social (q.v.).

FALADE, MAX PAUL WENCESLAS HEYESIPPE ADE NIRAN ALAO, 1927– . Architect. Born on September 28, 1927, in Porto Novo (q.v.), and educated in French primary and secondary schools, Faladé studied architecture and urban planning between 1951 and 1961. He was employed in a variety of posts in Paris, including the latter's Office of Architecture and Town Planning (1957–1960) and private firms, until appointed Economic Officer in the Town Planning Division of the Economic Commission for Africa, based in Addis Ababa. He has been in that position since 1973.

FANTODJI, AGATHE, 1947– . Educator. Born on February 5, 1987, and with degrees in oceanography (University of

Brest, 1974) and biology (Reims, 1977), Fantodji teaches animal biology at the National University of Benin (q.v.).

FANTODJI, COMLAN PIERRE, 1941– . Mathematician. Born in 1941 and obtaining degrees in mathematics at the University of Paris in 1968, 1972, and 1974, Fantodji teaches at the National University of Benin (q.v.).

FANTODNJI, PASCAL. Political aspirant. Little known head of the Parti Communiste du Dahomey, normally resident in Abidjan. In 1990 he returned to Cotonou (q.v.) to organize demonstrations against the convening of the National Reconciliation Conference (q.v.) (that was to usher in multipartyism) until Kérékou (q.v.) was ousted and in jail.

FASSASSI, ASSENI, 1944– . Lawyer and international administrator. Born in 1944, and educated in Paris in Political Science and Law, Fassassi first served as head of administration at the Ministry of Public Health (1976–1979) before joining the United Nations High Commission for Refugees based in Kigali, Rwanda. Fassassi returned to Benin to run in the 1992 Presidential elections, obtaining 0.9 percent of the vote.

FAVI, JOACHIM, 1948– . Economist. Born in 1948, and with a doctorate from Paris in Economics in Industrial Planning, Favi has been Director of the Centre de Formation Administrative et de Perfectionnement before being appointed to his current post as Head of Program Planning at the Department of State Planning.

FEDERATION DES ETUDIANTS DE L'AFRIQUE NOIRE EN FRANCE (FEANF). Militant union of Francophone Africa's students in France, with branches in various university cities. Several of Benin's intellectuals have played a role in the FEANF during their sojourn in France, notably Richard Dogbéh and Albert Tévoédjré (qq.v.).

FELIHO, ISIDORE, 1933– . Director of the National Library and National Archives in Porto Novo (q.v.). Born in Abomey (q.v.) on July 8, 1933, and educated in Porto Novo (q.v.) and in France (1961–1963), Feliho has been head librarian since November 1964.

FELIHO, JEAN FLORENTIN, 1932– . Former Minister of Defense. A Fon from Abomey (qq.v.), Feliho was born on November 24, 1932, and obtained a degree in law from the University of Dakar in 1963. He then continued his law studies at the University of Bordeaux (1963–1965), returning to serve as State Prosecutor in both Cotonou and Porto Novo (qq.v.) (1966–1967). In 1968 he entered private practice as an attorney registered at the Court of Appeals. Active in the civic rights movement in Benin, and founder of ACAT-Benin (Christian Action against Torture), Feliho was appointed to the transitional government of 1990 as Minister of Interior and Public Security, serving between March 1990 and July 1991. He was then appointed Minister of Defense, but resigned in March 1993 when President Soglo (q.v.) appointed new heads of the armed services without consulting him.

FETICHEURS. Priests of the various fetish cults, diviners of the Fa (q.v.) and venerators of spirits or deities. Still very prevalent in southern Benin. One of the prime centers of these cults has been Ouidah (q.v.), where the temple of the python cult (q.v.) stands across from the Catholic cathedral. The government of Kérékou (q.v.) went to great lengths to limit or destroy the role of féticheurs in Benin, to no avail. It utilized both educational campaigns and force to drive sorcerers into disgrace; it destroyed or uprooted "sacred" trees and/or boulders, imprisoned (on charges of fraud) recalcitrant *féticheurs,* and depicted them over the channels of communication as national traitors. This early zeal was tempered by moderation in the late 1970's, when the ingrained traditions and beliefs of Beninois proved to be simply irremovable. Consequently a subtle shift in policy developed; instead of punitive action, the government increasingly tried to work with these fetish priests, converting them, when possible, to allies in the developmental task.

FETISHISM see FETICHEURS

FETISHISTS see FETICHEURS

FIFATIN, AGOSSOU MAURICE, 1935– . Educator. Born on May 25, 1935, and educated at the University of Montpellier in political science (Ph.D., 1973), Fifatin teaches political sociology and maritime law at the National University of Benin (q.v.). He is also the owner of a food processing plant in Cotonou (q.v.).

FINANCIAL BANK. New commercial bank established in Cotonou (q.v.). Most equity (99 percent) is owned by Financial Bank Corporation of Geneva, Switzerland.

FOCCART, JACQUES, 1913– . Born on August 31, 1913, Foccart was raised in Guadeloupe where his father was a landowner. He joined the Resistance during the Second World War, emerging in its aftermath as a staunch Gaullist and important leader of the Rassemblement du Peuple Français (RPF). Foccart served in a variety of high-level governmental positions in France, including 14 years (1960–1974) as Secretary-General to the Presidency in charge of African and Malagasy Affairs. As architect of France's African policies, Foccart wielded enormous influence and has been the power behind several African political thrones. Hubert Maga (q.v.), the northern Dahomean leader, was widely regarded as one of his protégés. In 1970 Foccart was instrumental in helping set up the Presidential Council (q.v.) that ruled Dahomey between 1970 and 1972.

FON. Core ethnic group of the precolonial Dahomey kingdom (q.v.), one of West Africa's more powerful and better organized states. Culturally belonging to the Adja (q.v.) group of peoples and speaking on Ewe dialect (also spoken in neighboring Togo), the Fon currently number about 900,000 and are found throughout central and southern Benin. The Fon have been very upwardly-mobile and, during the colonial and postcolonial periods, occupied a high percentage of the civil service and professional positions. Many have emigrated and settled in other parts of Francophone Africa or in France. Between the mid-1940's and the 1972 coup d'etat (q.v.) the unchallenged political leader of the Fon was Justin Ahomadégbé (q.v.), a descendant from the Agonglo branch of the Dahomean royalty. See also ADJA; DAHOMEY, KINGDOM OF.

FONDS D'AIDE ET DE COOPERATION (FAC). French development fund, dispensing financial aid and technical assistance to former colonial territories. Among projects assisted by FAC in Benin were SONADER (q.v.) and the Port of Cotonou (q.v.). FAC is the successor, following the independence of much of Africa, of the Fonds d'Investissement para le Développement Economique et Social des Territoires d'Outre Mer (q.v.). In 1990 FAC's contribution to Benin was 3,128 million CFA francs.

FONDS D'INVESTISSEMENT POUR LE DEVELOPPEMENT ECONOMIQUE ET SOCIAL DES TERRITOIRES D'OUTRE MER (FIDES). Precursor of the contemporary Fonds d'Aide et de Coopération (q.v.). French development fund distributing economic and technical assistance to overseas colonies and associated territories. Between 1947–1957, over $750 million was allocated to French West Africa. Dahomey received $32 million during these years, for research on palm oil (q.v.) production, the development of a textile industry, etc.

FONDS EUROPEEN DE DEVELOPPEMENT (FED). The European Development Fund is an agency of the European Economic Community (q.v.) with which most of Africa is linked via the Yaoundé treaties of 1963 and 1969. The FED dispenses the Community's economic and technical assistance to member and associate states. Benin has received important sums from FED, including for the construction of the port of Cotonou (q.v.). Total sums allocated to Dahomey by 1973 amounted at $43.5 million, and nearly twice that by 1992. France's contribution to the FED has usually been around 24 percent of the latter's funds.

FONGBE. Language of the Fon (q.v.).

FORCE OMEGA. Code name for the mercenary assault (q.v.) on Cotonou airport in 1977.

FORCES ARMEES DU BENIN (FAB). Benin has always had relatively small security forces, a function of perennial budgetary pressures. Despite this the armed forces absorb as much as 22 percent of the entire national budget (11.4 billion CFA francs or $40 million); the officer corps has among the best salaries in the country; and the military has always been paid on time, even when other segments of the civil service (especially during 1987–1990) went unpaid for up to 12 months. On top of that, both during periods of civilian rule, and especially during the longer periods of military rule, the armed forces decreed themselves a variety of fringe benefits, perks (e.g. exemption from customs duties of personal vehicles) and gratuities, and have engaged in a variety of legitimate private enterprises (trucking, wholesale trade, urban and inter-urban transport) as well as illegitimate activities. Thus, for example, much of the historic two-way smuggling (q.v.) across the porous borders with both Nigeria and Togo (that results in Benin "exporting" large amounts of commodities such as coffee and cocoa that it does not produce) is done with the direct connivance of the border patrols and gendarmerie (q.v.). More ominously, during the latter years of the Kérékou (q.v.) era a number of military officers were engaged in the much more lucrative smuggling, onward transhipment, and to a lesser extent cultivation, of drugs including cocaine and heroin. Kérékou's former personal marabout and prime security aide, Mohamed Cissé (q.v.), for example, though tried in 1992 for embezzlement of large sums of State funds, was allegedly at the center of a major drug-smuggling network utilizing Benin as a transhipment point as all shipments from Nigeria (a former fulcrum) were internationally closely monitored.

The total size of the armed forces has slowly inched forward until by 1990 (when military rule collapsed) it stood at 4,350, up from 3,200 in 1984. The force is composed of an army of 3,800 (up from 3,100 in 1984) organized into three infantry battalions, an air force of 350 (up from 1984's 60, which was a decrease from 1972's force of 150), and a navy of 200 (up from 40). The army includes an engineering and two infantry battalions, a para-commando company, a reconnaissance squadron, an artillery battery and one armored squad. Most of the troops (circa 80 percent) and their non-technical NCO's have always been northerners, partly a function of the upward mobility, aspirations and greater educational qualifications of southern ethnic groups.

In October 1976 the FAB were structurally reorganized into three sections: (1) the National Defense forces—including the army, navy, airforce, gendarmerie, national police, fire-fighting forces, customs units and forest wardens; (2) the Public Security Force ("Section Deux"), involved in political indoctrination and surveillance; and (3) the People's Militia—the civilian armed corps with poorly defined "special" tasks and ad hoc "assignments."

The armed forces currently have approximately 150 officers (up from 90 in the early 1970's, but were in 1992 in the process of being severely pruned) of which, until the 1972 coup that brought Kérékou (qq.v.) and a northern hegemony to power, 80 percent were southerners, mostly Fon (q.v.) in operational command posts and Yoruba/Nagot and Mina (qq.v.) in technical ones. The number of southerners has declined considerably since. Nearly the entire top command of the army (of which only one was from the north) was retired in 1972, and many others fell afoul of Kérékou and were either imprisoned for plotting or attempted coups, liquidated (e.g. Major Aikpé [q.v.]) or appointed to non-military sinecures or administrative posts. At the same time a stranglehold of northerners slowly emerged in the officer corps, especially since 1984 when they began to assume middle rank. This new crop of young northern officers were either Somba (q.v.) (Kérékou's ethnicity, but by virtue of being among Benin's most laggard groups, still very few) or (especially) Fulani (q.v.)—a northern minority, not on good terms with the more numerous haughty northern Bariba (q.v.) whose cattle they tend, and who historically looked down on the Somba whom they used to raid for slaves. The slow ethnic matching of rank and file and officer corps brought the Kérékou regime a measure of stability unequalled in Benin's history, but only because of his willingness to use repression (via specialized units, such as the BGP, SDI and the Deuxième Bureau) that previous military regimes were reluctant to do, and because in choosing Marxism as a

State ideology (even though in reality whatever Socialism was attempted in 1974 was gone by 1982) a measure of civilian support was tapped.

In terms of materiel the FAB has an assortment of armored personnel carriers, 20 tanks, 60 mm and 81 mm mortars and 105 mm guns. Some of these, according to one source, are largely "ornamental." The Air Force consists of an assortment of non-combat aircraft (e.g. several C47's and Antonov 26 medium-transport planes, ten light transport planes, and six armed helicopters); only the latter are known to be operational. The navy (based in Cotonou) consists of nine patrol crafts, only one of which is operational; the others broke down years ago due to poor maintenance or were cannibalized for spare parts.

Military camps exist in several locations, the key ones being Cotonou, Porto Novo, Parakou and especially Ouidah (qq.v.) (see below) with the formerly small (60-man garrison) Natitingou (q.v.) camp greatly augmented by the Natitingou origin of Kérékou, and used among other things as a maximum security confinement center for either (southern) civilian political leaders or (southern) military plotters.

Until 1972 the army's elite corps was the 120-man Ouidah-based well-armed para-commando until that with superior esprit-du-corps was always mobilizable to topple civilian regimes. Being a largely Fon force, however, the unit was a threat to Kérékou, who could not disband it either. (In 1975 Captain Assogba's [q.v.] assault originated from there.) In the mid-1970's, therefore, Kérékou built up the overwhelmingly Fulani (northern) Bataillon de la Garde Presidentielle (BGP) (q.v.)—which during the pre-1972 era was a small largely ceremonial unit best known for its very colorful uniforms. Trained by North Korea, and with the best weapons in the country, it became the true military prop of the regime against domestic foes and mutinies from within the army itself.

To these forces should be added the greatly augmented (by Kérékou) gendarmerie (q.v.) (by law part of the armed forces), totalling 2,000 men (up from 1,200) and organized in four (six previously) mobile companies, well as 1,000 policemen (see POLICE FORCE), the Deuxième Bureau (Military Intelligence) part of a larger Public Security Force, and the elite all-northern Service de Documentation et de l'Information (SDI) (q.v.) secret police and a 2,000-man People's Militia (q.v.), the latter two disbanded in 1991.

The Chief-of-Staff of the Armed Forces under Kérékou was Colonel Vincent Ghézodie. Former occupants of the post have been General Kérékou himself, General Christophe Soglo, Col. Alphonse Alley, Col. Maurice Kouandété and Col. Paul Emile de Souza (qq.v.). In 1992 President Soglo appointed Colonel Aristide Awe Boni (q.v.) Chief-of-Staff and, in 1993, Colonel Marcellin Sinsin (q.v.) was appointed his Deputy. For the various military interventions see COUP OF 1963; COUP OF 1965(a); COUP OF 1965(b); COUP OF 1967; COUP OF 1969; COUP OF 1972.

With the eclipse of military, Marxist, northern rule, President Nicéphore Soglo (q.v.) initiated a number of reforms in the military forces. The several intelligence and/or secret services and BGP were disbanded, and their members largely dispersed among other military units. Their key commanding officers were either pensioned, dispersed to distant garrisons, or in a few cases (as with Captain Tawès [q.v.]) arrested for various civil crimes. In 1993, also, a number of key commands were reassigned to assure the fidelity of the armed forces to civilian rule.

FORCES POPULAIRES. Mimeographed newssheet, one of several appearing in Dahomey's pamphleteering tradition, utilized to publicize Justin Ahomadégbé's (q.v.) charges of corruption and demands for reform in the administration of Hubert Maga (q.v.) while the latter was chairman of the Presidential Council (q.v.). The paper was banned by Maga in March 1972, shortly after a mutiny in the Ouidah (q.v.) army garrison. Six months later, citing several of the same charges, the army overthrew the Presidential Council, by then under Ahomadégbé's Chairmanship.

FOREIGN AID. Benin has not been very successful in efforts to attract significant amounts of foreign financial infusions, either during the pre-1972 era, the "revolutionary" years, or after normalization in 1990. Indeed, levels of aid tended to be quite stable throughout at between $75–95 million per year, with up to 30 percent of this from France, 13 percent from the EEC, and 15 percent from Germany. At the same time little risk capital has come into the country, including in recent years, reflecting assessments that the economy has little attraction to entrepreneurs.

FORT ST. JEAN BAPTISTE D'AJUDA see OUIDAH; OUIDAH HISTORICAL MUSEUM.

FOURN, GASTON BERNARD. Former Attorney General of Benin. Previously a magistrate and President of the Association des Syndicats du Dahomey (ASYNDA), Fourn served as legal adviser to the Presidency (May–December 1967), demanding the maximum sentence (20 years) in the famous trial of Colonel Alley (q.v.). He was appointed Attorney General in 1968 and remained in that capacity until the coup of 1972 (q.v.) when he went to reside in France.

FRANC ZONE. Monetary transaction association formed by most of the territories once ruled by France, including the Communauté Financiére Africaine (q.v.). National or regional currencies, pegged to the French franc, are freely exchangeable and transferable within the Franc Zone.

FRANCISCO, MARIUS THEODULE, 1938– . Union pour la Liberté et le Développement (ULD) leader. Born in Ouidah (q.v.) on May 3, 1938, and trained in mathematics and mechanical engineering in Dakar, Francisco was imprisoned during 1975–1976 before serving (1978–1989) as Director of the Office Béninois d'Informatique. He joined the transitional cabinet of 1990, and was elected to the National Assembly (q.v.) on the ULD ticket, as part of the post-1991 pro-Soglo Union pour la Triomphe du Renouveau Démocratique (qq.v.).

FRANCO-DAHOMEAN CAMPAIGNS. The battles that led to the imposition of colonialism in Dahomey. There were three principal campaigns in the Franco-Dahomean War of 1890–1894 that led to the destruction of the military might of the Kingdom of Dahomey (q.v.). The first in 1890; the second, in

1892; and the third campaign in 1893–1994 (see DODDS, ALFRED-AMEDEE). While the conquest of Dahomey was consequent to crass colonial aspirations, the triggering cause for hostilities was Dahomey's non-recognition of a disputed treaty ceding Cotonou (q.v.) (then only a small coastal village), and of French suzerainty (Protectorate) over Porto Novo (q.v.)—Dahomey's traditional enemy.

FREEDOM VILLAGES. Large number of "independent" Gando (q.v.) villages, found especially in the Kandi and Nikki areas but also all over the Borgou and Atakora (qq.v.). The villages sprang up with the onset of colonialism and the abolition of internal slavery in Bariba (q.v.) society. A major outflux from Bariba villages resulted in the "freedom" villages. Currently some 15 percent of the population of Borgou and Atakora live in villages with such an origin.

FREEMAN, THOMAS BIRCH, 1809–1890. Founder of the Methodist Church in Benin. Born in England in 1809 of racially mixed parents, Freeman entered the Church in 1828. Much of his missionary work was in Ghana and Nigeria. In 1842 a Methodist mission was established not far from Porto Novo (q.v.) (in Badagry), and the next year Freeman visited King Ghézo in Abomey (qq.v.), obtaining permission to commence activities in Dahomey. In 1854 the British fort in Whydah (q.v.) was the scene of the first regular Methodist effort in the country. Most of the actual missionary work in Dahomey was done by Thomas Joseph Marshall (q.v.).

FRENCH UNION. Structure established under the French constitution of October 1946 allowing a measure of representation to French colonial territories in the policy-making process. The French Union was composed of metropolitan France and its overseas territories, classified as Overseas Departments, Overseas Territories, Associated Territories, Protectorates, and Associated States. The mainland African colonies fell under the heading of Overseas Territories.

The Union had a President (the French President), a High Council and an Assembly in which Deputies from the territories participated. The new provisions also allowed

African representation in the two houses of the French Parliament and in the Economic Council.

FRENCH WEST AFRICA see AFRIQUE OCCIDENTALE FRANCAISE (AOF)

FRONT D'ACTION COMMUNE DES ELEVES ET ETUDI-ANTS DU NORD (FACEEN). Breakaway student organization from the southern-dominated UGEED (q.v.). FACEEN organized in 1966 in order to promote northern interests, then very much neglected in Cotonou (q.v.) and the UGEED. During the Kérékou (q.v.) era FACEEN had been strongly supportive of the regime.

FRONT D'ACTION DEMOCRATIQUE (FAD). Temporary alliance against Sourou-Migan Apithy (q.v.), leader of the Nagot and Goun (qq.v.) of Porto Novo (q.v.), by Hubert Maga and his Rassemblement Démocratique Dahoméen (RDD) (qq.v.) and Justin Ahomadégbé and his Union Démocratique Dahoméene (qq.v.). The alliance lasted two months (February to March 1958), following which the RDD joined Apithy's Parti Républicain Dahoméen (q.v.) to form the anti-Ahomadégbé Parti Progréssiste Dahoméen (q.v.), Dahomean branch of the interterritorial party, the Parti du Regroupement Africain (q.v.).

FRONT DE LIBERATION ET DE REHABILITATION DU DAHOMEY (FLERD). Clandestine opposition to the Marxist regime in Cotonou (q.v.) in the 1970's and 1980's. Established in 1974 in Paris by Emile Derlin Zinsou (q.v.), FLERD had branches—supported by the large Beninois exile community—in Ivory Coast, Gabon, Senegal and Togo. FLERD claimed co-responsibility for the ill-fated 1977 mercenary assault (q.v.) on Cotonou airport. One of its supporters was Alphonse Alley (q.v.). By the mid-1980's the movement had become moribund.

FRONT UNIFIE DEMOCRATIQUE (FUD). Radical pressure group, formed in 1974 in Cotonou, composed of pupils, students, intellectuals and unemployed labor in particular. With branches in other urban centers, but mostly active in

Cotonou (q.v.), the FUD pressed for radicalization of Beninois society from "below," and for the creation of Soviets in the countryside and the elimination from the military regime of conservative and pragmatic elements. One of the "enemies" of the FUD was Colonel Barthelemy Ohouéns (q.v.), as well as the civilian minister Aboubakar Baba Moussa (q.v.), both pragmatic conservative leaders. The idol of the FUD was Captain Michel Aikpé (q.v.), murdered in 1975, leading to the mass upheaval in Cotonou that led to the pro-forma banning of the FUD. The Liguers (q.v.) were, in a sense, the ideological successors of the FUD (though their class composition was different, with unionists predominating). The FUD was a major threat to Kérékou's (q.v.) regime, since it polarized his cabinet and officer corps while gaining support of the revolutionary structures in the country.

FULANI. Muslim people, numbering possibly 12 million, scattered throughout West Africa but found especially in Nigeria, Mali, Guinea, Cameroun and Niger. Few Fulani made their way into Benin (where they are estimated at around 100,000), nor did the country experience any of the religious wars or Fulani invasions that Nigeria did. (This is attributed to the military bulwark provided in the Borgou [q.v.] by the powerful Bariba [q.v.] states.) In Benin the Fulani (better known as Peul, elsewhere, also, as Fulbé) are mostly pastoralists, having established symbiotic relationships with the Bariba Wasangari (q.v.), whose cattle they tended in exchange for protection. In Benin the Fulani's Islamic faith is of a non-puritanical variety and is strongly affected by prolonged contact with the surrounding animist (q.v.) population. The Fulani are especially found in the Kandi, Kouandé, Parakou and Djougou (qq.v.) regions. Politically and economically they have often formed alliances with the (also Muslim) Dendi (q.v.).

-G-

GA. Dendi (q.v.) word for animal pens, sites of Fulani (q.v.) settlements in precolonial Borgou (q.v.).

GABA (d. 1918). A Somba (q.v.) (also Natimba) chief who sparked an anti-French revolt in the Atakora (q.v.) at the time of the Borgou (q.v.) rebellion (see BIO GUERA). The leader of a village a few kilometers east of Kouandé (q.v.). Gaba mobilized a force of villagers to attack the French garrison of Natitingou (q.v.) while the latter's commander was on a tour of the district. Though the revolt spread, it was not as cohesive as its counterpart in Borgou, where the Bariba (q.v.)—whether or not involved in the hostilities—were fully sympathetic to Bio Guéra. The French gave low priority to the Atakora rebellion until they fully crushed the more dangerous one among the Bariba. The Somba (Natimba) revolt was finally contained in mid-1917, though Gaba and his last warriors were not captured until 1918. See also UPRISINGS OF 1915–1918.

GAN. Chief (or Head) among the Adja (q.v.) population of southern Benin, as in *"hennougan"*—head of a lineage group (*hennou*).

GANDO. One of the largest social strata in traditional Bariba (q.v.) society. Prior to the French occupation of Dahomey, the Gando were slaves of the *Wasangari* (q.v.) nobility, engaged in agricultural or herding activities in the Bariba villages of the Borgou and Atakora (qq.v.). Originally captured during warfare, razzias and intermittent strife, which typified Bariba life, the Gando—who were of various ethnic origins—constituted the lowest social strata in the quasi-feudal social hierarchy of the Bariba. Many were of Yoruba (q.v.) origin, while some Gando were actually slaves of the Fulani (q.v.) in the region, living in a symbiotic relationship with the Bariba. As much as 20 percent of the population of Borgou, at the time of the French entry, were Gando. The origin of the word itself is not clear, but the term universally implied servitude in "camps" as distinct from residence (i.e., with full status) in villages. After the abolition of internal slavery there was a major outflux of Gando from Bariba settlements to "freedom villages" (q.v.), forcing the Wasangari into unaccustomed manual labor and farming activities, destroying in the process traditional class lines in Bariba society.

GANGAN KISRA. The quasi-sacred royal trumpets of Bussa (q.v.), the parent state of all Bariba (q.v.) in Benin and Nigeria. According to tradition the Gangan Kisra were brought to Bussa from Bornu by either Kisira—the Bariba ancestor—or one of his sons.

GANI. Annual ceremonies among the Bariba of Borgou (qq.v.). The word "*gaani*" means "dancing," or any manifestation of rejoicing, though there are other theories of the semantic origins of the term. In origin and essence, a ceremony of the nobility *Wasangari* (q.v.) aimed at both cementing historic clan cleavages and personal antagonisms and paying allegiance to the Kisira (q.v.) foundation of Borgou, and repulsing its enemies. Calculated by the lunar calendar Gani falls between March and June and lasts three days. Having socioeconomic and religious functions, the ceremonies bring together all the nobility from the Bariba diaspora to pay fealty to the King of Nikki (q.v.). In precolonial times, gifts of slaves and food accompanied the pilgrimage of clan leaders to Nikki. A part of the ceremony—which symbolized the continued devotion of the Bariba to common ancestors despite their dispersal and friction—involves the use of the sacred trumpets of Nikki (the *Tufaro* [q.v.]) to call upon and assemble the souls of all Bariba ancestors. The King (*Sinaboko*) then visits on horseback the nine cult-centers of Nikki (including where major Bariba figures are buried) and also visits the Imam for his blessing (since many Bariba are becoming Muslim.)

GANI, OROU SOUBROUKOU, 1922– . Anthropologist and former curator of the Parakou (q.v.) museum. Born in 1922 in Boukombé in the Atakora (q.v.) province, Gani studied in Porto Novo (q.v.) and Senegal. He served in the French army for five years during the Second World War, following which he continued his studies at IFAN (q.v.) in Abidjan, Ivory Coast. Back in Dahomey, he accompanied a variety of anthropological research teams as interpreter-guide and was, for several years, curator of the Abomey (q.v.) museum and later, the Ethnographic Museum of Porto Novo (q.v.). In 1972, with the beginning of the construction of the Museum of the North in Parakou, Gani was appointed its Director, Orou Gani has published extensively on the customs and history of the northern populations. He is currently retired.

GANIER, FERDINAND, 1848–1900. Colonial officer. Born on December 24, 1848, in Switzerland, Ganier became a naturalized French citizen and served in France's colonial armies in Senegal and New Caledonia. He was dispatched to Dahomey in 1897 to pacify the northern part of the country and swing it into France's orbit. Treaties signed with Kouandé and especially Nikki (qq.v.) (on November 24, 1897) helped keep the Borgou (q.v.) out of British hands. Ganier died of yellow fever in Senegal in August 1900, having played a major role in the French absorption of Dahomey.

GANTIN, BERNARDIN, 1922– . Cardinal and former Archbishop of Cotonou (q.v.). Born on May 6, 1922, in Toffo, and on his mother's side of royal blood, Gantin completed seminary training at Ouidah (q.v.) in 1942. He continued his studies in Rome in 1953 and, after being ordained a priest, served in Cotonou. He was ordained Bishop in 1956—the youngest ever—and appointed Archbishop of Cotonou in 1961. He participated in various Vatican activities and committees and became Vice-President of the Peace and Justice Committee in 1976. In 1977 he was made Cardinal and relocated to Rome. In 1984 Gantin was appointed to the powerful post of Prefect of the Congregation of Bishops, one of the most senior in the Curia.

GANVIE. Stunningly scenic lacustral village of 12,000 people on Lake Nokoué 18 kilometers north of Cotonou (q.v.). Touted as Africa's Venice, it is one of Benin's major tourist attractions, though there are other, though smaller, lacustral villages in the area (So Zounko, So Tchanhoué, Vekky) with similar attractions though not as accessible to Cotonou.

Ganvié was established by the Tofinnu who were seeking refuge from military pressures of their neighbors. Paradoxically they also established a large slave-market at Kindji, where they sold slaves captured in their various battles. ''Ganvié'' is also the name of COBENAM's (q.v.) first cargo vessel, launched in 1978. There are an estimated 17,000 Tofinnu fishermen today.

GARCIA, LUC, 1937– . Academic and author. Born in 1937 Garcia was educated overseas, obtaining his Ph.D. in 1969 from the University of Paris. He is the author of several books, most on the history of the region's kingdoms, and has been attached to both IRAD and the National University of Benin (qq.v.).

GARDE PRESIDENTIELLE see BATAILLON DE LA GARDE PRESIDENTIELLE (BGP).

GAZETTE DU GOLFE. Benin's first major privately-owned journal. Established in March 1988, during the period of liberalization in the country but before the grant of total freedom of the press, the journal ran afoul of the administration with a critical article in September 1989 and was briefly banned. It is a bi-monthly covering socioeconomic and political issues.

GBAGUIDI, DAVID. As attested by his name of the Savalou (q.v.) royal family, Gbaguidi served as Ambassador to the EEC (q.v.), based in Brussels. In December 1982 he was brought back to Cotonou (q.v.) and was appointed Minister of Youth and Sports, a position he held until 1984.

GBAGUIDI, FAUSTIN, 1918– . Important early Mahi (q.v.) leader and journalist. Born on December 13, 1918, in Savalou (q.v.) and of chiefly descent, Gbaguidi played a key role in extending Maga's (q.v.) political reach to central Dahomey, swinging part of the Savalou vote behind the latter. Gbaguidi ran on the GED list (and its successors) both in 1952 and in 1956. In the late 1950's, while living in Senegal, he served as Cabinet Director to André Peytavin, the Senegalese Minister of Finance (1957–1961), following which he returned to Dahomey to fill the same position under Maga's Presidency (1961–1963). Briefly Cabinet Director of the Minister of Foreign Affairs (1963–1964), Gbaguidi was next appointed First Secretary at Dahomey's Embassy to West Germany between 1964 and 1969. Gbaguidi is currently in retirement. His multi-faceted career included journalism (he served for a while as editor of the important Dakar-based Catholic weekly, *Afrique Nouvelle*) and business (he served as director of the French shipping company Chargeurs Réunis).

GBAGUIDI, PLACIDE, 1927– . Former Cabinet Director of Victorien Gbaguidi, and public works engineer. Born in Savalou (q.v.) of the ruling Mahi (q.v.) clan (as signified by his name) on November 27, 1927, and educated in Porto Novo (q.v.) and the Public Works School in Bamako, Mali, and in Paris, Gbaguidi served as an administrator on ASECNA and the OCDN (q.v.), while also President of the Savalou Youth Group (1946–1952). He was appointed Party Secretary for the Savalou branch of the PDU (q.v.) and, after several years in Senegal, was repatriated to Cotonou (q.v.) and named Head of Construction in the Ministry of Public Works (1960), and Cabinet Director of the Minister of Public Works in 1961. In July 1968 he was appointed technical consultant in the Ministry of Public Works until his retirement in 1987.

GBAGUIDI, VICTORIEN, 1924– . Public works engineer and former Minister. Born in Savalou (q.v.) in 1924 of the local Mahi (q.v.) royal lineage, Gbaguidi was trained as a public works engineer. In 1960–1961 he served as head of the Dahomey Postal System as well as Cabinet Director of the Minister of Transportation. In 1960 he was elected to the National Assembly (q.v.) and immediately appointed Minister of Public Works, serving through 1963, when the coup (q.v.) of that year cut short his tenure. Temporarily detached from his ministry for research purposes, in 1965 he was appointed Cabinet Director to President Soglo (q.v.). Following the 1967 coup d'etat (q.v.), Gbaguidi was reintegrated into the Ministry of Public Works as technical consultant. He has been retired since 1986.

GBEDJINON AHOYO, VERONIQUE 1940– . Minister of Labor and Social Affairs. Born in Cotonou (q.v.) on January 20, 1940, and trained as a civil administrator in Paris, Abidjan and (in social service) in Toulouse, Mrs. Gbedjinon Ahoyo, who is widowed, served for 15 years as Deputy Director (1967–1975) and then Director of Social Affairs (1975–1990) before being appointed in March 1990 Minister of Labor and Social Affairs.

GBEGAN, ALABI ANTOINE, 1946– . Minister. Born in June 1946 and educated at a Catholic mission school (at Séhoué) and in Porto Novo (q.v.), during which time he was very active in student union activities, in 1969 Gbegan proceeded to the University of Provence at Marseilles to study mathematics, completing his doctorate in 1984 with a specialization in statistical analysis. There, too, he was active in FEANF (q.v.) activities. Concurrent with his studies Gbegan taught in schools in Abomey and Cotonou (qq.v.) (1971–1980), and since 1985 taught mathematics and statistics at the National University of Benin (q.v.). A leader of the Jeunesse du Dahomey branch of Allada (q.v.) until dissolved by the government in 1974, and other union and civic groups, Gbegan was one of the leaders invited to participate in the National Conference (q.v.) of February 1990. In May of that year he became interim Attaché at the Ministry of Interior in charge of assisting preparations for the elections. In February 1991 he was elected to the National Assembly, and in July 1991 was appointed Minister of Civil Service and Administrative Reform.

GBEHANZIN see BEHANZIN

GBENOU, GREGOIRE GILBERT, 1926– . Lawyer and Attorney General. Born on February 13, 1926, in Adjohoun and educated in Ivory Coast and France, Gbénou attended the University of Bordeaux (1950–1956), obtaining his law degree. After serving as an apprentice in France, Gbénou returned home and was appointed technical consultant to the Minister of Justice (1961–1962) and Cabinet Director to Sorou-Migan Apithy (q.v.). In 1962 he became Solicitor-General of the Cotonou Court of Appeals, serving in that capacity until 1966. In 1966 he was brought into the cabinet as Minister of Justice, serving until 1968, at which date he became legal consultant to the Supreme Court (q.v.). Since 1970 he has been Attorney General of the Supreme Court.

GBENOU, MARCEL HONORE SEMASSA, 1941– . Journalist. Born on January 16, 1941 in Cotonou (q.v.), and educated at home and in Paris in journalism and production, Gbénou served as journalist for Radio-Dahomey between 1963 and 1974, when he left the country. He then worked as a reporter for *Le Monde* and Radio-France Internationale (1974–1977), and since 1977 as reporter and producer for Radio Hilversum (Netherlands).

GBETOWOUENONMON, LUCIEN (Captain). Politician and Minister. A former aide-de-camp of Justin Ahomadégbé (q.v.), until 1972. After the coup that toppled the civilian triumvirate (q.v.), Gbetowouenonmon was brought into the Cometé Militaire Révolutionnaire (q.v.). Earlier he had served in a similar capacity during the previous military interregnum of 1968, when he had been for three months the Minister of Public Health. In 1975 Gbetowouenonmon, implicated in the Assogba attempted putsch, was sentenced to life imprisonment. He was released only as part of the general amnesty in 1990.

GBOUELE. Mahi (q.v.) settlement that was a prime target of the Dahomey kingdom's (q.v.) campaigns in the eighteenth century.

GENDARMERIE NATIONALE see POLICE FORCE.

GHEZO, KING (1818–1858) OF DAHOMEY. One of Dahomey's most famous kings, under whose reign the kingdom greatly expanded. Ghézo succeeded to the throne with the assistance of Francisco da Souza (q.v.), after a dynastic upheaval in which King Adandejan (q.v.) was deposed. One of his first acts was to throw off the restraining and humiliating tributary relationship with the Oyo Empire (q.v.), greatly weakened by now (see AGAJA). Restructuring the kingdom's armed forces, especially the elite Amazon (q.v.) units, Ghézo built up Dahomey to the position of preeminence in the zone between Yoruba power (Nigeria) and Ashanti power (in Ghana). During his reign, powerful drives were mounted against Abeokuta (in Nigeria), the Mahi (q.v.) and the coastal populations. In the economic field, several drives were mounted to diversify the sources of revenue by developing new palm plantations. See DAHOMEY, KINGDOM OF.

GIRIGISSOU, GADO. Former Minister. One of Mathieu Kérékou's (q.v.) closest cronies, Girigissou was appointed Minister of Trade in February 1987. It was under his aegis that Benin negotiated the ill-advised agreement with PANOCO regarding the Sémé (q.v.) oil field, which collapsed after criticisms, leaving Benin for some time with greatly reduced exports. Because of Girigissou's closeness to Kérékou he was not dismissed from his post for several months.

GLEHOUE. First quarter of what was eventually to become Ouidah (q.v.).

GLELE, KING (1858–1889) OF DAHOMEY. Glélé succeeded to the throne of Dahomey after King Ghézo's (q.v.) death, and both were strong kings at times of rapidly changing circumstances. His reign saw the continued expansion of Dahomey that had shaken off Oyo (Yoruba) (qq.v.) tributary status under Ghézo, two renewed offenses against Abeokuta (Nigeria), in 1864 and 1873, and various other campaigns against Ketou, the Mahi and Porto Novo (qq.v.). During his reign, both France and Britain were vying for a foothold along the coast and Glélé's difficulties with the French (see COTONOU; PORTO NOVO) were harbingers of the armed confrontation that was shaping up between the two powers and that was to erupt under his successor, Béhanzin (q.v.).

GLELE, ADRIEN AHANHANZO, 1936– . Agronomist. Born on March 5, 1936, in Zinvié, and possessing a diploma from ORSTOM in genetics, Glélé has served with IRAT (q.v.), conducting agronomical research in Niaouli. He joined Gen. Soglo's (q.v.) cabinet in July 1968 as Minister of Rural Development but reverted to research and administrative duties after the coup that was shortly to topple the regime. Implicated in the attempted coup of 1975 (q.v.), Glélé was arrested and imprisoned in the northern garrison town of Natitingou (q.v.). He was amnestied in August 1984. His brother, Capt. Lucien Glélé (q.v.), was arrested in 1972 for a plot against the government.

GLELE, DAA MELE. Head of all descendants of the lineage of King Glélé (q.v.).

GLELE, DAN LANGANFIN. Current administrative head of the Glélé (q.v.) royal family branch of Abomey (q.v.), one of three dominant ones: those of Glélé, Béhanzin and Guézo (qq.v.). He shares status with Daa Mélé Glélé, head of all descendants of the Glélé royal lineage.

GLELE, LUCIEN (Captain). Former leader of a small clique within the officer corps. Part of the elite para-commando Ouidah (q.v.) garrison, Glélé first came to prominence when he was named First Secretary of the military CRM (q.v.) in 1967–1968. He then served loyally as aide-de-camp to President Emile Derlin Zinsou (q.v.), forewarning him of the coup (q.v.) that toppled him and of several other attempts to oust him from power. He had also served as aide-de-camp to Chief-of-Staff De Souza (q.v.). Glélé was arrested in 1972 for his involvement in fomenting a mutiny at the Ouidah military garrison and sentenced to death. He was released from prison at the time of the coup (q.v.) that erupted a few months later and appointed to head a military unit in northern Benin.

GLELE, MAURICE AHANHANZO, 1934– . Historian, lawyer and diplomat. Born on January 15, 1934, in Allada (q.v.), and tracing his descent to the Glélé royal dynasty, Glélé was educated in Paris at the Lycée Louis-le-Grand and at the Faculty of Law of the University of Paris, where he obtained a law degree. Glélé worked with UNESCO in 1961, then at Union Afrique et Malyache in Cotonou (q.v.) (1962–1963) before being appointed Permanent Secretary to the Presidential Cabinet (1963–1965). He then became Adviser to the Office of the Presidency, serving until 1966 when he rejoined UNESCO as Program Specialist on African Cultures where he still works. Glélé is a noted historian who has written seminal work on the Abomey (q.v.) kingdom and on contemporary politics in Benin.

GLELE AHO, YEWABOU RENE, 1906–1966. Former Deputy to the Assemblée Territoriale (q.v.) and journalist. Born in Abomey (q.v.) in 1906, Glélé Aho issued two regional publications during the colonial era: *L'Eclaireur* and *Le Dahoméen*. Active in numerous cultural associations, especially Fon (q.v.), he was the guiding spirit behind the Rassemblement Populaire pour le Défense des Coutumes et Traditions du Dahomey, as well as its Secretary-General. Also secretary of the regional advisory council of the south during the colonial era, Glélé Aho served in independent Dahomey's first National Assembly (q.v.), between 1960 and 1965. He died shortly after the 1965 coup d'etat (q.v.).

GLELE AKPOKPO, REMY. Student leader. Glélé Akpokpo, who comes from the Abomey (q.v.) royal family, was arrested by Kérékou's (q.v.) units and beaten to death on January 18, 1988. This and other incidents played a role in triggering the largely Abomey Fon (q.v.) attempted coup of March 1988.

GNANIH, ROGATIEN, 1939– . Born in Athiémé on October 24, 1939, and a graduate of IHEOM, with a sociology degree as well, Gnanih has been Director of Labor and Social Law at the Ministry of Labor (1966–1968) and Secretary-General of the Civil Service between 1968 and 1973. In 1973 he was shifted to become Director of the Ministry of Labor. Since 1977 he has been Technical Advisor on Labor Legislation with the Ministry of Labor.

GNIDEHOU, JUSTIN. Former Minister. A Fon leader from Abomey who rallied to the Kérékou (qq.v.) regime, Gnidehou was brought into the cabinet as Minister of Youth and Sports, and between 1982–1984 as Minister of Rural Development and Cooperative Action. Though dropped in a 1984 reshuffle he was integrated into the PRPB (q.v.) Politburo in 1985, and in 1988 he once again rejoined the cabinet as Minister of Industry and Energy.

GNONNOU, ROBERT, 1897–1967. Industrialist, merchant and early supporter of Apithy (q.v.). Born in Djakotomé, Gnonnou supported the Apithy political candidacy and helped organize the Yoruba (q.v.) vote in the southeast. In 1952 he was persuaded to play a more active role and ran for the National Assembly (q.v.) elections in Athiémé. He was reelected several times and was Deputy until 1965.

GOHOUN, COHOVI AIME, 1950– . Physician. Born in 1950 and educated in France in medicine, Gohoun served as Senior Medical Officer at Bassila and Materi before being appointed in 1986 Chief Medical Officer at the Ouidah Health Center.

GOLD. Commercially exploitable gold ore was discovered in several sites in Benin during the colonial era. The most promising site is in the Perma river region in the north, and in 1939 SMDN (q.v.) started modest mining in the area. Quantities refined were small, the peak being in 1944 when 148 kgs. were processed. Though the veins were rich (9 grams per ton of rock compared to a global average of 4 grams) the low price of gold on the world market and the modest local reserves brought about the closure of SMDN operations in 1956, with the company shifting its efforts to its cassiterite plant in Niger.

In the late 1950's exploratory research and prospecting in the area revealed that its potential was greater than assumed and, with the sharp rise in global market prices for gold, the economic viability of exploiting the ore was confirmed. Currently estimated reserves are pegged at 1,250 kilograms and a modest annual working of this source would give any processing plant a 20-year life span. Other alluvial gold resources have likewise been confirmed, raising prospects of an ultimate commitment on the part of foreign capital in reviving the gold sector.

GOMEZ, CHARLES, 1936– . Veterinary doctor. Born in Ouidah (q.v.) on June 19, 1936, and trained in France, Gomez has been Deputy Head of Stockbreeding Services between 1963 and 1968. In 1968 he was appointed Secretary-General of the Ministry of Rural Development and Cooperation, a post he retained until 1973. In 1973 he assumed the post of Head of Stockbreeding Services, but later returned to his private practice, retaining only a consultantship with the Ministry effective 1977.

GOMINA, SANNI MAM. An influential PRPB (q.v.) Politburo member during the Kérékou (q.v.) regime, Gomina was appointed Minister of Trade in February 1980, following the elections.

GONCALVES, PAUL, 1933– . Inspector of Accounting. Born in Allada (q.v.) on January 18, 1933, and trained in law and accountancy, Goncalves was head of the Mobile Financial Accounting Service of Benin between 1963 and 1966, serving all the remote areas, especially in the north. In 1966 he was promoted to Inspector General of Finances and special fiscal consultant to the Presidency.

GOUDJO, COME, 1945– . Mathematician. Born on February 15, 1945, and with higher degrees in mathematics, Goudjo teaches at the National University of Benin (q.v.) where he is also Dean of the Faculty of Science.

GOUDOU, THOMAS. A professor at the National University of Benin (q.v.), Goudou was a Presidential candidate in the 1991 elections (q.v.), though obtaining miniscule percentage of the votes cast.

GOUN. A branch of the Adja (q.v.) population strongly affected by Yoruba (q.v.) cultural influences. According to one tradition, the Goun are descendants from an offshoot of the Allada (q.v.) kingdom, expelled after a succession dispute in the seventeenth century. Numbering around 163,000, they are found especially in the Ketou-Porto Novo (qq.v.) areas. They are the dominant group in Porto Novo and for over 25 years were strongly organized behind their political leader, Sourou-Migan Apithy (q.v.).

GOUNME, BADJO (Lt. Colonel) A close confidant of President Kérékou (q.v.), Gounmé was one of the key ringleaders in the 1987 attempted coup.

GOUTCHILI see AGOLI-AGBO

GOVERNORS, (CIVILIAN) OF DAHOMEY (1894–1960)

Jan. 1894–June 1900	Ballot
June 1900–Sept. 1906	Liotard
Dec. 1906–Sept. 1908	Marchal
Sept. 1908–April 1909	Peuvergne
May 1909–March 1911	Malan
July 1911–April 1912	Merwhardt
May 1912–April 1917	Noufflard
April 1917–Dec. 1928	Fourn
April 1929–Jan. 1931	Reste
February 1931–Jan. 1932	Tellier
Jan. 1932–July 1932	Blanchet
July 1932–June 1934	De Coppet
Jan. 1935–Jan. 1937	Bourgine
Jan. 1938–August 1940	Annet
Sept. 1940–August 1943	Truitard
August 1943–Sept. 1945	Assier de Pompignan
Sept. 1945–May 1946	De Villedeuil
June 1946–Jan. 1948	Legendre
Jan. 1948–Dec. 1948	Chambon
Jan. 1949–August 1949	Boissier
Nov. 1951–June 1955	Bonfils
June 1955–April 1958	Biros
April 1958–July 1958	Hepp
July 1958–August 1960	Tirant

GOVERNORS, FRENCH WEST AFRICA, (1895–1959).

1895–1900	J. B. Chaudié.
1900–1902	N. E. Ballay
1902–1906	E. N. Roume
1908–1916	W. Merlaud-Ponty
1916–1917	M. F. Clozel
1917–1918	J. Van Vollénhaven
1918–1919	G. L. Angoulvant
1919–1923	M. H. Merlin
1923–1930	J. G. Carde
1930–1936	J. Brevié
1936–1940	J. M. de Coppet
1940	L. H. Cayla
1940–1943	P. F. Boisson
1943–1946	P. C. Cournarie
1946–1948	R. V. Barthes
1948–1951	P. L. Bechard
1951–1956	B. Cornut-Gentille
1956–1958	G. Cusin
1958–1959	P. A. Messmer

GRAND POPO. Small island off the coast of Benin (distinct from Petit Popo, also in this area) that was historically a major center of the slave trade (q.v.) with European merchants and a place of refuge for the kings of Ouidah (q.v.) during the assaults from Dahomey. The Popos were never truly subdued by the Dahomey kingdom (q.v.), with the residents of this region of coastal lagoons and island spits often mounting raids on the latter's mainland outposts.

GRANDS MOULINS DU BENIN (GMB). Flour mills. Set up in 1971 in Cotonou (q.v.) as a joint economy enterprise with a Beninois 20-percent share, the GMB is capitalized at the level of 204 million CFA francs and has the capacity of producing, on a daily basis, 125 tons of processed flour.

GREAT ARDRA see AJASE IPO; ARDRA; PORTO NOVO

GRIMAUD, MAXIMILIEN, 1938– . Agricultural engineer. Born in Porto Novo (q.v.) on January 15, 1938, and educated abroad as an agronomist, Grimaud was appointed upon his return home to head agricultural services in Zou, with headquarters in Bohicon (qq.v.). In 1967 he was also named Deputy Prefect of Zou. Between September 1968 and 1973 he was also technical advisor at the Ministry of Rural Development in Cotonou (q.v.). Grimaud was promoted to head one of the Ministry's divisions in 1973.

GRIVOT, RENE, 1902– . Colonial administrator. Born in Hamburg on August 12, 1902, and qualified in African languages (Mandingo and Fulani) as well as law, Grivot joined the colonial administration and served in Morocco, Senegal, Upper Volta, Ivory Coast and Dahomey. There he served as head of the Athiémé cercle (1943–1945) and that of Parakou (q.v.) (1947) before being appointed Inspector of Administrative Services (1947–1952). He wrote extensively on Dahomey before being transferred to Madagascar. Grivot has been in retirement since 1968.

GROUPEMENT DES FON D'ABOMEY. Regional ethnic association of the Fon (q.v.) that became a nucleus of Dahomey's first political party, the Union Progréssiste Dahoméenne (q.v.). When, in 1946, Justin Ahomadégbé left the UPD to establish his own Bloc Populaire Africain (and later the Union Démocratique Dahoméenne) (qq.v.), he carried with him most elements of the Groupement des Fon d'Abomey.

GROUPEMENT DES INDEPENDANTS. Minor political faction set up in 1951 by dissidents of the Union Progréssiste Dahoméenne (q.v.), headed by Maximilien Quénum (q.v.). See also UNION PROGRESSISTE DAHOMEENNE.

GROUPEMENT ETHNIQUE DU NORD (GEN; also GEND). Proto-political movement established in northern Dahomey in 1951 to support Hubert Maga (q.v.) and his election as Deputy to the French National Assembly. The rise of the GEN spelled the doom of Dahomey's first political party, the Union Progréssiste Dahoméenne (q.v.), of which the GEN leaders had been members. The creation of the GEN completed the process of splintering the UPD into three major ethnic movements, corresponding to the ethnic regionalism (q.v.) of the country. The GEN organized the various Bariba (q.v.) and other northern notables behind Maga and, in 1953, gave birth to the Mouvement Démocratique Dahoméen (q.v.). One early GEN leader who frequently bolted the MDD and its successor, the Rassemblement Démocratique Dahoméen, was Paul Darboux (qq.v.).

GROUPEMENT ETHNIQUE DU NORD DAHOMEY (GEND) see GROUPEMENT ETHNIQUE DU NORD

GROUPEMENTS DE VIGILANCE REPUBLICAINS. Loose groups of supporters of Justin Ahomadégbé (q.v.), organized in 1971–1972 to protect their leader from any plots from militants of the other two leaders in the Presidential Council (q.v.).

GROUPEMENTS REVOLUTIONNAIRES DE VOCATION COOPERATIF (GRVC). Structures, gradually set up throughout Benin during the "revolutionary" era starting in 1977, aimed at providing a socialist base for agricultural production. Made up of smallholders and agricultural labor working on communal land; smallholders were entitled to retain ownership of their own plots, while landless peasants were allowed to cultivate their own plots, selling produce privately to the state purchasing boards. The GRVC were much less popular in South Benin than in the north, due to the strong individualist ethos in the south; there theft was inordinately high—in Mono up to 33 percent of communal produce regularly "disappeared" from GRVC warehouses. In the north access to credit and services via the GRVC made them more popular.

GUEDEHOUNGUE, SOSSA. One of the two Grand Priests of the Vodun (q.v.) cult in Benin.

GUEDOU GANGBE, ROBERT, 1929– . Civil administrator. Born in 1929 in Tidji-Abomey, Gúedou Gangbé was trained as an accountant. He served in a wide array of posts, starting with Comptroller of Financial Services (1949–1953) while simultaneously Deputy Head at the Ministry of Finance.

Between 1953 and 1959 he served as special consultant to the Ministry, between 1959 and 1961 he was Secretary-General of the Abomey Municipality, and in 1961 he was appointed Deputy Director of the Dahomean Budget Office. He served in the latter capacity until 1967 when he reverted to administrative duties in Ketou (q.v.) (as sousprefet) and in Abomey (q.v.) (as administrative head of the urban circon-scription) (1968–1973). In 1973 he was shifted back to the Ministry of Finance in the central government, where he was administrative head of one of its divisions.

GUEZO, ROMAIN VILON. Former President of the National Assembly (q.v.), trade union leader, long the central figure in Beninois labor and Secretary-General of the UGTD (q.v.), as well as labor representative to the Conseil Economique et Social (q.v.). A prince of the Fon royal lineage from Abomey (qq.v.), and with a measure of control over his ethnic kinsmen consequent to this, prior to the 1970 elections Guézo issued a pledge that organized labor would boycott any candidate who did not commit himself in advance to the total reform of socioeconomic conditions in the country. Despite his occasional radical rhetoric Guézo was very rapidly outflanked on the left by the Ligue (q.v.) and other arch-Left elements, and his control over the trade union (q.v.) movement increasingly came under challenge. Indeed, in 1975 he was ousted from the leadership of the trade union confederation (Union Syndicale Nationale [q.v.]) when he supported the then-embattled Kérékou (q.v.) regime vis-a-vis the urban reaction to the liquidation of Aikpé (q.v.). He was rewarded for his loyalty by being appointed secretary-general of the new trade union (UNSTB) [q.v.] that the government created on the ashes of the old one. Later he was also appointed President of the National Assembly (1980), a post he retained until the collapse of the Kérékou regime. In 1981 he was removed from his union leadership post, however, in an attempt by the government to heal the Left-Right rift within it.

GUEZODJE, VINCENT (Colonel). Long-time ally of Kérékou (q.v.) and Minister for 14 years as well as Chief-of-Staff of the Armed Forces (q.v.). Guézodjé—then only Lieutenant—first came to the national limelight when he was appointed Second Vice-president of the CRM (q.v.) and Minister of Justice in the interim government following the 1967 coup d'etat (q.v.). A Fon from Abomey (qq.v.), and a prince of royal lineage, he was promoted to Captain in 1972, and as a reward for rallying to the northern regime of Kérékou was integrated into the cabinet in September 1973 as Minister of Education, joining the PRPB (q.v.) Politburo several years later. In October 1974 his Ministry was split and he retained the Ministry of Primary Education. Twice promoted since, in February 1980 he was appointed Minister of Interior and Public Security, one of the most sensitive posts in Benin. Temporarily dropped from the cabinet in a December 1982 reshuffle, by August 1984 he was back as Minister of Public Health. After the upheavals in the educational establishment that caused Alladayé's (q.v.) dismissal, Guézodjé was appointed in a June 1985 cabinet reshuffle as Minister of Middle and Higher Education. However, as he too was unable to soothe student unrest, he left the cabinet in 1989 to become Chief-of-Staff of the Armed Forces.

GUIRIGUISSOU, GADO. Radical former Ligue (q.v.) leader and Minister. An Algerian-trained professor of mathematics with a Bariba (q.v.) mother and a part-Yoruba (q.v.) father, Guiriguissou was a close aide of Kérékou (q.v.) since the late 1970's, including as the latter's Presidential Cabinet Director. He was also one of the seven permanent PRPB (q.v.) Politburo members, with responsibility for Internal Affairs. He joined the government in February 1980 after the first military-sponsored elections and served as Minister of Public Works, Housing and Construction. In August 1984 he was shifted to head the Ministry of Equipment and Transport.

-H-

HACHEME, JEAN-BAPTISTE (Major). Fon military officer. Hachémé first came to national prominence when, in 1963, he brutally crushed popular demonstrations in Parakou (q.v.)

in support of deposed President Hubert Maga (q.v.). Between 1965 and 1967 he served as general Soglo's (q.v.) Cabinet Director and, in 1967, he briefly acted as Chairman of the Comité Militaire de Vigilance (q.v.). He was dismissed from the army in January 1968 as part of a purge of southern officers and as a consequence of allegations of his plotting a countercoup against the regime of colonels Alphonse Alley and Maurice Kouandété (qq.v.).

Reinstated in the army shortly thereafter, Hachémé was appointed Head of the Armed Forces Fifth Bureau and later (in mid-1970), Head of the Service Civique (q.v.), a non-operational command. Following the October 1972 coup by Major Mathieu Kérékou (q.v.), Hachémé was purged from the army, together with the entire senior southern officer corps. In the allocation of administrative posts in the State industries that accompanied the purge, Hachémé was named Commissioner of Dahomey's Ceramic Crafts industry (SONAC). He was arrested a few months later for plotting against Kérékou's regime, together with ex-Col. Alley and Pascal Chabi Kao (qq.v.), and sentenced to 20 years' hard labor. He was amnestied in August 1984.

HAITI. Much of Haiti's population is supposed to have originated in Benin, brought to the New World via the slave trade (q.v.). Rituals and fetish practices in Haiti are closely related to their counterparts in southern Benin, as are names, clothing and oral traditions. After Dahomey's independence, close cultural relations were established between the two countries. One of Haiti's few embassies in Africa is in Benin.

HAUT CONSEIL DE LA REPUBLIQUE DU BENIN (HCRB). Transitional quasi legislature set up by the National Conference (q.v.) on March 9, 1990, with special responsibilities to oversee the 1991 elections (q.v.). It was composed of the country's former living Presidents (Maga, Ahomadégbé, Zinsou, Congacou [qq.v], plus others deemed to have played a distinguished role in Benin: Isidore de Souza, Bishop of Cotonou (who persuaded Kérékou to accept his demise), Léopold Dossou, Secretary General of the Union of Teachers, Bertin Borna, a popular former Djougou Minister, and

Albert Tévoédjré (qq.v.), former Assistant Director of the International Labour Office.

HAZOUME, ADJOU FELIX, 1938– . Physician. Born on August 5, 1938, and trained in medicine at the University of Nancy (1969), Hazoumé teaches at the National University of Benin (q.v.) where he is also Dean of the Faculty of Health Sciences.

HAZOUME, FLORE. Author, Obtaining her degree from the University of Abidjan in 1984, Hazoumé published her first book—a collection of stories—the same year.

HAZOUME, GUY LANDRY. Former Foreign Minister. A graduate of the Institute of Political Science in Paris, Hazoumé was appointed Deputy-Director of Political Affairs in the Ministry of Foreign Affairs in February 1968. Later he was moved to become Ambassador to the United Nations, and in February 1987 was appointed Foreign Minister of Benin.

HAZOUME, MARC LAURENT. Professor of Linguistics at the National University of Benin (q.v.).

HAZOUME, PAUL, 1890–1980. Educator, editor, ethnologist, Benin's best-known author and an early political leader. Born in Porto Novo (q.v.) on April 15, 1890, of direct descent from the Porto Novo kingdom's nobility (his grandfather had been King Toffa's [q.v.] prime minister), Hazoumé studied locally and at the Ecole William Ponty (q.v.) in Senegal. One of the very first local fully-trained educators, Hazoumé was appointed in 1910 director of Ouidah's school system. During World War I he cooperated with Louis Hunkanrin (q.v.) in editing the newspaper *Le Messager du Dahomey,* while working in the African department of the Musée de l'Homme in Paris. In the interwar period, Hazoumé published two of his most famous works, *Le Pact du sang au Dahomey* (1937) and *Doguicimi* (1938), gaining recognition and prizes both as an ethnologist and as a novelist. Both works are still widely cited and available in reprinted editions. After the Second World War, Hazoumé became secretary of the most influential Comité Electoral (q.v.), that of Cotonou (q.v.), and was a co-founder of the country's first political party, the UPD (q.v.), in which he played an early prominent role. Though in retirement since 1947, Hazoumé served as Councillor of the French Union, from 1947 until its dissolution, and Deputy to the Assemblée Territoriale (q.v.) (1952–1957). In 1964 he became Chairman of the Association des Anciens du Dahomey (q.v.) and, in 1968, he was a candidate in the military-sponsored Presidential elections. In that contest, despite his international fame, he obtained only 11,091 of the 187,392 votes cast, a result of ethnic bloc voting. One of Benin's towering intellectuals, Hazoumé died on April 18, 1980, at the age of 90, having personally witnessed both the colonization and the independence of his country.

HENNOU. Kinship lineage, the head of which is the *hennougan* (*gan*-chief).

HENRY, HARRY YEDENOU, 1922– . Head of the Methodist Church of Benin. Born in Porto Novo (q.v.) on October 26, 1922, and indirectly linked to the royal clan of the Porto Novo Kingdom. Henry studied in Porto Novo for the priesthood and involved himself deeply in youth affairs. He has been Vice-President of the Protestant Youth Council of Dahomey and President of the Fédération des Associations Chrétiennes d'Etudiants Dahoméens.

HESSOU, THEODORE. Former Mayor of Cotonou (q.v.). A staunch supporter of Justin Ahomadégbé (q.v.), Héssou was arrested a number of times for activities aimed at furthering the latter's Presidential candidacy: in 1961 by President Maga (q.v.) and again, in May 1969, by President Zinsou (q.v.). Formerly also Mayor of Abomey (q.v.), Héssou was elected to the Consultative Assembly in 1970, serving until the 1972 coup d'etat (q.v.). He has not been active politically since the coup.

HOGBONOU. ''The Big House,'' an early name for the chiefly residence and surrounding settlement that was to become Porto Novo (q.v.).

HOHOUETO, FRANCOIS AYIKOUN, 1932– . Civil administrator. Born in 1932 in Grand Popo (q.v.), Hohouéto was educated in Paris where he received a degree at the IHEOM. Upon his return home he was appointed Deputy Prefect of Borgou (q.v.) (1965). Between 1961 and 1967 he also served as the Cabinet Director of the Minister of Foreign Affairs, later of Justice, and briefly as Urban Councillor of Cotonou (q.v.). In August 1968 he was brought into the Presidential staff of Zinsou (q.v.) as Deputy Director of the Cabinet, and assisted Zinsou in founding the short-lived URD (q.v.) party. With Zinsou's overthrow, Hohouéto was shifted to administrative duties in the Ministry of Interior and, following the 1972 coup d'etat (q.v.), he left the country.

HOLLI. A Yoruba (q.v.) sub-branch, residing south of Ketou (q.v.) and in Pobé, that figured prominently in several outbreaks of resistance against French rule (see HOLLI REVOLT; UPRISINGS OF 1915–1918). Their name derives from the Fon and Nagot (qq.v.) term meaning ''those who do not speak either Fon or Nago,'' though they call themselves Ijé (French scholars often combine the two terms into Hoidjé). Until the colonial era, the Holli villages were tributaries to the kingdom of Dahomey (q.v.) and were frequently raided by Porto Novo (q.v.). In 1894 they declared themselves ''independent'' of both powers. The Holli number around 15,000.

HOLLI REVOLT. A series of rebellions among the Holli (q.v.) villages in the Mono (q.v.) département, not fully quelled until the end of World War I. Inhabiting a region contested by both the kingdom of Dahomey and that of Porto Novo (qq.v.), the Holli declared themselves independent of both in 1894. The latter date coincided with the extension of French control over most of the new colony, and the Holli resented the encroachments on their newly gained independence by France's demands for corvée (q.v.) and porterage labor and military recruitment during World War I. The last major Holli insurrection occurred in 1915–1916, following which their king was deported to Mauritania.

HOLO, THEODORE, 1948– . Minister of Foreign Affairs. Born in Porto Novo (q.v.) on April 15, 1948, and educated in

Brazzaville, Orleans and Paris in law and political science, Holo taught between 1979 and 1985 at the Ecole Nationale d'Administration (ENA) before joining the National University of Benin (q.v.) in 1986 as professor of international relations and constitutional law. Between 1986–1989 he was also Deputy-Director of ENA, becoming its director in 1989. In 1990 Holo became Deputy Secretary-General of the Haut Conséil de la République du Bénin (q.v.) that supervised the transition to multiparty elections and a new political order, and on July 19, 1991 he was selected by President Nicéphore Soglo (q.v.) as Foreign Minister.

HON-ME PALACE. Former residence of the King Toffa of Porto Novo (qq.v.), until recently in an extremely run-down state. It was refurbished as a museum, becoming one of Porto Novo's few tourist attractions.

HONVO, AUGUSTIN (Captain). Former Minister. Chairman of the CMR (q.v.) in 1967, following the coup of that year, Honvo was outside the national limelight until the 1972 coup (q.v.) catapulted him into the cabinet. He served as Minister of Information, later of the Civil Service between 1973 and 1974, and in the latter year he was appointed Minister in charge of the National Plan and Coordination of Aid. In October 1976 he was shifted to head the Ministry of Higher Education, and he was returned to military duties in a reshuffle in 1978.

HOUDOU, ALI. Former Minister. A Dendi from Parakou (qq.v.), and a civil administrator by profession, Houdou was the Prefect of Atakora province, and earlier of Zou (qq.v.), before being appointed Minister of Information and Communications in August 1984. In a 1988 reshuffle he was appointed Minister of Culture, Youth and Sports, a post he held until the eclipse of the Kérékou (q.v.) regime.

HOUEDA. Small ethnic group, also known as Pédah, closely related to the Aïzo (q.v.) (indeed, sometimes confused with them) and engaged in fishing along the coastal lagoons and in Lake Ahémé. The Houéda were the founding group of the

Kingdom of Houéda (q.v.) (Ouidah). Currently they number around 18,000.

HOUEDA, KINGDOM OF. Small precolonial kingdom founded by the Houéda (q.v.), arriving along the coastal lagoons from Tado (q.v.) in the middle of the sixteenth century, becoming in essence the first of the Adja (q.v.) states in the area. Its political capital was Savi (q.v.) (called Xavier by French traders), though the Houéda kingdom became renowned for its seaport, Ouidah (q.v.) (Whydah or Juda to the early traders along the coast), that was consecrated to Dagbé (see CULT OF THE GREAT SERPENT). Intermittently tributary to the Allada (q.v.) kingdom, Houéda was the main intermediary between the European slave dealers along the coast and the African slave caravans arriving from the north. Without any resources (except fresh food for the traders), but controlling the middle-man function, Ouidah became the greatest slave port of the coast in the seventeenth century. In the eighteenth century Ouidah fell to Dahomey (q.v.) (1727) and lost its preeminent position. Its last king, Huffon, ascended the throne in 1708 at age 13, and died in exile in 1733. See also OUIDAH.

HOUEDA, KINGS OF. As with most king-lists, there is controversy about dates:

Haholo,	
Kpassé	?–1670
Agbangla	1670–1703
Ayohouan	1703–1704
Amah	1704–1708
Huffon	1708–1727

HOUEGNON, OLOU BERNARD, 1948– . Minister of Trade and Tourism. An Adja (q.v.) born in Ablomé in Mono (q.v.) province, and educated at home and in Paris where he obtained a doctorate in economics in 1979, Houegnon spent several years working in various banking activities before being appointed Minister of Trade and Tourism in 1991.

HOUESSOU, AURELIEN. Minister of Energy. A totally unknown politician, elected to the National Assembly (q.v.) in

1990 and appointed to Soglo's (q.v.) cabinet in July 29, 1991.

HOUESSOU, JEAN. Physician and Director of the Medical-Social Institute of Benin since 1968.

HOUNDEGLA, ALPHONSE (Captain). Ouidah-based officer involved in the 1975 attempted coup of Assogba (q.v.). Houndégla was subsequently arrested and sentenced to life imprisonment. He was only recently amnestied.

HOUNDETON NOUTAI, FREDERIC. Former Secretary-General of Justice. A magistrate with the Cotonou Court of Appeals, Houndéton Noutai was appointed Secretary-General of Justice on August 30, 1968. Prior to this he had held a wide variety of posts, including that of Deputy Director of Civil and Penal Affairs at the Ministry of Justice and Technical Counsellor on Legal Affairs to the Presidency. He is currently retired.

HOUNGBEDJI, ADRIEN, 1942– . Lawyer and Presidential hopeful. Born in Aplahoué on March 5, 1942, Houngbédji was educated at home and in France, acquiring a law degree in Paris. Upon his return home, he joined the Ministry of Justice as technical consultant (1967) and Attorney General to the Lower Court of Cotonou. He was President Zinsou's (q.v.) legal adviser between 1968 and 1970. He fell afoul of Kérékou (q.v.) when the latter seized power in 1972 and was briefly imprisoned, following which he left the country to practice law in France and Gabon. In the latter country he acquired backing for his political aspirations from President Omar Bongo. Though sentenced to death in absentia in Cotonou for subversive activities, Houngbédji was considered as a possible interim Prime Minister under Kérékou as the latter tried to retain power in the late 1980's. Houngbédji participated in the National Conference (q.v.) of 1990 and was one of the Presidential candidates in 1991. Elected to the National Assembly (q.v.) at the head of the party he set up, the Parti de la Rénouveau Démocratique (q.v.), he was elected Speaker, winning against Kéké (q.v.), President

Soglo's personal choice. Since then Houngbédji has turned out to be Soglo's most bitter foe in the Assembly.

HOUNGBEDJI, GATIEN. Presidential hopeful. By profession a freighter, Hounbédji participated in the 1991 Presidential elections though he secured a very small vote.

HOUNKPATIN, PAUL, 1918– . Early administrator. Born in Ouidah (q.v.) on December 22, 1918, and in his youth a civil servant in other French colonies, Hounkpatin returned home in October 1958 to become Deputy Director of Personnel and, in August 1961, Prefect of Mono (q.v.). He was then attached to the Presidential Office of Hubert Maga (q.v.) as Secretary-General of the Government (1962–1963) and, following Maga's overthrow, was reappointed in a prefectural post, this time as sous-préfet of Savalou (q.v.) (1963–1964) and Deputy Prefect of Atlantique (q.v.) (1964–1965). In October 1968—under the presidency of Emile Derlin Zinsou (q.v.)—he regained his old post of Director of Personnel, serving in that capacity until his retirement.

HOUNKPONOU, COSME. A law graduate, Hounkponou served for eight years as Director of Custom's Duties (1960–1967) before being dispatched to Brussels as legal advisor to the Benin Embassy to the EEC.

HOUNON, DAGBO. One of the two most important Grand Priests of the vodun (q.v.) cult in Benin.

HOUNSOU, JEAN. Medical head of the Abomey circonscription and head of the National School for Nurses since 1966. Hounsou has also served for several years (1968–1973) as technical director at the Ministry of Public Health in Cotonou.

HOUNTON, JOSEPH LOUIS. Ambassador of Benin to Nigeria since 1991.

HOUNTONDJI, PAULIN, 1942– . Minister of Culture and Communications. Born in Abidjan on April 11, 1942, and educated locally (Savé, Sakété and Porto Novo [q.v.]) and at the Sorbonne and Nanterre in France, Hountondji obtained a degree in philosophy. He then taught at the University of Besançon (1967–1970), Lovanium and Lubumbashi, Zaire (1970–1972), before joining the National University of Benin (q.v.) in 1972, where he was to become Dean of the Faculty of Letters between 1974–1975. He was integrated into the interim 1990 government as Minister of National Education, and in July 1991 was named Minister of Culture and Communications.

HOUNTONDJI, VICTOR, 1953– . Author. Born in Sakété to a father who was a pastor, on September 22, 1953, Hountondji was educated in France, and published some poetry as well as books, including one that extolled the Beninois "Revolution." He currently teaches in Gabon, and has won several literary prizes in France.

HOUNTOU, JOSEPH LOUIS, 1938– . Diplomat. Born in Cotonou (q.v.) on March 14, 1938, and possessing a degree in international studies from Georgetown University, Hountou has been Director of Economic Relations at the Ministry of Foreign Affairs (1964–1967), First Secretary at the Benin Mission to the United Nations (1967–1972) and, since 1972, back in an administrative capacity in the Foreign Ministry in Cotonou.

HOUNTOUNDJI, PASCAL (Captain). Co-leader with Lt. Col. Hilaire Badjagoumé and Lt. Col. François Kouyami (qq.v.) of the March 1988 military conspiracy to oust the Kérékou (q.v.) regime.

HOUSSOU, BARTHELEMY DENANGNON, 1925– . Civil servant. Born in Porto Novo (q.v.) on April 15, 1925 and educated in tropical agriculture in France, Houssou was promoted within the Finance Ministry until appointed Director of Weights and Measures in 1970. He is currently retired.

HOUSSOU, DJEDJE MOISE, 1938– . Educator. Born in Porto Novo (q.v.) on April 28, 1938, and educated in psychology in

Paris, Houssou Djédjé has been attached to IRAD in Porto Novo (qq.v.) and, since 1965, he has also been head of the Institut Pédagogique National.

HUANNOU, ADRIEN 1946– . Educator and poet. Born in 1946 in Azoolissé, and educated in Catholic schools at home and at the Universities of Dakar (1966–1968), Besançon (1968–1973) and Paris (1974–1979) where he obtained a doctorate in humanities, Huannou returned to Benin to teach at the National University of Benin (q.v.). He has been Dean of the Faculty of Letters (1981), Secretary-General of the Association of Writers and Literary Critics (1981–), and has published a number of volumes of poetry.

HUFFON, KING OF HOUEDA (c. 1695–1727). Last independent king of Houéda (q.v.). Contrary to tradition, Huffon acceded to the throne on the death of his father, although still a minor (12 years of age). This and other aspects of his rise to power polarized the population and contributed to the kingdom's eclipse despite the central role of Ouidah (q.v.) in the slave trade (q.v.) along the coast and the concomitant riches that accrued to it. During Huffon's reign, Houéda was involved in a long tug-of-war with Allada (q.v.) (1712–1722). Manipulated by his advisors and betrayed by his own wife, King Huffon suffered invasion by Dahomey, and Ouidah was occupied in 1727. King Huffon escaped, together with some of his followers, to Grand Popo (q.v.), and he mounted from that small kingdom a number of raids against the Dahomean garrison in Ouidah but never regained his throne. He was finally captured and executed in 1733. See also HOUEDA KINGDOM.

HUNKANRIN, LOUIS, 1886–1964. Publicist, journalist and early nationalist. Born in 1886 in Porto Novo (q.v.) to a distinguished family (his mother was of princely origins, his father, jeweler to the Kings of Porto Novo) Hunkanrin studied locally and at a Teachers College in Dakar, Senegal. One of Dahomey's very first indigenous teachers, he returned to teach in Ouidah (q.v.) in 1906, only to be dismissed from his job four years later after a dispute with his superior over the superior's arbitrariness with the pupils. Returning to Dakar, Hunkanrin engaged first in commerce and then journalism and political activity. During the First World War, he and Paul Hazoumé (q.v.) helped edit the newspaper *Messager du Dahomey.* At the same time Hunkanrin prepared tracts from abroad (especially from Nigeria) attacking France's treatment of Dahomean recruits to the war effort. He founded a Dahomean branch of the League for Human Rights and was a continuous thorn in the side of the French administration in Dahomey. Imprisoned in France for several months, Hunkanrin returned to Dahomey only to be arrested again by the French authorities for his militant nationalist views. Accused of pro-British sympathies (he had supported the legitimate claim to the Porto Novo throne by a branch resident in Nigeria), Hunkanrin also was penalized for his role in inciting the Cotonou (q.v.) and Porto Novo population not to pay taxes, resulting in a dock-yard strike referred to as "the Porto Novo disturbances." In the latter instance Hunkanrin cogently cited the 1882 treaty between Porto Novo and France in support of his claims. He was sentenced to ten years in exile, though he had been in prison at the time of the strikes and demonstrations.

Hunkanrin served his exile in barren Mauritania (1923–1933). For a while after his return he appeared to have been affected by his exile and turned to the study of Dahomean traditional customs. But in 1934 he again was brought to trial by the French authorities in Dahomey as co-defendant for two inflammatory articles in the local newspaper *La Voix du Dahomey* (q.v.). Following the trial Hunkanrin moved out of the anti-establishment limelight, supporting the Free French cause in the Second World War. In 1941 he was again arrested on the charge of spying for Britain, having sent recruits to the war effort in Nigeria. He was tried in Dakar, where he was sentenced to death, a sentence later commuted to eight years in exile, this time in Mali. Hunkanrin was freed and repatriated in 1947 at the age of 61. He again immersed himself in political activities, this time legal under the liberalized framework of France's 1946 constitution. He became an important member of the Porto Novo Comité Electoral (q.v.) in the brief period preceding the creation of Dahomey's first political party. In

1950 he was appointed chairman of the Union des Anciens du Dahomey, a powerful pressure group in Porto Novo, and in the same year he edited the local newspaper *L'Eveil.* After independence, too old to serve full time in a governmental capacity, Hunkanrin was appointed special consultant to both President Hubert Maga and Vice-President Sourou-Migan Apithy (qq.v.). Hunkanrin died in Porto Novo on May 28, 1964, having personally witnessed both the colonization and independence of Dahomey. At his funeral he was eulogized (by French speakers alike) for his courage in fighting France's colonial abuses and being Dahomey's first and foremost nationalist and anticolonialist.

-I-

IBRAHIM, SOURADJOU. Northern political broker. Appointed High Commissioner for the Plan in 1970 by President Maga (q.v.), Ibrahim reverted back to administrative duties until integrated into President Kérékou's (q.v.) office as Special Adviser on Planning. In February 1987 he was promoted to Minister of State attached to the Presidency in charge of Planning and Statistics, retaining the post until the August 1988 cabinet shuffle.

IDJE see HOLLI

IGNACIO-PINTO, LOUIS, 1903–1984. Well-known lawyer, diplomat and former member of the International Court of Justice. Born in June 21, 1903, in Porto Novo (q.v.), Ignacio-Pinto descended on his maternal side from the Abeoukuta (Nigeria) royal family. He studied in Abeokuta, Lagos, and Bordeaux, obtaining a law degree. He was an officer cadet in 1931–1932, involved himself in a starch manufacturing enterprise (1933–1936) and practiced law in Paris (1937–1939). In the interwar period he kept abreast of developments at home and lashed out in his writings against French colonial abuses. Together with Louis Hunkanrin (q.v.), Ignacio-Pinto was a co-defendant in the *La Voix du Dahomey* (q.v.) trial, accused of writing an inflammatory article, for which he was given a symbolic fine. During the Second World War Ignacio-Pinto served in the French forces, was wounded, and transferred to French Guinea where he was a member of the Resistance. At the conclusion of the war he was elected representative of Dahomey to the French Senate where he served between 1945 and 1956. During the 1930's and 1950's he also served on the editorial board of the extremely influential *Eveil du Benin* (together with Emile Derlin Zinsou (q.v.)), that had a wide readership in French Africa. In 1957 he was appointed Minister of Economics, Finance and Industry and, in 1958, he joined Justin Ahomadégbé's party Union Démocratique Dahoméenne (qq.v.), being transferred to head the Ministry of Justice and Civil Service (1958–1959). In 1959 he resigned from the cabinet over Dahomey's pullout from the projected Mali Federation (q.v.) and was appointed counsellor in the French Embassy to the Vatican. The next year he became Dahomey's first Permanent Representative to the United Nations and Ambassador to the United States. After seven years at the post, Ignacio-Pinto returned home to become President of Dahomey's Supreme Court (1967–1969). In 1968 he ruled that barring Dahomey's political triumvirate (q.v.) from the military-sponsored election (see ELECTORAL BOYCOTT, 1968) was unconstitutional, a ruling ignored by the junta in power. In 1969 Ignacio-Pinto was appointed to the International Court of Justice in The Hague, serving on it until 1979, when he retired, following an accident. He died in Paris on May 24, 1984.

INDEPENDANTS D'OUTRE MER (IOM). Political grouping in the Assembly of the French Union formed in 1948 by Léopold Sédar Senghor, future President of Senegal. The purpose of the IOM was to unify delegates from the colonial territories. In 1953 the IOM included 14 African delegates loosely allied with the left-of-center French Catholic party, the MRP (Mouvément Républicain Populair). Though attempts were made to transform the IOM into a viable African interterritorial party, it lacked support in the territories themselves and remained essentially a caucus of like-minded deputies in Paris. One of the IOM's more ardent supporters from Dahomey was Emile Derlin Zinsou (q.v.).

INDEPENDANTS DU NORD see DEFENSE DES INTERETS ECONOMIQUES.

INDIGENAT. Civil code established in 1924 and in existence until 1946, restricting the civil rights of the indigenous population that had not attained the status of *evolué* or *assimilé* (qq.v.). Restrictions on civil and political liberties included the obligation to perform *corvée* (q.v.) labor, including porterage, and legal jurisdiction under customary law with a French administrator presiding. The *indigénat* code was one of the greatest sources of friction in colonial French Africa. See also ASSIMILATION POLICY.

INDUSTRIE BENINOISE DES TEXTILES (IBETEX). Former textile enterprise formed by 48 percent State funds in conjunction with French private interests, producing textiles aimed primarily for the European market. Set up in 1971 in Parakou (q.v.) (as IDATEX before Benin's name change), originally capitalized at 600 million CFA francs, augmented to 2,400 million, the plant was involved in weaving, spinning, and textile and hosiery production. It had a capacity of 3,000 tons of finished goods, expanded with the erection of a second plant (called IBETEX II) at Bohicon (q.v.).

The company started operations in 1975 and was supplied with raw materials by SONAGRI. Employing 2,340 workers, production was erratic and often at 20 percent of capacity (rarely producing more than 1,000 tons of finished goods), and it closed down bankrupt in 1982.

INDUSTRIE COTONIERE DU DAHOMEY (ICODA). Mixed-economy enterprise, originally with a 13.33 percent state participation, founded in Cotonou (q.v.) in 1968. the company was renamed SOBETEX (q.v.) in 1975.

INDUSTRIE DAHOMEENNE DE TEXTILE (IDATEX) see INDUSTRIE BENINOISE DE TEXTILE (IBETEX).

INSTITUT DE RECHERCHES APPLIQUEES DU BENIN (IRAB). Successor to the "Dahomey" era IRAD, which itself was the local pre-independence branch of the Institut Français d'Afrique Noire (q.v.) established as a research institute in Porto Novo (q.v.) in 1944. One of IRAD's first directors was Stainislas Adotevi (q.v.). Publisher of the journal *Etudes Dahoméennes* (q.v.), which since 1969 has appeared very erratically (due to fiscal constraints), IRAD has also been in charge of the staffing and management of museums (Ouidah [q.v.], Porto Novo, Parakou [q.v.], and more recently the Porto Novo palace-turned-museum) and historical sites (Abomey [q.v.]) in Dahomey. It used to have one of the best libraries/ archives in Francophone Africa, but already by 1969 through lack of maintenance and upkeep (a function of inadequate fiscal allocations) the collection had seriously deteriorated with many priceless documents in tatters. In 1970 IRAD was merged with the University of Benin (q.v.).

INSTITUT DE RECHERCHES APPLIQUEES DU DAHOMEY see INSTITUTE OF RECHERCHES APPLIQUEE DU BENIN

INSTITUT DE RECHERCHES COTONIERES ET TEXTILES (IRACT). French experimental station and farm in the outskirts of Abomey (q.v.), involved in producing superior cotton seed and research on pest control.

INSTITUT DE RECHERCHES POUR LES HUILES ET OLEAGINEUX (IRHO). French-sponsored research center concerned with improving the state of Benin's aging palm oil (q.v.) plantations. In the late 1960's a master-plan was prepared and, after considerable delays, some 2,400 hectares of new plantations were planted, with some of the area also irrigated. Low water levels in Benin's lagoons, droughts, and weak State financing have scaled down work on some of these tracts. Indeed, the first 400 irrigated hectares were only operational in 1977 consequent to infusion of funds from the FAC (q.v.).

INSTITUT D'ENSEIGNEMENT SUPERIEUR DU BENIN (IESB). Joint Togolese-Dahomean institute for higher studies, in existence between 1965 and 1970. The school had a sciences section in Porto Novo (q.v.) and a humanities section in Lomé. Dahomey's 1970 decision to establish a humanities section in Abomey-Calavi (q.v.), as part of the new University of Dahomey, brought an end to the joint cooperation between Togo and Dahomey.

INSTITUT FRANCAIS D'AFRIQUE NOIRE (IFAN). Research institute with headquarters in Dakar, Senegal, and branches in most territories of French West Africa (AOF[q.v.]). The Dahomean branch was established in Porto Novo (q.v.) in 1944 and concentrated especially on anthropological and social studies. Among the distinguished roster of researchers attached to it at one time or another were the French scholars Jacques Lombard (q.v.), Paul Mercier, Edouard Dunglas (q.v.), and the Dahomean Tidjani Serpos (q.v.). The Institute developed one of the best libraries in Francophone Africa and in 1948 initiated the publication of the scholarly journal Etudes Dahoméennes (q.v.). After independence the Institute's name was changed to Institut de Récherches Appliquées du Dahomey (IRAD) (q.v.).

INSTITUT FRANCAIS DE RECHERCHES FRUITIERES OUTRE MER (IFAC). French experimental agricultural station and farm near Abomey (q.v.).

INSTITUT PEDAGOGIQUE NATIONAL (IPN). State teacher-training school, located in Porto Novo (q.v.). The school was charged in the mid-1970's with the near impossible task of supplying the educational system with qualified instructors after the massive exodus from the country of large numbers of teachers. Despite an increased output from the IPN, much of the teaching staff in the country remains unqualified.

INSURRECTIONS see BIO GUERA: HOLLI REVOLT: UPRISINGS OF 1915–1918

INTERTERRITORIAL PARTIES. There have been several efforts at establishing interterritorial political movements in Francophone Africa, with local branches in each country. Of these, five have been the most important in terms of the affiliation of Dahomean parties, though the local array of regional power-wielders seriously eroded the significance or longevity of such linkages.

(1) Rassemblement Démocratique Africain (q.v.). Francophone Africa's first and most important interterritorial political movement. The Union Progréssiste Dahoméenne (q.v.) was briefly affiliated with the RDA in 1946–1948; the Union Démocratique Dahoméenne (q.v.) next became the local section of the RDA (1955–1961).

(2) Indépendants d'Outre Mer (q.v.). Though individual Dahomean deputies aligned themselves in France with the IOM, the movement never developed a viable territorial section in Dahomey, as elsewhere, and remained essentially a strong caucus group in Paris. Emile Derlin Zinsou (q.v.) was the IOM's most ardent Dahomean supporter.

(3) Convention Africaine (q.v.). Successor of the Indépendants d'Outre Mer. Emile Derlin Zinsou founded a CA nucleus in Dahomey prior to the latter's transformation into the Parti du Regroupement Africain (q.v.).

(4) Parti du Regroupement Africain. Successor of the Convention Africaine. A local section was briefly (1958–1959) established in Dahomey—the Parti Progréssiste Dahoméen—a fusion of Sourou-Migan Apithy's Parti Républicain Dahoméen and Hubert Maga's Rassemblement Démocratique Dahoméen (qq.v.).

(5) Mouvement Socialiste Africain (q.v.). Though a local section of the MSA was established in Dahomey, it was essentially of minimal impact on local politics and quickly disappeared.

For more information on the interterritorial movements and their Dahomean sections see the individual entries. See also POLITICAL PARTIES.

IROKO, ABIOLA FELIX. Historian and educator. Educated in Paris, Iroko taught at the Department of History in the National University of Benin (q.v.) and is the author of many important articles on his country's history.

ISLAM. Islam is not very prevalent in Dahomey. Officially an estimated 13 percent of the population are Muslim, though this figure is growing and may be an underestimate. In the northern provinces, Dendi and Fulani (qq.v.) areas tend to be Muslim but the Bariba (q.v.) majority is largely animist. (The Fulani conquests and jihads in what is now Nigeria left Benin in general, and the Borgou (q.v.) specifically, largely untouched.) The spread of Islam has thus been peaceful. There are numerous Koranic schools in the northern provinces. In the south Islam has gained adherents mostly among the Nagot and Goun (qq.v.) and especially in the Porto Novo (q.v.) area among mercantile elements. The powerful stronghold of animism and *vodun* (qq.v.) cults over the southern populations, however, has prevented more serious Muslim inroads except via Yoruba and/or Hausa merchants. The bulk of Benin's Muslim community belongs to the Tidjaniya order, though the Quadriya is also present. Both came to Benin via north Nigeria; all other sects and orders are barely known in the country.

-J-

JACQUES, JEAN. Administrator and former Mayor of Porto Novo (q.v.). Jacques has served in a variety of administrative capacities including as Prefect of Lokossa (q.v.). In the 1980's he was also Mayor of Porto Novo. He was arrested by the Kérékou (q.v.) regime in February 1989 for negotiating with the urban rioters during the upheavals that were to finally lead to the National Conference (q.v.) of 1990.

JACQUIN. Main slave port of the Kingdom of Allada (q.v.), known also as Djekin. At the time, Allada was a competitor of the Houéda Kingdom and its port of Ouidah (qq.v.), but Jacquin never rivalled the latter. The port was captured by troops of the Kingdom of Dahomey (q.v.) during the the major expansion into the coastal areas that brought it also into Ouidah. Though conquered early in the eighteenth century Jacquin had constantly to be reconquered and, in 1761, it was finally razed to the ground because of the population's unwillingness to send the annual tribute to Abomey (q.v.). The area was only resettled in 1771.

JEUNESSE UNIVERSITAIRE DU DAHOMEY (JUD). Liberal nationalist movement opposing the northern bias and left-ward drift of Benin, spreading from the National University of Benin (q.v.) and appealing to segments of the junior officer ranks of the armed forces (q.v.). Established to counter the role of the northern FACEEN (q.v.) among students, the movement was predominantly, but not solely, Fon (q.v.). By the mid-1980's it was a serious counterweight to the extreme-Left Ligue (q.v.) and the Communist Party of Dahomey, the other two movements to compete for the political allegiances of students and intellectuals. Many of its early members went into exile after the liquidation of Aikpé (q.v.) though some—like Tiamiou Adjibadé and Kifuli Salami (qq.v.)—remained in Benin, rallying to the regime and tried stem the extreme Left from within.

JOACHIM, PAULIN, 1931– . Journalist and poet. Born on September 20, 1931, in Cotonou (q.v.), he was educated locally and in Gabon, briefly studying law at the University of Lyon (1950) before obtaining training as a journalist. Between 1958 and 1960 he was political editor of *France-Soir* and between 1960 and 1970 chief editor of *Bingo*. Since 1971 Joachim has been manager of the Parisian journal *Décennie 2*. He has also published two volumes of poetry.

JOHNSON, FERDINAND (Major). Controversial former head of the gendarmerie (q.v.). Director of Benin's Sûreté in 1967 and briefly one of the key members of the CMR (q.v.) established after the 1967 coup (q.v.), Johnson was purged from operational control of troops and was seconded to the Ministry of National Education in February 1968 to head a Commission investigating major fraudulent activities dealing with diploma graft. All along having problems with troops under his command who rejected his leadership (as was the case of a few other "Brazilian" (q.v.) creoles), Johnson was appointed director of the National Lottery in 1972. A year later he was removed from that office, allegedly because of his attempts to make the office profitable through the introduction of slot machines and other innovations. Johnson was finally purged from the armed forces (q.v.) in 1975.

JUDA. French name for the Kingdom of Houéda (q.v.) or Whydah. See also HOUEDA KINGDOM; OUIDAH.

-K-

KABA CAMP. Major garrison in Natitingou in the Atakora (qq.v.) province. Originally a small camp lodging 200 troops, Kaba was built up by various administrations as a detention center away from their ethnic regions for important southern political leaders, and the military nerve-center for the north. Under President Kérékou (q.v.), who also came from Natitingou, the camp was greatly augmented and became one of the prime recruitment and training camps of the Beninois army. It was to there that Kérékou-loyalist Captain Tawès (q.v.) fled in 1992 to declare himself "Commander-in-Chief" of die-hard loyalist Kérékou forces.

KAIAMA. One of the Bariba kingdoms in the Borgou (qq.v.), mostly in Nigeria, that asserted its independence of Nikki (q.v.) in the nineteenth century. Centered around the town of the same name, some 140 kilometers southeast of Nikki and south of the "parent" Bariba state of Bussa (q.v.), Kaiama was founded by one of the sons of the legendary Kisira (q.v.). Originally a Nikki dependency, in the nineteenth century Kaiama's military strength began to dwarf that of all kingdoms in the Nigerian Borgou and it disengaged from the latter's hegemony. At the height of Kaiama's strength, the town was a major caravan stop and had a population of 30,000. As with Bussa to the north, the onset of colonialism, and especially the end of the caravan trade, brought about a major decline to Kaiama, its urban population decreasing rapidly to just a couple of thousand.

KANA. Second seat of the Dahomean monarch during the precolonial era. Seat of the "Bush-King," as distinct from the role of the monarch as "Town-King," with his capital in Abomey (q.v.). Monarchs alternated residence and duplicated ceremonies in Abomey and Kana. Kana itself was a large town (also known to Europeans as Calmina) of up to 15,000 people, some 13 kilometers from Abomey. It contains the royal burial grounds, storage depots of the kingdom and large markets.

KANDI. In the precolonial era Kandi was one of the Bariba states in the Borgou attaining independence from Nikki (qq.v.) at the end of the nineteenth century. In the traditional Bariba hierarchy, Kandi ranks right after Nikki because of its continued fealty to the "parent" Bariba state. Not as strong as Kouandé (q.v.) to the west, nor as big a commercial center as either Parakou (q.v.) or Nikki, Kandi straddled the important traditional trade route from Kano (Nigeria) to Ashanti (Ghana) via Kouandé and Djougou (q.v.) and benefited from its location. Currently the town is a minor stop on the Cotonou-Niamey (Niger) road axis.

KAPKA, HENRI AMOUSSOU. Magistrate. A lawyer by training, Kapka occupied a variety of top positions under the Kérékou (q.v.) regime, notably First Counselor to the Central Popular Court. In April 1988 he was appointed head of the new State Security Court and Benin's representative to the Human Rights Commission in Geneva.

KARIMOU, MAMADOU. Civil administrator. Karimou has served in a variety of administrative posts, notably as Prefect of Borgou (q.v.) between 1963 and 1968 and Inspector of Administrative Affairs in the Ministry of Interior between 1968 and 1974. He is currently retired.

KARITE. Cash-crop grown mostly in the Borgou and Atakora (qq.v.) in north Benin. Production has been extremely erratic since the crop is especially susceptible to the periodic droughts that have afflicted the north in the 1970's. From 10,888 tons produced in 1974/75, production plummeted to 248 tons in 1978/79 back to 17,702 in 1979/80, down to 1,800 in 1982/83, and to a record 25,506 in 1983/84. It has been produced at the level of 12,000 tons in recent years.

KARL, EMMANUEL, 1926– Historian. Born on December 6, 1926, and educated in Dakar (in administration, 1965) and Toulouse (history, 1970), Karl taught at the National University of Benin (q.v.) where he was for several years head of the Department of History. He is currently retired and lives in Cotonou (q.v.).

KEKE, JOSEPH, 1927– . Former Minister of Justice and political leader. Born in Avrankou (near Porto Novo [q.v.]) on December 5, 1927, Kéké graduated with a law degree and rapidly entered the political arena, becoming Sourou-Migan Apithy's (q.v.) prime lieutenant. Between 1959 and 1960 Kéké was Vice-President of Apithy's PRD (q.v.) parliamentary party, having been elected Deputy between 1959 and 1965. In November 1960 he was appointed Minister of Justice, a position he occupied during Maga's (q.v.) first presidency. Following the 1963 coup d'etat (qq.v.) Kéké was temporarily eclipsed and did not occupy a ministerial post until the creation of the Presidential Council (q.v.) in 1970, when he became Minister of Economics and the Plan (1970–1973) as an Apithy appointee. During the Kérékou (q.v.) interregnum he practiced law in Cotonou (q.v.) and abroad, but reentered political life in 1990 with the onset of civilian competitive politics. After Apithy's death in 1989 he inherited the latter's mantle of leadership over part of the Porto Novo vote, and the MRD (q.v.) party, forming a compact with Justin Ahomadégbé (q.v.) to run on a joint RND (q.v.) platform. He contested the Presidential elections unsuccessfully, though was elected to the Assembly. There he was surprisingly defeated in his bid for the Speakership of the National Assembly by Adrien Houngbédji (qq.v.), even though Kéké was President Soglo's personal choice.

KENAF see SOCIETE DAHOMEENNE AGRICOLE ET IN-
DUSTRIELLE DU KENAF (SODAK) and SOCIETE
BENINOISE DU KENAF (SOBEK)

KEREKOU, MATHIEU (General), 1933– . Former Head of State
and Chief-of-Staff of the armed forces (q.v.). Born near
Natitingou (q.v.) (in either Kotopounga or Kouarfa according
to different sources) in the northwestern Atakora (q.v.) province on September 2, 1933, Kérékou is of Somba (q.v.) origins
and a former protégé of Col. Maurice Kouandété (q.v.). He was
educated in Kati, Mali, and Saint Louis, Senegal, following
which he received military training at Fréjus and at the Ecole
Militaire de Saint Raphael. He served in the French army for a
year and was then transferred to the budding Dahomean armed
forces in August 1961 with the rank of Second Lieutenant.
Kérékou served as President Hubert Maga's (q.v.) aide-de-
camp (1961–1962), was commander of two pioneering camps
(1962–1963) that were precursors of the Service Civique (q.v.),
and received his first operational command in March 1963. In
January 1965 he was promoted to Captain and during the
Soglo (q.v.) military regime he was widely regarded as Col.
Kouandété's protégé. In 1967 Kérékou was appointed a member of the Comité Militaire de Vigilance (q.v.) that tried to
supervise Soglo's policies. Following Kouandété's 1967 coup,
he became Vice-President and then President of the Comité
Militaire Révolutionnaire (q.v.). In 1968–1969 Kérékou was
attending senior staff officers courses in France and, therefore,
was not involved in Kouandété's 1969 coup d'etat (q.v.). Upon
his return he was promoted to Major, appointed commander of
the Ouidah-based elite para-commando force and, in July
1970, he became Deputy Chief-of-Staff under Col. Paule
Emile De Souza (q.v.). During the tense period of the Ouidah
garrison mutiny, the attempt against De Souza's life and the
abortive coup (1972), Kérékou played a moderating role,
cooling tempers and keeping intact the fragile organizational
structure of the armed forces, a fact that conferred upon him a
measure of grudging respect among the younger officer corps.
Though critical of the Presidential Council (q.v.), Kérékou
counselled patience to those disillusioned by the "politics as
usual" interregnum the latter ushered in.

When Maga handed over power to Ahomadégbé (q.v.), and the latter also proved either incapable or unwilling to weed out corruption (see KOVACS AFFAIR), the younger elements in the armed forces staged the October 26, 1972 coup (q.v.), prevailing in Kérékou (who had not been in the inner circle of the conspiracy) to join them. As the most senior of the putschists Kérékou ended up as Head of State. After he had seized control, one of his first actions was to purge the army's entire senior officer corps, all of whom were appointed to administrative sinecures at the head of the various state industries, later to be retired. An attempted countercoup took place early in 1973, engineered by Col. Alphonse Alley, Major Jean-Baptiste Hachémé and former Minister of Finance Pascal Chabi Kao (qq.v.), the first of many to punctuate Kérékou's 18-year long reign. In the interim he promoted himself Lieutenant Colonel in 1973, Colonel in 1977 and General in 1983.

In 1974 Kérékou wrenched Dahomey onto a path of radicalization, culminating in the declaration for Marxism-Leninism, massive nationalizations and the change in the country's name to Benin. In like manner, Church-State relations, the educational system, administration, commerce and political activity were radically altered. In 1977, a new Constitution (q.v.) set up a quasi-legitimated, semi-civilianized political order, though still under tight Kérékou and party control.

Kérékou faced several serious challenges to his authority, but his regime surprisingly was by far Benin's longest lasting one. In 1975 he had to ward off assaults from Captain Assogba and Major Aikpé (qq.v.) among the original con-spirators who recruited him in 1972. The latter's liquidation sparked trade unionist (q.v.) disturbances that nearly toppled the regime. In 1977 came the ill-fated mercenary assault (q.v.) on Cotonou, and since then Kérékou has been espe-cially hard-pressed from the extreme Left wing of his party (see CAPO-CHICHI, GRATIEN TONAICPON; LIGUE IN-TERNAZIONACE DE LA DEFENSE DES DROITS DES PEUPLES). Essentially a moderate, playing off the various factions surrounding him, including a "right wing" repre-sented by Ohouéns (q.v.) by the mid-1980's Kérékou was restricted in most of his political options. As economic conditions worsened in the country—a function of both Benin's inherent weakness and drainage of resources in the incompetent and corruption-ridden public sector—additional conspiracies and plots emerged, all nipped in the bud by Kérékou's hand-picked all-northern elite Presidential Guard (q.v.) and political spies. With up to 92 percent of the budget going to pay salaries of the bloated State sector, the latter's utter inefficiency and massive deficits required "correction"—at a time of increasing Left-wing militancy. Notwithstanding modest oil (q.v.) revenues from the Sem oil-deposits, the dismantling of part of the State sector and a virtual renunciation in all but domestic rhetoric of the radical option, the economic situation further deteriorated.

In 1988–1989 the banking sector collapsed and civil servants unpaid for up to 18 months commenced a series of demonstrations that, together with global pressures for democratization, led to the convening of a National Conference (q.v.) in 1990 in Cotonou. The latter arrogated to itself quasi-legislative rights and set the stage for the dismantling of Marxism-Leninism, single party and military rule in Benin. In the first round of the 1991 Presidential elections (q.v.) Kérékou obtained the second-highest vote entitling him to contest the second round which he lost to Nicéphore Soglo (q.v.). Kérékou is currently in retirement, having been granted immunity from prosecution for any acts committed under his aegis. Efforts to have him brought to account for a series of criminal acts (notably the murder of Aikpé) have been rejected by Soglo in order not to upset ethnic peace in the country.

KETOU. A former Yoruba (q.v.) kingdom north of Porto Novo (q.v.) and centered around the town of Ketou, its original territory and population divided by the Benin-Nigeria border. Very ancient tombs on its outskirts are venerated as the resting place of the founding fathers of Ketou, of Odudawa origin, possibly also of the leaders of the early Yoruba migrations into Dahomey. The original inhabitants can be traced back to the legendary migration from Ile-Ife that led most of the wave on to Tado (q.v.) and, several centuries later, back to Dahomey. Indeed, all but one of its long list of kings was chosen from the royal clans of the original Ile-Ife dispersal (see ADJA; ADJA-TADO). With the rise of Dahomean power in the nineteenth century, Ketou was the target of several military assaults. The city was finally sacked in 1883 and destroyed in 1885. Remnants of its fortification, one of the few in this area, attest to its turbulent history and its precarious location, straddling one of the military routes used by both King Ghézo and King Glélé (qq.v.) in their attacks against Abeokuta in Nigeria. Currently the village is largely isolated from the rest of the country by poor roads, but its traditional status as the cradle of the Yoruba remains unimpaired.

KIDJO, ANGELIQUE, 1964– . Singer. Kidjo's striking presence and songs has brought her celebrity in European music circles. She has had commercial successes with two of her albums *Parakou* and *Logazo*.

KIGERA III, MUSA MOHAMMED. King of Bussa (q.v.) in contemporary Nigeria, and spiritual head of all the Bariba (q.v.) in Benin and Nigeria. Kigera III ascended the throne in 1968 after the long reign of Babiki Mohamman Sani (1935–1968). In his efforts to revive the spiritual unity of the Bariba, he made several "state visits" to neighboring former Bariba states, including Nikki (q.v.). See also BARIBA; BUSSA; NIKKI.

KINDE, ARSENE, 1920– . High government official and former Minister. Born in Ouidah (q.v.) on April 2, 1920, Kindé was educated in his home town and entered the civil service in 1936 as a simple clerk. He was transferred to Dakar in 1948, where he completed his education in night classes. In 1958 he returned to Dahomey as technical advisor to the Ministry of Finance, occupying ever higher positions in the following years: Head of Cabinet of the Minister of Labor and Social Affairs (1959); Head of the Prime Minister's Cabinet (1959–1960); Secretary-General of the National Assembly (q.v.) (1961–1962); Head of National Security (1962–1963); Secretary of State for African and Malagasy Affairs (1963);

Head of Cabinet of the Provisional Government of Col. Christophe Soglo (q.v.) (1963–1964); President of the Administrative Committee of the Supreme Court (q.v.) (1964–1965); Minister of Justice (1965–1967); and Director-General of SNAHDA (q.v.) (1967). In 1968 Kindé relocated to France; he is currently retired.

KINDJI see GANVIE.

KINIFO, VALERE, 1930– . Physician. Born in 1930 and a physician by training, Kinifo teaches pathological surgery at the National University of Benin (q.v.). He is currently semi-retired.

KISIRA. Legendary ancestor of all the Bariba (q.v.) people of the Nigerian and Beninois Borgou (q.v.). A seventh-century warrior from Arabia (by legend) who refused to convert to Islam (q.v.), Kisira was forced into self-exile, crossed into Africa, trekked to Bornu (Chad, where Kisira legends also abound), and from there moved northwards (or his sons did so) to found Bussa (q.v.), the parent Bariba state of the Borgou. All other states were formed after splits from the latter, including Nikki (q.v.), the senior Benin state. Other societies in Africa hold similar Kisira legends, referring to origins from lineages originating in Arabia. With respect to the Bariba, alternate oral tradition refers to Kisira as being a Persian prince, defeated by the Byzantines, and, rejecting Islam, taking his followers south into Bornu (across the Garamantian caravan trail?), following which (much later) his sons founded Bussa and Nikki. See also BARIBA; BORGOU; BUSSA.

KITI, GABRIEL, 1900–1948. Early Catholic priest and author. Born around 1900 in Ouidah (q.v.), and of royal lineage (related to the Ouémé-Djigbé, Ketou, and Savé (qq.v.) ruling dynasties), Kiti studied at the Catholic mission in Ouidah and then undertook an apprenticeship with the de Souza family. In 1915 he was admitted to the Ouidah seminary (q.v.) and when ordained was Dahomey's second local priest. He was a prolific author, writing on Dahomey's various ethnic groups. He served his Church in particular in Cové and Abomey (q.v.). Suffering from diabetes, he died on November 20, 1948, and is buried in the graveyard of the Ouidah seminary.

KITOY, ARCADE ROMAULD (Lieutenant). Little-known northern military officer and member of the inner circle of officers and NCO's that coalesced around Col. Maurice Kouandété (q.v.) during the period from 1967 to 1972. In the 1969 attempted kidnapping of Kouandété (see ALLEY, ALPHONSE; KOUANDETE MAURICE), it was Kitoy who discovered and arrested the plotters. Following Kouandété's 1969 coup d'etat (q.v.) Kitoy became director of the Security Service, having also commanded the unit that arrested President Zinsou (q.v.). In 1972 he played a role in the unrest and mutiny of the Ouidah (q.v.) garrison and later that year he was sentenced to death, together with Kouandété and several other officers, for a plot against the Presidential Council (q.v.). The sentence was not executed and Kitoy, released from prison in the amnesty following the 1972 coup of Mathieu Kérékou (q.v.) went to live in Paris.

KLIKA, JOSEPH. Educator and early political figure. A former Councillor from Porto Novo (q.v.) and a teacher by profession, Klika was a pre-independence cabinet Minister (of the Plan and Rural Development) in the Sorou-Migan Apithy (q.v.) government of 1957–1959. He returned to teaching in 1960, though he was a member of the Counseil Economique et Social (q.v.) between 1968 and 1972 and a party branch leader in Ouémé.

KODIA, ANTOINE. Businessman and former Kérékou (q.v.) cronie. A large landowner, wholesale importer, and with investments in trucking and construction, Kodia was also the managing director of the joint Benin-Nigerian sugar refinery in Savé. With the eclipse of Kérékou's right-hand man

Mohamed Cissé (q.v.) (who eventually fled the country after absconding with State funds) Kodia became Kérékou's main business aide.

KODJA, GANDOUNOU (Colonel). Military officer integrated for the first time in Kérékou's (q.v.) cabinet in 1988 when appointed Minister of Rural Development and Cooperatives. Previously he had served in senior administrative posts, notably as Prefect of Borgou and of Atlantique (qq.v.).

KOKOU AZANDEGBE, EDOUARD. Director of Fisheries in the Ministry of Rural Development; by profession a veterinary inspector.

KOKPON (d. 1610?). King of Allada (q.v.). At this father's death, a succession struggle erupted between and him and his two brothers. Legend has it that Kokpon gained the Allada throne while the other brothers left to establish their own dynasties, one in Abomey, the Fon kingdom of Dahomey, the other in Porto Novo (qq.v.). Evidence suggests, however, that Porto Novo was founded much later, by refugees escaping the destruction of Allada by King Agaja (q.v.) of Dahomey in 1724.

KOSSOU, BASILE TOUSSAINT, 1944– . Educator. Born in 1944 and educated in Paris in philosophy, Kossou joined the National University of Benin (q.v.) before being appointed Head of the Institut Culturel Africain in Dakar, Senegal, where he still serves. He has written several academic works, and has served as a consultant for UNESCO and EEC (q.v.).

KOUANDE. One of the northern Bariba (q.v.) states in the precolonial era. Founded at the end of the eighteenth century by dissidents who lost out in a succession struggle in Nikki (q.v.) and rallied behind a self-exiled prince, Gaba (q.v.), Kouandé broke with its parent state a century later and, territorially expanding, established an alliance with Djougou (q.v.). In the traditional Bariba hierarchy Kouandé ranks below Kandi (due to Kouandé-Nikki friction and hostilities in the past), though ahead of Parakou (qq.v.). The state straddled important east-west caravan trails connecting Kano and Ashanti and exploited its location to its profit. At the time of the French conquest, Kouandé was by far the most powerful Bariba state, and generalized fear of the Bariba "threat" in the north was largely consequent to Kouandé's aggressive expansion in all directions. Currently Kouandé is greatly isolated from other Bariba centers in the north due to poor roads. Its economic neglect, and the preference given in Cotonou to Bourgou (q.v.), fomented a minor political shift toward southern candidates at election time during the civilian era (1960–1972). The neglect of Kouandé, and Atakora (q.v.) in general, ended with the rise to power of Kérékou (q.v.) (a Somba [q.v.] from Atakora) in 1972. The current king (a Bangana) is a retired ex-gendarmerie sergeant. See also CHABI GABA.

KOUANDETE, IROPA MAURICE (Colonel). Former chief of staff of Dahomey's armed forces (q.v.) leader of two military coups (q.v.) (1967, 1969), and briefly Head of State. Born in the Gaba district in the Atakora (qq.v.) département, Kouandété was the first Somba (q.v.) to reach national prominence. A professional soldier from his late teens, Kouandété attended France's Ecole Militaire and Saint Cyr, acquiring a haughty contempt for such colleagues promoted up the ranks as his superiors, Gen. Christophe Soglo and Col. Alphonse Alley (qq.v.). Resentful also of the heavy Fon (q.v.) predominance in the senior ranks of the armed forces, Kouandété tried during 1965–1967 to undermine the authority of the Fon military hierarchy in favor of the junior northern officers. He served for a year as General Soglo's adjutant and as commander of his Presidential Palace Guard (q.v.) (1965–1966). In 1966 he was appointed head of the Security Services. Allegedly caught falsifying reports in an effort to discredit Soglo, Kouandété was again transferred, in 1967, to become adjutant to Chief-of-Staff Col. Alley.

In April 1967 Kouandété was appointed Vice-President of the Comité Militaire du Vigilance (q.v.), set up to supervise Soglo's administration. Increasingly incensed at Soglo's "unmilitary" political style while in office (see COUP OF 1967), Kouandété utilized his popularity among the northern and junior ranks and his operational control over the Ouidah-based paracommando unit to topple Soglo's regime in December 1967. Unpopular and feared in the south, Kouandété was forced to cede primacy in the subsequent interim military regime to Alley, whom he had earlier placed under house arrest. Following the electoral boycott (q.v.) of 1968 and the appointment of Emile Derlin Zinsou (q.v.) as civilian president, Kouandété wrested control of the armed forces from Alley who was eventually imprisoned for an alleged kidnapping plot. In 1969 Kouandété once again mounted a coup d'etat, this time against Zinsou. Rigid, unsociable, condescending and ambitious, Kouandété was this time incensed by Zinsou's independence in office and the latter's unwillingness to heed much of the advice of his Chief-of-Staff.

Kouandété overestimated his control over the army, however, and his drive for the Presidency was blocked. Appointed to an interim three-man Military Directorate (q.v.) he was outflanked and outvoted by two southerners. Following a series of power struggles in the army command,Kouandété was eased out of operational control of troops, purged as Chief-of-Staff (in favor of Paul Emile De Souza [q.v.]) and attached as adjutant to Col. Alley (recently released from prison) as Deputy Secretary-General of National Defense. In 1972 Kouandété attempted a comeback but was arrested and sentenced to death for his role in a convoluted plot against the Presidential Council (q.v.). The sentence was not carried out and he was released shortly after the October 1972 coup d'etat by major Mathieu Kérékou (qq.v.), and retired from the army. His abrasive and arrogant personality had alienated him from other northern officers who no longer wished his leadership. Though for long retired Koundété's irascible temperament was again visible briefly in in 1990 when he urged fellow-northern officers in the armed forces to mount a coup rather than watch the National Conference (q.v.) strip

Kérékou of all his powers prior to a return to civilian rule. See also COUP OF 1967; COUP OF 1969.

KOUDJO, BIENVENU, 1952– . Born in 1952, and educated in Paris in comparative literature (1972–1976), Koudjo, a published author, teaches literature and theater at the National University of Benin (q.v.).

KOUDOGBO, ORED'OLA ETIENNE, 1932– . Educator and agronomist. Born in Porto Novo (q.v.) on August 3, 1932, and with a degree in agronomy from the University of Toulouse and another in tropical agronomy from the University of Paris, Koudogbo was appointed in 1959 as Head of Agricultural Services in the southern regions and shortly after also as Deputy Head of Agriculture (1959–1961). He taught at the Centre de Formation Rurale in Porto Novo and was active in regional conferences. In 1963 he was appointed Director of Rural Development and, in 1965, Director of Agricultural Teaching and Agronomic Research in the Ministry of National Education. Between 1973 and 1974 he served as ILO Acting Director for Central Africa, and since 1974 he has been in Yaoundé as ILO Advisor on Rural Questions.

KOUHOUNOU STADIUM. Showpiece of China's technical assistance to Benin. A multi-sport complex ("omnisports stadium") facility built by China, was transferred to the Benin government on November 25, 1983. Since the country is very sports conscious and the former facilities were quite primitive, the Stadium has garnered China much good will while meeting an important need in Benin.

KOUKOUNI, NOEL, 1931– . Architect. Born in Porto Novo (q.v.) on March 2, 1931, Koukouni has an architectural degree with a diploma in decorative arts from Paris. Upon his return to Cotonou (q.v.) he was appointed director of the new Centre National de l'Industrie Céramique du Dahomey, and he continues to serve in a similar capacity today.

KOUKOUNI, VALERE. Cotonou police (qq.v.) commissioner. Koukouni, normally engaged in routine investigatory police matters, acquired a measure of notoriety in 1975 when he was charged with the attempted kidnapping of Zinsou (q.v.) in Nigeria. The plot, aimed at bringing Zinsou to trial in Cotonou (for "treason"), failed.

KOURTEY. An ethnic group formed of a fusion of Dendi and Fulani (qq.v.), the Kourtey are found along the banks and islands of the Niger river. Originally only a few Kourtey lived in Benin, along the segment of the river that forms Benin's boundary with Niger. In the past three decades, however, there has been an increased Kourtey "migration" downstream, with the result that their numbers in Benin have noticeably increased. No estimates of total population exists.

KOUTON, ISSIAKOU. Senior agronomist officer. Trained in agronomy, and normally head of a division in the Ministry of Agriculture in Porto Novo (q.v.), Kouton was brought into the cabinet on two occasions in an interim capacity. During the period of January 1964 to December 1965, he served as President Ahomadégbé's (q.v.) Minister of Youth, Sports and Tourism, and between March and December 1967 as Minister of Rural Development and Cooperation. He is currently retired.

KOUYAMI, FRANCOIS (Colonel). Police officer, former Director of the Sûreté Nationale (q.v.) and the paramilitary forces, and since early 1993 commander of the gendarmerie (q.v.). Kouyami first came into prominence when he was integrated into the Military Tribunal (q.v.) charged with the 1972 trial of Colonel Kouandété (q.v.). Dropped from the panel at his own request, this stood in his favour when after the 1972 coup d'etat (q.v.), he was appointed head of the Sûreté Nationale. In 1974 he was also integrated into the Politburo of the new PRPB (q.v.) party set up. After the attempted coup of Assogba (q.v.), Kouyami was integrated into the cabinet as Minister of Labor and the Civil Service (Assogba's Ministry) and also promoted to Captain. In April 1975 he was shifted to head the ministry of Youth and Sports but reverted to his normal gendarmerie duties in 1976. He was twice promoted and by 1984 was in command of all of Benin's paramilitary forces. The fact that he was the ringleader of the dangerous plot of 1987 traumatized Kérékou (q.v.) since it indicated that even his hitherto loyal key military appointees were rebelling against his crumbling leadership. Coincidentally or not, and somewhat reminiscent of the story put out in 1975 with respect to the liquidation of Captain Aikpé (q.v.), Kouyami was also cited as Kérékou's rival for the affections of Valentine Gandonou, Second Vice-President of the National Assembly (q.v.). Kouyami was imprisoned in the Parakou military camp, tortured and probably targetted for execution. However, he had no difficulty in escaping (together with three other prisoners) by helicopter to Nigeria, something that further embarrassed the regime. Amnestied in 1990 by the post-Kérékou regime, Kouyami resumed his military duties. In 1993, in a move that led to the resignation of the Minister of Defense, who had not been consulted, Kouyami was appointed by President Soglo (q.v.) as Head of the Gendarmerie.

KOVACS AFFAIR. Indirectly the spark that ignited the 1972 coup by Major Mathieu Kérékou (qq.v.), the Kovacs Affair involved influence-peddling, bribery, fiscal irregularities and the de facto monopoly over the sale of official stationery to the government, resulting in alleged profits to Finance Minister, Pascal Chabi Kao (q.v.). When the scandal erupted (including allegations of embezzlement by Chabi Kao) Co-President Hubert Maga (q.v.) would not let his protégé be removed and Justin Ahomadégbé (q.v.) (who became chairman of the Presidential Council [q.v.] in May 1972) was unable to fire Chabi Kao over the veto of his two other colleagues on the Council. Kérékou (q.v.) cited this and other instances of government paralysis as justification for his coup. Paradoxically, Captain Janvier Assogba's 1975 coup against Kérékou was preceded by allegations that the latter had himself been involved in the Kovacs scandal, having accepted a bribe from Bertin Borna (q.v.). For whatever reason the latter became the bête noire of the Kérékou regime, and Assogba himself remained in prison for most of Kérékou's reign. See also CHABI KAO, COUP OF 1972; PASCAL.

KPAKPO, GILBERT. Politician and former First Vice-President of Dahomey. A graduate of Dakar's Ecole William Ponty (q.v.), Kpakpo was an early political figure and the UPD running-mate of Emile Derlin Zinsou (qq.v.) in the 1951 elections, when the once-united party split into three. Later his allegiances shifted to Justin Ahomadégbé (q.v.), and he became a prominent member of the latter's Union Démocratique Dahoméenne, later the Parti Démocratique Dahoméen (qq.v.). In May 1959 Kpakpo was appointed Secretary of State, attached to the Presidency, and in January 1960 Minister of Information. A teacher by profession, with a strong unionist power base in Cotonou (q.v.), Kpakpo was Mayor of the city in 1960. When President Maga banned the UDD (q.v.) in 1961, Kpakpo was briefly imprisoned but reemerged in the succeeding regime of Ahomadégbé and Sourou-Migan Apithy (qq.v.) as First Vice-President (1964–1965). He died soon after.

KPEGOUNOU, ISSA, 1923– . Thirty-ninth Emir (king) of Borgou (q.v.). Traditional rule of Nikki and head of the Bariba (qq.v.) hierarchy in Dahomey, owing fealty only to the Emir of Bussa in Nigeria (see BARIBA; BORGOU; BUSSA). Born in 1923 to one of the branches of the ruling hierarchy, Kpegounou served in the French navy, becoming a gendarme after Dahomey's independence and eventually attaining the rank of Sergeant. With the death of the preceding ruler of Nikki, a major succession struggle developed between the five royal clans from which the new Emir could be chosen, necessitating active intervention and mediation by a number of northern political figures, including Hubert Maga (q.v.). In 1969 Kpegounou was chosen as the new Emir. Though only a retired civil servant with a small government pension, he is one of the most important traditional chiefs in Benin.

KPENGLA (KING OF DAHOMEY), c. 1735–1789. Born around 1735, Kpéngla acceded to the throne in 1774 at the death of King Tegbésu (q.v.). Kpéngla was energetic but unsuccessful in his efforts to make Dahomey independent of Oyo (q.v.), nor was he very successful in the various slave raids he mounted that were aimed at reviving the port of Ouidah (q.v.), conquered in 1727. He died in 1789 of smallpox, to be succeeded by Agonglo (q.v.).

KPENOU, CECILE, 1937– . Lawyer. Born in 1937 and educated in law and literature, Kpenou was director of Benin College (Nigeria), later teaching at the University of Nigeria in Nsukka, before her appointment as Legal Advisor to the United Nations High Commission for Refugees in Geneva.

KPOFFON, PAUL. Former Minister and diplomat. Kpoffon joined the Kérékou (q.v.) cabinet in February 1980 and served for just over two years as Minister of Public Health. He was subsequently appointed Ambassador to Rumania.

KPOGNON, STANISLAS YEDOMON. Economist and former Minister. A graduate of IHEOM in Paris, and of Law School, Kpognon was attached to the Ministry of Labor and Finance in a variety of capacities including as Labor Inspector. Between 1963 and 1970 he also served as President of the Société Dahoméenne pour le Développement de l'Industrie et le Commerce (SODIAC) and of the Banque Dahoméenne de Développement (BDD) (q.v.). In 1968 he was brought into the Zinsou (q.v.) cabinet as Minister of Economics and Finance, reverting to his administrative duties in the same ministry after the coup of 1970 (q.v.).

KUTUKLUI AFFAIR. The affair involved Togo's request for the extradition from Dahomey of Noë Kutuklui, Togolese lawyer and politician, in exile in Cotonou (q.v.) since the late 1960's. While practicing law in Dahomey, Kutuklui—political heir of slain former Togolese President Sylvanus Olympio—had sponsored a series of plots against the Togolese military regime, headed by Olympio's assassin, General Etienne Eyadema. Togo's request for Kutuklui's extradition and Dahomey's decision to expel him (though not to hand him over to Eyadema) sparked off student and union protests in Cotonou. Before the regime could arrest him, Kutuklui was spirited out of the country under full military escort by Col. Alley (q.v.), one of those infuriated by the Presidential Council's (q.v.) decision to abide with the Togolese requests. The "affaire Kutuklui" seriously eroded the Council's popularity in the south, tarnishing its reputation because of both the decision to expel Kutuklui and the government's utter inability to execute the decision.

-L-

LAHIMI, THOMAS (Major). Former army officer and Minister. Prior to the 1972 coup (q.v.) a military attaché at the Dahomean Embassy in Paris, Lahimi joined the Kérékou (q.v.) cabinet in October 1972 as Minister of Finance and Economics. In April 1973 he was reassigned to military duties as Deputy Quartermaster General of the armed forces, and went into retirement in 1985.

LALEYE, ISIDORE (Lieutenant). During the Kérékou (q.v.) era Head of Military Intelligence, charged with monitoring the armed forces (q.v.) for subversive activities.

LATIN QUARTER. Term frequently applied to Dahomey during the colonial era. Such a comparison with the artistic-intellectual quarter in Paris drew attention to the disproportionate number of intellectuals, literary figures, pamphleteers, publicists, professionals and newspapers (over fifty in the period 1904–1955) produced by Dahomey.

LAWINI, ISSA RAIMI (Major), 1939– . Senior gendarmerie (q.v.) officer. Born in Porto Novo (q.v.) on April 13, 1939 of Goun (q.v.) parents, Lawani joined the gendarmerie after high school and was Commander of the Northern Region during 1962–1963. He then served as President Sourou-Migan Apithy's (q.v.) aide-de-camp between 1964–1965, becoming Commander of the Gendarmerie of Cotonou after Apithy's demise. Following the next coup (q.v.), in 1967, he was integrated in Gen. Soglo's (q.v.) cabinet as Minister of Posts, serving until May 1968 when he was reassigned to head the Southern Region Gendarmerie. After the 1972 coup (q.v.) he was promoted and reassigned to administrative duties, and was recently retired.

LEAGUE, THE see LIGUE INTERNATIONALE DE LA DEFENSE DES DROITS DES PEUPLES.

LE HERISSE, AUGUSTE, 1876–1953. Colonial administrator. Born in Antrain on March 29, 1876, Le Herissé served in the French armed forces for two years, following which he joined the colonial administration, arriving in Porto Novo (q.v.) in December 1900. He later served for six years in Abomey (q.v.), during which time he studied the customs of the Fon and the history of the former Kingdom of Dahomey (qq.v.). In the process he thoroughly mastered Fongbe, and his 1911 work *L'Ancien Royaume au Dahomey* is cited to this day as one of the classics. In 1914 Le Herissé was reassigned to Senegal until his retirement in 1924. He later served as Mayor of his home village, where he died in 1953.

LEMAN, IBRAHIM (Major), 1934– . Former Minister. Born in 1934 in Kandi (q.v.), Leman attended cadet officers schools at both Saint Maxient and St. Cyr, as well at the University of Dakar where he majored in the social sciences. While a Lieutenant he was brought into the 1965 interim military government as Minister of Interior, and during 1967–1968 he served as Minister of Education, Youth and Sports. Leman remained in military duties during most of the post-1972 era.

LEMON, IDELPHONSE. Economist. Educated in public administration, economics and law, Lemon served in a number of key capacities, including as member of the Counseil Economique et Social (q.v.), member of the Governing Board of the Société des Ciments du Dahomey, Director-General of the Société Dahoméenne de Banque (q.v.) and Technical Counselor to the Presidency. A well-known supporter of Emile Derlin Zinsou (q.v.), Lemon was arrested on several occasions, including in 1968. After the 1972 coup he resided in France, or as advisor to the Ivory Coast Minister of Agriculture, being twice sentenced to death in absentia by the Kérékou (q.v.) regime. He returned to Cotonou (q.v.) with the liberalization of the regime in 1989, when he served as interim Minister of Finance and Economics. As he tried to block the ascendance of Nicéphore Soglo (q.v.), and was also a Presidential candidate in the 1991 elections (q.v.), his old Ministry was reassigned after Soglo's electoral victory.

LETE ISLAND DISPUTE see DAHOMEY-NIGER BOUNDARY DISPUTE

LIBRARIES. The main library centers in Benin are: (1) the National Archives (see ARCHIVES NATIONALES) in Porto Novo (q.v.); (2) the Public Administration library in Cotonou (q.v.); (3) the National Library in Porto Novo; (4) the Provincial libraries, each in its provincial capital; (5) the Archives of the Chambre de Commerce et d'Industrie (q.v.) in Cotonou; (6) the library of the College Polytechnique Universitaire in Abomey-Calavi (q.v.); (7) the library of the Institut National de Formation et de Recherche en Education in Porto Novo; (8) the library of the National University of Benin (q.v.).

LIGUE INTERNATIONALE DE LA DEFENSE DES DROITS DU PEUPLES, LA. Powerful hard-line Leftist clique in both the administration and the trade union (q.v.) movement during the "revolutionary" era in Benin. Formed in 1973 to bolster, and nudge, Kérékou's (q.v.) Leftist resolve, despite its radical credentials the Ligue was the arch-enemy of the Parti Communiste Dahoméen (q.v.). Highly critical of Kérékou's pragmatic Marxism and of the pro-government leadership of the trade union movement (UNSTB [q.v.]), La Ligue nevertheless avoided confrontations with Kérékou, and for this reason was not very popular with youth, students and intellectuals of either Left or Right persuasion, remaining in essence a pragmatic elitist clique of civilian and military personnel. At the height of its influence the Ligue actually had four of its leaders in the PRPB (q.v.) Politburo—Captain Gratien Capochichi, Gado Guirigissou, Simon Ifédé Ogouma and Joseph Degla, the latter the prime ideologue of the regime. Apart from these, other key Ligue members were Manassé Ayayi, Captain Phillipe Akpo, Armand Monteiro, Grégoire Agbahé and David Gbaguidi.

LITTLE ARDRA see AJASE IPE; ARDRA; PORTO NOVO

LOI CADRE. The "enabling" act passed by the French National Assembly in June 1956. The Act expanded the legislative powers of the territorial assemblies of each colony at the expense of those of the two federations; it also gave the colonies internal autonomy, made suffrage universal and established a single electoral college. See also DOUBLE ELECTORAL COLLEGE.

LOI FONDAMENTALE, 1977. Benin's "Basic Law" or Constitution of 1977 (q.v.), under which it was administered until 1990. The Constitution had 11 chapters and 160 articles, all of which were allegedly widely debated by the population prior to submission to a referendum that ratified it. The Constitution set up an Assemblée Nationale Révolutionnaire (ANR) consisting of Commissaires du People (qq.v.) or Assembly of People's Commissioners, elected for three years, who elected the President of the Republic from Central Committee PRPB (q.v.) nominations for a three year term. The Constitution also specified the guiding principles of the State, its revolutionary structures and powers. Chapter 11, composed of Articles 13 to 29, specified the role of the State in the economy and the limits of private enterprise. Several articles of the Constitution were later set aside for reasons of expediency. For example, both the term of the Assembly and the President were extended without election on a variety of technicalities of a "temporary" nature. In February 1984 the Revolutionary National Assembly met in an Extraordinary Session, in essence "legitimating" these deviations by amending the Basic Law. Aside from recognizing several new classes for purposes of elections on corporatist principles, the ANR reduced its membership from 336 to 180, while extending its tenure, and that of the President, from three to five years. On the basis of these changes the new Revolutionary National Assembly was elected in June 1984.

LOKOSSA. Small town with a population of 7,800 that serves as the administrative headquarters of Mono (q.v.) province.

LOMBARD, JACQUES, 1926– . Former Director of Benin's IFAN (q.v.) center and important scholar of Beninois ethnology and history. Born in Paris on May 31, 1926, Lombard studied locally in the field of law. He was appointed to Dahomey in 1951 to succeed Paul Mercier (q.v.) as head of the Institut Français d'Afrique Noive center in Porto Novo (q.v.). He was for ten years its Director (1951–1960), and in many ways the center is Lombard's creation. He personally conducted a great deal of research in the north, publishing his seminal work on the Bariba (q.v.) in 1968. The latter study gained him a Ph.D. and, after leaving IFAN upon Dahomey's independence, Lombard began teaching at the Ethnology Department of the University of Lille, France.

LOZES, GABRIEL, 1917– . Physician, politician and former Foreign Minister. Born on August 18, 1917, and a graduate of the Dakar School of Medicine and Pharmacology, where he first met Justin Ahomadégbé (q.v.), Lozès has been one of Ahomadégbé's principal political lieutenants since the mid-1950's. First elected to the Assemblée Territoriale (q.v.) in 1957 as Deputy from his home town, Abomey (q.v.), Lozès also served as Senator to the Communauté Française (q.v.) (1959–1961). Lozès was also deputy between 1957 and 1964 and Municipal Councillor for Abomey between 1956 and 1965. Secretary-General of the Union Démocratique Dahoméenne (UOP) (q.v.) (1956–1961) and its leading theoretician and intellectual, Lozès was one of the UDD's leaders arrested and imprisoned by President Hubert Maga (q.v.) for an alleged plot against the regime in 1960. Released in 1962, Lozès became Technical Counselor in the Ministry of Public Health (November 1963–January 1964) during the Soglo (q.v.) interim regime, before being given the key posts of Foreign Minister in the new Sourou-Migan Apithy (q.v.)–Ahomadégbé administration (1963–1965) and Secretary-General of their new joint party, the Parti Démocratique Dahoméen (q.v.) (1964–1965). After the overthrow of that government, Lozès was locked out of any position of influence and served as Deputy Director of Public Health in the Ministry of Public Health. In 1969 he was imprisoned for a plot against President Emile Derlin Zinsou (q.v.). Released after the 1969 coup d'etat (q.v.) that toppled Zinsou, Lozès became Minister of Mines, Transport and Public Works in the 1970–1972 cabinet of the Presidential Council (q.v.). With the radicalization of politics after the 1972 coup (q.v.), Lozès lost all influence and retired into private life, practicing medicine in Cotonou (q.v.).

LUBBERT, ELIAS ODOUNTAN, 1935– . Educator. Born in 1935, and with a Ph.D. in political science and law from France, Lubbert was appointed a Lecturer of Public Law at the Ecole Nationaled Administration (1979–1982), following which he joined the National University of Benin (q.v.) to teach politics and public law. He has written several books, including two on Nigeria.

-M-

MABUDU, LEOPOLD. Civil administrator. An accountant by training, Mabudu is Head Treasury Inspector, and a former long-term member of the Counseil Ecominique et Sociale,

President of the Banque Dahoméenne de Développement and Director General of SNAHDA (qq.v.).

MACHUBE. A category of slaves in precolonial Fulani society in the Borgou, of Bariba (qq.v.), "witch-children" given to the Fulani (who do not believe in the phenomenon), by the Bariba who do. A variety of pre- and post-birth symptoms connote to the Bariba the intervention of witches at birth. In the nineteenth century such children were either killed, left to die in the bush or given to the Fulani. The practice persists to this day though the Marxist regime of Kérékou (q.v.) in particular issued strict edicts against it.

MAGA, COUTOUCOU HUBERT, 1916– . Former President of Dahomey and political leader of the north since the mid-1940's. Born in Parakou in 1916 to a Bariba (qq.v.) mother and Voltaic father, Maga was educated locally (studying under Emile Derlin Zinsou's [q.v.] father) and at the Ecole William Ponty (q.v.) in Dakar, where he first met future Niger President Hamani Diori. Born Muslim, Maga converted to Catholicism in Dakar and returned to Dahomey in 1935 to teach in a Natitingou (q.v.) school, becoming its Director in 1945. He married a "Brazilian" of Fon origins from Ouidah (qq.v.). One of the few educated men in the north at the time, Maga represented his region in the first Counseil Général (1947–1952) and became a member of Dahomey's first political party, the Union Progréssiste Dahoméenne (UPD) (qq.v.). Encouraged by the French administrator in the north, Peperty, Maga in 1950–1951 bolted the UPD, organized his Bariba (q.v.) support behind the Groupement Ethnique du Nord (q.v.) and won the second French National Assembly seat then allocated to Dahomey. He served as Deputy between 1951 and 1958, and President of the new MDD (later RDD) party, allied to the Indépendants d'Outre Mer (q.v.) faction, and between November 1957 and April 1958 he was Under-Secretary of State for Labor in Gaillard's government. During the same period he was also Councillor to the AOF Grand Council (1948–1957) and Deputy (later Vice-President) of the Assemblée Territoriale (q.v.) (1952–1957).

In 1958 Maga became Minister of Labor in Sourou-Migan Apithy's (q.v.) cabinet and, following the challenge to the latter's leadership, Prime Minister (1959–1960). Maga's party, the Mouvement Démocratique Dahoméen, merged in 1958 with Apithy's Parti Républicain Dahoméen to form the short-lived Parti Progréssiste Dahoméen (PPD), a section of the interterritorial party Parti du Régroupement Africain (qq.v.) led by Senegal's President Léopold Sédar Sénghor. Following Dahomey's decision not to join the projected Mali federation (q.v.), the PPD collapsed into its constituent parts and Maga's party was renamed Rassemblement Démocratique Dahoméen (q.v.). After independence Maga was again forced to move closer to Apithy in light of Justin Ahomadégbé's (q.v.) electoral challenge and 1960 power gambit. Maga's and Apithy's parties once again merged to form the Parti Dahoméen de l'Unite (q.v.), the electoral rules were changed, Ahomadégbé was imprisoned and his party banned, and in the new Presidential regime Apithy became Vice-President. Later Maga got rid of his Vice-President by appointing him Ambassador to France. His closest allies during this period were Mama Chabi and Mama Arouna (qq.v.).

Hubert Maga's first Presidency (1960–1963) was replete with fiscal extravaganzas, such as the construction of the Presidential Palace (q.v.). In 1963 mass demonstrations in southern Dahomey, sparked by Maga's austerity policies and by the Bohiki Affair (q.v.), brought in the armed forces under General Christophe Soglo (qq.v.) (see COUP OF 1963). Progressively eased out of power, Maga was finally placed under house arrest (1964–1965) for the duration of the next administration, that of Sourou-Migan Apithy and Justin Ahomadégbé. Following the 1965 coup d'etat (q.v.), Maga and the other members of the triumvirate (q.v.) went into exile in Paris.

In the 1968 military-sponsored Presidential elections, Maga appealed from abroad for an electoral boycott (q.v.), which was widely successful. Maga remained in exile until 1970 when the triumvirate was invited back to participate in that year's elections (q.v.). The elections were annulled before Maga could claim a victory due to his solid support in the north. Retreating to Parakou (q.v.), he organized an Assembly of the Peoples of the North (q.v.) that demanded his appointment as President and threatened the secession of the north.

In May 1970 a Presidential Council (q.v.) formula was agreed upon by the triumvirate, with a rotating chairmanship. Maga, as the potential victor in 1970, became the first Chairman. Maga's second Presidency (1970–1972) was distinguished by lavish expenditures and the scandal of the Kovacs Affair (q.v.). In 1972 two plots-cum-mutinies rocked the regime and the October 1972 coup of Col. Kérékou (qq.v.) came shortly after Maga had handed over the chairmanship to Justin Ahomadégbé. Under house arrest since 1972, Maga and the other two civilian leaders were not released until 1981. Maga then proceeded to Paris where he remained until the democratization of Benin in 1989, when he returned to set up a party under his co-leadership.

MAHI. Ethnic group that was a prime target in the precolonial era for Dahomey's raids for slaves for the Annual Customs (q.v.). Founders of the Savalou kingdom and, ethnically, a fusion of Adja and Nagot and hence close to the Fon (qq.v.), the Mahi reside north of Abomey, between the Ouémé river and the Dassa (qq.v.) hills in isolated but protected villages. Their systematic pulverization during annual Dahomean slave raids has resulted in a general animosity towards Fon political candidates in the contemporary era.

MALI FEDERATION. Projected union of Senegal, French Soudan, Dahomey, and Upper Volta, sponsored in 1959 by Léopold Sédar Senghor, President of Senegal, and Modibo Keita, President of French Soudan. Under pressure from both France and Ivory Coast's President Félix Houphouet-Boigny (who felt isolated by the projected federation), Upper Volta and then Dahomey decided not to join the union. The latter two, together with Niger, Ivory Coast, and later Togo, formed the Counseil d l'Entente (q.v.), while Senegal and the French Soudan merged into the Mali Federation. In mid-1960 the latter collapsed and the French Soudan inherited the name of Mali.

MALLAM-IDI, ABDOULAYE. Key economic advisor to President Kérékou (q.v.) in the mid-1980's. By training and occupation a teacher of physical education, Mallam-Idi became in 1985 Kérékou's Economic Technical Advisor, and one of the few aides the latter respected and relied on. It was he who in 1986 counselled Kérékou on the inevitability of a rapprochement with Benin's conservative Francophone African neighbors, and with the West, in light of the country's economic collapse.

MAMA DJOUGOU (Colonel). A northerner from Djougou (q.v.), Mama Djougou was Chief-of-Staff of the Benin armed forces (q.v.) between 1982 and 1991, and Commander of the Kandi (q.v.) garrison.

MAMAN, YACOUBA (Captain). Former key Kérékou (q.v.) military supporter, head of the country's Secret Service—Service de Documentation et d'Information (q.v.)—reporting directly to Kérékou.

MAMIE BENZ. Popular nickname for the "mamies" (rich women traders) who have attained the pinnacle of success, a Mercedes Benz car. The term is especially applied to those mamies engaged in textile sales.

MANASSE, AYIYI see AYIYI, MANASSE

MANKO, AYITE. Beninois poet.

MANUFACTURE BENINOISE DES CYCLES (MABECY). Mixed-economy bicycle-assembly plant in Cotonou (q.v.).

MARO. Strangers' quarters in north Dahomey towns. Also known as Wangara or Zongo (qq.v.).

MAROIX, JEAN EUGENE PIERRE, 1867–1942. Colonial officer. Born on March 4, 1867, in Teret, France, and commissioned in 1893, Maroix served in various capacities in Madagascar and Senegal before being dispatched to Dahomey in 1914 to help quell the Holli (q.v.) rebellions. Later he transported his battalion by rail to Savé (q.v.) and across Dahomey to German Togo and the powerful Kamina radio transmitters, leading to the collapse of the German administration in that colony. Promoted to Lieutenant Colonel in 1915, he was later named military commander of Togo. He died in Nice in July 1942.

MARSHALL, THOMAS JOSEPH, 1830–1899. Early Protestant evangelist and architect of the Methodist Church in Dahomey. Born in 1830 to an important fetishist (q.v.) family in Badagry, near Porto Novo (q.v.), Marshall was supposed to become a fetishist priest. However, he was converted to Christianity in 1846 after attending a missionary school on his own and resisting attempts by his parents to cure him of this "disease." Accepted into the Christian ministry, Marshall worked in Porto Novo, continuing the preliminary work of Thomas Birch Freeman (q.v.), founder of the Methodist Church in Dahomey. Under Marshall's direction, a number of missionary schools were set up in Porto Novo and evangelization was given a serious impetus. He personally translated portions of the Bible into Goun (q.v.). Marshall died in Porto Novo in 1899.

MARTINEZ, DOMINGO. A Brazilian slave trader (qq.v.) who was one of the most successful dealers along the coast in the 1740's and 1750's. With the opening of trade between the Dahomey Kingdom (q.v.) and European dealers in Ouidah (q.v.), his influence waned. Some of his descendants still play an important role in the economic life of Benin and Togo.

MAWU-LISSA CULT. Vodon cult, of Yoruba (qq.v.) origins—similar to that of Odudua and Obatala—introduced in ancient Dahomey at the time of King Agaja (q.v.). Conceived of as a pair of twins (Mawu, female and Lissa, male) symbolizing the moon, west, night; and the sky, east, sun, and day, respectively, and/or the duality of the world in general. Mawu and Lissa are the creators of the world, whose children—iron, earth, thunder, lightning, etc—form part of the extensive vodon pantheon.

MEDEIROS, FRANCOIS DE, 1941– . Historian. Born on April 29, 1941, and with a diploma in history, Medeiros teaches at the National University of Benin (q.v.).

MEHU. Second most important official in the former Dahomey Kingdom after the Migan (qq.v.), the Mehu traditionally sat on the left of the monarch and in time of war commanded the left wing of the army. He was in charge of protocol and administration of the Court and, immediately after the conquests of new territories, was in charge of their integration into the kingdom and interim administration. The Yevogan of Ouidah (qq.v.) reported directly to him. A similar official was to be found in the Porto Novo kingdom and in many of the other Adja (qq.v.) kingdoms along the coast.

MEKPON, SOHINGBE. Successor to the Porto Novo throne after the death of King Toffa (qq.v.), but denied his throne by the French administration. On King Toffa's death in 1908 the French named his brother, Adjiki, as Superior Chief, honoring a promise made to Toffa (in exchange for which he had signed the Protectorate agreement with France) to appoint chiefs only from his lineage. On Adjiki's death in 1913 Mékpon's candidacy—based on the accepted traditional rotational principle—was again denied. His cause was advocated by most of Porto Novo's Yoruba and by Louis Hunkanrin (qq.v.). Mékpon was nevertheless expelled from Dahomey (his residence was across the border in Nigeria), and the throne, by now symbolic, was retained by the Toffa lineage. Its succession was challenged in subsequent years as well.

MEKROU RIVER. A 250-kilometer long tributary of the Niger river (q.v.). Originating north of Kouandé (q.v.) it joins the Niger opposite Boumba in Niger.

MENAGER, ERNEST MARIE, 1848–1912. First Apostolic Vicar of Dahomey. Born in Vitre in 1848, and joining the Missions Africaines de Lyon, Menager was ordained in 1871. He worked in Porto Novo, Agoué (qq.v.) and

Abeokuta (Nigeria) and was named head of the church in the new Dahomean subdivision in 1883. Not very popular with the other missionaries in the colony, Menager was nevertheless supported by his superiors in France.

MENSAH, ANTOINE-BEAUCLAIR, 1916 – . Early political militant. Born in Adjaha on August 10, 1916, to an important "Brazilian" (q.v.) family, and educated locally, Mensah was active in a variety of low-level administrative posts in his home canton of Grand Popo (q.v.). With the political reforms after the Second World War, Mensah became very active in the political committees that were the origin of the political parties (q.v.) in the country, and in 1952 he was elected Deputy from Athiémé on the PRD (q.v.) ticket. He was then reelected and served in the National Assembly (q.v.) through 1965. He was the Assembly's Secretary between 1952 and 1959 and Vice-President of the Social Affairs Commission between 1957 and 1963. After the 1965 coup d'etat (q.v.) Mensah withdrew to local politics.

MENSAH, MOISE CHRISTOPHE, 1934– . International administrator. Born on march 22, 1934, in Sassandra (Ivory Coast) and educated as an agricultural engineer, Mensah obtained his degrees from Grignon and The Hague's Institute of Social Studies (diploma) and, later, from the School of Banking in Paris, completing an unusually variegated academic preparation. He served for a year as Minister of Rural Development and Cooperation (December 1965–December 1966) at the same time as his regular appointment as head of SONADER (q.v.). A southerner, Mensah resigned from General Soglo's (q.v.) cabinet over the latter's shift to a northern bias after 1966. In 1967 he left Dahomey to serve as regional representative (Africa) on the Rome-based FAO, with headquarters in Accra, Ghana. In 1970 he was promoted to FAO's Assistant Director-General in Africa (also based in Accra), and in 1978 was named Assistant President of the International Fund for Agricultural Development based in Rome. With the liberalization of politics in Benin in 1989 Mensah returned home and ran as a candidate in the Presidential elections of 1991 (q.v.).

MENSAH, NATHANAEL. Minister of Labor and Social Affairs between August 1984 and 1989.

MERCENARY ASSAULT ON COTONOU, 16 JANUARY 1977. A mercenary attack on Cotonou airport aimed at toppling the regime of Kérékou (q.v.). Engineered by Zinsou (q.v.) and other elements from abroad, the attack fizzled out despite its complete surprise and the absence of any resistance. After a few hours of haphazard firing in the air and looting the mercenary force, including Europeans and some Africans, flew away unscathed, leaving a dozen Beninois civilian and military dead and some $28 million worth of damage, which Benin tried to recover from France, Gabon, Morocco and other countries that were directly or indirectly involved in the attempted putsch. Relations with Gabon (where the plot was hatched, and where the French mercenary leader, Bob Denard, was based) in particular plummeted, leading to the latter's mass expulsion of all Beninois from the country. The force had been trained in the outskirts of Marakesh (Morocco) and received funds for its two planes from French sources. Codenamed Omega, details on the assault were obtained from several Africans left behind when the force withdrew, including Ba Alpha Oumara (q.v.). Later Zinsou's role in financing the plot was downgraded and Gratien Pognon (q.v.) (Ambassador to the EEC at the time of the 1972 Revolution) was given prime responsibility for the plot aimed at bringing him to power. On May 24, 1979, the Benin National Revolutionary Court formally condemned to death in absentia all those involved in the 1977 plot, including Zinsou, Denard, 60 European and 38 African mercenaries.

MESSE, KING (1752–1757) OF PORTO NOVO. One of the first kings to expand the dominions of the nascent Kingdom of Porto Novo (q.v.) into the Ouémé river valley with the assistance of the first rifles to reach Porto Novo. Messé organized the slave trade (q.v.) in his kingdom and clashed with Dahomey's King Tegbesu (qq.v.).

METHODIST MISSIONS see FREEMAN, THOMAS BIRCH; MARSHALL, THOMAS JOSEPH; PROTESTANT MISSIONS.

MIDAHOUEN, CLAUDE, 1928– . Senior accountant. Born in Cotonou (q.v.) on November 28, 1928, and trained as an accountant, Midahouén has served in a variety of senior posts within the State sector in Benin, notably as comptroller of SONADER (q.v.) since 1963, comptroller of the Port of Cotonou (1963–1968) and Director of Fiscal Accounts in the Ministry of Finance, also since 1963. Between 1963 and 1972 he also served as comptroller of SNAHDA (q.v.). In 1972 he left the country.

MIGAN. In the former kingdoms of both Dahomey and Porto Novo (qq.v.), the Migan was the chief minister of the kingdom, frequently with religious functions, a hereditary, lifetime appointment, and one of the most important. In the Dahomean Kingdom the Migan sat on the right side of the King and in battle commanded the right wing of the armies. The Migan played an important role in selecting a new King and also had religious and judicial functions (see also MEHU). Sorou-Migan Apithy's (q.v.) middle name signifies descent from the Porto Novo Migans, though in his case the link is distant if not spurious.

MIGAN, ALBERT MAX, 1923– . Administrator. Born in Porto Novo (q.v.) on August 4, 1923, and a graduate of the Ecole William Ponty (q.v.) (1943) and IHEOM (1960), Migan has served in a variety of administrative posts in Benin. He was *sous-préfet* of Sakété immediately upon his return from IHEOM training (1960–1962), followed by a similar appointment in Natitingou (q.v.) (1962–1963). In 1963 he became Director of Justice in the Ministry of Justice, followed by an appointment as *sous-préfet* of Adjohon (1964–1965) and Deputy-Prefect of Cotonou (q.v.) (1965–1966). In 1966 he was promoted to the post of Inspector of Administrative Affairs and, in 1968, assumed the post of Inspector General of Administrative Affairs, remaining in that position until 1973. In 1973 Migan became Senior Technical Consultant at the Ministry of Interior until his retirement in 1980.

MILITARY DIRECTORATE. Three-man ruling body created in the aftermath of Col. Maurice Kouandété's 1969 coup (qq.v.). Composed of the heads of the army (Col. Kouandété), the gendarmerie (Col. Benoit Sinzogan), and the Department of National Defense (Col. Paul Emile De Souza) (qq.v.), under the chairmanship of the most senior of the three, Colonel De Souza. The Military Directorate in effect boxed in the aggressive ambitions of Kouandété and paved the way for the civilian elections of 1970 (q.v.) and the Presidential Council (q.v.) administration of 1970–1972. See also COUP OF 1969.

MILITIA. The People's Militia, Section III of the reorganized Forces Armées du Benin (q.v.) under Revolutionary Benin, was the civilian armed branch of the Revolution, charged with very hazy, ill-defined "special" assignments. Though organizational charts assigned the militia a key role linking the masses with the professional armed forces, in reality the militia was highly disorganized and largely inactive.

MISON. Popular acronym for the "superministry"—le Ministère de l'Interieur, de la Securité et de l'Orientation Nationale— that, during the tenur of Captain Dohou Azonhiho (q.v.), dominated pronouncements and codifications of the Beninois Revolution. The term was often used pejoratively to refer to the pompousness of the ministry.

MISSION PERMANENTE D'AIDE ET DE COOPERATION. Permanent office of the French Technical Assistance Mission, in Cotonou (q.v.). The office, administratively separate from the French Embassy, monitors appeals for bilateral aid, approves in principle projects and monitors the effort of French coopérants in the country.

MITO-BABA TOHOSSOUSSI, KOOVI FLORENTIN, 1938– . Highly regarded technocrat and current Minister of Public Works and Transport. Born around 1938 in Abomey (q.v.), and educated in France between 1957 and 1964 as an engineer, Mito-Baba Tohossoussi was Head of the Division of Studies on Roads and Bridges (1965–1970), then Head of General Studies of Public Works (1971–1974) and Director of Roads and Bridges (1974–1975) in the Ministry of Public

Works. He then served two years in the Ministry of the Plan's Central Office, was Deputy Director General of the Ministry of the Plan between 1977–1978, and Director General between 1979–1982. He then served two years as Head of the Habitat Service at SONAGIM, and was Director of Land Transport between 1985–1988. In 1988 he was named Director of the Office of Studies of the Port of Cotonou (q.v.), and between 1990–1991 Director General of the Port itself. After Nicéphore Soglo's (q.v.) rise to power in 1991 Mito-Baba Tohossoussi was named Minister of Public Works and Transport.

MOKOLLE. A series of clans of Yoruba origin found in small numbers in the Borgou that participated in the formation of the Bariba state of Kouandé (qq.v.). They are also found east and north in Kandi (q.v.).

MONDJANNAGNI, COMLAN ALFRED, 1931– . Deputy Secretary-General of the Pan African Institute for Development. Born on October 6, 1931, educated in geography in Abidjan and Dakar, and with a Ph.D. (1969) from France, Mondjannagni is the author of an acclaimed book on south Benin. His current post is based in Buéa, Cameroun.

MONO. One of Dahomey's provinces with administrative headquarters in Lokossa and encompassing the sub-prefectures of Athiémé, Aplahoué, Bopa, and Grand Popo (q.v.). Its 1992 population of 521,221 is mostly composed of Adja (q.v.), Mina, Pedah (q.v.) and Aizo (q.v.).

MONO RIVER. A 35-kilometer-long river originating in and flowing mostly in Togo, emptying in Grand Popo (q.v.) into the Gulf of Guinea. Navigable for some 100 kilometers upstream to Togodo, the river forms, for 125 kilometers, part of the Benin-Togo border.

MONO RIVER PROJECT. Joint Benino-Togolese cooperation in the development of the resources of the Mono river (q.v.) region that forms part of the boundary between the two countries. On January 31, 1979, an agreement was initialled approving the construction of a hydroelectric dam at Nangbéto (q.v.) that would lessen the CEB's (q.v.) dependence upon Ghanaian electricity. The dam, since completed, can generate 130 million KwH of electricity, and allows the irrigation of 42,000 hectares of land. Other dams are planned under a master plan developed by the UNDP and World Bank.

MONTEIRO, ARMAND. Former Minister. Previously a diplomat who had attained ambassadorial rank, Monteiro, who is a Fon (q.v.), joined the Kérékou (q.v.) cabinet in February 1980 as Minister of Higher Education. He was a member of the PRPB (q.v.) Politburo and Central Committee. He was the author of a collection of revolutionary poems, some written before the 1972 radicalization of politics, published by ONEPI (q.v.) in 1981.

MONTEIRO, BRUNO, 1934– . Director of the School of Nurses. Born on October 6, 1934, and trained abroad in tropical medicine, Monteiro was appointed in 1971 Coordinator of the anti-TB effort in Benin and Director of the School of Nurses of Benin based in Cotonou (q.v.).

MOUMOUNI, BASILE ADJOU see ADJOU MOUMOUNI, BASILE.

MOUVEMENT BENINOIS POUR LA LIBERTE ET LA DEMOCRATIE (MBLD). Underground movement that sprung up within Benin to reverse the 1972 coup d'etat (q.v.). Some of the conspirators of 1987 were members of the MBLD.

MOUVEMENT DE LA RENOVATION DU DAHOMEY (MRD). Clandestine movement, based in Paris and with membership in Togo, Benin (clandestine) and Gabon. It was headed by Gratien Pognon (q.v.) and other personalities who refused to acknowledge the Marxist regime of Kérékan (q.v.).

MOUVEMENT DE LIBERATION NATIONAL (MLN). Porto Novo (q.v.)-based, short-lived, left-leaning political party.

Established in 1958 by Albert Tévóedjré and Jean Pliya (qq.v.), the party, being ideological and bereft of traditional sources of support, appealed to few but intellectuals and students. In 1960 the MLN leadership joined the traditionalist parties they had opposed in the past to form the Parti Dahoméen de l'Unité (q.v.). Although Tévoédjré received a cabinet post in the new government, he became disenchanted shortly after and resigned.

MOUVEMENT DEMOCRATIQUE DAHOMEEN (MDD). Political party of the Bariba (q.v.) north, an outgrowth of the 1951–1952 Groupement Ethnique du Nord (GEN) (q.v.) that coalesced behind the leadership of Hubert Maga (q.v.) Originally affiliated with the Indépendants d'Outre Mer, in 1958 the MDD—which in August 1957 had changed its name to Rassemblement Démocratique Dahoméen—merged with Sourou-Migan Apithy's Parti Républicain Dahoméen (PRD) to form the Parti Progréssiste Dahoméen (PPD) (qq.v.), the Dahomean section of Senegal President Senghor's interterritorial party, the Parti du Regroupement Africain (PRA) (q.v.). Disagreements between the PPD leadership, and between the latter and PRA headquarters, led to a schism in the PPD with Hubert Maga's faction opting out in 1959.

Always a congeries of powerful local leaders and nobility with limited fiefdoms in the north, the MDD and its successor the PDD were continuously beset by rifts. Thus the historic Nikki-Parakou (qq.v.) friction plagued the northern leadership during the formation of the GEN, predecessor of the MDD. The opposition of Dendi notables to Bariba (qq.v.) leadership also affected the MDD's unity and a number of challenges to Maga's leadership translated themselves, especially in Djougou (q.v.), into the form of splinter parties. Among the most important of the latter was the Indépendants du Nord (q.v.) led by Djougou's Paul Darboux (q.v.), which cooperated with Sourou-Migan Apithy's PRD. Moreover, historic friction between the former Bariba kingdoms allowed Justin Ahomadégbé's Union Démocratique Dahoméenne (q.v.) to gain local blocs of votes in the north, especially in the Kouandé (q.v.) region.

MOUVEMENT DEMOCRATIQUE REPUBLICAIN (MDR). Political party set up in 1989 by Joseph Kéké (q.v.). In May 1990 the MDR merged with Justin Ahomadégbé's FND to form the RND party, part of the broad political front RFD (qq.v.).

MOUVEMENT NATIONAL POUR LA DEMOCRATIE ET LE DEVELOPPEMENT (MNDD). A Left-of-center power formation set up in 1990 as the political vehicle of the popular northern leader Bertin Borna (q.v.).

MOUVEMENT POUR LA LIBERTE ET LE DEVELOPPEMENT SOCIAL (MLDS). Southern political party under the leadership of Marcelin Dégbé that joined in 1991 in a parliamentary alliance—the UTR (q.v.)—in support of the Soglo (q.v.) Presidency.

MOUVEMENT SOCIALISTE AFRICAIN (MSA). Dahomean section of the interterritorial party of the same name. Established in 1957 and headed by Flavien Campbell and Hyacinthe de Silva, the party, appealing only to intellectuals and students, had little effect on Dahomean politics and withered away shortly after it was officially founded.

-N-

NA WANJILE (d. 1797). The assassin of King Agonglo (q.v.) of Dahomey. A member of the opposing faction that violently opposed the adoption of Christianity, demanded by Portuguese traders along the coast as a precondition to expanded trade, Na Wanjilé was buried alive with other members of her faction after the murder of Agonglo.

NAGOT (also NAGO). Benin's Yoruba (q.v.) population is locally called Nagot (or Nago). They are to be found especially in Ketou (qq.v.), in the Fon/Mahi (qq.v.) country (Savé), north of Abomey (q.v.), and in Porto Novo (qq.v.) where they are mixed with the heavily Yoruba-influenced Goun (q.v.). Yoruba elements are also found in smaller numbers in the northern provinces. Many of the Porto Novo Nagot are Muslim. Like the Fon, Benin's Nagot have been highly upwardly mobile and have played an important role in the country's economy and administration. Politically the Nagot have been allied in the past with the Goun to support the Presidential candidacies of Sourou-Migan Apithy (q.v.).

NANGBETO DAM. Important dam and hydro-electric complex on the Mono river (q.v.), a joint Benin-Togo project built with funds approved by CCCE (q.v.) in mid-1984 and inaugurated in 1988. The total cost of the project was 34 billion CFA francs. The dam allows regulation of water flow on the Mono, in the past causing flooding in both Benin and Togo, and the production of up to 150 kWh of electricity for the CEB (q.v.). See also COMMUNAUTE ELECTRIQUE DU BENIN; MONO RIVER PROJECT.

NATA, THEOPHILE, 1947– . Minister of Foreign Affairs. Born in 1947 in Sinkouatahei and educated in Natitingou and Ouidah (qq.v.), Nata studied at Togo's university, University of Abidjan and the Sorbonne between 1967–1976 obtaining degrees, including a doctorate in comparative literature. In 1977 he joined the National University of Benin (q.v.) teaching literature and linguistics, in 1978 concurrently also Head of the Asia Desk at the Foreign Ministry. In 1982 he was appointed Ambassador to Algeria, serving in that capacity until 1988. In 1988 he was shifted to become Ambassador to the USA. In 1990 he became Foreign Minister of Benin. He is the author of numerous linguistic studies.

[LA] NATION. The post-May 1990 name of the government daily newspaper *Ehuzu,* itself previously *Daho-Express* and *l'Aube Nouvelle* (qq.v.). *La Nation* was unable to compete effectively with the multitude of newspapers that emerged when press freedom arrived in 1990, went bankrupt and closed down.

NATIONAL ASSEMBLY see ASSEMBLEE NATIONALE.

NATIONAL CONFERENCE (or CONFERENCE DES FORCES VIVES). The National Conference of the Active Forces of the Nation was a nine day conference that opened on February 19, 1990, and ushered in democratization, contrary to Kérékou's (q.v.) original intent of a tamer meeting to discuss Benin's burning economic issues. Robert Dossou was Chairman of the Organizing Committee. Between 488 and 524 delegates participated in the Conference that was broadcast live on radio and TV. Membership originally was determined rather strictly, but eventually made more flexible so that all the "living forces of Benin" were represented, including groups the regime had sought to completely exclude at the outset. The government sent 22 members; the Assemblée Nationál Revolutionnaire (q.v.) 13; the PRPB (q.v.) 15; the military dispatched 21 participants; the trade unions (q.v.) 36; non-government parties were allowed 2 delegates each; the exiled community 25; the university 14, etc.

On the 21st the Conference declared its sovereignty with the power to set up a commission to draft a new constitution, dismiss the existing national assembly, appoint an interim Prime Minister and release all political prisoners including the military mutineers of 1987. Only the persuasive skills of the Archbishop of Cotonou, Isidore de Souza (q.v.), and pressure from France prevented the military from disbanding the Conference and reverting to the status quo ante. A new interim government ensued with Nicéphore Soglo (q.v.) as Prime Minister; the latter appointment was again a slap in the face of Kérékou who had preferred Adrien Houngbédji (q.v.). Indeed Kérékou's own interim leadership during the transition was only reluctantly agreed to, and not by all the delegates. Soglo was later to defeat Kérékou in the 1991 Presidential elections (q.v.).

NATIONAL UNIVERSITY OF BENIN see UNIVERSITE NATIONALE DU BENIN

NATITINGOU. Northern garrison town and administrative capital of the Atakora (q.v.) province. Natitingou is the home town of Hubert Maga, Col. Maurice Kouandété, and General Mathieu Kérékou (qq.v.), and is in an area populated by the Somba (q.v.) ethnic group, which benefitted most from Kérékou's long political tenure (1972–1990). For this reason the town scored some socioeconomic advances, including agro-industry, and in 1986 the opening of an ultra-modern hospital. The name of the town is a corruption of the words Nanto (name of the original founder) and Tinngou (village, country). The area is north Benin's major tourist attraction due to the unique building style of the Somba (see SOMBATATA) and is on the main dry-season route to the "W" wildlife park and the Penjari National Park, (see PARC NATIONAL), both straddling the Dahomey-Burkina Faso border. The population of Natitingou shot up since the 1972 coup (q.v.), with the first serious and sustained development of the region. Its population is currently estimated at 60,000, making Natitingou—a sleepy village in the 1960's—Benin's fourth-largest town. As recently as 1972 it had ranked seventh.

NEHAM, ROCH, 1929– . Chemist and early Apithy (q.v.) supporter. Born in Porto Novo (q.v.) on September 10, 1929, and educated in Paris where he worked for some time (1953–1956) as a chemist. On his return to Dahomey, Neham became Secretary-General to the Mayor of Porto Novo (q.v.) (1957–1960) and was a major supporter of Sourou-Migan Apithy. He served as Secretary of the PND between March and November 1960, and Deputy Treasurer of the PDU after November 1960, in charge also of the PDU youth activities and branches. He served as Apithy's Cabinet Director between 1960 and 1962 and, after the latter's eclipse, departed for Yaoundé, Cameroun, where he served as Director of the Foreign Commerce section of the OAMCE.

N'GOMA, EUGENE, 1945– . Linguist. Born on July 9, 1945, and educated at the University of Bordeaux, where he obtained degrees in English, N'Goma joined the National University of Benin (q.v.) where he is now Deputy-Head of the Department of English and Head of the Department of Foreign Languages.

NICOUE, URBAIN, 1924– . Publisher and former Minister. Born in Cotonou (q.v.) on October 29, 1924, and with a degree in journalism (1948), Nicoué is a prominent Cotonou publisher today. At independence, he also served as a member of the Commission of Finance of the Conséil

Général of the South, and as the latter's President between 1959 and 1965. Technical consultant with the Ministry of Finance in 1959–1960, he was also briefly Minister of Information and Tourism between 1968 and 1969.

NIGER RIVER. Africa's third-longest river, rising in Guinea's Fouta Djallon highlands and spiraling in a great half circle that passes through Mali, Niger, Burkina Faso, Benin and Nigeria, and empties in the Atlantic Ocean. The Niger's length is 4,200 kilometers and its drainage basin is 1.5 million square kilometers. During the colonial scramble for territories in Africa the northern Nigerian part of the river was subject to intense Anglo-French competition. A small portion of the river forms the boundary between Benin and Niger with Malanville on the Benin side, the main crossing point on the Cotonou-Niamey axis. One of the Niger river's half-submerged islands (Lété) was in 1964 the cause of friction between the two countries. See also DAHOMEY-NIGER BOUNDARY DISPUTE.

NIKKI. Traditional center of Benin's Bariba in the Borgou (qq.v.) province. Established by Sunon Séro (q.v.) at the end of the fourteenth century after a dynastic feud in Bussa (q.v.)—see KISIRA—Nikki is the parent state of the other Bariba kingdoms in Benin and second in the traditional hierarchy, after Bussa (q.v.) and its dependencies in Nigeria. Prior to the French occupation, the Nikki dynasty numbered 28 kings. After a sharp nineteenth-century defeat of Bariba cavalry—allied to the Yoruba against Ilorin and Muslim encroachments (see SERO KPERA ILORINKPUNON)—Nikki suffered major secessions and rivalries as Parakou, Kouandé, and Kandi (qq.v.) declared their independence. Following the French occupation, Nikki—which was the subject of intense Anglo-French rivalry—found itself geographically at the extremity of the new colony and hence away from the emerging modern commercial routes. Partly for this reason, Nikki was administratively subordinated to Parakou, its former commercial rival, political vassal and ethnic inferior (due to Parakou's mixture of ethnicities). In 1911, contrary to a custom forbidding him to do so, the king of Nikki was compelled to travel to Parakou to greet Governor General William Ponty. This was regarded by the Wasangari (q.v.) as a major humiliation and fueled Bariba grievances that erupted with the rebellions in the Borgou several years later (see UPRISINGS OF 1915–1918). Currently Nikki is a small town connected by a dirt road to Benin's main north-south axis. Though Nikki's traditional importance has been eroded, it is still sufficient to assure that all northern candidates seeking election pay their ritual respects to the head of this former state.

NIKKI-WENU. The old sanctuary and sacred quarter of Nikki (q.v.), traditional parent state of the Bariba (q.v.) of Benin. Its royal tombs (including that of Sunon Séro [q.v.], founder of Nikki) and ritual centers are located here, seven kilometers from Nikki proper, and are venerated on ceremonial occasions, especially when a new king is enthroned. At Wooré, seven kilometers from Nikki on the Péréré road, is the site where Nikki's Woru-Tokura resided, the village currently inhabited solely by a caste of royal griots who communicate in a secret dialect. See also NIKKI.

NOKOUE, LAKE. Southern lagoon by oral tradition formed by Chango (the deity of punishment) who razed a fetishist's house and the surrounding forests to create the lake. The name is a composite of *"non"* which is mother and *"kue"* which is house, referring to the incident.

NOTRE CAUSE COMMUNE (NCC). Political party set up by Albert Tévoéjdré (q.v.) that tried to obtain political support for his candidacy in 1990–1992 from the northern prefectures.

NOUDEHOU, MICHEL, 1897–1968. Educator and early political militant. Born in Adjaha in 1897, and an independent schoolmaster of a local school of some repute, Noudehou was part of the powerful Athiémé political group that coalesced behind the PRD (q.v.) ticket in that region. He was elected to the Assemblée Territorial (q.v.) in 1952 and remained the Athiémé Deputy until the 1963 coup (q.v.), serving on the Assembly as its Vice-President between 1957 and 1959.

NOUFFLARD, CHARLES, 1872–1936. Former Governor of Dahomey. Born on September 7, 1872, Noufflard became Governor of Dahomey in 1912 after serving in similar high posts in Congo, Gabon and the New Hebrides. His period of administration saw the construction of the Cotonou-Porto (qq.v.) Novo railroad as well as major road and infrastructure building. On the other hand, the eruption of the First World War and France's strict demands on its colonies sparked serious rebellions in Dahomey during Noufflard's administration. The Holli in 1914, the Bariba in 1916 and the Somba (qq.v.) in 1917 took up arms over the taxation, military conscription and porterage demands enforced by Noufflard. His harsh punitive expeditions raised a hue and cry until Noufflard was finally recalled to Paris in 1917 in full disgrace, to retire in 1925.

NOUVELLE REPUBLIQUE. Coalition of parties controlling 21 seats forged in support of President Nicéphore Soglo. (q.v.) The coalition was formed when the original pro-Soglo UTR (q.v.) of 12 deputies was joined by nine additional ones from other parties. In mid-1993 the alliance was jointed by an additional ones from other parties. In mid-1993 the alliance was jointed by an additional 13 members (six ex-Convergence, seven ex-USD) and it changed its name to Le Rénouveau (q.v.).

NTCHA, JEAN (Major). Kérékou (q.v.) loyalist from the latter's home village, who was rapidly promoted within the Presidential Guard until assuming its command in 1988.

NUCLEAR WASTE AFFAIR. Major scandal that came into the open in 1988. The fiscally hard-pressed Kérékou (q.v.) regime signed a 30-year contract with France to dispose of French nuclear waste in Benin, and a similar offer from a Gibraltar firm was also accepted. The terms of the deals were extremely disadvantageous to Benin—$2.50 per ton compared to the $40 per ton, for example, that Guinea-Bissau was able to secure. On top of this the Kérékou regime planned to bury the highly toxic waste in the densely populated area of Abomey, perceived by the Fon as the ultimate plot of the northerners to eliminate them through nuclear poisoning. The widespread publicity generated by this affair led to the cancellation of the contracts.

-O-

ODOULAMI, HONORE, 1941– . Physician. Born in 1941 and obtaining an M.D. with specialization in surgical pathology, Odoulami teaches Medicine at the National University of Benin (q.v.) and is Dean of the School of Health Sciences.

OFFICE BENINOIS D'AMENAGEMENT RURAL (OBAR). State organ set up on May 1984 under the Ministry of Rural Development and headed by Zachary Saloufou. Capitalized at 500 million CFA francs, OBAR took over some of the functions of the financially ailing SONAGRI and SO-BEPALH (q.v.). It was charged with promoting agricultural projects in the countryside alongside the provincial CARDER's, and especially developing a comprehensive system of hydroagriculture. Originally set up in 1982 under a slightly different name, OBAR's functions were redefined in 1984. Like SONAGRI and SOBEPALH, and other parastatals, OBAR ran up major deficits and was liquidated in 1987.

OFFICE BENINOIS DES ARTS (OBA). Segment of the Ministry of Alphabetization and Popular Culture charged with encouraging the traditional arts and assisting in the marketing of local output abroad and, through several outlets for tourists, at home. The structure was very costly and its activities were closed down in the mid-1980's.

OFFICE BENINOIS DES MANUTENTIONS PORTUAIRES (OBEMAP). State organ, attached to the Ministry of Transportation and Communications, with a monopoly over loading and unloading of ships in the port of Cotonou (q.v.).

OFFICE BENINOIS DES MINES (OBEMINES). State organization under the Ministry of Industry, Mines and Energy, responsible for monitoring all mining activities in Benin and assisting in the requests for development capital for new mining projects. One project of OBEMINES was the reactivation of mining of the modest gold ore deposits in the Perma river area.

OFFICE D'APPROVISIONNEMENT DE L'ETAT (OAE). . State organization set up in 1974 to serve as a clearing house and supply agency for the office needs of the State sector in Benin. Its activities were wound down in 1987.

OFFICE DE COMMERCIALISATION AGRICOLE DU DAHOMEY (OCAD) see SOCIETE DE COMMERCIALISATION ET DE CREDIT AGRICOLE DAHOMEENNE (SOCAD)

OFFICE DE LA RADIODIFFUSION ET DE TELEVISION DU BENIN (ORTB). State communications agency under Director General Lucien Maghonkou that until 1990 operated the "Voix de la Révolution" (q.v.) station. ORTB offered radio broadcasts in French, English and 18 local languages, and seven hours of TV weekly, in three languages.

OFFICE NATIONAL DE CEREALES (ONC). State organ set up in 1984 to regularize marketing, assure stable prices and organize the export to neighboring countries of surplus cereals grown by Benin. The ONC had 7,000 tons of storage space that it planned to expand to a total of 35,000 tons. The ONC's storage needs were given high priority because the previous three maize harvests in Ouéme (q.v.) were largely devoured by predators.

OFFICE NATIONAL DE LA PHARMACIE (ONP). State organ under the Ministry of Public Health with a total monopoly over all purchases, sales and imports of pharmaceuticals in Benin, aiming to facilitate marketing and distribution. The office piled up significant deficits through high overheads, and was also systematically looted by its directors and staff. Totally bankrupt, it was closed down in 1987.

OFFICE NATIONAL D'EDITION, DE PRESSE ET D'IM-PRIMERIE (ONEPI). State publishing and printing office. Founded in 1975 to replace a previous organ, its headquarters were in Cotonou (q.v.) and it was headed by Director General Laléyé Abiodun.

OFFICE NATIONAL DU BOIS (ONAB). State organ set up in 1983 to develop the timber industry and resources in Benin and to tackle the problem of deforestation going on from precolonial days. ONAB supervised the planting of new commercial species, including some 7,000 hectares mostly with teak.

OFFICE NATIONAL DU TOURISME ET DE L'HOTELLERIE (ONATHO). State company with headquarters in Cotonou (q.v.) and in 1984 capitalized at 275 million CFA francs. ONATHO assumed in 1974 the role of sole renter of cars to tourists, organizer of tourist circuits, manager of hotels and promoter of arts and crafts for the tourist trade. After the mass nationalization of hotels in Benin in 1974, ONATHO became responsible for the operation of hotels including the Hotel Croix du Sud, Hotel de la Plage, Hotel du Port (always national) and Hotel Dana, as well as several camping places. Later the Benin Sheraton and the Hotel Aledjo came under ONATHO's wing.

ONATHO was specifically charged with setting up tourist facilities wherever they did not exist, especially hotels "more in accord with socialist revolutionary principles" (defined as "for the masses"). Since the masses did not engage in intercontinental globe-trotting, part of ONATHO's mission was always in dispute and was even the subject of debate at cabinet level, the result of which was the (1982) Sheraton hotel. The latter, together with the Aledjo (ex-OCAM Village) greatly boosted the country's tourist capacity, adding 350 rooms to the existing 300 international class rooms, with a further expansion to 900 rooms (quadrupling the 1972 capacity) by 1986. The "socialist" principles were maintained via moderate rates: the Sheraton commenced operations with suites priced at less than 15,000 CFA francs ($50).

ONATHO has also expanded Abomey's (q.v.) tourist facilities from six to 30 rooms, constructed Dassa-Zoumé's first (30-room) hotel, doubled Parakou's (q.v.) tourist capacity and developed those in Natitingou (q.v.) to international levels. A project to develop a Club Méditerranée village at Zoungbodji-Kpavi, however, did not materialize.

OGAN BADA, BARNABE, 1935– . Former civil servant. Born in Cotonou (q.v.) in 1935, and a graduate of Law Schools, Ogan Bada was with the Ministry of Economics and Finance in a variety of capacities until assuming the post of Director of Taxes and Registrations in November 1968. Since 1973 Ogan Bada has been outside the country.

O'GOUMA, SIMON IFEDE. Former Minister and key member of the Ligue (q.v.). A radical economist in the Ministry of Economics and Finance, O'Gouma had been administrator of SNAHDA (q.v.) and Director of Statistics in the Ministry between 1967 and 1972. Following the 1972 coup d'etat (q.v.), he became co-leader of the radical Ligue, and, in February 1980 was appointed Foreign Minister. His tenure was only two years as the financially hard-strapped regime found it expedient to moderate its international stance and rhetoric. O'Gouma was also regarded as intrinsically more concerned with ideological purity than with loyalty to Kérékou (q.v.). With the eclipse he reverted back to his old post in the Ministry of Economics and Finance, but was soon appointed Ambassador to the United Nations. In August 1988 he was reintegrated in the cabinet as Minister of the Plan and Statistics until the end of the Marxist option and the Kérékou reign swept him out of office.

OGOUNDELE-TESSI, JEAN, 1927– . Librarian and political militant. Born on 28 September 1927 in Porto Novo (q.v.), to a mercantile family (and grand-daughter of the Chief Fetish-ist of Porto Novo), Ogoundélé-Tessi completed his studies at home before proceeding to Ivory Coast for further schooling. He worked as a schoolteacher between 1946 and 1951 and then principal until 1961. In 1961 he was the co-founder of the militant Mouvément de Libération Nationale (q.v.), though nothing came of the latter party. Between 1962 and 1963 he studied librarianship in Paris and upon his return to Porto Novo was named librarian of the new National University of Benin (q.v.). Since 1968 he has also been its Registrar. Ogoudélé-Tessi has also written and published several songs and poems in Goun (q.v.), Mina, and French. He retired in 1987.

OHOUENS, BARTHELEMY (General), 1930– . Former Minister and head of the gendarmerie (q.v.). Born in Porto Novo (q.v.) on February 15, 1930, of Goun (q.v.) origins, and educated at the University of Paris (in criminology) and at the Melun Ecole Supérièure, on his return home Ohouéns was appointed Commander of the Mobile Gendarmerie and technical consultant to the Minister of Interior (June 1966–January 1967). He first entered the political limelight when he was appointed to the Comité Militaire Révolutionnaire (q.v.) and became Minister of Interior and Security in the interim military government of Col. Alphonse Alley and Major Maurice Kouandéte (qq.v.) (see COUP OF 1967) in 1967–1968. In May 1968 Ohouéns was appointed Minister of Justice, returning in his military duties with the onset of the civil administration of Emile Derlin Zinsou (q.v.). In 1970 he became Deputy Chief of the Gendarmerie. Following the 1972 takeover by Col. Mathieu Kérékou (q.v.), Ohouéns was reappointed Minister of Justice and in October 1973 became Chief-of-Staff of the Gendarmerie, being promoted to Lieutenant Colonel in February 1974.

Under fire from the extreme Left for his accumulated wealth, Ohouéns resigned from the Political Bureau of the Conséil National de la Révolution (q.v.) late in 1974, shortly after he was appointed to it. Yet his role and status remained unimpaired. Indeed, he was the longest surviving member of Kérékou's regime. His capitalist, pro-French, anti-Marxist credentials were used to counterbalance the strong Left pressures on Kérékou, making him indispensable. Since

January 1976 Minister of Industry, Mines and Energy, he was promoted to General—together with Kérékou—in January 1982, and remained in the cabinet until 1984. Well regarded in the USA—he frequently takes his holidays in Texas—and in France, where he has a handsome house, pressures on Kérékou from the ultra-Left to remove the arch-conservative Ohouéns were not successful. Ohouéns reached mandatory retirement age in 1990 but was retained in the armed forces (q.v.) as a loyal technocrat until a complete reorganization could be affectuated by the new Soglo (q.v.) regime.

OIL. Modest off-shore oil shales were discovered near Sémé (q.v.) as early as 1968 by Union Oil of California, but they were not regarded at that time as being of sufficient size to justify exploitation. When the price of oil went up dramatically in the 1970's, the oil field became an economic proposition. In 1979 contracts were finally signed between Benin and two Norwegian companies (Union Oil having renounced its claims), and exploitation commenced in 1982 at the rate of 4,000 barrels of oil a day, rapidly increasing to around 10,000. Though the deposits are small (some 3 million tons of proven reserves, enough for ten years exploitation), they cover all of Benin's domestic needs (some 3,000 barrels a year) and provide the Beninois economy a gross income of $150,000 per day.

In August 1985 the government of Benin cancelled its contract with the Norwegian consortium, transferring the right of exploitation to the Swiss-based Pan Ocean Oil Company (PANOCO). The latter had pledged a major speed-up in pumping, to reach the rate of 25,000 barrels a day by late 1986, and joint development (with the Benin government) of refinery and fertilizer plants as well as other projects. The cancellation of the contract with the Norwegian consortium was challenged in court, however, leading to an international freeze of investments and guarantees, and PANACO also did not deliver on its original pledges, so that by the late 1980's oil production actually seriously declined rather than going up. In 1988, with output less than 4,000 barrels a day, Benin broke the impasse and appointed another developer, Ashland Oil, and production has slowly normalized. The fields currently have three wells onstream.

OKE, ASSOGBA, 1903–1973. Born in Adjohon on February 3, 1903 to a Goun-Yoruba (qq.v.) chiefly family, Oké studied at Dakar's Ecole William Ponty (q.v.), returning home as a high school instructor. Rapidly developing a personal following in the Ouémé (q.v.) region, Oké was elected to the first and second Assemblée Territoriale (q.v.) (1952–1957; 1957–1959). An early lieutenant of Sourou-Migan Apithy (q.v.) and a prominent member of the latter's Parti Républicain Dahoméen (PRD) (q.v.), Oké occupied a succession of ministerial posts in Dahomey's early governments. He served as Minister of Education and Youth (1958–1960), during which time he was also designated Vice-Prime Minister of Dahomey under Hubert Maga (q.v.) (May 1959–November 1960). From 1956 to 1961 he was also Secretary-General of the PRD and the choice of a significant section of the party to replace Apithy during the latter's temporary eclipse that year. He assumed the portfolios of Defense (November–December 1960) and Foreign Affairs (December 1960–February 1962). In February 1962 Oké was shifted to head the Ministry of Civil Service. Following the 1963 overthrow of Maga (see COUP OF 1963), Oké was arrested and imprisoned for fomenting subversion in his personal fiefdom of Ouémé aimed at restoring Maga to power. His pro-Apithy credentials tarnished by his long association with Maga, Oké did not occupy ministerial positions in the Ahomadégbé-Apithy regime (1963–1965) though he had an advisory role. In 1968 he was appointed to the Counseil Economique et Social (q.v.). He died several years later.

OKPARA. Tributary of the Ouémé river passing through Parakou (qq.v.). For about 100 kilometers the river forms the border with Nigeria.

OLAOGOUN, ADEYE BASILE, 1935– . Topographer. Born in 1935 and educated in France as a topographer, Olaogoun served as a senior surveyor in Nigeria before joining the

University of Ile-Ife as senior lecturer in the Center for Training in Aerial Survey Techniques.

OLIVIER, NICHOLAS. Early French trader in the Slave Coast. Establishing himself in Ouidah (q.v.) in 1623, Olivier acted in a variety of middleman roles for the French slave traders along the coast. He married a ''Brazilian'' (q.v.) woman and founded what were to become the Ganvé and Boya quarters of town. His descendants are the d'Oliveiras of contemporary Benin and Togo.

OLOGOUDOU, EMILE DESIRE, 1935– . Journalist and former director of ''Radio-Dahomey.'' Born in Savalou (q.v.) on June 17, 1935, and educated at home and at the University of Dakar in sociology and economics (later also at the University of Cologne) where he was involved in student movements, Ologoudou returned to Benin and served as a consultant in the Ministry of Foreign Affairs (1966–1968) before becoming government delegate to the National Lottery and Director of ''Radio-Dahomey'' in September 1968. Technical consultant to the Ministry of Information in 1972, he then launched into secondary and higher education before leaving Benin in 1978 for a career in international journalism. He is the author of several books of poems.

OMEGA. ''Force Omega'' was the code name for the mercenary assault (q.v.) on Cotonou airport in 1977.

ORGANISATION COMMUNE AFRICAINE, MALGACHE ET MAURITIENNE (OCAMM). A grouping of most of Francophone Africa, later joined by Mauritius, for purposes of economic, social and cultural cooperation. It was an indirect successor to the Brazzaville Group, the UAM—Union of African and Malagasy States—and OAMCE—Organisation Africaine et Malgache de Cooperation Economique. The organization's most successful venture to date has been the creation of Air Afrique—the multinational airline of French Africa—as well as a joint telecommunications system and cooperation on joint technical colleges. Since 1970 the organization has suffered attrition as several states have withdrawn.

ORGANISATION COMMUNE BENIN-NIGER DES CHEMINS DE FER ET DES TRANSPORTS (OCBN). Joint Benin-Niger transportation organization (formerly OCDN), founded in 1959 with a Beninois majority (63 percent) of the total shares. OCBN's main activity is running the railroad from Cotonou to Parakou (qq.v.) and the Parakou-Niamey transshipment by trucks of goods destined for Niger. The OCBN is for Niger the country's main, and preferred, outlet to the sea, except for peanut exports that go via Nigeria. Indeed between 73–81 percent of the OCBN cargo traffic is imports for Niger arriving at Cotonou. (See COTONOU, PORT OF.) The Cotonou-Parakou line is 438 kilometers long. Laying track over the remaining 500-kilometer section to the Niger border (at Malanville) has been projected for decades, with some international commitment in the 1980's, but has not come to fruition due to the World Bank's preference for road transport. The OCBN has a turnover of 11–12 billion CFA francs and employs some 2,400 employees, nearly all Beninois, and is one of the country's main sources of employment. Benin has two other railway lines in operation, connecting Cotonou with Pobé near the Nigerian border via Porto Novo (107 kilometers), and the Cotonou-Ouidah-Segboroué line in the west (34 kilometers). Since 1979 the acquisition of new locomotive engines has cut travel time on the Cotonou-Parakou line to five hours, down from the 12 required in the past. In 1989 fully 66 percent of the OCBN's 389,000 tons of cargo carried was in transit to/from Niger, but tonnage has been declining progressively.

ORGANISATION COMMUNE DAHOMEY-NIGER DES CHEMINS DE FER ET DES TRANSPORTS (OCDN). Former name of the ORGANISATION COMMUNE BENIN-NIGER DES CHEMINS DE FER ET DES TRANSPORTS (OCBN), which see.

ORGANISATION DE LA JEUNESSE REVOLUTIONNAIRE DU BENIN (OJRB). Youth organization, set up in late 1982, that like the OFRB (q.v.), was an ancillary support organization for the Marxist regime in Cotonou.

ORGANISATION DES FEMMES REVOLUTIONNAIRES DU BENIN (OFRB). Organization for militant women set up in 1982, and holding its first congress in December 1983. The OFRB was involved in the selecting of a number of delegates to run for election to the National Assembly (q.v.) and spreading the militant ethic among the women of Benin.

OTOUTOU-BI-ODJO, KING, (1882–1939). Last King of the Holli (q.v.). Born in Iwoyé and succeeding to the throne in November 1912, Otoutou-Bi-Odjo was unable to bridge the gap between the traditional independence of his people—pressed and harassed by both Porto Novo and Dahomey (qq.v.)—and the dictates of French colonialism that had recently imposed itself in the region. In January 1914 a general revolt was triggered in Holli areas (see HOLLI REVOLT) over various abuses of the colonial authorities. This was crushed by May but commenced again in August 1915, at the instigation of Outou-Bi Odja, who was stripped of his throne in 1916 and exiled to Mauritania, where he died in 1939.

OUASSA, ALBERT. Former Minister. Long-standing political ally and supporter of Hubert Maga (q.v.), Ouassa has been a senior administrator and Prefect of Atakora (q.v.). He was in Zinsou's (q.v.) cabinet of 1968–1969 as Minister of the Civil Service, but he deserted Zinsou in favor of Maga in the 1969 elections. He was integrated in the subsequent cabinet as Minister of Health and Social Affairs and served in that capacity until the 1972 coup d'etat (q.v.). He was then accused of embezzlement while in office and retired from the civil service.

OUEME. One of Benin's provinces, with administrative headquarters in Porto Novo (q.v.) and consisting of the *sous-préfectures* of Porto Novo (q.v.), Adjohon, Avrankou, Ketou (q.v.) Pobé, and Sakété. Ouémé's 1992 population of 724,000 is composed mostly of Goun, Yoruba, Nago and Holli (qq.v.).

OUEME RIVER. Benin's biggest river, 450 kilometers long and navigable for 200 kilometers. Its two major tributaries are the Okpara and the Zou. Its source is in the Atakora (q.v.) mountains in the northwest. The river splits into two branches in the south, the western (So) emptying in Lake Nokué near Cotonou, the eastern in Porto Novo's (qq.v.) coastal lagoon.

OUEMENOU. Mixture of Yourba (q.v.) and non-Yoruba ethnic groups formed of various clans arriving in the vicinity of the Ouémé river (q.v.) at various times during the eighteenth and nineteenth centuries. Chased out of their original lands west of Abeokuta (currently, Nigeria), the groups migrating eastwards were mostly Egba. Larger groups migrated to the Ouémé river valley from the northwest seeking refuge from the Kingdom of Dahomey (q.v.). Speaking Fongbe and other original languages, Goun (q.v.) became the dominant language of the Ouemenou ethnic amalgam. They are concentrated in the Adjohoun district northwest of Porto Novo (q.v.), in villages engaged mostly in fishing. During the precolonial era their lands were badly pillaged by both Porto Novo and Dahomey.

OUIDAH. Main port of the precolonial Houéda kingdom (q.v.) and major historical town on the Atlantic Ocean in the Atlantique province, some 32 kilometers east of Cotonou (qq.v.). Ouidah was considered the intellectual capital of Benin due to the large number of "Brazilians" (q.v.) who settled here in the nineteenth century, descendants from whom have played a very active role in the political and cultural life of the country. Among Ouidah's remaining historical attractions are the python fetish cult temple (see CULT OF THE GREAT SERPENT), the cathedral opposite the latter and several old domiciles and forts. The most important of the latter was the Portuguese fort known as Fort Saint-Jean-Baptiste d'Ajuda (see OUIDAH HISTORICAL MUSEUM).

Ouidah, established by the King of Savi (q.v.) in the sixteenth century as Gléhoué, was intermittently independent or tributary to Allada (q.v.) as part of the Houéda kingdom (though effectively independent by the 1680's). Ouidah, then known as Whydah, or Juda, was first contacted by European traders in the 1580's. By 1670 the British and French had established forts, and Ouidah rapidly became one of the greatest and most prosperous slave-trading ports in the Gulf of Guinea, much coveted by various foreign companies. When conquered by Dahomey (q.v.) in 1727, it became the main port of the latter kingdom. Subsequent to its fall to Dahomey, Ouidah's decline commenced. Pounded by heavy surf, it had become the preferred port of call on the coast solely because of the competitiveness of slave prices. The constant assaults by Dahomey, the latter's imperious mannerisms after Ouidah's conquest, and a decline in the number of slaves offered drove many merchants to Badagry, Porto Novo (q.v.), or elsewhere. In 1893 the town came under French control after two centuries of competition for it among the French, British, Dutch, Danish and Portuguese. The Portuguese fort was vacated only after Dahomey's independence, on July 31, 1961.

In the twentieth century the town has slowly declined in importance, though it is a tourist attraction of the south. Ouidah is the garrison base of several units of the Benin armed forces, including the crack para-commando force that has participated in several coups (q.v.) to date. Ouidah's population has not increased much over the years, since many of its native sons have migrated to Cotonou (q.v.). Currently it is Benin's sixth-largest town, with a population of 33,000.

OUIDAH HISTORICAL MUSEUM. The Ouidah Historical Museum, originally maintained by the Institute de Récherches Appliquées du Dahomey (q.v.), is housed in the remains of the old Portuguese fort in that city. The fort was built in 1721 and was known for some time as Fort Saint-Jean-Baptiste d'Ajuda. Twice occupied and burned to the ground by Dahomean troops, the fort was administered since 1806 by Francisco Felix da Souza (q.v.). Abandoned in 1862 and alternately the center of Protestant and Catholic missionary efforts, it was reoccupied by the Portuguese in 1865 and vacated only on July 31, 1961, one year after Dahomey's independence. Before relinquishing the fort, the Portuguese set fire to the main building in an effort to destroy it. The Museum has a collection of artifacts, photographs and drawings depicting the slave trade (q.v.)—in which Ouidah was a preferred port of call for European traders—as well as a documented exhibit of the similarity of ritual and dress in Benin and in Brazil, Haiti and Cuba, areas to which most slaves from Ouidah were transported. The Portuguese fort of Ouidah is actually one of three in this port. The others were William's Fort (British) and Fort St Louis (French).

OUMARA, BA ALPHA. Key witness (one of several who were captured) of the 1977 mercenary assault (q.v.) on Cotonou airport. A Senegalese of Guinean origin, Oumarou directly implicated Gabon as having knowledge of the conspiracy. Morocco was also directly implicated since the mercenaries were trained in a camp near Marakesh.

OYO EMPIRE. One of the most powerful Yoruba (q.v.) Kingdoms, based in contemporary Nigeria and establishing suzerainty over most of the Adja (q.v.) states in what was to become contemporary Benin, as well as over the Bariba regions of the Borgou (qq.v.). Founded by Oranyan, a prince from Ile Ife, the Oyo cavalry was much feared throughout the area and was the key to Oyo success in the region. Oyo defeated the Ashanti in 1764, twice invaded Allada (q.v.) (1600, 1698) and periodically razed Dahomey, exacting a heavy tribute for 70 years, until shaken off in 1818. The Oyo Empire fell into a major decline in the nineteenth century, due to a variety of factors, ushering in Dahomey's golden century of expansion, unfettered by the hitherto constraining Oyo.

-P-

PABEGU. Small village in the area of Djougou (q.v.), a major center of Benin's Taneka (q.v.) ethnic group.

PADONOU, GABRIEL. Director of the OICMA based in Accra, Ghana. Trained as an agronomist, Padonou was Deputy

Director of Rural Development (1965–1968) before his appointment to the regional locust commission in Accra. He has continued his career overseas and has been involved in a variety of other international bodies as well.

PALM OIL. One of Benin's principal export commodities. Palm trees were systematically planted by the kings of Dahomey in the nineteenth century, in an effort to generate new sources of revenue consequent to the drastic decline in state income with the abolition of the slave trade (q.v.). In the contemporary era the industry suffered a decline in both quality and number of trees planted between 1956 and 1963, with exports booming only in the late 1960's. Indeed, in the 1970's, Benin briefly ranked fourth in Africa in production of palm oil (13,661 tons) and palm kernels (58,000 tons) after Nigeria, Ivory Coast and Zaire. Production and exports plummeted in 1976, however, with the exhaustion of the old plantations, the non-mature nature of those planted in the 1960's and a series of droughts that affected even the normally humid coastlands. In 1961 a State corporation, SNAHDAH (q.v.), was formed to promote the development of the industry and to extract and process palm tree products via three palm-oil presses. SNAHDAH was replaced, after the 1972 coup, by SOBEPALH (q.v.) which was itself dissolved in 1982 after revelations of utter mismanagement and corruption. The organ that took over SOBEPALH's plant and activities, was SONICOG (q.v.), that was also wound up several years later.

PANCRAS, BRATHIER (Major). Minister of Interior and Public Security in the liberalized interim cabinet erected in August 1989 to oversee the transition to multiparty competitive politics. Prior to this Pancras had been Kérékou's (q.v.) military cabinet chief, and had personally ferreted out several plots against the regime.

PAOLETI-BEHANZIN THEOPHILE. Militant trade union (q.v.) leader and co-founder of the (1959) short-lived Parti de la Révolution Socialiste (q.v.). Paoleti-Béhanzin assumed a major political role in 1961 when he was appointed by

President Hubert Maga (q.v.) to head the newly established single trade union federation, the Union Générale de Travailleurs du Dahomey (UGTD) (q.v.). Despite being Maga's hand-picked appointee he led unionist strikes against Maga in 1963, indirectly leading to the latter's overthrow. For some time then Paoleti-Béhanzin exacerbated the turmoil by establishing "Revolutionary Committees" with militant demands. His bid for power was blocked by Major Alphonse Alley (q.v.) though, to appease the unions, he was brought into Ahomadégbé-Apithy's (qq.v.) government as Minister of Labor, 1964–1965. In 1964–1965 he also served on the Executive Committee of the governmental party, the Parti Démocratique Dahoméen (q.v.). In 1970 Paoleti-Béhanzin joined the cabinet as an Ahomadégbé appointee as Minister of Information and Tourism in the Presidential Council (q.v.) government, a position he occupied until the 1972 coup d'etat by Major Mathieu Kérékou (qq.v.). Inquiries following the coup found Paoleti-Béhanzin guilty of embezzlement of funds while in public office. He returned to Benin after the 1989 normalization to help set up a new political party, the RND (q.v.), together with Joseph Kéké (q.v.) and Justin Ahomadégbé, and he was elected on its ticket to the National Assembly (q.v.). There, in 1992, he forged an ad hoc inter-party alliance supportive of President Nicéphore Soglo (q.v.), who until then did not have the active support of the majority of the deputies, that in 1992 was renamed Le Rénouveau (q.v.).

PARAISO, EMILE, 1932– . Technocrat and former Minister. Born in Porto Novo (q.v.) on May 4, 1932, and a hydraulic engineer by profession, Paraiso also studied law and economics at the University of Grenoble. He was appointed Head of Hydraulic Services in 1960, with additional consultative duties for the government through 1968. In August 1968 he was hand-picked as an ideal apolitical technocrat to sit in Zinsou's (q.v.) cabinet as Minister of Public Works. Following Zinsou's eclipse, Paraiso was appointed Director General of SOBEK (q.v.) and he served on several other parastatal boards. Since the 1972 coup (q.v.) he has been abroad.

PARAKOU. Major town in north Benin, administrative capital of the Borgou (q.v.) province, and under the Kérékou (q.v.) regime (1972–1990) a rapidly growing town that reached a population of 120,000 in 1993. Parakou is also the terminus of the Benin-Niger railroad (see ORGANISATION COMMUNE BENIN-NIGER DES CHEMINS DE FER ET DES TRANSPORTS), and point from which long-distance trucks proceed north with transhipped goods for Niger.

Parakou (from "*Kpara Klou*") was probably settled by Wangar (q.v.) traders in the fifteenth or sixteenth century, before the influx of Bariba (q.v.). The founder of the Parakou dynasty was a descendant of the Yoruba kingdom of Savé (q.v.) some 200 kilometers to the south. Oral tradition refers to his growing up in Nikki as a Bariba *Wasanangari* (qq.v.), but being rejected socially due to his mixed origins.

Leaving Nikki with its followers, to found Parakou, the new dynasty retained its disenchantment with—and distance from—Nikki, though nominally one of the Bariba states in the region. Parakou became a major slave market town in the nineteenth century, straddling one of the Bussa (Nigeria)-to-Ashanti (Ghana) routes. As the city prospered and grew (because of its liberal policies toward slave traders), friction developed with Nikki, the Bariba parent state to the northeast. Always distant from Nikki and subject to diverse and outside influences, including Yoruba, Dendi (qq.v.), and Hausa, Parakou did not send troops for the Ilorin battle (see NIKKI; SERO KPERA ILORINKPUNON) and broke with Nikki during a local succession dispute in which Nikki tried to intervene. An unsuccessful Nikki punitive expedition and the record of friction and hostilities between the two states were only further aggravated when, in the colonial era, Parakou, the former vassal state, became the administrative center of the Borgou, overseeing Nikki affairs.

Prior to the 1972 coup Parakou was politically, like the rest of the Borgou, allied behind Hubert Maga, though its true power-wielder was Chabi Mama (qq.v.). In reality, political power was much more diffused in Parakou itself due to its mixed ethnic base, and the pro-Maga sentiment was more part of an anti-south syndrome. Indeed, as the least

Bariba town in Borgou, Parakou has had a certain "anti-Benin" maverick tradition.

PARC NATIONAL DE LA PENDJARI. Wildlife reserve straddling the Benin-Burkina Faso border along the Pendjari river (a tributary of the Oti and Volta in Togo and Ghana). Entry into the park is from Natitingou (q.v.) to Porga, accessible only in the dry season. The main tourist facilities are within Burkina Faso.

PARC NATIONAL DU W. Wildlife reserve along the Benin-Burkina Faso border, taking its name from the shape of the Niger river in that area. Access, in the dry season, is via Kérémou.

PAQUI, ROGER DAVID, 1934– . Diplomat. Born on January 11, 1934 in Porto Novo (q.v.) and educated locally and at the Universities of Dakar and Paris (1954–1961) Paqui served for two years as Cabinet Chief of the Office of the Director-General of the French Ministry of Health (1961–1963) followed by two years as Secretary at the Benin Embassy in Paris before joining the Ministry of Foreign Affairs as Assistant Chief of Protocol. In 1969 he was reassigned as Assistant Director of the Political and Legal Department in the Ministry, and in 1971 moved to a similar role in the Department of International Organizations and Technical Assistance. He then moved to New York as Counselor at the Benin Mission to the United Nations.

PARTI AFRICAIN DE L'INDEPENDENCE. (PAI) Pro-Soviet faction within the ruling PRPB party of Kérékou (qq.v.), aiming at radicalizing further PRPB policies and placing its members in key posts of importance. The faction was most inimical to the Parti Communiste Dahoméen (q.v.), an externally based movement that was making inroads among youth and intellectuals.

PARTI COMMUNISTE DAHOMEEN (PCD). Minuscule pro-Albanian Stalinist party founded in 1978 with a mostly Fon (q.v.) intellectual membership. It published a periodical, *En*

Avant, printed in Canada and smuggled into Benin where the party was clandestinely organized. The PCD was sharply critical of the Kérékou (q.v.) leadership that it felt presented a caricature of Marxism-Leninism, and tried to create a non-ethnic anti-Kérékou front. It was the Ligue's (q.v.) main competitor, but developed some grass-roots support among students at the local university more than the Ligue that was deeply compromised due to its participation in Kérékou's cabinet. Involved in many of the student strikes in Benin in the 1980's, nearly 150 of its members were in prison in 1987. Its head was Professor Pascal Fatondji, normally resident in Abidjan. Participating in the National Conference (q.v.) of 1990, the party urged a rejection of the draft constitution in the referendum that year.

PARTI DAHOMEEN DE L'UNITE (PDU). A 1960 merger of Sourou-Migan Apithy's Parti des Nationalistes de Dahomey, representing the Yoruba and the Nagot of the southeast, the Rassemblement Démocratique Dahoméen of the north, headed by Hubert Maga (qq.v.), and several splinter movements. At the 1960 election, the PDU ticket won 468,002 votes to the 213,564 of the Union Démocratique Dahoméenne (UDD), opposition party of the Fon, led by Justin Ahomadégbé (qq.v.). The election confirmed in power Hubert Maga as president and Apithy as Vice-President. Shortly after that, the UDD was banned and Ahomadégbé was arrested and imprisoned on trumped-up charges. In 1963 the PDU was dissolved with the overthrow of Maga and a new "parti unique" (q.v.) was formed; the Parti Démocratique Dahoméen (q.v.) of Ahomadégbé and Apithy. From 1960 to 1963 the Secretary-General of the PDU was Chabi Mama (q.v.). See also POLITICAL PARTIES.

PARTI DE LA REVOLUTION POPULAIRE DU BENIN (PRPB). Benin's Marxist-Leninist ruling, and sole, party until 1990. Established by General Kérékou (q.v.) on November 30, 1975, to assume the role of the revolutionary avant-garde in Benin. The PRPB's first ordinary Congress was held in December 1979 when a Central Committee of 45 was formally elected, from which 13 were coopted into the

Political Bureau (Politburo). Until these elections, both the Central Committee and the Politburo had been significantly smaller, standing at 25 and 7 respectively, and much more in the hands of their military membership. At the time Captain Dohou Azonhihon (q.v.), the regime's number-two man and primary of official ideologue, was the guiding spirit of the Politburo; he was subsequently purged and posted to prefectural duties, only to be rehabilitated in the waning days of the Kérékou regime when his iron fist was once again needed. The Political Bureau was elected by the Central Committee of the party, a body itself nominated by the Party Congress.

Despite official rhetoric, the PRPB was both largely elitist, with few roots in the countryside or significant support among the masses, and a very divided party, where factionalism—especially on the Left—was rife. Its total membership was 2,000 in 1986, and rhetoric apart, it is doubtful if it ever stood at a much higher number. By far the most aggressive group within the PRPB was the Ligue (q.v.), an arch-Left Maoist clique trying to prod the centrists—under Kérékou—into more orthodox policies. A small group of orthodox communists were also members of the party, divided into "Stalinists" and "Muscovites," and there was also a small pro-Western "capitalist" faction, headed by Colonel Ohouéns (q.v.), very much on the defensive but retained in positions of influence by Kérékou as a counterweight to the Left hard-liners. On many occasions internal splits were so intense and positions so rigid that the party virtually ceased to operate cohesively. With the collapse of global Marxism and the return to competitive politics the PRPB dissolved itself (April 30, 1990), with Kérékou and its leading members setting up a new party, the Union des Forces du Progrés (UFP) (q.v.).

PARTI DE LA REVOLUTION SOCIALISTE DU BENIN (PRSB). Still-born political party founded in 1959 by two cousins Louis Béhanzin, a Marxist-Leninist instructor in Guinea, and Theophile Paoletti-Béhanzin (q.v.), a Dahomean trade union leader. The PRSB drew inspiration from the neo-Marxist parti Africain de l'Indépendance in Senegal and was supposed to operate in Togo and Dahomey. Its ideological platform included immediate independence, socialist economic policies and militant pan-Africanism. Though it appealed to a few intellectuals and students in the south, the PRSB had no real effect on the Dahomean political picture.

PARTI DE RENOUVEAU DEMOCRATIQUE (PRD). Party of Adrién Houngbédji (q.v.) set up in 1991, and within the current National Assembly in alliance with Hubert Maga's Parti National pour la Démocratie et le Développement (PNDD) to form a bloc of nine against Soglo's leadership (behind which was ranged the UTR) (qq.v.). Of the nine the PRD won five.

PARTI DEMOCRATIQUE DAHOMEEN (PDD). The joint "parti unique" (q.v.) of Sourou-Migan Apithy and Justin Ahomadégbé, formed after the 1963 overthrow of President Hubert Maga (qq.v.). The party mainly represented the Yoruba and Nagot of the southeast and the Fon and Adja (qq.v.) of the center and southwest of the country. In 1965 a governmental deadlock occurred as a consequence of increasing friction between President Apithy and Vice-President Ahomadégbé. Following the Supreme Court Affair (q.v.), Ahomadégbé, having a stronger following in the PDD, succeeded in obtaining a party censure of his rival. The resultant political stalemate and growing civic unrest brought in the armed forces and the first coup of 1965 (qq.v.). The collapse of the PDD led to the rebirth of the three-party pattern of the past, each party supporting its ethnic-regional candidate. On December 22, 1965, Gen. Christophe Soglo (q.v.) again intervened in the political area (see COUP OF 1965 (b)), dissolving all political movements and establishing his military regime.

PARTI DEMOCRATIQUE DAHOMEEN (PDD). Small, pro-Western political opposition movement to the Marxist regime of General Kérékou (q.v.), with links to other groups in exile. With branches in Gabon, Togo, Senegal and France, the PDD was under the leadership of Emile Derlin Zinsou (q.v.) and should not be confused with the earlier PDD party (see preceding entry).

PARTI DES NATIONALISTES DAHOMEENS (PND). Successor to Sourou-Migan Apithy's Parti Républicain Dahoméen established in 1960 and joined by Emile Derlin Zinsou (qq.v.) and his splinter party. At independence the PND merged with the northern-based party of Hubert Maga, the Rassemblement Démocratique Dahoméen, and with the militant short-lived Mouvement de Libération Nationale of Jean Pliya and Albert Tévoédjré to form the governing party of 1960–1963, the Parti Dahoméen de l'Unité (qq.v.). The alliance essentially left out only one major formation, the Fon Adja-based Union Démocratique Dahoméenne of Justin Ahomadégbé (qq.v.), banned on trumped-up charges in 1961. Following the overthrow of Hubert Maga in 1963 Ahomadégbé and Apithy joined forces and set up a new "parti unique", the Parti Démocratique Dahoméen (qq.v.), the ruling party during 1964–1965. See also POLITICAL PARTIES.

PARTI DU REGROUPEMENT AFRICAIN (PRA). Successor interterritorial party to the Convention Africaine (q.v.). Established in March 1958 in Dakar by Léopold Sédar Senghor, the PRA had its founding Congress in Cotonou (q.v.) on July 25–27, 1958. Attended by Dahomean leaders Emile Derlin Zinsou, Hubert Maga and Sourou-Migan Apithy (qq.v.), the Congress called for immediate independence, with Zinsou trying to moderate some of its demands. The 1958 referendum on the future of Francophone Africa went against the PRA in Dahomey, as elsewhere, since it had few strong roots in the countryside and no powerful local leaders willing to back it. In Dahomey the PRA branch was the Parti Progressiste Dahoméen, a 1958 fusion of the political parties of Maga (Rassemblement Démocratique Dahoméen) and Apithy (Parti Républicain Dahoméen) (qq.v.). The party was short-lived, however, collapsing in 1959 over issues dealing with the nature of future relations with France. See also POLITICAL PARTIES.

PARTI NATIONAL POUR LA DEMOCRATIE ET LE DEVELOPPEMENT (PNDD). Political party set up in 1989 by Hubert Maga (q.v.), forming an electoral alliance for the legislative elections with the Parti de la Rénouveau Démocratique of Adrien Hounbédji (qq.v.). The PNDD won four seats of the compact's total of nine of the 65 seats in opposition to President Soglo's (q.v.) leadership behind which were then ranged the 12 Deputies of the UTR (q.v.).

PARTI PROGRESSISTE DAHOMEEN (PPD) Short-lived 1958 merger of the Parti Républicain Dahoméen of Sourou-Migan Apithy and the Rassemblement Démocratique Dahoméen of Hubert Maga, affiliated to the interterritorial Parti du Régroupement Africain (qq.v.). The PRA was the successor of the Conventional Africaine (q.v.) and was founded in Dakar, Senegal, in March 1958, having its first Congress in Cotonou (q.v.) in July of that year. The PPD promptly collapsed in 1959 over the issue of the future of relations between France and Francophone Africa, with the two main formations reemerging only to reunite in 1960 as the Parti Dahoméen de l'Unité (q.v.). See also POLITICAL PARTIES.

PARTI REPUBLICAIN DAHOMEEN (PRD). Political party of Sourou-Migan Apithy, representing the Yoruba and Nagot of the southeast, and especially the Porto Novo (qq.v.) region. Established in 1951, following the split in the Union Progréssiste Dahoméenne (q.v.), of which Apithy had been a member. The PRD won 35 of the 60 Assemblée Territoriale (q.v.) seats in 1957 and formed a ruling coalition with the northern-based party of Hubert Maga, the Mouvement Démocratique Dahoméen (qq.v.). In 1958 the two political parties briefly merged under the name of Parti Progréssiste Dahoméen (PPD), constituting the local section of the interterritorial Parti du Regroupement Africain (PRA) (qq.v.) led by Senegal's future president, Léopold Sédar Senghor. In 1959 differences of opinion between the MDD and PRD leaders and between them and the PRA leadership, led to the collapse of the PPD coalition and the reemergence of the Apithy and Maga parties. In the 1959 elections, the PRD was found to have won 37 seats with 144,038 votes while Justin Ahomadégbé's opposition Union Démocratique Dahoméenne (UDD) (qq.v.) had obtained only 11 seats with

172,119 votes. The resultant charges of electoral fraud forced the PRD to concede to the UDD nine seats, following which the PRD, under its new name, Parti des Nationalistes Dahoméens (q.v.), joined a government headed by Hubert Maga and his also newly named Rassemblement Démocratique Dahoméen (q.v.). See also POLITICAL PARTIES.

PARTI UNIQUE. Single Party. The quest for unity of Dahomey's various political movements has dominated the country's political history since parties were allowed shortly after the end of the Second World War. Though Benin has had several instances of such partis uniques as the UPD or PDU (qq.v.), in all instances prior to 1972 such experiments collapsed under the pressures of personalities or regionalism (q.v.) in the country. Moreover, when single party rules was made legally part of the political system (as in 1961 during Hubert Maga's presidency or during the Second Republic of Sourou-Migan Apithy and Justin Ahomadégbé [q.v.]), the country's fragmented political tendencies were simply temporarily subsumed under the structural umbrella of the single party without any erosion in their strength or quest for individual expression. The creation of the PRPB (q.v.) in 1975 was the first attempt at an ideological parti unique. The new experiment survived for 18 long years, but largely due to the coercive force yielded by Kérékou (q.v.), with the party rarely having more than 2,000 members.

PATINVOH, EPIPHANE, 1930– . Trade union leader. Born in Porto Novo (q.v.) on January 6, 1930, and an accountant by profession, Patinvoh has been attached to the Caisse des Allocations Familiales et des Accidents du Travail since 1957. He has been prominent in union activities and served as Deputy Secretary-General of the Catholic union in Dahomey until the latter was forcibly merged. He continued his unionist activities until his retirement in 1990.

LA PATRIE DAHOMEENNE. Fortnightly publication that expressed Sourou-Migan Apithy's (q.v.) views and positions during his tenure on the Presidential Council (q.v.) between 1970 and 1972. It was banned in 1971 after publicizing an

incident in neighboring Togo where three political oppo-
nents of General Etienne Eyadema, the President, were
liquidated in prison.

PEDAH see HOUEDA

PEDRO, SALIFOU BONI, 1923– . Born in Natitingou (q.v.) on
May 24, 1923, and an educator by profession, Pedro played
an important early political role in reorganizing the electoral
vote in the north. In March 1952 he was elected (at the age of
29) as Deputy from Savalou on the MDD (qq.v.) ticket, and
he continued being reelected through 1963. He served as
Secretary of the National Assembly (q.v.) between 1957 and
1959 and as Vice-President between 1959 and 1960. He was
both President of the Economic and Finance Committee and
Chairman of the Common Funds Savings Bank of the
Entente (see CONSEIL DE L'ENTENTE). In 1957 he was
elected as Dahomey's delegate to the AOF Grand Council in
Dakar (serving through 1959), and, between 1959 and 1961,
he also represented Dahomey at the Senate of the Commu-
noute Francaise (q.v.) (1959–1961). Since 1963 he has been
living in France.

PELOFY, ISIDORE, 1874–1953. Early missionary, regarded by
some as "Father of Agoué." Born in Belcaire in 1874 and
ordained a priest in 1900, Pelofy joined the Missions Africaines du Lyon and was sent out to Dahomey. Attached to
the Lokosso (q.v.) cercle of Athiémé, Pelofy was named head
of the church in Agoué (q.v.) in 1911 and stayed on in this
capacity for 36 years. He developed an easy working relationship with all the chiefs and fetishists (q.v.) in the area, a
fact that greatly facilitated his missionary effort in the region.
He died in Ouidah (q.v.) in 1953.

PEOPLE'S COMMISSIONERS. Title of the Deputies to the
Assemblée Nationale Révolutionnaire (ANR) (q.v.) during
the Revolutionary era. In French they were called Commissaires du Peuple (q.v.).

PERERE. Currently a small village in the Borgou, southwest of
Nikki (qq.v.). Immediately prior to the French occupation of

Dahomey, Péréré—a province of Nikki—was rapidly asserting its independence of Nikki and developing into a "new" Bariba (q.v.) kingdom.

PERMA RIVER. Small river in north Benin, site of current gold (q.v.) mining and of early colonial gold-panning under the SMDN (q.v.). The site is currently under the jurisdiction of OBEMINES (q.v.). See also GOLD.

PERMANENT NATIONAL INVESTIGATORY COMMISSION ON STATE SECURITY see FORCES ARMEES DU BENIN.

PERRIN, GUSTAVE, 1919– . Long Benin's Director of Social Affairs in the Ministry of Public Health and Social Affairs. Born in Abomey (q.v.) on November 19, 1919, and a graduate of the University of Dakar Medical School, specializing in ophthalmology, Perin established a practice in Dakar where he worked from 1944 until shortly after Dahomey became independent. He then returned home and was appointed Director of Social Affairs in 1963, serving in that capacity until 1972, when he went into retirement.

PEUL see FULANI

LE PHARE DU DAHOMEY. Influential weekly published in Cotonou between 1929 and 1949, edited by Augustin Nicoué. Essentially catering to the "Brazilian" (q.v.) readership in Benin, Le Phare was very active in attacking the abuses of colonialism, carrying articles by many of the colony's first intellectuals and nationalists.

PILA PILA. Small ethnic group found mostly in the vicinity of Djougou, south of Natitingou in the Atakora (qq.v.) province. They number around 24,000 and speak a dialect close to the More of the Burkina Faso Mossi. The Pila Pila call themselves Yowa (or Yao) and reside in the key villages of Barey, Subruku and Zugu.

PINTO, LOUIS IGNACIO see IGNACIO-PINTO, LOUIS

PLIYA, JEAN, 1931– . Politician, author and educator. Born in Djougou (q.v.) on July 31, 1931, of a chiefly Fon (q.v.) family, Pliya studied in Dahomey, Ivory Coast, Senegal and France between 1957 and 1967, training as a teacher, and specializing in geography. He taught at Lycée Béhanzin in Porto Novo (q.v.) and at Lycée Coulibaly in Cotonou (q.v.), as well as at the National University of Benin (q.v.). In the 1960's Pliya published several highly acclaimed novels, including *Kondo le Réquin* and *L'Arbre Fétiche*, the latter work winning him the *Grand Prix de la Nouvelle Africaine*.

Politically militant, Pliya in 1959 co-founded, together with Albert Tévoédjré, the Mouvement de Libération Nationale (MLN) (qq.v.). The party was a loose association of progressive intellectuals (Pliya himself wanted an MLN link with the Marxist-Leninist Parti Africain d'Indépendance (PAI) in Dakar, Senegal), and hence had little success at the polls and rapidly withered. In the 1960 creation of the Parti Dahoméen de l'Unite (PDU) (q.v.), the MLN merged with the PND and RDD (qq.v.), and MLN leaders were given several important posts in the new regime. Pliya became a PDU officer and Director of the Ministry of National Education (1961–1963). In 1964 he became a party militant of the successor parti unique, the PDD (qq.v.), on whose ticket he was elected as Deputy, serving as First Secretary of the National Assembly (q.v.) (1964–1965) and Secretary of State for Information and Tourism (1963–1965). After the military takeover of Gen. Christophe Soglo (q.v.), Pliya taught for several years in France before becoming a professor of geography at the University of Benin in Lome, Togo. In 1980 he was invited home to assume the post of Rector of the National University of Benin, a post he held until the mid-1980's when he returned to France.

POGNON, GRATIEN LAZARE. Former Ambassador to the EEC (q.v.) and self-exiled leader of the anti-Kérékou (q.v.) opposition. Educated at home and abroad, Pognon completed a degree in history and joined the Foreign Ministry, where he rose very fast. At independence, as Secretary of Foreign Affairs, Pognon was sent in 1961 to serve as Dahomey's First Counselor at the Embassy to France, and in 1963 he went to Washington, D.C., in a similar capacity. In 1964 he was elected Deputy Secretary-General of the Organization of African Unity, based in Addis Ababa. After the expiry of his term of office, he returned to Cotonou to be later appointed Ambassador to Benelux and the EEC. Following the 1972 coup d'etat (q.v.) and the establishment of a People's Republic, Pognon publicly broke with Cotonou and remained in self-exile in Brussels and Paris, founding an opposition group—Mouvement de la Rénovation du Dahomey (q.v.)—that claimed credit for the ill-fated mercenary assault (q.v.) on Cotonou airport in 1977. Captured documents from that raid indicate that the attempted coup aimed at bringing Pognon to power. Pognon and Zinsou (q.v.) (leader of the other major anti-Kérékou force in exile at the time) did not see eye-to-eye on many issues and were divided in terms of personality. After the return of civilian rule Pognon returned and won election to the National Assembly on the NCC (qq.v.) ticket.

POGNON, GUY, 1935– . Economist. Born in Cotonou (q.v.) on November 3, 1935, and a graduate of the University of Paris in economics, Pognon was appointed Secretary-General, then Director of Studies, of the Banque Dahoméenne du Développement (BDD) (q.v.) (1965–1968). Previously he had been attached to the World Bank as liaison officer with the African Development Bank. In 1968 Pognon was promoted to General Director of the BDD, becoming also Rapporteur of the Counseil Economique et Social in Cotonou. After the 1972 coup d'etat (q.v.), Pognon relocated to France to live in Paris.

POISSON, EMILE, 1905– . Educator, politician, elder statesman and diplomat. Born in Ouidah (q.v.) on May 25, 1905, Poisson was one of Dahomey's earliest political leaders. Educated in Dakar and Aix-en-Provence, and trained as a teacher, Poisson taught and founded schools in Porto Novo (1936) and Ouidah (qq.v.) (1958). In 1945 he created a pressure group to protect the interests of local traders vis-a-vis French expatriates, a fact that gave him political clout later. He was elected to the Counséil Général (q.v.)

(1946–1952) while a member of the Union Progréssiste Dahoméenne (q.v.), Dahomey's first political party. In 1950 he bolted the party in opposition to Apithy's leadership and, together with Justin Ahomadégbé, formed the Bloc Populaire Africain (qq.v.), of which Poisson was President and which in 1955 became the Union Démocratique Dahoménne (UDD) (q.v.). Poisson was also Mayor of Ouidah (1956–1959) and Senator to the Communauté Française (q.v.). While a UDD member, he was appointed to Hubert Maga's (q.v.) cabinet in May 1959 as Minister of Justice. In 1962 he was dispatched to Brussels to represent Dahomey with the European Economic Community (q.v.), and from 1964 to 1967 Poisson was also Ambassador to France (as well as to Great Britain, Italy and Benelux). When the Presidential Council (q.v.) was set up in 1970, Poisson ran as candidate from Ouidah and was elected to the Assemblée Consultative (q.v.), a position he held until the 1972 coup d'etat (q.v.). Following the coup, he was attached to the Foreign Ministry in a consultative capacity until his recent retirement.

POLICE FORCE. The police force is composed of two structures, both of colonial origin: the Gendarmerie Nationale and the Sûreté Nationale. Historically the gendarmerie (q.v.) was the first to be established. The origins of the Sûreté were the gardes-cercle established in administrative centers to support the gendarmerie, whose numbers were then too few. Thus, in origin, the sûreté was a local police force. Functionally and structurally the gendarmerie is separate and distinct from the sûreté, though both undertake police work. The gendarmerie, however, is primarily concerned with maintaining order and is, by law, a regular branch of the Benin armed forces (q.v.). Though under the jurisdiction of the Minister of Defense, it has a separate command hierarchy and acts as a national police, primarily charged with civic order and administratively part of the armed forces. Until the mid-1970's it had six companies with 1,500 men; the Kérékou regime augmented its strength to 2,000 within a few years, and reorganized the force into four mobile companies. Its last pre-1990 commander was Captain Mathieu Tchétou; Kérékou's last Police head was Commissioner F. Guinikoukou, a northerner. The Surété Nationale is the national headquarters of the country's police force and directly subordinated to the Minister of Interior. It is much more involved with criminal and investigatory work. The Surété Nationale and its local units normally numbered 1,000 men but the force was augmented under the Kérékou regime. The administrative reorganization of the Benin armed forces, after the 1972 coup (q.v.), brought the surété and especially the gendarmerie under tighter military control, in light of policy divergencies in the past.

POLITICAL PARTIES. Organized political activity commenced in Dahomey following the Second World War. The precursors of the country's political parties were the electoral committees that sprang up in the urban areas to nominate and support candidates for the forthcoming elections (see COMITES CENTRALES D'ORGANISATION ELECTORALE). The coalescence of the leaders of the committees resulted in the creation of Dahomey's first political party, the Union Progréssiste Dahoméenne (UPD) (q.v.). Intense personality frictions and personalist ambitions within the UPD rent it asunder and, together with the country's history of interregional cleavages, produced the threefold array of power that characterized Dahomean politics into the 1970's. (See also UNION PROGRESSISTE DAHOMEENNE.)

(1) The first faction to organize itself outside the UPD was the Bloc Populaire Africain led by Emile Poisson and Justin Ahomadégbé, depending upon Fon and Adja (qq.v.) support in the south and center of the country. The party merged in 1955 with the by-then greatly diminished rump of the UPD party, headed by Emile Derlin Zinsou, to form the Union Démocratique Dahoméenne (UDO), the Dahomean section of the interterritorial Rassemblement Démocratique Africain (qq.v.) (see INTERTERRITORIAL PARTIES). Except for a few months when the UDD participated in a government coalition, the UDD was Dahomey's "opposition party" par excellence. The party was

banned by President Hubert Maga (q.v.) in 1961 but reemerged following Maga's overthrow (see COUP OF 1963) to form a coalition with the Yoruba/Nagot based party of Sorou-Migan Apithy (the PRD), called the Parti Démocratique Dahoméen (qq.v.). After Gen. Christophe Soglo's (q.v.) second coup (see COUP OF 1965 (a)), which came on the heels of a sharp break in the coalition, the UDD reemerged under the name Alliance Démocratique Dahoméenne (ADD) (q.v.). On December 22, 1965, all political parties were banned (see COUP OF 1965 (b)), including the ADD.

(2) The second group to opt out of the UPD were the northern members, who in 1951 organized the Groupement Ethnique du Nord, precursor of the Mouvement Démocratique Dahoméen (qq.v.), established in 1953. The party suffered a number of minor schisms (see paragraph 5 below) and in 1957 changed its name to Rassemblement Démocratique Dahoméen (RDD) (q.v.). In 1958 the RDD temporarily joined with the Parti Républicain Dahoméen of Sourou-Migan Apithy to form the Parti Progréssiste Dahoméen (PPD), Dahomean section of the interterritorial movement Parti du Régroupement Africain (qq.v.). See INTERTER-RITORIAL PARTIES. In 1959 the merger collapsed and the RDD was reconstituted only to coalesce again (in 1960) with the PRD, since renamed the Parti des Nationalistes Dahoméens (q.v.). The new joint party (which also included several other factions)—the Parti Dahoméen de l'Unité (q.v.)—emerged as the ruling party from 1960 to 1963. Following Maga's overthrow in 1963, northern politicians were forced to join the new southern-based parti unique of 1963–1965, the Parti Démocratique Dahoméen (qq.v.). After the first 1965 coup of Gen. Christophe Soglo (q.v.), Maga's northern supporters briefly organized themselves under the name of the Union Nationale Dahoméenne (UND) (q.v.). On December 22, 1965, all political parties were banned, including the UND.

(3) The third political movement previously encompassed by the UPD were Yoruba and Nagot members that coalesced around Sourou-Migan Apithy and established in 1951 the Parti Républicain Dahoméen (PRD) (qq.v.). After several years of dominating the Assemblée Territoriale, the PRD formed an alliance with the northern-based Mouvement Démocratique Dahoméen (MDD) (qq.v.). In 1958 the two parties briefly merged (the MDD now called the Rassemblement Démocratique Dahoméen) to form the Parti Progréssiste Dahoméen, local branch of the interterritorial Parti du Régroupement Africain (qq.v.). See INTERTERRITORIAL PARTIES. In 1959 the alliance collapsed and the PRD reemerged as the Parti des Nationalistes Dahoméens (q.v.). The party failed to capture the majority of the Assembly seats in 1959, following rectification of electoral irregularities, and in 1960 coalesced with the RDD to form the 1960–1963 parti unique, the Parti Dahoméen de l'Unité (PDU) (qq.v.). The PDU was banned following the collapse of the Maga regime (see COUP OF 1963) and Apithy and Justin Ahomadégbé combined forces to form the 1964–1965 ruling coalition with their joint Parti Démocratique Dahoméen (PDD) (qq.v.). The PDD was banned after Gen. Soglo's first coup of Fall 1965, which came right after a sharp break among the leaders of the coalition, and Apithy's supporters reorganized themselves under the banner of the Convention Nationale Dahoméenne (CND) (qq.v.). On December 22, 1965, Gen. Soglo took over all political power, and all political parties, including the CND, were declared dissolved.

Apart from the original UPD party and the three personalist/regional formations with their variations in nomenclature and coalitions, the Dahomean political scene has been cluttered by a variety of other splinter groups. The following are the most important:

(4) Mouvement de Libération Nationale (q.v.), a short-lived small leftist party led by Albert Tévoédjré and

Jean Pliya (qq.v.). It merged with the PDU (q.v.) coalition in 1960.

(5) The several splinter groups from the MDD and RDD, invariably led by Djougou-based Paul Darboux (qq.v.). Among these were the Defense des Intérêts Economiques, Indépendants du Nord and Union des Indépendants du Dahomey (q.v.).

(6) The Rassemblement de l'Impératif National, 1965 still-born political party of Valentin Djibodé Aplogan in Allada (qq.v.).

(7) Parti de la Révolution Socialiste du Bénin, a still-born party founded in 1959 with links to the Marxist-Leninist Parti Africain d'Independance (qq.v.), based in Dakar, Senegal.

(8) Mouvement Socialist Africain (q.v.), Dahomean branch of the interterritorial party of the same name. Established in 1958, the party never succeeded in striking roots in Dahomey.

(9) Union pour le Rénouveau du Dahomey (URD) established in May 1969 to support the regime of President Emile Derlin Zinsou (qq.v.). Since the latter was deposed six months later, the URD was mostly a paper structure during its brief life. There were no official political parties in Dahomey between Zinsou's overthrow in December 1969 and the foundation in 1975 of the Marxist-Leninist PRPB (q.v.). With the establishment of the latter's parti unique (q.v.) system (see below), a number of opposition groups sprouted abroad that existed until the dismantling of Marxism and the PRPB in 1990.

The Government Party (1975–1990): (10) Parti de la Révolution Populaire du Bénin (PRPB) (q.v.). Established as the ruling Marxist-Leninist party of Benin, the party elected in a Congress its Central Committee, which in turn elected a 13-man Political Bureau. As with other uniparty systems in

Benin, but much more so due to the military and ideological nature of the regime, the PRPB was highly factionalized, with sharp ideological and personality clashes manifesting themselves continuously. Regional and ethnic cleavages, always a feature of the past, were not so pronounced as before since numerous (especially junior) Fon (q.v.) officers jointed the Marxist bandwagon, though the rank and file did not. Indeed, membership of the PRPB, admittedly a ''vanguard'' party, normally gravitated around 2,000. Southern elements predominated in the leadership of the PRPB, as they have in the leadership of other parties as well, though key posts were controlled by Kérékou (q.v.) and his loyalists. See also PARTI DE LA REVOLUTION POPULAIRE DU BENIN. His role within the PRPB has been that of a juggler, trying to maintain the middle course of the ''revolution,'' while warding off powerful ideological challenges, especially of arch-Left factions including the Ligue (q.v.) and the Parti Communiste Dahoméen (PCD) (qq.v.)

Opposition (1972–1990): (11) The Parti Démocratique Dahoméen (PDD), based in Paris and led by Emile Derlin Zinsou (q.v.), that included various other political figures self-exiled in France and elsewhere. The party had cells in Gabon, Ivory Coast, Senegal and Togo, as well as in France, and sponsored a variety of antigovernment activities in Benin. However, by the mid-1980's it was moribund; indeed, it was never a very viable opposition movement.

(12) The Mouvement de la Rénovation du Dahomey (MRD), set up in Brussels, and then transferred to Paris, by self-exiled Gratien Pognon (q.v.), who was at the time Benin's Ambassador to Benelux and the EEC (q.v.). It included a variety of younger elements and Amadou Assouma (q.v.) as co-leader. The MRD was behind the 1977 mercenary assault (q.v.) on Cotonou, but as with the PDD was moribund a few years later.

(13) The Parti Communiste du Dahomey (PCD). With cells in Benin, but guided from both Canada (its

inspirational and fiscal base) and Ivory Coast (where its leader was based), the PCD was a pro-Albanian ultra-Left movement, that unlike the other opposition movements did strike roots among Beninois students and intellectuals. It was behind much of the student unrest at the National University of Benin (q.v.), supported two of the military mutinies that threatened Kérékou (q.v.), campaigned against the holding of a National Conference (q.v.) unless Kérékou was ousted, and against the ensuing Constitution (q.v.) of Benin.

Post-1990 parties. With the lifting of the ban on political parties in 1990 a large number of political parties emerged, at one count 36, and an additional 12 purely personalist ephemeral formations existed at one time or another. The picture was further complicated by the party fluidity in the period leading up to the various elections as several inter-party electoral compacts were formed and dissolved, and splinters seceded from original groups. Most groups in one guise or another contested the municipal, legislative and/or Presidential, elections (q.v.), and ultimately 21 of these shared the 64 seats in the new National Assembly (q.v.), though some as part of electoral alliances.

The largest formation to emerge was the 12-man ''governmental'' compact, the Union pour la Triomphe du Rénouveau (UTR) (q.v.), an alliance originally between three southern parties—Ananlin Timothée's Union Démocratique des Forces du Progrès, Marcelin Degbé's Mouvement pour la Démocratie et le Progrès Social (MDPS) (qq.v.) and Francisco Marius' Union pour la Liberté et le Développement (ULD)—to support Nicéphore Soglo's (q.v.) Presidential candidacy. The compact later grew to a 21-deputy Nouvelle République and, in July 1993, to the 34-vote Rénouveau under Paoleti-Béhanzin (qq.v.).

The second group in size was the anti-Soglo ''Opposition'' compact of nine seats of Hubert Maga's (q.v.) Northern Parti National pour la Démocratie et le Développement (PNDD) and the ex-Apithy (who died in 1989) Porto Novo vote ranged behind the ambitious Adrien Houngbédji and his

Parti de Rénouveau Démocratique (PRD) (qq.v.). The third alliance in terms of strength was the eight-man bloc of Bruno Amoussou's (q.v.) Parti Social-Démocrate (PSD) and Eustache Sarre's Union Nationale pour la Solidarité et le Progrès (UNSP). Most of these joined to form Rénouveau in 1993. Then there is a seven-man group of Justin Ahomadégbé and Joseph Kéké's Rassemblement National pour la Démocratie (RND) and an equal bloc held by Albert Tévoédjré's Notre Cause Common (NCC) (qq.v.) with the remaining 21 seats divided by ten smaller party machines, one bloc of which—Convergence (q.v.)—also joined Rénouveau in 1993.

The most important of these political formations/alliances are listed separately in the Dictionary. They include: (14) the Rassémblement Démocratique Dahoméen (RDD), later the Parti National pour la Démocratie et le Développement (PNDD) of Hubert Maga: (15) the Mouvement Démocratique Républicain (MDR) of Joseph Kéké who inherited part of the recently deceased Sourou-Migan Apithy power base, but see also (23) below; (16) the Front National pour la Démocratie (FND) set up by Justin Ahomadégbé, but see also his own party within in (23) below; (17) the Union National pour la Démocratie et le Progrès (UNDP) of Emile Derlin Zinsou; (18) the Union des Forces du Progrès (UFP), formed by pro-Kérékou members of the now dissolved Marxist PRPB under Machoudi Dissoudi; (19) the Union Démocratique pour le Développement Economique et Social (UDES) of Gatien Houngbédji (q.v.); (20) Mouvement National pour la Démocratie et le Développement (MNDD) of the popular northerner Bertin Borna (q.v.), formerly a Maga supporter; (21) the radical Alliance Démocratique pour le Progrès (ADP) of Gedéon Dassoundo (q.v.), popular in student circles; (22) Notre Cause Commune (NCC) of maverick Albert Tévoédjré who was expelled from the RND for prematurely declaring his Presidential candidacy and captured Catholic support; (23) Rassemblement National pour Démocratie (RND), essentially comprising the former southern parties (UDD and PRD) of Ahomadégbé and Apithy/Houngbédji grouped under Secretary General Joseph Kéké; (24) the Union pour la Démocratie et la Solidarité of

Adamou N'Diaye, a Minister in the Interim Government; (25) the Rassemblement des Démocrates Libéraux (RDL) of Sévérin Adjovi (q.v.); (26) the three-party southern electoral alliance behind Nicéphore Soglo (q.v.), the Union pour la Triomphe de Rénouveau (UTR), to become in July 1992 Nouvelle République and, in 1993, Le Rénouveau under Théophile Paoletti-Béhanzin: the original three parties of UTR were Ananlin Timothée's Union Démocratique des Forces du Progrès (UDFP); Marcelin Dégbé's Mouvément pour la Démocratie et le Progrès Social (MDPS); Francisco Marius' Union pour la Liberté et le Développement (ULD); (27) the Parti de Rénouveau Démocratique (PRD) of Adrien Houngbédji, Speaker of the Assembly; (28) Bruno Amoussou's Parti Social-Démocrat (PSD), (29) Eustache Sarre's Union Nationale pour le Solidarité et le Progrès (UNSP) and; (30) the Convérgence.

POPOS. Small precolonial coastal lagoon kingdoms (Great or Grand Popo; Small or Petit Popo) west of Ouidah (q.v.). Small Popo is the contemporary Aného, just across the border in Togo. Populated by a variety of ethnic groups, especially Mina, the communities played an important historical role during the slave era in this area of the coast. Grand Popo (q.v.) in particular was a vibrant slave center, and the traditional place of refuge of the Kings of Ouidah (Houéda Kingdom) whenever attacked by Dahomean columns advancing from the north. See also GRAND POPO.

PORTO NOVO. Capital and second-largest city of Benin. Contradictory oral tradition refers to Porto Novo's foundation in the sixteenth century (see ADJA-TADO; ALLADA) or in the year 1730, following Allada's conquest by Dahomey and the population's relocation to Ajasé Ipo. (qq.v.). Once established, Porto Novo became an Oyo (q.v.) tributary and one of Oyo's outlets to the ocean. Porto Novo prospered during the slave trade (q.v.) in dealings with the Portuguese. After the conquest of Ouidah (q.v.) by Dahomey, Porto Novo became the preferred port of call for slave-traders. In the nineteenth century the French superseded the Portuguese and became the protectors of Porto Novo against perennial Dahomean military thrusts. Since Porto Novo and Dahomey had long been traditional rivals and in an intermittent state of war, a Dahomean attack on Porto Novo inevitably ushered in the Franco-Dahomean campaigns (q.v.) and the establishment of French authority over the entire country. The last Porto Novo king—see TOFFA—died in 1908 and no new kings were enthroned since. Instead, the Toffa lineage, contrary to customary tradition, was given hereditary rights to the new post of superior chief of the Porto Novo canton (q.v.). This caused considerable unrest in the region, right through the 1940's (see MEKPON SOHINGBE).

Since Porto Novo had been the French point of entry into the entire country, as well as an ally, the town became the capital of the new colony. With time, however, Cotonou (q.v.) became the de factor capital. Currently the latter is the center of all modern trade, foreign embassies and most government offices. Prominent institutions still in Porto Novo are gendarmerie headquarters, IRAD and the National Archives (qq.v.). Porto Novo is the administrative capital of Ouémé (q.v.) province and is situated on a coastal lagoon at the extreme southeast of the country. It has an estimated population of 180,000, most of whom are Nagot, Goun and Yoruba (qq.v.). The town is connected by rail and road to Cotonou (some 30 kilometers to the west), by road to Nigeria and by a secondary road to Ketou (q.v.). Though it has a certain charm, the town has been largely bypassed by modernization and urban renewal and is quite seedy with few paved roads and/or modern facilities. King Toffa's (q.v.) palace compound—for long in an acute state of decay and neglect—was refurbished in the 1980's as a National Museum. It possesses many fine Fon and Yoruba (especially Gélédé) sculptures and masks, doors from the palace of Ketou, replicas of those from Abomey (q.v.) and musical instruments. Politically the entire area has been the electoral fiefdom of Sourou-Migan Apithy (q.v.) until his death in 1989.

PORTO NOVO INCIDENTS see HUNKANRIN, LOUIS

PORTO NOVO, KINGS OF. As with all king-lists, there is controversy about some of the dates, and even succession may be in doubt. The following is, therefore, but one of several possible king-lists:

1688–1729	Té Agbanlin
1729–1739	Hiakpon
1739–1746	Lokpon
1746–1752	Houdé
1752–1757	Messi
1757–1761	Houyi
1761–1775	Gbeyon
1775–1783	Ayikpé
1783–1794	Ayaton
1794–1807	Houffon
1807–1816	Adjohan
1816–1818	Toyi
1818–1828	Houzé
1828–1836	Toyon
1838–1848	Meyi
1848–1864	Sodji
1864–1872	Mikpon
1872–1874	Méssi
1874–1908	Toffa
1908–1913	Gbedissin

PORTO NOVO NATIONAL MUSEUM. The premises of the old palace of King Toffa (q.v.), until the 1980's in an acute state of decay, restored with foreign funds as a national museum.

PREFET (PREFECT). Head of the administrative hierarchy at the prefectural (i.e. regional) level in Continental administrative practice. In Benin there were traditionally six prefectures, renamed after 1974 as provinces (q.v.). Overseeing the administrative functions in these units, with broad executive powers as personal delegates of the Minister of Interior, were the *préfets*. After the change in nomenclature of the districts, the name of the *préfets* remained unchanged, though their subservient officials in the subdistricts had their title changed from *sous-préfet* (i.e. sub-prefect) to Chef du District. In accord with the new administrative practice in Benin, the mostly civilian Prefects are assisted by advisory councils at the prefectural/provincial levels (during 1974–1990 by the

Conseil Provincial Revolutionnaire) as are the *chefs du district* (see ADMINISTRATIVE ORGANIZATION). The Prefects in turn sit at the national level in a policy-making body, providing for structural unity from top to bottom.

PRESIDENTIAL COUNCIL. Three-man executive that was to rule Dahomey from May 1970 to May 1976. The structure was decided upon after intense bargaining among Dahomey's triumvirate (q.v.), following the annulment of the results of the 1970 Presidential elections (q.v.) by the interim Military Directorate (q.v.). See COUP OF 1969. According to the agreement, Hubert Maga (q.v.), forerunner in the elections, was to serve as Chairman of the Presidential Council until May 1972, followed by Justin Ahomadégbé (to May 1974), and then Sourou-Migan Apithy (q.v.). Cabinet Ministries were to be apportioned equally among the triumvirate's followers. The Council was not a successful formula for it multiplied executive costs, entrenched regionalism (q.v.) and narrow interests, froze the status quo, and resulted in governmental deadlocks as a fluid and ever changing balance of power developed in it with two members (not always the same) ganging up on the third. The Council was toppled by the 1972 coup d'etat mounted by Mathieu Kérékou (qq.v.), several months after Justin Ahomadégbé had acceded to the Chairmanship.

PRESIDENTIAL ELECTIONS, SECOND ROUND 1992. The results of these elections follow.

Region	Kérékou (%)	Soglo (%)
Atakora	93.6	6.4
Borgou	97.6	2.0
Zou	10.0	90.0
Mono	18.5	81.5
Atlantique	6.8	93.2
Ouémé	9.0	91.0

PRESIDENTIAL PALACE. The extravagant building dominating the esplanade of Cotonou (q.v.), built in 1963 by

President Hubert Maga (q.v.) at a cost then deemed exhorbitant of \$3 million. Designed by the French architect Chomette, who had a penchant for pebble dash walls, multicolored mosaic staircases, marble and golden balconies, construction of the palace at a time of intense austerity and economic hardship was one of the grievances that helped lead to the coup that ousted Maga. The Palace was very much a white elephant, being used only intermittently between 1963 and 1970. In 1970 Maga's return to power brought about its expensive renovation and redecoration.

PRESIDENTS OF DAHOMEY, 1960–1994.

Dec. 1960 to Oct. 1963	Hubert C. Maga
Oct. 1963 to Jan. 1964	Col. Christophe Soglo
Jan. 1964 to Nov. 1965	Sourou-Migan Apithy
Nov. 1965 to Dec. 1965	Tahirou Congacou
Dec. 1965 to Dec. 1967	Gen. Christophe Soglo
Dec. 1967 to June 1968	Lt. Col. Alphonse Alley
July 1968 to Dec. 1969	Emile Derlin Zinsou
Dec. 1969 to May 1970	Lt. Col. Paul Emile de Souza
May 1970 to May 1972	Hubert C. Maga
May 1972 to Oct. 1972	Justin T. Ahomadégbé
Oct. 1972 to April 1991	General Mathieu Kérékou
April 4, 1992–	Nicéphore Soglo

PROTESTANT MISSIONS. The Protestant effort in Benin dates from the middle of the nineteenth century, arriving in the country from the neighboring Anglophone colonies. Indeed, most of the Protestant missionaries in Benin were not French but English. In 1842 a Methodist mission was established in Badagry, Nigeria, near Porto Novo, and the next year Thomas Birch Freeman visited Abomey (qq.v.) to obtain permission to proselytize in Dahomey. The British fort in Whydah (q.v.) became in 1954 the setting for the Methodist mission. Several years later Thomas Marshall (q.v.), son of a fetishist (q.v.) from Badagry, established a Methodist mission in Porto Novo. He was expelled in 1867, after concerted pressure by local fetishists, and only returned in 1876 with the rise of King Toffa (q.v.), who had much more liberal views. By the 1870's other missionaries had arrived in the country, continuing the Protestant proselytizing effort, always aware that Catholicism was very much the majority sect of the Christian religion. In the early 1940's, the Protestant effort started shifting to the north with the establishment of the Djougou (q.v.) mission in 1942. Others sent by the American Sudan Interior Mission followed in 1946 and 1947. Just prior to the nationalization of private religious schools in 1975, there were 257 Protestant mission centers (including schools) in all of Benin, with some 1,200 personnel. Roughly three percent of the population professes to be Protestant, compared to 12 percent who are Catholic. Most of the rest (a growing Muslim minority notwithstanding) hold a wide variety of animist (q.v.) beliefs.

PROVINCE. Post–1974 name of Benin's six prefectures—Atakora, Atlantique, Borgou, Mono, Ouémé and Zou (qq.v.)—further divided into rural and urban districts and a large number of *communes* (qq.v.). The number of districts and *communes* has varied over the years; currently it stands at 84 districts (formerly 39) and 404 *communes*. See also ADMINISTRATIVE ORGANIZATION; PREFET. The administrative system, and nomenclature, are scheduled for imminent change by the new regime of Nicéphore Soglo (q.v.), with provinces specifically slated to revert back to being prefectures.

PRUDENCIO, EUSTACHE WILFRID, 1924– . Teacher, politician and author. Born in Bopa in Mono province (q.v.) on September 20, 1924, Prudencio is a descendant from the Oyo (q.v.) (Nigerian) royal family. He studied in Porto Novo and at the Ecole William Ponty (qq.v.) in Senegal. He stayed on in Senegal as a schoolteacher, becoming involved in Senegalese politics and being appointed Secretary-General of Senegal's RDA (q.v.) branch in Dakar, the MPS. Prudencio returned to Dahomey prior to independence to become Head of the Cabinet of the Minister of Interior, Director of

Information (1957–1958) and Secretary-General of Sourou-Migan Apithy's PRD (qq.v.) party. After a short sojourn in Senegal, Prudencio again returned to Dahomey in 1961 to teach at Cotonou's (q.v.) Lycée Coulibaly, following which he was appointed Principal Inspector of Primary Education in the Ouidah (q.v.) region. In 1964 he served as Propaganda Secretary in the PDD party and was Justin Ahomadégbé's (qq.v.) technical counselor in 1964–1965. During 1964–1965 Prudencio also served on the Municipal Council of Ouidah and presented his candidacy in the 1968 Presidential election, in which he obtained 11,359 of the 287,392 votes cast. He was then appointed to supervise all teaching activities in Cotonou, serving in that capacity between 1968 and 1972. He joined the Presidential Council (q.v.) regime briefly in 1972 as Press Attaché, and was appointed after the coup that year as Head of Press services of the Kérékou (q.v.) regime. In 1975 he was appointed Ambassador to Nigeria and Cameroun, serving in that capacity until 1981, at which time he retired. Prudencio has also written numerous books of poetry and history.

PUBLIC SECURITY FORCE. Section II of the post–1976 reorganized Forces Armées (q.v.) du Benin, charged inter alia with political indoctrination and surveillance.

PYTHON CULT See CULT OF THE GREAT SERPENT.

-Q-

QUENUM, AUGUSTE ALFRED, 1926–1984. Physician and international cult servant. Born in Ouidah (q.v.) on January 10, 1926, Quénum attended Porto Novo's (q.v.) Lycée Victor Ballot and the Ecole William Ponty (q.v.) in Senegal. Between 1948 and 1952 he studied medicine in Dakar, following which he continued his studies in Bordeaux (1954–1957) and taught histology and embryology in Dakar until 1964. Since 1965 Quénum has been Regional Director for Africa of the World Health Organization, based on

Brazzaville (Congo). He has written about 60 articles on his scientific research.

QUENUM, GLETTON IDELPHONSE, 1927– . Magistrate. Born in Ouidah (q.v.) on June 25, 1927, Quénum was educated in law in France, and he practiced law in a private capacity in Benin. He was then appointed Magistrate and, in 1964, Deputy Director of Justice in the Ministry of Justice. He served in this capacity until December 1965 and again between 1967 and 1968. In 1968 he was appointed Deputy Director of the Ministry of Justice in charge of Personnel and Materials, serving until 1974, when he migrated abroad. He is currently in retirement.

QUENUM, MAXIMILIEN POSSEY BERRY, 1911– . Anthropologist. Born in 1911, Quénum was educated locally before continuing anthropological studies in France. His nephew is author Olympe Bhely-Quénum (q.v.). Quénum's most outstanding study—*Au Pays du Fons: Usages et Coutumes de Dahomey*—was widely acclaimed and was chosen by the French Academy as one of 1938's outstanding books. Quénum was elected to the Assemblée Térritoriale (q.v.) in 1957, serving as a Deputy and its Vice-President until 1960. He was also a senator to the Commanauté Francaise (q.v.). Quénum has been in retirement since 1971, in which year he submitted to the electorate an unsuccessful independent party list.

QUIRINO-LANHOUNMEY, JULIEN, 1936– . Economist. Born on February 16, 1936 in Abomey (q.v.), and educated in Catholic schools at home and at the University of Dakar, the Sorbonne and EPHE, Quirino-Lanhounmey served as Technical Adviser to the Presidency in 1963, followed by two years as a journalist in Paris during which he continued his studies at the EPHE. In 1968 he was appointed Head of the Integrated Rural Development program of the UN Economic Commission for Africa and, in 1971, was assigned to be Gabon President Bongo's UN Advisor on Rural Development. In 1975 he was made Chief, Village Technology, and in 1976 Coordinator, African Data Bank Program at the ECA Executive in Addis Ababa, where he still serves.

-R-

RAFIATOU, KARIMOU. Interim Minister of Public Health in the liberalized 1989 cabinet. A teacher by profession, Mrs. Rafiatou had been President of the PRPB (q.v.) Revolutionary Women's organization.

RAILROADS see ORGANISATION COMMUNE DAHOMEY-NIGER DES CHEMINS DE FER ET DES TRANSPORTS (OCDN)

RASSEMBLEMENT DE L'IMPERATIF NATIONAL (RIN). Short-lived opposition party, largely on paper, set up in Allada (q.v.) in 1965 by Valentin Djibodé Aplogan (q.v.), then President of the Supreme Court (q.v.). The party was banned and all those involved in it, including Aplogan, were arrested. See also COMITE DES 104.

RASSEMBLEMENT DEMOCRATIQUE AFRICAIN (RDA). Francophone Africa's first and most influential political movement, with branches in all of France's African territories. Founded in 1946 at the Bamako, Mali, Congress by Ivory Coast's Felix Houphouët-Boigny, the movement was initially militantly nationalist and until 1950 was allied in the French Assembly with the French Communist Party. Its territorial affiliate in Dahomey was Justin Ahomadégbé's Union Démocratique Dahoméenne (UDD) (qq.v.), though in a major 1960 policy shift Houphouët-Boigny recognized Hubert Maga's Rassemblement Démocratique Dahoméen (qq.v.) as the official RDA branch, removing his support from the UDD.

RASSEMBLEMENT DEMOCRATIQUE DAHOMEEN (RDD). Successor to Hubert Maga's Mouvement Démocratique Dahoméen (MDD) (qq.v.), established in August 1957, following a merger of the MDD with Paul Darboux's Indépendants du Nord (qq.v.). Shortly after, Darboux once again bolted the party, setting up his Union des Indépendants du Dahomey (q.v.). Like its predecessor, the RDD was rent by cleavages originating from the historic Nikki-Parakou (qq.v.) friction in the north and by challenges to the Bariba leadership by localized Dendi (qq.v.) groups. In 1958 the RDD merged with the Yoruba (q.v.)-based party of Sourou-Migan Apithy, the Parti Républicain Dahoméen (PRD), to form the Parti Progréssiste Dahoméen (PPD) (qq.v.), local branch of Sénghor's interterritorial movement, the Parti du Régroupement Africain (q.v.). Disagreements between the leadership of the new party regarding the future relationship of Francophone Africa with France brought the collapse of the PPD in 1959 and the reemergence of the old parties. In 1960 the RDD merged again with Apithy's PRD, by now renamed the Parti des Nationalistes Dahoméens, to form the ruling parti unique of 1960–1963, the Parti Dahoméen de l'Unité (PDU) (qq.v.). Besides Maga, leading figures in the PDU were the northerners Chabi Mama and Arouna Mama (qq.v.). With the overthrow of Hubert Maga in 1963, the odd man-out during 1960–1963, Justin Ahomadégbé (q.v.), joined forces with Sourou-Migan Apithy to form a new southern-based parti unique, the Parti Démocratique Dahoméen (q.v.) that was the ruling party during 1964–1965. After General Christophe Soglo's first 1965 coup (q.v.), the RDD reemerged briefly as the Union Nationale Dahoméene (q.v.). On December 22, 1965, Soglo again intervened in the political arena and all political parties were banned. The RDD was resurrected in 1990 as the name of Hubert Maga's political party in the era of competitive elections. See also POLITICAL PARTIES.

RASSEMBLEMENT DES FORCES DEMOCRATIQUES (RFD). A coalition of several political formations with common goals set up on January 15, 1990, at Vankrou by Justin Ahomadégbé's FND party, Hubert Maga's RDD party, Alexandre Adandé and Emile Derlin Zinsou's UNDP party and Joseph Kéké's (ex-Apithy, who had just died) MDR party (qq.v.). Later some of these formations moved closer to set up a political party, while others opted out. See also POLITICAL PARTIES.

RASSEMBLEMENT NATIONAL POUR LA DEMOCRATIE (RND). Post-1990 southern coalition party, a merger of the UDD of Justin Ahomadégbé and the Sourou-Migan Apithy (who had died) PRD power-base, under Joseph Kéké (qq.v.) as its Secretary General. In September 1990 the RND expelled from its ranks Albert Tévoédjré (q.v.) who announced his plans to compete in the Presidential elections against his own party's nominee.

REFERENDUM OF DECEMBER 2, 1990. Referendum on the new civilian semi-Presidential constitution (q.v.), that also approved the elimination from future Presidential elections (via an age clause) of the older generation of politicians (specifically, the triumvirate and Zinsou [qq.v]) that had dominated Beninois political life for 30 years. The turnout was 63.6 percent of 2,056,353 eligible voters, including for the first time Beninois living abroad, with only 6.8 percent rejecting in its totality the new constitution.

The turnout was uniformly high in all regions, from a low of 60.5 percent in both Borgou and Mono, to a high of 69.6 percent in Atlantique (qq.v.), exceeded only by the 76.2 percent (10,697 votes) cast by Beninois registered abroad. Voters had three choices: a "No" red card, to reject the constitution outright (85,717 or 6.8 percent did so, most in Atakora [q.v.]); a "Yes-but" green card, accepting the constitution but without the "below-70" clause for Presidential candidates (250,196 or 19.9 percent voted thus, most in Borgou and Atakora); and a "Yes" white card, ratifying the constitution in full (922,256 or 73.3 percent, the highest percentage being in Zou [q.v.]).

REFUGEES. In 1984 it had been estimated that over 100,000 Beninois were political refugees, residing abroad in opposition to the Marxist regime in Cotonou. (This group of political refugees is distinct from the 250,000 Beninois traditionally resident abroad due to better economic opportunities in other Francophone countries or in France.) Roughly half of the political refugees have returned home since the normalization of politics in Benin, but the other half has been deterred from doing so due to the harsh economic conditions after 17 years of Marxism and mismanagement. Most of the politically disaffected pool of personnel left Benin in 1974–1975 after the liquidation of Michel Aikpe (q.v.), and the harshening of the ideological tenor in Cotonou; indeed, so heavy was the outflow in 1975 that travel controls had to be imposed at all border gates.

Many of the political refugees were intellectuals, civil servants, and professionals. A very high percentage of Benin's teachers deserted the revolution, for example, when private (i.e., church) schools were nationalized and the curricula was officially modified. Some other governmental divisions (besides education) virtually collapsed due to this massive exodus of personnel; since Benin has always had a high percentage of skilled labor and professionals, the personnel shortages (except in the area of education) were only temporary, especially since the periodic expulsions of ''aliens'' in neighboring countries periodically brought back to Benin large numbers of nationals. This outflow of personnel was dramatically reflected in Benin's population growth in the 1970's, which would have been much higher were it not for the net outflow of people.

REGIE DE RAVITAILLEMENT DES NAVIRES (RAVINAR or RNN). Founded in 1976 under the Ministry of Interior and Public Security, RAVINAR was a state company capitalized at 10 million CFA francs and charged with loading and unloading all ships calling at Cotonou port (q.v.).

REGIE DES TRANSPORTS DE LA PROVINCE DE L'AT-LANTIQUE (RTPA). One of the biggest state transportation companies set up in each of Benin's six provinces after the 1972 coup d'etat (q.v.). The RTPA had its headquarters in Cotonou and serviced the Atlantique (qq.v.) province, providing passenger and freight transport. Most companies collapsed economically and/or were privatized starting in 1987.

REGIONALISM. The intense regionalism that has characterized Beninois politics has been the result of the interaction between historic ethnic conflict and animosities (e.g., Fon/Mahi or Dahomey/Porto Novo [qq.v.]) and the geographical and socioeconomic neglect of certain groups (Somba, Bariba [qq.v.]) and their isolation from the rest of the country. The uneven spread of education, politicization and economic development in Benin, to the detriment of the northern regions, has likewise driven a wedge between the various ethnic groups. All these have been exploited by Benin's early political leaders, especially the triumvirate (q.v.), in their quest for political power. In the process, no single "national" candidate or leader emerged but rather regional politicians with electoral fiefdoms in their respective ethnic strongholds.

RELIGIOUS AFFILIATION. The 1961 census, viewed as the most authoritative, noted that 15 percent of the population of Dahomey professed to be Christian (12 percent Catholic, 3 percent Protestant), 13 percent were Muslim, and 65 percent held a variety of animist beliefs. These percentages probably still obtain today, with the possible slow accretion in Muslin adherents. The 1972 coup d'etat (q.v.) and the declaration of a People's Republic rapidly affected the various established churches and religious life in Benin. Catholic, Protestant and Muslim schools were nationalized, triggering an exodus of teachers and principals unwilling to abide by this policy. In June 1976 the government delegalized such traditional religious holidays as Christmas, Pentecost, Easter, Tabaski and others, replacing them with secular holidays that included National Day (November 30), Feast of Production (December 31), New Year's Day (January 1), Labor Day (May 1) and Armed Forces Day (October 26). The government also mounted a major campaign against traditional religion, sorcery and fetishism (q.v.), destroyed sacred trees and sites, and denounced belief in such practices. See also ANIMISM; CATHOLIC MISSIONS; ISLAM; PROTESTANT MISSIONS.

RENOUVEAU, LE. Coalition of parties controlling 34 of the 64 seats formed in July 1992 in Benin's legislature supportive of Nicéphore Soglo's (q.v.) Presidency. The main architect and leader of the coalition was Théophile Paoletti Béhanzin (q.v.). The Rénouveau emerged when the former Nouvelle République alliance, with 21 seats, was jointed by 7 UDS and 6 Convergence (qq.v.) Deputies.

REPATRIATIONS. Prior to the independence, Dahomey, with a large upwardly mobile population and few domestic opportunities, had been a prime exporter of skilled manpower to the various Francophone states of Africa. With the approach of independence, many of these states proceeded with the indigenization of their civil services and/or economies. In the process, thousands of Dahomeans had to be repatriated to their homeland. In October 1958, for example, some 17,000 Dahomeans were expelled from Ivory Coast alone. In October 1962, Gabon expelled 674 and in December 1963 (partly as a result of the deterioration in Dahomey-Niger relations) Niger expelled 16,000 Dahomeans (see DAHOMEY-NIGER BOUNDARY DISPUTE). The total number of Dahomeans outside their homeland is not known but they are estimated at possibly 250,000, residing in France or in other African states, contributing to the functioning of the economy and bureaucracy or enriching the intellectual life of their adopted countries.

REVENDEUSES. Retail merchants, most of whom (290,000 of 297,000) are women, constituting almost one third of Benin's working population. Women also control most of Cotonou's (q.v.) taxicabs and hold half of the commercial bank accounts. Men, by contrast, control much of the smuggling (q.v.) activity across (especially) the Nigerian border, that already by the late 1960's had become an aggravating problem, and is in the 1990's directly or indirectly a major source of employment of Beninois.

RODRIGUEZ, RICHARD (Lt. Colonel) Former senior military officer with a checkered career. Rodriguez first came into national prominence in 1969 when, as Commander of the Ouidah artillery battery and Deputy Commander of the base, his leadership position was "rejected" by troops under his control. Though reinstated by the military, he was shunted from operational control of troops. In 1972 he briefly emerged as Director of the Port of Cotonou Cargo Handling Office but was involved in a very nasty personal dispute with another officer (Captain Béhéton [q.v.]), who encouraged the trade unions (q.v.) to strike against Rodriquez. As a result of this, both officers were purged in August 1973, though Rodriguez did emerge once again as Deputy Chief-of-Staff in March 1974, with the rank of Major. Promoted to Lieutenant Colonel in August 1975, he was brought into the cabinet in January 1976 as Minister of Mines and Equipment and was finally retired from the army and government—again allegedly due to opposition to his leadership among troops—in 1978.

-S-

SABE, ZACHARIE, 1938– . Agricultural engineer. Born in 1938 in Séméré, Sabé was educated at home and in France and graduated as an agricultural engineer. He returned home and was attached to the Natitingou (q.v.) agricultural service and, in 1967, was brought into the cabinet of the Minister of Rural Development as Cabinet Director. In 1970 he returned to agricultural service duties in Atakora (q.v.), and in 1976 he was appointed head of a division in the Ministry of Rural Development.

SAGA PETROLEUM see OIL; SOCIETE SAGA PETROLEUM BENIN.

SAGBO, CYRILLE GUY ROGER, 1938– . Veteran Foreign Ministry officer and Ambassador to France. Born in Ouidah (q.v.) on July 7, 1938, and a lawyer by profession, having been trained in Law in Toulouse (1961, 1972), and in diplomacy at IHEOM (Paris, 1962), Sagbo served as Deputy-Director of International Organizations and Technical Assistance at the Foreign Ministry (1964–1969), then as Director of Political and Judicial Affairs (1969–1971) and Cabinet Director of the Minister of Foreign Affairs (1971–1971). In 1973 he was appointed Secretary General of Foreign Affairs in that Ministry, but in 1975 was seconded to the Ministry of Interior for one year, before moving to an educational career as the Beninois revolution moved into high gear. He then taught for 14 years at both the National University of Benin (q.v.) and Ecole Nationale d'Administration (1976–1990) before being named by the normalized regime in Cotonou Ambassador to France, the top diplomatic post of his country. Sagbo has filled numerous other diplomatic posts, including representing Benin at the UN's General Assembly in 1965, 1968, 1970 and 1973.

SAINT JEAN-BAPTISTE D'AJUDA. Name of the Portuguese fort in historic Ouidah. See also OUIDAH HISTORICAL MUSEUM.

SAKE. Title of the king of the precolonial Bariba state of Kandi (qq.v.).

SALAMI, KIFULI. Minister of the Plan, Statistics and Economic Analysis between 1984 and 1987. A conservative Yoruba (q.v.) economist with important personal and trade connections with Nigeria, Salami had been a former JUD (q.v.) member in his youth.

SAMBO, SOULEY MAMA. Fulani (q.v.) former commander of the nearly all Fulani Bataillon de la Garde Presidentielle (BPI) (q.v.) that protected the Kérékou (q.v.) regime. Sambo has also been Prefect of Atlantique, and in February moved to Parakou in Borgou (qq.v.). Following the civilianization of Benin Sambo was assigned to normal military duties.

SANI AGATA, AMZAT, 1901–1970. Powerful Porto Novo (q.v.) merchant and early National Assembly (q.v.) figure. Born in Porto Novo on March 20, 1901, to an established trading family with extensive connections in Nigeria, Sani Agata was drawn into the Sourou-Migan Apithy (q.v.) political network and was elected to the Assemblée Territorial (q.v.) in 1952. He served as Deputy from Porto Novo for 11 years, becoming a powerful figure within it. He was Speaker of the House between 1957 and 1963 and member of several of committees, including Vice-President of the powerful Economic Affairs Committee and Rapporteur of the Finance and Budget Committee. After the 1963 coup d'etat (q.v.), Sani Agata retired from politics.

SANTOS, JOSE FIRMIN. Early publisher who clashed with the French colonial administration in the 1930's. Born in Agoué in 1893 to a "Brazilian" (q.v.) family, Santos worked for the postal service but tendered his resignation when a European was appointed to a similar post at a much higher salary. In 1927 he assisted in the establishment of the *Voix du Dahomey* (q.v.), which was to become one of Dahomey's early influential newspapers, and became its Directing Editor after the departure of Jean da Matha Sant'Anna. In the early 1930's he ran afoul of the French colonial administration on a host of grounds, including a series of inflammatory articles in his paper in 1932 that lambasted the economic exploitation of the country. Put on trial he was sentenced to a stiff financial fine of 200 francs in 1936.

SARRE, EUSTACHE, 1939– . Minister of Environment, Habitat and Urbanization. Born in Porto Novo (q.v.) on March 29, 1939, Sarre studied in his home town and Parakou (q.v.) before proceeding to the University of Dakar (1961–1963) and Reims (1964–1965), followed by two years at a specialized meteorology college. He then returned to Dakar in 1973 as meteorologist and, in 1976, joined the Cotonou Meteorological Center. Between 1976 and 1980 he served as General Director of the Ministry of Transport, returning to the former Center in 1980, eventually becoming its Head. In 1985 he was appointed Head of Benin's meteorological services and in 1988 was ASECNA's official representative in Benin. Brought into Nicéphore Soglo's (q.v.) cabinet in 1990 as Minister of Transport, in 1991 he was reassigned to his current post.

SAVALOU. Small town north of Abomey (q.v.), historically center of a Mahi (q.v.) kingdom during the precolonial era. Founded by Ahossou Soha (Gbaguidi I) in the seventeenth century, the area was constantly pillaged by Dahomean troops in search of slaves: indeed, the Mahi areas in general were the favored hunting grounds of Abomey for slaves for the coastal trade and for the Annual Customs (q.v.). The Mahi resisted furiously all these encroachments but shortly before the arrival of French force of arms in the area, Savalou finally became a tributary of Dahomey (q.v.). The town itself is in a region that has been sadly neglected by both the colonial administration and all post-independence governments.

SAVE KINGDOM. Small Yoruba (q.v.) kingdom centered around the town of the same name, not to be confused with Savi (q.v.). There are quite contradictory oral traditions about its foundation and tumultuous history, located as it is at the crossroads of Fon, Oyo, Abeokuta, and Bariba (qq.v.) expansionist pressures. The population was always quite small and was periodically reinforced by influxes of refugees from other regions. The kingdom controlled some of the territory between the Okpara and Ouémé rivers (qq.v.). Presently Savé is a small village, much neglected, but finally benefitting from some industrial activity, namely the Savé sugar complex, that has brought the area badly needed modern jobs.

SAVI. Capital of the small precolonial Kingdom of Houéda (q.v.), some 16 kilometers from its more famous (abroad) port of Ouidah (q.v.). The Houéda kingdom was vanquished and absorbed with some difficulty by Dahomey in the 1720's. Ouidah then became Dahomey's main slave port, while Savi—the former seat of Houéda royal authority—fell into total decay.

SE. One of the biggest villages of Mono (q.v.) province, some 80 kilometers northwest of Cotonou on the road to Lokossa (qq.v.). Famous for its excellent pottery, its founders were from Togo, possibly part of the Notsé migration.

SECTION DEUX. Popular appellation for the feared Second Section of the Forces Armée (q.v.) du Benin, the Public Security Force charged inter alia with political surveillance and indoctrination.

SECULAR HOLIDAYS. Following the June 1976 delegalization of all traditional Christian and Muslim holidays (including Christmas and Tabaski), a series of secular holidays was declared in effect, including January 1—New Year's Day; May 1—Labor Day; October 26—People's Armed Forces

Day; November 30th—National Day; December 31—Feast of Production.

SEME. Location of Benin's offshore oil shales, close to the maritime border with Nigeria. See also OIL.

SEMINARY OF OUIDAH. Important seminary situated in the historic port of Ouidah (q.v.) that is also the center of Beninois fetishism (q.v.). Opened on February 17, 1914, but inactive until 1919 due to the absence of instructors consequent to dislocations caused by the First World War, many of the current facilities were built in 1929–1930 by the Swiss Saint Gallen diocese. The first local priest to be ordained was Moulero in 1928. The seminary played a major role in the socioeconomic development of the colony of Dahomey.

SERO KPERA ILORINKPUNON (d. 1831). Legendary King of Nikki (q.v.) who died at the gates of Ilorin (in Nigeria) in the battles against the Fulani (q.v.), who mobilized large armies of Yoruba of the Oyo Empire (qq.v.) in an alliance with the Bariba from Borgou (qq.v.). Sero Kpéra ("*Ilorinkpunon*" = died in Ilorin) rose to power at a time when the original Nikki hegemony over outlying Bariba states was being challenged by secessions. He is credited with temporarily crushing many of the attempted secessions, especially that of Kouandé (q.v.). The traditional friction between Nikki and Parakou (q.v.) was greatly exacerbated by the fact that Parakou was the only Bariba state not to dispatch an army against Ilorin, a fact that is still remembered among the Bariba and that played a role in post-independence politics in separating Parakou from Nikki in the common northern political front against the south. At the same time, historic Yoruba fears of the Bariba divided the nineteenth century military alliance against the Fulani. The Bariba cavalry was betrayed by these erstwhile allies, and unsupported by the promised Yoruba troops, was soundly defeated at Ilorin. Memories of this "historic" betrayal has also been carried into the modern era in the form of a deep mistrust of southerners in general and Yoruba in particular.

SERVICE CIVIQUE. A branch of the armed forces of Dahomey training (with Israeli assistance and some instructors until 1972) ex-servicemen (later, reservists, still later unemployed rural youth) in modern agrarian techniques, following which trainees established their own camps, raised their own crops and undertook various other projects. The precise structure of the Service Civique has varied over the years, as has its official name. In the past (and under a different structure and name), it was subordinated to both the Ministry of Agriculture and of Defense and was very much an inter-ministerial football. The program at all times suffered from high desertion rates, poor financing (sometimes picked up by Israel), and counter-pressures from the traditional social ethos once trainees were on their own farms. Following the radicalization of politics in 1974, the Service Civique promptly acquired a new impetus, and in October 1977 legislation creating a new Commission Nationale du Service Civique was enacted, aimed at encompassing a much wider and larger group of youth in civic action projects.

SERVICE DE DOCUMENTATION ET D'INFORMATION (SDI). Kérékou's (q.v.) secret police, much feared and involved in a variety of atrocities and torture, while under Captain Yacouba Maman (q.v.). See FORCES ARMEES DU BENIN.

SINANDE. Sacred Bariba (q.v.) village some 35 kms. from Bémbéréké where konde, the sacred crocodile, is located.

SINSIN, MARCELLIN. (Colonel) Deputy-Commander of the armed forces since March 1993.

SINZOGAN, BENOIT (Colonel), 1930– . Former head of the gendarmerie (q.v.) and member of the 1970 Military Directorate (q.v.). Born in Abomey (q.v.) on July 14, 1930, and of Fon (q.v.) origins, Sinzogan was part of the powerful Fon clique of officers that controlled the armed forces of Dahomey from 1965 to 1967 and that Major Maurice Kouandété (q.v.) worked to discredit and tried to purge. Sinzogan joined the French colonial armies in 1953 and, after being commissioned in 1960, served as Gen. Christophe Soglo's (q.v.) aide-de-camp, commander of the First Battalion (Cotonou), and chairman of the Comité Militaire de Vigilance (q.v.) when the latter was set up in April 1967. Following Kouandété's 1967 coup d'etat (q.v.), Sinzogan was under house arrest for two days until the Kouandété-Alphonse Alley (q.v.) compromise resulted in an interim military administration headed by the latter two, with Sinzogan as Minister of Foreign Affairs (December 1967–July 1968). After the army appointed Emile Derlin Zinsou (q.v.) as civilian President of Dahomey, Kouandété displaced Alley as Chief-of-Staff and in a rearrangement of senior positions Sinzogan was moved to head the National Police. He occupied that post between September 1968 and August 1970, at which time he became head of the gendarmerie. Following Kouandété's 1969 coup (q.v.), a three-man ruling Military Directorate (q.v.) was formed in which Sinzogan was a member (1969–1970) in charge of the Ministries of Foreign Affairs, Justice, and Education. In the 1972 conspiracy trial, Sinzogan served as alternate president of the military court that issued the death sentences of Kouandété and two other officers. Following the 1972 coup by Mathieu Kérékou (q.v.), Sinzogan was purged together with the entire senior hierarchy of the army. In the subsequent allocations of sinecures at the head of Dahomey's State industries, he was appointed government Commissioner in charge of the Société Nationale pour le Développement Forestier (SNAFOR) (q.v.), and later he was retired on a government pension. Though Sinzogan has often wielded considerable power, apart from one minor power gambit in 1970, he has been too timid to mount a coup, one of Benin's very few senior officers not to attempt to.

SITEX. Chinese-Beninois textile factor inaugurated in May 1987 in Lokossa (q.v.) near the Togolese border. Constructed at the cost of 7.5 billion CFA francs, the plant is expected to process 2,500 tons of cotton a year, employing 1,120 people.

SLAVE COAST. Geographic stretch of the coast of West Africa which a large number of slave ships visited to purchase slaves from native middlemen. The Coast is conventionally defined as the region between the Volta river (in contemporary Ghana) and Lagos (in Nigeria), and more specifically the coastal regions controlled by the Adja (q.v.) and Ewe peoples, whose main kingdoms were Ouidah and Allada (qq.v.). See also SLAVE TRADE.

SLAVE TRADE. With the advent of the slave trade, the villages and ports along Dahomey's coast became important calling places for slave ships. Among them Ouidah (q.v.) became a major entrepot for slaves, and domination of this port— nominally independent (see HOUEDA KINGDOM) but more usually under the control of the kingdom of Allada and later Dahomey (qq.v.)—was the goal of various foreign companies. With the conquest of Ouidah by Dahomey in 1727, higher taxes levied on all ships anchoring in the port raised the attractiveness of alternate sources of supply such as Porto Novo (q.v.) and ports along the Gold Coast.

Some of the most important interior long-distance routes for slave caravans ran from Kano in Nigeria via Nikki to Parakou (qq.v.) and thence either through Mahi (q.v.) country to Allada and Ouidah, or to the Ashanti country and then to the Gold Coast ports. Other major supplies were the Dahomey kingdom (q.v.), that sold its excess of war captives not needed for the Annual Customs (q.v.) rites, as well as local ethnic groups in the interior. In 1807 Britain declared the slave trade illegal and started patrolling the coast, intercepting slave ships. The trade continued for several decades, however, since many of the kingdoms along the coast or controlling the caravan routes had a vested interest in it. Dahomey, in particular, required a constant import of guns and ammunition for its perennial military campaigns, which could be purchased only through the sale of slaves. See also ALLADA; DAHOMEY, KINGDOM OF; OUIDAH.

SMUGGLING. A major problem in most African states, the illegal transport of goods across state boundaries is a sign of (1) the permanence of traditional precolonial trade routes, (2) informal market activities in action, (3) the lack of control of African governments over their fissiparous borders, and (4) the profit motive—especially enhanced when neighboring countries have substantially different import/export tariffs, taxes and state commodity purchasing policies. While traditional patterns of trade have continued in Benin, smuggling activities are heightened by neighboring Nigeria's high import tariffs alongside Dahomey's low tariff policy. Hence large quantities of printed wax, cigarettes and liquor are smuggled into Nigeria from Benin and, conversely, Nigerian cocoa and palm kernels reach Benin where they are bartered for consumer goods which are smuggled back to Nigeria. So important are smuggling activities to sectors of Benin's population residing along the Nigerian border (and especially in Porto Novo [q.v.]), that one important cause for the urban unrest under President Emile Derlin Zinsou (q.v.) was the latter's decision to try to clamp down on this illicit trade. Complicating matters is the fact that the frontiers are long, the populations either sympathetic to or engaged in smuggling, and the patrolling frontier guards are both understaffed and paid by smugglers to turn a blind eye to the illicit trade. In the 1970's more effective patrolling of the border regions on the part of Nigeria has brought about a sharp fall in Beninois exports of coffee and cocoa—crops Benin does not grow! Cocoa exports, for example, dropped from 20,000 tons in 1973 to 2,750 in 1975, and coffee exports from 2,772 tons in 1973 to 572 in 1975. However, by the 1980's Benin's economic decline under the Marxist regime of Kérékou (q.v.) triggered a massive spurt in smuggling activities (including by military personnel in the Beninois government) so that by the mid-1980's it was regarded as Benin's "national vocation."

SO see OUEME RIVER

SOCIETE AGRO-ANIMALE BENINO-ARABE-LIBYENNE (SABLY). Joint company set up in 1979. Capitalized at 430 million CFA francs, with Benin holding 51 percent of the capital and Libya the remainder, SABLY in effect took over the operations of SONAPA (q.v.).

SOCIETE BENINO-ARABE-LIBYENNE DE PECHE MARITIME (BELIPECHE). Joint company set up in 1979, commencing activities in 1981. The original capital of 450 million CFA francs was put up by Benin (51 percent) and

Libya (49 percent). BELIPECHE was involved in offshore fishing, utilizing modern trawlers and technology, the catches being destined for the smoking plant at Jacko and for sale via Benin's national AGB supermarkets. BELIPECHE, in effect, took over many of the functions of the previous SONAPECHE (q.v.) state company.

SOCIETE BENINO-ARABE-LIBYENNE DES MINES (BE-LIMINES). Joint company set up in 1979 and operational since early 1982. It was capitalized at $2 million, with Benin putting up 51 percent of the funds and Libya 49 percent. The company aimed at exploiting Benin's marble deposits and developing other mineral deposits, including gold (q.v.).

SOCIETE BENINOISE DE PALMIER A HUILE (SOBEPALH). Much mismanaged company that used to control Benin's prime cash crop, palm oil (q.v.). Founded in 1961 as SONADER (q.v.), and fully nationalized in 1975, its capitalization remained unchanged at 150 million CFA francs. The company was involved in the production of palm and cottonseed oil, with a 28,000 hectare palm forest and three (later six) palm-oil presses at Grand Hinvi, Agouvy, Houin Agamé, Gbada, Avrankou and Abomey-Calavi (q.v.). The latter had a capacity of 215,000 tons per year. SOBEPALH was closely linked to another state company, SONICOG (q.v.), to which it transferred palm oil and palm products.

The company was so badly mismanaged in the late 1970's and early 1980's that it was incapable of meeting any contracted delivery schedules, which caused disruptions all along the marketing chain, local and foreign. In 1976 drought and other natural calamities piled up further problems, causing major cash flow bottlenecks, idling much of the company's large truck fleet and triggering the cannibalization of parts from up to one half of the fleet. The company was unable to pay its labor force with any regularity, triggering strikes and sabotage. Its financial problems showing no end, and its deficits progressively larger, SOBEPALH was finally dissolved in April 1982. Its facilities were taken over by SONICOG, which also undertook some of the operations of SOBEPALH.

SOCIETE BENINOISE DE SIDERURGIE (SBS). One of the few new private industrial ventures since the 1990 economic liberalization. A steel wire and corrugated sheet mill plant set up by an American entrepreneur in 1991 (who operates a similar factory in Togo) in the abandoned Bata shoe factory near Cotonou (q.v.). Though Benin has only a limited (7,000 tons) demand for these products, the plant expects to export to Nigeria and Burkina Faso.

SOCIETE BENINOISE D'EAU ET D'ELECTRICITE (SBEE). Name of the State company that in 1973 replaced the privately owned SDEE. SBEE operated six diesel thermal stations in Cotonou, Porto Novo, Bohicon, Parakou, Natitingou, and Lokossa (qq.v.) with a capacity of over 21,000 KVA, which is only a small percentage of Benin's needs. The company imports electricity from Ghana, and from the Benin-Togo Nangbéto Dam (q.v.) complex via the joint Togo-Benin Compagnie Eléctrique du Benin (CEB (q.v.). In 1984 Ghana caused a major electricity crisis in both Benin and Togo when electricity exports were drastically curtailed with the fall in the water levels of the Volta Lake, A consequence of the drought in West Africa.

SOCIETE BENINOISE DES CIMENTS ET DES MATERIAUX ANNEXES (SOBECIMA) see SOCIETE BENINOISE DES MATERIAUX DE CONSTRUCTION (SOBEMAC)

SOCIETE BENINOISE DES GAZ INDUSTRIELS (SOBEGI). Bottling and manufacturing plant for oxygen, acetylene and a few other industrial gases, with a capacity of 350,000 cubic meters of oxygen and 60,000 cubic meters of acetylene per year. The company was fully nationalized in 1975.

SOCIETE BENINOISE DES MATERIAUX DE CONSTRUCTION (SOBEMAC). Successor in 1976 to the Société Béninoise des Ciments et des Materiaux Annexes (SOBECIMA). SOBEMAC was set up to market locally cement produced by the Société des Ciments d'Onigbolo (q.v.), and other construction products imported from abroad.

SOCIETE BENINOISE DES TEXTILES (SOBETEX). Successor to the Industrie Cotonière du Dahomey (q.v.) known as ICODA. A mixed-economy enterprise in which Benin possessed 49 percent of equity, SOBETEX was involved in bleaching and printing of cloth imported from Ghana. Originally established in Cotonou (q.v.) (1968), the company was capitalized at 900 million CFA franc, had a 20 million meter capacity and an original 13.3 percent State participation. The company was privatized in 1991.

SOCIETE BENINOISE DU GAZ (SOBOGAZ). State company set up in 1975, with a plant in Cotonou (q.v.), to extract juice from an array of fruits and to manufacture soft drinks. Capitalized at 5 million CFA francs, the company has a capacity of 16,000 hl.

SOCIETE BENINOISE DU KENAF (SOBEK). State company, successor to the Société Dahoméenne Agricole et Industrielle du Kenaf (SADAK) (q.v.), which had been established in 1965. SOBEK is capitalized at 343 million CFA francs, cultivates jute and kenaf, exports kenaf fiber and manufactures twine, sacks and other related products. It has factories in Bohicon (q.v.) for the manufacture of twine sacks and in Parakou (q.v.) for the manufacture of jute, kenaf and related products. Its Director General is Emile Paraiso and its Deputy Manager is Antoine Boya (qq.v.). The company employs some 460 employees. It was badly hurt in the mid-1970's by extreme variations in crop harvests.

SOCIETE BON-HIA. Mixed-economy enterprise involved in the production of cattle feed that was marketed inter alia to Benin's State and experimental farms. Capital investments have amounted to 148 million CFA francs and the company has the capacity to produce 12,000 tons per year.

SOCIETE DAHOMEEN D'IMPORTATION ET DU COMMERCE (SODAIC). State company with a limited monopoly over the import and local marketing of a number of commodities. In 1974 SODAIC's functions were redefined and expanded, and its name changed to Société Nationale d'Importation de Bénin (SONIB) (q.v.).

SOCIETE DAHOMEENNE AGRICOLE ET INDUSTRIELLE DU KENAF (SODAK). Former joint Italian-Dahomean company founded in 1963 with a capitalization of 343 million CFA francs. It was involved in the cultivation and export of kenaf and the manufacture of twine and sacks. With headquarters in Cotonou (q.v.) the company employed 460 workers. Serious lags in domestic cultivation of kenaf in the late 1960's reduced SODAK's output and created fiscal problems. In the reorganization that followed, kenaf cultivation operations were turned over to another company— Société des Fibres Textiles—with SODAK retaining its main manufacturing plant in Bohicon (q.v.) until 1981. However, following the 1972 coup d'etat (q.v.), this agreement was annulled. SODAK was nationalized, and its name changed to Société Béninoise du Kenaf (SOBEK) (q.v.).

SOCIETE DAHOMEENNE DE BANQUE (SDB) see BANQUE COMMERCIALE DU BENIN (BCB)

SOCIETE DAHOMEENNE DE TEXTILES (SODATEX). Cotonou-based textile production company. Established originally with a capitalization of 500 million CFA francs and Dahomean State participation. The company was renamed SOBETEX (q.v.) in 1975 and its base of operations was expanded.

SOCIETE DAHOMEENNE D'ELECTRICITE ET D'EAU (SDEE) see SOCIETE BENINOISE D'ELECTRICITE ET D'EAU (SBEE)

SOCIETE D'ALIMENTATION GENERALE DU BENIN (AGB). State company set up in 1978, consisting of a series of food stores throughout the country. The chain has received both financial and technical assistance from abroad, especially Switzerland. It included 17 supermarkets and ten wholesale stores. It had a total monopoly over the import and marketing of foodstuffs in Benin, including the marketing of soft drinks and tobacco products. Within a few years the company was bankrupt, plundered by its State administrators and mismanaged to boot. The company's operations were taken over in 1984 by the Swiss consortium.

SOCIETE D'AMENAGEMENT ET DE DEVELOPPEMENT DE LA VALLEE DE L'OUEME (SADEVO). Established on July 1, 1972, SADEVO was involved primarily in the development of the Ouémé river (q.v.) valley's 1,200 hectares of irrigated rice lands, a pilot project. The company was superseded in April 1975 by SONIAH (q.v.), which had a countrywide mandate, and SONIAH itself was dissolved (and some of its functions taken over by another State company) in 1982 as part of the streamlining of the State sector necessitated by the awesome deficits being piled up by State companies.

SOCIETE DE COMMERCIALISATION ET DE CREDIT AGRI-COLE DAHOMEENNE (SOCAD). State organization that on June 30, 1972, succeeded the Office de Commercialisation Agricole du Dahomey (OCAD). Its main function was to help agrarian development through grants of loans and machinery. After the 1972 coup d'etat (q.v.) the former Chief-of-Staff, Paul Emile De Souza (q.v.), was appointed government Commissioner of SOCAD. The activities of SOCAD were terminated in 1975 when the company was merged with the new Caisse Nationale de Credit Agricole (CNCA) (q.v.).

SOCIETE DE DISTRIBUTION DE FOURNITURES, MATE-RIEL ADMINISTRATIF ET SCOLAIRE (SODIMAS). State company under the Ministry of Commerce, with a monopoly over the provision of furniture to the State and parastatal sectors.

SOCIETE DE GESTION DES MARCHES AUTONOMES (SOGEMA). State company under the Ministry of Interior and Public Security, charged with the centralization and administration of all existing traditional (i.e., private) markets in the country and the planning and erection of new ones. Its activities, originally regarded as threatening private traders, have in fact greatly benefited small cultivators and private vendors, especially outside the main large markets.

SOCIETE DE TRANSIT ET DE CONSIGNATION DU BENIN (SOTRACOB). Mixed-economy enterprise set up in 1975 and capitalized at 100 million CFA francs with 49 percent State equity and 51 percent private capital. SOTRACOB groups together all the hitherto private customs brokers in the country and is the private sector's equivalent of SON-ATRAC (q.v.), providing brokerage services.

SOCIETE DES BRASSERIES DU DAHOMEY (SOBRADO). Brewing and bottling industry with a plant just outside Cotonou (q.v.), producing beer, soft drinks and ice. Founded in 1957, with a capitalization of 550 million CFA francs, 94 percent of SOBRADO's shares were owned by the French holding company SOGEPAL, before nationalization in 1975, when its name changed to the Société Nationale de Brasseries de la République Populaire du Bénin (La Béninoise). After nationalization the company piled up huge deficits; it was de-nationalized in 1992.

SOCIETE DES CIMENTS D'ONIGBOLO (SCO). Originally a joint Nigeria (41 percent) Benin (49 percent) enterprise, with a minority Danish interest (10 percent). The latter delivered and assembled the complete factory at Onigbolo, just north of Pobé, near the Nigerian border, in mid-1982. Initiated by the two countries as far back as 1975, the project costs reached 25 billion CFA francs, including such infrastructure improvements as roads to the border with Nigeria. The company, which never reached full production, has a capacity of producing 500,000 tons of cement, with 60 percent of this amount pledged to the Nigerian market. The plant taps mineral reserves exploitable for 110 years, and employed 350 workers and six expatriate experts. Within Benin its products are marketed by SOBEMAC. However, cost overruns, reductions (up to 35 percent) in the supply of electricity from Ghana and mismanagement have made SCO's products much more expensive than comparable imports, so that Nigeria has reneged on most of its purchase commitments, while Benin, which consumes its products, consequently ends up with overly high construction costs. The company, virtually bankrupt since inception, was saved several times by infusions of State funds.

SOCIETE DES CIMENTS DU BENIN (SCB). Formerly the Société des Ciments du Dahomey, the SCB is a mixed-economy enterprise set up in 1971 with 80 percent Sate participation (previously only 20 percent). It runs a clinker plant in Cotonou (q.v.), with a capacity of 240,000 tons, though it has operated for long at only 50 percent of capacity. In 1978 a second cement factory was erected in Benin, the fully State-owned Société Nationale des Ciments (SONACI) (q.v.), in order to pick up the slack in cement production. It too worked at half capacity, and yet there continued to be a shortage of cement in Benin. In 1980 the joint Nigerian-Beninois Onigbolo cement complex (see SOCIETE DES CIMENTS D'ONIGBOLO) was initiated to assure the local market of cement supplies and to supply Nigeria with some of its needs. Only with the erection of the latter company—also working at only 60 percent of capacity!!—has the local market been assured adequate supplies, though at high cost. Cement products in Benin are marketed exclusively via two state-owned companies: the Société Beninoise des Matériaux de Construction (q.v.) and the Société Provinciale des Matériaux de Commercialisation de Produits Manufacturés.

SOCIETE DES CIMENTS DU DAHOMEY see SOCIETE DES CIMENTS DU BENIN

SOCIETE DES FIBRES TEXTILES (SOFITEX) see SOCIETE DAHOMEENNE AGRICOLE ET INDUSTRIELLE DU KENAF (SODAK)

SOCIETE DES PRODUITS PLASTIQUES DU BENIN (SPB). Joint company set up in 1982 and operational in 1984, charged with manufacturing a wide array of plastic ware for the local market.

SOCIETE DES TRANSPORTS ROUTIERS DU BENIN (TRANSBENIN). Parastatal organization set up in 1977 in Cotonou (q.v.) with 300 million CFA francs in capital and 49 percent State equity. The company centralized all long-distance transport of goods and passengers, previously fragmented in the hands of a variety of private companies.

SOCIETE DU CAR DU BENIN (SOCAB). Mixed-economy enterprise comprising 20 percent State participation and 80 percent from private French sources. The company, in existence before the adoption of Marxism, was not nationalized in the 1974–1975 spate of nationalizations. It assembled Citroen vehicles, the parts being dispatched from France, and had the capacity of producing 800 vehicles a year.

SOCIETE GENERALE DU COMMERCE DU BENIN (SOGE-COB). Former State company charged with the import and internal marketing of an array of products not specifically allocated to other State importing agencies. SOGECOB in essence took over part of the functions of the former SONACEB (q.v.). Its activities were wound down in 1987.

SOCIETE MINIERE DU DAHOMEY-NIGER (SMDN). Cassiterite mining company currently involved solely in Niger where it mines cassiterite and exports its entire output to Nigeria. Founded in 1941, the company was involved during the colonial era in mining gold (q.v.) in the Perma river region in Dahomey as well. Its activities lasted between 1941 and 1955, at which time the company withdrew from Dahomey, due to the unprofitability of what were in essence very modest gold reserves. See also GOLD.

SOCIETE NATIONALE D'ASSURANCES ET DE REASSURANCES (SONAR). State company set up in Cotonou (q.v.) under the Ministry of Finance with a monopoly over commercial insurance activities in Benin. Capitalized at 300 million CFA francs, the company replaced a number of large foreign (French) insurance companies and nationalized several local ones.

SOCIETE NATIONALE DE BRASSERIES DE LA REPUBLIQUE POPULAIRE DU BENIN (LA BENINOISE). Successor in name to the pre-1975, privately owned Société des Brasseries du Dahomey (SOBRADO) (q.v.), which was nationalized. The company has two plants, producing a variety of drinks, beer, sodas and juices. The oldest factory is in Cotonou (q.v.) (set up in 1959), with a capacity of producing 450,000 hl of beer and 150,000 of other drinks. In June 1981 a new factory was opened in Parakou (q.v.), with a capacity of 150,000 hl of beer and 80,000 of other drinks, and capable of doubling this capacity with minor infrastructure changes. La Béninoise also has a bottling plant at Possotomé, under license from Coca Cola, and originally had plans to set up a third plant in Abomey (q.v.), to be financed by Czechoslovakia. Current capitalization of the company stands at 693 million CFA francs. It was privatized in 1992.

SOCIETE NATIONALE DE COMMERCIALISATION DES PRODUITS PETROLIERS (SONACOP). Former State company founded in 1974 following the nationalization of petroleum marketing networks in Benin. It has a monopoly over all petrol imports and distribution.

SOCIETE NATIONALE DE COMMERCIALISATION ET D'EXPORTATION DU BENIN (SONACEB). Former State company set up in Cotonou (q.v.) in 1972 with a monopoly over the collection of agricultural products, with the exception of palm-related items, cotton and tobacco. Its functions were reorganized several times, however, the latter commodities being its last responsibilities. In the reorganization of the State sector in the late-1970's, the company was dissolved and most of its duties allocated to SONAPRA (q.v.).

SOCIETE NATIONALE DE CONSTRUCTION ET DES TRAVAUX PUBLICS (SONACOTRAP). Centralized construction arm of the Ministry of Public Works, which has a monopoly over all building activities in the public and parastatal sector in Benin.

SOCIETE NATIONALE DE GESTION IMMOBILIERE (SONAGIM). Former State company set up in 1978 under the Ministry of Public Works and responsible for the administration and maintenance of all State buildings. Grossly mismanaged and unprofitable, it was one of the first to be closed down in the bout of savings and privatizations that began in 1984.

SOCIETE NATIONALE DE MATERIEL ELECTRIQUE ET ELECTROMENAGER (SONAMEEM). State company set up in 1978 with responsibilities over the import and domestic maintenance of specialized electrical and electronic equipment. In 1982 the company was liquidated as a separate entity and its functions taken over by other State organs.

SOCIETE NATIONALE DE PAPETERIE ET DE LIBRAIRIE (SONAPAL). State company set up in 1974 with a monopoly over the import of books, paper products, and school textbooks as well as office supplies. The company was merged in 1982 with the Société de Distribution de Fournitures, Matériel Administratif et Scolaire (SODIMAS), (q.v.) and closed down a few years later.

SOCIETE NATIONALE DE PECHE (SONAPECHE). Former parastatal company set up in 1971 to sponsor fishing cooperatives, improve fish supplies on Benin markets and provide technical assistance with marketing. Overfishing and poor climatic conditions, however, resulted in declining yields, from 6,592 tons in 1972 to 2,028 tons in 1978. SONIPECHE became redundant once BELIPECHE (q.v.) was created in 1979.

SOCIETE NATIONALE DE TRANSIT ET CONSIGNATION (SONATRAC). First State company to be set up after the 1972 coup d'etat (q.v.) and the radicalization of politics in 1974. Formed under the Ministry of Transportation and Communications in March 1974, SONATRAC was charged with being the sole customs broker, transport agency and clearing house for the State and parastatal sector. A parallel structure—SOTRACOB (q.v.)—was set up for the private sector. In 1979 a major embezzlement scandal, involving millions of CFA francs, rocked the company and required new infusions of funds. The company was dissolved in 1989.

SOCIETE NATIONALE D'EQUIPEMENT (SONAE). State company established in 1975 in Cotonou (q.v.) with 300 million CFA francs in capitalization. The company controlled all imports and exports of capital goods. It is now defunct.

SOCIETE NATIONALE DES CIMENTS (SONACI). Former State company established in Cotonou (q.v.) in 1978 and operating a clinker factory. Total capacity of the plant is 200,000 tons per year, though it has been working at half capacity. SONACI was set up specifically to satisfy the local need for cement that had not been met by the previously existing SCB (q.v.). In 1981 a new large plant was erected at Onigbolo (see SOCIETE DES CIMENTS D'ONIGBOLO), as a joint Nigeria-Benin enterprise, and only then was the Beninois market fully sated. Distribution of SONACI's products were, until the economic liberalization, in the hands of two state distributing companies, the Société Béninoise des Matériaux de Construction (q.v.) and the Société Provinciale de Commercialisation des Produits Manufacturés. SONACI was privatized in 1992, coming under the control of the Scandinavian Skansen Group and changing its name to CIMBENIN. The State distribution companies disappeared.

SOCIETE NATIONALE DES HUILERIES DU DAHOMEY (SNAHDA). State industry founded in Cotonou (q.v.) in 1961, with a capitalization of 600 million CFA francs to manage the production of palm oil (q.v.), palmetto and oilcakes in the domestic palm-oil mills (in Ahozan, Avrankou, Bohicon, Cotonou, and G'bada) constructed with FIDES (q.v.) funds. The company was also involved in the export of its oil products and cooperated with the Société Nationale pour le Développement Rural SONADER (q.v.) in the management of palm plantations from which it buys its raw materials. Following the 1972 coup Col. Alphonse Alley (qq.v.) was appointed government Commissioner of SNAHDA. Alley was later arrested in connection with an anti-Kérékou (q.v.) conspiracy. Following the change in Dahomey's name, SNAHDA became SONICOG (q.v.).

SOCIETE NATIONALE D'IMPORTATION DU BENIN (SONIB). Former State import monopoly. It was set up in 1963 in Cotonou (q.v.) under a different name and with a modest list of items under its control. SONIB's post-1972 activities were progressively enhanced until it became the country's major import agency and wholesale distributor. In the mid-1970's it also switched much of its trading from West to East Europe and took over SODAIC's installations. SONIB held monopolies over the import of rice, wheat, sugar, milk, alcohol, tobacco and a number of fabrics. Until 1978 it allowed private companies to import under license a limited amount of some of these products. The company maintained 20 stores and depots.

SOCIETE NATIONALE D'IRRIGATION ET D'AMENAGE-MENT HYDROAGRICOLE (SONIAH). Former State company set up on Porto Novo (q.v.) on April 23, 1975, as the successor—though with nationwide responsibilities—of the Société d'Aménagement et de Développement de la Vallée de l'Ouémé SADEVO (q.v.). SONIAH continued SADEVO's pilot rice growing activities in the Ouémé river (q.v.) valley, with assistance of the CARDERs, and has also been involved in new irrigated rice projects all over the country. In the reorganization of the State sector in April 1982, SONIAH was dissolved and its activities were redistributed among several other State companies.

SOCIETE NATIONALE POUR LA PRODUCTION ANIMALE (SONAPA). State company set up in 1975 and charged with organizing the commerce of live cattle and administering Benin's abbatoirs. SONAPA had a monopoly over the import and export of cattle and was involved in raising meat supplies by developing pasturelands in south Borgou (q.v.) for the grazing and fattening up of its own cattle. In 1979 SONAPA transferred some of its activities to the Benino-Libyan SABLY (q.v.) and, in 1982, when it was dissolved, to SONAPRA and OBAR (qq.v.).

SOCIETE NATIONALE POUR LA PROMOTION AGRICOLE (SONAPRA) see SOCIETE NATIONALE AGRICOLE POUR LA PROMOTION AGRICOLE POUR LE COTON (SONACO).

SOCIETE NATIONALE POUR LE COTON (SONACO). Former State society that in 1974 replaced marketing activities of the Compagnie Française pour le Développement des

Fibres Textiles (CFDT). SONACO took over the CFDT plants in Parakou, Savalou, Bohicon, Kandi (qq.v.), and Glazoué, and had the capacity of producing 67,500 tons of cotton fiber per year. The eviction of CFDT and its expert staff coincided with a series of natural disasters that brought about a sharp decline in cotton production in Benin, significantly alleviated since.

In the 1982 reorganization of the parastatal sector SONACO took over the activities of SONAGRI and SONACEB (qq.v.). Under the Ministry of Rural Development and Cooperative Action, it is charged with aiding farmers in rural areas to increase their productivity, assisting in the spread of new crops, developing more effective methods of seed distribution and assisting in increasing the country's cattle herds.

The 1990 SONACO's ginning capacity was expanded from 78,000 to 120,000 tons, with two new gins established at Banikoara and Bembéréké.

SOCIETE NATIONALE POUR LE DEVELOPPEMENT DES FRUITS ET LEGUMES (SONAFEL). Former State company with headquarters in Cotonou and Parakou (qq.v.), charged with the development of fruit and vegetable production in Benin. It also had a monopoly over all exports of these products. The company managed a tomato canning plant in Natitingou (q.v.) and a juice extracting plant at Allahé. It built a tomato paste factory in Mallanville on the Niger border and had a master plan of constructing several agro-industries aimed at encouraging the increased production of fruits and vegetables in each province.

SOCIETE NATIONALE POUR LE DEVELOPPEMENT FORESTIER (SONAFOR). Former State company created in 1969 to develop Dahomey's weak forestry industry and related products. The company invested funds in the planting of several species of trees and in developing a large (100,000 hectares) cashew plantation and cashew-processing plant in Parakou (q.v.). Results were quite disappointing, however, with less than 400 tons produced in 1976. After serious management problems and financial pressures, SONAFOR was formally dissolved in May 1982 as part of the reorganization of the State sector.

SOCIETE NATIONALE POUR LE DEVELOPPEMENT RURAL (SONADER). State corporation established in Porto Novo (q.v.) in 1961 with a capitalization of 150 million CFA francs. Its multifaceted functions were to promote agricultural production and rural modernization and to supply specialized personnel where needed in lagging agrarian sectors. One of SONADER's main preoccupations was to revitalize the palm oil (q.v.) industry that suffered following a decline in palm tree planting and palm plantation quality during 1956–1963. In 1967 the company began to manage extensive palm plantations in the southern part of the country in coordination with the Société Nationale des Huileries du Dahomey (SNAHDA) (q.v.). SONADER's directors have included Moïse Mensah (q.v.) (1964–1965). Following the change in Dahomey's name, SONADER became SO-BEPALH (q.v.).

SOCIETE NATIONALE POUR L'INDUSTRIE DES CORPS GRAS (SONICOG). Former State company, the post–1975 successor of the Société Nationale des Huileries du Dahomey (SNAHDA) (q.v.) that in April 1982 absorbed the inefficient and deficit-ridden Société Béninoise de Palmier à Huile (SOBEPALH) (q.v.). Capitalized at 600 million CFA francs, SONICOG was responsible for the production of palm oil, palm kernel and groundnut oil, as well as palm cakes, palm butter and palm soaps. Its five plants were in Avrankou, Cotonou (q.v.), Gbada, Bohicon (q.v.) and Ahoza; Bohicon is the largest, capable of processing 115 tons of cotton seed daily.

Recent low levels of palm supplies led SONICOG to convert its Bohicon plant to one treating and manufacturing cottonseed oils. The financial and other mismanagement aspects of SOBEPALH (q.v.)—from which SONICOG was supposed to receive its palm oil for processing—brought about SOBEPALH's ultimate dissolution in 1982, and the absorption of the latter's activities, plants and workers by SONICOG. SONICOG consequently became a mammoth enterprise involved in the entire vertical sequence, from planting and maintaining palm trees, to the collection of the crop via a large fleet of trucks and then the processing and delivery of the final product.

SOCIETE SAGA PETROLEUM DU BENIN. Mixed-economy enterprise under the Ministry of Industry, Mines and Energy. Saga Petroleum, a Norwegian company, was engaged in exploitating the Sémé (q.v.) oil field 20 kilometers off the Benin shore near the maritime boundary with Nigeria. It employed eight expatriates at sea and 29 on the coastal installations, plus 130 local workers, some of whom were trained to undertake sea operations. By the mid-1980's production was roughly 9,000 barrels a day, of which 5,000 were exported. However, Benin's fiscal straits forced it to break with the Norwegian consortium that was paying only a 2.08% export tax, and to link up with the Swiss-based Pan Ocean Oil Company (PANOCO), which offered a host of fringe attractions. The action cost Benin heavily. Not only did the deal fall through when a long legal battle ensued during which all donor agents froze their loans and pledges, but without any management team production at the oilfield declined dramatically, with the drop in revenues compounded by the fall in global oil prices. In 1988 Benin passed the management contract to Ashland Oil, and production has since slowly normalized. See also OIL.

SOCIETE SUCRIERE DE SAVE (SSS). Former joint company originally set up by Benin (49 percent), Nigeria (46 percent) and British private interests (Lonrho Group 5 percent) in 1975, and since 1989 privatized. Operational only in 1984, and constantly plagued by problems, the complex was capitalized at 7,500 million CFA francs, making it one of the largest enterprises in Benin. Lonrho was retained in a technical capacity and managed the complex for a few years. The agroindustrial complex is at Savé (q.v.), hitherto a neglected region in central Benin, 260 kilometers north of Cotonou. SSS includes 5,200 hectares of irrigated plantations that were supposed to produce 500,000 tons of sugar cane, with most of the processed sugar scheduled to be exported to Nigeria, where the latter's huge needs (635,000 tons) are hardly touched by internal production (25,000 tons). At the same time, Benin's more modest needs, running at 15,000 tons per year, were to be fully met from internal production at SSS. The capacity of the complex is 40,000 tons of refined sugar per year, though it has been producing only a fraction of that. SSS provides employment for some 2,000 Beninois.

SODJI, KING (1848–1864) OF PORTO NOVO. Sodji ascended the throne on September 8, 1848, and his reign was marked by a long war with the Yoruba (q.v.) of Oke Odan and difficulties with British vessels and British territorial encroachments. These pressures resulted in Porto Novo's (q.v.) request for a French Protectorate, established on February 22, 1863. Under Sodji's successor, Dé Mikpon, France withdrew, only to return again, definitively, under Toffa I (q.v.).

SOGLO, CHRISTOPHE, 1909–1983. Former Chief-of-Staff of the armed forces (q.v.) and President of Dahomey. Born in Abomey (q.v.) on June 28, 1912, to a Fon (q.v.) chiefly family, Soglo volunteered to serve in the French army in 1931. He saw action during the Second World War, serving in Morocco and taking part in the Allied landings in Corsica, Elba and southern France. Promoted through the ranks to Lieutenant, he served on the General Staff of the Colonial Forces and, in 1947, became Military Advisor at the Ministry for French Overseas Territories. Promoted to Captain in 1950, he took part in the Indochina campaigns and, in 1956, was awarded the Croix de Guerre. After the French defeat in Indochina, Soglo was promoted to Major and served in Senegal until 1960. With Dahomey's independence he returned home to serve as President Hubert Maga's (q.v.) military advisory and Chief-of-Staff of the Dahomean army, with the rank of Lieutenant Colonel.

In 1963 Soglo staged his first coup d'etat (see COUP OF 1963) and presided over the shift of power to Sourou-Migan Apithy and Justin Ahomadégbé (qq.v.). He was promoted to General in February 1964. In 1965 Soglo had to intervene twice (see COUP of 1965(a); COUP OF 1965(b)), the second time establishing a military regime that lasted until 1967. With the growing politicization and polarization of the armed forces, the laxity of his administration and the emergence of personal ambitions within the officer corps, Soglo suffered a serious erosion of authority and was finally toppled from office in 1967 (see COUP OF 1967). In exile in France, Soglo played an intermediary role following the 1969 coup d'etat (q.v.) when the country's triumvirate (q.v.) was invited back to form the Presidential Council (q.v.). Having gone into retirement, in Rochefort, France, the hometown of his French wife, Soglo died there in 1983.

SOGLO, NICEPHORE D., 1934– . President of Benin. Born in Lomé, Togo on November 29, 1934, and educated at the University of Paris in private law and also a graduate of the Ecole Nationale of d'Administration, Soglo served as Inspector of Finances before being brought into General Soglo's (q.v.) cabinet as Minister of Finance and Commerce. He served in that capacity between December 1965 and December 1966. A nephew of the head of state, his appointment to the cabinet was increasingly criticized as nepotism, though commentators were unanimously impressed by Nicéphore Soglo's personal performance in office. After a stint at the National University of Benin (q.v.), Soglo left the country to join the World Bank in Washington, D.C., in 1979, and between 1983 and 1986 he was an Administrator representing 24 African states. In 1987 Soglo returned to Benin to assume the function of Inspector of Finances, only to be selected Interim Prime Minister by the National Conference (q.v.) in 1990. In the 1991 Presidential elections (q.v.) he emerged victorious on the second ballot, defeating former President Kérékou (q.v.). In a poor state of health all along, Soglo caught typhoid during the electoral campaigns, which was aggravated by sciatica, and had to be flown to France several times for hospitalization.

SOGLOHOUN, JEROME (Captain). Head, during the Kérékou (q.v.) era, of the dreaded intelligence agency, the Service de Documentation et d'Information (SDI) (q.v.). Soglohoun was formerly the director of Kérékou's military cabinet.

SOLIDARITY TAX. Chronic budgetary imbalances, in part caused by excessive administrative costs for a bloated civil service, have resulted in a variety of "solidarity taxes" on personal incomes in urban areas. The first instance of such a tax was President Hubert Maga's (q.v.) so-called 10-percent "austerity tax" of 1961. Prime Minister Justin Ahomadégbé (q.v.) lowered the tax to 5 percent in 1964, shortly after he came to power, only to raise it in July 1965 to 25 percent for employees in the public sector of the economy and 20 percent for those in the private sector. Gen. Christophe Soglo (q.v.) applied the 25 percent tax to the private sector as well, in mid-1966. The tax was then reduced to 20 percent by his successor Emile Derlin Zinsou (q.v.) and was completely eliminated with the creation of the 1970 Presidential Council (q.v.) regime. The tax in all its guises has been a major source of discontent and unrest among unionists.

SOMBA. Ethnic group found in the Atakora (q.v.) mountains, in northwestern Benin, and in adjoining parts of Togo. In reality three related ethnic groups of Voltaic origins, the Somba have been extensively studied. Benin's Somba number approximately 72,000 and are best known to the laymen by their two-storied castle-like domiciles (see SOMBATATA). The noted anthropologist Frobenius called them Africa's Burgbauern—"castle peasants." Inhabiting an area of poor soil, and in general taciturn, the Somba are among the least advanced groups in Dahomey. They figured in the Atakora uprisings under French colonial rule (see UPRISINGS OF 1915–1918) and have become disenchanted—to the extent that they are at all politicized—with government policies. Two of their best known representatives on the national scene were colonels Maurice Kouandété and Mathieu Kérékou (qq.v.): under the latter a considerable improvement of socioeconomic conditions was visible in Atakora (q.v.), though this only marginally affected the average Somba.

SOMBATATA. The thatched-mud turreted "castles" characteristic of the Somba (q.v.) domiciles in the northwestern Atakora (q.v.) département of Benin. Roughly 3.7 to 4.2 meters high and 9 meters in diameter, they possess round turrets and two floors. The lower one is used for stables and storage and the upper one constitutes the living quarters. The turrets are also used for storage. A shrine near the entrance of each unit honors the place of origin of the lineage.

SOTA RIVER. Some 320 kilometers long, and originating between Nikki (q.v.) and Ndali in the Borgou (q.v.), it flows northward to join the Niger river (q.v.) near Malanville.

SOUS-PREFECTURE. Administrative local units into which Dahomey's pre-1974 *départements* (q.v.) were divided. They were renamed districts (q.v.) in 1974. See also ADMINIS-TRATIVE ORGANIZATION; DEPARTEMENT.

SOUS-PREFET. Sub-prefect. Title of the administrative officer on the *sous-préfecture* level, responsible for his unit to the Prefect (q.v.) above him and assisted in his tasks for an advisory committee. With the 1974 administrative reforms (q.v.), greater powers were granted to these committees (Conseil Révolutionnaire du District [q.v.]) and the name of the *sous-préfet* was changed to *chef du district,* with the *sous-préfectures* also becoming *districts* (q.v.). See also PREFECT; ADMINISTRATIVE ORGANIZATION.

SOZONLIN, HYACINTHE, 1953– . Physician. Born in 1953 and trained in medicine in France, Sozonlin is the Chief Medical Officer of the Tori-Bossito Health Center in Benin.

STATE COMPANIES. With the 1972 coup d'etat (q.v.) and especially the 1974 radicalization of ideology in Benin, most sectors of the economy were gradually nationalized. Though the regime was cautious not to overly alienate France (and pledged compensation—the tab picked up by France!), many existing private companies were either taken over by or fell under the control or influence of the State through joint companies or mixed-economy companies. Within a few years virtually all of these enterprises were losing money: some because of natural calamities that had nothing to do with nationalization; others after losing their expert expatriate staff to suffer a period of technical and administrative chaos (as when the French CFDT was crudely evicted and replaced by SONACO [q.v.]). But most became unprofitable because of crass mismanagement, fiscal embezzlement, corruption and the utilization of the payrolls for the creation of sinecure posts that could not but drain whatever profitability existed in the first place. (There were 26,733 persons employed in the parastatal sector in 1979.) Among the new State companies set up during this period, many were entrusted with sectors that were too limited so that the administrative costs of State control (assuming no mismanagement) swallowed up any profits centralization might have resulted in. Others were charged with rather monumental tasks, resulting in inefficiency. And still others were simply incompetent, the best example being Air Bénin (q.v.), which was established and commenced flights without even conducting feasability studies. All these companies were, moreover set up at a time when large numbers of skilled manpower were deserting the country, disenchanted with the radical drift of ideology, the oppressiveness of the northern military regime and the worsening economic conditions.

Possessing under the best of circumstances one of the weakest economies in Africa, not surprisingly by the early 1980's the country was bankrupt, with the deficits piled up by the State sector exerting a strong negative impact upon the entire economy. A restructuring and reorganization of the parastatal sector followed, with 15 companies either dissolved or privatized in April 1982. Among these were some of the giants of yesteryear—SONIAH, SOBEPALH, SONAGRI, SONAFOR (qq.v.), etc. In the process of the country's sole political party, the PRPB (q.v.), declared that in the future Benin would demand exclusive control only over banking (q.v.) and energy, while in other fields the State would be willing to coexist with private enterprise or not to intervene at all. This was a major retreat from previous stances demanding either total control or leadership of all segments of the economy. In foreign trade, for example, where in the past a major effort had been made to bring all commodities under State monopolies (nationalizing ''middleman'' profits), Benin allowed private traders to operate except for a narrow specific list of commodities.

Following the April 1982 reorganization of the state sector, the following companies remained in existence, under the jurisdiction of the Ministries as specified. The vast majority of them were to close in the next scaledown of the parastatal sector and/or with economic normalization in 1990 ending the saga of State companies in Benin. During 1987–1989, moreover, the banking sector, virtually in its entirety in State hands, completely collapsed.

BENIN: PUBLIC AND SEMI-PUBLIC COMPANIES IN THE MID-1980'S GROUPED UNDER THE RESPONSIBLE MINISTRY

MINISTRY OF RURAL DEVELOPMENT

1. Office Béninois d'Aménagement Rural (OBAR)
2. Société Nationale pour la Production Agricole (SON-APRA)
3. Centres d'Action Régionale pour le Développement Rural (CARDER)

MINISTRY OF STATE FARMS, STOCKBREEDING AND FISHERIES

4. Société Nationale des Fruits et Légumes (SONAFEL)
5. Société Agro-Animale Bénino-Arabe-Libyenne (SA-BLY)
6. Société Bénino-Arabe-Libyenne de Pêche (BELIP-ECHE)

MINISTRY OF MINES, ENERGY AND INDUSTRY

7. Société Nationale pour l'Industrie des Corps Gras (SONICOG)
8. Société Béninoise d'Eléctricité et d'Eau (SBEE)
9. Société Nationale de Brasserie (La Béninoise)
10. Société Béninoise des Textiles (SOBETEX)
11. Office Béninois des Mines (OBEMINES)
12. Société des Ciments du Bénin (SCB)

13. Société Nationale des Ciments (SONACI)
14. Société des Ciments d'Onigbolo (SCO)
15. Société Sucrière de Savé (SSS)
16. Société Saga Petroleum, Benin
17. Société Bénino-Arabe-Libyenne des Mines (BELIM-INES)

MINISTRY OF PUBLIC WORKS AND CONSTRUCTION

18. Société Nationale de Construction et des Travaux Publics (SONACOTRAP)
19. Société Nationale de Gestion Immobiliére (SON-AGIM)
20. Institut National de Cartographie (INC)
21. Centre National d'Essais et de Recherches des Travaux Publics (CNER-TP)

MINISTRY OF TRANSPORT AND COMMUNICATIONS

22. Office Béninois des Manutentions Portuaires (OBEMAP)
23. Société Nationale de Transit et de Consignation (SONATRAC)
24. Société de Transit et Consignation du Bénin (SOTRACOB)
25. Port Autonome de Cotonou (PAC)
26. Office des Postes et Télécommunications (OPT)
27. Société des Transports du Bénin (TRANS-BENIN)
28. Organisation Commune Bénin-Niger (OCBN)
29. Compagnie Béninoise de Navigation Maritime (CO-BENAM)

MINISTRY OF COMMERCE

30. Société d'Alimentation Générale du Bénin (AGB)
31. Société Béninoise de Matériaux de Construction (SO-BEMAC)

32. Société Nationale d'Equipement (SONAE)
33. Société Nationale de Commercialisation de Produits Pétrolier (SONACOP)
34. Société de Distribution de Fournitures, Matériel Administratif et Scolaire (SODIMAS)
35. Société Générale du Commerce du Bénin (SOGE-COB)

MINISTRY OF TOURISM AND ARTISAN ARTS

36. Office National du Tourisme et de l'Hôtellerie (ONATHO)

MINISTRY OF LABOR AND SOCIAL AFFAIRS

37. Office Béninois de Sécurité Sociale (OBSS)

MINISTRY OF PUBLIC HEALTH

38. Office National de Pharmacie (ONP)

MINISTRY OF INFORMATION AND PROPAGANDA

39. Office Béninois de Cinéma (OBECI)
40. Office de Radiodiffusion et Télévision du Bénin (ORTB)
41. Office National d'Edition, de Presse et d'Imprimerie (ONEPI)

MINISTRY OF INTERIOR AND PUBLIC SECURITY

42. Régie de Ravitaillement des Navires (RAVINAR)
43. Société de Gestion des Marchés Autonomes (SOGEMA)

MINISTRY OF NATIONAL DEFENSE

44. Transports Aériens du Bénin (TAB)

MINISTRY OF FINANCE

45. Société Nationale d'Assurances et de Réassurances (SONAR)
46. Loterie Nationale du Bénin (LNB)
47. Office Béninois d'Informatique (OBI)
48. Caisse Autonome d'Amortissement (CAA)
49. Fonds National d'Investissement (FNI)
50. Banque Commerciale du Bénin (BCB)
51. Banque Béninoise pour le Développement (BBD)
52. Caisse Nationale de Crédit Agricole (CNCA)

MINISTRY OF ALPHABETIZATION AND POPULAR CULTURE

53. Office Béninois des Arts (OBA)

MINISTRY OF REGIONAL ADMINISTRATIONS

54. Société des Transports de l'Atacora (STA)
55. Société des Transports de la Province de l'Atlantique (STPA)
56. Société des Transports du Borgou (STB)
57. Société Provinciale de Transports du Mono (SOTRAMO)
58. Société Provinciale des Transports de l'Ouémé (TRANS-OUEME)
59. Société Provinciale des Transports du Zou (SOTRAZ)

STATE SECURITY COURT. Special tribunal created by President Emile Derlin Zinsou (q.v.) in 1969. Its function was to try all cases of crimes against the state, meting out punishments for conspiracies and attempted coups (q.v.). The court was set up after several attempts on Col. Maurice Kouandété's (q.v.) life and the discovery of plots against Zinsou's administration by supporters of the triumvirate (q.v.).

STEINMETZ, FRANCOIS, 1868–1952. Catholic missionary. Born in Strasbourg on January 10, 1868, Steinmetz arrived in Dahomey in 1892, residing for the next 60 years in Ouidah (q.v.) and becoming Apostolic Vicar in 1906. His work in Ouidah was important: he was the first translator of the catechism into the Fon (q.v.) language; the construction of Ouidah's imposing cathedral was begun under this direction; and he assisted in the erection of numerous schools in the region as well as Ouidah's seminary (q.v.). He established good relations with the fetishist (q.v.) chiefs in the area, allowing him to achieve maximum efficiency in his evangelical work. Steinmetz died in Ouidah on March 19, 1952.

SUBRUKU. Small village in the Djougou (q.v.) area that, together with its immediate countryside, contains one of the largest concentrations of the Pila Pila (q.v.) ethnic group in Benin.

SUNON SERO. Founder of Nikki (q.v.) in the late fourteenth century. He is reputed to have left the Bariba "parent state" of Bussa (qq.v.) following a succession dispute. Sunon Séro's alleged tomb is found in the old and sacred part of Nikki, Nikki-Wenu (q.v.)

SUPREME COURT. Created on October 18, 1961. The following have been Presidents of the Supreme Court:
Oct. 18, 1961 to March 1, 1962 Emile Derlin Zinsou (q.v.)
March 1, 1962 to Nov. 12, 1963 Sebastien Dassi (q.v.)
June 11, 1964 to June 5, 1965   Valentin Aplogan-Djibodé (q.v.)
Dec. 8, 1965 to Jan. 13, 1967   Cyprien Ainandou (q.v.)
Jan. 13, 1967 to Nov. 19, 1969 Louis Ignacio-Pinto (q.v.)
    In May 1977 the Supreme Court was formally renamed the Cour Populaire Suprême, with Léandre Amlon (q.v.) as President.

SUPREME COURT AFFAIR. One of a series of disagreements between President Sourou-Migan Apithy and Vice-President Justin Ahomadégbé (qq.v.) in 1965 that brought about a governmental paralysis and Col. Christophe Soglo's (q.v.) eventual military takeover (see COUP OF 1965(a)). The matter at issue was Ahomadégbé's competence and constitutional authority to appoint personnel to the Supreme Court (q.v.) over Apithy's objections. Since the Supreme Court was charged with determining the political succession in the executive in case of any disputes, the issue was an explosive one. Apithy's refusal to promulgate Ahomadégbé's nominations—partly because the President of the Court was Valentin Aplogain-Djibodé (q.v.), one of Apithy's supporters—brought about a governmental deadlock and constitutional crisis that could not be resolved. As demonstrations broke out in the cities in support of one or another of the protagonists, Col. Soglo intervened, suspended both from office, and called on the President of the National Assembly, Tahirou Congacou (q.v.), to form the next government.

SURETE NATIONALE see POLICE FORCE

SYNDICAT NATIONAL DES COMMERCANTS ET INDUSTRIELS AFRICAINS DU BENIN (SYNACIB). Post-1975 name of SYNACID (q.v.) under President Urbain da Silva.

SYNDICAT DES COMMERCANTS ET INDUSTRIELS AFRICAINS DU DAHOMEY (SYNACID). Cotonou (q.v.)-based organization of all the private African traders in the country. The organization was renamed SYNACIB (q.v.) in 1975, following the country's name change.

SYNDICAT DES COMMERCANTS IMPORTATEURS ET EXPORTATEURS DU BENIN (SCIEB).Trade organization of Benin's private import/export entrepreneurs. Its headquarters are in Cotonou (q.v.).

SYNDICAT DES ENSEIGNANTS DU SUPERIEUR (SYNES). Trade union (q.v.) of the higher education sector that was at the forefront of anti-government demonstrations and salary agitations of January and May 1989. Many of its members had also been in opposition to the regime, in their private capacities (and some as underground members of the Parti Communiste Dahoméen [q.v.]) for years. In August 1989 the union broke from the former unified union syndicate, and later that year threatened a general strike for December 8th if a National Convention were not held to usher in civilian rule. SYNES was headed by Léopold Dossou (q.v.).

SYNDICAT DES TRANSPORTEURS ROUTIERS DU BENIN (STRB). Organization of all independent passenger and cargo transporters in Benin.

-T-

TADO. Currently a small village 96 kilometers from the Atlantic coast, in Togo's Atakpamé district. Founded around 1300, it was the dispersal point of much of Benin's Adja (q.v.) population.

TANEKA (also TONGBA). Small ethnic group found in the vicinity of Djougou (q.v.), speaking a Voltaic dialect. The Taneka are often confused with the Pila Pila (q.v.) to their southeast. The Taneka live in chiefless, stateless lineage clans, and number 32,000 in Benin. Their key villages are Taneka Koko and Taneka Beri (q.v.), both of which have ritual importance, and Pabégu.

TANEKA BERI. Largest, oldest and most sacred of the Taneka (q.v.) villages in northwest Benin. In 1981 there were only 150 permanent residents, mostly notables, in Taneka Beri.

TAOFIQUI, BOURAIMA. Former Minister of Transport and Communications. A Yoruba (q.v.) from the north, Taofiqui served as Director General of the Department of Posts and Telecommunications before joining Kérékou's (q.v.) cabinet in December 1982, serving through 1986.

TAWEMA, DANIEL. Interim Foreign Minister during the August 1989 Kérékou (q.v.) administration. Tawema was a trusted aide and head of Kérékou's civilian Presidential staff prior to joining the cabinet.

TAWES, PASCAL (Captain). Former Deputy Commander, under Major Jean Thia (q.v.), of the much dreaded Bataillon de la Garde Présidentielle of General Kérékou (q.v.). Tawès, as most members of the battalion, is from the northern Atakora (q.v.) region. Fiercely loyal to Kérékou, and the latter's liaison with the Permanent National Investigation Commission on State Security charged with ferreting out subversive activity, Tawès on several occasions during the 1990 National Conference (q.v.) counselled disbanding the Conference, cracking down on the assembled opposition elements or firing into the demonstrating crowds. Unreconciled with the transition to civilian rule, in May 1992 he was involved in a mutiny and/or attempted coup. More prosaically, however, Tawès was implicated in a host of illegal dealings—some allegedly related to Mohamed Cissé (q.v.)—and was about to be placed on trial for trafficking in drugs. Though arrested, he managed to escape from custody (due to the large number of northerners in the armed forces and gendarmerie [qq.v.]) and reaching his home region, Natitingou (q.v.), he captured the important local Kaba camp (q.v.) with some supporters and raised the banner of the residual pro-Kérékou forces. The rebellion was over in two days.

TCHABE see SAVE KINGDOM.

TCHETOU, MATHIEU (Captain). Until 1990 General Kérékou's (q.v.) staunchly loyalist head of the gendarmerie (q.v.).

TCHIBOZO, ANATOLE, 1931– . Administrator. Born on June 30, 1931, a meteorologist who taught science at the Lycée de Porto Novo (1958–1961), Tchibozo was selected to head the Agence pour la Sécurité de la Navigation Aérienne en Afrique et a Madagascar (ASECNA) and to represent Benin at the World Meteorology Organization. He has also served in a wide variety of other administrative posts, as on the Board of Air Afrique (both as Benin's delegate and as technical expert).

TCHIBOZO, PIERRE (Colonel). President Nicéphore Soglo's (q.v.) Head of the Gendarmerie (q.v.).

TE-AGBANLIN. First King of Porto Novo (q.v.), after the dispersal from Allada (q.v.).

TEGBESU, KING (1740–1774) OF DAHOMEY. Tegbesu's long reign was replete with pressures from the powerful Oyo Empire (q.v.), whose suzerainty he had to acknowledge in 1742 and to whom Dahomey had to pay a heavy tribute, especially in later years. Tegbesu's efforts to increase the kingdom's share of the slave trade in order to bring about a pickup of the economy were not successful. He was brutal in dispersing dissent and is credited with assisting in the routinization of the succession procedures to the throne.

TEKYETE see SOMBATATA

TEVOEDJRE, ALBERT, 1929– . Politician and international civil servant. Born in Porto Novo (q.v.) on November 10, 1929, Tévoédjré studied locally, in Ouidah (q.v.), and also at the Universitie of Dakar, Toulouse and Fribourg (Switzerland, graduating with a Ph.D. in social and economic sciences. As a student in France, he was the radical editor of *L'Etudiant d'Afrique Noire,* the publication of the militant Fédération des Etudiants de l'Afrique Noire en France (FEANF). He taught at the Lycée Delafosse in Dakar (1952–1954) and at the teachers college of Cahors (1957) before returning home to Cotonou. Upon his return, Tévoédjré plunged into politics with zeal. He was a co-founder of the Mouvement de Libération Nationale (q.v.), a radical quasi-interterritorial party that survived in Dahomey for two years (1958–1960). Tévoédjré also immersed himself in trade union (q.v.) activities while teaching at Lycée Victor Ballot, becoming in 1959 Assistant Secretary-General of the National Teachers Union and, later, member of the Council of the Union Générale de Travailleurs Dahoméens (UGTD) (q.v.).

Though he had violently opposed the emergence of Sorou-Migan Apithy (q.v.) as one of Dahomey's key leaders and representative to France's structures, with independence, Tévoédjré compromised on most of his ideological planks, joining the joint Hubert Maga (q.v.)/Sourou-Migan Apithy government as Secretary of State for Information (1961–1963), and merging his party with the Parti Dahoméen de l'Unité (q.v.). Rapidly disillusioned with Maga's policies and political style, and recognizing the paucity of viable political alternatives, Tévoédjré changed careers, moving into international administration. He served as Secretary-General of the African and Malagasy Union (UAM) (1962–1963), taught at the Geneva Africa Institute (1963–64) and at Georgetown University (1964), and was a research associate at Harvard University's Center for International Affairs (1964–1965). In 1965 he joined the International Labour Office (ILO) in Geneva where he was promoted to Regional Director for Africa (March 1966) and Assistant Director General (January 1969). Early in 1975 Tévoédjré was appointed Director of the ILO's Institute for Labour Studies in Geneva, a position he still holds. In March 1983 he was reappointed for another term as ILO Deputy Director General. Tévoédjré returned to Benin after the eclipse of the Kérékou regime and joined the new RND (qq.v.) party. His unwillingness to adhere to party discipline, and early announcement of his candidacy for the 1991 Presidential elections (q.v.), led to his expulsion from the party. He came in a strong third (after Nicéphore Soglo and Kérékou [qq.v]) though his support vote was concentrated in his native Ouémé (q.v.). Later his new party, Notre Cause Commune, (q.v.) gained a number of seats in the new legislature.

TEVOEDJRE, VIRGILE-OCTAVE, 1931– . Former diplomat and international civil servant. Born in Porto Novo (q.v.) on November 27, 1931, Tévoédjré was educated locally and at the University of Bordeaux, where he majored in political science. He taught for several years in France (Collège Classique et Moderne de Nerac) and headed the French section of Radio Ghana in 1959–1960. On his return home he served for one year as Cabinet Director for the Minister of Foreign Affairs (1961); he also served as UN Security Advisor in Zaire and on behalf of Ghana as member to the

UN at the 15th Session. In the mid-1960's, while working as information officer for the FAO in Africa, Tévoédjré was appointed Counselor at the Benin Embassy to the United States in November 1967. In 1972 he served in a similar capacity in Brussels but left the diplomatic corps in the mid-1970's to become an international civil servant with ancillary organizations of the UN, based in Paris.

THIA, JEAN, (Major). Former Commander of the much dreaded Bataillon de la Garde Présidentielle of General Kérékou (qq.v.) disbanded in 1991. Thia, like most personnel of the entire battalion, is from the northern Atakora (q.v.) region.

TIAMYOU, ALI, 1922– . Agricultural engineer. Born in Porto Novo (q.v.) in 1922, and trained as an agricultural engineer abroad, Tiamyou served as head of the Agricultural Apprenticeship Center between 1954 and 1957, before becoming Cabinet Director of the Minister of Agriculture (1957–1959). After independence, he served as Director of Weights and Measures in the Ministry of Economics and Finance. Later, he worked as Agricultural Pioneer Farms advisor in the Ministry of Rural Coperation, until his retirement from the civil service in 1982.

TIDJANI, ABDOU SERPOS, 1918–1981. Ethnologist, historian, author, librarian, union leader and, until his death, Director of the National Archives (q.v.) of Dahomey. Born in Djougou (q.v.) in 1918 to Muslim Yoruba (q.v.) parents, Tidjani studied in Allada, Ouidah, Porto Novo and, finally, at Ecole William Ponty (qq.v.) in Senegal. He did his military service in Senegal and upon his discharge joined the Porto Novo branch of the Institut Français d'Afrique Noire (q.v.). A prolific author, he has written on Dahomey's history and ethnology. A member of Dahomey's first political party, the Union Progréssiste Dahoméenne (q.v.), he was for a time Secretary-General of its Porto Novo branch. Tidjani has also been involved in trade union (q.v.) activities, serving as President of the Union des Syndicats Libres du Dahomey and Vice-President of the Conféderation Dahoméenne des Travailleurs Croyants (q.v.) between 1945 and 1960. He was appointed Director of the

National Archives in Porto Novo in 1967 and served in that capacity until his death on August 20, 1981.

TIMOTHEE, ANANLIN. Leader of the Union Démocratique des Forces du Progrès (UDFP) (q.v.) political party that was an original partner of the UTR (q.v.) parliamentary alliance that formed in 1991 in support of President Nicéphore Soglo (q.v.). Timothée is a deputy at the National Assembly.

TOFFA, KING (1874–1908) OF PORTO NOVO. Last independent king of Porto Novo (q.v.). In part owing his rise to power to King Glélé (q.v.) of Dahomey, Toffa's reign was marked by anti-Dahomean policies that pitted the two kingdoms against each other. Boastful and tending to exaggerate his military power (which was meager), Toffa signed a treaty of protection with France on July 24, 1883. The latter treaty resulted in Porto Novo-Dahomean hostilities, dragging France into the ongoing hostilities and precipitating the Franco-Dahomean campaigns (q.v.). The French several times considered deposing Toffa, who was quite inept, but allowed him to complete his reign. When he died in 1908, no successor was allowed, though his brother was recognized as superior chief, contrary to custom that would have given the succession to a branch then resident in Nigeria (see MEKPON, SOHINGBE). The same deviation from tradition occurred in 1913 at Adjiki's death, when another of Toffa's brothers was appointed chief, causing significant unrest in Porto Novo.

TOFINNU. Adja inhabitants of the lacustral fishing villages of the lower So and Lake Nokoué, including Ganvié (qq.v.), Benin's prime tourist attraction. Little is known of their origins (their name means "water-people") except that they sought refuge in the shallow lake from assaults all around them. They arrived in their current habitat in the seventeenth or eighteenth century from Tado (currently in Togo) and settled on huts on stilts in the water. A considerable number has migrated to Nigeria since the 1970's.

TONGBA see TANEKA.

TOSSOU, KOMLAN, 1939– . Bank director. Born in 1939 in Cotonou, and educated in Porto Novo (qq.v.) and Grenoble, Tossou obtained a Ph.D. in Economics. He taught several years in France (1968–1972) before joining the Banque Nationale in Paris where he served for the next four years. In October 1976 Tossou was appointed Director General of the Togolese Bank for Commerce and Industry in Lomé, a post he still holds.

TOSSOU, MARCELLIN (Captain). Former Ouidah (q.v.) garrison officer who participated in the 1975 anti-Kérékou (q.v.) attempted putsch of Captain Assogba (q.v.). He was subsequently given a life sentence and purged from the armed forces (q.v.).

TOURISM see ONATHO.

TOVALOU-HOUENOU, MARC, 1877–1935. Author and editor. Born in 1877 and educated abroad, Tovalou-Houénou obtained a law degree from Bordeaux. He published a number of his own works and served as the editor in Paris in *Les Continents* journal. He was arrested in 1925 in Lomé, Togo, for conspiring to set up a nationalist movement in Dahomey and exiled to Senegal, where he worked in anti-Blaise Diagne circles in attempts to defeat the "collaborationist" Senegalese leader.

TOVALOU-QUENUM, GEORGES, 1897–1943. Merchant, entrepreneur and early nationalist. Born in 1897 Tovalou-Quénum first served in the administration—briefly being head of a *canton*—before establishing himself in Cotonou (q.v.) as an independent merchant. Bypassing the big French importers and retailers, Tovalou-Quénum developed a direct commercial links with France, employing Casimir Agbo (q.v.) as his assistant. He also subsidized the journal *La Voix du Dahomey* (q.v.), which lashed out at the administration's colonial policy; in 1935 he was a co-defendant in the administration's suit against the newspaper. In financial difficulties during the Second World War, Tovalou-Quénum died in 1943.

TOVALOU-QUENUM, JOSEPH, 1855–1925. Traditional Dahomean notable and founder of the village of Gbodjé. Born in Zado (Abomey) in 1855, and established as a merchant in Porto Novo (q.v.), Tavalou-Quénum prospered with the arrival of the French in that kingdom by supplying livestock and other commodities in large quantities to the colonial troops. By virtue of his contacts with the French authorities he became the intermediary between the French and the local rulers of Ouidah, Allada, and Abomey (qq.v.), in the process shielding Abomey in particular from possible punitive actions after the Franco-Dahomean campaigns (q.v.). His efforts to stem the early colonial abuses bore fruit when a colonial inspector visited Dahomey, and Abomey specifically, and recommended the dismissal of numerous inept and masochistic officials, including the Governor of the colony himself. Tavalou-Quénum was regarded as the "protector" of the Adja (q.v.) kingdoms, and, on his death at the age of 70, he was given great traditional honors.

TOVODUN. Deified clan-ancestors, usually founding fathers of major lineages or kingdoms but also of smaller clans or villages. Symbolizing the origins of the clan, they are normally honored to this day in annual ceremonies that also unite the clan/village through ritual. See, for example, ADJAHOUTO, the *tovodun* of the Adja (qq.v.) population of Benin.

TOUTEE, GEORGES-JOSEPH, 1855–1927. Colonial officer and explorer. Born in Saint-Fargeau on February 26, 1855, Toutée joined the colonial armies and was commissioned on October 1, 1877, and first served in Indochina. In 1894 he was charged with an expedition to reach Tombouctou (Timbuktu) via the Niger river (q.v.), starting from Dahomey. He carried out the expedition, though only reaching Gao, in the process verifying that the British presence in the hinterland was not as widespread as had been thought in Paris. Upon his return, he played a role in the delimitation of the Dahomey-Nigeria boundary lines, spending his last few years in Algeria and France. He has written works on his expedition to Gao.

TRADE UNIONS. Until the 1972 coup (q.v.), Dahomey had four main trade unions, listed below in descending order of strength and/or importance.

(1) Union Générale des Travailleurs du Dahomey (UGTD) (q.v.) with 10,000 members. Founded in 1961 and affiliated to the World Federation of Labor, the UGTD's Secretary-General was Jacob Padonou.
(2) Union Générale des Syndicats du Dahomey (q.v.) with 8,000 members. Reestablished in 1964 after being forcibly merged in 1961 with the UGTD. Its Secretary-General was Honorat Ogoubiyi-Akilotan.
(3) Confédération Nationale des Syndicats Libres (q.v.) with 2,250 members. Founded in 1964 its Secretary-General was Etienne Ahouangbé.
(4) Confédération Dahoméenne des Travailleurs Croyants (CDTC) (q.v.) with 1,000 members. Founded in 1952 and forcibly merged during 1961–1964 into the UGTD, the CDTC's Secretary was Gabriel Ahoué. Affiliated with the International Federation of Christian Trade Unions.

The 1972 coup d'etat was greeted equivocally by the country's trade unionists, including those with left-wing inclinations. At the time, the unions, grouped under the umbrella structure of the Union Syndicale Nationale (USN) (q.v.), were deeply divided on a multiplicity of planes, including ideological. The 1974 declaration of the Kérékou (q.v.) regime for a Marxist state did not appeal to many unionists, who were suspicious of both the military and northern credentials of most of the ruling clique. Soon after came the murder of Major Aikpé (q.v.)—who had been extremely popular in the south—which led to a massive societal upheaval spearheaded by the unions. After quelling the disturbances, Kérékou moved harshly to suppress the independence of the unions and to subjugate them to the state. In the purges that followed, several popular leaders lost office, thousands of civil servants fled into self-exile abroad (see REFUGEES), and a new trade union structure was created—the Union Nationale des Syndicats des Travailleurs du Benin (UNSTB)—under Vilon Romain Guézo (qq.v.), who had proven himself loyal to the regime and had been ousted from his leadership post in the unions because of this. Despite all these measures, the unionists never remained securely in the government camp. Radicals supported the Ligue (q.v.) or the Parti Communiste Dahoméen (qq.v.), while conservatives plotted for the collapse of the Marxist state. During the mid-1980's the deteriorating Beninois economy triggered numerous wildcat strikes, demonstrations and social unrest, to the degree that the UNSTB could no longer be regarded a cohesive or viable confederation. In 1989 its disintegration came about as several branches formally seceded, and the remanant disintegrated a year later.

TRANS-BENIN see SOCIETE DES TRANSPORTS ROUTIERS DU BENIN.

TRANSPORT AERIEN DU BENIN (AIR BENIN or TAB). State-owned national airline, better known as Air Bénin (q.v.). Set up in 1978 with headquarters in Cotonou and under the directorship of Manasse Ayayi (q.v.), the airline was sharply criticized in cabinet in 1980 for running massive deficits. In the process, it was revealed that the company had been set up with hardly any feasibility studies, cost-analysis projections or preplanning, so that most of the operations of the "international" airline (it had one foreign destination, Lagos) were ad hoc matters. In the reorganization of the State sector in 1982, the airline was allowed to continue its loss-making operations under stricter accounting guidance, but was soon closed down. See also AIR BENIN.

TRAORE, ALI MOUSSA. Former cabinet minister. A Parakou Dendi (q.v.), Traoré was originally a diplomat accredited to Libya, and was later brought into Kérékou's (q.v.) cabinet, first as Minister of Nursery and Primary Education (February 1980) and, in June 1984, as Minister of Culture, Youth and Sports. He was purged following the 1985 student upheavals.

TRIUMVIRATE. The term frequently used to refer to the three Dahomean leaders who have directly or indirectly controlled events in the country from the mid-1940's to the early 1970's, two of whom, still alive, are also indirectly currently influential in Beninois political life. The original trio was Sourou-Migan Apithy, who died in 1989, Hubert Maga and Justin Ahomadégbé (qq.v.).

TUFARO. The royal trumpets of Nikki (q.v.). Of major religious and political significance, the *tufaro* are used to this day in various ritual ceremonies, especially during the Gani (q.v.) celebrations when they assemble the souls of the ancestors of the Bariba clans for the pledge of unity of the living *Wasangari* (q.v.).

TYPAMM, ANDRE. Beninois poet.

-U-

UNION DEMOCRATIQUE DAHOMEENNE (UDD). Successor to the Bloc Populaire Africain (q.v.), following the latter's 1955 merger with Emile Derlin Zinsou's Union Progréssiste Dahoméenne (qq.v.). The UDD was essentially the political party of Justin Ahomadégbé (q.v.), powerful in Fon and Adja (qq.v.) districts in the south and central parts of the country and in such non-Yoruba (q.v.) urban constituencies as Cotonou and Ouidah (qq.v.). Apart from Justin Ahomadégbé and Emile Derlin Zinsou, the UDD leadership included Alexandre Adandé and Gabriel Lozès (qq.v.), Secretary-General of the party and Foreign Minister in the Ahomadégbé-Apithy 1964–1965 regime. The party was affiliated to the Rassemblement Démocratique Africain (q.v.). Except for two months (see FRONT D'ACTION DEMOCRATIQUE), the UDD was Dahomey's opposition party with political power held, or shared by, the two other formations, the northern Rassemblement Démocratique Dahoméen (RDD) led by Hubert Maga, and the Parti Républicain Dahoméen (PRD) of the Yoruba and Nagot south, led by Sourou-Migan Apithy (qq.v.). In the 1959 elections the UDD polled the largest vote but won only 11 seats in the National Assembly (q.v.) while Apithy's party got 37 seats. Electoral fraud was charged and the UDD obtained 9 more seats. In 1960 the PRD, now renamed the Parti des Nationalistes Dahoméens (q.v.), merged with the RDD to form the Parti Dahoméen de l'Unité (q.v.). In the 1960 elections the PDU received 468,002 votes to the UDD's 213, 564. Under the new electoral rules, this gave the PDU total control of both the executive (Maga became President and Apithy, Vice-President) and the legislature. When demonstrations flared up in the south against the regime (as well as over economic grievances) the UDD was banned on flimsy grounds on April 10, 1961. It reemerged, following President Maga's overthrow in 1963, within the joint party of the new Apithy-Ahomadégbé leadership, the Parti Démocratique Dahoméen (q.v.). Following the first 1965 coup d'etat and until the second 1965 coup (qq.v.) that banned all political activity, the UDD reemerged under the name Alliance Democratique Dahoméenne (q.v.). See also POLITICAL PARTIES.

UNION DEMOCRATIQUE DES FORCES DU PROGRES (UDFP). Fon (q.v.) political party headed by Ananlin Timothée (q.v.) that in 1991 joined with two other southern parties in support of the Soglo (q.v.) Presidency.

UNION DES FORCES DE PROGRES (UFP). Political party set up on April 30, 1990, when the former Marxist-Leninist government party PRPB (q.v.) dissolved itself, under the provisional leadership of Machoudi Dissoudi (q.v.), Professor of Economics at the National University of Benin (q.v.).

UNION DES INDEPENDANTS DU DAHOMEY (UNIDAHO). Splinter group, composed of supporters of Paul Darboux (q.v.), established in April 1958 after the latter's withdrawal from Hubert Maga's Rassemblement Démocratique Dahoméen (qq.v.) party. See also DEFENSE DES INTERETS ECONOMIQUES; INDEPENDANTS DU NORD; RASSEMBLEMENT DEMOCRATIQUE DAHOMEEN.

UNION FRANCAISE. Temporary 1951 electoral ticket on which Sourou-Migan Apithy campaigned together with Edouard Dunglas (qq.v.), prior to Apithy's creation of his own political movement, the Parti Républicain Dahoméen (q.v.). See also UNION PROGRESSISTE DAHOMEENNE.

UNION GENERALE DES ETUDIANTS ET ELEVES DA-HOMEENS (UGEED). Militant student union dissolved by President Hubert Maga (q.v.) in 1961, its membership absorbed by the government-sponsored Union Nationale des Etudiants et Elèves Dahoméens (UNEED) (q.v.). After the fall of Maga, the UGEED was resurrected. It participated in a series of student strikes, especially against the regime of Emile Derlin Zinsou (q.v.), following which several schools were closed for varying periods of time. On November 4, 1971, the UGEED called a strike against the policies of the Presidential Council (q.v.), leading to governmental retaliation, including closure of all schools and the banning of the union. Regarded by that time as subversive and infiltrated by radical and/or aspiring politicians, the ban on the activities of the UGEED continued until after the military takeover by Major Mathieu Kérékou (q.v.) in 1972. In mid-1974 the UGEED was once again banned, charged by the military regime with "verbalism and infantile Left-wingism." The disenchantment of the UGEED was complete after the liquidation of Captain Michel Aikpé (q.v.) who was very popular among students.

UNION GENERALE DES SYNDICATS DU DAHOMEY (UGSD). Militant trade union (q.v.), forcibly merged in 1961 with the Union Générale des Travailleurs des Dahomey (q.v.). The UGSD reemerged in 1964 following the coup that toppled President Hubert Maga (q.v.). Internationally nonaligned to any trade union federation, the UGSD had a platform of economic socialism. Until 1972 Dahomey's second-largest union with 8,000 members, the UGSD was under the leadership of Secretary-General Honorat Ogoubiyi Akilotan.

UNION GENERALE DES TRAVAILLEURS D'AFRIQUE NOIRE (UGTAN). Interterritorial trade union (q.v.) movement founded in Cotonou (q.v.) in January 1957 in an effort to break the links of African trade unions with the various French- or European based trade union confederations.

Headed by Guinea's President Sékou Touré, UGTAN later split at the 1959 Conakry, Guinea, Congress—for all practical purposes disappearing as an effective movement—with the All-African Trade Union Federation assuming the militant leadership.

UNION GENERALE DES TRAVAILLEURS DU DAHOMEY (UGTD). Unified trade union (q.v.) set up by law in 1961 when President Hubert Maga (q.v.) moved to destroy unionist forces in opposition to his regime. The principal union to suffer was the militant Union Nationale des Syndicats des Travailleurs du Dahomey (UNSTD) (q.v.), which had been under the control of Hubert Maga's opponent Justin Ahomadégbé (q.v.). Despite Maga's selection of its Secretary-General, Theophile Paolétti (q.v.), the UGTD became progressively more radical and its call for a general strike on October 26, 1963, over a variety of issues, including the Bohiki Affair (q.v.), led to Maga's overthrow (see BOHIKI AFFAIR; COUP OF 1963). After the coup the UGTD pressed for the purge of corrupt officials and the creation of a new party, the PDD, in the new administration of Ahomadégbé and Sourou-Migan Apithy (q.v.). After the 1963 coup (q.v.), the UGTD lost some of its membership to other unions, now legal. In 1967 it participated again in a series of strikes against Gen. Christophe Soglo (q.v.), which also led to the collapse of the regime (see COUP OF 1967). The UGTD was led by Secretary-General Jacob Padonou and was internationally linked with the World Federation of Labor. Its socioeconomic platform called for major reforms of the country's investment code and profit repatriation statutes, "normalization" of Dahomey's relations with the East, a break with the Conseil de l'Entente (q.v.) and revision of Dahomey's treaties with France. The union was Dahomey's largest, with 10,000 members.

UNION GENERALE POUR LE DEVELOPPEMENT D'OUIDAH (UGDO). Cultural organization set up in 1984 with former President Kérékou's (q.v.) strong support in an effort to split Ouidah's Fon from the mainstream Abomey (qq.v.) groups. The UGDO was headed by Barthelemy Anagon.

UNION NATIONALE DAHOMEENNE (UND). Northern political party set up by Hubert Maga, Paul Darboux and Arouna Mama (qq.v.) on December 10, 1965, after Gen. Christophe Soglo's November 29, 1965, coup (qq.v.) and the appointment of Speaker of the House Tahirou Congacou (q.v.) as Interim President. When Soglo dismissed the latter on December 22, 1965 (setting up his military administration), all parties, including the UND, were banned. The short-lived UND was successor to the Mouvement Démocratique Dahoméen and the Rassemblement Démocratique Dahoméen (qq.v.). See also COUP OF 1965(b).

UNION NATIONALE DES ETUDIANTS ET ELEVES DAHOMEENS (UNEED). The unified organization into which all other student unions were forcibly merged by President Hubert Maga (q.v.) during his first Presidency (1960–1963). Among the unions to be dissolved at that time was the militant Union Générale des Etudiants et Elèves Dahoméens (UGEED) (q.v.), which was reestablished after the fall of Maga.

UNION NATIONALE DES SYNDICATS DES TRAVAILLEURS DU BENIN (UNSTB). Sole trade union (q.v.) organization in "revolutionary" Benin. Set up by the government in 1978 after the previous union—the Union Syndicale Nationale (q.v.)—beset by factionalism, had ousted Secretary-General Vilon Romain Guézo (q.v.) under pressure from the extreme Left. Regarded as loyal to the State, Guézo was appointed Secretary-General of the new UNSTB, which remained as polarized as its epistemological predecessor, with the rank and file unhappy with its role as partner of the government in the process of which unionist interests are sacrificed. The first congress of the UNSTB was held in May 1981. Later the leadership of the UNSTB passed to Philippe Adjo, as Guézo was promoted within the PRPB (qq.v.) party. The UNSTB slowly disintegrated in the late 1980's as the government was unable to pay labor salaries; despite "breaking" with the government and the PRPB in 1989 this was not sufficient to save it; in 1989 two component unions and, in

1990, another three seceded from it, leading to its dissolution in 1990.

UNION NATIONALE DES SYNDICATS DES TRA-VAILLEURS DU DAHOMEY (UNSTD). Pro-Justin Ahomadégbé and pro-Union Démocratique Dahoméenne trade union (qq.v.) that led the October 1960 general strike and demonstrations in the south, in the wake of which Ahomadégbé tried to come to power. The demonstrations were broken up by troops and police, the UNSTD was banned, and in 1961 its membership was forced to join the government-sponsored Union Générale des Travailleurs Dahoméens (q.v.). UNSTD factions remained within the UGTD and, in 1963, they helped spark the general strike that brought the collapse of the Maga (q.v.) regime. See also COUP OF 1963; UNION GENERALE DES TRA-VAILLEURS DAHOMEENS.

UNION POUR LE RENOUVEAU DU DAHOMEY (URD). Emile Derlin Zinsou's "parti unique" (qq.v.), established in May 1969 to support his Presidential policies. In light of the shortness of Zinsou's term in office and his meager sources of popular support in the country, the URD was much more a paper structure than a viable political movement. The party disappeared with the overthrow of Zinsou in December 1969.

UNION POUR LE TRIOMPHE DU RENOUVEAU DE-MOCRATIQUE (UTR). A three-party parliamentary coalition of 12 deputies formed in 1991 in support of the Presidential candidacy, and later leadership, of Nicéphore Soglo (q.v.). The group slowly expanded, changing names first to Nouvelle République and, in 1993, to Le Rénouveau (qq.v.) when it included 34 deputies. The original UTR partners were Amnanlin Timothée's Union Démocratique des Forces du Progrès (UDFP), Marcelin Dégbé's Mouvement pour la Démocratie et le Progrès Social (MDPS) (qq.v.) and Francisco Marius' Union pour la Liberté et le Développement (ULD).

UNION PROGRESSISTE DAHOMEENNE (UPD). First Dahomean political party, established in July 1946 following a merger of several of the earlier Comités Electoraux (q.v.). Affiliated with the SFIO (the French Socialist party), the UPD included at the outset most of the then best-known politicians in the country—Augustin Azango (q.v.), Victor Patterson, Sourou-Migan Apithy (q.v.) and Emile Derlin Zinsou (q.v.). Personal rivalries rent the party several months later and led to the defection of an important faction that coalesced in 1947 to form the Bloc Populaire Africain (BPA) under Emile Poisson and Justin Ahomadégbé (qq.v.). The BPA was the precursor of the Union Démocratique Dahoméenne (q.v.). The UPD was initially affiliated with the Rassemblement Démocratique Africain (q.v.), but, under strong Catholic pressure, it disengaged itself in 1948 (providing yet another impetus for the secession from the party of the more militant members) and became affiliated with the Indépendants d'Outre Mer (q.v.). In May 1951 the UPD broke up completely with the secession of the northern members organized under Hubert Maga in the Groupement Ethnique du Nord (qq.v.)—shortly to become the Mouvement Démocratique Dahoméen (q.v.)—and with the withdrawal of the Porto Novo and Yoruba (qq.v.) members organized under Apithy in the Parti Républicain Dahoméen (qq.v.). The rump of the UPD remained under Zinsou until the party merged in 1955 with Justin Ahomadégbé's Union Démocratique Dahoméenne. One major issue that led to the collapse of the ''national'' UPD party was the impossibility of accommodating the political ambitions for office of three or four regional leaders at a time when Dahomey was only entitled to send two delegates to Paris. Also, there was increasing resistance against Apithy's leadership in the party and, in the north, resentment against the ''domination'' of the party by southerners. The origin of the tripartite division of power in Dahomey resides in the tensions that tore apart the UPD. See also POLITICAL PARTIES.

UNION SYNDICALE NATIONALE (USN). Principal trade union (q.v.) confederation set up after the 1972 coup d'etat (q.v.) to centralize all existing structures. Beset by cleavages on a multiplicity of planes, in 1975 the union adopted a confrontational stand vis-a-vis the government, consequent to a series of actions that antagonized part of the membership, including the liquidation of the popular Major Aikpé (q.v.). A new union was subsequently set up—the UNSTB(q.v.)—under the leadership of Guézo (q.v.), who had previously been ousted from the USN leadership due to his pro-government line. The UNSTB replaced the USN in 1978.

UNIVERSITE DU DAHOMEY see UNIVERSITE NATIONALE DU BENIN.

UNIVERSITE NATIONALE DU BENIN (UNB). National university established with French assistance in 1970–1971 in Abomey-Calavi, a few miles away from Cotonou (qq.v.). Prior to its foundation, Dahomey and Togo had shared a common institution, the Institut d'Enseignement Supériéur du Bénin, with a sciences section in Porto Novo (q.v.) and a humanities branch in Lomé, Togo. The new university had, in 1972, 52 instructors and 1,097 students; a year later the student body had increased to 1,800. Its first rector was Edouard Adjanohoun and its Secretary-General, Michel Assogba. The location of the University in Abomey-Calavi, essentially in the political fiefdom of Justin Ahomadégbé (q.v.)—contrary to the recommendation of a French mission to locate it in Porto Novo—caused a serious rift in the Presidential Council (q.v.), alienating the Porto Novo leader Sourou-Migan Apithy (q.v.). Following Dahomey's change in name in 1975, the university was renamed Université Nationale du Bénin (UNB), a name similar to that of the University in Togo and in Benin City in Nigeria.

Direct French contributions to the UNB have fluctuated between 165 and 350 million CFA francs per year. Since its establishment, the university has expanded dramatically: in 1981 it enrolled 5,515 students; in 1991, nearly 10,000. Its library had, in 1993, some 40,000 volumes. The educational reforms (q.v.) of 1976 brought about curriculum revisions and a projected syphoning off of students into three new polytechnics at Pobé, Bohicon, and Natitingou (qq.v.). The unpopular reforms and measures cutting student bursaries caused serious student unrest on campus during 1979, 1981, 1984–1985, and virtually annually since. Unrest and rioting over poor food and living conditions, low bursaries or their non-payment on time and a host of other issues, have continued even after the transition to civilian rule, to plague the regime of Nicéphore Soglo (q.v.).

UPRISINGS OF 1915–1918. Scattered series of uprisings in Borgou, Atakora and Mono (qq.v.), ignited in part by the higher taxation, porterage and recruitment policies necessitated by the onset of the First World War. Contributing factors were the colonial disruption of traditional caravan and trade routes, grievances with respect to the French administrative organization of Dahomey (see NIKKI), excesses by local administrators (see GABA) and historic unrest (see HOLLI REVOLT). Also involved was anti-white agitation by Muslims from Nigeria (where the Sokoto Moslem revolts had recently occurred), the spread of malaise among Dahomean Bariba (q.v.) chiefs (especially in Nikki) over the British deposal in 1915 of a Bussa (q.v.) chief in nearby Nigeria, and a general reassertion of traditional chiefly authority against the restrictions placed upon it by France. While the uprisings tended to be localized and never actively pitched against the administration, the entire population of the region was involved, and suppression of the revolts was hampered by the terrain and the understaffed nature of France's forces in Dahomey. In the process of subduing the areas in revolt, many local chiefs had their traditional powers further whittled down.

The Holli Revolt (q.v.) in the Mono erupted in 1914 and was not quelled until 1918. It occurred in a region historically contested by both the Porto Novo and Dahomey kingdoms (q.v.), at a time when the local population was asserting its freedom from both. The French overlordship was thus highly resented while the swampy terrain made repression more difficult.

The uprising in Borgou was sparked in 1916 by Bio Guéra (q.v.), a minor local chief, over abuses of power by French administrators, increased taxation, military recruitment and *corvée* (q.v.) labor. In the process, the revolt spread to other parts of the Borgou. It was crushed in 1918. The Somba (q.v.) rebellion in the Atakora was also sparked by resentment at recruitment policies (possibly hated here more than elsewhere) and occurred in a region of Dahomey not yet fully "pacified" or effectively occupied. The Somba rebellion was given rather low priority by the French administration until the Borgou rebellion was fully crushed.

URBAN CENTERS. Benin's urban population stands at 32 percent of the population, with the country having six main urban centers. These are, arranged by rank and estimated population, as of 1992: (1) Cotonou, 400,000; (2) Porto Novo, 160,000; (3) Abomey, 80,000; (4) Natitingou, 75,000; (5) Parakou, 74,000; and (6) Ouidah 32,000 (qq.v.).

-V-

VIDEGLA, PAMPHILE, 1936– . Former civil administrator. Born in Cotonou (q.v.) on August 21, 1936 and educated at IHEOM in Paris, Videgla returned to Dahomey to occupy a variety of administrative posts, including Deputy-Prefect (later Prefect) of Ouémé (q.v.). In October 1968 he was appointed head of the Cotonou urban circonscription. He left the country for France in 1974.

VIEYRA, CHRISTIAN, 1930– . Lawyer, politician and international civil servant. Born in Porto Novo (q.v.) on March 30 1930, Viéyra studied in France, including the Paris School of Economics, graduating in law and economics. Returning to Dahomey, he briefly served as Assistant Judge, Public Prosecutor and Legal Advisor to President Hubert Maga (q.v.) (1962). In 1961 he was appointed Secretary-General of the African and Malagasy Union (UAM) by the Tananarive, Malagasy, Conference of Heads of State. His tenure in that post was brief, following which he served as Director of the African Institute for Economic Development and Planning (IDEP), at the United Nations, and as head of the UNESCO planning mission in South Vietnam. Gen. Christophe

Soglo's (q.v.) cousin by marriage, Viéyra was brought into Soglo's government in December 1965 as High Commissioner for Planning and Tourism. He resigned from this post a year later in opposition to Soglo's inclusion in his government of several former politicians from the north. In December 1966 he was dispatched to New York as Dahomey's Permanent Delegate to the UN and since 1967 has been with UNESCO on various missions including one to Zaire (1968–1973).

VIEYRA, DESIRE. Minister of Defense and international civil servant. Born in Ouidah (q.v.) on January 18, 1928, and educated in law and politics in France, Viéyra served as the Head of the Cabinet of the Minister of Labor between 1956 and 1958, and then headed the Ministry of Foreign Affairs as Secretary-General (1960–1961). In 1961 he joined UNESCO as representative of the organization to the four Francophone equatorial states with a base in Brazzaville. In 1963 he went on behalf of UNESCO as representative to Cameroun (1963–1965) and, in 1967, joined the Niger River Commission based in Niamey. Throughout his career as an international civil servant he was acting as a member of the French civil service attached to the Office of the Prime Minister of France. With the return of civilian rule to Benin Viéyra returned home and was appointed by Nicéphore Soglo (q.v.) (while interim Prime Minister under Kérékou [q.v.]) as Minister of State in charge of Government Coordination. He was appointed Minister of Defense in March 1993. Viéyra is Soglo's brother-in-law.

VIEYRA, JUSTIN. Senior editor of the influential *Jeune Afrique* and editor of *Entente Africaine.*

VIEYRA, PAULIN SOUMANOU, 1925–1987. Film-maker. Born in Porto Novo (q.v.) on January 30, 1925 to a "Brazilian" (q.v.) family, and educated in France in cinematography, Viéyra was Director and Editor-in-Chief of the Senegalese Cinema and News service between 1957 and 1972, producing numerous films during this period. One of the pioneers of African film, Viéyra died in 1987 after a long illness.

VIGBE, PROSPER. Director of the Treasury in the Ministry of Finance and Economics.

VILON-GUEZO, ROMAIN see GUEZO, ROMAIN VILON.

VODOUNOU, OKE MARCELLIN (Lt. Colonel). Former Director of the Gendarmerie (q.v.) (1967), Second Vice-President of the Conseil Militaire Révolutionnaire (q.v.) (1967–1968) and Defense aide-de-camp to President Emile Derlin Zinsou (q.v.) (1968–1970). A neutral in the regional political struggle in Benin, Vodounou supervised (on behalf of the armed forces [q.v.]) the elections of 1969, serving as President of the Electoral Commission. He was retired from the armed forces in 1972, with all the senior hierarchy of the officer corps.

VODUN or VOODOO. Various ancestral and spirit cults, deities and fetishes (q.v.) encompassing cosmological beliefs and myths. Once the powers of the *vodun* are proven effective, they are venerated and worshipped. Many such cults have come to Benin from Togo (also a major center of *vodun* beliefs) from whence the Adja (q.v.) dispersal to what is now Benin took place, and/or have been strongly influenced by Yoruba (q.v.) beliefs. (Of note is that the Adja themselves trace their origins to Ketou [q.v.] and further back to Ile-Ife in current Nigeria.) These practices have been exported, via the slave trade (q.v.), to Cuba, Brazil and Haiti (q.v.), and there are striking similarities between several contemporary practices/rituals in Benin/Togo and those currently in Haiti and Brazil especially. This is a topic researched by several scholars, and the historical museum in Ouidah (q.v.) has a collection of photos of New World *vodun* practices and their Beninois equivalent. In 1993 it was estimated that 62 percent of Beninois practice *vodun,* and during February 8–18 of that year the First International Festival of Vodun Art and Culture took place in Ouidah (a major *vodun* center and home to the Temple of the Great Serpent), opened by President Nicéphore Soglo, officiated by High Priests Sossa Guedehoungué (q.v.) and Dagbo Hounon, and attended by delegations from Benin, Nigeria, Ghana, Haiti and Trinidad and Tobago.

"LA VOIX DE LA REVOLUTION." The post-1972 name of Benin's radio station previously known as "Radio-Dahomey" and "La Voix du Dahomey" (q.v.). The station broadcasted in French, Fon, Yoruba, Bariba, Mina, Fulani, Dendi (qq.v.), and several other dialects. Television broadcasts (seven hours weekly) were initiated in 1978.

"LA VOIX DU DAHOMEY." (a) "The Voice of Dahomey," previously "Radio-Dahomey," which transmitted in French, Fon, Yoruba, Mina, Bariba, and Dendi (q.v.). After the 1972 coup d'etat (q.v.) the station's name was changed to "La Voix de la Revolution" (q.v.). (b) Also, *La Voix du Dahomey* was the Dahomean newspaper sued by the French administration for publishing seditious and inflammatory articles by Louis Hunkanrin and Louis Ignacio-Pinto (qq.v.) in 1935.

VOODOO. see VODUN

-W-

WANGARA. The name given to the northern urban quarters inhabited by non-local populations. Also sometimes known as Maro or Zongo (qq.v.).

WANILO, PRINCE, 1882–1928. Son of King Béhanzin (q.v.) and a former Nagot (q.v.) war-slave. At the age of 12 Wanilo accompanied his father to exile in Martinique and Algeria. After his father's death he was forced to remain abroad in order not to form a focal point for the resurrection of the Abomey (q.v.) dynasty. Though educated in modern schools, a request for a St. Cyr commission was turned down in order not to give him military credentials, but also because he had manifested anti-French (and pro-British) sentiments. He obtained a law degree instead in 1914, and opened an office in Paris. During the first World War he joined the army and secured French citizenship. He lived in Bordeaux mostly, together with his French wife, visiting his homeland only in 1921 when he arranged the repatriation of his father's remains, dying in 1928 on his way back to France where he is buried.

WASANGARI. Generic name of the Bariba (q.v.) nobility. Also, term applied to princely and royal lineages, all of which trace their descent to the Bussa (q.v.) kingdom in Nigeria or to its dependencies, Wawa and Ile. The name has a slightly pejorative meaning in Bariba, signifying vagabonds or adventurers. Classically, *Wasangari* was involved in warfare, pillage, and hunting, but rarely sedentary work. After the onset of the colonial era the *Wasangari* lost control over their Gando (q.v.) serfs and had to revert to cultivation of land in order to survive. See also BARIBA; BORGOU; NIKKI.

WEGBADJA, AHO, KING OF DAHOMEY (d. 1685). First king of Dahomey (q.v.), Dogbagri (q.v.) had earlier led the migration from Allada (q.v.) with his son Dako, consolidating the outer bounds of the new colony. Dako's son, Wegbadja, assumed the royal title as he expanded the small kingdom after a struggle with the indigenous populations among which they had settled. He also introduced many customs and innovations, including the Annual Customs (q.v.), brought over from Allada.

WHYDAH see OUIDAH.

WOROU. First King of Kouandé (q.v.). See CHABI GABA.

-X-

XAVIER. Name by which Savi (q.v.), the political capital of the precolonial kingdom of Houéda (q.v.), was known by French traders along the Slave Coast (q.v.).

XWEDA. Original spelling of Houéda (q.v.).

-Y-

YANDJOU, HOUSSOU DAVID, 1921- . Former Director of Water and Forests. Born in Porto Novo (q.v.) in 1921, and a water and forests engineer by training, Yandjou progressed in his career until appointed Director in December 1967. He served in that post until he retired in 1981.

YAO or YOWA. Original name of the Pila Pila (q.v.).

YAYA, MOUSSA DEDE. Former Minister. Trained as a teacher, Yaya taught English at Lycée Béhanzin and served briefly in 1965 (December 1–31) as Interim Minister of Education and Health. In 1967 he was appointed Superintendant of the Lycée in Parakou (q.v.) and, in 1972, Superintendant of Schools in Borgou (q.v.). He is currently in retirement.

YEHOUESSI, D. YVES, 1940– . Minister of Justice. Born in Grand Popo (q.v.) on May 24, 1940, and educated locally and in Dakar, Tehouéssi studied law at both the University of Dakar and Paris. Between 1970–1972 he served as a lower court judge in Cotonou (q.v.). He then worked in a variety of posts within the Beninois legal system, including four years as President of the Social Court (1973–1977) and seven years as Director of Civil and Penal matters at the Ministry of Justice (1981–1988). In 1988 he was appointed President of the Court of Appeals of Atlantique Province (q.v.) and, in 1990, was nominated by Nicéphore Soglo (q.v.) as Minister of Justice. His appointment was somewhat controversial since he was "tainted" by prolonged association with the previous Kérékou (q.v.) regime. Moreover, during the 1992 trial of Kérékou's marabout and prime security aide, Mohamed Cissé (q.v.), for embezzlement of State funds, Yehouéssi, two magistrates and one lawyer, were accused by seven Beninois lawyers of soliciting a 300 million CFA franc bribe in exchange for Cissé's acquittal.

YEHOUESSI, GILLES FLORENT. Economist. Yehouéssi was educated in France as an economist; he also obtained a banking diploma. He has been on the adminstrative board of the BCEAO, as well as on the governing board of the Société Dahoméenne du Banque (qq.v.). Since 1967, and until his retirement in 1981, he was technical consultant on banking relations with international organizations in the Ministry of Economics and Finance.

YEKPE, MAXIMILIEN, 1925– . Physician. Born in Cotonou (q.v.) on April 3, 1925, and a graduate of the University of Dakar Medical School, with several specializations, Yekpé has been Chief Physician of Epidemic Diseases at Cotonou Hospital since 1967.

YERIMA, PIERRE YAROU, 1922– . Administrator. Born in Kandi (q.v.) in 1922, and a deputy to the National Assembly (q.v.) between 1957 and 1963, Yerima has been Secretary of State for Rural Action between January and November 1960. Briefly also Minister of Social Affairs (for two months in 1960) he then commenced his administrative career as the *sous-préfet* of Banikoara, and later as Deputy Prefect of Borgou (q.v.), serving through 1968. In that year he was promoted to head the civil administration of Borgou as Prefect: in 1971 he was appointed in a similar capacity to the prefecture of Ouémé (q.v.). Briefly appointed to another prefectural post in 1975, Yerima served as head of a division in the Ministry of Interior until his retirement in 1982.

YEVOGAN. Sometimes erroneously referred to as Viceroy of Ouidah (q.v.), the *yevogan* was the "Chief of the White Men," according to one Dahomean source. The *yevogan* was appointed by the court of the Kingdom of Dahomey (q.v.) to supervise trade in Ouidah and to report on contacts with Europeans via the Mehu (q.v.). Abomey's loose control over Ouidah led many *yevogans* astray, and many are recalled in disgrace or executed for enrichment while in office. King Tégbésu alone had five such state officials executed. The duties of the *yevogan* included collecting "landing" taxes from all ships, selling the king's slaves first and at a higher price, collecting a variety of other duties on behalf of the kingdom, provisioning the various vessels, forwarding safely to Abomey (q.v.) all monies (i.e., cowries and/or other species) collected, and submitting to the Court samples of the new goods being introduced by slavers on the coast. The role of the *yevogan* was created in 1733, after condensing into that official the functions of several previous Dahomean dignitaries. By far the most famous, trustworthy and powerful *yevogan* was the Brazilian Francisco de Souza (q.v.).

YEYE, AMOUSSOU DENIS, 1948– . Psychologist. Born in 1948 and educated in France in psychology, Yéyé is at the National University of Benin (q.v.) as Head of the Psychology Laboratory; he also has a private practice in Cotonou (q.v.) as a psychotherapist.

YORUBA. An ethnic group found mostly in southwestern Nigeria and numbering over six million. Also scattered in Togo and Dahomey, the latter's Yoruba community numbers around 400,000 and is locally called Nago or Nagot (q.v.). Although most are either Christian or Muslim, belief in traditional religion continues. Yoruba religion and culture has had a strong influence on other ethnic groups in southern Dahomey (see GOUN). Dahomey's Yoruba are mostly found in Ouémé (q.v.) province and in the past were supportive of the presidential candidacies of Sourou-Migan Apithy (q.v.).

YOWA see PILA PILA.

-Z-

ZAKARI, IBRAHIMA. Powerful unionist. Head of the Postal and Telecommunications workers union (Synespostel), it was Zakari who raised the banner of rebellion against continued affiliation with the PRPB party and the UNSTB (qq.v.) trade union (q.v.) confederation. Though arrested for his role in further calling upon the railway workers to join the strikes, his action spelled the end to both state bodies.

ZANGBETO. Male animist secret initiation society in parts of southern Benin.

ZINKPO. Royal thrones of the Kings of Dahomey, symbols of authority. Quite similar in shape to the better known Ashanti stools, the Dahomean thrones are partly inlaid with metal (silver and/or copper) with one—Agonglo's—fully plated with silver. After the death of each king, the throne became part of the ceremonies celebrating the kingdom's ancestors. All the thrones are found in the important Abomey Palace Museum, just outside Abomey (q.v.).

ZINSOU, ABEL JUSTIN, 1940– . Born in Ouidah (q.v.) on August 22, 1940, Zinsou has served in a series of mid-echelon administrative capacities. Between 1962 and 1964 he was Administrative Secretary to the Supreme Court (q.v.), followed by four years as Personal Secretary to the Minister of Foreign Affairs. In 1968 he was attached to the presidential cabinet of Emile Derlin Zinsou (q.v.), serving until the 1969 coup d'etat (q.v.) and leaving the country for France in 1972.

ZINSOU, EMILE DERLIN, 1918– . Physician, prominent early politician, former President and main opposition leader (in exile) to the Marxist regime. Born in Ouidah (q.v.) on March 23, 1918, Zinsou was educated in Porto Novo, the Ecole William Ponty (qq.v.) in Senegal and the Dakar Medical College, where he qualified as a doctor. He served as a physician in the French army (1939–1940) and then practiced in Dahomey. Rapidly involving himself in politics, Zinsou was one of the founders of Dahomey's first political party, the Union Progréssiste Dahoméenne (UPD) (q.v.) and fought against its affiliation with the interterritorial Rassemblement Démocratique Africain (q.v.). In 1945 he was personal assistant to Sourou-Migan Apithy (q.v.), and Dahomey's Deputy to the French National Assembly. He later (1947–1953) became Councillor to the Assembly of the French Union, and its Vice-President. His control over the UPD never too strong, Zinsou witnessed its collapse from within as ethnic/regional factions, led by Justin Ahomadégbé, Hubert Maga (qq.v.), and finally Sourou-Migan Apithy, deserted it to set up their own particularistic parties (see POLITICAL PARTIES.) In 1955–1956 he led the remainder of the UPD into a brief merger with Justin Ahomadégbé's Bloc Populaire Africain, their new party named Union Démocratique Dahoméenne (qq.v.).

In 1955 Zinsou was elected Senator of the French Republic (1955–1959), joining there the Indépendants d'Outre Mer (q.v.) and beginning his close association with Senegal's future President Léopold Sédar Senghor. Deputy to Dahomey's Assemblée Territoriale, and later the Assemblée Nationale (qq.v.), Zinsou joined the Apithy government set up under the "loi cadre" (q.v.) liberalization and served as Minister of Commerce (1958–1959). A convinced federationist, unwilling to see the post-independence splintering of Francophone Africa, and in 1959 founder of a Convention Africaine (q.v.) caucus in Dahomey, Zinsou was at that time Secretary of the interterritorial Parti du Regroupement Africain (PRA) (q.v.), based in Dakar, and Secretary-General of the latter's Dahomean affiliate, the Parti Progréssiste Dahoméen (q.v.)—a merger of Apithy's PRD (q.v.) and Maga's MDD (q.v.) parties. In 1959 Zinsou broke with Apithy over the latter's change of heart regarding Dahomey's joining the then-projected Mali Federation (q.v.), which was a basic PRA plank.

After Dahomey's independence, Zinsou joined the Maga/Apithy government as President of the Supreme Court (q.v.) then Ambassador to France and finally Minister of Foreign Affairs (1962–1963). Shortly before Maga's overthrow in 1963 Zinsou was abruptly dismissed. During the Ahomadégbé/Apithy administration, he was Francophone Africa's 1964 candidate for the position of Secretary-General of the Organization of African Unity (OAU) and, later, advisor on African affairs to the South African Anglo-American Corporation in Paris. Late in December 1965 he was recalled to Dahomey to again head the Foreign Ministry, following the establishment of Gen. Christophe Soglo's (q.v.) government (1965–1967).

A staunch antimilitarist, Zinsou was paradoxically chosen by the army—following the 1967 coup and the electoral boycott of 1968 (qq.v.)—to become president of Dahomey. He provided the country with a strong no-nonsense administration which, however, attracted the ire of powerful groups hurt by some of his policies (i.e., antismuggling crackdowns, more efficient tax collection, stronger countermeasures against student strikes, etc.) and his independence in office drove a wedge between him and his Chief-of-Staff, Col. Maurice Kouandété, who toppled him in December 1969. In the 1970 Presidential elections (q.v.), Zinsou garnered only a handful of votes (3 percent of the total cast) since he had no traditional, ethnic or regional power base. Rejecting a half-hearted offer that he join the Presidential Council (q.v.),

Zinsou eschewed political activity and relocated to Paris. On March 17, 1975, following Captain Assogba's (q.v.) attempted coup in January, Zinsou was accused of complicity and sentenced to death in absentia. He declared his total opposition movement in exile that was involved in several attempts to destablizie the Kérékou (q.v.) regime. With the onset of civilian rule and multipartyism in Benin Zinsou returned from his 17-year exile and set up a political party, the Union National pour la Démocretie et le Progrés (UNDP), that called for the rejection of the proposed constitution in the 1990 referendum (q.v.). Unsuccessful in his efforts, and politically weak, Zinsou is semi-retired today.

ZINZINDOUHE, CLEMENT (Lt. Colonel). Former brutal and much feared Commissioner of the Permanent National Investigatory Commission on State Security during the Kérékou (q.v.) era. His torture of political prisoners brought the regime much international condemnation, and he was replaced in 1988 by Commissioner of Police Justin Attakpa (q.v.).

ZODEHOUGAN, EDOUARD (Lt. Colonel). Former commander of the Military Police and the Benin navy. In January 1975 Zodehougan was appointed to head the Sureté Nationale (q.v.) and, in February 1980, he joined the cabinet as Minister of Technical Education. His appointment in 1984 as Minister of Interior, Public Security and Territorial Administration and simultaneously a member of the PRPB (q.v.) Politburo made him in essence the second most powerful man in Benin, especially in light of Alladayé's (q.v.) eclipse in the 1980's. Though in November 1985 Zodehougan was dropped from the Politburo, he remained in his cabinet office until the transition to civilian rule.

ZOLNER, MAXIME LEOPOLD, 1935– . Diplomat and international administrator. Born to a German Alsatian father and his Dahomean wife on October 4, 1935, in Porto Novo (q.v.), Zollner was educated locally and at the elitist Lycée Louis-le-Grand and the Ecole Nationale de la France Outre Mer in

Paris (1953–1960), obtaining a degree in law and political science. Since the completion of his studies, he has served in a succession of important positions: Delegate to the UN and Counselor at Dahomey's Embassy to the U.S. (1960–1963); member of the UN Commission of Inquiry on New Guinea (1962) and Congo/Leopoldville (1962). In July 1963 Zollner succeeded Tévoédjré (q.v.) as Secretary-General of the African and Malagasy Union (UAM), and in 1966 he was appointed Amabassador to the U.S., a position he occupied until 1971. He retired from the Foreign Ministry following the 1972 coup (q.v.) and is currently in Geneva. He has served as Secretary-General of Volunteer Services of the U.N. and is currently Deputy Secretary-General of the World Refugee Organization.

ZONGO. Term used in northern Dahomey referring to the "strangers" (visitors') quarters in urban areas. The term is often reserved exclusively for Yoruba (q.v.) or Hausa quarters. Other terms used include *Wangara* and *Maro* (qq.v.).

ZOU. One of Dahomey's provinces with administrative headquarters in Abomey (q.v.), including the sous-préfectures of Abomey, Dassa-Zoumé, Savalou (q.v.), Savé and Zagnanado. Its estimated population of 520,556 is composed mostly of Fon, Adja, Nagot and Yoruba (qq.v.). Zou used to be the center of Justin Ahomadégbé's (q.v.) political fiefdom. It is also the name of a river in the area, a tributary of the Ouémé (q.v.), which for a long time marked the boundary of the Dahomey kingdom's (q.v.) area of prime influence.

ZOUMAROU, WALLIS IBRAHIM (Major). Former Commander of the Northern Zone. A gendarmerie (q.v.) officer, Zoumarou supported Colonel Alphonse Alley (q.v.) in the "Easter Plot" in 1968, and he was arrested and fined for his role in it. He was subsequently appointed Military Prefect of Bembéréké and Commander of the Northern Zone. Following the 1972 coup d'etat (q.v.), he was retired from the armed forces (q.v.), together with the entire senior command. Prior to his dismissal, he was appointed to a temporary sinecure as head of the state company SONOCO.

ZOUME RIVER. Another name for the So river (see OUEME RIVER).

ZOUNON, JEAN. Little-known Deputy Leader of the Parti Communiste Dahoméen that incited anti-Kérékou (q.v.) demonstrations among students at the National University of Benin (q.v.), and in 1990 tried to sway public opinion not to participate in the National Conference (q.v.) until Kérékou was ousted.

BIBLIOGRAPHY

INTRODUCTORY NOTES

Francophone Africa, and its smaller components like Benin, still suffers from a dearth of scholarly work in the English language, though this has slowly been corrected in several fields. Apart from the early pioneering work of Herskovits (Herskovits 1938, 1958), only in the mid-1970's did the first books appear (Ronen 1975; Manning 1978, 1981) dealing exclusively with Dahomey/Benin. Their number has not been significantly augmented since, but a steady stream of books has appeared that include chapters on Dahomean history or recent Beninois developments. The first of this genre tended to be either overly general (Thompson 1963) or dealt with specific phenomena such as military coups (Skurnik 1970; Bebler 1973; Decalo 1976, 1990). But with time the result has been—especially after Allen's contribution (Allen et. al., 1989)—that there is a basic, if disciplinarily uneven, corpus of books, or chapters in books, on Benin in English.

The interested reader can also tap a by-now not insignificant number of articles published in English, though many of these are in a variety of weeklies, academic periodicals, or annuals. Though, for all practical purposes, French language sources are indispensable for any serious in-depth analysis (one significant exception being current affairs, but others are slowly emerging) the bleak picture outlined in the 2nd edition of this volume for those only versant in English is no longer true. A synthesis of English and French sources would be ideal, of course. This is by now also true for French scholars who—judging by their claims to originality, and their footnotes—are woefully unaware of their Anglophone counterparts' research.

The bibliographical section of this volume endeavours to simplify the quest for data. However, in order to include literature that has accrued since the 2nd edition without making the volume too long (and costly), the thrust has somewhat changed. Hitherto, omissions notwithstanding, the goal was comprehensiveness, even at the cost of including ephemeral material or short articles. Most of these have now been dropped and a degree of selectivity has been exercised in compiling the bibliography. As a further aid, the following comments serve in pinpointing some of the principal work in several fields.

SOCIOLOGY, ANTHROPOLOGY, AND HISTORY. The best single work in this broad field remains Robert Cornevin's massive *Histoire du Dahomey* (1962), revised and updated to appear in 1981 as *La République Populaire du Bénin* (1981). The volume surveys in great detail the country's topography, socioeconomic infrastructure, ethnic groups, colonial conquest, and history, but is quite bland, and of little use for the postindependence era, or politics in general. The work is ideally complemented by Maurice Glélé's *Naissance d'un Etat Noir* (1969), which traces in minute detail Dahomey's evolution up to 1965 (see next section), and François de Medeiros' *Peuples du Golfe du Bénin* (1984) that through individual chapters provides fresh insights into the origins and histories of the region's coastal ethnic groups.

Other noteworthy studies in these fields include Jacques Lombard's classic work on the Bariba of the north, *Structures du type "féodal" en Afrique Noire* (Lombard 1965), and the works on Dahomey's Fon by Argyle (1966), Akinjogbin (1967), Le Hérisse (1911), Polanyi (1966), and M. Quénum (1938). One should also mention the study of the colonial competition for this region (Obichere 1971), Casimir Agbo's work on Ouidah (Agbo 1959), and the valuable study of Akindélé and Aguessy on Porto Novo (Akindélé and Aguessy 1953), Grivot's *Réactions Dahoméennes* (Grivot 1954), and the many solid articles of Paul Mercier and Jacques Lombard (both of whom served in Porto Novo's Institut Français d'Afrique Noire), Robert Cornevin, Jacques Bertho, Melville Herskovits' books and articles, and the historical and ethnological research of Edouard Dunglas, Pierre Verger (especially on the Dahomey-Brazil slave trade), and Jacques Bertho. Maurice's work on Atakora, recently reprinted (Maurice 1985) with its painstakingly assembled sketches and clan-lists, is likewise a very useful though inevitably dated contribution. To these should be added the numerous, and refreshingly revisionist, historical studies of Robin Law and Ross, indispensable, of course, for students limited to English-language literature. These studies are only a handful of the many fine works in these sections. Being one of Africa's better-known countries, Benin has attracted considerable interest, and indigenous scholars have begun to contribute to our knowledge, as especially attested by the work of Hélène d'Alméda-Tupor and Félix Abiola Iroko.

POLITICS AND CONTEMPORARY AFFAIRS. The first thorough, full-length studies of Dahomey's political evolution were Maurice Glélé's *Naissance d'un Etat Noir,* referred to above, and Dov Ronen's *Dahomey Between Tradition and Modernity.* The former is a minutely detailed analysis of the period 1945–1965, incredibly rich in original data and information about the dominant political personalities and the evolution of the country's unique political style, and has no rival to date. Written by a Beninois at a time when the military was in power, the study is lean on the political role of the armed forces. Since the latter topic has attracted much English-language research, this gap can easily be filled by the works of Skurnik (1968, 1970), Bebler (1973), Lemarchand (1968), Matthews (1966), and Decalo (1968, 1970, 1971, 1973, 1979, 1990).

Ronen's book, leaner on detail than Glélé's, carries the political analysis into the "Revolutionary" (post-1972) period, providing valuable insights into the nature of politics in transitional societies. Ronen's other articles in this section (including his chapter in Harbeson 1988), together with Decalo's on the rhetoric-reality cleavage of Beninois Marxism, are ideally complemented by Chris Allen's monograph-length chapter (Allen et al. 1988) that provides a fairly contemporary survey of the Kérékou era, and an analysis of several policy initiatives rarely touched upon, at least by English-language authors. Allen's subsequent articles on contemporary Benin are also among the best in the English language.

Other important sources on the political and economic evolution of Benin include Manning's twin economic-history studies (Manning 1978, 1981), Virginia Thompson's (1963, 1972), Robert Cornevin's various articles, and the annual sections on Benin in *Africa Contemporary Record* until its recent demise. *West Africa* (London) and *Africa Report* also intermittently publish brief reports on Benin (most of these are the kind dropped from this Bibliography) while the monthly issues of the two series of *Africa Research Bulletin* (Exeter) and the Banque Centrale de l'Afrique de l'Ouest's quarterly "Indicateurs Economiques" and other bulletins (that being mostly statistics require little French) provide more than adequate and utterly indispensable primary data on ongoing political and economic developments. The biweekly *Africa Confidential* also periodically publishes brief reports on Benin that despite their brevity have detail not easily obtainable in any other source.

Finally, three works from the other sections need be mentioned: Huannou's guide to the fairly voluminous Beninois literature (Huannou 1984) that discusses the literary role and themes of each main author; Etienne-Nugué's *Artisanats traditionnels.* (Etienne-Nugué 1984) that is detailed study, replete with several hundred photos, of artisanal and other markets in Benin; and for students of traditional architecture several works have recently appeared of which a real gem is Alain Sinou and Bachir Oloudé's *Porto Novo* (Sinou & Oloudé 1988) if only for its voluminous sketches, photos and architecural layouts on the palace of the Kings of Porto Novo, recently refurbished and transformed into a national museum.

The books and articles are organized under the following subjects:

1. General Works
2. Early (Nineteenth-Century) Historical and Exploration Accounts
3. Historical Studies
4. Anthropology, Ethnology, and Sociology
5. Politics, Administration, and International Relations
6. Economics, Agriculture, Trade and Commerce
7. Education
8. Scientific Studies
9. Religion
10. Literature, Poetry, Theater and Cinematography
11. Linguistics
12. Art
13. Tourism
14. Reference and Bibliography

1. GENERAL WORKS

Afrique Occidentale Française. 2 vols. Paris: Encyclopédie Coloniale et Maritime, 1949.

Agboton, Gaston. *Voulez-vous Connaître la République populaire du Bénin?* Paris: ACCT, 1983.

Amin, Samir. *L'Afrique de l'Ouest Bloquée: l'économie politique de la colonisation, 1880–1970.* Paris: Editions de Minuit, 1971.

"Benin" in Moroney, Sean. *Africa.* New York: Facts on File, 1989, vol. 1, pp 25–34.

Betts, Raymond F. *Assimilation and Association in French Colonial Theory, 1890–1914.* New York: Columbia University Press, 1961.

Blanchet, André. *L'Itinéraire des Partis Africains depuis Bamako.* Paris: Plon, 1958.

Borella, F. *L'Evolution politique et juridique de l'Union Française depuis 1946.* Paris: R. Pichon & R. Durand-Auzias, 1958.

Brass, William. "The Demography of French-Speaking Territories," in A. J. Coale (ed.), *The Demography of Tropical Africa.* Princeton, N.J.: Princeton University Press, 1968, pp. 342–439.

Note that articles (the, a, an, le, la, les) in French and English and in French, "au" and "à" and "de"—were ignored in any position in alphabetizing the lists that follow.

Carpenter, John Allen. *Benin.* Chicago: Children's Press, 1978.

Chailley, Marcel. *Histoire de l'Afrique Occidentale Française.* Paris: Berger-Levrault, 1968.

Cohen, William B. *Rulers of Empire: The French Colonial Service in Africa.* Stanford: Hoover Institution Press, 1971.

Comité d'Etudes Historiques et Scientifiques de l'Afrique Occidentale Française. *Coutumiers Juridiques de l'Afrique Occidentale Française III: Mauritanie, Niger, Côte d'Ivoire, Dahomey, Guinée Française.* Paris: Larose, 1939.

Constitutions of the New African States. Cairo: Egyptian Society of International Law, 1962.

Cooke, James J. *New French Imperialism, 1880–1910: The Third Republic and Colonial Expansion.* Hamden, Conn.: Archon Books, 1973.

Corbett, Edward M. *The French Presence in Black Africa.* Washington, D.C.: Black Orpheus Press, 1972.

Cornout-Bentille, B. ''The Development of Social Legislation in French West Africa,'' *Inter-African Labour Institute Bulletin* (Brazzaville), vol. 3 (May 1956), pp. 8–17.

Le Dahomey. Paris: Société d'Editions Géographiques, Maritimes et Coloniales, 1931.

Delavignette, Robert. *Freedom and Authority in French West Africa.* New York: Oxford University Press, 1957.

Deloncle, Pierre. *L'Afrique occidentale française: découverte, pacification, mise en valeur.* Paris: Editions Ernest Leroux, 1934.

Deschamps, Hubert J. *Afrique noire pré-coloniale.* Paris: Presses Universitaires de France, 1962.

———— *Les Méthodes et doctrines de colonisation de la France.* Paris: Armand Colin, 1953.

D'Horel, P. *Afrique occidentale: Sénégal, Guinée, Côte d'Ivoire, Dahomey.* Paris, 1905.

Fage, J. D. *An Introduction to the History of West Africa.* Cambridge: Cambridge University Press, 1959.

Foltz, William J. *From French West Africa to the Mali Federation.* New Haven: Yale University Press, 1965.

Françoise, Louis, and R. Mangin. *La France et les territoires d'outre-mer.* Paris: Hachette, 1959.

Gérardin, Hubert. *La Zone Franc.* Paris: Harmattan, 1989. 2 vol.

Gonidec, P. F. *Constitutions des états de la Communauté.* Paris: Sirey, 1959.

Guernier, Eugène (ed.) *Encyclopédie de l'empire français.* Paris: Encyclopédie Coloniale et maritime, 1949. 2 vol.

Hadfield, Percival. *Traits of Divine Kingship in Africa.* London: Watts, 1949.

Hallet, Robin. *Africa to 1875: A Modern History.* Ann Arbor: University of Michigan Press, 1970.

Hardy, George. *Histoire sociale de la colonisation française.* Paris: Larose, 1953.

———. *La Politique coloniale et le partage de la terre aux XIXe et XXe siècles.* Paris: Albion Michel, 1937.

Hargreaves, J. D. *West Africa: The Former French States.* Englewood Cliffs, N.J.: Prentice-Hall, 1967.

Hempstone, Smith. *Africa—Angry Young Giant.* New York: Praeger, 1961.

Histoire et épopée des troupes coloniales. Paris: Presse Moderne, 1956.

Hodgkin, Thomas, and Ruth Schachter. "French-Speaking West Africa in Transition," *International Conciliation,* no. 528 (May 1960), pp. 375–436.

International Institute for Strategic Studies. *The Military Balance.* London: International Institute for Strategic Studies, annual.

Jalloh, A. A. *Political Integration in French-Speaking Africa.* Berkeley: Institute of International Studies, University of California, 1973.

Johnson, G. Wesley. "The Archival System of Former French West Africa," *African Studies Bulletin,* vol. 8, no. 1 (April 1965), pp. 48–58.

Kimble, George H. T. *Tropical Africa.* New York: Twentieth Century Fund, 1960, 2 vol.

Lavroff, Dimitri, and G. Peiser. *Les Constitutions africaines.* Paris: A. Pedone, 1961–63.

Leroi-Gourhan, André, and Jean Poirier. *Ethnologie de l'Union Française (Territoires Extérieurs)* vol. I: Afrique. Paris: Presses Universitaires, 1953.

LeVine, Victor T. *Political Leadership in Africa: Post-Independent Generational Conflict in Upper Volta, Senegal, Niger, Dahomey and the Central African Republic.* Stanford: Hoover Institution, 1967.

Lusignan, Guy. *French-Speaking Africa Since Independence.* New York: Praeger, 1969.

Marshall, D. Bruce. *The French Colonial Myth and Constitution-Making in the Fourth Republic.* New Haven: Yale University Press, 1973.

Meyers Handbuch über Afrika. Mannheim: Bibliographisches Institut, 1962.

Morgenthau, Ruth Schachter. *Political Parties in French-Speaking West Africa.* Oxford: Oxford University Press, 1964.

Mortimer, Edward. *France and the Africans 1944–1960.* London: Faber and Faber, 1969.

Newbury, C. W. "The Formation of the Government General of French West Africa," *Journal of African History,* vol. 1, no. 1, 1960, pp. 11–128.

Nowzad, Bahram. "Economic Integration in Central and West Africa," *International Monetary Fund Staff Papers,* vol. 16, no. 1 (March 1969), pp. 103–139.

Pedler, F. J. *Economic Geography of West Africa.* London: Longmans, Green, 1955.

Pedrals, Denis Pierre de. *Dans la brousse Africaine au Dahomey-Borgou.* Paris: La Nouvelle Edition, 1946.

Priestly, Herbert Inghram. *France Overseas: A Study of Modern Imperialism.* New York: Appleton-Century, 1938.

Richard-Molard, Jacques. *Cartes ethno-démographiques de l'Afrique Occidentale (Feuilles No. 1).* Dakar: Institut Français d'Afrique Noire, 1956.

Robinson, Kenneth. "Constitutional Reform in French Tropical Africa," *Political Studies,* vol. 6 (Feb. 1958), pp. 45–69.

―――. "The Public Law of Overseas France Since the War," *The Journal of Comparative Legislation,* vol. 32 (1950).

Salacuse, Jeswald W. *An Introduction to Law in French-Speaking Africa, I: Africa South of the Sahara.* Charlottesville, Va.: Michie, 1969.

Santos, Anani. *L'Option des indigènes en faveur de l'application de la loi française (en A.O.F. et au Togo).* Paris: Maurice Lavergne, 1943.

Saurrat, Albert. *La Mise en valeur des colonies françaises.* Paris: Payot, 1923.

Schnapper, Bernard. *La Politique et le commerce français dans le golfe de Guinée de 1838 à 1871.* Paris: Mouton, 1961.

Scholefield, Alan. *The Dark Kingdoms.* London, 1975.

Schramm, Josef. *Westafrika.* Buchenhain: Volk und Heimat, 1976.

Simon, Marc. *Souvenirs de Brousse, 1905–1918—Dahomey, Côte d'Ivoire.* Paris: Nouvelles Editions Latines, 1965.

Spitz, George. *L'Ouest Afrique Français*. Paris: Société d'éditions géographiques, maritimes et coloniales, 1947.

Stride, G. T., and Caroline Ifeka. *Peoples and Empires of West Africa*. New York: Africana, 1971.

Suret-Canale, Jean. *Afrique noire: occidentale et centrale*, 2 vol. Paris: Editions Sociales, 1964 and 1968.

————. *French Colonialism in Tropical Africa*. London: Hurst, 1971.

————. and Djibril Tamsir Nian. *Histoire de l'Afrique occidentale*. Paris: Présence Africaine, 1961.

Trimingham, John Spencer. *Islam in West Africa*. London: Oxford University Press, 1959.

Tymowski, Michal. *Le Développement et al régression chez les peuples de la boucle du Niger à l'époque précoloniale*. Warsaw: University of Warsaw, 1974.

Vignes, K. "Etude sur la rivalité d'influence entre les puissances européennes en Afrique équatoriale et occidentale depuis l'acte général de Berlin jusqu'au seuil du XXe siècle," *Revue Française d'Histoire d'Outre-Mer*, vol. 48, no. 1 (1961), pp. 5–95.

Wallerstein, Immanuel M. "How Seven States Were Born in Former French West Africa," *Africa Report*, vol. 4, no. 3 (March 1961).

Westermann, Diedrich, and Margaret A Bryan. *The Languages of West Africa*. New York: Oxford University Press, 1952.

Weygand, Général Maxime. *Histoire de l'armée française.* Paris: Flammarion, 1953.

2. EARLY (NINETEENTH-CENTURY) HISTORICAL AND EXPLORATION ACCOUNTS

Adams, John. *Remarks on the Country Extending from Cape Palmas to the River Congo.* London: Frank Cass, 1966 (repr. of 1823 ed.)

————. Sketches Taken During Ten Voyages to Africa Between the Years 1786 and 1800. London: Hurst, Robinson & Co., 1822.

Albéca, Alexandre Librecht d'. *La France au Dahomey.* Paris: Hachette, 1895.

————. *La Conquête du Dahomey, 1893–1894,* vol. 2. Paris: Berger-Levrault, 1895.

Aublet, Edouard Edmund. *La Guerre au Dahomey 1888–1893, d'après les documents officiels,* vol. 1. Paris: Berger-Levrault, 1894.

Augeard, A. *Etude sur la traite des noirs avant 1790.* Nantes, 1901.

Avril, Adolphe d'. *La Côte des esclaves.* Paris, 1889.

Barbot, John. *A Description of the Coasts of North and South Guinea.* London: Churchill, 1732.

Bartet, A. ''Colonne expéditionnaire dans le haut Dahomey,'' *Archives de Médicine Navale,* Aug.–Sept. 1898.

————. "Les Rois du Bas-Dahomey," *Bulletin de la Société de géographie de Rochefort,* vol. 30 (1908), pp. 179–216.

Barthelemy, Edouard. *Notice Historique sur les Etablissements français des côtes occidentales d'Afrique 1364–1840.* Paris: A. Bertrand, 1848.

Bayol, J. "Les forces militaires du Dahomey," *Revue Scientifique,* vol. 49, no. 17 (1892), pp. 520–524.

Béraud, Médard. "Note de séjour au Dahomey," *Bulletin de la Société de géographie,* vol. 14 (1866), pp. 224–232.

————. "Note sur le Dahomé," *Bulletin de la Société de Géographie,* 5th ser., vol. 12 (1866), pp. 371–386.

Bern, A. *L'Expédition du Dahomey.* Sidi-bel-Abes: Lavenne, 1893.

Bertin, Capt. *Renseignements sur le royaume de Porto Novo et le Dahomey.* Paris: Baudoin, 1890.

Bettencourt, Vasconcellos Corte Real do Canto, Vital de. *Descripcao historica, topographica e ethnographica do dictricto de S. Joao Baptista d'Ajuda e do reino de Dahomena Costa da Mina.* London, 1869.

Binet, Edouard. "Observations sur les Dahoméens," *Société d'Anthropologie: Bulletins et Mémoires,* vol. 1 (1990), pp. 244–252.

Borelli, Georges. "Voyage au Dahomey," *Bulletin de la Société de géographie de Marseilles,* vol. 26 (1902), pp. 153–165.

Bosman, Willem. *A New and Accurate Description of the Coast of Guinea.* London, 1809.

Bouche, Pierre Bertrand. "Le Dahomé," *Bulletin de la Société de Géographie,* June 1874.

⸻. *Le Dahomey et Porto Novo.* Paris: A. Colin, 1893.

⸻. *Les Noirs peints par eux-mêmes.* Paris: Poussielgue Frères, 1893.

⸻. *Sept Ans en Afrique Occidentale: La Côte des esclaves et le Dahomey.* Paris: Plon, 1885.

Brousseau, Georges. "Le Cercle du Borgou," *La Géographie,* 1904.

Brué, A. de. "Voyage à Abomey," *Revue Coloniale,* vol. 4, Sept. 1845.

⸻. "Voyage fait en 1843 dans le royaume de Dahomey," *Revue Coloniale,* vol. 7 (1845), pp. 55–68.

Brunet, J. L., and Louis Giethlen. *Dahomey et dépendances: Exposition Universelle de 1900—les colonies françaises.* Paris: Augustin Challamel, 1900.

Burét, Joseph. "Aperçu politique-agricole et commerciale sur le royaume de Konkobiri," *Journal Officiel Dahomey,* no. 16, Aug. 15, 1895, pp. 9–14.

Burton, Sir Richard F. *A Mission to Gelele, King of Dahome.* London: Routledge and Kegan Paul, 1966 (rep. of 1864 ed.).

Buzon. *Une visite à la Cour du roi du Dahomey.* Paris: Revue bleue, 1893.

Chappet, E. "Quatre années au Dahomey," *Bulletin de la Société de Géographie,* vol. 4 (1881), pp. 33–58.

Chautard, A. *Le Dahomey*. Lyon, 1890.

———. *Dahomey*. Paris: Challamel, 1910.

Cortez da Silva Curado. *Dahomé*. Lisbon, 1888.

Courdioux, R. *Manuel Dahoméen*. Paris: Leroux, n.d.

Courtet, H. ''Aperçu historique de la colonisation au Dahomey,'' *Bulletin de la Société Nationale d'acclimatation de France*, vol. 51 (1905), pp. 377–389.

Dalzel, Archibald. *The History of Dahomey, an Inland Kingdom of Africa; Complied from Authentic Memoirs: With an Introduction and Notes*. London: Cass, 1967 (repr. of 1793 ed.).

De la Harpe, M. *Abrégé de l'histoire générale des voyages*. Paris: Hôtel de Thou, 1780.

D'Elbée. *Journal de Voyage du Sieur d'Elbée en 1669*. Paris, 1671.

Describes, Emmanuel. *L'Evangile au Dahomey et à la Côte d'esclaves*. Clermont, 1877.

Desplantes, F. *Le Général Dodds et l'expédition du Dahomey*. Rouen: Magard et Cie, 1894.

———. *Le Sergeant Fritz au Dahomey*. Limoges, 1894.

Dex. Léo. *Du Tchad au Dahomey en ballon*. Paris: Hachette, 1930.

Drake, Richard. *Revelations of a Slave Smuggler*. New York, 1860.

Drault, J. *Chapuzot au Dahomey.* Paris, 1895.

Drot, A. "Notes sur le haut Dahomey," *La Géographie,* 1904.

Dubarry, Armand. *Voyage au Dahomey.* Paris: Dreyfous, 1879.

Duncan, John. *Travels in Western Africa in 1845–1846, Comprising a Journey from Whydah, Through the Kingdom of Dahomey, to Adofoodia in the Interior.* London: R. Bentley, 1847.

Ellis, Alfred Burton. *The Yoruba-Speaking Peoples of the Slave Coast of West Africa; Their Religion, Manners, Customs, Laws, Language, etc.,* 1894. Facsimile repr., Oosternout (Netherlands), Anthropological publications, 1966.

Ferris, Basile. "La Côte des Esclaves," *Archives de Médicine Navale,* vol. 31, 1879.

Foa, Edouard. *Le Dahomey; histoire, géographie, moeurs, coutumes, commerce, industrie, expéditions françaises (1891–1894).* Paris: A. Hennuyer, 1895.

———. "Le Dahomey et ses habitants," *Revue Scientifique,* vol. 47, 1895, pp. 366–68.

———. *Sur le Fleuve Whémé, limite entre Dahomey et Porto Novo.* Paris, 1888.

Fonssagrives, J. B. *Au Dahomey, souvenir des campagnes 1892–93.* Paris, 1894.

———. *Notice sur le Dahomey publiée à l'occasion de l'Exposition universelle.* Paris: Alcan-Levy, 1900.

Forbes, Frederick E. *Dahomey and Dahomans: Being the Journals of Two Missions to the King of Dahomey, and Residence at His Capital, in the Years 1849 and 1840.* London: Longmans, 1851, 2 vols.

"Français, anglais et allemands dans l'arrière-pays du Dahomey," *Bulletin du Comité Afrique Française,* vol. 2 (1895).

Freeman, Thomas Birch. *Journal of Various Visits to the Kingdoms of Ashanti, Aku and Dahomi in Western Africa.* London: Cass, 1968 (3d ed. of 1844 pub.).

Gallois, E., and R. Arnette. "La Dernière convention coloniale franco-allemande Dahomey-Togoland," *Bulletin de la Société de Géographie,* Dec. 1897.

Gandoin. *Trois Mois de captivité au Dahomey.* Paris, 1890.

Grandin, L. *A l'Assaut du pays des Noirs: Le Dahomey,* 2 vols. Paris, 1895.

Guillevin, R. "Voyage dans l'intérieur du royaume du Dahomey," *Nouvelles Annales des Voyages,* June 1862, p. 258–299.

Guy, C. "Résultats géographiques et économiques des explorations du Niger," *Bulletin du Comité Afrique Français,* 1899.

Hadjukiewicz de Pomian. "Dahomey," *Land och Ymer* (Stockholm), vol. 15, 1895, pp. 89–131.

Hagen, A. "La Colonie de Porto Novo et le roi Toffa," *Revue d'ethnologie,* vol. 6 (1887), pp. 81–116.

Hansen-Blangsted. *Le Dahomey*. Paris: L'Exploration, 1885.

Hartmann, Robert. "Uber die Amazonen des Königs von Dahomey," *Verh. Berlin, Geschichte für Anthropologie, Ethnologie und Vergeschichte*, 1891, pp. 64–71.

Hentsch, Henry. *Deux années au Dahomey, 1903–1905, d'après ses lettres*. Nancy: Berger-Levrault, 1916.

Heudebert, Lucien. *Promenades au Dahomey*. Paris: Librairie des Mathurins Dujarric et Cie, 1902.

Hulot, Baron. *Les Relations de France avec la Côte des Esclaves jusqu'en 1891*. Paris, 1894.

Huré, C. *L'Expansion française au Dahomey*. Paris: Challamel, 1891.

Jacolliot, A. *Le Pays des Nègres et la Côte des esclaves*. Tours: Editions Mame, 1873.

———. *Voyages en Guinée, au Niger, au Bénin et dans le Borgou*. Paris: Mapon et Flammarion, 1871.

Laffitte, R. *Le Dahomé*. Tours: Editions Mame, 1873.

Lara, H. Adolphe, and Ouanilo Béhanzin. *Pour Béhanzin*. Lyon, 1905.

Le Hérissé, René. *Voyage au Dahomey et à la Côte d'Ivoire*. Paris: H. Charles-Lavauzelle, 1903.

Lemoine, Frédéric. *Le Dahomey*. Melum, 1911.

Livingstone, David. *Un prince nègre ou les victimes du roi du Dahomé*. Lyon: Bulletin da la Société de Géographie 1886.

Lorho, Comte. *Historique de notre expansion dans l'hinterland dahoméen* Paris: Lavauzelle, 1904.

MacLeod, John. *A Voyage to Africa: With Some Account of the Manners and Customs of the Dahomian People.* London: John Murray, 1820.

Maire, A. *Dahomey.* Besançon, 1905.

Malavialle, L. "Le Dahomey," *Bulletin de la Société Languedocienne de Géographie,* vol. 13 (1890), pp. 267–309.

Marienval, A. *La Guerre du Dahomey.* Paris: Hatier, 1893.

Masse, Daniel. "Au Dahomey, 1892," *Revue de Paris,* vol. 5 (1892), pp. 169–196.

Mattei, A. *Bas Niger, Bénoué, Dahomey.* Grenoble: Vallier, 1890.

Merruau, Paul. "Le Dahomey et le roi Guézo," *Revue des Deux Mondes,* Dec. 15, 1851, pp. 1036–1062.

Mimande, Paul. *L'Héritage de Béhanzin.* Paris: Didier, 1898.

Monléon, M. de. "Le Dahomey en 1844," *Revue Coloniale,* vol. 6 (May–Aug. 1845), pp. 64–75.

Ned-Noll. "La Mission du Capitaine Vermersch à Borgou," *Bulletin de la Société de Géographie de Lyon,* vol. 14, 1838.

Nicolas, Victor. *L'Expédition du Dahomey en 1890.* Paris: Lavauzelle, 1892.

Noir, Louis. *Au Dahomey; une amazone de Béhanzin.* Paris: 1892.

Norris, Robert. *Memoirs of the Reign of Bossa Ahadie King of Dahomey, an Inland Country of Guiney, to Which Are Added the Author's Journey to Ahomey [sic] the Capital, etc.* London: Cass, reprint of 1789 ed.

Nuelito, F. *Au Dahomey, Journal d'un officier de spahis.* Abbéville, 1897.

Pied, A. "De Porto Novo à Oyo," *Missions Catholiques,* July 1892, pp. 1198–1207.

Piruz, V. F. *Viagem de Africaem o Reino de Dahomé.* Rio de Janeiro, 1800.

Planque, R. "Funérailles à Porto Novo," *Missions Catholiques,* no. 341–42, Dec. 1876.

Plé, James. "Exposé sommaire des opérations de délimitations entre le Dahomey et le Togo," *Revue des troupes coloniales,* Paris, 1902.

————. "La Mission Plé au Togo-Dahomey," *Revue Française,* 1900.

Poirier, Jules. *Campagne du Dahomey.* Paris: Lavauzelle, 1895.

Preil, Friedrich. *Deutsch-französische Waffenbruderschaft im Hinterlande von Togo und Dahomey.* Leipzig: Engelman, 1909.

Reclus, E. *Côte des Esclaves.* Paris: Hachette, 1887.

Renard Louis. *Porto Novo.* Paris, 1862.

Renaud J. *Le Général Dodds.* Paris, 1931.

Repin, A. "Voyage au Dahomey," *Etudes Dahoméennes,* vol. 3 (1950), pp. 89–95 (orig. pub. in 1863).

Riols, J. de. *La Guerre de Dahomey 1889–94.* Paris: Le Bailly, 1893.

Roqués, A. *Le Génie au Dahomey en 1892.* Paris: Berger-Levrault, 1895.

Rossi, A., and R. Meaulne. *Aventures au Dahomey: l'Homme aux yeux de verre.* Tours, 1893.

Rouard du Card, A. *Traités de délimitations concernant l'AOF.* Paris: Geuthner, 3 vol. 1910, 1913, 1926.

————. *Les traités de protectorat conclus par la France en Afrique.* Paris: Pedone, 1897.

Salinis, P. A. de. *Le quet-apens de Ouidah.* Paris: Perrin, 1890.

————. *La Marine au Dahomey, campagne de la "Naiade,"* Paris: Perrin, 1893.

————. *Le Protectorat français sur la côte des esclaves; la campagne du "Sané" 1889–1890.* Paris: Perrin, 1908.

Sampaio, A. *Sao Joao Baptista d'Adjuda.* Lisbon, 1895.

Sarmento, Augusto. *Portugal no Dahomé.* Lisbon: Livraria Tavares Cardoso, 1891.

Savinhiac, Louis. "La guerre sur Dahomey," *Spectateur Militaire,* vol. 4 (1890), pp. 457–472; vol. 1 (1891), pp. 33–43, 131, 142, 228–238, 328–343, 420–430, 485–491.

Schelameur, Frédéric. *Souvenirs de la campagne du Dahomey.* Paris: Lavauzelle, 1898.

Simond, C. *Les Français en Afrique, Les Missions françaises au xix siècle, Le partage de l'Afrique.* Paris, 1900.

Skertchly, A. J. *Dahomey As It Is.* London: Chapman and Hall, 1874.

Snelgrave, William. *A Full Account of Some Parts of Guinea and the Slave Trade.* London: Knapton, 1734.

Terrier, Auguste, "Délimitation de la frontière du Togo et du Dahomey," *Ouinzaine Coloniale,* vol. 11, 1907.

Toutée, Georges Joseph. *Du Dahomé au Sahara.* Paris: A. Colin, 1907.

————. *Dahomé, Niger, Toureg: récit de Voyage.* Paris: A. Colin, 1917.

————. "Principaux résultats géographiques de la mission Toutée," *Annales de Géographie,* March 1897.

————. *Du Sahara au Niger,* Paris: Colin, 1897.

Valdez, Francisco de. *Six Years of a Traveller's Life in Western Africa.* London, 1862. 3 vol.

van Looy. *En Reisje in Dahomey Naar het verhaal der Geloofzendelin en andere Reizigers, verzamelt en Gerangsschikt door.* Mechelen: H. Dessain, 1892.

Vermeersch, C. *Historique de la Mission Baud-Vermeersch.* Paris, 1897.

Vigne d'Octon, P. *Au Pays des Fétiches.* Paris: Lemerre, 1890.

————. *Terre de Mort (Soudan et Dahomey).* Paris: Lemerre, 1890.

3. HISTORICAL STUDIES

Abayomi, G. "Les investissements étrangers au Dahomey 1945–60." Thesis, University of Paris, 1974.

Adediran, Biodun. "The formation of the Sabe Kingdom in central Benin republic," *Africana Marbungensia*, vol. 16, no. 2 (1983), pp. 60–74.

————. "From constitutional troubles to civil war in Sabe: internal wars in a 19th century Yoruba community," *Africana Marbugensia*, vol. 17, no. 2 (1984), pp. 3–21.

————. "Idaisa: the making of a frontier Yoruba state," *Cahiers d'Etudes Africaines*, vol. 24, no. 1 (1984), pp. 71–85.

————. "Kings, traditions and chronology in pre-colonial Africa: conjectures on the Yourba kingdom of Ketu," *Afrika Zamani*, vol. 18/19 (1987), pp. 74–87.

Adeyinka, Augustus A. "King Ghezo of Dahomey, 1818–1858: A Reassessment of a West African Monarch in the Nineteenth Century," *African Studies Review*, vol. 17, no. 3 (Dec. 1974), pp. 541–48.

Adissoda, Marie-Antoinette. "La Presse au Dahomey 1890–1939." Thesis, University of Dakar, 1973.

Adjanohoun, Charles Elisha. "Armées et guerres dans l'Ouest africain médiéval." Thesis, University of Paris, 1976.

Adu Boahen, A. "Asante-Dahomey Contacts in the 19th Century," *Ghana Notes and Queries*, no. 7, January 1965.

"Les Afro-américains," *Mémoires de l'Institut Français d'Afrique Noire*, 1952–53, pp. 13–17.

Agbo, Casimir. *Histoire de Ouidah du XVIe au XXe siècles.* Avignon: Aubanel Père, 1959.

Aguessy, C., and A. Akindélé. "Esclavage, colonisation et tradition au sud-Dahomey," *Présence Africaine,* no. 6 (Feb.–March 1956), pp. 58–67.

Aguessy, Honorat. "Le Dan-Homé du XIXe siècle était-il une société esclavagiste?," *Revue Française d'Etudes Politiques Africaines,* no. 50 (Feb. 1970), pp. 71–91.

————. "De Mode d'existence de l'Etat sous Ghézo, 1818–1859." Thesis, University of Paris, 1970.

Akindélé, A., and C. Aguessy. *Contribution à l'étude de l'histoire de l'ancien royaume de Porto Novo.* Dakar: Mémoires de l'Institut Français d'Afrique Noire, no. 25 (1953).

————. and ————. *Le Dahomey.* Paris: Editions Maritimes et Coloniales, 1955.

Akinjogbin, I. A. "Agaja and the Conquest of the Coastal Aja States 1724–1730," *Journal of the Historical Society of Nigeria,* vol. 2, no. 4 (Dec. 1963), pp. 545–566.

————. "Archibald Dalzel: Slave Trader and Historian of Dahomey," *Journal of African History,* vol. 7, no. 1 (1966), pp. 67–68.

————. *Dahomey and Its Neighbors 1708–1818.* London: Cambridge University Press, 1967.

————. "Dahomey and the Yoruba in the Nineteenth Century" in J. C. Anene and G. Brown (eds.), *Africa in the Nineteenth and Twentieth Centuries.* Ibadan: Ibadan University Press, 1966, pp. 255–269.

Akiwowo, Akinsola. ''Varieties of Military Establishment in Pre-Colonial West African States,'' *Ghana Journal of Sociology,* vol. 10, no. 1, 1976, pp. 5–31.

Albéca, Alexandre d'. *L'Avenir du Dahomey.* Paris, 1895.

———. *Le Dahomey en 1894.* Paris, 1895.

———. *Les Populations indigènes de la côte occidentale d'Afrique.* Paris, 1889.

Almeida, Leslie d'. ''Le Dahomey sous le règne de Dada Glélé 1859–89.'' Thesis, University of Paris, 1973.

Almeida Prado, J. F. de. ''Les Relations de Bahia (Brésil) avec le Dahomey,'' *Revue de l'Histoire des Colonies Françaises,* vol. 41 (1954), pp. 167–226.

Almeida-Topor, Hélène d'. *Les Amazones: Une armée de femmes dans l'Afrique pré-coloniale.* Paris, 1984.

———. ''Un aspect des rivalités impérialistes: la liquidation des firmes allemandes au Dahomey pendant la guerre mondiale,'' in *Entreprises et entrepreneurs en Afrique,* vol. 2, Paris: Harmattan, 1983, pp. 165–177.

———. ''Naga et la fin des amazones du Dahomé,'' in C.A. Julien (ed.), *Les Africains.* Paris: Editions Jeune Afrique, 1977, pp. 241–271.

———. ''Les Populations dahoméennes et le recrutement militaire pendant la première guerre mondiale,'' *Revue Française d'Histoire d'Outre-mer,* vol. 60, no. 219 (1973), pp. 196–241.

————. "Une société paysanne devant la colonisation: la résistance des Holli du Dahomey," in *Sociétés paysannes du Tiers Monde*. Lille: Presses Universitaires de Lille, 1980.

————. "Les termes de l'échange du Dahomey 1890–1914," in G. Liesegang et al., (eds.), *Figuring African Trade: Proceedings of the Symposium on the Quantification and Structure of the Import and Export and Long-distance Trade in Africa 1800–1913.* Berlin: Reimer, 1986.

Amegboh, Joseph. *Béhanzin, Roi d'Abomey.* Paris: APC, 1975.

Amoussou, Cocou. "Gigla et le protectorat d'Alada." Cotonou: Mémoire, Ecole Normale Supérieure, 1978.

————. "Les Travailleurs du chemin de fer au Dahomey sous la colonisation des origines à 1952." Thesis, University of Paris, 1977.

Anignikin, S. C. "Les facteurs historiques de la décolonisation au Dahomey," in C. R. Ageron (ed.), *Les chemins de la décolonisation de l'empire colonial français,* Paris, CNRS, 1986.

Arnold, Rosemary. "A Port of the Trade: Whydah on the Guinea Coast" in K. Polanyi et al. (eds.), *Trade and Market in the Early Empires.* Glencoe, Ill.: Free Press, 1957.

Asiwaju, A. I. "The Anti-French Resistance Movement in Ohoriije," *Journal of the Historical Society of Nigeria,* vol. 7, no. 2, 1974, pp. 255–269.

————. *Western Yorubaland Under European Rule 1889–1945. A Comparative Analysis of French and British Colonialism.* London: Longmans, 1976.

Ayandele, E. A. "The Yoruba Civil Wars and the Dahomean Confrontation," *Nigerian Historical Studies,* 1979, pp. 43–64.

Babagheto, Bai. "La rivalité des puissances européennes au Dahomey 1876–88." Thesis, University of Paris, 1974.

Baldus, Bernd. "Social Structure and Ideology. Cognitive and Behavioral Responses to Servitude Among the Machube of Northern Dahomey," *Canadian Journal of African Studies,* vol. 8, no. 2.

Ballard, John A. "Les Incidents de 1923 à Porto Novo: la politique à l'époque coloniale," *Etudes Dahoméennes,* no. 4 (May 1965), pp. 83–87.

Barbou, Alfred. *Histoire de la Guerre au Dahomey.* Paris, 1893.

Barrois, Auguste. *Les Etapes d'un volontaire au Dahomey.* Paris, 1893.

Bay, Edna G. "On the trail of the bush king: a Dahomean lesson in the use of evidence," *History in Africa,* vol. 6, 1979, pp. 1–15.

―――. "The royal women of Abomey," Ph.D. Thesis, Boston University, 1977.

―――. "Servitude and worldly success in the palace of Abomey," in Claire C. Robertson and Martin A. Klein (eds.) *Women and Slaves in Africa,* Madison, University of Wisconsin Press, 1983, p. 340–367.

Berbain, Simone. *Etudes sur la traite des noirs au golfe de Guinée. Le Comptoir français de Juda (Ouidah) au XVIIIe siècle*. Dakar: Mémoires de l'Institut Français d'Afrique Noire, 1942.

Bibi, Alice. "L'Administration française dans le cercle de Ouidah, 1892–1914," Cotonou: Mémoire, Ecole Normale Supérieure, 1978.

Braga, Julio Santana. "Anciens esclaves brésiliens au Dahomey." *Etudes Dahoméennes*, no. 20, April–June 1970, pp. 91–103.

————. "Em torno de um documento em que se da noticia de uma investida politica dos exescravos Brasileiros no Daome," *Afro-Asia* (Salvador, Brazil), vol. 12, 1976, pp. 167–75.

Brasseur, Paul Marion. "Cotonou, porte du Dahomey," *Les Cahiers d'Outre Mer*, no. 24, Oct.–Dec. 1953, pp. 364–378.

Campion-Vincent, Véronique. "L'image du Dahomey dans la presse française (1890–1895); les sacrifices humains," *Cahiers d'Etudes Africaines*, no. 25 (1967), pp. 27–58.

Célarié, Henriette. "Au Dahomey," *Revue des Deux Mondes*, vol. 7, no. 8 (1932), pp. 861–882.

————. *Nos frères Noirs—Cameroun-Dahomey*. Paris: Librairie Hachette, 1932.

Challenor, H. S. "Dahomeyans and Stranger Elites in Former French West Africa," *Africa Urban Notes*, no. 1, 1975, pp. 35–48.

Cluzot-Martinot. "Une tournée de police au Dahomey en 1923," *Revue Militaire de l'AOF*, no. 28, Jan. 15, 1936, pp. 53–71.

Codo, Bellarmin C. "L'Evolution de la presse dahoméenne face aux aspirations des 'évolués' 1927–57." Thesis, University of Paris, 1978.

————. and Sylvain C. Anignikin, "Pouvoir Colonial et tentatives d'intégration africaine dans le système capitaliste: le cas du Dahomey entre les deux guerres," *Canadian Journal of African Studies,* vol. 16, no. 2, 1982, pp. 331–342.

Classen, Henri J. M. "Kings, chiefs and officials: the political organization of Dahomey and Buganda compared," *Journal of Legal Pluralism and Unofficial Law,* no. 25/26 (1987), p. 203–241.

Couéry, M. "Origines historiques des Cantons de la subdivision d'Athiémé," *Etudes Dahoméennes,* no. 8, 1952, pp. 90–101.

Coquery-Vidrovich, Catherine. "Le Blocus de Whydah (1876–1877) et la rivalité franco-anglaise au Dahomey," *Cahiers d'Etudes Africaines,* vol. 2, no. 7 (1962), pp. 373–419.

————. "La fête des coutumes au Dahomey," *Civilisations,* vol. 19, no. 4 (1964), pp. 696–716.

————. "Gezo," in *Les Africains.* Paris: Editions Jeune Afrique, 1977.

————. "Le Royaume d'Abomey," *Histoire* (Paris), vol. 16, 1979, pp. 46–54.

Cornevin, Robert. *Le Dahomey.* Paris: Presses Universitaires de France, 1965, 1970.

————. "Les divers épisodes de la lutte contre le royaume d'Abomey 1887–1894," *Revue Française d'Histoire d'Outre Mer,* vol. 47 (1960), pp. 161–212.

————. *Histoire du Dahomey.* Paris: Berger-Levrault, 1962.

————. "A Propos de l'histoire du Dahomey," *Etudes Da-homéennes,* no. 3 (Dec. 1964), pp. 123–125.

————. *La République Populaire du Bénin.* Paris: Maisonneuve, 1981.

Cote, C. "Les origines de la conquête du Dahomey." Thesis, University of Paris, 1974.

Coyssi, Anatole. "Un Règne de femme dans l'ancien royaume d'Abomey," *Etudes Dahoméennes,* no. 2 (1948), pp. 5–8.

Crowder, Michael, "The 1916–17 Revolt Against the French in Dahomeyan Borgou," *Journal of the Historical Society of Nigeria,* vol. 8, no. 1 (Dec. 1975), pp. 99–115.

————. *Revolt in Bussa: A Study of British 'Native Administration' in Nigerian Borgu 1902–1935.* Evanston, Ill.: Northwestern University Press, 1973.

————. *West Africa under Colonial Rule.* Evanston: Northwestern University Press, 1968.

Dan, Rosine. "Cotonou des origines à 1914." Thesis, National University of Benin, 1973.

Da Silva, Marcellin D. "Démographique historique du Bénin 1930–1950," Thesis, University of Paris, 1988.

Davidson, Basil. "Dahomey in the 17th and 18th Century," in *A History of West Africa 1000–1800.* London: Longmans, 1967.

Davis, Shelby Cullom. *Reservoir of Men: A History of the Black Troops of French West Africa.* Westport, Conn.: Negro Universities Press, 1970.

Débourou Djibril, Mama. "Commerçants et Chefs dans l'ancien Borgou." Thesis, University of Paris, 1973.

Degbeto, Amélie, "Les Amazones." Thesis, Abomey-Calavi, National University of Benin, 1977.

Deloncle, Pierre. *L'Afrique occidentale française: découverte, pacification, mise en valeur.* Paris: Editions Ernest Leroux, 1934.

Demanche, G. "Dahomey," *Revue Française de l'Etranger et des Colonies,* vol. 18, pp. 397–406.

Desanti, H. *Du Danhomé au Bénin-Niger: L'oeuvre de la France au Dahomey.* Paris: Larose, 1945.

De Souza, Norberto Francisco. "Contribution à l'histoire de la famille de Souza," *Etudes Dahoméennes,* no. 13 (1955), pp. 15–22.

Devaulx, B. "Les protectorats de la France en Afrique," Thesis, University of Dijon, 1903.

Djivo, Joseph Adrien, "Les chants et la résistance du Roi Gbéhanzin à la colonisation, 1890–1906," in C. H. Perrot, *Sources orales de l'Histoire de l'Afrique.* Paris: CNRS, 1989.

―――. "Gbéhanzin et Agoli-Agbo, le refus de la colonisation dans l'ancien royaume du Dauxome 1875–1900." Thesis, University of Paris, 1980.

————. *Guézo: la rénovation au Dahomey.* Paris: NAE-ABC 1977.

————. "Le protectorat d'Abomey: Ago-Li-Agbo, 1894–1900. La Fin de la monarchie Danxomé," Thesis, National University of Benin, 1985.

Dramani-Issifou, Z. "Les origines de la dynastie royale de Tylika-Djougou," *Revue Française d'Histoire d'Outre Mer,* vol. 69, no. 257 (1982), pp. 275–277.

Duignan, Peter, and Lewis Henry Gann. *Colonialism in Africa, 1870–1960.* New York: Cambridge University Press, 1973.

Dunglas, Edouard. "Adjohoun: Etude historique," *Etudes Dahoméenes,* no. 8 (Oct. 1966), pp. 57–73.

————. "La Chacha Francisco Felix da Souza," *Etudes Dahoméennes,* May–June 1959.

————. "Contribution è l'étude du Moyen-Dahomey; royaumes d'Abomey, de Kétou, et de Ouidah," *Etudes Dahoméennes,* no. 19 (1957), pp. 9–185; no. 20 (1957), pp. 3–152; no. 21 (1958), pp. 7–118.

————. "La Deuxième attaque des Dahoméens contre Abéokouta (15 mars 1864)," *Etudes Dahoméennes,* no. 2 (1949), pp. 37–58.

————. "L'Histoire Dahoméenne à la fin du XIXe siècle à travers les textes," *Etudes Dahoméenes,* no. 9 (1953), pp. 1–156.

————. "La Première attaque des Dahoméens contre Abéokouta (3 mars 1851)," *Etudes Dahoméennes,* no. 1 (1948), pp. 7–19.

Echenberg, M. ''Military Conscription in French West Africa,'' *Canadian Journal of African Studies,* vol. 9, no. 2, 1975, pp. 171–192.

Ehouzou, Jean Marie. ''Etude du journal colonial France-Dahomey.'' Abomey-Calavi: Mémoire, National University of Benin, 1978.

Ekué, Albert. ''La presse et les événements: la conquête française au Dahomey jugée à travers la presse de la Haute Garonne.'' Thesis, University of Paris, 1976.

Elwert, Georg. ''History, humour and social control: genres of oral history and registers of speech among the Ayizo, Benin'' in Elizabeth Linnebuhr (ed.), *Transition and Continuity of Identity in East Africa and Beyond.* Bayreuth: Eckhardt Breitinger, 1989, pp. 67–110.

————. *Wirtschaft und Herrschaft von Daxome im 18 Jahrhundert.* Munich: Klaus Renner, 1973.

''End of an Empire [Jukum],'' *Nigeria,* March 1960, pp. 56–71.

L'Evolution sociale et économique du Dahomey. Paris: Léon Bassou, 1914.

Fassassi, Osseni. ''La Conquête du Dahomey par la France ou l'histoire d'un malentendu.'' Thesis, University of Provence, 1976.

Faure, Claude. ''Deux anciens comptoirs français de la côte de Guinée: Amokou et Juda,'' *Bulletin du Comité d'Etudes Historiques et Scientifiques de l'AOF,* 1922, pp. 128–137.

Folayan, Kola. ''Egbado and the Expansion of British Power in Western Nigeria,'' *Geneva-Africa,* vol. 13, no. 2 (1974) pp. 70–93.

France. "Traités avec les Royaumes d'Abomey et d'Allada des 29 Janvier et 4 Février 1894," Porto Novo: Imprimerie du Gouvernement, 1894.

————. Agence de Colonies. "Afrique occidentale française; le Dahomey." Paris, 1948.

————. Agence Economique de l'Afrique Occidentale Française. "Le Dahomey," 1931.

François, Georges. *Notre colonie du Dahomey; sa formation, son développement, son avenir.* Paris: Emile Larose, 1906.

————. "Le Royaume de Porto Novo," *Bulletin du Comité d' Afrique Française,* no. 4, April 1904, pp. 97–103.

Freyre, Gilberto. *A Dynastia dos xaxa de Souza.* Rio de Janeiro: O. Cruzeiro, 1951.

Fuglestad, Finn. "Quelques réflexions sur l'historie et les institutions de l'ancien royaume du Dahomey et de ses voisins," *Bulletin de l'Institut Français d'Afrique Noire,* vol. 39, no. 3, July 1977, pp. 493–517.

Ganier, Geneviève. "Les Rivalités franco-anglaise et franco-allemande de 1894–98. Dernière phase de la course au Niger: la mission Ganier dans le Haut Dahomey 1897–98," *Revue Française d'histoire d'outre mer,* vol. 49, no. 175 (1962), pp. 181–261.

Garcia, Luc. "L'Administration Française au Dahomey, 1894–1920." Thesis, University of Paris, 1969.

————. "La France et la conquête du Dahomey." Thesis, University of Paris, 1970.

———. "La genèse de l'administration française au Dahomey." Thesis, EPHE, 1969.

———. "Les Mouvements de résistance au Dahomy 1914–1917," *Cahiers d'Etudes Africaines,* vol. 10, no. 37 (1970), pp. 144–178.

———. *Le royaume de Dahomé face à la pénétration coloniale 1875–1894.* Paris, Karthala, 1988.

Gaudron, Pierre, "Le Dahomey: les possibilités futures," Paris: CHEAM Report, No. 2095 (Dec. 19, 1952).

Gavoy, (Admin.). "Note historique sur Ouidah," *Etudes Dahoménnes,* vol. 12 (1955), pp. 47–70.

Gayibor, Nicoue. "Agokoli et la dispersion de Notsé," in François de Medeiros, *Peuples du Golfe du Bénin.* Paris: Karthala, 1984.

———. "L'Aire culturelle ajatado des origines à la fin du XVIII siècle," Thesis, University of Paris, 1985.

———. "Les Gényi, 1680–1884." Thesis, University of Benin, 1976.

———. "Les origines du royaume de Glidji," *Bulletin de l'Université du Bénin,* vol. 3 no. 1 (1976), pp. 75–102.

Geay. "Origine, formation et histoire du royaume de Porto Novo, d'après une légende orale des Porto Noviens," *Bulletin du Comité d'Etudes Historiques et Scientifiques de l'O.A.F.,* vol. 8, no. 4 (Oct.–Dec. 1924), pp. 619–634.

Ghézo, R. "Le Commerce sur la côte des esclaves au xixe siècle." Abomey-Calavi: Mémoire, National University of Benin, 1977.

Gifford, Prosser and William R. Louis. *France and Britain in Africa: Imperial rivalry and colonial rule.* New Haven: Yale University Press, 1971.

Glélé, Kakai. "Du Dan-Ho-Min: un royaume en mutation 1789–1900." Thesis, University of Paris, 1988.

Glélé, Maurice. *Le Danxomé: du pouvoir aja à la nation fon.* Paris: Nubia, 1974.

Goerg, Odile. "Le Dahomey 1918–1933: De la Convention du Niger à l'assimilation douanière." Thesis, University of Paris, 1972.

Gouzien, Paul. *Notice sur Dahomey.* Paris, 1899.

Grivot, R. *Réactions Dahoméennes.* Paris: Berger-Levrault, 1954.

Guyon, A. "D'Abomey à Porto Novo par Zagnando, Hollis et Sakété," *Bulletin du Comité d'Etudes Historiques et Scientifiques de l'AOF,* no. 1, March 1907, pp. 18–27.

Hargreaves, John D. "The French Conquest of Dahomey," *History Today,* vol. 30, 1980, pp. 5–9.

Hazoumé, Guy Landry. "La presse dahoméenne et le système coloniale." Thesis, University of Paris, 1978.

Henige, D., and M. Johnson. "Agaja and the slave trade: another look at the evidence," *History in Africa,* vol. 3, 1976, pp. 57–67.

Hentsch, Henry. *Deux années au Dahomey.* Paris, 1905.

Heudebert, Lucien. *Promenades au Dahomey.* Paris: Dujarne, 1902.

Houseman, Michael et al. "Note sur la structure évolutive d'une ville historique: l'exemple d'Abomey," *Cahiers d'Etudes Africaines,* vol. 26, no. 4 (1986), pp. 527–546.

Iroko, Abiola Félix. "Les cavaliers Djerma et le commerce des esclaves dans l'Atacora au XIXe siècle," *Le Mois en Afrique,* no. 243/4 (1986), p. 129–40.

————. "Le commerce des esclaves sur le marché d'Abomey-Calavi aux XVIIIe-XIXe siècles. *Africa* (Rome), vol. 43, no. 3 (1988), pp. 378–393.

————. "Les forges et ateliers d'Adjaha: une entreprise Béninoise post-coloniale née en France," Actes du Colloque Entreprise et Entrepreneurs en Afrique, XIXe et XXe siècles. Paris: Harmattan, 1983.

————. "Le marché d'esclaves de la cité lacustre de Ganvié sur la Côte des Esclaves," *Le Mois en Afrique,* no. 213/4 (Oct.–Nov. 1983), pp. 143–55.

————. "Notice historique sur les Kufaloyinma de l'Atacora," *Le Mois en Afrique,* no. 221/2 (June-July 1984), pp. 121–129.

————. "Le spectre de la mort à Cotonou des origines à nos jours," *Le Mois en Afrique,* no. 227/8 (1985), pp. 133–144.

————. "Survivances du troc en République Populaire du Bénin dans le dernier quart au XXe siècle," *Le Mois en Afrique* no. 223/4 (1985), pp. 72–80, 97–108.

————. "Les vestiges d'une ancienne industrie de métallurgie du fer dans la région d'Abomey," *West African Archeological Review* (Ibadan), vol. 19 (1989) pp. 1–20.

Jérôme-Fourmence, Carlos. "L'Action de la France sur la côte des Popo." Dakar: Mémoire, University of Dakar, 1970.

Johnson, Marion. "Polanyi, Peukart and the Political Economy of Dahomey," *Journal of African History,* vol. 21, no. 3, 1980, pp. 395–398.

Kalous, Milan. "Some Correspondence Between the German Empire and Dahomey in 1882–1892," *Cahiers d'Etudes Africaines,* no. 32 (1968), pp. 635–641.

Karl-August, Emmanuel. "La population du Mono béninois," in François de Medeiros, *Peuples du Golfe du Bénin.* Paris: Karthala, 1984.

———. "Les traités de protectorats français dans le Dahomey." Thesis, University of Toulouse, 1970.

Katz, Naomi. "The Kingdom of Dahomey: political organization and ecological relations in a slave trading state." Thesis, UCLA, 1976.

Kiki Sagbo, Cosmé, "L'Etablissement de la frontière Dahomey-Nigéria." Mémoire, University of Dakar, 1970.

Kilkenny, Roberta Walker. "The slave mode of production: precolonial Dahomey," in Donald Conmey (ed.), *Modes of Production in Africa.* Beverly Hills: Sage, 1981, pp. 157–173.

Klein, Norman. "Karl Polanyi's Dahomey," *Le Journal Canadien des Etudes Africaines,* vol. 2, no. 2 (Autumn 1968), pp. 210–222.

Kossi-Djihento, "Chefferie supérieure d'Allada." Cotonou: Mémoire, Ecole Nationale Supérieur, 1978.

Kouandété, Iropa Maurice. *Kaba: un aspect de l'insurrection nationaliste au Dahomey.* Cotonou: Editions Silva, 1971.

Krasnowolski, Andrzej. "Independence or equality of rights: the movement of protest in colonial Dahomy between 1894 and 1946," *Africana Bulletin* (Warsaw), no. 24 (1987), pp. 121–131.

————. "Status and function of Slave Coast creols in the pre-colonial and colonial periods: the case of Dahomey," *Hemispheres*, no. 1 (1985), pp. 249–258.

Law, Robin. "The common people were divided: monarchy, aristocracy and political factionalism in the Kingdom of Whydah 1671–1727." *International Journal of African Historical Studies,* vol. 23, no. 2, 1990, pp. 201–229.

————. "Dahomey and the slave trade: reflections on the historiography of the rise of Dahomey," *Journal of African History,* vol. 27, no. 2 (1986), pp. 237–267.

————. "The Fall of Allada, 1724—an ideological revolution?" *Journal of the Historical Society of Nigeria,* vol. 5, no. 1 (1969), pp. 157–163.

————. "Further light on Bulfinch Lambe and the 'Emperor of Pawpaw': King Agaja of Dahomey's letter to King George I of England," *History in Africa,* vol. 17 (1990), pp. 211–26.

————. "History and legitimacy: aspects of the use of the past in precolonial Dahomey," *History in Africa,* vol. 15 (1988), pp. 431–456.

————. "Human sacrifice in pre-colonial West Africa," *African Affairs,* vol. 84, no. 334 (1985), pp. 53–87.

————. "Ideologies of royal power: the dissolution and reconstruction of political authority on the 'slave coast' 1680–1750," *Africa,* vol. 57, no. 3 (1987), pp. 321–44.

————. "My head belongs to the King: on the political and ritual significance of decapitation in pre-colonial Dahomey," *African History,* vol. 30, no. 3 (1989), pp. 399–415.

————. "A neglected account of the Dahomean conquest of Whydah, 1727: the 'Relation de la guerre de Juda' of the Sieur Ringard of Nantes," *History in Africa,* vol. 15 (1988), pp. 321–338.

————. "Problems of plagiarism, harmonization and misunderstanding in contemporary European sources: early (pre-1680's) sources for the 'Slave Coast' of West Africa," *Paideuma* (Frankfurt), vol. 33 (1987), pp. 337–358.

————. "Royal monopoly and private enterprise in the Atlantic trade: the case of Dahomey," *Journal of African History,* vol. 18, no. 4, 1977, pp. 555–577.

————. "Slave raiders and middlemen, monopolists and freetraders: the supply of slaves for the Atlantic trade in Dahomey, c. 1715–1850," *Journal of African History,* vol. 30, no. 1 (1989), pp. 45–68.

————. "The slave trader as historian: Robert Norris and the history of Dahomey," *History in Africa,* vol. 16 (1989), pp. 219–235.

LeFaivre, Henri. "Dictateurs noirs: les derniers rois du Dahomey, 1610–1894," *Revue d'Histoire des Colonies,* vol. 25, no. 1 (1937), pp. 25–76.

Le Garrères, R. "Dahomey, cercle de Borgou," *Revue Coloniale,* vol. 8, 1908, pp. 513–530.

Le Hérissé, A. *L'Ancien royaume du Dahomey; moeurs, religion histoire.* Paris: Larose, 1911.

Lemoine, Frederic. *Le Dahomey.* Melun, 1911.

Lima, V. "Economie et Société dans le Bas Dahomey." Thesis, University of Paris, 1974.

Lokossou Kondessa, Clément. "La Presse au Dahomey." Thesis, University of Paris, 1976.

Lombard, Jacques. "Contribution à l'histoire d'une ancienne société politique du Dahomey: la royauté d'Allada," *Bulletin de l'Institut Français d'Afrique Noire,* no. 1–2, Jan.–April 1967, pp. 40–66.

———. "Cotonou, ville africaine," *Bulletin de l'Institut Français d'Afrique Noire,* no. 3–4, vol. 16, July–Oct. 1954.

———. "The kingdom of Dahomey," in Daryll Forde and P. M. Kaberry (eds.), *West African Kingdoms in the 19th Century.* London: Oxford University Press, 1967, pp. 70–92.

Lovejoy, P. E. *Caravans of Kola: The Hausa Kola Trade 1700–1900.* Kano: Ahmadu Bello University Press, 1980.

———. "Kola in the History of West Africa," *Cahiers d'Etudes Africaines,* vol. 20, no. 77–78, pp. 97–134.

Lupton, Kenneth. "The partitioning of Borgou in 1898 and the French enclaves in Nigeria 1900–1960," *Journal of the Historical Society of Nigeria* (Ibadan), vol. 12, no. 3/4 (1984/5), pp. 77–94.

McDougall, E. A. "Setting the story straight: Louis Hunkanrin and *Un Forfait colonial,*" *History in Africa,* vol. 16 (1989), pp. 285–310.

Manning, Patrick. "L'Affaire Adjovi," in *Entreprise et entrepreneurs en Afrique,* Paris: Harmattan, 1983.

————. "Coastal society in the Republic of Benin: reproduction of a regional system," *Cahiers d'etudes Africaines,* no. 114 (1989), pp. 239–257.

————. "Merchants, porters and Canoeman in the Bight of Benin," in Catherine Coquery-Vidrovitch and Paul E. Lovejoy (eds.), *The Workers of African Trade.* Beverly Hills: Sage Publications, 1985, pp. 51–74.

————. "The slave trade in the Bight of Benin, 1640–1890," in Henry A. Gemery and Jan S. Hogendorn (eds.), *The Uncommon Market.* New York, 1979, pp. 107–147.

————. "Slave trade, 'legitimate' trade, and imperialism revisited: the control of wealth in the Bights of Benin and Biafra," in *Africans in Bondage,* 1986, pp. 203–233.

Maroukis, Thomas C. "Warfare and Society in the Kingdom of Dahomey 1818–1894." Unpub. Ph.D. diss., Boston University, 1974.

Matthews, A. B. "The Kisra Legends," *African Studies,* vol. 9, no. 3, Sept. 1950.

Mauny, R. "Etat actuel de nos connaissances sur la préhistoire du Dahomey et du Togo," *Etudes Dahoméennes,* no. 4 (1950).

Medeiros, François de (ed.). *Peuples du Golfe du Bénin.* Paris: Karthala, 1984.

Mercier, Paul. *Civilisations du Bénin*. Paris: Société Continentale d'Editions Modernes Illustrées, 1962.

Merlo, Pierre and Christian Vidaud. "Dangbé et le peuplement houéda," in François de Medeiros, *Peuples du Golfe du Bénin*. Paris: Karthala, 1984.

Merlo, Thomas. "Histoire et légende: la bataille d'Ilorin," *Notes Africaines*, no. 47, July 1950.

Metinhoué, G. "Regard de l'administration coloniale sur le chef indigène: l'exemple de Kpalassi, chef de canton des adjas de Sé, Bénin," *Le Mois en Afrique*, vol. 21 no. 245/6 (1986), pp. 158–64.

Meyn, Matthias et al. *Der Aufbau der Kolonialreiche*. Munich: Beek, 1987, 3 vol.

Michel, Marc. "Les recrutements de tirailleurs en AOF pendant la première Guerre mondiale," *Revue Française d'Histoire d'Outre Mer*, vol. 60, no. 221, 1973, pp. 644–660.

Morton-Williams, Peter. "The Oyo Yoruba and the Atlantic Trade," *Journal of the Historical Society of Nigeria*, vol. 3, no. 1, 1964, pp. 25–45.

Moseley, Katherine Payne. "Indigenous and External Factors in Colonial Politics: Southern Dahomey to 1939." Ph.D. Thesis, Columbia University, 1975.

Moulero T. "Conquête de Kétou par Glélé et conquête d'Abomey par la France," *Etudes Dahoméennes*, no. 4 (May 1965), pp. 61–68.

———. "Guézo ou Guédizo Massigbé," *Etudes Dahoméennes*, no. 4 (May 1965), pp. 51–60.

————. *Histoire de Kétou.* Paris: La Reconnaissance Africaine, 1926.

Moulinie, M. *La Conquête du Dahomey.* Paris, 1893.

Moussa, Albert. ''La Résistance des Bariba du Nord Dahomey à l'instauration de l'autorité française 1897–1918.'' Thesis, University of Paris, 1974.

Mulira, Jessie Gaston. ''A history of the Mahi peoples from 1774 to 1920.'' Ph.D. Thesis, UCLA, 1984.

Nardin, Jean-Claude. ''La Reprise des relations franco-dahoméennes du XIXe siècle: la mission d'August Bout à la cour d'Abomey,'' *Cahiers d'Etudes Africaines,* vol. 7, no. 25 (1967), pp. 59–126.

Newbury, Colin W. ''The Development of French Policy on the Lower and Upper Niger 1880–98,'' *Journal of Modern History,* vol. 31, no. 1 (March 1959), pp. 16–26.

————. ''An Early Enquiry into Slavery and Captivity in Dahomey,'' *Zaïre: Revue Congolaise,* vol. 14, no. 1 (1960), pp. 53–67.

————. ''A Note on the Abomey Protectorate,'' *Africa,* vol. 29, no. 2 (April 1959), pp. 146–155.

————. *The Western Slave Coast and Its Rulers: European Trade and Administration Among the Yoruba and Adja Speaking Peoples of South-Western Nigeria, Southern Dahomey and Togo.* Oxford: Clarendon Press, 1961.

Obichere, Boniface. ''Change and Innovation in the Administration of the Kingdom of Dahomey,'' *Journal of African Studies,* vol. 1, no. 3 (Fall 1974), pp. 235–251.

————. *West African States and European Expansion: The Dahomey-Niger Hinterland, 1885–1898.* New Haven: Yale University Press, 1971.

————. "Women and slavery in the Kingdom of Dahomey," *Revue Française d'Histoire d'Outre Mer,* vol. 65 (1978), pp. 5–20.

Oké, Raymond. "L'ancien Danhomé: des origines à la formation territoriale du royaume." Thesis, University of Paris, 1972.

————. "Les siècles obscurs du royaume aja du Danxomé," in François de Medeiros, *Peuples de Golfe du Bénin.* Paris: Karthala, 1984.

Oumar Sy, Moussa. "Le Dahomey: le coup d'état de 1818," *Folia Orientalia,* vol. 6 (1964), pp. 205–238.

Pagnon, André. *Dans le tourment du Destin.* Cotonou, 1971.

Palau-Marti, Montserrat. "Note à propos d'un ancien récit de voyage au Dahomey (1797)," *Revue Française d'Histoire d'Outremer,* vol. 50, no. 1 (1963), pp. 53–63.

————. "Notes sur les Rois de Dassa," *Journal de la Société des Africanistes,* vol. 27, no. 2, 1957.

Parrinder, Geoffrey, E. *The Story of Ketu.* Ibadan: Ibadan University Press, 1956.

Parti Communiste de Dahomey. *Les Sociétés pré-coloniales au Dahomey.* Paris: Presses Jeunesse du Monde, 1980.

Pazzi, Roberto. "Aperçu sur l'implantation actuelle et les migrations anciennes des peuples de l'aire culturelle ajatado," in

François de Medeiros, *Peuples du Golfe du Bénin.* Paris: Karthala, 1984.

Pelissier, Paul. "Réflexions sur l'occupation des littoraux ouest-africains," in *Pauvreté et développement dans les pays tropicaux: hommage à Guy Lasserre.* Paris: Institut de Géographie, 1989, pp. 122–134.

Person, Yves. "Chronologie du royaume gun de Hogbonu," *Cahiers d'Etudes Africaines,* no. 58, 1976, pp. 217–38.

————. "Les grandes compagnies Zarma au Dahomey et au Togo," *Le Mois en Afrique,* no. 203/4 (Dec. 1982–Jan. 1983) pp. 136–159; and no. 204/5 (Feb.–Mar. 1983), pp. 127–144.

————. "Les monarchies africaines," *Revue Française d'Etudes Politiques Africaines,* no. 200, Aug.–Sept. 1982; and no. 201/2, Oct.–Nov. 1982, 104–121.

————. "Note sur les Nyantruku," *Etudes Dahoméennes,* no. 16, 1951.

Peukert, Werner. *Der Atlantische Sklavenhandel von Dahomey 1750–97.* Wiesbaden: Steiner, 1978.

Pineau-Jamous, M. J. "Porto-Novo: royauté, localité et parenté," *Cahiers d'Etudes Africaines,* vol. 26, no. 4 (1986) pp. 547–576.

Pliya, Jean. *Le Dahomey.* Porto Novo: Imprimerie Nationale, 1969.

————. *Les Rois d'Abomey.* Paris: A.U.D.E.C.A.M., 1972.

Polacek, Josef. *Dahome.* Prague: Nakladeteswi Svoboda, 1967.

Polanyi, Karl. "Sortings and Ounce Trade in the West African Slave Trade," *Journal of African History,* vol. 5, no. 3, pp. 381–393.

———. (in collab. with Araham Rotstein). *Dahomey and the Slave Trade; An Analysis of an Archaic Economy.* Seattle: University of Washington Press, 1966.

Preil, Friedrich. *Deutsch-französische Waffenbruderschaft im Hinterlande von Togo und Dahome.* Leipzig: Ed. Engleman, 1909.

Prudencio, Eustache. *Les Rois d'Abomey, 1625–1898.* Dakar: Editions Saint Paul, 1957.

Quénum, Maximilien. *L'Afrique Noire rencontre avec l'Occident.* Paris: Nathan, 1956.

Ralston, Richard. "The return of the Brazilian freedmen to West Africa in the 18th and 19th centuries," *Canadian Journal of African Studies,* vol. 3, no. 3 (Autumn 1969), pp. 577–592.

Rawley, H. A. "Further light on Archibald Dalzel," *International Journal of African Historical Studies,* vol. 17, no. 2 (1984), pp. 317–323.

Renaud, J. *Le Général Dodds.* Paris, 1931.

Reste, J. F. *Le Dahomey, réalisations et perspectives d'avenir.* Paris: Comité de l'Afrique Française, 1934.

Rondeau, Georges. "Sociétés et Associations du Bas et du Moyen Dahomey." Paris, CHEAM Mémoire no. 4287, 1969.

Ronen, Dov. "The Colonial Elite in Dahomey," *African Studies Review,* vol. 17, no. 1 (April 1974), pp. 55–76.

————. "On the African Zone in the Trans-Atlantic Slave Trade in Dahomey," *Cahiers d'Etudes Africaines,* vol. 11, 1971, pp. 5–13.

————. *The State in Precolonial Africa: Dahomey.* London: Frank Cass, 1979.

————. *Traditional Dahomey: a search for the 'state' in precolonial Africa.* Jerusalem: Hebrew University, 1975.

Roqués, A. *Le Génie au Dahomey en 1892.* Paris: Berger-Levrault, 1895.

Ross, David. "The anti-slavery trade theme in Dahomean history: an examination of the evidence," *History in Africa,* vol. 9, 1982, pp. 263–271.

————. "The Autonomous Kingdom of Dahomey 1818–1894." Thesis, University of London, 1967.

————. "The Career of Domingo Martinez in the Bight of Benin," *Journal of African History,* vol. 6, no. 1, 1965, pp. 79–90.

————. "The Dahomean middleman system, 1727–c.1818," *Journal of African History,* vol. 28, no. 3, 1987, pp. 357–375.

————. "Dahomey" in Michael Crowder, *West African Resistance to Europe.* New York: Africana Publishing Corp., 1972, pp. 144–169.

————. "European Models and West African History," *History in Africa,* vol. 10, 1983, pp. 293–305.

————. "The First Chacha of Whydah: Francisco Felix de Souza," *Odu,* no. 2 (October 1969), pp. 19–28.

————. "Mid-nineteenth century Dahomey: recent views vs. contemporary evidence," *History in Africa,* vol. 12 (1985), pp. 307–323.

————. "Robert Norris, Agaja and the Dahomean conquest of Allada and Whydah," *History in Africa,* vol. 16 (1989), pp. 311–324.

Rouard du Card, A. *Traités de délimitation concernant l'AOF.* Paris: Geurthner, 3 vols. 1910, 1913, 1926.

Rouget, Gilbert. "Court songs and traditional history in the ancient Kingdoms of Porto Novo and Dahomey," in K. P. Wachsmann (ed.), *Music and History in Africa.* Evanston: Indiana University Press, 1971, pp. 27–64.

Sanvi, Annie "Métis et Brésiliens dans la colonie du Dahomey 1880–1920." Abomey-Calavi: Mémoire, National University of Benin, 1978.

Sidokpo, Hou. "Le Commerce de l'huile de palme au Dahomey au xixe siècle." Abomey-Calavi. Mémoire, National University of Benin, 1977.

Sintodji, Cécile. "Le Protectorat de Toffa." Cotonou: Mémoire, Ecole Nationale d'Administration, 1976.

Sinou, Alain, and Bachir Oloudé. *Porto Novo: ville Africaine.* Marseilles: ORSTOM, 1988.

Soumonni, E. A. "Dahomean economic policy under Ghézo 1818–58," *Afrika Zamani* (Yaounde), vol. 10/11, Dec. 1979, pp. 50–62.

————. "Porto Novo, between the French and the British 1861–1884," *Journal of the Historical Society of Nigeria* (Ibadan), vol. 12, no. 3/4 (1984/5), pp. 53–60.

Souza, Germain de. ''De Francisco Felix de Souza et la côte des Esclaves à la croisée des civilisations.'' Thesis, University of Paris, 1973.

Stewart, Marjorie Helen. ''The Borgou people of Nigeria and Benin: the disruptive effect of partition on traditional political and economic relations,'' *Journal of the Historical Society of Nigeria* (Ibadan) vol. 12, no. 3/4 (1984/5), pp. 95–120.

―――. ''The Kisra Legend as Oral History,'' *International Journal of African Historical Studies.* vol. 13, no. 1, 1980, pp. 51–57.

Suret-Canale, Jean. *The Colonial Era in French West and Central Africa, 1900–1945.* London: C. Hurst, 1970.

―――. ''Un Pionnier méconnu du mouvement démocratique et national en Afrique: Louis Hunkarin,'' *Etudes Dahoméennes,* no. 3 (Dec. 1964), pp. 5–30.

―――. ''An unrecognized pioneer of the democratic and national movement in Africa: Louis Hunkanrin, 1887–1964,'' in his *Essays on African History: from the Slave Trade to Neocolonialism,* London: Hurst, 1988.

Tidjani, Abdou Serpos. ''Notes sur la migration humaine à la côte du Bénin,'' *Bulletin de l'Institut Français d'Afrique Noire,* vol. 22, no. 3–4, 1960, pp. 509–530.

Turner, J. Michael. ''Les Brésiliens: The Impact of Former Brazilian Slaves upon Dahomey.'' Ph.D. diss., Boston University, 1975.

Ukpabi, S. C. ''The Anglo-French Rivalry in Borgu: A Study of Military,'' *African Studies Review,* vol. 14, no. 3 (Dec. 1971), pp. 447–462.

Vallet, Jacqueline. "La femme dans l'ancien Royaume du Dahomey." Thesis, University of Benin, 1969.

Van Dantzig, Albert. "Les hollandais et l'essor de l'Ashanti et du Dahomey." Thesis, University of Paris, 1970.

Verger, Pierre. *Bahia and the West African Trade 1549–1851.* Ibadan: Ibadan University Press, 1964.

————. "Les Côtes d'Afrique occidentale entre 'Rio Volta' et 'Rio Lagos' 1535–1773." *Journal des Africanistes,* vol. 38, no. 1968, pp. 35–58.

————. "Echanges de cadeaux entre Rois d'Abomey et Souverains Européens aux XVIIIe et XIX siècles," *Bulletin de l'Institut Français d'Afrique Noire,* vol. 32, no. 3, 1970, pp. 741–754.

————. *Flux et reflux de la Traite des nègres entre le golfe du Bénin et Bahia de todos os Santos du 17e au 19e siècles.* Paris: Mouton, 1968.

————. "Le Fort portugals de Ouidah," *Etudes Dahoméennes,* no. 4 (May 1965), pp. 5–50; no. 5 (Oct. 1965), pp. 5–50.

————. *Le Fort St. Jean Baptiste d'Ajuda (Ouidah) 1721–1961,* Mémoire no. 1. Porto Novo: IRAD, 1966.

————. *L'Influence du Brésil au Golfe du Bénin,* Mémoire no. 27. Dakar: Institut Français d'Afrique Noire, 1953.

————. "Retour des 'Brésiliens' au Golfe du Bénin au XIXe siècle," *Etudes Dahoméennes,* no. 8 (Oct. 1966), pp. 5–28.

————. "Yoruba influence in Brazil," *Odu* (Ibadan), no. 1, 1955, pp. 3–11.

Vermeersch, A. *Historique de la Mission Baud-Vermeersch au Dahomey 1894–1895.* Paris, 1897.

Videgla, Dadjo, and Michel W. Videgla. "Réactions africaines devant les rivalités européennes dans le golfe du Bénin 1860–90." Thesis, University of Paris, 1973.

————. and Abiola Félix Iroko. "Nouveau regard sur la révolte de Sakété de 1905," *Le Mois en Afrique,* no. 229/30 (1935), pp. 139–145.

Videgla, Michel W. "Quelques aspects des frontières coloniales en pays aja, ewé et yoruba 1863–1892," in François de Medeiros, *Peuples du Golfe du Bénin.* Paris: Karthala, 1984.

Waldman, L. K. "An Unnoticed Aspect of Archibald Dalzel's The History of Dahomey," *Journal of African History,* vol. 6, no. 2 (1965), pp. 185–192.

Walker, S. S. "The History of an African Kingdom in Symbols," *Current Bibliography of African Affairs* (Washington), vol. 9, no. 2, 1976/7, pp. 130–139.

Ward, Dennis Earl. "The Dahomean campaign of 1892." M.A. Thesis, Mississippi State University, 1982.

Wawoeke, A. "Les P.T.T. dans la colonie du Dahomey, 1880–1940," Abomey-Calavi: Mémoire, National University of Benin, 1977.

Wigboldus, Jouke S. "Trade and agriculture in coastal Benin c. 1470–1660," *A.A.G. Bijdragen* (Wageningen), vol. 28 (1986), pp. 299–383.

Yoder, John. "Fly and Elephant Parties: Political Polarization in Dahomey 1840–1870," *Journal of African History,* vol. 15, no. 3, 1974, pp. 417–432.

Zanfougnon, A. "La Révolte de Hetti-Sotta." Cotonou: Mémoire, Ecole Normale Supérieur, 1976.

Zech, Comte von. "Pays et populations de la frantière Nord-Ouest du Togo," *Etudes Dahoméennes* vol. 2 (1949), pp. 9–36.

Zimmer, Baldwin. *Dahomey.* Bonn: Kurt Schröder, 1969.

Zossoungho, J. "Les rapports entre l'administration coloniale et les chefferies traditionnelles au Dahomey 1890–1920, et le cas du Bariba." Thesis, University of Paris, 1974.

4. ANTHROPOLOGY, ETHNOLOGY, AND SOCIOLOGY

Adagba, Comlan. "Les Migrations historiques dans le pays adja." Thesis, University of Paris, 1969.

Adjahi, Christine. "Etude de géographie humaine, économique et urbaine de deux villes moyennes du Dahomey." Thesis, University of Toulouse, 1973.

Adrian, Hannelore. *Ethnologische Fragen der Entwicklungsplanung: Gbeniki-Die ethnologische Erforschung eines Bariba-Dorfes als Grundlage für Planung und Aufbau eines Projectes der Entwicklungshilfe im Nord-Dahomey.* Meisenheim am Glan: Anton Main, 1975.

Agbanrin, Victoire. "La femme en droit coutumier dahoméen," *Revue Juridique et Politique,* no. 4, Oct.–Dec. 1974, pp. 639–662.

Agbo, Casimir. *La philosophie mortuaire au Dahomey.* Cotonou: ABM, 1969.

Aguenou, Jérôme Célestin. "La dot au Benin." Thesis, University of Paris, 1981.

Ahouanou, Denis Fagla. "Recherche sur l'histoire et l'émigration des Alladahonou." Thesis, University of Paris, 1974.

Ajovon, Pierre-Lawuétey. "La mort chez les Guins du Sud Togo." Thesis, University of Bordeaux, 1980.

Akindélé, A. "La Collectivité actuelle chez les Gouns du royaume de Porto Novo," *Bulletin de l'Institut Français d'Afrique Noire,* no. 4, vol. 15, Oct. 1953.

————. "La collectivité chez les gouns de l'ancien royaume de Porto Novo." *Coutumiers de l'AOF,* vol. 3. Paris: Larousse, 1939.

————. and Aguessy, C. "Données traditionnelles relatives aux Fons Dovinou de Savalou," *Bulletin de l'Institut Français d'Afrique Noire,* vol. 17, no. 3–4 (1955), pp. 551–560.

Améga, L. Koffi. "La situation juridique de la veuve en droit coutumier mina," *Penant,* no. 694, 1962; no. 695, 1963, pp. 31–49.

Argyle, W. J. *The Fon of Dahomey: A History and Ethnography of the Old Kingdom.* Oxford: Clarendon Press, 1966.

Asiwaju, A. I. "The aja-speaking peoples of Nigeria," *Africa,* vol. 49, no. 1, 1979, pp. 15–28.

————. "Les peuples parlant aja en Nigéria," in François de Medeiros, *Peuples du Golfe du Bénin.* Paris: Karthala, 1984.

Audric, M. F. "Coutumes Aïzo, Fon, Nago, coutumiers juridiques de l'A.O.F.," *Bulletin du Comité historique et scientifique de l'AOF,* no. 10 (1939), pp. 459–473.

Aupiais, Francis. "La Société indigène au Dahomey," *Compte Rendu de l'Académie des Sciences Coloniales,* vol. 10 (1927–28), pp. 511–521.

Bagado, R. "Le royaume de Nikki-Borgou dans la première moitié du xixe siècle." Thesis, National University of Benin, 1974.

Baldus, Bernd. "Social Structure and Ideology: Cognitive and Behavioral Responses among the Machube of Northern Dahomey." *Canadian Journal of African Studies,* vol. 8, no. 2 (Summer 1974).

Bartel, M. "Origine des noms de villages—cercle de Natitingou," *Etudes Dahoméennes,* no. 7, 1952, pp. 76, 82; no. 8, 1952, pp. 82–86.

Bastide, R. and P. Verger. "Contribution à l'étude sociologique des marchés Nago du bas-Dahomey," *Cahiers de l'Institut de Science Economique Appliqué,* no. 95 (Nov. 1959), pp. 33–65.

Beaudet, A. "Origine des noms de village—cercle de Ouidah," *Etudes Dahoméennes,* no. 8, 1952, pp. 58–60.

Berge, J. "Etudes sur le Pays Mahi, 1926–1928. (Cercle de Savalou, Colonie du Dahomey)," *Bulletin du Comité d'Etudes Historiques et Scientifiques de l'Afrique Occidentale Française,* vol. 11, no. 4, (1928), pp. 708–755.

Bernolles, Jacques. "Un Mythe nago de Dassa-Zoumé," *Etudes Dahoméennes,* no. 2 (1964), pp. 33–50.

———. "Note sur le cycle végétatif et humain des danses du pays dompago," *Etudes Dahoméennes,* no. 3 (1964), pp. 91–105.

————. "Note sur les enfants anormaux dans le nord du Dahomey," *Etudes Dahoméennes*, no. 4 (Oct. 1965), pp. 51–67.

————. "Notes sur les masques de la société Guélédé de Savé." *Etudes Dahoméennes*, 1966, pp. 23–25.

————. "Note sur l'ornementation d'un chapeau Peul en usage dans la région de Djougou," *Notes Africaines*, no. 98 (April 1963), pp. 47–50.

————. "Première étude sur les rites et danses funéraires des Pila-Pila de Belefoungou, arrondissement de Djougou (Dahomey)," *Etudes Dahoméennes*, no. 1 (1963), pp. 125–134.

Bertho, Jacques. "Adja-Tado: races et langues du Bas-Dahomey et du Bas-Togo," *Notes Africaines*, no. 26 (April 1945), pp. 22–24.

————. "Aperçu d'ensemble sur les dialactes de l'Ouest de la Nigéria," *Bulletin de l'Institut Français d'Afrique Noire*, vol. 14, no. 1, 1952.

————. "Le bain rituel du roi d'Abomey Houé li'lé," *Notes Africaines*, no. 7, July 1947, pp. 14–15.

————. "La Case des morts chez les Yoruba de la région de Natitingou," *Notes Africaines*, no. 36, Oct. 1947, pp. 28–29.

————. "Le Gbadou chez les adja du Togo et du Dahomey," *Première Conférence Internationale des Africanistes de l'Ouest. Comptes Rendus*, vol. 2 (1951), pp. 331–350.

————. "Notes concernant les rois de Nikki," *Notes Africaines*, no. 35 (July 1954), pp. 8–10.

———. "Notice sur les Pila-Pila du Dahomey," *Notes Africaines,* no. 43 (July 1949), pp. 74–77.

———. "Parenté de la langue Yourba de la Nigéria du Sud et la langue Adja de la région côtière du Dahomey et du Togo," *Notes Africaines,* no. 35 (July 1947), pp. 10–11.

———. "La Parenté des Yoruba aux peuplades de Dahomey et Togo," *Africa,* vol. XIX, no. 2 (April 1949), pp. 121–132.

———. "Quatres dialectes mandé au Nord Dahomey," *Bulletin de l'Institut Français d'Afrique Noire,* vol. 13, no. 4, 1951.

———. "Races et langues du bas Dahomey et du bas Togo," *Bulletin de l'Institut Français d'Afrique Noire,* vol. 13, no. 4 (Oct. 1951), pp. 1265–1271.

———. "Races et langues du bas Dahomey et du bas Togo," *Grands Lacs,* Special issue, July 1946.

———. "Rois d'origine étrangère, *Notes Africaines,* no. 28, Oct. 1945.

———. "Les sièges des rois d'Abomey," *Notes Africaines,* no. 30, April 1946, pp. 7–9.

———. Trois îlots linguistiques du Moyen Dahomey," *Bulletin de l'Institut Français d'Afrique Noire,* vol. 12, no. 2 (1951), pp. 872–892.

Blier, Suzanne Preston. "Field Days: Melville Herskovitz in Dahomey," *History in Africa,* vol. 16 (1989), p. 1–22.

Bohannan, Laura. "Dahomean Marriage: A Reevaluation," *Africa,* vol. 19, no. 4 (Oct. 1949), pp. 273–287.

Bourgoignie, Georges Edouard. "Ethno-écologie d'une collectivité régionale: les cités lacustres du Dahomey," *Canadian Journal of African Studies,* vol. 6, no. 3 (1972), pp. 403–432.

————. *Les hommes de l'eau, ethno-écologie du Dahomey lacustre.* Fribourg: Editions Universitaire, 1972.

Brand, Roger-Bernard. "Les hommes et les plantes: L'Usage des plantes chez les Wéménou du Sud Dahomey," *Genève-Afrique.* vol. 15, no. 1, 1976, pp. 15–44.

Brasseur, G. "Un type d'habitat au Bas Dahomey," *Bulletin de l'Institut Français d'Afrique Noire,* vol. 14, no. 2, April 1952, pp. 669–71.

Brousseau, Georges. *Un Pays d'avenir? Le Cercle du Borgou Haut-Dahomey.* Paris: Masson et Cie, 1904.

Bruneau, Jean-Claude et al. *Travaux de géographie urbaine: Zaïre, Côte d'Ivoire, Bénin.* Talence: CNRS, 1987.

Cadier, Pierre. "Les Fons du Dahomey," *Journal des Missions Evangéliques,* no. 9 and 10 (Nov.–Dec. 1967), pp. 238–242.

Ceccaldi, Pierrette. *Essai de nomenclature des populations, langues et dialectes de la République Populaire du Bénin.* Paris: Cardan, 1979, 2 vol.

Codo, Lydia. "Problèmes posés par l'Aménagement des nouveaux quartiers périphériques au Nord de la ville de Porto Novo." Thesis, National University of Benin, 1979.

Comlan Mondjannagni, Alfred. *Campagnes et Villes au sud de la République Populaire du Bénin.* Paris: Mouton, 1977.

Coquery-Vidrovich, Catherine. "La Fête des coutumes au Dahomey: historique et essai d'interprétation," *Annales, Economies, Sociétés, Civilisations,* vol. 19, no. 4 (July–Aug.
1964), pp. 696–716.

Cornevin, Robert. "Contributions à l'étude des populations parlant des langues Gouang au Togo et au Dahomey," *Journal
of African Languages,* no. 3 (1964), pp. 226–230.

―――. and Y. Person. "Au Sujet de Bazantchéou Gbazantché de
Seméré (Cercle de Djougou-Dahomey)," *Bulletin de l'Institut Français d'Afrique Noire,* vol. 24, no. 3/4 (July–Oct.
1963), pp. 627–632.

"Coutumes Nago et Djedj (Cercle de Porto Novo)." *Coutumiers
Juridiques de l'AOF,* vol. 3, Paris, Larousse, 1949.

Coutumier du Dahomey. Porto Novo: Imprimerie du Governe-
ment, 1923.

Coyssi, Anatole. "L'Arrivée des Alladahonout à Ouanoué,"
Etudes Dahoméennes, no. 13, 1953, pp. 33–34.

―――. "Un règne de femme dans l'ancien royaume d'Abomey,"
Etudes Dahoméennes, no. 2, 1949, pp. 5–8.

―――. "Savalou," *Paris-Outre Mer,* Sept. 1933, pp. 227–285.

Cresta, M., et al. "Croissance et type d'hémoglobine chez les
enfants du Bénin," *Bulletins et Mémoires de la Société
d'Anthropologie du Paris,* vol. 9, no. 4, 1982, pp. 247–55.

Cyrille, Guillaume. "Ethnographie dahoméenne," *Paris Outre-
Mer,* no. 2–3 (June–Sept. 1932), pp. 144–155.

Dahomey, Traditions du Peuple Fon. Genève, Musée d'Ethnographie, 1975.

Da Silva, Guillaume. "Un aspect des systèmes de mariage chez les Fons de l'ancien royaume d'Abomey," in C. Oppong et al., *Marriage, Fertility and Parenthood in Africa.* Canberra: Australian National University, 1978, pp. 177–186.

————. "Notes sur les éléments de l'horoscope dans l'ancien Dan-Homé," *Etudes Dahoméennes,* no. 20, April–June 1970, pp. 69–84.

————. "Savalou," *Paris Outre-Mer,* Sept. 1933, pp. 227–285.

Delafosse, M. "Organisation de la famille, fiançailles et mariage dans les régions de Zagnanado, Kétou." *Enquête Coloniale dans L'AOF.* Paris: Société d'Editions Géographiques, Maritimes et Coloniale, 1948.

Diamond, Stanley. "Dahomey: A proto-state in West Africa," Ph.D. Dissertation, Columbia University, 1951.

Dissou, Machioudi Idriss. "Essai de reconnaissance et de détermination de l'origine des principales familles Yoruba de Porto Novo à partir de leur 'Oriki'," *Etudes Dahoméennes,* no. 13 (June 1969), pp. 35–88.

Dory, Isabelle. *Femmes et développement rural,* Paris: Karthala, 1990.

Dozon, J. P. "Ce que valoriser la médecine traditionnelle veut dire," *Politique Africaine,* no. 28 (1987), pp. 9–20.

Dresch, J. "La pêche dans le bas Ouémé, '*Bulletin du Comité d'Etudes Historiques et Scientifiques de l'AOF,* vol. 10, no. 3, July-Sept. 1937, pp. 350–359.

Eades, J. S. *The Yoruba Today.* Cambridge, Cambridge University Press, 1968.

Elegbe, Afiji. ''Aménagement et urbanisation des petites villes du centre Dahomy; Savé.'' Thesis, University of Paris, 1975.

Elwert, Georg. ''Animation zur Selbsthilfe: von Bauern getragene Alphabetisationsgemenschaften in Benin,'' in B. Engels and U. Laaser (eds.), *Deutsche Bildungshilfe in der zweiten Entwicklungdekad.* Munich: Weltforum, 1977, pp. 353–387.

————. ''Die Elemente der traditionellen Solidarität: ein Fall studie in Westafrika,'' *Kölner Zeitschrift für Soziologieyund Soziopsychologie,* vol. 32, no. 4, 1980, pp. 681–704.

————. ''Uberleben in Krisen, Kapitalistiche Entwicklung und traditionelle Solidarität,'' *Zeitschift fur Soziologie,* vol. 9, no. 4, 1980, pp. 343–365.

Engelbert, Victor. ''Somba,'' in *Primitive Worlds,* Washington, D.C., National Geographic Society, 1973, pp. 112–139.

Evénamia, A. ''Les Fons dans la souspréfecture d'Abomey-Calavi.'' Abomey-Calavi: Mémoire, National University of Benin, 1973.

Etude socio-urbaine: Bénin. Paris: URBANOR, 1984.

Fett, Roland. *Zwei Frauen sind zuviel.* Saarbrucken, 1978.

Fuglestad, Finn. ''Quelques réflexions sur l'histoire et les institutions de l'ancien royaume du Dahomey et de ses voisins,'' *Bulletin de l'Institut Français d'Afrique Noire,* vol. 39, no. 3, July 1977, pp. 493–517.

"Les Funérailles chez nous," *La Voix de St. Gall* (Ouidah), 52 pp.

"Gaillard, R. "Etude sur les lacustres du bas Dahomey," *L'Anthropologie*, vol. 18 (1907), pp. 99–125.

———. "Le Lac Nokoué," *La Géographie*, vol. 17, 1908, pp, 281–284.

Gani, Orou, "Une coutume quotidienne née du respect des morts," *Notes Africaines*, no. 63, 1954.

———. "Le lieu sacré d'intronisation des Rois de Nikki," *Notes Africaines*, no. 72, July 1953.

———. "Notes sur les coutumes funéraires des Pila," *Etudes Dahoméennes*, no. 4 (1950), pp. 13–21.

———. "Origine de la dynastie de Kandi," *Notes Africaines*, no. 72, (Oct. 1956), pp. 123–124.

———. "Origine de la dynastie de Parakou," *Notes Africaines*, no. 66, April 1955.

———. "Superstitions nord-dahoméennes," *Notes Africaines*, no. 65, Jan. 1955.

Gbénou, Grégoire. "La Famille dahoméenne," *Revue Juridique et Polotique*, vol. 21, no. 1 (Jan.–Mar. 1967), pp. 48–63.

Gibbal, Jean-Marie. "Loin de Mango: les Tiokossi de Lomé," *Cahiers d'Etudes Africaines*, vol. 21, no. 81–3, 1981, pp. 25–51.

Giesecke, M., and G. Elwert. "Literacy and Emancipation," *Development and Change*, April 1983, pp. 255–276.

Glélé, M. A. *Le Phénomène urbain au Dahomey.* Aix-en-Provence Congress, Brussels: INCIDI, 1967.

Glokpon, Kokou, "Le culte des jumeaux chez les Adja." Thesis, University of Paris, 1989.

Greuter, S. *Paysans dans l'impasse: étude de cas dans le sud du Bénin.* Bern: Peter Lange, 1984.

Grivot, R. "La pêche chez les Pédah du Lac Ahémé," *Bulletin de l'Institut Français d'Afrique Noire,* vol. 11, Jan.–April 1949.

Guédou, Georges. "Xo et Gbé. Langage et culture chez les Fons." Thesis, University of Paris, 1976.

————. and C. Coninckx, "La dénomination des couleurs chez les Fons," *Journal des Africanistes,* vol. 56, no. 1 (1986), pp. 67–86.

Guillou, Anne. *Corps utile, corps fertile.* Nantes: University of Nantes CNRS no. 7 (Jan 1985), 128 p.

"L'Habitat rural en Afrique." *Etudes Scientifiques,* Sept.–Dec. 1975, pp. 1–70.

Hazoumé, Paul. *Le Pacte du sang au Dahomey.* Paris: Institut d'Ethnologie, 1937.

Heath, D. F. "Bussa Regalia," *Man,* May 1937.

Herskovits, M. J. "The Best Friend in Dahomey" in Nancy Cunard (ed.), *Negro Anthology.* London: Wishart Books, 1934, pp. 627–632.

————. *Dahomey: An Ancient West African Kingdom.* Evanston, Ill.: Northwestern University Press, 1967, 2 vols. (repr. of 1938 ed.)

———. "Some Aspects of Dahomean Ethnology," *Africa,* vol. 5, no. 3, (July 1932), pp. 266–296.

———. and Frances S. Herskovits. *Dahomean Narrative: A Cross-cultural Analysis.* Evanston, Ill.: Northwestern University Press, 1958.

Houndjahoué, M. "Le décret Jacquinot et les questions de fiançailles des dots et de mariages dans le bas-Bénin," *Africa* (Sao Paolo, Brazil), no. 7 (1984), pp. 3–16.

Houngbédji, Adrien. "Le Chef de Clan et le droit de la femme dans les coutumes du Bas-Dahomey," *Revue Juridique et Politique,* no. 4, (Oct.–Dec. 1967), pp. 603–620.

Housman, M. et al. "Note sur la structure évolutive d'une ville historique: l'exemple d'Abomey," *Cahiers d'Etudes Africaines,* vol. 26, no. 4 (1986), pp. 527–546.

Huber, Hugo. "L'Existence humaine en face du monde sacré: rites domestiques chez les Nyendé du Dahomey," *Anthropos,* vol. 68, 1973, pp. 3–4, 377–441.

———. *Tod und Auferstehung: organisation rituelle, symbolic und ehrprogram einer westafrikanischen Initiationsfeier.* Freiburg (Switz.): Universitätsverlag, 1979.

Hurault, Jean. *Les principaux types de peuplement du Sudest du Dahomey.* Paris: Imprimerie de l'institut géographique nationale, 1965.

Huttel, Wladimir. "Contribution à l'Anthropologie générale des Gounsou Djédjé du cercle de Porto-Novo," *Revue des Sciences Tropicales,* vol. 2, no. 1 (1954), pp. 69–80.

Igué, John Ogounsola. "Contribution à l'étude de civilisation Yoruba." Thesis, National University of Benin, 1980.

———. "L'Habitat holli au Dahomey," *Odu* (lle-lfe), no. 14, July 1976, pp. 89–107.

———. "Sur l'origine des villes yoruba," *Bulletin de l'Institut Français d'Afrique Noire,* vol. 41, no. 2, April 1979, pp. 248–280.

Iroko, Abiola Félix. "Notice historique sur les Kufaloyinma de l'Atacora," *Le Mois en Afrique,* no. 221/22 (1984), pp. 121–129.

———. "Regards extérieurs et saisie interne des ethnies et des ethnonymes: République Populaire du Bénin," in J. P. Chrétien and G. Prunier (eds.), *Les Ethnies ont une histoire.* Paris: Karthala, 1989.

———. "Le spectre de la mort à Cotonou des origines à nos jours," *Les Mois en Afrique* no. 227/8 (Dec. 1985–Jan. 1986), pp. 133–144.

Karl, Emmanuel. *Traditions Orales au Dahomey-Bénin.* Niamey: Centre Régional de Documentation pour la Tradition Orale, 1974.

Kiti, Gabriel. "Quelques coutumes des Goun," *Anthropos,* vol. 32, 1937.

———. "Quelques rites expiatoires au Dahomey," *Anthropos,* vol. 32, 1937, pp. 75–86; vol. 32, 1937, pp. 283–287; vol. 32, 1937, pp. 419–434; vol. 32, 1937, pp. 978–980.

———. "Rites funéraires," *Revue des Missions Catholiques,* Nov. 1, 1929, pp. 502–503; Jan. 16, 1930, pp. 52–53; Feb. 1, 1930, pp. 72; Feb. 16, 1930, pp. 92–96.

————. "Rites funéraires chez les Alladahonou au Dahomey," *Echo des Missions Africaines de Lyon,* March 1932, pp. 65–68; April 1932, pp. 93–94; June–July 1932, pp. 140–144; Aug.–Sept. 1932, pp. 162–163.

————. "Rites funéraires des Goun (Dahomey)," *Suisse Revue internationale d'Ethnologie et de Linguistique.* 1937.

Kordes, Hagen. "Funktionen und Wirkungen Europäischer Entwicklungshelfer im der rolle von Sozialarbeiten . . . Dahomey," *Sociologus,* vol. 21, no. 2 (1971), pp. 138–168.

Kotchikpa, Dossou. "Cotonou: étude portuaire," Thesis, University of Aix-en-Marseilles, 1973.

Koudjo, Bienvenu. "Le chanson populaire dans les cultures fon et goun de Bénin," Ph.D. Thesis, University of Paris, 1989.

————. "Parole et musique chez les Fons et les Gun du Benin: pour une nouvelle taxonomie de la parole littéraire" *Journal des Africanistes,* vol. 58, no. 2 (1988), pp. 73–97.

Krasnowolski, Andezej. "Les problèmes de la formation des liens supraethniques en Afrique Noire," *Revue Française d'Histoire d'Outre Mer,* vol. 68, no. 250/53, 1981, 388–393.

Lafage, Suzanne, and Laurent Duponchel. *Murmures des lagunes et des savanes.* Paris: Conseil international de langue française, 1983.

Langevin, Christine. "Peuples et échanges économiques à Djougou," Thesis, Paris, 1975.

Lombard, Jacques. *Autorités traditionnelles et pouvoirs européens en Afrique Noire—le déclin d'une aristocracie sous le régime colonial.* Paris: Armand Colin, 1967.

―――――. "Les bases traditionnelles de l'économie rurale Bariba," *Bulletin de l'Institut Français d'Afrique Noire,* vol. 23, no. 1/2, 1961.

―――――. "Chieftancy Among the Bariba of Dahomey" in Michael Crowder (ed.), *West African Chiefs.* New York: Africana, 1971, pp. 124–133.

―――――. "Contribution à l'histoire d'une ancienne société politique du Dahomey: la royauté d'Allada," *Bulletin de l'Institut Français d'Afrique Noire,* vol. 29, no. 1–2 (Jan.–April 1967), pp. 40–66.

―――――. "Cotonou: ville africaine," *Etudes Dahoméennes,* no. 10 (1953), pp. 4–210.

―――――. "L'Expression actuelle de la vie politique dans une ancienne société de type féodal: les Bariba du Haut Dahomey," *Cahiers d'Etudes Africaines,* no. 3 (1960), pp. 5–45.

―――――. "L'intronisation d'un roi Bariba," *Notes Africaines,* no. 62, April 1954.

―――――. "The Kingdom of Dahomey" in Daryll Forde and P. M. Kaberry, *West African Kingdoms in the Nineteenth Century.* London: Oxford University Press, 1967, pp. 70–92.

―――――. "Les Moyens de contrôle social dans l'ancien Dahomey. Survivances actuelles et formes nouvelles," *Le Monde Non-Chrétien,* no. 38 (April–June 1956), pp. 145–157.

―――――. "Notes sur la préhistoire du Dahomey, *Etudes Dahoméennes,* no. 17 (1957).

———. "Quelques notes sur le Peul du Dahomey," *Notes Africaines.* no. 73 (Jan. 1957), 4–7.

———. *Structures de type "féodal" en Afrique Noire: étude des dynamismes internes et des relations sociales chez les Bariba du Dahomey.* Paris: Mouton, 1965.

———. "Un Système politique traditionnel de type féodal: les Bariba du Nord-Dahomey," *Bulletin de l'Institut Français d'Afrique Noire,* 19 (13), 3/4 (July–Oct. 1957), pp. 464–506.

———. "La Vie politique dans une ancienne société du type féodal: les Bariba du Dahomey," *Cahiers d'Etudes Africaines,* vol. 1, no. 3, (Oct. 1960), pp. 5–45.

Lopez-Escartin, N. *Données de base sur la population.* Paris: Centre Français sur la population et le développement, 1991.

Lounes, Balkacem. "Cotonou: ville-dortoir?" *Cités Africaines,* no. 3 (1985), pp. 8–10.

Maiwald, Jurgen. *Noch herrschen Fetisch und Phantom. Entwicklungsdienst in Dahomey.* Scheinfled: Verlag der Lutheran Mission Erlangen, 1971.

Marchesseau, J. "Sur la découverte d'un gisement à industrie paléolithique dans le nord ouest du Dahomey," *Bulletin de l'Institut Français d'Afrique Noire,* vol. 28, no. 3/4, July–Oct. 1966, pp. 575–594.

Marin, J. "Etude de moyens de pêche dans la basse et moyenne vallée de l'Ouémé," *Etudes Dahoméennes,* vol. 16, 1964, pp. 17–20.

Maurice, A. *Atakora, Otiau, Otammari, Osuri: Peuples du Nord Bénin, 1950,* Paris: Académie des Sciences d'Outre Mer, 1986.

———. "Les Châteaux Somba," *Tropiques,* vol. 55, no. 395 (May 1957), pp. 59–66.

Medeiros, François de (ed.). *Peuples du Golfe du Bénin.* Paris: Karthala, 1984.

Mercier, Paul. *Civilisations du Bénin; connaissance de l'Afrique.* Paris: Société Continentale d'Editions Modernes Illustrées, 1962.

———. "Conception d'orientation chez les Bé-Tammaribé," *Notes Africaines,* no. 41, Jan. 1949.

———. "Le consentement au mariage et son évolution chez les Bétammadébé," *Africa,* vol. 20, no. 3, July 1950.

———. "The Fon of Dahomey" in Daryll Forde (ed.), *African Worlds; Studies in the Cosomological Ideas and Social Values of the African Peoples.* New York: Oxford University Press, 1954, pp. 210–234.

———. "L'habitat et l'occupation de la terre chez les Somba," *Bulletin de l'Institut Français d'Afrique Noire,* vol. 15, no. 2, April 1953.

———. "L'Habitation à l'étage dans l'Atakora," *Etudes Dahoméennes,* no. 11 (1951), pp. 29–86.

———. "Notes sur les Kivayaribé, *Etudes Dahoméennes,* no. 1, 1948.

———. "Notice sur le peuplement Yoruba au Dahomey-Togo," *Etudes Dahoméennes,* no. 4 (1950), pp. 29–40.

———. "Les Royaumes Nago," *Etudes Dahoméennes,* no. 4 (1950).

————. *Tradition-changement—histoire: les "Somba" du Dahomey Septentrional.* Paris: Anthropos, 1968.

————. "Travail et Service Public dans l'Ancien Dahomey," *Présence Africaine,* no. 13 (1952), pp. 84–91.

————. "Vocabulaire de quelques langues du Nord-Dahomey," *Etudes Dahoméennes,* no. 2, 1948.

Midiohouan, T. "La femme dans la vie politique, économique et sociale en République Populaire du Bénin," *Présence Africaine,* no. 141 (1987), pp. 59–70.

Montserrat, Palau-Marti. "Notes sur les noms et les langues chez les Sabé," *Journal de la Société des Africanistes,* vol. 38, no. 1, 1968, pp. 59–88.

Morel, Alain. "Un exemple d'urbanisation en Afrique occidentale: Dazza-Zoumé," *Cahiers d'Etudes Africaines,* no. 46, 1974, pp. 727–748.

Moulero, T. "Histoire et légende de Chabé (Savé)," *Etudes Dahoméennes,* no. 2 (June 1964), pp. 51–92; no. 14–15 (Sept.–Dec. 1969), pp. 29–58.

————. "Histoire et légendes des Djékens," *Etudes Dahoméennes,* no. 8, Oct. 1966, pp. 39–56.

N'Bessa, Benqit. "La fonction urbaine de Cotonou." Thesis, University of Bordeaux, 1973.

Nicholson, W. E. "Notes on some of the customs of the Busa and Kyenza tribes of Ilo," *Journal of the African Society,* vol. 26, 1926–27.

N'Tcha, Kouagou Jean. ''Anthropologie économique de Bétammarbé dans l'Atacora.'' Thesis, National University of Benin, 1982.

Oké, Finagnon Mathias. ''Notice sur les villages lacustres du Dahomey,'' *Etudes Dahoméennes,* no. 13 (June 1969), pp. 89–93.

Okou, C. ''L'Urbanisation face aux systèmes naturels: le cas de Cotonou,'' *Cahiers d'Outre Mer,* no. 168 (1989), pp. 425–37.

Oliveira, Alexandre de. ''Monographie Régionale. La région de Kouandé (Natitingou-Cercle de l'Atacora),'' *Bulletin de l'Enseignement AOF,* no. 31 (March 1917), pp. 122–200.

Onokerhoraye, A. G. ''The influence of different cultures on the patterns of change in traditional Africa,'' *Cultures et Développement,* no. 4, 1976, pp. 623–645.

Orou, Yorouba Robert. ''Le Gani et ses implications socioéconomiques.'' Thesis, National University of Benin, 1982.

Palau-Marti, Montserrat. ''Notes sur les noms et les langages chez les Sabé,'' *Journal Société des Africanistes,* vol. 38, no. 1, 1968, pp. 59–88.

————. ''Problèmes juridiques du mariage et du divorce dans le Dahomey moderne'' in Jean Poirier, *Etudes de droit africain et de droit malgache.* Paris: Cujas, 1965, pp. 391–406.

Parrinder, Geoffrey. ''Yoruba-Speaking Peoples in Dahomey,'' *Africa,* vol. 17, no. 12 (1947), pp. 122–129.

Perron, Michel. ''Le Pays Dendi,'' *Bulletin du Comité d'Etudes Historiques et Scientifiques de l'Afrique Occidentale Français,* vol. 7, no. 1 (Jan.–March 1924), pp. 51–83.

Person, Yves. "La Dynastie de Tyilixa (Djougou)," *Perspectives Nouvelles sur le passé de l'Afrique Noire et Madagascar.* Paris: Publications de la Sorbonne, 1956, pp. 201–212.

———. "Note sur les Nyantroukou," *Etudes Dahoméennes,* no. 16, (1956), pp. 23–45.

———. "Première esquisse de peuple Biyobé," *Bulletin d'l'Institut Français d'Afrique Noire,* vol. 17 (July 1955).

———. "Le système des classes d'âge chez les Tangba et les Yowa, cercle de Djougou," *Cahiers d'Etudes Africaines,* vol. 19, no. 73–76, 1979, pp. 25–54.

Peterli, Rita. *Die Kultur eines Bariba-Dorfes im Norden von Dahomé.* Basel: Pharos-Verlag Hansrudolf Schwabe AG, 1971.

Pétrequin, Anne-Marie, and Pierre Pétrequin. *Habitat lacustre du Bénin,* Paris: Editions recherches sur les civilisations, 1984.

Pineau-Jamous, Marie-Josee. "Porto Novo: royauté, localité et parenté," *Cahiers d'études africaines,* vol. 26, no. 4 (1986), pp. 547–576.

Pontié, Danielle. "Les Moba de Lomé," *Cahiers d'Etudes Africaines,* vol. 21, no. 81–3, 1981, pp. 53–65.

Quénum, Alphonse. "Leisure in a developing Country: The case of Lower Dahomey," *Culture* (Paris), vol. 1, no. 2, 1973, pp. 67–86.

Quénum, Maximilien. "Au pays des Fons," *Bulletin du Comité d'Etudes Historiques et Scientifiques de l'A.O.F.,* vol. 18, no. 2–3 (April–Sept. 1935), pp. 143–337.

————. *Au pays des Fons: usages et coutemes de Dahomey.* Paris: Larose, 1938.

Renaud (Cdt.), and A. Akindélé. "La Collectivité actuelle chez les Goun du royaume de Porto Novo," *Bulletin de l'Institut Français d'Afrique Noire,* vol. 15, no. 4 (1953), pp. 1690–1709.

Rondeau, Georges. "Sociétés et associations du bas et moyen Dahomey," Paris: Mémoires du CHEAM, 1969.

Rouget, Gilbert. "La Voix, la cloche et le pouvoir du roi," in Ganay Solange et al (eds.). *Ethnologies: hommage à Marcel Griaule.* Paris: Hermann, 1989, pp. 313–332.

Sacramento, Leon. "Cotonou: Etude urbaine." Thesis, University of Toulouse, 1976.

Salvaing, Bernard. "La femme Dahoméenne vue par les missionnaires: arrogance culturelle, ou antiféminisme clérical," *Cahiers d'études Africaines,* vol. 21, no. 4 (1981), pp. 507–21.

Sargent, Carolyn Fishel. "Between death and shame: dimensions of pain in Bariba culture," *Social Science and Medicine* (Oxford), vol. 19, no. 12 (1984), pp. 1299–1304.

————. "Born to die: witchcraft and infanticide in Bariba culture," *Ethnology,* vol. 27, no. 1 (Jan. 1988), pp. 79–95.

————. *The Cultural context of therapeutic choice: obstetrical care decisions among the Bariba of Benin.* New York: Reidel, 1982.

————. "Factors Influencing Women's Choices of Obstetrical Care in a Northern District in the People's Republic of Benin." Ph.D. diss., Michigan State University, 1979.

————. "Obstetrical choice among urban women in Benin," *Social Science and Medicine* (Oxford), vol. 20, no. 3 (1985), pp. 287–292.

————. "Prospects for the professionalization of indigenous midwifery in Benin," in Murray Last and G. L. Chavanduka (eds.), *The Professionalization of African Medicine*. Manchester: Manchester University Press, 1986.

————. "Utilization of national health maternity services in a northern district of the People's Republic of Benin," *Rural Africana*, vol. 8/9, Fall/Winter 1980–81, pp. 77–89.

Savary, C. *La pensée symbolique des Fons du Dahomey*. Geneva: Editions Médicine et Hygiène, 1976.

Schramm, J., and W. Keuper. *Die Sozio-ökonomische Stellung der Frau in Elfenbeinküste, Ghana, Dahome*. Freiburg: Institut für soziale Zusammenarbeit, 1969.

Silva, G. da. "Un aspect des systèmes du mariage chez les Fons de l'ancien royaume d'Abomey," in C. Oppong, et al. (eds.), *Marriage, Fertility and Parenthood in West Africa*. Canberra: Australian National University Press, 1978, pp. 177–86.

Sodo Gandji, Martial. "Le Développement urbain de Cotonou," Thesis, University of Paris, 1967.

Solken, Heinz. "Innerafrikanische Wege nach Benin," *Anthropos*, vol. 49 (1954), pp. 809–933.

Sossouhonto, M. F. "Les anciens rois de la dynastie d'Abomey; essai généalogique et historique," *Etudes Dahoméennes*, no. 13 (1955), pp. 25–30.

Souza, Germain de. "Conception de vie chez les Fons." Thesis, University of Rennes, 1971.

Stamm, Volker. "Sollen alle Stühle die gleiche Höhe haben? Beobachtungen zu Disziplin und Autoritat in Sudbenin," *Sociologus* (Berlin), vol. 39, no. 2 (1989), pp. 161–171.

Steel, James Carelton. "The Memory subsystem of the Dahomey Kingdom," M. S. Thesis, University of Louisville, 1977.

Stewart, Marjorie Helen. "The Borgu people of Nigeria and Benin: the disruptive effect of partition on traditional political and economic relations," *Journal of the Historical Society of Nigeria* (Ibadan), vol. 12, no. 3/4 (1984/5), pp. 95–120.

―――. "Kinship and Succession to the Throne of Bussa," *Ethnology,* vol. 17, April 1978, pp. 169–182.

Tardits, M. Claude. "Parenté et classe sociale à Porto Novo, Dahomey" in P. C. Lloyd (ed.), *The New Elites of Tropical Africa.* London: Oxford University Press, 1966, pp. 184–198.

―――. *Porto Novo: les nouvelles générations africaines entre leurs traditions et l'Occident.* Paris: Mouton, 1958.

Terreau and Huttel, "Monographie du Hollidjé," *Etudes Dahoméennes,* no. 2 (1948).

Tiando, A. "Le Peuple Woaba Takamba." Thesis, National University of Benin, 1974.

Tidjani, Serpos Abdou. "Calendrier agraire et religieux au Bas Dahomey," *Première Conférence Internationale des Afri-*

canistes de l'Ouest. Comptes Rendus, vol. 2, Dakar, 1951, pp. 290–298.

———. "Un Exemple d'émigration: la tribu de Quin-vi, Aihonvi ou Adikoum-vi de Cové," *Bulletin de l'Institut Français d'Afrique Noire,* vol. 22, no. 3–4 (July–Oct. 1960), pp. 514–530.

———. "Notes sur le mariage au Dahomey," *Etudes Dahoméennes,* no. 6 (1951), pp. 27–107; no. 7 (1952), pp. 5–80.

———. "Un procédé de divination au Dahomey: la gourdependule," *Bulletin de l'Institut Français d'Afrique Noire,* vol. 5 (1943), no. 1–4, pp. 122–135.

Tingbe-Azalou, Albert. "Rites de dation du nom, initial de naissance chez les Aja-Fon du Bénin," *Anthropos,* vol. 85, no. 1/3 (1990), pp. 187–192.

Verger, Pierre. "Contribution à l'étude sociologique des marchés nago au Bas Dahomey," *Les Cahiers de l'Institut de Science Economique Appliqués,* no. 95, Nov. 1959, pp. 33–65.

———. "Rôle joué par l'état d'hébétude au cours de l'initiation des novices aux Cultes des Orishas et Vodun," *Bulletin de l'Institut Français d'Afrique Noire,* vol. 16, no. 3–4 (1954), pp. 332–340.

———. "Tam-Tam Avohoun," *Notes Africaines,* no. 59, July 1953, pp. 72–76.

Vernière, Marc. "A propos de la marginalité: réflexions illustrées par quelques enquêtes en milieu urbain et suburbain africain," *Cahiers d'Etudes Africaines,* no. 51, 1973, pp. 587–605.

Vignon, Roger. "Etude sociologique d'une région agricole de Sakété," *Etudes Dahoméennes,* no. 3 (1964), pp. 77–89.

Welcomme, R. L. "Les Moyens de pêche dans les eaux continentales du Dahomey," *Etudes Dahoméennes,* no. 20, April–June 1970, pp. 5–36.

Wheatley, Paul. "The Significance of Traditional Yoruba Urbanism," *Comparative Studies in Society and History,* vol. 12, no. 4, 1970, pp. 393–423.

Wittrant, Liliane. "La Croissance urbaine de Cotonou: Etude d'un quartier périphérique." Thesis, University of Paris, 1971.

Wolo, F. "Le jeu de l'escargot au Dahomey," *Etudes Africaines,* no. 109–110, 1944–45.

Yérimé, Pierre. "Conflit du commandement africain dans le Borgou, royaume des Sako de Kandi," *Notes Africaines,* no. 83, July 1959, pp. 91–94.

Zachariah, K. C., and J. Condo. *Migration in West Africa.* Washington, D.C.: World Bank, 1981.

Zimmer, Baldwin. *Dahomey.* Bonn: Kurt Schroeder, 1969.

5. POLITICS, ADMINISTRATION, AND INTERNATIONAL RELATIONS

Adamou, Agnide Amidou. "L'Evolution de l'administration locale en Bénin de 1960 à 1974." Thesis, National University of Benin, 1983.

Adandé, Alexandre. "L'Organisation Judiciare et l'évolution legislative générale au Dahomey," *Penant,* no. 708–709, (Oct.–Dec. 1965), pp. 429–445.

Adesina, A. "Nigeria-Benin relations." Thesis, University of Ife, 1976.

Adjanahoun, C. E. "Le Coup d'état d'octobre 1972 au Dahomey." Thesis, University of Paris, 1974.

Afrique, April 1967. Special issue on Dahomey.

Afua, Akjemado. "Etude comparative de deux régimes militaires: cas du Bénin et du Togo." Mémoire, Académie de Paris, Ecole des hautes études internationales, 1988.

Alberich, Julio Cola. "La Pertinaz inestablidad politica del Dahomey," *Revista de Politica Internacional,* no. 124 (Nov.–Dec. 1972), pp. 155–167.

Albert Tévoédiré, compagnon d'aventure, Paris: Berger-Levrault, 1988.

Alladaye, Michel. "Les mécanismes juridiques de protection des droits de la personne en République Populaire du Bénin," *Revue Juridique et Politique,* no. 1, Jan–March 1982, pp. 41–47.

Allen, Chris et al. *Benin, The Congo, Burkina Faso.* London: Pinter, 1989.

————. " 'Goodbye to all that': the short and sad history of socialism in Benin," *Journal of Communist Studies,* vol. 8, no. 2 (June 1992), pp. 63–81.

———. "Restructuring an authoritarian state: 'Democratic renewal' in Benin," *Review of African Political Economy*, no. 54 (July 1992), pp. 43–58.

Almeida, E. d'. "La coopération soviéto-béninoise 1972–1979." Thesis, University of Paris, 1979.

Alodo, André K. "Les institutions de la République populaire du Bénin," *Revue Juridique et Politique*, vol. 32, no. 2 (Apr.–June 1978), pp. 759–792.

American Council on Voluntary Agencies for Foreign Service. "Development Assistance program of U.S. non-profit organizations, Benin," Washington, 1976.

Amzat, Adamaou. *Debout—au service de la révolution*. Cotonou: ONEPI, 1976.

Anignikin, S. C. "Les origines du mouvement national au Dahomey." Ph.D. diss., University of Paris, 1980.

L'Année Africaine. Paris: Pedone, annual.

L'Année Politique Africaine. Dakar: Société Africaine d'édition, annual.

Annene, J. C. "The Nigeria-Dahomey Boundary," *Journal of the Historical Society of Nigeria*, vol. 11, no. 4 (Dec. 1963), pp. 479–485.

Apithy, Sourou-Migan. *Face aux impasses*. Cotonou: Editions A.B.M., 1971.

———. *Au Service de mon pays*. Montrouge, France: Etablissements Dalex, 1957.

————. *Telle est la vérité.* Paris: Présence Africaine, 1968.

————. *La Vérité sur l'éclatement de l'U.P.D.* Porto Novo: Imprimerie Silva, 1951.

Assaba, Claude. ''Pouvoir Yoruba: Bénin.'' Thesis, University of Paris, 1989.

Assikidana A., and B. Adjeyigbe. ''Un aspect des échanges commerciaux entre le Bénin et la Nigéria.'' Thesis, National University of Benin, 1980.

Ayo, S. Bamidele. ''Ideology, local administration and problems of rural development in the Republic of Benin,'' *Public Administration and Development,* Oct.–Dec. 1984, pp. 361–372.

Baynham, S. J. ''Praetorian politics and the Benin raid,'' *Army Quarterly and Defence Journal,* vol 107 (Oct. 1977), pp. 422–434.

Bebler, Anton. *Military Rule in Africa: Dahomey, Ghana, Sierra Leone & Mali.* New York: Praeger, 1973.

''Benin,'' in Colin Legum (ed.), *Africa Contemporary Record,* New York, Africana Publishing Co., annual, 1966+.

''Bénin,'' Special issue of *Europe-Outremer,* no. 669/70 (1985).

''Benin,'' in Dante A. Caponera (ed.), *Water Law in Selected African Countries.* Rome: FAO, 1979, pp. 43–62.

''Bénin: le dossier de l'agression mercenaire,'' *Afrique Asie,* Supplement to no. 37, 1977, pp. 31–82.

"Benin: ending isolation," *Africa Confidential,* vol. 20, 1979, pp. 3–5.

"Benin: Keeping the Lid On," *Africa Confidential,* vol. May 6, 1981, pp. 45.

"Bénin—La Loi fondamentale," *Afrique Contemporaine,* no. 93, Sept.–Oct. 1977, pp. 23–35.

"Benin: Test tube democracy," *Africa Confidential,* April 4, 1990, pp. 4–5.

Beynel, Jean. "Dahomey: de l'Assemblée territoriale à l'Assemblée nationale," *Penant,* no. 742 (Oct.–Nov.–Dec. 1973), pp. 456–476.

———. "L'Organisation judiciare au Dahomey," *Penant,* no. 740 (April–May–June 1973).

———. *Répertoire alphabétique des textes législatifs et des principaux textes réglementaires du Dahomey (1958–1971).* Université de Dakar: Faculté des Sciences Juridiques et Economiques, 1972.

———. "Réponses dahoméennes à quelques problèmes en matière pénale, civile et sociale," *Revue Juridique et Politique,* no. 2, April–June 1972, pp. 247–270.

Bhêly-Quénum, Olympe. "Le Dahomey: ou en sommes-nous après huit ans d'indépendance?" *Afrique Actuelle,* no. 24 (Jan. 1968), pp. 5–14.

Biarnes, Pierre. "Dahomey: le prix de la banqueroute." *Revue Française d'Etudes Politiques Africaines,* no. 25 (Jan. 1968), pp. 29–31.

———. *Les Français en Afrique noire de Richelieu à Mittérand.* Paris: Armand Colin, 1987.

———. "Les Militaires au Dahomey et au Togo," *Revue Française d'Etudes Politiques Africaines,* Dec. 1968, pp. 65–84.

Bierwirth, G. "Ideologische Funktion und praktische Konsequenz der Evaluierung von Entwicklungshilfeprojecten—Ein Erklärungsversuch am Beispiel von Massenmedienprojecten zur Unterstutzung landlicher Entwicklung in der Volksrepublik Benin," in D. Kantowsly (ed.), *Evaluierungsforschung und Praxis in der Entwicklungshilfe.* Zurich: Verlag der Fachvereine, 1977, pp. 347–393.

Bonzon, Suzanne. "Les Dahoméens en Afrique de l'Ouest," *Revue Française de Science Politique,* vol. 17, no. 4 (1967), pp. 718–726.

Bossou, M. "Dossier de presse sur l'agression impérialiste du 16 janvier contre la République populaire du Bénin." Thesis, University of Paris, 1977.

Bovy, Lambert. "La Nature du mouvement syndical ouest africain d'après la législation," *Revue Juridique et Politique d'Outre Mer,* July–Sept. 1963, pp. 365–384.

Brand, Roger. "Structures Révolutionnaires au Bénin." *Genève-Afrique,* vol. 16, no. 1, 1977–78, pp. 67–88.

Chambard, Paul, and Geneviève Sigisbert. "L'Aide publique bilatérale à l'Afrique noire francophone," *Europe-Outremer,* no. 564, Jan. 1977, pp. 13–54.

"La Chambre de réflexion," *Afrique Contemporaine,* no. 15 (Sept.–Oct. 1964), pp. 12–13.

Chasme, Louis. "L'Armée nationale dahoméenne 1960–72." Thesis, University of Rouen, 1977.

Codo, Léon C. *Le Bénin dans les rapports ouest-africains: stratégie d'insertion, bilatéralisme sous-régional et engagements régionaux.* Bordeaux: Université de Boardeaux, Centre d'Etudes Politiques, 1987.

Cola Albrich, Julio. "La Pertinez Inestablidad Politica del Dahomey," *Revista de Politica* (Madrid), 1972, no. 124, pp. 155–165.

Comte, Gilbert. "Le Dahomey au sein de l'Entente; la réconciliation avec le Niger," *Europe-France-Outremer,* vol. 42, no. 426–427 (July–August 1965), pp. 22–24.

————. "Dahomey: une élection pour rien," *Revue Française d'Etudes Politiques Africaines,* no. 29 (May 1968), pp. 6–7.

Conac, Gérard (ed.). *Les institutions administratives des Etats Francophones d'Afrique Noire.* Paris: Economica, 1979.

Constantin, François. "Dahomey," in *Année Africaine 1971.* Paris: Editions A. Pedone, 1972, pp. 422–426.

————. "Dahomey," in *Année Africaine 1972.* Paris: Editions A. Pedone, 1973. pp. 397–406.

————. and C. Coulon. "Des casernes aux chancelleries," *Canadian Journal of African Studies,* no. 1975, pp. 17–49.

————. "La Constitution du gouvernement de M. Hubert Maga et le programme du Conseil présidentiel," *Bulletin de l'Afrique Noire,* no. 598 (May 6, 1970), pp. 12059–12062.

Corbett, Edward M. *The French Presence in Black Africa.* Rockville, Md.: New Perspectives, 1972.

Cornevin, Robert. "Le Bicéphalisme dahoméen, *Europe-France-Outre-Mer,* July 1965, pp. 19–21.

————. "Coups d'état en chaine au Dahomey," *Revue Française d'Etudes Politiques Africaines,* no. 99 (March 1974), pp. 52–65.

————. "Dahomey," *Année Africaine.* Paris: Editions A. Pedone 1964–1970.

————. "Dahomey: Das frühere Königreich und die heutige Republik (von Danhome bis Dahomey)," *Afrika Forum,* no. 7/8 (July–Aug. 1967), pp. 397–400.

————. "Les Difficultés des jeunes nations africaines: L'exemple du Dahomey," *Bulletin de la faculté des lettres de Strasbourg,* March 1964, pp. 355–362.

Cowan, L. Gray. "Benin joins the pragmatists," *CSIS Africa Notes,* no. 54, 1986.

————. *Local Government in West Africa.* New York: Columbia University Press, 1958.

Crowder, Michael. *Revolt in Borgou.* London, 1974.

"Dahomey," in *Africa South of the Sahara.* London: Europa Publications Ltd., annual. (After 1975, as "Benin.")

"Dahomey," in *Europe-France-Outremer,* annual issue on "L'Afrique d'expression française et Madagascar," 1960–1987.

"Dahomey," in Donald George Morrison et al., *Black Africa: A Comparative Handbook.* New York: Free Press, 1972, pp. 227–233.

"Dahomey," in Amos J. Peaslee (ed.), *Constitutions of Nations.* The Hague: Martinus Nijhoff, 1965, pp. 148–166.

"Dahomey: l'armée au pouvoir," *Europe-France-Outremer,* special issue no. 515 of December 1972.

"Dahomey: The Army Again," *Africa Confidential,* vol. 13, no. 23, (Nov. 24, 1972), pp. 6–7.

"Dahomey: Cent-quarante et un jours de crise," *Revue Française d'Etudes Politiques Africaines,* no. 53 (May 1970), pp. 12–16.

"Dahomey—les élections de mars 1970, leur annulation, le nouveau gouvernement," *Afrique Contemporaine,* no. 49 (May–June 1970), pp. 14–15.

"Dahomey: Eternal Triangle," *Africa Confidential,* vol. 9, no. 14, (July 12, 1968), pp. 3–5.

"Dahomey: The Full (and Bizarre) Story," *Africa Confidential,* vol. 11, no. 3 (Jan. 30, 1970), pp. 3–6.

"Dahomey Gropes," *Africa Report,* April 1970, pp. 6–7.

"Dahomey: More Rumblings," *Africa Confidential,* Feb. 7, 1975.

"Dahomey, Our Next Door Neighbor," *Nigeria Magazine,* no. 70 (Sept. 1961), pp. 225–240.

"Dahomey: Règlements de comptes entre officiers supérieurs," *Revue Française d'Etudes Politiques Africaines,* no. 47 (Nov. 1969), pp. 10–13.

"Dahomey: Still No Solution," *Africa Confidential,* vol. 11, no. 9 (May 1, 1970), pp. 4–5.

"Dahomey: The Troika and the Military," *Africa Confidential,* vol. 11, no. 18 (Sept. 4, 1970), pp. 6–7.

"Dahomey Will the Army Keep Quiet?" *Africa Confidential,* vol. 13, no. 14 (July 14, 1972), pp. 2–4.

"Dahomey's Revolution," *Africa Confidential,* Nov. 2, 1973, p. 3.

Dangou, Issaka. "L'Organisation judiciaire Dahoméenne en matière pénale," *Revue Juridique et Politique,* Oct. 1969, pp. 769–778.

Decalo, Samuel. "The Army in a Praetorian State: Dahomey," in *Coups and Army Rule in Africa: Studies in Military Style.* New Haven: Yale University Press, 1976.

————. "Benin: Radical Military Rule in a Praetorian State," in *Coups and Army Rule in Africa: Motivations and Constraints.* New Haven: Yale University Press, 1990.

————. "Dahomey 1968–1971: Return to Origins," *Geneva-Africa,* vol. 10, no. 1 (1971), pp. 76–91.

————. "Full Circle in Dahomey," *African Studies Review,* vol. 13, no. 3 (Dec. 1970), pp. 445–458.

————. "Ideological Rhetoric and Scientific Socialism in Two People's Republics: Benin and Congo/B," in Carl Rosberg and Tom Callaghy (eds.), *Socialism in Subsaharan Africa.* Berkeley: Institute of International Studies, 1979, pp. 231–264.

————. "The People's Republic of Benin," in B. Sjakowski (ed.), *Marxist Governments: A World Survey,* vol. 1. London: Macmillan, 1980, pp. 87–115.

————. "The Politics of Instability in Dahomey," *Geneva-Africa,* vol. 7, no. 2 (1968), pp. 5–32.

————. "Regionalism, Politics and the Military in Dahomey," *Journal of Developing Areas,* vol. 7, no. 3 (April 1973), pp. 449–478.

Decheix Pierre. "La Charte du Conseil présidentiel dahoméen du 7 Mai 1970," *Revue Juridique et Politique,* vol. 24, no. 3 (July–Sept. 1970), pp. 517–526.

————. "Le Code de la nationalité dahoméenne," *Revue Juridique et Politique,* no. 4 (Oct.–Dec. 1965), pp. 605–624.

————. "La Nouvelle constitution du Dahomey," *Revue Juridique et Polotique,* vol. 22, no. 3 (July–Sept. 1968), pp. 919–935.

Decraene, Philippe. "Dahomey: la France en accusation," *Revue Française d'Etudes Politiques Africaines,* no. 87 (March 1973), pp. 18–20.

————. "Dahomey: une succession sans heurts," *Revue Française d'Etudes Politiques Africaines,* no. 78 (June 1972), pp. 31–32.

————. "Les Répercussions au Dahomey de la Crise du Nigéria," *Comptes Rendus Mensuels des Séances de l'Ac-*

adémie des Sciences d'Outre Mer, XXVII (Oct.–Nov. 1967), pp. 468–476.

Deguenon, Barthélémy. ''Le Mouvement réformateur de l'administration territoriale au Bénin.'' Dakar: E.N.D.A., 1984.

De Lusignan, Guy. *French-speaking Africa since Independence.* New York: Praeger, 1969.

''Did Morocco aid coup attempt?'' *Africa Confidential,* vol. 18, no. 6, 1977.

Didier, Jean. ''Dahomey: la perspective de jours meilleurs,'' *Revue Française d'Etudes Politiques Africaines,* no. 81 (Sept. 1972), pp. 15–16.

Diop, David. ''Le Congrès de Cotonou: Interview de M. Bertin Borna,'' *Présence Africaine,* no. 20 (June–July 1958), pp. 117–119.

Djivo, Adrien Guézo. *La rénovation du Dahomey.* Paris: ABC, 1978.

Doh, Dominique. ''La Trahison des élites,'' *Africasia,* no. 16 (May 25, 1970), pp. 15–18.

Dossa, Raymond. ''Le constitutionalisme Marxiste: Bénin.'' Thesis, University of Bordeaux, 1988.

Duic, Walter Z. *Africa Administration, Directory of public life, administration and justice in the African States.* 3 vols. Munich: Verlag Dokumentation, 1978. [Benin, vol. 1, pp. 243–294]

Edwige, Videgla M. M. ''Le Maître en Histoire, rôle des intellectuels dans le mouvement de la décolonisation de l'ex-Dahomey.'' Thesis, National University of Benin, 1980.

Elwert, Georg. "Notizen zur Mikropolitik des Bauern Staats-Verhältnisses in der V. R. Benin," *Afrikanische Eliten zwanzig Jahre nach Erlangung der Unabhängigheit.* Hamburg: Buske, 1983, pp. 81–96.

France. Ambassade de France au Bénin. "L'Aide publique française au Bénin." Cotonou, 1990.

France. La Documentation Française. "Constitution de la République du Dahomey (Janvier 1964)," in *Les Nouvelles Constitutions Africaines,* Notes et Etudes Documentaires, no. 3175, (March 25, 1965), pp. 42–51.

————. ————. "Constitution du Dahomey (31 mars 1968)," Notes et Etudes Documentaires, no. 3625 (Oct. 2, 1969), pp. 1–14.

————. ————. "Dahomey. Constitution du 25 Novembre 1960" in *Les Constitutions des Républiques Africaines et Malgache d'expression Française,* Notes et Etudes Documentaires, no. 2994 (May 27, 1963), pp. 45–51.

————. ————. "La République du Dahomey." Notes et Etudes Documentaires, no. 2620 (Dec. 31, 1959).

————. ————. "La République du Dahomey." Notes et Etudes Documentaires, no. 2629 (1959).

————. ————. "La République du Dahomey." Notes et Etudes Documentaires, no. 3307 (Aug. 7, 1966).

Garcia, Luc. "L'Evolution politique récente au Dahomey." Paris: Mémoire, Ecole Pratique des Hautes Etudes, 1966.

"Général Soglo prend le pouvoir!" *Afrique Contemporaine,* no. 23, (Jan.–Feb. 1966), pp. 7–9.

Genne, Marcelle. ''La tentation du Socialisme au Bénin,'' *Etudes Internationales* (Montréal), vol. 9, no. 3, 1978, pp. 383–404.

Germany. Statistisches Bundesamt. ''Statistik des Auslandes, Benin.'' Wiesbaden, irregular.

Glélé, Maurice A. ''Des Institutions politiques dahoméennes,'' in *Les Constitutions et institutions administratives des états nouveaux.* Brussels: INCIDI, 1965.

———. *Naissance d'un état noire: révolution politique et constitutionelle du Dahomey, de la colonisation à nos jours.* Paris: R. Pichon et R. Durand Auzias, 1969.

———. *La République de Dahomey.* Paris: Editions Berger-Levrault, 1969.

Globerson, Aryeh. ''Problems of Public Administration in West African Countries with Special Reference to Dahomey,'' *Public Administration in Israel and Abroad,* 1963, pp. 85–95.

Godin, Francine. *Bénin 1972–1982: la logique de l'état africain.* Paris: Harmattan, 1986.

———. ''Le crise d'état au Dahomey 1960–1972. Genèses et fondement.'' M.A. Thesis, University of Quebec, 1981.

———. ''Etat, accumulation de capital et luttes de classes au Bénin, 1972–1982.'' Ph.D. thesis, University of Montreal, 1984.

Golan, Tamar. ''The Counseil de l'Entente.'' Ph.D. diss., Columbia University, 1980.

Guérivière, Jean de la. "Dahomey: un coup d'état 'en toute cordialité'," *Revue Française d'Etudes Politiques Africaines.* no. 83 (Nov. 1972), pp. 23–25.

Guichard, Martine. "L'ethnisation de la société peule du Borgou (Bénin)," *Cahiers d'Etudes Africaines,* vol. 30, no. 1 (1990), pp. 7–44.

Hazoumé, Guy Landry. *Idéologies tribalistes et nation en Afrique: le cas dahoméen.* Paris: Présence Africaine, 1972.

Herzog, Chaim. "UN at Work: The Benin Affair," *Foreign Policy,* no. 29, Winter 1977–78, pp. 140–159.

Holo, T. "Etude d'un régime militaire: le cas du Bénin 1972–77." Ph.D. Thesis, University of Paris, 1979.

Houndjahoué, Michel. "Aide alimentaire étrangère et force de travail au Bénin," *Le Mois en Afrique,* no. 223/4 (1984), pp. 146–151.

———. "Bénin: révolution socialiste et politique étrangère à l'ère de la diplomatie nouvelle," *Le Mois en Afrique,* no. 225/6 (1984), pp. 31–36.

———. "Le Bénin socialiste et le bon voisinage, 1971–1986," *Le Mois en Afrique,* no. 253/4 (1987), pp. 28–41.

———. "Le différend américano-béninois: genèse, évolution, et fin d'un malentendu, 1976–1983," *Le Mois en Afrique,* no. 219/20 (1984), pp. 25–31.

———. "Notes sur les relations internationales du Bénin socialiste 1972–1986," *Etudes Internationales,* vol. 18, no. 1 (1987), pp. 371–388.

Houngavou, Patrice. "Les Intellectuels dahoméens et la construction nationale." Grenoble: Mémoire d'Institut d'études politiques, 1968.

Houigbedji, Adrien. "Le Chef de clan et le droit de la femme dans les coutumes du Bas Dahomey," *Revue Juridique et Politique.* no. 4, Oct.–Dec. 1967, pp. 603–624.

Howe, Russell Warren. "A Talk with President Zinsou," *Africa Report,* Dec. 1968, pp. 31–32.

Huannou, Adrien. "L'Image du Dahomey et des Dahoméens en occident à travers la litterature et la presse françaises," *L'Afrique Littéraire,* no. 58, 1981, pp. 140–147.

Ignatio-Pinto, Louis. "Discours prononcé lors de son installation à la Cour Suprême," *Penant,* no. 720 (April–May–June 1968), pp. 141–145.

Iroko, Abiola Feliz. "Survivances du troc en République Populaire du Bénin dans le dernier quart du Vingtième siècle," *Revue Française d'Etudes Politiques Africaines,* no. 223–4, Aug.–Sept. 1984, pp. 72–108.

Jouffrey, Roger. "Le Bénin depuis 1981," *Afrique Contemporaine,* no. 127, July–Sept. 1983, pp. 34–43.

Jouhaud, Y. "La Nouvelle constitution de la République du Dahomey; note et texte," *Revue juridique et politique,* vol. 18, no. 1 (Jan.–Mar. 1964), pp. 157–172.

Kassim, Momodu. "Extradition: the treaty between Benin, Ghana, Nigeria and Togo," *Nigerian Current Law Review* (Lagos) (1985), pp. 155–166.

Kayossi, Raymonde. "Les rôles des délégués syndicaux et des Comités de défense de la Révolution en Bénin." Thesis, National University of Benin, 1983.

Kérékou, Mathieu. *Base et tâches de mobilisation consignées aux C.R.L.* Cotonou, Office National d'Edition, 1974.

———. *Dans la voie de l'édification du Socialisme.* Cotonou, Office National d'Edition, 1979.

Laleye, O. Mouftao. "Urban local government in Benin, the case of Cotonou urban district 1," *Public Administration and Development,* vol. 12, no. 1 (Feb. 1992), pp. 53–70.

Lavroff, Dimitri-Georges. "La République populaire du Bénin: la constitution du 9 septembre 1977," *Année Africaine 1977.* Paris: Pedone, 1979, pp. 109–158.

Lemarchand, René. "Dahomey: Coup Within a Coup," *Africa Report,* June 1968, pp. 46–54.

LeVine, Victor T. "The Coups in Upper Volta, Dahomey and the Central African Republic," in Robert I. Rothberg and Ali A. Mazrui (eds.), *Power and Protest in Black Africa.* New York: Oxford University Press, 1970, pp. 1035–1071.

———. "Independent Africa in Trouble," *Africa Report,* Dec. 1967, pp. 19–24.

Leymarie, P. "Bénin: une démocratie populaire qui s'estime constamment menacée," *Revue Française d'Etudes Politiques Africaines,* vol. 12, no. 135, Mar. 1977, pp. 52–58.

"La Loi fondamentale," *Afrique Contemporaine,* no. 93, Sept.–Oct. 1977, pp. 23–35.

"Loi fondamentale de la République Populaire du Bénin." Cotonou: OPEPI, 1983.

Makedonsky, Eric. "Nouvelles tentatives de création d'un parti unique au Dahomey," *Revue Française d'Etudes Politiques Africaines,* no. 45 (Sept. 1969), pp. 62–72.

Mangin, G. "L'Evolution du Droit: Dahomey," *Annuaire de Législation Française et Etrangère,* 1966, pp. 161–178.

Manouan, A. "L'Evolution du Conseil de l'Entente," *Penant,* no. 746, Oct.–Dec. 1974, pp. 447–497; no. 747, Jan.–Mar. 1975, pp. 19–92; no. 748, Apr.–June 1975, pp. 211–236.

Martin, Michel. "Note sur le changement politique et constitutionnelle en République populaire du Bénin depuis l'indépendence," *Année Africaine 1982,* Paris: Pedone, 1982, pp. 91–127.

————. "The rise and 'thermidorization' of radical praetorianism in Benin," *Journal of Communist Studies,* vol. 1, no. 3/4 (1985), pp. 58–81.

Matthews, Ronald, "Dahomey," in *African Powder Keg: Revolt and Dissent in Six Emergent Nations.* London: Bodley Head, 1966, pp. 134–160.

Mavoungou, Valentin. "Le syndicalisme dans les pays d'Afrique à l'idéologie marxiste-léniniste," *Penant,* no. 803 (1990), pp. 268–298.

Medieros, F. d'. "Armée et stabilité: les partis militaires au Bénin," in Alain Rouquie (ed.), *La Politique de Mars.* Paris: Sycamore, 1981, pp. 125–135.

Melin, P. F. "L'expérience institutionnelle et politique du Dahomey." Mémoire DES, Science Politique, Paris 1972.

Mensah, Nathanael G. *Evolution politique et constitutionnelle de la République populaire du Bénin.* Cotonou: Centre de Formation administrative et de perfectionnement, 1982, 217 p.

Mondjannagni, Alfred. "Quelques aspects historiques, économiques et politiques de la frontière Dahomey-Nigeria," *Etudes Dahoméennes,* no. 1 (1963), pp. 17–57.

Neavoll, George. "Benin: a victory for democracy," *Africa Report,* May–June 1991, pp. 39–42.

Nicolas, A. "Un pays Africain à option socialiste," *Cahiers du Communisme,* May 1983, pp. 88–94.

Novicki, Margaret A. "Msgr. Isidore de Souza: building a new Benin," *Africa Report,* May–June 1991, pp. 43–45.

Noukoumiantakin, A. "Le contrat clé en main conclu au Bénin entre la Société Nationale pour la Production Agricole et la société française 'Le Silos du Sud-Ouest,' " *Revue Juridique et Politique,* vol. 42, no. 2/3 (1988) pp. 177–184.

"La Nouvelle Constitution et réélection présidentielle," *Afrique Contemporaine,* no. 37 (May–June 1968), pp. 18–19.

Nwokedi, Emeka. "Nigeria-Benin relations: the joy and anguish of bilateralism," *Genève-Afrique,* vol. 29, no. 1 (1991), pp. 33–52.

———. "Strands and strains of 'Good Neighbourliness': the case of Nigeria and its Francophone neighbours," *Genève-Afrique,* no. 1 1985, pp. 39–60.

Nzongola, Georges. *Essai sur le Dahomey.* Brussels: Cahiers du CEDAF, no. 5, 1971.

Nzongola, N. "Les chefs traditionnels dans l'administration locale coloniale au Dahomey et au Sierra Léone," *Cahiers Zaïrois d'études politiques,* no. 1, 1973, pp. 95–116.

Obukhov, L. A. "The Ideological and political platform of the Revolutionary democracy of Benin," in *The Most Recent Tendencies in the Socialist Orientation of Various African and Arab States.* Prague: 1979, pp. 13–45.

Oke, Finagnon Mathias. "La Chefferie traditionnelle et l'évolution politique de Dahomey." Ph.D. Thesis, University of Paris, 1967.

————. "Des Comités électoraux aux partis politiques dahoméens," *Revue Française d'Etudes Politiques Africaines,* no. 45 (Sept. 1969), pp. 45–57.

————. "L'Influence du tribalisme sur les régimes politiques africains," *Revue Française d'Etudes Politiques Africaines,* no. 55 (July 1970), pp. 63–72.

————. "Les Partis politiques dahoméens." Paris: Mémoire, Ecole Pratique des Hautes Etudes, 1964.

————. "Reflections on the Political Parties of Dahomey," *Africa Quarterly,* vol. 8, no. 1 (April–June 1968), pp. 38–43.

————. "Réflexions sur les partis politiques Dahoméens," *Revue Française d'Etudes Politiques Africaines,* no. 28 (April 1968), pp. 95–102.

————. "Le rôle de la presse dans le mouvement nationaliste," in J. Dofny and A. Akiwowo (eds.), *National and Ethnic Movements.* Beverly Hills: Sage, 1980.

————. "Survivance tribale ou problématique nationale en Afrique noire: un cas concret, celui de la réalité dahoméenne," *Etudes Dahoméennes,* vol. 12, no. 1 (Apr. 1968), pp. 5–8.

Olodo, André K. "Les institutions de la République Populaire du Bénin," *Revue Juridique et Politique,* vol. 32, no. 2, Apr.–June 1978, pp. 750–792.

Ologoudou, Emile. *Les Intellectuels dans la nation: l'examen de conscience d'un jeune Dahoméen.* Cotonou: Les Editions du Bénin, 1967.

Omelewa, M. A. "Dahomean immigrants in Nigeria," *Nigerian Magazine* (Lagos), no. 126/7, 1978, pp. 60–65.

Onwuka, Ralph. *Development and Integration in West Africa.* Ife: University of Ife Press, 1982.

Oumar Sy, Moussa. "Le Dahomey, gouvernement et administration," *Acta Ethnographica Academiae Scientiarum Hungaricae* (Budapest), vol. 12, no. 3–4 (1963), pp. 333–365.

Pageard, R. "La réforme des juridictions coutumières et musulmanes dans les nouveaux Etats de l'Afrique de l'Ouest," *Penant,* no. 6989, Dec. 1963, pp. 462–493.

Paraiso, Alexandre. "Au Bénin, une juridiction exceptionnelle de droit commun: la Cour criminelle d'exception," *Penant,* no. 765, July–Sept. 1979, pp. 289–308.

————. "La loi fondamentale et les Nouvelles constitutions de la République Populaire du Bénin," *Penant,* no. 770, Oct.–Dec. 1980, pp. 403–440.

————. "La protection des libertés en République Populaire du Bénin," *Revue de Droit International et de Droit Comparé,* vol. 65, no. 1/2 (1988), pp. 58–75.

Pfeffer, Ruppert. "Dahomey," *Internationales Afrika Forum*, 7 (Dec. 1971), pp. 705–711.

Port Novex, Alain de. *Le Dossier est Ouvert*. Cotonou, 1974.

Quirino-Lanhoumey, Julian. "Le Développement communautaire en Afrique Noire: leçons d'une expérience au Dahomey," *Politique Etrangère*, 1965, pp. 161–180.

République du Dahomey. "Constitution du 14 février 1959." *Journal Officiel de la République du Dahomey*. Feb. 16, 1959.

————. "Constitution du 26 novembre 1960." *Journal Officiel de la République du Dahomey*. Nov. 26, 1960.

————. "Constitution du 11 janvier 1964." *Journal Officiel de la République du Dahomey*. Jan. 12, 1964.

————. "Ordonnance No. 20/PR du 8 avril portant constitution de la République du Dahomey, no. 9, April 15, 1968.

————. Ministère de Défense Nationale. *Le Service civique*. Porto Novo: Imprimerie Nationale, 1971.

————. Service d'Information. Connaissez-vous le Dahomey? Paris, 1962

————. ————. Le Dahomey: naissance d'une nation. Porto Novo, 1963.

————. ————. Le Dahomey des temps anciens au jour d'hui [sic] Lomé: Editogo.

————. ————. The Truth About the Dispute Between Dahomey and Niger. Porto Novo, 1963.

Reuke, L. "Die Eingriffe des dahomeischen Militärs in die Politik," *Vierteljahresberichte,* no. 48 (June 1972), pp. 141–155.

Répertoire des pouvoirs publics africains. Paris: Ediafric, 1975.

"La Révolution Béninoise a dix ans," *Europe-Outre Mer,* Special Issue, no. 631, Aug. 1982.

"La Révolution Béninoise en 1977," *Europe-Outre Mer,* Special Issue, no. 566, March 1977.

Ronen, Dov. "Benin: the role of the uniformed leaders," in I. J. Mowe (ed.), *The Performance of Soldiers as Governors.* Washington, D.C.: University Press of America, 1980, pp. 101–150.

———. *Dahomey Between Tradition and Modernity.* Ithaca: Cornell University Press, 1975.

———. "People's Republic of Benin: the military, Marxist ideology and the politics of ethnicity," in John Herbeson (ed.), *The Military in African Politics.* New York: Praeger, 1987, pp. 92–122.

———. "Political Development in a West African Country: The Case of Dahomey." Ph.D. Thesis, Indiana University, 1969.

———. "Preliminary Notes on the Concept of Regionalism in Dahomey," *Etudes Dahoméennes,* vol. 12, no. 1 (April 1968), pp. 11–14.

———. "The Two Dahomeys," *Africa Report,* June 1968, pp. 55–56.

Salacuse, Jeswald. *An Introduction to Law in French-speaking Africa*, Charlottesville, Va.: Michie Co., 1969, vol. 1.

Sanda, A. O. "Ethnic pluralism and inter-class conflicts in four West African societies," *Civilisations*, 1977, vol. 27, no. 1/2, pp. 65–80.

Satchivi, F. "Dépendence ou autonomie: Bénin." Mémoire, University of Amiens, 1978.

Sekpon, A. P. "La politique extérieure du Bénin." Mémoire, University of Bordeaux, 1980.

Sinou, Alain et al. *Les villes d'Afrique Noire: politique et opérations d'urbanisme et d'habitat entre 1650 et 1960.* Paris: Ministère de la coopération et du développement, 1989.

Skurnik, W. A. E. "The Military and Politics: Dahomey and Upper Volta," in Claude E. Welch, Jr. (ed.), *Soldier and State in Africa.* Evanston, Ill.: Northwestern University Press, 1970, pp. 62–123.

Sordet, Monique. "La Loi martiale," *Europe-France-Outremer,* no. 515 (Dec. 1972), pp. 10–13.

Sossou-Gloh Maximilien. "La Conscience politique au Dahomey, à partir d'une enquête d'attitudes à Cotonou." Thesis, University of Paris, 1970.

Staniland, Martin. "Regionalism and political parties of Dahomey." M.A. Thesis, University of Ghana, 1964.

———. "The Three-Party System in Dahomey," *Journal of African History,* vol. 14, nos. 2, 3, 1973, pp. 291–312, 491–504.

Stanley, G. E. "Military Involvement in Dahomey 1963–75." M.A. Thesis, University of Birmingham, 1976.

Terray, Emmanuel. "Les Révolutions congolaise et dahoméenne de 1963; essai d'interprétation," *Revue Française de Science Politique,* vol. 14, no. 5 (Oct. 1964), pp. 917–942.

Tévoédjré, Albert. *L'Afrique révoltée.* Paris: Présence Africaine, 1958.

————. *Contribution à une synthèse sur le problème de la formation des cadres africains en vue de la croissance économique.* Paris: Diloutremer, 1965.

————. *Pan Africanism in Action.* Cambridge: Harvard University Center for International Affairs, 1965.

Tévoédjré, Eric. "The limits and uses of deviance in Franco-African Relations: Guinea, Congo and Benin, 1958–1981," Ph.D. Thesis, Johns Hopkins University, 1990.

Thibault, Jean. "Dahomey: le Général Soglo à Paris," *Revue Française d'Etudes Politiques Africaines,* no. 24 (Dec. 1967), pp. 8–10.

Thompson, Virginia. "Dahomey," in Gwendolen M. Carter (ed.), *Five African States: Responses to Diversity.* Ithaca, N.Y.: Cornell University Press, 1963, pp. 161–262.

————. and Richard Adloff. "Dahomey," in *French West Africa.* London: George Allen & Unwin, 1958, pp. 139–145.

————. *West Africa's Council of the Entente.* Ithaca, N.Y.: Cornell University Press, 1972.

Tirolien, F. "Les Premiers élus africains et l'évolution politique du RDA." Thesis, University of Paris, 1974.

Tixier, Gilbert. "Les Etats du Conseil de l'Entente," *Penant,* no. 686 (Apr.–May 1961).

"Togo and Dahomey: The Kutuklui Affair," *Africa Confidential,* vol. 12, no. 25 (Dec. 21, 1971), pp. 4–5.

Toko, Michel Bamenou. "La Dévolution successorale au Dahomey," *Revue Juridique et Politique,* no. 4 (Oct./Dec. 1972), pp. 687–704.

Touval, Saadia. "Dahomey and Niger," in *The Boundary Politics of Independent Africa.* Cambridge: Harvard University Press, 1972, pp. 198–203.

Vienney, Cl. "Nouvelles institutions juridiques dans l'organisation coopérative dahoméenne," *Archives Internationales de Sociologie et de la Coopération,* no. 16 (1964), pp. 63–92.

Viou, Michel. "La légalité administrative en République Populaire du Bénin," *Revue Juridique et Politique,* no. 1 (Jan. 1984), pp. 26–52.

Weiss, Danielle. "Interview du Colonel Mathieu Kérékou," *Europe Outre Mer,* no. 631, Aug. 1982, pp. 7–13.

———. "Le Socialisme en marche," *Europe Outre Mer,* no. 566, March 1977, pp. 9–12.

Welch, Claude. "Obstacles to disengagement and democratization: military regimes in Benin and Burkina Faso," in Constantine P. Danopoulos (ed.), *The Decline of Military Regimes.* Boulder, Col.: Westview Press, 1988, pp. 25–44.

Zatsfpine, Alexandre. "L'Evolution du droit de la nationalité des Républiques francophones d'Afrique et de Madagascar," *Penant* no. 748, Apr.–June 1975, pp. 147–201; no. 749, July–Sept. 1975, pp. 346–380.

Zinsou, Emile Derlin. "La Politique étrangère du Dahomey," *Europe-France-Outremer*, vol. 45, no. 453 (Oct. 1967), pp. 16–17.

————. *Pour un socialisme humaniste*. Yverdon, Switzerland: Editions Kesselring, 1975.

6. ECONOMICS, AGRICULTURE, TRADE, AND COMMERCE

"L'Accord de cession par le Ghana d'énergie électrique au Dahomey et Togo," *Industries et Travaux d'Outre Mer*, no. 192, Nov. 1969, pp. 967–970.

Adandé, Alexandre Senou. *Le maïs et ses usages au Bénin méridional*. Paris: ACCT, 1984.

————. "Regard rétrospectif sur l'économie africaine et perspective de développement agricole au Dahomey," *Etudes Dahoméennes*, no. 1 (1963), pp. 7–16.

Adandé, Christian. "La politique économique du développement pour le Dahomey." Thesis, University of Paris, 1974.

Adjar-Ahouansou, Joseph. "Du développement des productions bovins au Dahomey." Toulouse: Imprimerie Toulousaine, 1972.

Africascope: guide économique des pays francophones. Paris: Editions Mermon, 1986, annual.

Agbadjé, Augustine. "Restructuration des sociétés d'état en Bénin: absorption de la SOBEPALH par le SONICOG." Thesis, National University of Benin, 1984.

Agnilo, Raymond. "Les dépenses militaires dans les finances publiques des pays du Tiers Monde: le cas du Bénin." Thesis, National University of Benin, 1984.

"L'Agriculturé-Objectif no. 1; produire pour parvenir à l'autosuffisance," *Europe-Outre-Mer.* no. 566, March 1977, pp. 20–23.

"L'Agriculture—Un potentiel agricole sousutilisé et une autosuffisance alimentaire théorique," *Europe-Outre-Mer.* no. 631, Aug. 1982, pp. 37–39.

Ahouansou, Nicolas. "Secteur commercial et financement du développement économique. Elements de réponse pour le Dahomey." Thesis, IEDES, Paris, 1971.

Ahounou, Nicaise. "La segmentation du marché du travail en milieu urbain." Thesis, University of Bordeaux, 1988.

Ahoyo, Jean-Roger. "Les marchés d'Abomey et de Bohicon," *Cahiers d'Outre Mer,* no. 110, April–June 1975, pp. 162–184.

Akpo, Gilbert. "Associationnisme et développement, Sociologie rurale d'un département dahoméen; le département du Zou." Thesis, University of Paris, 1974.

Alao-Fary, S. K. "L'Action de la FAO en faveur du développement agricole au Benin." Yaoundé, Cameroun: IRIC, 1983.

Alfo, Frédéric. "Rapports dynamiques réciproques entre éducation et la production économique au Dahomey." Thesis, IEDES, Paris, 1971.

Amegnagbo, Blaise. "Investissement humain et les ressources humaines du Dahomey." Thesis, IEDES, Paris, 1971.

Amoussou, B. "Le Développement du palmier à huile au Dahomey," *Oléagineux,* no. 4, April 1967, pp. 205–214.

Anson-Meyer, Monique. "Les illusions de l'autosuffisance alimentaire: Bénin, Ghana, Niger, Togo," *Mondes et Développement,* vol. 11, no. 41–2, 1983, pp. 51–79.

Antheaume, Benoît. "La Palmeraie du Mono: approche géographique," *Cahiers d'Etudes Africaines,* no. 47, 1972, pp. 458–484.

Apithy, Sourou-Migan. "A propos du port common Togo-Dahomey," *France-Outremer,* no. 297–8, Sept. 1954, pp. 16–20.

Apovo, Christophe. *Cuirs et peaux au Dahomey.* Lyon, 1970.

Arnould, E. J. "The Dahomean *dokpe:* some effects of recent evolutionary changes in an archaic cooperative association," *Ikenga* (Nsukka), vol. 3, no. 1/2, 1975, pp. 1–6.

Assikidana, O.E., and B. Adjeyigbe. "Un aspect des échanges commerciaux entre le Bénin et le Nigéria: le commerce clandestin," Mémoire, National University of Benin, 1980.

Assogba, Marc Napoléon. *Contribution à l'étude des besoins en protéine d'origine animale de la population de la République populaire du Bénin.* Paris: Agence de Coopération culturelle et technique, 1979.

Atchaca, G. "Tontines et développement en République populaire du Bénin," *Communautés,* no. 81 (1987), pp. 89–94.

Atohoun, Patrick, and Léocadie Awounou. "Le secteur public industriel en République Populaire du Bénin." Thesis, National University of Benin, 1988.

Ayo, S. Bamidele. "Ideology, local administration and problems of rural development in the Republic of Benin," *Public Administration and Development,* vol. 4, no. 4 (1984), pp. 361–372.

————. "Rural cooperatives in the Republic of Benin since independence," *Odu* (Ilorin), no. 23 (1983), pp. 71–84.

Azagoun, Mathieu, and Marie Françoise Affouda. "La coopération Sud-Sud: cas du Bénin avec les pays Arabes." Thesis, National University of Benin, 1984.

Bankolé, Gabriel O. "Etude critique de la contribution du système bancaire au développement de l'agriculture depuis l'indépendence." Thesis, National University of Benin, 1984.

Banque, Africaine de Développement. "Etude des possibililtés de co-opération économique entre le Ghana, la Côte d'Ivoire, la Haute Volta, le Niger, le Dahomey et le Togo." Paris, 3 vol., mimeo, 1970.

Banque Centrale des Etats de l'Afrique de l'Ouest. "L'Anacarde au Dahomey," Indicateurs économiques no. 187 (Aug.– Sept. 1971).

————. "La Balance des Paiements du Dahomey, années 1965– 1966–1967," Indicateurs économiques no. 163 (June 1969).

————. "Balance des paiements du Dahomey, années 1965 à 1970," Indicateurs économiques no. 205 (April 1973).

————. "Balance des paiements extérieurs du Dahomey Années 1965 à 1969," Indicateurs économiques no. 187 (Aug–Sept. 1971).

————. "Les Budgets généraux des états de l'Union Monétaire," annual.

————. "Chronologie Economique et Politique," 3 times annually.

————. "Indicateurs économiques", 3 times annually.

————. "Indicateurs économiques dahoméens," annual.

————. "Statistiques Economiques et Monétaires," 3 times annually.

Baron, S. "Dahomey: Deep Sea Fishermen," *Geographical Magazine,* vol. 40 (August 1968), pp. 1335–1342.

"Benin: political risk for extractive industries." Syracuse: Political Risk Services, 1991.

"Bénin: la stratégie du développement repose sur l'expansion de l'agriculture et les exportations," *Bulletin de l'Institut Français d'Afrique Noire,* vol. 7, no. 6, March 1978, pp. 89–91.

"Benin struggles for market-led recovery," *Africa Recovery,* vol. 6, no. 3 (Nov. 1992), pp. 18–23.

Bernard. "Les Cocotiers dans le golfe du Bénin," *Etudes Dahoméennes,* no. 1 (1949), pp. 20–46.

Beynel, Jean. "Réponses dahoméennes à quelques problèmes en matière pénale, civile et sociale," *Revue Juridique et Politique,* no. 2, April–June 1972, pp. 247–270.

―――. "Revue des différentes solutions dahoméennes aux problèmes du développement de l'agriculture," *Penant,* no. 736, Apr.–June 1972, pp. 209–245.

Bierschenk, T. "Baumwolleanbau und gesellschaftliche Entwicklung in Benin," *Sociologus,* vol. 37, no. 2 (1987), pp. 155–174.

―――. "Development projects as arenas of negotiation for strategic groups," *Sociolgia Ruralis,* vol. 28, no. 2/3 (1988), pp. 146–160.

Booker Agricultural International. *Benin: Review of the Save Sugar Project.* New York: Booker International Ltd., 1982.

Bouraima, R. "Le Naira dans le commerce intérieur et extérieur en Bénin." Thesis, National University of Benin, 1984.

Brasseur, Gérard. "Réflexions nouvelles sur la palmeraie de Porto Novo," *Annales de l'Ecole des Lettres,* (Lome) vol. 1, 1972, pp. 197–225.

Brasseur-Marion, Paule. "Cotonou, capitale économique du Dahomey," *Encyclopédie Mensuelle d'Outre Mer,* no. 38 (June 1955).

―――. "Cotonou, porte du Dahomey," *Les Cahiers d'Outre Mer,* no. 24 (Oct.–Dec. 1953), pp. 364–378.

―――. and G. Brasseur. *Porto Novo et sa palmeraie.* Dakar: Institut Français d'Afrique Noire, 1953.

Caputo, E. "Nuovo politiche agricole: il caso de Benin," *Africa* (Rome), vol. 41, no. 1 (1986), pp. 89–106.

Catoire, M. B. "Le Port de Cotonou," *Afrique Contemporaine*, no. 20 (July–Aug. 1965), pp. 19–20.

Chaillard, H., C. Daniel and V. Houeto, "L'Irrigation du palmier à l'huile et du cocotier," *Oléagineux*, vol. 38, no. 10 (Oct. 1983), pp. 519–528.

Clemens Ursula, W. Hillebrand and Thomas Kessler. *Dahomey und seine wirtschaftsräumliche Gliederung.* Hamburg: Deutsches Institut fur Afrikaforschung, 1970.

Clerc, Joseph, et al. *Société paysanne et problèmes fonciers de la palmeraie Dahoméenne: étude sociologigue et cadastrale.* Paris: Office de la Recherche scientifique et technique outre mer, 1956.

Clifford, Paul. *Francophone West Africa.* London: Metra Consulting Group, 1982.

Codjia, Edith. "Le port de Cotonou et son rôle dans l'économie dahoméenne." Thesis, University of Paris, 1973.

Codo, Léon César. "Incidence économiques des flux transfrontaliers clandestins: le cas du Nigéria et du Bénin," *Afrique Contemporaine*, no. 140, Oct–Dec. 1986, pp. 11–23.

Costa, E. "Back to the Land: The Campaign Against Unemployment in Dahomey," *International Labour Review*, vol. 93, no. 1 (Jan. 1966), pp. 29–49.

La culture cotonnière dans le nord-est du Dahomey: source de richesse. Paris: Jouvé, 1966.

Daane, Jon R. V., and J. A. Fanou. "Faculty-building in a small francophone African state: the case of Benin," in W. van den Bor et al. (eds.), *South-North partnership in strengthening higher education in agriculture.* Wageningen: Centre for Agricultural Publishing and Documentation, 1989, pp. 153–177.

———. and Roch L. Mongbo. "Peasant influence on development projects in Benin: a critical analysis," *Genève-Afrique,* vol. 29, no. 2 (1991), pp. 49–76.

Dagba, Eugène. "Une Etude sur le maïs dans la région d'Allada," *Etudes Dahoméennes,* no. 1, 1963, pp. 91–100.

Dahomey, *Plan de Développement économique et social 1966–70.* Cotonou: 1965, 498 pp.

———. Ministère des Finances. *Code d'Investissements.* Porto Novo: 1965.

"Dahomey," in International Monetary Fund, *Surveys of African Economies,* vol. 3, Washington, D.C., 1970, pp. 143–219.

"Le Dahomey," special issue of *Marchés Tropicaux et Méditerranéens.* Nov. 1965.

"Dahomey," in *Momento de l'Economie Africaine.* Paris: Ediafric. 1966+ (Annual).

"Dahomey, Niger, Togo: le décollage économique est commencé," *Moniteur du Commerce International,* no. 1083, Aug. 26, 1971. pp. 3387–3401.

"Dahomey: Radio in the service of rural development," *Entente Africaine,* Jan. 1975, pp. 35–45.

"Le Dahomey et son port," special issue of *Europe-France-Outremer,* vol. 42, no. 426–427 (July–Aug. 1965), pp. 9–59.

"Dahomey's economic review," *New York Times*, annual, January.

Dakpogan, Nestor. "Dimensions économiques et sociales de la société béninoise de textiles." Thesis, National University of Benin, 1984.

Delarue, Philippe. "Les Ports africains: Port Etienne (Nouadhibou) et Cotonou," *Afrique Contemporaine*, no. 46 (Nov.–Dec. 1969), pp. 2–8.

De Surgy, Albert. *La Pêche traditionnelle sur le littoral Evhé et Mina (de l'embouchure de la Volta au Dahomey)*. Paris: Groupe de Chercheurs Africanistes, 1966.

"Développement économique et social du Dahomey 1966–1970," *Nations Nouvelles* (Yaoundé), no. 10 (Dec. 1966), pp. 18–27.

"Le Développement rural au Dahomey." Addis Ababa: Economic Commission for Africa, 1970.

"Le Développement spectaculaire de la culture du coton," *Europe-France-Outremer*, no. 515 (Dec. 1972), pp. 27–28.

Dissou, Machioudi Idriss. "Développement et mise en valeur des plantations de palmier à huile au Dahomey," *Cahiers d'Etudes Africaines*, vol. 12, no. 47 (1972), pp. 485–499.

Domingo, Aboudou Moutiou. *Contribution à l'étude de la poulation bovine des Etats de golfe du Bénin*. Paris: ACCT, 1980.

Donnenfeld, Janine. "Etude d'un marché urbain africain: Dantokpa." Thesis, University of Abidjan, 1973.

Dossou-Yovo, Roger. "Le marché béninois des assurances: évolution et perspectives d'avenir," *Revue Juridique et politique,* no. 2 (May–Sept. 1992) pp. 183–192.

Dreschel, P., and S. Schmall. "Mineral deficiencies and fertilization of coastal reafforestation in Bein," *Fertilizer Research,* vol. 23, no. 1 (1990), pp. 125–133.

Droy, Isabelle. *Femmes et développement.* Paris: Karthala, 1990.

Durand, A. "Les Collectivités locales de base au Dahomey: le village et la commune," *Revue Juridique et politique,* vol. 22, no. 2 (April–June 1968), pp. 379–390.

Dutaillis, Jean. "Le chemin de fer du Dahomey," *Revue de Géographie,* vol. 53, 1903, pp. 421–31.

"Les échanges commerciaux entre les pays de l'Union Monétaire Ouest Africaine 1969–78," Banque Centrale des Etats de l'Afrique de L'Ouest, Indicateurs Economiques, no. 292, March 1981.

L'Economie Africaine. Dakar: Société africaine d'édition, annual.

"L'Economie dahoméenne," special issue of *Les Echos,* June 24, 1969.

"L'Economie dahoméenne," *Nations Nouvelles,* no. 37, Apr. 1972, pp. 16–22.

Ediafric. *L'Economie des pays d'Afrique Noire.* Paris: 1982.

———. *Les Plans de développement des pays d'Afrique Noire.* Paris: 1979.

Edon, O. André. "Le Pouvoir financier du trésor public: Bénin," Thesis, National University of Benin, 1984.

"L'électricité au Dahomey," *Actualités* (Cotonou), Apr. 1968, pp. 15–22.

Elwert, Georg, and R. M. Segbenou. "Urbanisation sans bidonvilles: le röle des structures économiques décentralisées pour le développement urbain de Cotonou, "*Journal des Africanistes,* vol. 53, no. 1/2 (1983), pp. 119–45.

————. et al. "Von des Subsistenzökonomie zur staatskapitalistschen Production," *Arbeitsgruppe Bielefelder Entwicklungssoziologen* (Saarbrucken), no. 1, 1979, pp. 13–60.

Elwert-Kretschmer, and Georg Elwert. "Mit den augen der Beniner: eine evaluation von 25 Jahren in Benin," *Afrika-Spectrum,* vol. 26, no. 3 (1991), pp. 335–350.

Etienne-Nugué, Jocelyne. *Artisanats traditionnels en Afrique Noire, Bénin,* Dakar: Institut culturel africain, 1984.

"L'Evolution économique et financière de la République Populaire du Bénin," *Banque Centrale des Etats de l'Afrique de l'Ouest,* annual.

"Une expérience radiophonique rurale réussie au Dahomey," *Entente Africaine,* no. 19, Jan. 1975, pp. 34–37, 40–45.

"Expériences de la République Populaire du Bénin en matière de réforme agro-foncière," *African Perspectives,* no. 1, 1979, pp. 27–43.

Fair, Denis. "The ports of West Africa: Benin, Togo, Ghana and Côte d'Ivoire," *Africa Insight,* vol. 19, no. 4 (1989), pp. 241–247.

Finance, échange et monnaie des pays d'Afrique noire, Paris: Ediafric, 1975.

France, Institut National de la Statistique et des Etudes Economiques. *Commerce extérieur des états d'Afrique et de Madagascar, 1949 à 1960, rétrospectif.* Paris, 1962.

————. Ministère des Travaux Publics et de Transports. "Mission d'étude des structures agraires dans le sud Dahomey," Paris, 1963. (Prepared by Jean Hurault and Jacques Jallet.)

France. Ministére de la Coopération. "Bénin: données statistiques sur les activités économiques." Paris, 1978.

————. Secrétariat du comité monétaire de la Zone Franc. *La Zone Franc en 1978.* Paris, 1979, 404 pp.

————. SEDES. "Le Développement de la pêche au Dahomey: Etude Socioéconomique." Paris, Nov. 1962.

Francophone West Africa: Business Opportunities. London: Metra Consulting Group Ltd., 1982.

Gaudemey, Sabin. "La Production et la commercialisation du maïs au Dahomey." Thesis, EPHE, 1974.

Gbégbékegbé, Patrice Dofonsou. "Perspectives de développement de l'économie dahoméenne face aux contraintes de la balance des paiements," M.Sc. Thesis, Laval University, 1974.

Gbégbo, C. et al. "La coopération économique entre la République populaire du Bénin et la République fédérale du Nigéria." Thesis, National University of Benin, 1981.

"Généralités économiques et mise en valeur," *Europe-Outre Mer*, no. 557–8, Sept. 1976, pp. 38–46.

Genné, M. "La voie paysanne de développement au Bénin," *Cultures et Développement*, no. 3, 1979, pp. 457–463.

Giesecke, J., and A. B. Simon. "Rénovation de la route Parakou Malanville," *Routes*, no. 509, May 1975, pp. 53–60.

Gomez, Charles. "Rural Dimension in regional development: the Beninois experience," in A. L. Mabogunje and A. Faniran (eds.), *Regional Planning and National Development in Tropical Africa*. Ibadan: Ibadan University Press, 1977, pp. 166–71.

Gosselin, G. "Traditional collectivism and modern associations: the example of southern Benin," in J. Nash, et al (eds.), *Popular Participation in Social Change*. The Hague: Mouton, 1976.

Grivot, R. "La Pêche chez les Pédah du lac Aheime," *Bulletin de l'Institut Français d'Afrique Noire*, 1949, pp. 106–128.

Guelly Cooni, Pierre Clavier. "Difficultés économiques du Dahomey: éléments et contributions au développement concerté de productions animales." Thesis, University of Toulouse, 1970.

Guendéhou, Macaire. "Le Deuxième Plan d'état (1983–1987) face à l'expérience du premier plan triennal (1977–1980)." Thesis, National University of Benin, 1984.

Guinard, A. "La Mise en valeur hydro-agricole du delta de l'Ouème," *Agronomie Tropicale*, vol. 12 (July–Aug. 1957), pp. 441–493.

Haubert, Maxime, Christiane Frelin and Nguyen Trong Nam Tran. *Politiques alimentaires et structures sociales en Afrique Noire.* Paris: Presses Universitaires de France, 1985.

Hetzel, Wolfgang, *Studien zur geographie des Handels in Togo und Dahomey.* Cologne, 1974.

Houdet, J. "Le projet d'extension du réseau de l'OCDN de Parakou à Dosso," *Industries et Travaux d'Outre Mer,* no. 163, June 1967, pp. 525–528.

Houndjahoue, Michel. "Aide alimentaire étrangère et force de travail au Bénin," *Le Mois en Afrique,* no. 223/4 (1984) pp. 146–151.

Hounso, Remy. "La compétivité du port de Cotonou comme axe de transit sous-régional." Thesis, National University of Benin, 1984.

Hounton, R. "L'OCBN, un outil de la coopération régionale." Ph.D. Thesis, University of Paris, 1977.

Hungbo, François. "Les cultures vivrières au Dahomey." Thesis, EHESS, 1975.

Hurault, Jean, and Jacques Vallet. *Mission d'étude des structures agraires dans le Sud Dahomey.* Paris: Institut Géographique Nationale, 1963.

Igué, John Pierre. "Organisation de l'espace agricole en pays tchabé." Thesis, University of Dakar, 1968.

Igué, Ogunsola John. "Un aspect des échanges entre le Dahomey et le Nigéria: le commerce du cacao," *Bulletin de l'Institut Français d'Afrique Noire,* vol. 38, no. 3, 1976.

————. ''Evolution du commerce clandestin entre le Dahomey et le Nigéria depuis la guerre du Biafra,'' *Canadian Journal of African Studies,* vol. 10, no. 2, pp. 235–257.

International Labour Office. *Jobs Skills programme for Africa.* Addis Ababa, 1982.

————. *La planification de la main-d'oeuvre.* Addis Ababa, 1985.

————. *Rapport au gouvernement de la République du Dahomey sur le développement de la coopération en milieu urbain.* Geneva, 1963.

————. *Rapport au gouvernement de la République sur la réglementation et l'administration de l'assurance-pensions.* Geneva, 1966.

————. *Rapport au gouvernement de la République du Dahomey sur l'emploi rural.* Geneva, 1970.

Iroko, Abiola Felix. ''Survivances du troc en République Populaire du Bénin dans le dernier quart du XXe siècle,'' *Le Mois en Afrique,* no. 223/4 (May–Sept. 1984), pp. 72–80, 97–108.

Janin, B. ''Le Nouveau port de Cotonou,'' *Revue de Géographie Alpine,* no. 52, 1964, pp. 701–712.

Kimpe, Paul de. ''Les Facteurs de production piscicole des lagunes de l'Est Dahomey et leur évolution récente,'' *Bois et Forêts Tropiques,* no. 111, Jan.–Feb. 1967, pp. 53–62.

Kingbo, Isaac. *La SONADER.* Abidjan: I.N.A.D.E.S., 1969.

Kirsch, Martin. "Le Dahomey posséde désormais un nouveau code de travail," *Industries et Travaux d'Outre-Mer*, no. 171 (Feb. 1968), pp. 119–121.

Kissenzounon, Vincent Cossi. "Benin: economic change and industrial prospects," *Industry Africa*, no. 6 (Sept. 1992), pp. 31–35.

Kouadio, F. "L'Adhésion du Benin à la Communauté économique de l'Afrique de l'Ouest et perspectives d'élargissement de la Communauté," *Le Mois en Afrique*, no. 237/8 (1985), pp. 66–80, 97–104.

Koudokpon, Valentin, Zacharie Martin et al. *Pour une recherche participative: stratégie et développement d'une approche de recherche avec les paysans au Bénin*, Amsterdam: KIT, 1992.

Kpodjédo Sossou, Mathias. "Aspirations paysannes, réalités villageoises de développement dans des coopératives de la région de Tori (Allada)." Thesis, EPHE, 1974.

Lachenmann, Gudrun. "Volksrepublik Benin: Schwierigkeitenvauf dem Wag zu einer eigenständigen Entwicklung," *Afrika Spectrum*, vol. 16, 1981, pp. 205–219.

Ladjonan, Mamadou Mouftaou. "Le palmier à huile dans l'économie dahoméenne." Thesis, EPEHE, 1974.

Laleye, O. M. "Urban local government finance in Benin: the case of Cotonou," *Public Administration and Development*, vol. 12, no. 1 (Feb. 1992), pp. 53–70.

Lamarche R. "Situation économique du Dahomey," *Colonies et Marine*, Jan. 1921, pp. 51–57.

492 / Bibliography

Latrémolière, Jacques. "Bénin: des économies parallèles," *Marchés Tropicaux et Mediterranéens,* May 1981, pp. 1225–1228.

Laurent, P. "Les Problèmes d'un pays sous-développé: le Dahomey," *Economie et Politique,* no. 125, Dec. 1964, pp. 99–114.

Lawson, I. M. "La République du Bénin dans la voie du développement socialiste," *Entente Africaine,* no. 33, Aug. 1978, pp. 12–17.

Leclerc, Michel. "Akpo, village de palmeraie porto-novienne." Thesis, University of Bordeaux, 1971.

Lelart, Michel. "L'épargne informelle en Afrique: les tontins béninois," *Tiers Monde,* no. 118 (Apr.–June 1989), pp. 271–298.

————. and S. Gnansounou. "Tontines et tontiniers sur les marchés Saint-Michel de Cotonou," in *African Review of Money, Finance and Banking,* no. 1 (1989), pp. 69–90.

Les 500 produits clés du marché africain. Paris: Ediafric, 1977.

Ligan-Paraiso, Gisèle. "LA SONADER, un instrument de promotion rurale," *Entente Africaine,* no. 1, July 15, 1969, pp. 57–63.

Loko, D. A., and W. Bankole. "Les échanges du Bénin avec les états Africains." Mémoire, National University of Benin, 1979.

Lombard, J. "Les Bases traditionnelles de l'économie rurale Bariba et ses fondements nouveaux," *Bulletin de l'Institut Français d'Afrique Noire,* vol. 23, no. 12 (Jan.–Apr. 1961).

Magnès, Bernard. "Les Champs collectifs au Dahomey," *Coopération et Développement,* no. 5, Mar.–Apr. 1965, pp. 44–51.

Manning, Patrick. "L'Affaire adjovi," in *Entreprises et entrepreneurs en Afrique.* Paris: Harmatton, 1983, pp. 241–67.

————. *Economic History of Dahomey.* New York: Praeger, 1978.

————. "An Economic History of South Dahomey 1880–1914." Thesis, University of Wisconsin, 1970.

————. "Public Finance and Capital Investment: A National Perspective on Colonial Dahomey," *Canadian Journal of African Studies,* vol. 14, no. 3, 1980, pp. 519–524.

————. *Slavery, Colonialism and Economic Growth in Dahomey 1840–1960.* Cambridge: Cambridge University Press, 1981.

————. "Slaves, Palm Oil and Political Power on the West African Coast," *African Historical Studies,* vol. 2, no. 2, 1969, pp. 279–288.

————. "The Technology of production in Southern Dahomey," *African Economic History,* no. 9, 1980, pp. 49–67.

"Le Marché dahoméen," *Marchés Tropicaux et Mediterranéens,* special issue, no. 1046 (Nov. 27, 1965).

Mensah, Moïse. "L'Expérience dahoméenne en matière de coopératives de production dans la cadre des périmètres d'aménagement rural," *Etudes Dahoméennes,* no. 6–7 (Apr. 1966).

————. "Problèmes du développement de l'agriculture dahoméenne," *Etudes Dahoméennes,* no. 1 (1963), pp. 59–78.

————. and Alfred C. Mondjannagni. *Contribution à l'étude des paysages végétaux du Bas-Dahomey.* Abidjan: Annales de l'Université d'Abidjan, 1970.

Mondjannagni, Alfred Comlan. *Campagnes et Villes au Sud de la République Populaire du Bénin.* The Hague: Mouton, 1977.

————. "Participation paysanne dans le cadre de la restructuration des compagnes du Sud-Bénin," in *La Participation populaire au développement en Afrique Noire,* Paris: Karthala, 1984.

Munier, P. *Mission d'étude technique et économique sur les cultures fruitières en République du Dahomey.* Paris: IFAC 1962.

Naigeon, Christophe. "La Pêche sur la côte ouest," *Afrique Agriculture,* no. 47, July 1979, pp. 22–48.

N'Bessa, Benoît D. *Akpakpa: quartier industriel de Cotonou.* Dakar: Université de Dakar, 1981.

Noukoumiantakin, Alexis. "Le contrat clé en main conclu au Bénin," *Revue Juridique et Politique,* vol. 42, 2/3 (Mar.– June 1988), pp. 177–184.

————. "Limite des pouvoirs des chefs d'entreprise: le cas du Bénin," *Revue Juridique et Politique,* vol. 43, no. 3/4 (1989), pp. 349–360.

Obermeier, Heinrich. *Dahomey als Wirtschaftpartner.* Cologne: Bundesstelle für Aussenhandelsinformation, 1967.

O'Connor, James. "A review of a pilot project for soybean promotion in Benin." M.S. Thesis, University of Illinois, 1984.

Office Statistique des Communautés Européennes. "Commerce Extérieur: République du Dahomey annuaire 1959–1966." Luxembourg, 1969.

Okou, Christophe. "Analyse des activités primaires et occupation du sol au sud-est du Bénin," Cotonou: SONAGIM, 1983.

————. "Genèse et évolution d'une spéculation nouvelle: les cultures maraichères dans la région de Cotonou-Porto Novo." Thesis, Strasbourg, 1982.

————. "Problèmes d'approvisionnement de Cotonou et de Porto Novo en produits maraichers et mauvaise gestion de l'espace périphérique," in Géographie humaine tropicale. Strasbourg: Association géographique d'Alsace, 1981.

Ologoudou, Emile. Intellectuels dans la nation. L'Examen de conscience d'un jeune Dahoméen. Cotonou: Editions du Bénin, 1967.

————. Introduction aux réalités économiques et sociales au Dahomey. Paris: Nouveau Bureau d'Edition, 1979.

Onodje, Kayossi. "Les coopératives agricoles et le développement économique du Dahomey." Thesis, University of Paris, 1973.

————. "L'Huile de palme dans l'économie dahoméenne." Thesis, University of Paris, 1970.

"Le Parrainage de l'Union Suisse des coopératives au Dahomey," Coopération, Oct. 1964, pp. 27–32.

Pécaud, A. L'Elevage et les animaux domestiques aux Dahomey. Gorée, Sénégal, 1912.

"La pêche maritime artisanale en République Populaire du Bénin: état actuel et perspective d'avenir." Dakar: E.N.D., 1984.

Pédrals, Dennis Pierre de. *Dans la brousse africaine au Dahomey-Bourgou*. Paris: La Nouvelle Edition, 1946.

Pelissier, Paul. "Les Pays du Bas Ouème, une région témoin du Dahomey méridional," *Cahiers d'Outre-Mer*, vol. 15, no. 59 (July–Sept. 1962), pp. 204–254.

Peter Jean. "Le Fonds Africain de Solidarité," *Revue Juridique et Politique*, no. 1, Jan.–Mar. 1977, pp. 30–42.

"Le port de Cotonou," *Europe-Outre Mer*, no. 566, March 1977, pp. 35–38.

"Le port de Cotonou," *Europe-Outre Mer*, no. 631, Aug. 1982, pp. 32–34.

Prévaudeau, Marie-Madeleine. *Narhi, femme de blanc, moeurs dahoméennes*. Paris, 1928.

"Les principales industries et les projets du Bénin," *Europe-Outre Mer*, no. 566, Mar. 1977, pp. 29–33.

Quénum, François-José. "Problèmes de mise en valeur agricole dans la région de Sakété-Pobé," in *Géographie humaine tropicale*. Strasbourg: Association géographique d'Alsace, 1981.

Quirino-Lanhoumey, Julien. "Le Développement communautaire en Afrique Noire: les 50 ans d'une expérience au Dahomey," *Politique Etrangère*, vol. 29, no. 2 (1964), pp. 161–189.

"Le Redressement dahoméen," special issue of *Europe-France-Outremer,* vol. 44, no. 453 (Oct. 1967), pp. 12–46.

République du Dahomey. Direction de la Statistique. *Cing Années de Commerce Extérieur du Dahomey 1961–1965.* Cotonou, Dec. 1969.

————. Ministère de l'Economie et du Plan. *Inventaire économique et social du Zou.* Cotonou, 1972.

————. Présidence de la République. Secrétariat Général au Plan. *Plan de développement économique et social 1966–1970.* Cotonou, 1966.

République Populaire du Bénin. Ministère du Plan. *Recensement des Entreprises.* Cotonou, 1981.

"La restructuration des entreprises publiques et semi-publiques," *Europe-Outre Mer,* no. 631, Aug. 1982, pp. 22–24.

Reste, G. *Le Dahomey, Réalisations et perspectives.* Paris: Comité de l'Afrique Française, 1934.

————. *La production pastorale et agricole au Dahomey.* Paris: Comité de l'Afrique Française, 1933.

Rivallain, Josette. "Le sel dans les villages côtiers et lagunaires du Bas Dahomey," *West Africa Journal of Archaelogy.* vol. 7, 1977, pp. 143–167.

Rocca, M. "Le Karité au Dahomey," *Chronique d'Outre Mer,* no. 44 (Apr 1958), pp. 13–17.

Rodary, Pierre. "L'Organisation Commune Dahomey-Niger des chemins de fer des transports," *Industries et Travaux d'Outre Mer,* no. 116, July 1963, pp. 634–638.

Russell, Sharon Stanton et al. *International Migration and Development in subsaharan Africa, vol 2: Country Analyses.* Washington, D.C.: World Bank, 1990.

Saliou, Mifoutaou, and K. Jean Tchougbé. "La coopération Bénino-Arabo Libyenne." Thesis, National University of Benin, 1982.

Samson, Didier. "L'Agriculture au Bénin," *Afrique Contemporaine,* no. 134, Apr.–June 1985, pp. 44–48.

Santos, R. "Du rôle de la monnaie et des échanges internationaux dans le processus de planification pour le développement au Dahomey." Thesis, University of Paris, 1973.

Sarlie, Joe Yanquoi. "The design of an agricultural credit system for small farm families in Benin." Thesis, University of Illinois, 1985.

Savariau, N. *L'Agriculture au Dahomey.* Paris: Challamel, 1906.

Schissel, Howard. "Getting in the oil act," *West Africa,* Feb. 7, 1983, pp. 317–318.

Schramm, J., and W. Kneper. *Die Sozio-ökonomische Stellung der Frau in Elfenbeinküste.* Fribourg: Institut für Soziale Zusammenarbeit, 1969.

"Séminaire international sur la réforme agro-foncière aux pays du Conseil de l'Entente, Lama Kara, Oct. 1978; Expérience de Bénin," *African Perspectives,* no. 1, 1979, pp. 27–43.

Sénou, Louise. "Problèmes de gestion dans les entreprises publiques et semi-publiques en Bénin." Thesis, National University of Benin, 1984.

Serreau, Jean. *Le Développement à la base au Dahomey et au Sénégal.* Paris: R. Pichon et R. Durand-Auzias, 1966.

Société Nationale pour le Développement Rural. "La SONADER et la gestion des palmeraies selectionnées et huileries," miméo, 1971.

Sociétés et fournisseurs d'Afrique Noire. Paris: Ediafric, 1983.

Sokal, R. "Une étude de micro-centrales hydroélectriques au Togo et au Bénin," *Académie Royale des Sciences d'Outremer,* vol. 32, no. 3 (1986), pp. 479–497.

Sory, Sinda. "Les groupements villageois et leurs problèmes dans l'Atakora (Dahomey)." Thesis, EPHE, 1974.

"Tableau économique du Bénin," *Bulletin d'Afrique Noire,* no. 1283, August 1, 1985, pp. 4–13.

Tardits, Claudine and Claude. "Traditional Market economy in South Dahomey," in Paul Bohannan and George Dalton (eds.), *Markets in Africa.* Evanston: Northwestern University Press, 1962, pp. 89–102.

Tchaboné, Yacoubou. "Formation Technique et développement économique: L'exemple du Dahomey." Thesis, University of Toulouse, 1970.

Tomagnimena Gbodja, Pierre. "Contribution à l'étude du développement et des perspectives de l'agriculture au Dahomey." Toulouse: Imprimerie Toulousaine, 1969.

Tossou, A. "Développement du palmier à huile au Dahomey— Rentabilité des palmeraies modernes." Thesis, University of Paris, 1968.

Vallet, Jacques. *Région du grand Hinvi: étude de géographie agraire, rapport de synthèse.* Paris: Institut geographique, 1968.

Vanbercie, R. "Avenir de la culture du tabac au Dahomey," *Agronomie Tropicale,* no. 11, Nov. 1963, pp. 1105–1119.

Varissou, Salon Dini. "Coopératives d'aménagement rural au Dahomey." Thesis, University of Paris, 1970.

Verschuren, J, et al. "Conservation in Benin, with the help of the European Economic Community," *Oryx* vol. 23, no. 1 (1989), pp. 22–26.

Wartena, Dorothéa. "Comme le monde évolue . . ." une historie agronomique du plateau d'Aplahoué, Bénin, 1894–1986." Mémoire, Wageningen Agricultural University, 1988.

Zekpa, Laurent R. "Benin: a long-tradition of tradeswomen," *Entente Africaine,* July 1979, pp. 40–43.

————. and Antoine Dossou. "Impact du contre-choc pétrolier au Nigéria sur l'économie béninoise," *Tivers Monde,* vol. 30, no. 120 (1989), pp. 893–905.

La Zone Franc et l'Afrique. Paris: Ediafric, 1981.

7. EDUCATION

Adamou, A. "Enseignement, formation professionnelle et évolution économique du Dahomey." Thesis, University of Paris, 1973.

Adejunmobi, S. A. "Problems of Education in Dahomey—A Nigerian View," *Journal of Negro Education,* Vol. 45, no. 3, Summer 1976, pp. 275–283.

Adjalla, Adrien, "Stratégie de l'éducation pour un développement endogène," UNESCO, 1982.

Agboton, Gaston. *Le citoyen dans la nation.* Cotonou: Editions Silva, 1968 [civics textbook].

———. *Le Citoyen et le Gouvernement.* Cotonou: Editions A.B., 1968 [civics textbook].

Allassounouma, Boumbera. "La reconversion des mentalités et les problèmes de l'unité nationale," *Etudes Togolaises,* no. 15–18, Dec. 18, 1976, pp. 7–15.

Asiwaju, A.I. "The Colonial Education Heritage and the problem of Nation-Building in Dahomey," *Bulletin de l'Institut Français d'Afrique Noire,* 1975, vol. 37, no. 2, pp. 340–357.

Auroi, C. "L'alphabétisation rurale au nord Bénin: la fin de l'exploitation commerciale des paysans," *Genève-Afrique,* vol. 16, no. 1, 1977/8, pp. 92–108.

Beynel, Jean. "De la Réglementation au Dahomey, de l'exercice des professions," *Revue Juridique et Politique,* no. 1 (Jan.–Mar. 1973), pp. 179–198.

Bohr, Elsie. "Implantation de l'institution scolaire dans l'ancienne colonie du Dahomey: les écoles des missions chrétiennes 1843–1923. Histoire, pédagogie, société." Thesis, University of Strasbourg, 1982.

Bouche, Denise. *L'Enseignement dans les territoires française de l'Afrique occidentale de 1817 à 1920.* 2 vols. Lille, 1975.

Codo, C. B. "L'Enseignement au Dahomey entre les deux guerres." Thesis, University of Paris, 1973.

Coureau, Jean Claude. "Planification de l'éducation et de l'enseignement en pays sous-développé." Thesis, EPHE, 1973.

"Dahomey," in Helen Kitchen (ed.), *The Educated African*. New York: Praeger, 1962, pp. 474–478.

"Dahomey," in Sasnett, Martena and Inez Sepmeyer, *Educational systems in Africa*. Berkeley: University of California Press, 1967, pp. 639–648.

Da Silveira, Yvonne I., and Josiane F. Hamers. "Scolarisation et bilingualité en contexte africain: Un défi?" *Language et Société*, vol. 52 (June 1990), pp. 23–58.

Djrekpo, C., and Johanes A. Toudonou. "La formation des magistrats au Bénin," *Afrique Contemporaine*, no. 156 (1990), pp. 135–139.

Dogbeh, Richard. "Les difficultés intellectuelles du Noir," *Etudes Dahoméennes*, no. 1 (1963), pp. 101–104.

———. "Les grandes lignes de la scolarisation au Dahomey," *Afrique*, April 1967, pp. 15–17.

———. *Voix d'Afrique*. Paris: Istra, 1962.

L'enfance et la jeunesse dans le développement national du Dahomey. Paris: S.E.D.E.S., 1966.

Farine, Avigdor. "The development of education in three francophone countries." Ph.D. Thesis, University of Pittsburgh, 1968.

Flator, Joan Adele. "Problems in the restructure of education to meet economic needs in Dahomey." Ed.D. Thesis, Columbia University Teachers College, 1975.

France. Ministère de la Coopération. Société d'Etudes pour le Développement Economique et Social. *Education et développement au Dahomey.* 3 vols. Paris, 1962.

Gandaho, P. "La formation des professionnels de l'information documentaire: l'expérience béninoise," *Afrique Contemporaine,* no. 151 (1989), pp. 217–223.

Garcia, Luc. "L'organization de l'instruction publique au Dahomey 1894–1920," *Cahiers d'Etudes Africaines,* vol. 11, no. 41, 1971, pp. 59–100.

Gbaguidi, Nestor. "Education et emploi au Dahomey." Thesis, EPHE, 1973.

Gomez, M.R.E. *Le Livre béninois à la 40e Foire de Francfort,* Cotonou: Nouvelles Messageries du Bénin, 1988.

Guézodjé, Vincent. "Educational Reform in Benin," *Prospects: Quarterly Review of Education,* vol. 7, no. 4, 1977, pp. 455–471.

Guilhem, Marcel, and Joel Daffa. *Dahomey: Récits Historiques.* Paris: Ligel, 1964 [textbook].

Housson, Moise. "L'Enseignement et la formation en Afrique francophone de l'Ouest; L'expérience dahoméenne depuis 1960." Thesis, University of Paris, 1970.

———. "Les problèmes psycho-pédagogiques de l'enseignement du français au Dahomey." Thesis, University of Paris, 1970, 2 vols.

International Labour Office. *Rapport sur l'éducation ouvière à la République du Dahomey.* Geneva, 1963.

Kordes, Hagen. "Curriculum Evaluation Concerning Dependent Societies: The Contradictory Experiment of Ruralized Primary Education in Dahomey and Its Evaluation," *Studies in Educational Evaluation,* vol. 3, no. 2, Summer 1977, pp. 77–86.

Kuenstler, P. *Politiques et problèmes concernant la jeunesse: rapport sur une visite au Dahomey du 31 Octobre au 8 novembre 1965.* New York: United Nations, March 29, 1966.

Lanhounney, J. Quirino. "La Planification de l'éducation au Dahomey," *Tiers Monde,* vol. 6, no. 22 (Apr.–June 1965), pp. 405–429.

Lawson, Raphael. "Intervention éducative et utilisation des médias au Bénin: Borgou," Thesis, University of Paris, 1989.

Midiohouan, G. O. "Le programme des études de Lettres Modernes à l'Université du Bénin," *Peuples Noirs—Peuples Africains,* vol. 9, no. 52 (1986), pp. 41–55.

Nekpo, Célestin. "Problèmes institutionnels et politiques de l'école au Dahomey (période coloniale et post-coloniale)." Thesis, Sorbonne, 1976.

Ologoudou, Emile. "L'Education-Consommation au Dahomey," *Terre Entière,* no. 29–30 (May–Aug. 1968), pp. 71–90.

Pliya, Jean. "The fundamental reform of education in Benin," in *Educational Reform and Innovations in Africa.* Paris: UNESCO 1978, pp. 31–37.

———. *Histoire du Dahomey.* Porto Novo: Imprimerie Nationale de Porto Novo, 1967 [textbook].

Ramin, J. C., V. Koubeff and M. Guilhem. *Histoire du Dahomey.* Paris: Ligel, 1964 [textbook].

Sims, B. J. "The ruralization of primary school education in Dahomey." Thesis, Columbia University Teachers College, 1975.

Sossou, Benoit. "Analyse coût-efficacité de la production scolaire: le cas de Bénin," Thesis, University of Dijon, 1988.

Tardits, M. Claude. "Réflexions sur le problème de la scolarisation des filles au Dahomey," *Cahiers d'Etudes Africaines,* vol. 3, no. 10 (1962), pp. 266–281.

Tossou, Lucien. "Structures agraires et développement: le cas de la région Sud du Dahomey." Thesis, University of Grenoble, 1972.

8. SCIENTIFIC STUDIES

Adjanohoun, E. J., V. Ajakidjé and M. R. Ahyi. *Contribution aux études ethnobotaniques et floristiques en République populaire du Bénin.* Paris: Agence de Coopération culturelle et technique, 1989.

Aicard, Pierre. "Le précambrien du Togo et du nord-ouest du Dahomey: Etude géologique et pétrographique." Thesis, University of Nancy, 1953.

Antheaume, Benoît. "La Palmeraie du Mono: approche géographique." *Cahiers d'Etudes Africaines,* vol. XII, no. 3 (1972), pp. 458–485.

Assani Skoda, Marie-Noëlle. "Contribution à l'étude de l'état sanitaire du Dahomey." Thesis, University of Marseille, 1968.

Assogba, Dossa Honoré. *La dermatophilose.* Paris: Agence de coopération culturelle et technique, 1979.

Assogba, Marc Napoléon. *Contribution à l'étude de la couverture des besoins en protéine d'origine animale.* Paris: Agence de coopération culturelle et technique, 1979.

Aubreville, A. "Les Forêts du Togo et du Dahomey," *Bulletin du Comité d'Etudes Historiques et Scientifiques de l'A.O.F.,* vol. 20, no. 1–2 (Jan.–June 1937), pp. 1–112.

Baudin, P. "Pathologie de la canne à sucre au Dahomey et Togo," *L'Agronomie Tropicale,* no. 8–9, Aug.–Sept. 1964, pp. 747–755.

Béneyton, A.M.J. "Les chemins de fer du Dahomey et du Togo: 1922–3," *Géographie,* vol. 45, no. 1/2, Jan.–Feb. 1926.

———. "Hydrologie et hydrographie de l'estuaire de l'Ouémé," *Géographie,* vol. 44, no. 4/5, Nov.–Dec. 1925.

Biondi, G., et al. "Distribution of S and C hemoglobins in Atakora district," *Human Biology,* vol. 52, no. 2, May 1980, pp. 205–213.

Boko, Michel. "Climat et communautés rurales du Bénin: rhythmes climatiques." Ph.D. Thesis, University of Dijon, 1988.

———. "La plaine côtière du Dahomey à l'ouest du Nokoué." Thesis. Dijon University, 1973.

Bradiké, Jean. "Etude géographique sur le Bas Dahomey." Thesis, University of Montpellier, 1971.

Brand, Roger. *Plantes médicinales en usage chez les Gun.* Cotonou: ABM, 1972.

Brasseur, G. "Réflexions nouvelles sur la palmeraie de Porto Novo," *Annales de la Faculté des Lettres* (Dakar), vol. 1, 1972, pp. 197–255.

Braumoulle, Adrien. *Les problèmes de la pêche en lagune.* Porto Novo: Institut Français d'Afrique Noire, 1959.

————. and P. M. Brasseur. *Porto Novo et al palmeraie.* Dakar: Institut Français d'Afrique Noire, 1954.

Chraibi, Larbi. "Essai de géographie médicale du Bas Dahomey." Thesis, University of Montpellier, 1951.

Daget, J. "Poissons d'eau douce de la région côtière du Togo et du Dahomey," *Notes Africaines,* no. 46, April 1950.

Dozon, J. P. "Ce que valoriser la médicine traditionnelle veut dire," *Politique Africaine,* no. 28 (1987), pp. 9–20.

Drot. "Notes sur le haut Dahomey," *Géographie,* vol. 10 (1904), pp. 267–286.

Dubroecq, D. Carte pédologique de reconnaissance de la République Populaire du Bénin." Paris: ORSTOM, 1977.

Faure, P. "Cartes pédologiques." Paris: ORSTROM, 1977.

Fishpool, L. D. C., and G. P. Popov. "The grasshopper faunas of the savannahs of Mali, Niger, Benin and Togo," *Bulletin d'Institut Français d'Afrique Noire,* vol. 43, no. 3/4 (1981).

France. Ministère de la Coopération. *Etude Monographique de trente et un pays africains,* 4 vols. Paris, 1965.

————. ————. "Rapport de mission au Dahomey," Paris, 1961.

————. Ministère de la Coopération pour le Développement. Société d'Etudes. *Enquête démographique au Dahomey 1961, Résultats définitifs.* Paris, 1964.

————. Secrétariat d'Etat aux Affaires Etrangères. *Nature et Chasse au Dahomey.* Paris, 1969.

Gaillard, Charles Etienne. "Le Lac Nokoué," *Géographie,* vol. 17 (1908), pp. 281–284.

Galan, P. et al. "Iron absorption from typical West African meals containing Fe," *British Journal of Nutrition,* vol. 64, no. 2 (1990), pp. 541–546.

Gayibor, Nicoue Lodjou. "Ecologie et histoire: les origines de la savane de Bénin," *Cahiers d'Etudes Africaines,* vol. 26, no. 1/2 (1986), pp. 13–42.

Grubben, G. "L'Amarante et sa culture au Dahomey," *Agronomie Tropicale,* no. 1, Jan. 1974, pp. 97–100.

————. "The cultivation of Amaranath as a tropical leaf vegetable." Amsterdam: Royal Tropical Institute, Department of Agricultural Research, 1976.

Guilcher, André. "La Région côtière du Bas-Dahomey occidentale: étude de géographie physique et humaine appliquée," *Bulletin de l'Institut Français d'Afrique Noire,* vol. 21, no. 3–4 (July–Oct. 1959), pp. 357–418.

Hasle, H. "Les cultures vivrières au Dahomey," *Agronomie Tropicale,* no. 8, Aug. 1965, pp. 725–746.

Hazoumé, Félix Adjai. "Préliminaire d'une étude longitudinale de la croissance et du développement de l'enfant au Dahomey." Thesis, Sorbonne, 1969.

Herschberg, S. et al. "Evaluation of the iron status of a rural population in south Benin," *Nutrition Research,* vol. 6, no. 6 (1986), pp. 627–634.

―――. "Nutritional anaemia in pregnant Beninese women: consequences on the haematological profile of the newborn," *British Journal of Nutrition,* vol. 57, no. 2 (1987), pp. 185–193.

―――. "Prévalence de l'anémie ferriprive dans un district rural du Sud-Bénin," in D. Lemonnier and Y. Ingenbleek (eds.), *Les malnutritiations dans les pays du Tiers Monde.* Paris: INSERM, 1986.

―――. "Prevalence of iron deficiency and iron deficiency anaemia in Benin," *Public Health,* vol. 102, no. 1 (1988), pp. 73–83.

Heywood, Arthur. "Primary care in the Atacora, Benin." *KIT: Bulletin of the Royal Tropical Institute* (Amsterdam), 1991.

Hostern, Joseph. "Le paysan et la terre au Dahomey." Thesis, University of Paris, 1973.

Hubert, Henry. "La 'Barre' au Dahomey," *Annales de Géographie,* vol. 17 (1908), pp. 97–104.

―――. *Mission Scientifique au Dahomey.* Paris: Larose, 1908.

Journaux, A. "Contribution à l'étude de la géographie physique du Dahomey," Thesis, University of Paris, 1968.

Kimpé, Paul de. "Les facteurs de production piscicole des lagunes de l'Est Dahomey et leur évolution récente," *Bois et Forêts des Tropiques,* no. 111, Jan.–Feb. 1967, pp. 53–62.

Lachenmann, Gudrun. "Bedingungen einer partizipatorischen Gesundheitspolitik: das Beispiel der Dorfgesundheitsarbeiter in der Volksrepublik Benin," *Grundbedürfnisorientierte ländliche Entwicklung.* Berlin: Deutsches Institut für Entwicklungspolitik, 1980, pp. 115–154.

Lang, J. et al. "Le domaine margino-littoral du Bénin," *Journal of African Earth Sciences,* vol. 7, no. 5/6 (1988), pp. 829–834.

Maslin, J. "The salinity tolerance of Corbula trigona from a West African lagoon and its variations." *Archiv für Hydrobiologie,* vol. 117, no. 2 (1989), pp. 205–223.

Mauny, R. "Tableau géographique de l'Ouest africain au Moyen Age, d'après les sources écrites; la tradition et l'archéologie," *Mémoires de l'Institut Français d'Afrique Noire,* vol. 61 (1961).

Mondjannagni, Alfred Comlan. *Campagnes et villes au Sud de la République Populaire du Bénin.* The Hague: Mouton, 1977.

Muelder, K., and A. Nourou. "Buruli ulcer in Benin," *The Lancet,* no. 8723 (1990), pp. 1109–1111.

Okkioh, O. "Recherches sur les dômes cristallines dans le Dahomey central." Thesis, University of Paris, 1972.

Oyédé, L. M. et al. "Un exemple de sédimentation: le lac Ahémé," *Journal of African Earth Sciences,* vol. 7, no. 5/6 (1988), pp. 835–872.

Pécaud, Georges. "L'élevage et les animaux domestiques au Dahomey." Thesis, University of Paris, 1927.

Pelissier, Paul. "Les pays du Bas Ouémé." Thesis, University of Dakar, 1963.

Pliya, Jean. *La pêche dans le sud-ouest du Bénin.* Paris: Agence de coopération culturelle et technique, 1980.

Pougnet, Robert. *Le pré-cambrien du Dahomey.* Dakar: Grande Imprimerie Africaine, 1957.

Poujade, R. "Les huileries de palme en Afrique," *Oléagineux,* no. 11, Nov. 1974, pp. 521–524.

————. "Le traîtement rationnel des régimes de palmier à huile au Dahomey," *Oléagineux,* July 1963, pp. 499–501.

Profizi, J. P. "Swampy area transformations by exploitation of Raphia hookeri in Southern Benin," *Human Ecology,* vol. 16, no. 1 (1988), pp. 87–94.

Rancoule, A. "Notices sur la culture et l'exploitation du palmier à huile au Dahomey." Porto Novo, Imprimerie du Gouvernement, 1934.

Raunet, M. "Contribution à l'étude pédo-agronomique des 'terres de barre' du Dahomey et du Togo," *Agronomie Tropicale,* no. 11, Nov. 1973, pp. 1049–1069.

Reynaud, Jean, and Guy Georgy. "Nature et Chasse au Dahomey." Paris: Secrétariat d'Etat aux Affaires Etrangères, 1969.

Rivallain, Josette. "Le sel dans les villages côtiers et lagunaires du Bas-Dahomey," *Annales de l'Université d'Abidjan,* vol. 8, 1980, pp. 79–127.

Sargent, Carolyn Fishel. *The Cultural Context of Therapeutic Choice: The Bariba of Benin.* Dordrecht: D. Reidel, 1982.

———. "Factors influencing women's choices of obstetrical care in a northern district in the People's Republic of Benin," PhD. Thesis, Michigan State University, 1979.

———. *Maternity, medicine, and power: reproductive decisions in urban Benin.* Berkeley: University of California Press, 1989.

———. "Obstetrical choice among urban women in Benin," *Social Science and Medicine* (Oxford), vol. 20, no. 3 (1985), pp. 287–292.

———. "Prospects for the professionalization of indigenous midwifery in Benin," in M. Last and G. L. Chavunduka (eds.), *The Professionalization of African Medicine.* Manchester: Manchester University Press, 1986.

Sireyjol, Pierre. "Transit littoral et conception des ports: Cotonou," *Bulletin du Comité d'Etudes d'Outre Mer,* no. 27, 1977, pp. 3–27.

Slansky, Maurice. "Contribution à l'étude géologique du bassin sédimentaire côtier du Dahomey et du Togo." Thesis, University of Nancy, 1959. Also, Paris, Editions Techniques, 1963.

Szmigielski, Basile. "Histoire médicale de la campagne du Dahomey en 1892." Thesis, University of Paris, 1897.

Viennot, M. *Carte pédologique de Kandi et Bimbéréké.* 2 vols. Paris: ORSTOM, 1978.

Volkoff, B., and P. Willaime. *Feuille de Porto Novo et d'Abomey.* 2 vols. Paris: ORSTOM, 1976.

White, H. P. "Dahomey—the Geographical Basis of an African State," *Tijdschrift voor economische en sociale Geografie,* vol. 57, no. 2 (Mar.–Apr. 1966), pp. 61–67.

Zinzindohoué, Stanislas C. "Contraception et avortement: étude psycho-sociologique d'information et d'attitudes en Afrique Noire, enquête au Dahomey." Thesis, University of Bordeaux, 1970.

Zon, A. P. M. van der. "Les légumes-feuilles spontanés et cultivés du Sud-Dahomey." Amsterdam: Royal Tropical Institute, Department of Agricultural Research, 1976.

9. RELIGION

Adediran, Biodun. "The Ketu Mission 1853–1859: An abortive experiment by the CSM in Western Yorubaland," *Journal des Africanistes,* vol. 56 no. 1 (1986), pp. 89–104.

Adoukonou, Barthélémy. *Jalons pour une théologie africaine: essai d'une herméneutique chrétienne du Vodun dahoméen.* Paris: Lethielleux, 1980.

———. "Syncrétism dans le Elaja et le Faéxi à Cotonou." Thesis, University of Paris, 1973.

Agossou, Jacob-Médéwalé. *L'Homme et le Dieu créateur selon les sud dahoméens.* Paris: Editions Beauchasme, 1972.

Aguessy, Honorat. "Convergences religieuses dans les sociétés aja, éwé et yoruba sur la côte du Bénin," in François de Medeiro, *Peuples du Golfe du Benin.* Paris: Karthala, 1984.

———. "Essai sur le mythe de Legba." Thesis, University of Paris, 1974.

Alapini, Julien. *Les Initiés.* Paris: Aubanel, 1953.

———. *Les noix sacrées, études complètes de Fa-Ahidégoun.* Monte Carlo: Ed. Regain, 1950.

Alladayé, Jérôme C. "Les missionnaires catholiques au Dahomey à l'époque coloniale." Thesis, University of Paris, 1978.

Allégret, A. *Les idées religieuses des Fons.* Paris: Leroux, 1929.

André, P. J. L'Islam Noire: Contribution à l'Etudes des confréries religieuses Islamiques en Afrique Occidentale, suivie d'une étude sur l'Islam au Dahomey. Paris: Paul Geuthner, 1924.

Aupiais, Francis. "Le cérémonialisme religieux au Dahomey." *Compte Rendu du XVe Congrès International d'Anthropologie et d'Archéologie Préhistorique.* Paris, 1933, pp. 776–880.

———. "Cérémonies fétichistes dites Ahuandido de Bohicon," *Anthropos,* vol. 21, no. 1, Mar. 1936, pp. 239–241.

———. "La lumière qui luit dans les ténèbres: aspirations religieuses des non-civilisés dans les missions catholiques et l'oeuvre de civilisation," in *Conférence donnée à l'Istitut Catholique de Paris.* Paris: Bloud et Gay, 1929, pp. 37–66.

Ayivi, E. "Joint Apostolic Action in Dahomey," *International Review of Missions,* April 1972, pp. 144–149.

Azam, P. "L'Islam au Dahomey-Togo," *L'Afrique et l'Asie,* 1948.

Bach, Marcus. *Voudou; Religion, sorcellerie, magie.* Paris: Librairie Hachette, 1955.

Bamumba, Y. K., and Barthelemy Adoukonou. *La Mort dans la vie africaine.* Paris: Présence Africaine, 1979.

Barbé, Richard. "Magie au Bénin," *Revue de Paris,* vol. 56, Apr. 1949, pp. 127–139.

Bastide, Roger. "Réflexions sans titre autour d'une des formes de la spiritualité africaine. Polythéisme des Nigériens ou Dahoméens," *Présence Africaine,* no. 17–18 (Feb.–May 1958), pp. 9–15.

———. *Les Religions africaines du Brésil.* Paris: Presses Universitaires de France, 1960.

Baudin, Noël. *Fétichisme et féticheurs.* Lyons: Séminaire des missions africaines, 1884.

Bertho, Jacques. "La science du destin au Dahomey," *Africa,* vol. 9, no. 3 (July 1936), pp. 359–373.

Bonfils, Jean. "La mission catholique en République populaire du Bénin aux XVIIéme et XVIIIème siècles," *Neue Zeitchrift für Missionswissenschaft* (Immensee), vol. 42, no. 3 (1986), pp. 161–174.

Boucher, R. *A travers les Missions du Togo et du Dahomey.* Paris: Librairie P. Téqui, 1926.

Brand, R. "Dynamisme des symboles dans les cultes Vodun au sud Dahomey." Thesis, University of Paris, 1973.

———. "Initiation et consécration de deux voduns dans les cultes vodun." *Journal de la Société des Africanistes,* vol. 44, no. 1, 1974, pp. 71–91.

———. *Population Dynamics of Persons Practicing Vodun in Southern Dahomey.* Washington, D.C.: Smithsonian Institution, 1975.

Cadieu, A. "Au pays des Adja," *Echo des Missions Africaines de Lyon,* 1952, pp. 86–89; June 1953, pp. 60–63.

———. "Débuts d'une jeune mission," *Echo des Missions Africaines de Lyon,* July–Aug. 1954, pp. 71–81.

Castanchoa, J. B. "Telle était notre tendresse pour vous: le Père Aupiais (1877–1945)," *Spiritus,* no. 26 (Feb. 7, 1966), pp. 21–30.

Chazal, Maxime. "Peines et joies d'un missionnaire constructeur." *Echo des Missions Africaines de Lyon,* Mar. 1952, pp. 20–23.

Chesi, Gert. *Voudou.* Paris: Arthaud 1980.

Chopard, R. "Dahomey Interdit," *Echo des Missions Africaines de Lyon,* no. 6, 1958, pp. 127–129.

———. "Mosque et cathédrale," *Echo des Missions Africaines de Lyon,* no. 1, 1958, pp. 11–41.

———. "Nord Dahomey," *Echo des Missions Africaines de Lyon,* 1960, pp. 12–15.

Chopard-Lallier, Robert. *Chrétiens du Nord Dahomey.* Lome: Imprimerie Ecole Professionnelle, 1963.

Codjo, Denis Dohou. "La Mort, sa conception, les cérémonies chez les Fons et le Yoroubas de Ouidah," *Africa: Revista de Centro de Estudos Africanos* (Saô Paolo), vol. 2, 1979, p. 13–44.

Comhaire-Sylvain, Jean. "Survivances africaines dans le vocabulaire religieux d'Haiti," *Etudes Dahomeennes,* no. 14, 1954.

Comlan, William. "Des moyens d'evangélisations aux projets de développement." Thesis, University of Paris, 1989.

Covi, Mensah. "Le culte des fétiches dans la région de Zangnanado," *Bulletin de l'Enseignement en AOF,* no. 85, Jan.–Mar. 1934, pp. 9–23.

Da Silva, Guillaume. "Le mythe du Fa et ses dérivés patronymiques," *Etudes Dahoméennes,* no. 1 (1963), pp. 115–124.

―――. "Les rites funéraires et l'expression de la mort au Bas Dahomey: Fon-Mahi-Agowmou, Gunnet Nago." Thesis, University of Paris, 1971.

Describes, Abbé. *L'Evangile au Dahomey—Missions de Lyon.* Lyon: Missions Africaines.

Desmangles, Leslie G. "African Interpretations of the Christian Cross in Vodun," *Sociological Analysis,* vol. 38, no. 1, 1977, pp. 13–24.

Ellingworth, P. "Christianity and Politics in Dahomey 1843–1867," *Journal of African History,* vol. 5, no. 2 (1964), pp. 209–220.

―――. "Methodism on the Slave Coast; 1842–1870," *Society for African Church History Bulletin,* vol. 2, no. 3 (1967), pp. 239–248.

Etienne, Abel. *Le Père Dorgère, ancien missionnaire au Dahomey, récit et souvenirs: conquête du Dahomey.* Toulon, 1909.

Falcon, Paul. "Religion du Vodun." *Etudes dahoméennes,* no. 20, 1970.

Faroud, A. "Sur les routes du haut Dahomey," *Echo des Missions Africaines de Lyon,* Dec . 1953, pp. 117–120.

Farrant, François. "Essai d'ethnologie religieuse à Savalou." Thesis, University of Paris, 1968.

Favier, A. "Mgr. Parisot," *Echo des Missions Africaines de Lyon,* no. 1, 1960, pp. 6–12.

Gaudron, Pierre. "Dan-Homé, 1952, l'évolution du fétiche." Paris: CHEAM Report, No. 2097 (Dec. 1952).

————. "Dan-Homé, 1952, pays du fétiche." Paris: CHEAM Report, no. 2096 (Dec. 1952).

Gordon, Jacob. "Yoruba Cosmology and Culture in Brazil: A Study of African Survivals in the 'New World,' " *Journal of Black Studies,* vol. 10, no. 2, Dec. 1979, pp. 231–244.

Guilcher, René F. *Au Dahomey avec le Père Dorgère: l'activité pacificatrice d'un missionnaire.* Lyon: Missions Africaines, 1902.

Hardy, Georges. *Un apôtre d'aujourdhui: le Révérand Père Aupiais, Provincial des Missions Africaines de Lyon.* Paris: Larose, 1949.

Hazoumé, Paul. "L'Ame du Dahomeén animiste révélée par sa religion," *Présence Africaine,* no. 14–15 (June–Sept. 1957), pp. 243–251.

————. "Braves et chers catéchistes," *Echo des Missions Africaines de Lyon,* 1953, pp. 50–53.

————. *Cinquante Ans d'Apostolat.* Lyon: Procuré des Missions Africaines, 1937.

————. "Jours de Soleil," *Echo des Missions Africaines de Lyon,* Apr.–May 1953, pp. 37–39.

————. "Le Père Dorgère," *Echo des Missions Africaines de Lyon,* no. 31, 1956, pp. 49–52.

————. "Physionomie d'une histoire Yétoupo," *Echo des Missions Africaines de Lyon,* Apr.–May 1951, pp. 44–48.

————. "La première pierre du collège 'Père Aupiais' à Cotonou," *Echo des Missions Africaines de Lyon,* Sept.–Oct. 1950, pp. 10–15.

————. "Routes et pistes," *Echo des Missions Africaines de Lyon.* July–Aug. 1952, pp. 75–79.

Hazoumé, Roger A. "Ethnocide et religions traditionnelles au Dahomey." Thesis, University of Paris, 1975.

Herskovits, Melville J., and Frances S. Herskovits. *An Outline of Dahomean Religious Beliefs.* New Haven: Memoirs of the American Anthropological Association, no. 41, 1933.

Houénassou-Houangbé, L., Kayissan Dravie and Claude Rivière. "Les gestionnaires du monde: vodun et tro chez les Evhé du Togo," *Etudes Togolaises,* no. 15–18, Dec. 1981, pp. 49–101.

Hounwanou, Remy T. *Le Fa, une géomancie divinatoire du golfe du Bénin.* Dakar: Nouvelles Editions Africaines, 1984.

Huber, Hugo. "L'existence humaine en face du monde sacré; rites domestiques chez les Nyondé du Dahomey," *Anthropos,* vol. 68, no. 3–4 (1973), pp. 377–441.

Igwe, E. "Thomas Birch Freeman: Pioneer Methodist Mission to Nigeria," *Nigeria Magazine*, no. 77 (June 1963), pp. 79–89.

Izevbigie, Alfred Omokaro. "Olokun: A Focal Symbol of Religion and Art in Benin." Thesis, University of Washington, 1978.

Khane, I. "Au pays des Orisha et des Vodun," *Afrique en Marche*, no. 12–13, Jan.–Mar. 1958, pp. 12–16; no. 14, Mar.–Apr. 1958, pp. 10–13; no. 17, Aug.–Sept. 1958, pp. 10–13.

Kiti, Gabriel. "Consécration à un fétiche," *Anthropos*, vol. 32, 1937, pp. 283–287.

———. "Sagesse dahoméenne," *Etudes Dahoméennes*, no. 11 (1968), pp. 5–72.

Kossou, Basile. "Sê et Gbé: dynamisme de l'existence chez les Fons." Thesis, University of Paris, 1971. Also, published by Pensée Universelle, Paris, 1983.

Labouret, Henri, and Paul Rivet. *Le royaume d'Arda et son évangélisation au 17e siècle*. Paris: Institut d'Ethnologie, 1929.

Laffitte, M. *Le Dahomé: souvenirs de voyage et de mission*. Tours: A. Mame, 1876.

Laléyé, Issiaka Prosper. *La Conception de la personne dans la Pensée traditionnelle Somba: Approche phénoménologigue*. Paris: Herbert Lang, 1970.

———. *Pour une anthropologie repensée Ori Onisha ou la personne comme histoire*. Paris: La Pensée Universelle, 1977.

————. ''Du rite au mythe et du mythe au rite: une phénoménologie de la transcendance—contribution à une approche non-positiviste du sacré dans les religions africaines traditionnelles,'' *Cahiers des religions Africaines,* vol. 20/21, no. 39/42 (1986/87), pp. 29–47.

Lucas, J. Olumide. *The Religion of the Yorubas.* Lagos, 1948.

Lucien, F. ''A propos du culte des anciens,'' *Bulletin d'Enseignement Supérier du Bénin,* no. 8, Jan. 1967, pp. 63–87.

McClelland, E. M. *The Cult of the Ifa among the Yoruba.* London: Ethnographica, 1982.

Maiwald, Jurgen. *Nach herrschen Fetisch und Phantom.* Erlangen: Verlag der Evangelisch Lutheran Mission, 1971.

Marty, Paul. ''Etudes sur l'Islam au Dahomey,'' *Bulletin du Comité d'Etudes Historiques et Scientifiques,* vol. 6 (1928).

————. *Etudes sur l'Islam au Dahomey: le Bas Dahomey; le Haut Dahomey.* Paris: Ernest Leroux, 1926.

Maupoil, Bernard. ''Contributions à l'étude de l'origine musulmane de la géomancie dans le Bas-Dahomey,'' *Journal de la Société des Africanistes,* vol. 13 (1943).

————. *La Géomancie à l'ancienne côte des esclaves.* Paris: Institut d'Ethnologie, 1943.

Mensa, Nathanaél. ''L'Influence islamique sur les coutumes dahoméennes.'' Thesis, University of Paris, 1970.

Merlo, Christian. ''Hiérarchie fétichiste de Ouidah,'' *Bulletin de l'Institut Français d'Afrique Noire,* vol. 2, no. 1–2 (Jan.–Apr. 1940), pp. 1–86.

———. "Synthèse de l'activité fétichiste aux Bas Togo et Dahomey," *Bulletin de l'Institut Français d'Afrique Noire,* vol. 12, no. 4 (Oct. 1950).

Metraux, Alfred. "Origines e historia de los cultos vodu," *Casa de las Americas* (Havana), 1966, vol. 6, no. 36/7, pp. 42–62.

Milum, John. *Thomas Birch Freeman: Missionary Pioneer to Ashanti, Dahomey and Egba.* London, 1881.

Montilus, Guérin. "Le Voudou dahoméen." Thesis, University of Paris, 1970.

Mouterde, Nicolas. "Dahomey Nord-Ouest: Tanguiéta," *Echo des Missions Africaines de Lyon,* no. 5, 1962, pp. 101–104.

Nascimento, Abdias do. "African Culture in Brazilian Art," *Journal of Black Studies,* vol. 8, no. 4, 1978, pp. 389–422.

"Notes sur le fétichisme dahoméen," *Bulletin de l'Enseignement AOF,* no. 96 (1937), pp. 23–41.

Olomola, Isola. "Ipade: An extinct aspect of traditional burial rite among Yoruba hunters," *Africana Marburgensia,* vol. 23, no. 2 1990, pp. 24–35.

Palau-Marti, Montserrat. *Le Roi-Dieu au Bénin, Sud-Togo, Dahomey, Nigéria Occidentale.* Paris: Berger-Levrault, 1964.

Parisot, A. "L'Eglise au Dahomey de 1900 à nos jours," *Echo des Missions Africaines de Lyon,* no. 6, 1958, pp. 130–133.

———. "Tournée pastorale dans le district de Savé," *Echo des Missions Africaines de Lyon,* Nov. 1950, pp. 4–7.

Parrinder, Geoffrey. "Dahomey half a century ago." *Journal of Religion in Africa,* vol 19, no. 3 (1989), pp. 264–273.

―――. "Theistic Beliefs of the Yoruba and Ewe Peoples of West Africa," in Edwin W. Smith (ed.), *African Ideas of God.* London: Edinburgh House Press, 1950, pp. 224–240.

―――. *West African Religions; Illustrated from the Beliefs and Practices of the Yoruba, Ewe, Akan and Kindred Peoples.* London: The Epworth Press, 1949.

Pognon, André. *Dans le tourment du Destin: Essai d'histoire et de documentation sur les us, coutumes et religions.* Cotonou: ABM, 1971.

Price-Mars, Jean. "Les Origines du Voudou," *Revue de la Société Société Haïtienne d'Histoire, de Géographie et de Sociologie,* vol. 29, no. 102 (July–Oct. 1956).

Ramin, J. C. "Au pays des châteaux," *Echo des Missions Africaines de Lyon,* Mar. 1954, pp. 32–36.

Rivert, Paul. *Le Royaume d'Ardra et son Evangélisation au xvii siècle.* Paris: Institut d'Ethnologie, 1929.

Rousse-Grosseau, Christiane. "Methodes d'evangélisation: les Missions Africaines de Lyon au Dahomey." Ph.D. Thesis, University of Lyon, 1967.

Rublon, Victor. "Une coutume chez les Peuls: bastonnade jusqu'au sang," *Echo des Missions Africaines de Lyon,* Mar. 1954, pp. 34–36.

―――. "Les Pila Pila," *Echo des Missions Africaines de Lyon,* Mar. 1953, pp. 27–30.

Salvioni, Giovanna. "Une Die a testa," *Nigrizia*, vol. 85, no. 3 (Mar. 1967), pp. 16–19.

Sargent, Carolyn F. "Born to die: witchcraft and infanticide in Bariba culture," *Ethnology*, vol. 27, no. 1 (1988), pp. 75–95.

Saulnier, P. "Recherches sur le vodun à partir des noms individuels de ses vodunsi," *Bulletin de l'Institut Français d'Afrique Noire*, vol. 37, no. 2, Apr. 1975, pp. 358–387.

Savary, Claude. "Instruments de Magie Dahoméenne," *Musées de Genève*, vol. 12, no. 120, 1971, pp. 2–5.

Sempore. S. "Popular religion in Africa: Benin as a typical instance," *Concilium*, no. 186 (1986), pp. 44–51.

Sohchon, T. "Croyances et superstitions dans le Bas Dahomey," *Bulletin du Comité Historique et Scientifique de l'AOF*, Oct. 1921, pp. 667–671.

Souza, Germain. *Conception de la vie chez les Fons*. Cotonou: Edition du Bénin, 1975.

Tidjani, Abdou Serpos. *Le Dilemme*. Paris: Silex, 1983.

———. "Un procédé de divination au Dahomey," *Bulletin de l'Institut Français d'Afrique Noire*, vol. 5, no. 1–4, 1943.

Tossa, Augustin, "Un village soudainement et presque complètement converti," *Echo des Missions Africaines de Lyon*, 1951, pp. 125–130.

Tossou, Yao Hovanna. "Les clefs de Fa." *Etudes Togolaises*, vol. 27/30, pp. 51–68.

Trautman, René. *La Divination è la Côte des esclaves et à Madagascar*. Paris: Librairie Hachette, 1940.

Trouiuot, Henock. "Le Créole et le voudou," *Revue de Louisiane*, vol. 11, no. 2, Winter 1972, pp. 100–108.

Valente, Waldemar. *Survivances dahoméennes dans les groupes de cultes africains du nord-est du Brésil*. Dakar: Centre de hautes études afro-ibéro-americaines de l'Université de Dakar, no. 9 1969.

Vendeix, J. "Etudes sur les couvents fétichistes au Dahomey," *Bulletin du Comité d'Etudes Historiques et Scientifiques*, no. 4, Oct.–Dec. 1928, pp. 640–646.

Vendeix, Marie-Joseph. "Etudes sur les couvents fétichistes au Dahomey," *Bulletin de Comite d'Etudes Historiques et Scientifiques de l'O.A.F.*, vol. 11 no. 4 (Oct.–Dec. 1968), pp. 640–646.

Verger, Pierrre. "Le culte des Vodun d'Abomey aurait-il été apporté à Saint Louis de Maranhao par la mère du roi Ghézo?," *Etudes Dahoméennes*, no. 8 (1952), pp. 19–24.

———. *Dieux d'Afrique: culte des Orishas et Voduns à l'ancienne Côte des esclaves en Afrique à Bahia, la baie de tous les saints au Brésil*. Paris: P. Hartmann, 1954.

———. "Notes sur le culte des Orisa et Vodun à Bahia, la baie de tous les saints, au Brésil et à l'ancienne Côte des esclaves en Afrique." Dakar: Mémoires de l'Institut Français d'Afrique Noire, no. 51, 1957.

———. "Oral tradition in the cult of Orisha and its connection with the history of the Yoruba," *Journal of the Historical Society of Nigeria*, vol. 1, no. 1, 1956, pp. 61–63.

526 / Bibliography

―――. "Première Cérémonie d'initiation au culte des orisha nago à Bahia au Brésil," *Revista do Museu Paulista* (Saô Paulo, Brazil), 1955, pp. 269–291.

―――. "Un rite expiatoire 'Omé,' " *Notes Africaines,* no. 58, Apr. 1953, pp. 41–46.

―――. "Une sortie de 'iyawo' dans un Village nago au Dahomey," *Etudes Dahoméennes,* no. 6, 1951, pp. 11–26.

―――. "Trance and Convention in Nago-Yoruba Spirit Mediumship," in John Beattie et al., *Spirit Mediumship and Society in Africa.* London: Routledge & Kegan, 1969, pp. 50–66.

Vermeersch, C. *Historique de la mission Baud-Vermeersch (1894–95).* Paris, 1897.

Williams, F. *Africa's God: Dahomey.* Anthropological Series of the Boston College Graduate School, vol. 1, no. 2, 1936.

Williams, P. Morton. "The Atinga cult among the Southwestern Yoruba," *Bulletin de l'Institut Français d'Afrique Noire,* vol. 18, no. 3–4, 1956.

Wood-Lainé, Paul. *Le Missionnaire Freeman et les débuts de la mission protestante au Dahomey-Togo.* Porto Novo, 1942.

Zadji, Joseph "L'Alliance divine et les alliances coutumières au Bas Dahomey." Cotonou: Mémoire, Institut Catholique, 1968.

Zimmerman, Joseph. "Porto Novo: le fétiche Onsé," *Annales de Propagation de la Foi,* vol. 53, 1981, pp. 58–66.

10. LITERATURE, POETRY, THEATER, AND CINEMATOGRAPHY

Acogny, Gervais. "Le Couteau de fétiche yéwa," *Notes Africaines*, no. 38, Apr. 1948.

Adandé, Alexandre. "A propos de la critique de théâtre dahoméen," *Outre Mer*, vol 9, no. 4 (Dec. 1937), pp. 318–321.

―――. "Paul Hazoumé, écrivain et chercheur," *Présence Africaine*, no. 114 (1980), pp. 197–203.

Adandéjan, Louis. *Au Coeur de la colline*. Paris: La Pensée Universelle, 1979.

Adanhoumey Agbogba, Paul. *Tam-Tams et flambeaux*. Cotonou: Editions du Bénin, 1970.

Agbo, Casimir. "Chant fétichiste dahoméen," *Notes Africaines*, July 1946.

Agbossahessou, Louis. *Ai Dia, J'ai vu*. Yaoundé: Editions C.L.E., 1969. (Alias for Martin Gutenburg Vinakpon.)

―――. *Les Haleines sauvages*. Yaoundé, Cameroun: Editions C.L.E., 1972.

―――. "Mythes et réalités dahoméens dans l'oeuvre de Julien Alapini." Thesis, University of Paris, 1973.

Agnomyan, Guy Bespo. *Le Messager*. Cotonou: ABM, 1971.

Agyemang, Akeb. "La résurrection du passé dans 'Doguicimi' de Paul Hazoumé." Thesis, University of Montpellier, 1978.

Akando, Severin. *Echo d'une révolution.* Cotonou: ABM, 1973.

———— *Révolution Africaine.* Cotonou: Typopresse, 1975.

Alapini, Julien. *Acteurs noirs.* Avignon: Les Presses Universelles, 1965.

————. *Les Dahoméens et Togolais au centenaire des apparitions.* Avignon: Aubanel, 1959.

————. *Les Initiés.* Avignon: Aubanel, 1953.

————. *Les Noix sacrées.* Monte Carlo: Regain, 1950.

————. *Le Petit dahoméen.* Avignon: Les Presses Universelles, 1950.

Almeida, A. d'. "Doguicimi: image de la femme dahoméenne." Thesis, University of Paris, 1976.

Almeida, Damien d'. *Le Jumeau ou mon enfance à Agoué.* Cotonou: Editions du Bénin, 1966.

Almeida, Fernando d'. *Au seuil de l'exil.* Paris: L'Harmattan, 1981.

————. *En Attendant verdict.* Paris: Silex, 1982.

Apovi Cossi, Jean-Marie. *Les Equatoriales.* Cotonou: ABM, 1974.

Barreau, P. *Contes et légendes du Dahomey.* Namur: Collection Grands lacs, n.d.

Bazou, Gibrilla. *Rencontres et passions.* 1962.

Bhêly-Quénum, Olympe. *Le Chant du lac.* Paris: Présence Africaine, 1965.

————. *L'initié.* Paris: Présence Africaine, 1979.

————. "The Laws of the Forest," *New African,* vol. 6, no. 2 (Oct. 1967), pp. 16–18.

————. *Liaison d'un été.* Paris: L'Afrique Actuelle, 1968.

————. "La Littérature du pays profound," *Revue Française d'Etudes Politiques Africaines,* no. 190/1 (Oct.–Nov. 1981), pp. 140–150.

————. *Un Piège sans fin.* Paris: Librairie Stock, 1960.

————. *Snares without End.* London: Heinemann, 1981.

"Bibliographie de la littérature Béninoise," *Notre Librairie,* no. 69, 1983, pp. 119–126.

Bogniaho, Ascension. "A la découverte de la chanson populaire au Bénin," *Itinéraires et Contacts de Cultures,* vol. 8 (1988), pp. 81–88.

————. "Littérature orale au Bénin: essai de classification endogène des types de parole littéraire," *Ethiopiques* (Dakar), vol. 4, no. 3/4 (1987), pp. 53–64.

Boughédir, Ferid. "Le cinéma dahoméen: un cinéma qui libère," *Cinéma Ouebec,* vol. 3, no. 9/10 (1973), pp. 38–39.

Brench, A. C. *The Novelists' inheritance in French Africa: Writers from Senegal to Cameroun,* London: Oxford University Press, 1967.

Byll Cataria, J. B. *L'Hôte des Drance, suivi de Une pensée pour la veuve.* Paris: Akpagnon, 1983.

Carlos, Jérôme Tovignon. *Cri de Liberté: contribution à la révolution dahoméenne.* Cotonou: ABM, 1973.

Chemain, R. "Vision du monde et structure de l'imaginaire dans l'oeuvre d'Olympe Bhêly-Quénum," *Annales de l'Université de Brazzaville* (Brazzaville), vol. 9, 1973, pp. 23–48.

Cornevin, Robert. "Un écrivain dahoméen méconnu: l'abbé Gabriel Kiti," *L'Afrique Littéraire et artistique,* Oct. 13, 1970, pp. 9–10.

———. "Félix Couchoro (1900–1968), premier romancier régionaliste africain," *France-Eurafrique,* no. 196 (June 1968), pp. 35–36.

Cosentino, Donald. "Who is that fellow in the many-colored cap? Transformations of Eshu in Old and New World Mythologies," *Journal of American Folklore,* vol. 100, no. 397 (July–Sept. 1987), pp. 261–275.

Couchoro, Félix. *Accusée levez-vous.* Lomé: Togo-Presse, 1967.

———. *D'Aklakou à El Mina.* Lomé: Togo-Presse 1970.

———. *Amour de féticheuse.* Ouidah: Almeida, 1941.

———. *Amour de féticheuse au Togo.* Lomé: Togo-Presse, 1967.

———. *Béa et Marilou.* Lomé: Togo-Presse, 1963.

———. *Les Caprices du destin.* Lomé: Togo-Presse, 1966.

———. *Les Dix plaies de l'Afrique.* Lomé: Togo-Presse, 1968.

———. *Le Dot, plaie sociale.* Lomé: Togo-Presse, 1966.

———. *Drame d'amour à Anecho.* Ouidah: Almeida, 1950.

———. *L'Esclave.* Ouidah: Almeida, 1930.

———. *Fille de nationaliste.* Lomé: Togo-Presse, 1969.

———. *Gangsters et policiers.* Lomé: Togo-Presse, 1967.

———. *Les Gens sont méchants, ici bas tout se paie.* Lomé: Togo-Presse, 1968.

———. *L'Héritage, cette peste, ou les secrets d'Eléonore.* Lomé: Editogo, 1963.

———. *L'Homme à la Mercédès-Benz.* Lomé: Togo-Presse, 1963.

———. *Max Mensah.* Lomé: Togo-Presse, 1962.

———. *Le Passé ressurgit.* Lomé: Togo-Presse, 1966.

———. *Pauvre Alexandrine.* Lomé: Togo-Presse, 1964.

———. *Le Secret de Ramsnou.* Lomé: Togo-Presse, 1968.

———. *Les Secrets d'Eléonore.* Lomé: Togo-Presse, 1963.

———. *Sinistre d'Abidjan.* Lomé: Togo-Presse, 1965.

Da Cruz, Clément. "Notes sur la littérature fon-mahi (région d'Abomey et Savalou—Dahomey)," *Notes Africaines,* no. 77 (Jan. 1958), pp. 16–20.

Dagba, Juvencio. "L'Orphelin Zinsou," *Reconnaissance Africaine,* no. 15, Apr. 15, 1926, pp. 6–8.

Dideh, Elie. "Pourquoi la tortue porte une carapace," *Notes Africaines,* no. 41, May 1949.

Dogbeh, Richard. *Cap Liberté.* Yaoundé: Editions C.L.E., 1969.

―――. *Les Faux du Mono.* Vire: Société Lec-Vire, 1963.

―――. *Enfant du Bénin.* Cotonou: Editions du Benin, 1969.

―――. *Rives mortelles.* Porto Novo: Editions da Silva, 1964.

―――. *Voyage au pays de Lénine.* Yaoundé: Editions C.L.E., 1967.

Dossou-Yovo, Cossi Philibert. *Echos du Bénin: Poèmes.* Porto Novo: Direction d'Enseignement et de Base, 1980.

Dovignon, Jérôme Carlos. *Cri de Liberté.* Cotonou: ABM, 1973.

Dramani, Bazani Zakari. *Le Nouveau Cri.* Brussels: Editions Remarques Congolaises, 1965.

Edebiri, U. "Jean Pliya: portraitist of Benin society," *Ba Skiru* (Madison, Wisc.), vol. 8, no. 1, 1977, pp. 1–10.

Elwert, Georg. "History, humour and social control—genres of oral literature and registers of speech among the Ayizo," in E. Linnebuhr (ed.), *Transition and continuity of identity in East Africa and beyond.* Bayreuth: Bayreuth University, 1989.

Fabo, Paul. *Ombrages.* Brussels: Wellens-Pay, 1948.

Fadairo-Kedil, Dominique. ''Proverbes Fon du Bénin: une approche anthropologique,'' *Cahiers de Littérature Orale*, vol. 13 (1983), pp. 109–126.

Fadhloum, Essya. ''Libérer le psychisme africain colonisé,'' *7e Art* vol. 34 (1979), pp. 26–28; vol. 41 (1981), pp. 12–15.

Feuser, Willfried F. ''L'Oeuvre d'Olympe Bhêly-Quénum,'' *Présence Africaine*, no. 125, 1983, pp. 186–201.

François, Agonvinon D. *Cri et paroles.* Cotonou: L. D. Whannou, 1974.

Funke, Emil. ''Die Sprachverhäiltnisse in Sugu Dahome,'' *Zeitschrift für Kolonialsprachen*, vol. 5 (1914–1915), pp. 257–269.

Gbégnonvi, Roger. *Paroles Interdites.* Paris: Editions Silex, 1981.

Gonçalves, Evelyne. *Poésie du Bénin.* Paris: Silex, 1982.

Hazoumé, Flore. *Rencontres.* Abidjan: N.E.A., 1984.

Hazoumé, Guy L. *La Vie et l'Oeuvre de Louis Oussou Hounkarin.* Cotonou: Librairie Renaissance, 1977.

Hazoumé, Paul. *Doguicimi.* Paris: Larose, 1938.

―――――. *Fleurs Africaines.* Paris: La Revue Moderne, 1967.

Herskovits, Melville and Frances. ''Contes haïtiens et tradition littéraire dahoméenne,'' *Bulletin du Bureau d'Ethnologie d'Haïti*, Series no. 3, no. 15.

Houéto, Colette Sénami. *L'Aube sur le cactus.* Porto Novo: INFRE, 1981.

Hountondji, Gisèle. *Une citronnelle dans la neige.* Abidjan: Nouvelles Editions Africaines, 1986.

Hountondji, Paulin. *Liberté.* Cotonou: Librairie Renaissance, 1973.

————. *Sur la philosophie africaine.* Paris: Maspéro, 1976.

Hountondji, Victor M. *Couleur de rêves.* Paris: La Pensée Universelle, 1977.

————. *Deux filles; un rêve fugutif.* Cotonou: Editions ABM, 1973.

————. *Les vestiges du Person Grand-Vet.* Paris: ABC, 1975.

Huannou, Adrien. "Deux écrivains béninois," *Recherche, Pédagogie et Culture,* vol. 6, no. 33, Jan.–Feb. 1978, pp. 17–23.

————. "Histoire de la littérature écrite de langue française dans l'ex-Dahomey." Thesis, University of Paris, 1979.

————. "L'Image du Dahomey et des Dahoméens en occident à travers la littérature et la presse françaises," *L'Afrique Littéraire,* vol. 58 (1981), pp. 140–147.

————. "L'Influence de la littérature orale sur l'écrivain béninois," *Itinéraires,* vol. 1 (1982), pp. 81–96.

————. *La littérature béninoise de langue française, des origines à nos jours.* Paris: Karthala, 1984.

————. "Le thème de la destinée dans la littérature oral Fon," *Afrique Littéraire et Artistique,* no. 36 (1975), pp. 62–69.

————. *Trois poètes béninois.* Yaoundé (Cameroun): C.L.E., 1980.

Huchet, A. Miriam. *Datine le Berba.* Lyon: Missions Africaines du Lyon, 1960.

————. *Reine Fétiche.* Lyon: Missions Africains du Lyon, 1957.

————. *Tena: jeune fille de la brousse dahoméenne.* Lyon: Missions Africaines de Lyon, 1959.

Ibitokun, B. M. "A Yoruba oral poet in Benin Republic: an appraisal of Cyrille Olaleye's art," *African Notes* (Ibadan), vol 11, no. 1 (1987), pp. 8–17.

Iroko, Abiola Félix, "Une littérature orale: La Panégyrique clanique du souvenir," *Notre Librairie,* vol. 69 1989, pp. 26–31.

————. "La place des oeuvres d'Aimé Césaire dans l'enseignement en République populaire du Bénin," in Jacqueline Leiner (ed.), *Soleil éclaté: mélanges offerts à Aimé Césaire.* Tubingen: Narr, 1984, pp. 233–238.

Jahn, Janheinz, Ulla Schild and Almut Nordmann. *Who's Who in African Literature,* Tubingen, 1972.

Joachim, Paulin. *Anti-grace.* Paris: Présence Africaine, 1967.

————. *Oraison pour une renaissance.* Paris: Silex, 1983.

————. *Paroles sur des langues.* Paris: Présence Africaine, 1962.

Kom, Ambroise. *Dictionnaire des oeuvres littéraires négro-africaines de langue française.* Sherbrooke: Editions Naaman, 1983.

Kondjo, Bienvenu. "Théâtre, rites et folklore au Dahomey." Thesis, University of Paris, 1976.

La Pin, Deirdre. "Narrative as precedent in Yoruba oral tradition," in John Miles Foley (ed.), *Oral Traditional Literature*. Columbus, Oh.: Slavica, 1981, pp. 347–374.

Lebel, A. Roland. *L'Afrique occidentale dans la littérature française depuis 1870.* Paris: Emile Larose, 1925.

Lecherbonnier, Bernard. "Introduction à la littérature négro-africaine d'expression française," *Français dans le Monde,* vo. 12, no. 94, Jan.–Feb. 1973, pp. 6–10.

La littérature africaine francophone. Lausanne: Bibliothèque cantonale et universitaire, 1991.

Lordereau, Paulette. *Littératures africaines à la Bibliothèque Nationale 1920–1972.* Paris: Bibliothèque Nationale, 1991.

———. *Littératures africaines à la Bibliothèque Nationale 1973–1983.* Paris: Bibliothèque Nationale, 1991.

Mane, Robert, and Adrien Huannou (eds.). *Doguicimi de Paul Hazoume: essais rassemblés et présentés par Robert Mane et Adrien Huannou.* Paris: Harmattan, 1987.

Maupoil, Bernard. "Le théâtre dahoméen," *Outre Mer,* no. 4, Dec. 1937.

Mercier, Paul, and Jean Rouch. *Chantes du Dahomey et du Niger.* Paris: GLM, 1950.

Mercier, Roger, and M. Battestini (eds.). *J. Olympe Bhêly-Ouénum: écrivain dahoméen.* Paris: Nathan, 1964.

Monteiro, Armand. *La Part du Feu: Poèmes.* Cotonou: Office National d'Edition, 1979.

Montilua, Guerin C. "The myth of Dahomey in Haiti," *Journal of Caribbean Studies,* vol. 2, no. 1 (Spring 1981), pp. 73–84.

Muzi, Jean. *Contes des rives du Niger.* Paris: Flammarion, 1986.

Nourrit, Chantal, and Bill Prutt. *Musique Traditionnelle de l'Afrique Noire, Benin, 1978.* Paris: Radio-France Internationale, 1985.

Okioh, François Sourou. *Le cinéma au Bénin.* Brussels: OCIC, 1988.

———. "Problems of African Cinema," *Young Cinema and Theatre,* vol 3 (1982), pp. 24–30.

Oliveira, C. A. d'. "Bossus et foudroyés au Dahomey," *Notes Africaines,* no. 26, Apr. 1945, pp. 7–8.

Ologoudou, Emile. *Eloge d'un royaume éphémère.* Paris: Silex, 1983.

Padonou, Ambroise Agboton. *Le Cardier.* Porto Novo: Imprimerie Rapidex, 1970.

Pliya, Jean. *L'Arbre fétiche.* Yaoundé: Editions Preuves, 1963; Editions C.L.E., 1971.

———. *Le Chimpanzé amoureux.* Paris: Imprimerie Saint Paul, 1977.

———. *La Conquête du bonheur.* Dakar: Nouvelles Editions Africaines, 1983.

———. *La fille têtue, contes et récits traditionnels du Bénin.* Abidjan: Nouvelles Editions Africaines, 1982.

———. *Kondo le reguin*. Porto Novo: I.R.A.D., 1966.

———. *La Secrétaire particulière*. Yaoundé: C.L.E., 1973.

Prudencio, Eustache. *Ailleurs . . . un jour peut-être*. Cotonou: UNEP, 1982.

———. *Océanides*. Cotonou: American Cultural Center, 1971.

———. *Ombres et soleils*. Cotonou: Editions du Bénin, 1968.

———. *Quelle tempête ravage mon âme*. Cotonou: ABM, 1979.

———. *Vents du Lac*. Cotonou: Editions du Bénin, 1967.

———. *Violence de la race*. Cotonou: ABM, 1971.

———. *Violence de la Race*. Paris: Harmattan, 1980.

Quénum, Maximillien. *Légendes Africaines, Côte d'Ivoire, Soudan, Dahomey*. Rochefort-sur-mer: A. Thoyon-Theze, 1946.

Regards sur la Littérature Dahoméenne. Cotonou: AMB, 1971.

Ricard, Alain. "Littérature coloniale et littérature africaine: Félix Couchoro," *Itinéraires et Contacts de cultures,* no. 12 (1990), pp. 67–70.

"Richard de Medeiros jeune cinéaste béninois," *Bingo* no. 289 (1977), pp. 32–35.

Rouget, Gilbert. "Une chante-fable d'un signe divinatoire," *Journal of African Languages,* 1962, pp. 273–92.

Saulnier, Pierre, and Gérard Guillet. *Regard sur la littérature dahoméenne,* 2 vol. Cotonou: Pro Manuscripts, 1971.

Schmidt, Nancy. *Sub-saharan African Films and Filmmakers.* London: Hans Zell, 1990.

Tchitchi, T. Y. "Littérature en langues africaines ou littérature de minorité: la situation en République Populaire du Bénin," *International Journal of the Sociology of Language,* no. 80 (1989) pp. 69–81.

Tidjani-Serpos, Noureini. *Agban'la.* Paris: Harmattan, 1981.

———. *Le Dilemme.* Paris: Silex, 1983.

———. *Maïté.* Cotonou: ABM, 1968.

Trautman, René. *La Littérature populaire à la Côte des esclaves, contes, proverbes, devinettes.* Paris, 1927.

Vignonde, Jean-Norbert. "La littérature orale Fon du Benin." Thesis, University of Paris, 1978.

Yao, Henri. "Sept films africains à Paris," *Bingo,* no. 308 (1978), pp. 53–56.

11. LINGUISTICS

Alapini, Julien. *Le petit Dahoméen: grammaire vocabulaire lexique en langue du Dahomey.* Paris: Les Presses Universelles, 1950.

Arnott, D. W. "Some features of the Nominal Class System of Fula in Nigeria, Dahomey and Niger." *Afrika und Ubersee,* vol. 43, no. 3, Mar. 1960, pp. 241–278.

Bascom, W. "John Clarke's unidentified Nago dialect," *African Languages,* vol. 2, 1976, pp. 14–18, 31.

Baudin, P. *Dictionnaire yoruba-français.* Porto Novo: Centre Catéchétique, 1966.

————. *Grammaire Yoruba.* Porto Novo: Centre Catéchétique, 1967.

Bertho, P. J. "Langues rituelles du Dahomey," *Notes Africaines,* no. 43, July 1949.

————. "Langues Voltaïques du Togo nord et du Dahomey nord," *Notes Africaines,* vol. 44 (Oct. 1949), pp. 124–126.

————. "Quatre dialectes Mandés du Nord Dahomey et de la Nigéria anglaise," *Bulletin de l'Institut Français d'Afrique Noire,* vol. 13, no. 4, Oct. 1951.

Bole-Richard, Rémy. *Systématique phonologique et grammaticale d'un parler Ewé: le Gen Mina du Sud-Togo et Sud-Bénin.* Paris: Harmattan, 1983.

Bonnaventure, A. *Eléments de grammaire de la langue fon ou dahoméenne suivis d'un vocabulaire et d'un recueil de conversations.* Paris: Lavauzelle, 1895.

Bouche, Pierre. "Alphabet Nagot," in *Les Noirs Peints par eux-mêmes.* Paris: Librairie Poussiélgué, 1883.

————. "Côte des esclaves et la Dahomey," in *Les Noirs Peints par eux-mêmes.* Paris: Librairie Poussiélgué, 1883.

————. *Etude sur la langue Nago.* Paris: Etudes Catholiques, 1880.

————. "Rôle des proverbes d'après les Nagots," in *Les Noirs Peints par eux-mêmes.* Paris: Librairie Poussiélgué, 1883.

Brousseau, Anne-Marie et al. ''Morphological processes in Haitian Creole,'' *Journal of Pidgin and Creole Language* (Amsterdam), vol. 4, no. 1 (1989), pp. 1–36.

Bruckner, Kathrin. ''The particle of contrast maa in Waama,'' *Journal of West African Languages,* vol. 17, no. 2 (1987), pp. 119–134.

Capo Hamkpati, B. C. *Renaissance du Gbé: réflexions critiques et constructions sur l'Evé, le Fon, le Gen, l'Aja, le Gun,* Hamburg: Buske, 1988.

Ceccaldi, Pierette. *Essai de nomenclauture des populations, langues et dialectes de la République Populaire du Bénin.* 2 vols. Paris: CARDAN, 1979.

Cherchari, Amar. *Réception de la littérature africaine d'expression française jusqu'en 1970.* Paris: SILEX Editions, 1982.

Courdioux, Ph. E. *Dictionnaire abrégé de la langue fongbé ou dahoméenne.* Paris, 1879.

Craene, Robert de. ''Le verbe conjugué en tem,'' *Studies in African Linguistics,* vol. 17, no. 1 (1986), pp. 1–37.

Crunden, Sheila. ''Une comparaison entre les systèmes phonologiques du Kabiyé, de l'éwé et du bassar du point de vue pédagogique,'' *Etudes Togolaises,* no. 15–18, Dec. 1981, pp. 102–116.

Da Cruz, Clément. ''Essai de petit vocabulaire française-fongbé,'' *Etudes Dahoméennes,* no. 11, 1951, pp. 15–19.

Da Silveira, Yvonne. ''Rôle de la valorisation des langues par le milieu dans le développement de la compétence langagière en contexte Africain,'' *Revue Ouébécoise de Linguistique*

Théorétique et Appliquée, vol 8, no. 2 (Apr. 1989) pp. 115–132.

Delafosse, Maurice. *Manuel dahoméen, grammaire, chrestomathie dictionnaire français-dahoméen et dahoméen-français*. Paris: Ernest Leroux, 1894.

Dujarlier, R. *Manuel progressif de conversation en langue fon*. 3 vols. Ouidah: 1964.

Duthie, A. S., and R. K. Vlaardingerbroek. *Bibliography of Gbe*. Basel: Basler Afrika Bibliographien, 1981.

Funk, Emite, "Die Sprache von Bussa am Niger," *Mittelungen des Seminars für Afrikanischen und Ozeionischen Sprachen* (Berlin), vol. 18 1915, pp. 52–84.

———. "Die Sprachverhältnisse in Sugu Dahome," *Zeitschrift für Kolonialsprachen*, vol. 5 (1914–5), pp. 257–269.

Giesecke, Michael, and Geirg Elwert. "Literacy and Emancipation: The Literacy Process in Two Cultural Revolutionary Movements," *Development and Change*, vol. 14, no. 2, April 1983, pp. 293–305.

Gouzien, Paul. *Contribution à l'étude des dialectes du Dahomey*. Paris: A. Chauamel, 1889.

Guédou, Georges G. Gangbé. "Tonalité et nature des consonnes en fongbé," *Zeitschrift für Phonefik, Sprachwissenschaft und Kommunikationsforschung*, vol. 33, 1980, pp. 715–724.

Heine, B. "A preliminary survey of the noun classes of Basila," *Journal of African Languages*, vol. 7, no. 1, 1968, pp. 1–13.

Hoftmann, H. "Le dévelopement des langues nationales et la politique linguistique en République Populaire du Bénin," in Siegmund Brauner and N.V. Ochotina (eds.), *Studien zur nationalsprachlichen Entwicklung in Afrika*. Berlin: Akademie-Verlag, 1982, pp. 201–212.

————. "Le statut phonologique des sons 'complexes' en langue Fon," *Zeitschrift fur Phonetik, Sprachwissenschaft und Kommunikationsforschung*, vol. 40, no. 4 (1987), pp. 525–37.

Huannou, Adrien. *Essai sur l'arbre fétiche et le chimpanzé amoureux de Jean Pliya*. Abidjan: Editions Africaines, 1983.

————. *La littérature béninoise de langue française*. Paris: Karthala, 1984.

Joulard, R. P. *Manuel de conversation française-Dahoméenne*. Paris: Albi, 1914.

————. *Manuel franco-dahoméen*. Lyon: Veuve Paquet, 1907.

Kenstowicz, M. et al. "Tonal polarity in two Gur languages," *Studies in the Linguistic Sciences*, vol. 18, no. 1 (1988), pp. 77–103.

Lafage, S. "Le Dictionnaire des particularités du français au Togo et au Dahomey," *Annales de l'Université d'Abidjan*, vol. 9, no. 1, 1976, pp. 131–141.

————. "Facteurs de différenciation entre le français d'Afrique," *Cahiers Ivoiriens de Recherche Linguistique* (Abidjan), no. 1, Apr. 1977, pp. 1–49.

Lefebvre, C. "Instrumental take-serial constructions in Haitian and Fon," *Journal of Linguistics*, vol 34, no. 3 (1989), pp. 319–337.

Lewis, Marshall. "Aspect-marking in Gegbe prepositions," *Papers from the 25th Regional Meeting of the Chicago Linguistic Society.* Part 1 (1989), pp. 272–287.

Manessy, G. "Le français d'Afrique Noire," *Langue Française,* no. 37, Feb. 1978, pp. 91–105.

————. "Note sur le niéndé, langue de l'Atakora," *Bulletin de l'Institut Français d'Afrique Noire,* vol. 38, no. 4, Oct. 1976, pp, 861–871.

Mercier, Paul. "Créateurs de mots nouveaux (Somba)," *Notes Africaines,* no. 41, Jan. 1949.

————. "Vocabulaire de quelques langues du nord Dahomey," *Etudes Dahoméennes,* no. 2 (1949), pp. 72–83.

Ndikuriyo, Albéric. "Pour une didactique contrastive sur le plan phonologique entre deux langues, le kirundi (langue bantu) et le fongbé (langue kwa)," *Culture et société* (Bujumbura), vol. 9 (1987), pp. 93–103.

Ourso, Meterwa Akayhou. "Critères de distribution des affixes en Lama," *Journal of West African Languages.* vol. 19, no. 1 (1989), pp. 35–56.

————. "Lama phonology and morphology." Ph.D. Thesis, University of Illinois at Urbana-Champagne, 1989.

————. "Root control, underspecification and ATR Harmony," *Studies in Linguistic Sciences* (Urbana), vol. 18, no. 2 (1988), pp. 111–127.

Prost, André. "Essai de description grammaticale de la langue boko ou bousa de Segbana (Dahomey)," *Annales de l'Université d'Abidjan* (Abidjan), vol. 9, no. 1, 1976, pp. 143–246.

————. "Les Langues de l'Atakora," *Bulletin de l'Institut Français d'Afrique Noire,* 3 parts, vol. 34, no. 2 (1972), pp. 299–392; vol. 34, no. 3 (1972), pp. 617–682; vol. 35, no. 2 (1973), pp. 443–511.

Reineke, B. "Zu einigen Charakteristika der grammatischen Struktur der Gur-Sprachen, dargestellt am Beispiel des Nateni," *Zeitschrift fur Phonetik, Sprachwissenschaft und Kommunikationsforschung,* vol. 38, no. 2 (1985), pp. 166–174.

Rouget, Gilbert. "Analyse des tons goun par le détecteur de mélodie," *Langage et comportement,* no. 1 (1965), pp. 31–48.

————. "Un chromatisme africain," *L'Homme,* vol. 1, no. 3 (Sept.–Dec. 1961), pp. 32–46.

————. "La nasalisation et le système des consonnes en goun," *Langues et techniques. Nature et Société.* Paris: Klincksieck, 1972, pp. 209–219.

————. "Tons de langue en goun et tons du tambour, *Revue de Sociologie,* vol. 50 (1964), pp. 3–29.

Saulnier, Pierre. *Manuel progressif de conversation en langue gun.* 2 vols. Porto Novo: Centre Catéchétique de Porto Novo, 1967.

Segurola, Abbé. *Dictionnaire fon-français.* Cotonou: Editions Procure de l'Archidiocèse, 1963.

————. and Dujarrier. *Grammaire élémentaire et exercices pratiques pour une première approche de la langue fon.* Ouidah: Editions Seminaire Saint-Jeanne d'Arc, 1963.

Smith, Jennifer L. "Rhetorical questions in Waama," *Afrikanistische Arbeitpapiere* (Cologne), vol. 12 (1987), pp. 37–51.

Tossa, Zépherin et al. *Langues, alphabétisation culturelles: Bibliographie sélective sur les langues béninoises.* Cotonou: Centre National de linguistique appliquée, 1990.

Welmers, W. E. "Notes on the Structure of Bariba," *Language,* vol. 28, no. 1 (1952), pp. 82–87.

Westermann, D. "Die Bargu Sprache," in *Die Sprache des Guang in Togo und auf der Goldküste.* Berlin, 1922.

Zima, Petr. "Research in the Territorial and Social Stratification of African Languages," *Zeitschrift für Phonetik,* vol. 28, no. 3–4 (1975), pp. 311–23.

Zinsou, Jean Francis. "Le Français au Benin," *Modern Sprachen,* vol. 30, no. 1–2 (Jan.–June 1986), pp. 37–39.

12. ART

Adama, Monni. "Fon Appliqued Cloths," *African Arts* (Los Angeles), vol. 13, no. 2, Feb. 1980, pp. 28–41.

Adandé, Alexandre. "Protection et développement de l'artisanat d'art du Dahomey," *Etudes Dahoméennes,* no. 2 (1964), pp. 93–100.

———. *Les Récades des Rois du Dahomey.* Dakar: l'Institut Français d'Afrique Noire, 1959.

Adandé, Joseph. "Les grandes tentures et les Bas-reliefs du Musée d'Abomey." Thesis, National University of Benin, 1974.

Aguéssi, W. "Emblèmes et chants," *Anthropos*, vol. 27, 1932, pp. 417–422.

Anquetil, Jacques. *L'Artisanat créateur au Bénin*. Paris: Agence de coopération culturelle et technique, 1980.

Bay, Edna. *Asen: Iron altars of the Fon people of Benin*. Atlanta: Emory Museum of Art and Archaeology, 1985.

Ben Amos, P. "Owina n'Ido: royal weavers of Benin," *African Arts* (Los Angeles), vol. 11, no. 4, July 1978, pp. 95–96.

Bertho, Jacques. "Instruments de musique des roi de Nikki au Dahomey," *Notes Africaines*, no. 52 (Oct. 1951), pp. 99–101.

Bhêly-Quénum, Olympe. "Théâtre et rites initiatiques au Dahomey," *Communauté France-Eurafrique*, no. 135, Oct. 1962, pp. 38–40.

Blackmum, Monica Lee. "The Asen of Dahomey: Iron altars from the People's Repubic of Benin." M.A. Thesis, University of California, Santa Barbara, 1978.

Blier, Rudolph. "Songs on Crisis; Songs of Heart. Tamberma Music and Community Consciousness," African Studies Conference paper, 1982.

Blier, Suzanne Preston. *The Anatomy of Architecture: ontology and metaphor in batammaliba architectural expression*. New York: Cambridge University Press, 1987.

Brand, Roger. *Regard sur l'art dahoméen*. Cotonou: Pro Manuscripto, 1971.

———. "Yesufu Asogba, modeleur dahoméen," *Anthropos*, vol. 67, no. 3–4 (1972), pp. 337–386.

Bruelle-Bauer, A. "L'Ecole d'art d'Askogbo et les temples vodun du sud-Bénin," *Expressions d'Afrique*, 1982.

Carroll, Kevin. *Yoruba Religious Sculpture: Pagan and Christian Sculpture in Nigeria and Dahomey*. New York: Praeger, 1967.

Crowley, Daniel J. "Bêtises: Fon brass genre figures," *African Arts*, vol. 15, no. 2, Feb. 1982, pp. 56–58.

———. "Fon brass tableaux as historical documents," *African Arts*, vol. 20, no. 1 (Nov. 1986), pp. 54–59.

———. and Doran H. Ross. "The Bahian market in African-influenced art," *African Arts*, vol. 14, no. 11 (Nov. 1981), pp. 56–62.

Crozet, J. "Dahomey: Etude de la restauration et la mise en valeur de palais royaux d'Abomey." Paris: UNESCO, 1968.

Cunha, Marrianno Carneiro da. *Da senzala ao sobrado: arguitetura brasileriana Nigeria e na Republica Popular do Benim*. Sao Paolo: Nobel, 1985.

Da Cruz, Clément. "Les Instruments de musique dans le bas Dahomey," *Etudes Dahoméennes*, vol. 12 (1952), pp. 11–79.

———. "Notes sur l'habitat dans le cercle de Porto Novo," *Etudes Dahoméennes*, vol. 11, 1954, pp. 5–15.

"Dahomey: Traditions du peuple Fon." Geneva: Musée d'Ethnographie, 1975.

Darbois, Dominique, and V. Vasut. *Afrika tanzt.* Prague: Artia, 1963.

De Beauchêne, Guy. "Prehistory and Archeology in Niger, Togo, Upper Volta, Dahomey and Ivory Coast," *West African Archeological Newsletter,* Nov. 5, 1966, pp. 6–8.

Denyer, Susan. *African traditional architecture: an historical and geographical perspective.* London: Heinemann, 1978.

Drewal, Henry John. "Beauty and Being: Aesthetics and Ontology in Yoruba Body Art," in Arnold Rubin (ed.), *Marks of Civilization: Artistic Transformation of the Human body.* Los Angeles: Museum of Cultural History, 1988.

———. "Pageantry and Power in Yoruba costuming," in Justine M. Cordell and Ronald A. Schwarz (eds.), *The Fabrics of Culture: The Anthropology of Clothing and Adornment.* The Hague: Mouton, 1979, pp. 189–230.

———. and Margaret Thompson. *Gelede: art and female power among the Yoruba.* Bloomington: Indiana University Press, 1983.

Etienne-Nugué, Jocelyne. *Artisanats traditionnels en Afrique Noire: Bénin.* Dakar: Institut Culturel Africain, 1984.

Fassassi, Masudi Alabi. *L'Architecture en Afrique noire: cosmoarchitecture.* Paris: Maspéro, 1978.

Frazer, J. G. "Statues of Three Kings of Dahomey," *Royal Anthropological Society Journal,* 1908, pp. 130–132.

Garner, Nancy. "Dahomean portable altars." M.A. Thesis, Columbia University, 1978.

Guédou, Georges A. G., and Claude Coninckx. "La dénomination des couleurs chez les Fon," *Journal des Africanistes,* vol 56, no. 1 (1986), pp. 67–85.

Hardy, Georges. *L'art nègre: l'art animiste des noirs d'Afrique.* Paris: Laurens, 1927.

Haselberger, Herta. "Gemalter, gravierter und modellierter Bauschmuck in Dahomey," *Tribus,* no. 10 (Sept. 1961), pp. 33–56.

Humbert-Sauvageot, M. "Quelques aspects de la vie et de la musique dahoméennes," *Zeitschrift für Vergleichende Musikwissenschaft,* vol. 2, no. 4 (1934), pp. 76–83.

Iroko, Abiola Félix. "Les forges et ateliers d'Adjoha," in *Entreprises et entrepreneurs en Afrique.* Paris: Harmattan, 1983, pp. 553–557.

Karl, Emmanuel. "Les Récades témoins d'une civilisation," *Etudes Dahoméennes,* no. 1 (1963), pp. 107–114.

Lawal, Babatunde. "New light on Gélédé," *African Arts,* vol. 11, no. 2 (Jan. 1978), pp. 65–70.

Livingstone, Thomas W. "Ashanti and Dahomean Architectural Bas Reliefs," *African Studies Review,* vol. 17, no. 2 (Sept. 1974), pp. 435–448.

Lobsiger-Deuenbach, Marguerite. "Figurines en terre modelée du Dahomey," *Archives suisses d'anthropologie générale,* vol. 11 (1945), pp. 215–238.

Locke, David, and Goduni Kwasi Agbeli. "A Study of the Drum Language in Adzogbo," *African Music* (Roodeport), vol. 6, no. 1, 1980, pp. 32–51.

Lombard, Jacques. "Aperçu sur la technologie et l'artisanat Bariba," *Etudes Dahoméennes*, no. 18 (1957), pp. 5–50.

Maurice, A. "Au Dahomey, les châteaux Somba," *Tropiques*, May 1957, pp. 59–66.

Mercier, Paul. *Les Ase du musée d'Abomey.* Dakar: Institut Français d'Afrique Noire, 1952.

————. "Evolution de l'art dahoméen," *Présence Africaine*, no. 10 & 11 (1951), pp. 185–193.

————. "L'Habitation à étage dans l'Atakora," *Etudes Dahoméennes*, vol. 11, 1954, pp. 28–86.

————. "Images de l'art animalier au Dahomey," *Etudes Dahoméennes*, vol. 5, 1950, pp. 93–109.

————. and Jacques Lombard. *Guide du Musée d'Abomey.* Porto Novo: Etudes Dahoméennes, 1959.

————. and J. Rouch. *Chants du Dahomey et du Niger.* Paris, 1950.

Merlo, Christian, "Un chef-d'oeuvre d'art nègre," *Anvers sur Oise Archer*, 1966.

Nooteboom, C. "The Coustere collection of African art from Dahomey, Benin and Nigeria." London: O'Hana Gallery, 1967.

Ombu, Jigekuma A. "Bibliography of art and material culture of the Benin Kingdoms from the earliest time to 1969," *Abhandlungen und Berichte* (Dresden), no. 34 (1975), pp. 171–213.

Owerko, Carolyn. *A Bibliography of Yoruba Art.* New York: Pace Editions, 1982.

Palau-Marti, Montserrat. "Calendriers dahoméens du Musée de l'Homme," *Objets et Mondes,* vol. 4, no. 1 (Spring 1964), pp. 29–38.

————. "Musée de l'Homme—Calendriers dahoméens," *Objets et Mondes,* vol. 4, no. 1, 1966, pp. 29–38.

————. "Sabres décorés du Dahomey," *Objets et Mondes,* vol. 7, no. 4, 1967, pp. 279–306.

"Pottery in Dahomey," *I.L.O. News,* no. 12 (March 1965), pp. 3–7.

Réal, Daniel. *Notes sur l'art dahoméen.* Paris: Art Vivant, 1926.

————. "Note sur l'art dahoméen," *L'Anthropologie,* vol. 30, no. 3–4 (1920).

Répertoire culturel: le Bénin. Paris: Agence de coopération culturelle et technique, 1983.

Rouget, Gilbert. "Mission d'ethnomusicologie au Dahomey en 1958–1959," *Cahiers d'Etudes Africaines,* no. 2 (May 1960), pp. 198–200.

————. "Tons de la langue en Gun (Dahomey), et tons du tambour," *Revue de musicologie,* vol. 50 (July 1964), pp. 3–29.

Savary, Claude. "Dahomey 1973: Un retour aux sources," *Musées de Genève,* vol. 15, no. 143, 1974, pp. 9–15.

————. "Notes à propos du symbolisme de l'art dahoméen,"

Bulletin annuel du Musée d'ethnographie de Genève, no. 10 (1967), pp. 69–98.

Shaw, Thomas McDonald. "Taneka Architecture and Village Structure in Northwestern Benin." Thesis, Columbia University, 1981.

Sinou, Alain, and Bachit Oloude. *Porto Novo: ville d'Afrique Noire.* Paris: ORSTOM, 1989.

Sydow, Eckart. *Handbuch des Afrikanischen Plastik.* Berlin: Dietrich Reimer, 1930, pp. 121–138.

Thompson, Robert Farris. *Black Gods and Kings: Yoruba Art at UCLA.* Bloomington: Indiana University Press, 1976.

Tiberini, Elvira Stefania. "La recade del Dahomey: messagio simbolo di potere," *Africa* (Rome), vol. 37, no. 1–2, Mar.–June 1982, pp. 54–74.

Turnbull, C. M. "Tribal Art from Africa: Dahomean Sculptures," *Natural History,* vol. 73, no. 3, pp. 46–53.

"Under the Sign of the Voodou," *Entente Africaine,* Jan. 1975, pp. 46–49.

Verger, Pierre. "The Bas-Reliefs in the Royal Palace of Abomey," *Odu* (Ibadan), no. 5 (1957), pp. 3–13.

———. "Painted Palaces of Dahomey: An Illustrated Commentary," *Geographical Magazine,* Mar. 1942.

———. and Clément Da Cruz. "Musée historique de Ouidah," *Etudes Dahoméennes,* no. 13 (June 1969), pp. 6–26.

Waterlot, E. M. G. *Les Bas-reliefs des bâtiments royaux d'Abomey.* Paris: Institut d'Ethnologie, 1926.

Wessenberg, Kristi Lee. "Dahomean Appliquee folk art." *M.A. Thesis, University of California, Berkeley, 1974.*

13. TOURISM

L'Afrique Noire Francophone. Paris: Editions Jeune Afrique, 1979.

Afrique Occidentale. *Guide Poche Voyage.* Paris: Marcus, 1984.

Allen, Philip M. "Dahomey," in Philip M. Allen and Aaron Segal, *The Travelers Africa: A Guide to the Entire Continent.* New York: Hopkinsons and Blake, 1973, pp. 455–468.

"L'Avenir du Tourisme," *Europe-Outre Mer,* no. 566, Mar. 1977, pp. 43–46.

Beautés du Monde: L'Afrique Occidentale. Paris: Larousse, 1980, pp. 1–9.

"Bénin," in Geoff Crowther, *Africa on a Shoestring,* Hawthorne (Australia): Lonely Planet Publications, 1989, pp. 97–106.

"Bénin," in Glaser, Sylvie, *Guide du voyageur en Afrique de l'Ouest.* Paris: Ediafric, 1984, pp. 33–46.

"Benin," in Newton, Alex, *West Africa: A survival kit.* Berkeley: The Lonely Planet Publications, 1988, pp. 93–110.

Blumenthal, Susan, *Bright Continent: A Shoestring Guide to Subsaharan Africa.* New York: Doubleday & Co. 1974.

Catrisse, Benoît. "Hôtellerie et tourisme," *Afrique Industrie*, no. 203, Mar. 1980. pp. 42–69.

"Cotonou and Porto Novo," in Sylvia Ardyn Boone, *West African Travels: A Guide to People and Places*. New York: Random House, 1974, pp. 289–308.

Le Dahomey. Boulogne: Delroisse, 1970.

"Dahomey," in *Guide Ouest Africain*. Paris: Diloutremer, annual, 1948+.

"Dahomey," in Robert S. Kane, *Africa A to Z*. Garden City: Doubleday, 1961.

"Dahomey," in *Le Moniteur du Tourisme Africain*. Dakar: Société Africaine d'Edition, annual 1971+.

"Dahomey," in *Travel Guide to Western and Central Africa*. Paris: UTA French Airlines, Tourism Department, 5th ed., 1989, pp. 23–38.

Glaser, Sylvie. *Guide de voyageur en Afrique de l'Ouest*. Paris: Ediafric, 1984.

Gosset, Pierre, and Renée Gosset. *L'Afrique, les Africains*. Paris: R. Juillard, 1958, vol. 1.

Greenfield, L. "Benin-Africa's royal roots," *Travel/Holiday*, Oct. 1980, pp. 52–57.

Hudgens, Jim and Richard Trillo. *West Africa: The Rough Guide*. London: Harrap-Columbus, 1990.

"Lions et hippotamus de la Pendjari," *Balafon* (Paris), no. 17, 1971.

"La Mise en valeur des attraits touristiques," *Europe-France-Outremer,* no. 515 (Dec. 1972), pp. 38–39.

"Un objectif nouveau—le tourisme," *Europe-Outre Mer,* no. 631, Aug. 1982, pp. 47–50.

Pedrals, D. Pierre de. *Dans la brousse africaine: Dahomey, Borgou.* Paris: La Nouvelle Edition, 1946.

Rake, Alan (ed.). *Travellers Guide to West Africa.* London: IC Publishers, 7th ed. 1988.

Tescaroli, Ciriuo. "Ganvié: una piceda Venezia africana," *Nigrizia,* vol. 87, no. 5 (Mar. 1969), pp. 23–25.

"Tourism in Africa," *Afro-Asian Economic Review,* no. 148/9, Jan. Feb. 1972, pp. 7–23.

Vieyra, J. *Conseil de l'Entente, Ivory Coast, Dahomey, Upper Volta, Niger, Togo: Five countries still to be discovered.* Paris: Presses Africaines Associées, 1969.

14. REFERENCE AND BIBLIOGRAPHY

Africa Research Bullettin. Series A: Political Social and Cultural. Series B: Economic Financial and Technical. Exeter, Eng., monthly, 1963+.

Africa South of the Sahara. London: Europa Publications, annual, 1971+.

Africa South of the Sahara: index to periodical literature. Washington: Library of Congress, Africa and Middle East Division, 1985.

Afrique Contemporaine. Paris: La Documentation Française, quarterly.

Allen, Chris. ''The People's Republic of Benin: a bibliography,'' Edinburgh: Edinburgh University Centre of African Studies, 1985.

Année Africaine. Paris: Pedone, annual, 1963+.

Anée Politique Africaine. Dakar: Société Africaine d'Edition, annual, 1966+.

L'Annuaire d'Afrique Noire. Paris: Ediafric, annual.

Asamani, J. O. *Index Africanus. Catalogue of articles in Western Languages published from 1885 to 1965.* Stanford: Hoover Institution Press, 1975.

Aube Nouvelle (Porto Novo), daily, 1961–1969.

Ballantyne, James, and Andrew Roberts. *Africa: a handbook of film and video resources.* London: British Universities Film and Video Council, 1986.

Banque Centrale des Etats de l'Afrique de l'Ouest. ''Indicateurs économiques dahoméens.'' Paris, quarterly.

Bibliographie des travaux en langue française sur l'Afrique au sud du Sahara. Paris: CARDAN, 1982.

Blackhurst, Hector (ed.). *Africa Bibliography.* Manchester: Manchester University Press, annual.

Blake, David, and Corola Travis. *Periodicals from Africa: a bibliography and Union list of periodicals publishers in Africa.* Boston: G. K. Hall & Co., 1984.

Bourges, Hervé, and Claude Wauthier. *Les 50 Afriques.* Paris: Le Seuil, 1979.

Brasseur, P., and J. F. Maurel. ''Les Sources bibliographiques de l'Afrique de l'ouest et de l'Afrique équatoriale d'expression française.'' Dakar: Bibliothèque de l'Université, 1970.

Carson, P. *Materials for West African History in French Archives.* London: Athlone Press, 1968.

Chauveau, J. P., and F. Verdeaux (eds.). *Bibliographie sur les communautés de pêcheurs d'Afrique de l'Ouest.* Cotonou: DIPA, 1989.

Chronologie Politique Africaine. Paris: Fondation Nationale des Sciences Politiques, Centre d'Etudes des Relations Internationales, bimonthly, 1960–1970.

Conover, H. F. *Official Publications of French West Africa, 1946–1958.* Washington, D.C.: Library of Congress, 1960.

Cornevin, Robert. ''Bibliographie,'' in Robert Cornevin, *Histoire du Dahomey.* Paris: Berger Levrault, 1962, pp. 533–556.

''Dahomey,'' in John Dickie and Alan Rake, *Who's Who in Africa.* London: African Development, 1973, pp. 87–95.

Da Silva, Guillaume. ''Contributions à la bibliographie du Dahomey,'' *Etudes Dahoméennes,* vol. 2, no. 12 (June 1968).

Decalo, Samuel. *Historical Dictionary of the People's Republic of Benin.* Metuchen, N.J.: Scarecrow Press, 2nd edition, 1977.

Deutsche Afrika-Gesellschaft. *Afrika-Bibliographie: Verzeichnis des wissenschaftlichen schrifttums in deutscher Sprache aus dem Jahr 1964.* Bonn.

Dictionary of African Biography, 2d ed. London: Melrose Press, 1971.

Dictionnaire bio-bibliographique du Dahomey. Porto Novo: I.R.A.D., 1969.

Directory of African Experts, 1989. Paris: U.N. Economic Commission for Africa, 1989.

Duignan, Peter. *Handbook of American Resources for African Studies*. Stanford: Hoover Institution Press, 1967.

The Economist Intelligence Unit. *Former French Tropical Africa*. London, quarterly, 1961+.

Les Elites africaines. Paris: Ediafric, 1970.

"Europe d'Expression Française et Madagascar," *Europe-Outre Mer*. Special Annual issue, 1960+.

Europe-France-Outremer. Paris. Monthly to 1987, including the annual June survey of all African states.

Gaignebet, Wanda. *Inventaire de thèses africanistes de langue française*. Paris: CARDAN, 1977.

————. "Répertoire de thèses africanistes françaises. Paris: CARDAN, 1982.

————. *Répertoire de thèses africanistes françaises 1988–1989*. Paris: CARDAN, 1991.

Gorman, G. E., and M. M. Mahoney. *Guide to Current National Bibliographies in the Third World*. Munich: Hans Zell, 1983.

Herdeck, Donald E. *African Authors: A Bio-Bibliographical Companion to Black African Writing, 1300–1972.* Esplanade, Md.: Black Orpheus Pres, 1972.

Hertefelt, Marcel d', and Anne-Marie Bouttiaux-Ndiaye. *Bibliographie de l'Afrique sud-Saharienne: Sciences humaines et sociales 1986–87.* Tervuren: Musée Royal de l'Afrique centrale, 1990.

Hommes et Destins. 5 vols. Paris: Académie des Sciences d'Outre Mer, 1977–1979.

Hoover Institution. *U.S. and Canadian Publications and Theses on Africa, 1961–1966.* Stanford: Hoover Institution Press.

International African Institute. *Africa* bibliographic section quarterly 1929.

Jahn, Janheinz. *Who's Who in African Literature.* Tubingen: Horst Erdmann Verlag, 1972.

Jakande, L. K. (ed.). *West Africa Annual.* Lagos: John West Publications.

Jeune Afrique. Paris and Tunis, weekly.

Johnson, G. Wesley. "The archival system of former French West Africa," *African Studies Bulletin,* vol. 8, no. 1 (1965), pp. 48–58.

Joucla, E. *Bibliographie de l'Afrique occidentale française.* Paris: Société d'Editions Géographiques, Martimes et Coloniales, 1937.

Kohl, Ernst. "Bibliographie der Zeitschriften aus Dahomey," *Afrika Archiv,* vol. 1 (Jan. 1970), pp. 1–4.

Kohler, Jochen. *Deutsche Dissertationen über Afrika: ein Verzeichnis für die Jaohre 1918–1959.* Bonn: K. Schroeder für Deutsche Afrika-Gesselschaft, 1962.

Lafond, Mireille. *Recueil des thèses africanistes 1967–1984.* Paris: Centre d'Etudes Juridiques et Comparatives, 1984.

Lauer, Joseph et al. *American and Canadian doctoral dissertations and Master's theses on Africa 1974–1987.* Atlanta: Crossroads Press, 1990.

Legum, Colin (ed.). *Africa Contemporary Record.* London: Rex Collings, 1968–1989.

Lipschutz, Mark R., and R. Kent Rasmussen. *Dictionary of African Historical Biography.* Berkeley: University of California Press, 1986.

Martineau, Alfred et al. *Bibliographie d'histoire coloniale 1900–30.* Paris: Société de l'histoire des colonies françaises, 1932.

Mercier, Paul. "Bibliographie," *Etudes Dahoméennes,* no. 4 (1950).

———. *Carte Ethno-Démographique de l'Afrique Occidentale.* Dakar: l'Institut Français d'Afrique Noire, no. 5, 1954, p. 4.

Le Mois en Afriqué, Revue Française d'Etudes Politiques Africaines. Dakar and Paris, monthly, to 1990.

Momento de l'Economie Africaine. Paris: Ediafric, irregular 1966 to 1987.

Pawloski, A. de Launay. *Bibliographie raisonnée des ouvrages concernant le Dahomey.* Paris: Baudoin, 1895.

Personnalités Publiques de l'Afrique de l'Ouest, 1969. Paris: Ediafric, 1969.

Peter, J. *Annuaire des états d'Afrique noire—gouvernements et cabinets ministériels des républiques d'expression française.* Paris: Ediafric, 1961.

Rake, Alan. *Africa's Top 300.* New York: Africa File, 1990.

Regelsperger, G. "Essai de bibliographie des Etablissements français de la Côte des esclaves et du Dahomey," Paris, 1985.

Répertoire des centres de documentation et bibliothèques. Abidjan: Conseil de l'Entente, Service de documentation, 1980.

Répertoire des Enseignants et Chercheurs Africains. Montreal: Association des Universités partiellement ou entièrement de langue française, 1984.

République du Dahomey. *Journal Officiel de la République du Dahomey.* Porto Novo, semi-monthly, 1958+ [superseded the *Journal Officiel de la Colonie du Dahomey,* pub. under various titles since 1890, and since 1985 published as *Journal Officiel de la République Populaire du Bénin*].

Revue des Marchés Tropicaux et Méditerranéens. Paris, weekly.

Roese, P. M., and A. R. Rees. "A Bibliography of Benin: A commentary on published and unpublished sources written in German," *Africa Research and Documentation,* no. 45 (1987), pp. 15–26; no. 46 (1988), pp. 31–39; no. 48 (1988), pp. 23–36.

Scheven, Yvette. *Bibliographies for African Studies 1970–1986.* London: Hans Zell, 1988.

Schmidt, Nancy J. *Subsaharan African films and filmmakers: a preliminary bibliography.* Bloomington: Indiana University African Studies program, 1986.

Segal, Ronald. *Political Africa: A Who's Who of Personalities and Parties.* New York: Praeger, 1961.

"Serials of Cameroun, Dahomey, Togo, Mali, Ethiopia and the Somali Republic," *Africana Newsletter,* Hoover Institution, vol. 2, no. 1 (1964), pp. 33–41.

Sims, Michael, and Alfred Kagan. *American and Canadian doctoral dissertations and Master's theses on Africa, 1886–1974,* Waltham, Mass.: African Studies Association, 1976.

Standing Conference on Library Materials on Africa. *United Kingdom Publications and Theses on Africa.* Cambridge: Heffer, 1963+.

Sternberg, Ilse, and Patricia M. Larby (eds.). *African Studies.* London: SCOLMA, 1986.

Stewart, John. *African States and Rulers,* Jefferson N.C.: MacFurland, 1989.

Taylor, Sidney (ed.). *The New Africans.* London: Hamlyn, 1967.

Tenaille, Franck. *Les 56 Afriques.* Paris: Maspero, 1979. 2 vols.

West Africa. London, weekly.

Witherell, Julian W. *Africana Resources and Collections,* Metuchen N.J.: Scarecrow Press, 1989.

———. *French Speaking West Africa: A Guide to Official Publications.* Washington, D.C.: Library of Congress, 1967.

Wiseman, John A. *Political Leaders in Black Africa.* Aldershot: Edward Elgar Publishing, 1991.

Yaranga, Zofia. *Bibliographie des Travaux en langue française sur l'Afrique au sud du Sahara.* Paris: Ecole des Hautes Etudes en Sciences Sociales, 1982, 1983, 1989.

Zell, Hans (ed.). *The African Studies Companion: A Resource Book and Directory.* New York: Zell, 1989.

———. and Helene Silver (eds.). *A Reader's Guide to African Literature.* New York: Africana Pub. Co., 1971.

ABOUT THE AUTHOR

Samuel Decalo (B.Sc., Ottawa University; M.A. and Ph.D. University of Pennsylvania) is an Israeli citizen, long resident in the USA. He has taught at various universities including the University of Rhode Island; The Graduate Faculty, New School for Social Research, and Emory University, as well as at several universities abroad including the University of Botswana and the University of the West Indies. He is currently Professor of Political Science at the University of Natal, South Africa, and Visiting Professor at the University of Florida in Gainesville. He has conducted research in some twenty African states, including Benin, on numerous occasions, and is the author of eleven books and some sixty articles on Africa and the Middle East.